PERGAMON GENERAL PSYCHOLOGY SERIES
EDITORS
Arnold P. Goldstein, Syracuse University
Leonard Krasner, Stanford University & SUNY at Stony Brook

HANDBOOK OF CHILD AND ADULT PSYCHOPATHOLOGY

(PGPS-161)

Pergamon Titles of Related Interest

Hersen/Kazdin/Bellack THE CLINICAL PSYCHOLOGY HANDBOOK
Johnson/Goldman DEVELOPMENTAL ASSESSMENT IN CLINICAL
CHILD PSYCHOLOGY: A Handbook
Schwartz/Johnson PSYCHOPATHOLOGY OF CHILDHOOD:
A Clinical-Experimental Approach, Second Edition
Van Hasselt/Hersen HANDBOOK OF ADOLESCENT PSYCHOLOGY

Related Journals
(Free sample copies available on request.)

BEHAVIOUR RESEARCH AND THERAPY
CLINICAL PSYCHOLOGY REVIEW
JOURNAL OF BEHAVIOR THERAPY AND
   EXPERIMENTAL PSYCHIATRY
JOURNAL OF CHILD PSYCHOLOGY AND PSYCHIATRY
   AND ALLIED DISCIPLINES

HANDBOOK OF CHILD AND ADULT PSYCHOPATHOLOGY

A Longitudinal Perspective

Edited by

MICHEL HERSEN
University of Pittsburgh School of Medicine

CYNTHIA G. LAST
Nova University

PERGAMON PRESS

Member of Maxwell Macmillan Pergamon Publishing Corporation
New York • Oxford • Beijing • Frankfurt
São Paulo • Sydney • Tokyo • Toronto

Pergamon Press Offices:

U.S.A.	Pergamon Press, Inc., Maxwell House, Fairview Park, Elmsford, New York 10523, U.S.A.
U.K.	Pergamon Press plc, Headington Hill Hall, Oxford OX3 0BW, England
PEOPLE'S REPUBLIC OF CHINA	Pergamon Press, 0909 China World Tower, No. 1 Jian Guo Men Wei Avenue, Beijing 100004, People's Republic of China
FEDERAL REPUBLIC OF GERMANY	Pergamon Press GmbH, Hammerweg 6, D-6242 Kronberg, Federal Republic of Germany
BRAZIL	Pergamon Editora Ltda, Rua Eça de Queiros, 346, CEP 04011, Paraiso, São Paulo, Brazil
AUSTRALIA	Pergamon Press Australia Pty Ltd., P.O. Box 544, Potts Point, NSW 2011, Australia
JAPAN	Pergamon Press, 8th Floor, Matsuoka Central Building, 1-7-1 Nishishinjuku, Shinjuku-ku, Tokyo 160, Japan
CANADA	Pergamon Press Canada Ltd., Suite 271, 253 College Street, Toronto, Ontario M5T 1R5, Canada

Library of Congress Cataloging-in-Publication Data

Handbook of child and adult psychopathology : a longitudinal
  perspective / edited by Michel Hersen, Cynthia G. Last.
       p.   cm. -- (Pergamon general psychology series : 161)
    ISBN 0-08-036101-3 :
    1. Mental illness—Longitudinal studies. 2. Child
psychopathology. 3. Psychology, Pathological.   I. Hersen, Michel.
II. Last, Cynthia G. III. Series.
    [DNLM: 1. Longitudinal Studies. 2. Mental Disorders. 3. Mental
  Disorders—in infancy & childhood.   WM 100 H23363]
  RC454.4.H35 1990
  616.89—dc20
  DNLM/DLC
  for Library of Congress   89-26673
                                                                CIP

Printing: 1 2 3 4 5 6 7 8 9 10   Year: 0 1 2 3 4 5 6 7 8 9

Printed in the United States of America

⊚™ The paper used in this publication meets the minimum requirements of
American National Standard for Information Sciences—Permanence of
Paper for Printed Library Materials, ANSI Z39.48-1984

CONTENTS

OBESITY

PREFACE

Most books that tackle the issue of psychopathology tend to focus exclusively on either children or adults. Indeed, we feel that the flow and continuity between child and adult presentations of similar disorders are lost in such separation. With increased data being adduced, there now is very good evidence showing the relationship between child and adult psychopathology for a good many disorders, albeit symptomatic pictures may vary at different developmental levels.

The purpose of this new *Handbook of Child and Adult Psychopathology: A Longitudinal Perspective,* therefore, is to bridge the gap between what we know about childhood and adult disorders. To accomplish this task we have recruited a large group of eminent authorities who have been most gracious to share their expertise with us, and we are most appreciative of their contributions.

The book contains 28 chapters presented in 14 parts. Part I presents introductory material, setting the tone for the volume. The bulk of the book appears in Parts II through XIV (Chapters 3 through 28). Each of these sections presents the child version and the adult version of the disorders, preceded by our editorial commentary to underscore the similarities and dissimilarities. To ensure comparability across the various parts of the book, contributors to the child and adult sections were instructed to follow a precise outline, with authors of child chapters considering adult manifestations in the Continuity and Discontinuity with Adult Presentation section of their reviews and the authors of adult chapters considering childhood and familial antecedents of adult psychopathology in the Childhood and Familial Antecedents section of their reviews. (See the accompanying outline.) Finally, after Chapter 28 our concluding comments are presented.

In addition to the contributors we wish to thank our technical experts: Mary Newell, Mary Anne Frederick, and Kim Sterner. Most of all, however, we wish to thank Jerome B. Frank, our editor and friend at Pergamon Press, who understood the timeliness of the project.

Michel Hersen, Pittsburgh, PA
Cynthia G. Last, Ft. Lauderdale, FL

CHILD	ADULT
1. Description of the Disorder	Description of the Disorder
2. Clinical Presentation	Clinical Presentation
3. Epidemiology	Epidemiology
4. Natural History	Natural History
5. Impairment and Complications	Impairment and Complications
6. Differential Diagnosis	Differential Diagnosis
7. Case Example	Case Example
8. Continuity and Discontinuity with Adult Presentation	Childhood and Familial Antecedents
9. Summary	Summary

INTRODUCTION

EDITORS' COMMENTS

In the two introductory chapters to this book the basis for the longitudinal study of psychopathology is examined first from a historical perspective and then from a developmental perspective. In Chapter 2, the focus is on the individual, the context, and the relationship between the two over the life span (i.e., the longitudinal approach).

As clearly articulated, the longitudinal perspective in psychopathology is quite new. Indeed, for the longest time, study of adult psychopathology predominated the field, with children initially conceptualized as miniature adults and given little specific consideration. Gradually since the beginning of the 20th century, study of childhood psychopathology has been accorded increased attention by psychopathologists. The independent and growing importance of childhood psychopathology can be nicely traced by contrasting DSM-I, DSM-II, DSM-III, and DSM-III-R, wherein each succeeding revision has increased the number of childhood categories.

In the last decade or two clinical researchers have been intrigued by the possible links between child and adult psychopathology, carrying out studies to evaluate effects of early experiences on adult behavior and looking at the continuities between child and adult manifestations of the disorder. However, as will be apparent as the reader goes through the succeeding chapters, the relationship between child and adult psychopathology is not always isomorphic, with a variety of permutations manifesting themselves over time. But despite the inconsistencies in some instances between child and adult manifestations of the same disorder, the importance of the longitudinal approach is underscored by detailing the relationship between the two.

CHAPTER 1

INTRODUCTION

Lori A. Sisson
Michel Hersen
Cynthia G. Last

HISTORY

The history of description and intervention related to adult psychopathology can be traced back to the ancient Greeks and Romans, who held organic theories about mental disorders. These theories mostly dealt with the balance of humoral substances in the body. Somatic treatments, such as bloodletting and laxatives, were applied to individuals who engaged in deviant behavior. In medieval times, the Greek physical theories of psychopathology were replaced by religious ones that viewed insanity as the work of the devil. Accordingly, treatments included humiliation, imprisonment, torture, and burning at the stake.

It was not until the late 1700s that more humane treatment of mentally ill persons was actively promoted by Philippe Pinel in France, William Tuke in England, and Benjamin Rush in America. These more enlightened mental health pioneers developed the system that has come to be termed "moral treatment." In such programs, patients were cared for with kindness and dignity in pleasant environments referred to as "retreats." Moral treatment was believed to cause an im-

provement in psychological well-being, with corresponding positive changes in impaired organic structures. Initial reports of "incredible" cure rates with this approach led to a "cult of curability" that replaced the former hopelessness about mental disorders.

Beginning in 1833, a large number of state legislatures erected institutions for the moral treatment of indigent mentally ill individuals. This show of public responsibility was prompted by (1) the new optimism about improved prognosis for persons with mental illness and (2) the work of militant crusaders such as Dorthea Dix, who exposed the cruelty suffered by poor individuals with mental disorders. However, only three decades after the opening of the first state hospital, it became apparent that the new system was unable to produce the miracle cures that once were predicted. As a result, medical leaders again became pessimistic about treatment for mental illness and state institutions became explicitly custodial.

The advent of widespread hospital care for mentally ill patients created a need for classification. Persons who exhibited violent aggression required housing and management different from those who were dysphoric. Although several attempts at classification preceded the comprehensive taxonomy developed by Emil Kraepelin (1883), his system is credited as the first to provide mental health professionals with detailed accounts of etiology, symptoms, and the course of a variety of psychogenic problems and personality disorders. It was the explicit hope that classification of mental disease entities could begin with the description of symptom syndromes and culminate in the eventual discovery of specific physical causes.

At the turn of the century, very little attention was paid to psychopathology in children. Kraepelin did not include any disorders specifically related to childhood in his nosological scheme. The first considerations of child behavior were in the context of understanding and treating adult disorders, and these appeared at the beginning of the twentieth century. First, Sigmund Freud rejected the notion of an organic basis for all pathology. Instead, he posited conflicts between unconscious desires and conscious values as contributing to psychological problems. Specifically, childhood sexual experiences, and particularly unresolved sexual desires toward parents, were hypothesized as important causes of neuroses (Freud, 1905). Early childhood experiences and desires were considered to have been pushed out of consciousness because of their perceived unacceptability, but they presumably exerted a widespread effect on adult behavior. Accordingly, Freud's method of treatment was to expose the unconscious childhood material through free association, and then conflicts were identified and resolved.

A second major force in clinical psychology and psychiatry in the early 1900s was behaviorism. John Watson (1913) attacked the psychoanalytic school for its preoccupation with the study of consciousness and proposed that observable behavior become the subject matter for psychology. However, like Freud, Watson believed that nearly all adult behavior had been shaped by early childhood experiences. Rather than reviewing these experiences with adult clients, Watson and his students began to observe and treat children themselves. He prescribed regimented parental behavior and environmental conditions that were carefully designed to develop self-sufficient, fearless, and unemotional children, who would eventually become well-functioning adults.

Although the psychoanalytic and behavioristic schools had many prominent followers, the impact of these approaches to understanding and treating mental illness was increased through the Mental Hygiene movement. Founded by Clifford Beers, a recovered psychiatric patient, a major goal of this movement was to prevent adult mental disorder through early detection and intervention. Thus, in addition to establishing improved, accessible services for adults, the Mental Hygiene movement provided an impetus for establishing child guidance clinics to assist with school problems and juvenile delinquency.

THE IMPACT OF CHILDHOOD EXPERIENCE

It is clear that early theorists and clinicians espoused the notion that an identifiable link existed between a child's experience and behavioral disturbance exhibited in adulthood. As previously noted, the activities of children were of interest from a theoretical and clinical standpoint primarily because they were thought to shed light on the etiology of adult psychopathology. Alternatively, they represented the key to prevention of adult pathology. This belief in the connectedness of childhood experience and adult disorder generally was accepted without challenge, although it initially was unsupported by empirical evidence. Kagan (1980) argues that the general popularity of this view is consistent with a Western partiality toward "inventing invisible essences that provide a continuity between the preceding and succeeding phenomena" (p. 26). Indeed, the belief in the importance of childhood experiences also is reflected in the often-repeated maxim that one must prepare for the future, which highlights parental responsibility to provide the proper early environment and training. Further, Western society's egalitarian ethic requires that "all infants are equally skilled or unskilled at birth" and regards "experience as unbiased tutor to all" (Kagan, 1980, p. 53).

Rutter (1981; Sroufe & Rutter, 1984) suggested a number of ways in which early experience might be connected to later disorder, in that (1) experience leads to disordered behavior at the time, and maladaptive responding persists; (2) experience leads to physical changes that influence later functioning; (3) there are altered patterns of behavior at the time that only later take the form of psychopathology. Other connections are less direct: (4) early events may change the family circumstances, and these altered circumstances produce disorder; (5) sensitivities to stress or coping styles are modified, thus "predisposing" the person to later disorder; (6) experiences alter the individual's self-concept or attitudes, and this in turn influences response to later situations; and (7) experience influences behavior through effects on the selection of environments or on the availability of opportunities.

Several lines of research have attempted to evaluate the impact of early childhood experiences on later behavioral response. For example, Sroufe (1979) described research on attachment of infants to their mothers, demonstrating that sheer numbers of stressful life events experienced by the family were related to the quality of attachment between child and caregiver. Less environmental stress was associated with more secure attachments. In addition, other studies found securely attached infants to be persistent, positive, and compliant as toddlers. They were described as "peer leaders, socially involved, attracting the attention of others, curious, and actively engaged in their surroundings" (p. 839) at ages $3\frac{1}{2}$ and 5 years. In contrast, insecurely attached infants were easily frustrated, oppositional, inhibited in social situations, and anxious.

What about the longer-term effects of early experiences on adult behavior? Possible environmental influences on conduct disorder in children and antisocial personality disorder in adults have been studied extensively. The results of these investigations are in agreement and show that several family variables are associated with juvenile delinquency and adult criminality. These include deviant parental behavior; poor parental supervision; cruel, passive, or neglectful attitudes; erratic or harsh discipline; family discord; and large family size (see Rutter, 1986; and Chapters 21 and 22 in this volume).

CONTINUITY OF CHILD AND ADULT PSYCHOPATHOLOGY

Adultomorphism

Perhaps because childhood behaviors were viewed simply as precursors to adult psychopathology, Kraepelin's (1883) classification scheme made no provision for diagnosing disorders that were specific to children. Rather, adult diagnoses could also be applied to this group. In fact, it was not until the 1960s that a variety of attempts to describe and categorize childhood disorders appeared (Achenbach & Edelbrock, 1978; American Psychiatric Association, 1968; Group for the Advancement of Psychiatry, 1966). With the exception of the empirically derived systems (Achenbach & Edelbrock, 1978), most were simply downward extrapolations of adult symptomatology and terminology. This tendency to see in the disorders of children the replicas and predecessors of analogously named conditions in adults is known as "adultomorphism" (Phillips, Draguns, & Bartlett, 1975). Kagan (1980) pointed out that the idea of stability across ages, like connectedness between ages, also is consistent with Western philosophy. In general, our language fails to distinguish between infants, children, and adults. Words like "intelligent" or "passive" are used to describe individuals of all ages as if their meanings were not altered by development and maturation. It is not surprising that our psychiatric diagnostic system followed this same pattern.

Unfortunately, the bias toward treating children like miniature adults has been an obstacle to understanding the developmental course of behavioral problems (Garber, 1984; Ollendick & Hersen, 1983; Sroufe & Rutter, 1984). It has been argued that adultomorphic classification does not work for children because (1) there is no guarantee that child and adult forms of a disturbance will be manifested in the same fashion (Peterson, Burbach, & Chaney, 1989); (2) the adult-based criteria for various disorders may be overinclusive, particularly for the very young, since there is a wider range and variety of normal behaviors available to this group in comparison with adults (Achenbach, 1980); and (3) psychopathology usually is relative to the age of the individual in question (Garber, 1984).

In the area of childhood depression, for example, early attempts at classification applied adult concepts directly to children. This is probably an appropriate initial strategy for studying the phenomenon, since there appear to be some similarities between child and adult forms of the disorder. Several investigators have presented evidence that the constellation of symptomatology diagnosed as depressive disorders in adult life also occurs in childhood (e.g., Carlson & Cantwell, 1982; Puig-Antich, 1980). However, the risk of adultomorphism with childhood depression is illustrated by the following points. First, the list of feelings and behaviors associated with depression has been found to characterize almost all children at one time or another during development; the symptoms of depression overlap with conduct disorder, separation anxiety, and poor peer relationships; and the problems tend to remit spontaneously as a function of time (Lefkowitz & Burton, 1978). In addition, biological correlates, such as response to the dexamethasone suppression test, sleep patterns, and response to antidepressant medications, appear to differ in children and adults with depression (Puig-Antich, 1985). Finally, while it is apparent that dysthymic mood can arise at any age, feelings of depression (in which there are the cognitive components of self-devaluation and feelings of hopelessness) are less frequent in early childhood than in adolescence or adulthood. Indeed, puberty is associated with a substantial rise in depression and suicide, as well as mania, especially in females (Rutter, 1986; see also Chapters 3 and 4 in this book for discussions of depression in children and adults).

Developmental Psychopathology

Developmental psychopathology represents an approach to the study of maladaptive responding that takes into account the problems just introduced. It has been defined as *"the study of the origins and course of individual patterns of behavioral maladaptation*, whatever the age of onset, whatever the causes, whatever the transformations in behavioral manifestation, and however complex the course of the developmental pattern may be" (Sroufe & Rutter, 1984, p. 18). There are a number of defining characteristics of this approach. These include a focus on description and cataloging of disordered behavior, especially but not exclusively as presented by children (who are growing and changing), with reference to normal developmental patterns (Garber, 1984). In addition, developmental psychopathology attempts to identify congruences between early and later dysfunction (Sroufe & Rutter, 1984). In this regard, there are no a priori assumptions that disordered behavior in childhood continues into adulthood, that adult problems are preceded by child problems, or that the antecedents or consequences of maladaptive behavior at one point in time will be phenotypically similar to that behavior. Indeed, recent research has shown that each of these assumptions represents too simplistic an approach to the problem (Puig-Antich, 1985; Rutter, 1986). Rather, the task of the developmental psychopathologist is to be sensitive to more complex relationships between child and adult disorder, taking into account the continuities and discontinuities between childhood and adult life.

Follow-up Studies

One of the primary research tools of developmental psychopathologists is the follow-up study. The essential concept of the follow-up study is that it includes measures at two or more points in time. Such an investigation can resemble a laboratory experiment if, during the elapsed time, some intervention has taken place (e.g., treatment). Thus, follow-up studies are uniquely adapted to assessing the results of therapy. However, elapsed time also may be evaluated as a period of spontaneous change and development only. As such, this method can provide important information on who is most likely to develop a psychopathological disorder and what is the outcome of behavior disturbances. Often, follow-up studies start with children and then locate information about their adjustment at some later point in time. However, research investigating the likelihood that the disorders of childhood will be carried over into adulthood also have begun with persons known to have psychopathological problems as adults, with retrospective study of childhood records to learn whether such adults also exhibited disordered behavior when they were children.

The first major follow-up studies (Kagan & Moss, 1962; Macfarlane, Allen, & Honzik, 1954; Thomas & Chess, 1976) were initiated in the 1920s and 1930s, when Freudian ideas were gaining popularity. It has been argued that the scientists who initiated these unique investigations did not adopt a developmental approach but instead were intent on gathering enough information on the growing child to uncover his or her life course (Kagan, 1980; McCall, 1977). The influence of the psychoanalytic school was reflected in the belief that pathology in the young was a product of internal conflict, resistant to change, and therefore a harbinger of the future. The studies involved extensive and continuing assessments, beginning in infancy, and focusing on the following variables: dependence, aggression, passivity, fearfulness, achievement, dominance, and irritability. Interestingly, results were consistent in finding that the majority of symptoms experienced by preschool-aged children were transient developmental phenomena. Such findings led several authors (Kagan, 1980; Robins, 1979) to conclude that patterns of symptoms appearing before age 6 were of little predictive significance.

A more recent review of several short-term follow-up studies of young children found, however, that early externalizing problems (aggression, hyperactivity) persist into elementary school and can worsen over time (Campbell, 1989). Convergent results also are emerging from follow-up studies of school-aged youngsters tracked into adolescence and adulthood. Children with conduct disturbances appear to be more likely than children with emotional problems (and much more likely than those without disorders) to show ongoing psychiatric and social impairment in adulthood (Robins, 1966). This picture is complicated by several observations. First, a follow-back approach indicates that adult antisocial personality disorders almost always are preceded by conduct disturbances in childhood. Yet, at least 50% of youngsters with conduct disorder do become reasonably well-functioning adults. Further, the adult sequelae of conduct disorder symptoms also include problems other than antisocial behavior, such as depression and schizophrenia (Robins, 1966; see also Rutter & Garmezy, 1983; Chapter 21).

The outcome of conduct disorders in children is relatively well researched. Limited data also have been accumulated for other disorders. The above brief review of pertinent findings illustrates that the tie between childhood disorder and the same type of behavior disturbance in adulthood can be direct, as in the case of conduct disorder and antisocial personality disorder. However, the developmental link often is more complex. It is not the shy, withdrawn child who tends to manifest schizophrenia in adulthood. Rather, it is the child characterized by impulsiveness, aggression, and antisocial behavior who is overrepresented in the schizophrenia group. As a result of these observations, it has been suggested that broad-based indicators of adaptational failure (inadequate peer relations, antisocial behavior, achievement problems) during the school years predict adult disorders broadly, rather than specifically (Sroufe & Rutter, 1984).

SUMMARY AND CONCLUSIONS

A longitudinal perspective is new in the study of psychopathology. Historically, an interest in adult disorders predominated, with consideration of childhood behavior problems beginning at the start of the twentieth century. From this point on, clinicians and researchers have attempted to identify links between child and adult psychopathology. Investigations have taken two directions:

(1) exploring the impact of early experience on adult behavior and (2) identifying continuities between child and adult disorders.

Unfortunately, early conceptualizations of psychopathology portrayed children as miniature adults experiencing the same disorders as their adult counterparts. These conceptualizations hindered attempts to understand the long-term course of behavioral problems, primarily because they did not account for the normal changes evinced by developing human beings. The popularization of developmental psychopathology, first comprehensively described by Achenbach in 1974, contributed significantly to the longitudinal study of disordered behavior, in part by explicitly rejecting the notion of isomorphism between disturbances in childhood and adulthood.

Currently, some data are available from follow-up studies about the relationship between child and adult psychopathology. Therefore, contrary to prior books that focused exclusively on child or adult psychopathology, the contributors to this volume have been asked to examine the evidence in support of connections between childhood and adult disorders. It will become apparent that research is warranted, not only documenting the tie between child and adult behavioral disturbances, but also the familial and environmental antecedents of psychological malfunctioning. This is a priority if we are to progress beyond the level of the description and classification of problems to an understanding of developmental processes and preventative factors (e.g., Pfeffer, 1985). Only with such understanding can clear guidelines for prevention and intervention be established.

REFERENCES

Achenbach, T. M. (1980). DSM-III in light of empirical research on the classification of child psychopathology. *Journal of the American Academy of Child Psychiatry, 19*, 395–412.

Achenbach, T. M. (1974). *Developmental psychopathology*. New York: The Ronald Press.

Achenbach, T. M., & Edelbrock, C. S. (1978). The classification of child psychopathology: A review and analysis of empirical efforts. *Psychological Bulletin, 85*, 1275–1301.

American Psychiatric Association. (1968). *Diagnostic and statistical manual of mental disorders* (2nd ed.). Washington, DC: Author.

Campbell, S. B. (1989). Developmental perspectives. In T. H. Ollendick & M. Hersen (Eds.),

Handbook of child psychopathology (2nd ed.). New York: Plenum Press.

Carlson, G. A., & Cantwell, D. P. (1982). Diagnosis of childhood depression: A comparison of the Weinberg and DSM-III criteria. *Journal of the American Academy of Child Psychiatry, 21*, 247–250.

Freud, S. (1905). Three essays on the theory of sexuality. In *Standard edition of the complete psychological works of Sigmund Freud* (Vol. 7, pp. 125–243). London: Hogarth Press, 1953.

Garber, J. (1984). Classification of childhood psychopathology: A developmental perspective. *Child Development, 55*, 30–48.

Group for the Advancement of Psychiatry, Committee on Child Psychiatry. (1966). *Psychopathological disorders in childhood: Theoretical considerations and a proposed classification* (Vol. 6, Report No. 62). New York: Author.

Kagan, J. (1980). Perspectives on continuity. In O. G. Brim & J. Kagan (Eds.), *Constancy and change in human development* (pp. 26–74). Cambridge, MA: Harvard University Press.

Kagan, J., & Moss, H. A. (1962). *Birth to maturity*. New York: John Wiley & Sons.

Kraepelin, E. (1883). *Compendium der psychiatrie* [Compendium of psychiatry]. Leipzig: Abel.

Lefkowitz, M., & Burton, N. (1978). Childhood depression: A critique of the concept. *Psychological Bulletin, 85*, 716–726.

Macfarlane, J. W., Allen, L., & Honzik, M. P. (1954). *A developmental study of the behavior problems of normal children between twenty-one months and fourteen years*. Berkeley: University of California Press.

McCall, R. B. (1977). Challenges to a science of developmental psychology. *Child Development, 48*, 333–344.

Ollendick, T. H., & Hersen, M. (1983). A historical overview of child psychopathology. In T. H. Ollendick & M. Hersen (Eds.), *Handbook of child psychopathology* (pp. 3–11). New York: Plenum Press.

Peterson, L., Burbach, D. J., & Chaney, J. (1989). Developmental issues. In C. G. Last & M. Hersen (Eds.), *Handbook of child psychiatric diagnosis*. New York: John Wiley & Sons.

Pfeffer, C. R. (1985). Suicidal fantasies in normal children. *Journal of Nervous and Mental Diseases, 173*, 78–84.

Phillips, L., Draguns, J. G., & Bartlett, D. P. (1975). Classification of behavior disorders. In N. Hobbs (Ed.), *Issues in the classification of children*. San Francisco: Jossey-Bass.

Puig-Antich, J. (1980). Affective disorder in childhood: A review and perspective. *Psychiatric Clinics of North America, 3*, 103–424.

Puig-Antich, J. (1985). Effects of age and puberty on psychobiological markers of depressive illness. In M. Rutter, C. E. Izard, & P. Read (Eds.), *Depression in childhood: Developmental perspectives* (pp. 341–396). New York: The Guilford Press.

Robins, L. N. (1966). *Deviant children grown up*. Baltimore: Williams & Wilkins. (Reprinted and published by Robert E. Krieger Publishing, Huntington, NY, 1974)

Robins, L. N. (1979). Follow-up studies. In H. C. Quay & J. S. Werry (Eds.), *Psychopathological disorders of childhood* (2nd ed.). New York: John Wiley & Sons.

Rutter, M. (1981). Stress, coping and development: Some issues and some questions. *Journal of Child Psychology and Psychiatry, 22*, 323–356.

Rutter, M. (1986). Child psychiatry: The interface between clinical and developmental research. *Psychological Medicine, 16*, 151–169.

Rutter, M., & Garmezy, N. (1983). Developmental psychopathology. In E. M. Hetherington (Ed.), *Carmichael's manual of child psychology: Vol. 4. Social and personality development*. New York: John Wiley & Sons.

Sroufe, L. A. (1979). The coherence of individual development: Early care, attachment, and subsequent developmental issues. *American Psychologist, 34*, 834–841.

Sroufe, L. A., & Rutter, M. (1984). The domain of developmental psychology. *Child Development, 55*, 17–29.

Thomas, A., & Chess, S. (1976). Evolution of behavior disorders into adolescence. *American Journal of Psychiatry, 133*, 539–542.

Watson, J. B. (1913). Psychology as the behaviorist views it. *Psychological Review, 20*, 158–177.

CHAPTER 2

A DEVELOPMENTAL PERSPECTIVE ON PSYCHOPATHOLOGY

Richard M. Lerner
Laura E. Hess
Katherine Nitz

INTRODUCTION

No instance of psychopathology, or indeed any functional attribute of a person, exists preformed or predetermined in the genome. All functional characteristics of a person, and in fact all structural ones as well, are developmental phenomena. As such, any attempt to describe or explain psychopathology must eventually deal with the topic of development. Development, however, is a complex concept.

While development always involves change, not all changes are developmental ones. Typically, developmentalists reserve the term "development" for application only to particular sets or types of changes. The specific changes held to be developmental ones vary in relation to different philosophical and theoretical positions or, in other words, models of development. Historically, definitions of development have been derived from "organismic" and "mechanistic" models (Lerner, 1976, 1986; Overton & Reese, 1973; Reese &

Overton, 1970). The organismic model is associated with conceptions of development that stress (1) movement toward a final end-state (i.e., teleology) and (2) the predetermined bases (usually hereditary or maturation in character) of developmental changes (e.g., Erikson, 1959; Freud, 1949; Gesell, 1946). The mechanistic model is associated with approaches to development that stress (1) the primacy of organism-extrinsic (e.g., environmental) determinants of behavior and (2) elementaristic influences (e.g., S-R units) that, through continuous, quantitative additions, shape behavior. These influences may be either proximal environmental events (e.g., conditioning processes; Bijou & Baer, 1961) or distal, macrosociological institutional effects (Meyer, 1988).

The history of the field of developmental psychology has seen, especially over the last two decades, increasing criticism of conceptions of development associated with organismic and mechanistic models. For instance, organismic conceptions have been criticized for philosophical

The writing of this chapter was supported in part by a grant to Richard M. Lerner and Jacqueline V. Lerner by the William T. Grant Foundation and by NIMH Grant MH39957.

problems associated with teleology (Nagel, 1957) and accordingly with a nonempirically supportable belief in unidirectionality in development (Baltes, 1987; Lerner & Kauffman, 1985); an empirically inappropriately rigid, nonplastic view of biological processes (Gollin, 1981; Gottlieb, 1970, 1983; R. M. Lerner, 1984; Tobach & Schneirla, 1968); a lack of needed attention to social, cultural, and historical variations in development (e.g., Bronfenbrenner, 1977, 1979); and an inappropriately pessimistic, too limited view of the potential for intervention to alter undesired or maladaptive behavior patterns (Baltes & Baltes, 1980; Brim & Kagan, 1980; R. M. Lerner, 1984). In turn, mechanistic conceptions have been criticized for a philosophical and theoretical elementarism and reductionism that have been inadequate to deal with qualitative changes across life (Piaget, 1950; von Bertalanffy, 1933, 1968); an inability to deal with phenomena at multiple levels of analysis (Riegel, 1975, 1976a, 1976b); and an inattention to the active, constructivist role of the person in his or her own development (Liben, 1981; Lerner, 1982; Lerner & Busch-Rossnagel, 1981).

Because of the philosophical, theoretical, and empirical problems with conceptions of development associated with the organismic and the mechanistic models, increasing attention has been given to other models, for example, dialectical and contextual ones (Lerner, Hultsch, & Dixon, 1983). Developmentalists have considered conceptions of development associated with these latter models (e.g., Dixon, 1986; Riegel, 1976a, 1976b). In addition, some developmentalists have forwarded conceptions involving integrations of ideas associated with two or more models (e.g., Overton, 1984). These latter, integrative efforts have attempted to overcome limitations of the respective models when they are employed separately. Through a synthesis of selected features of each model, attempts have been made to develop a potentially more useful concept of development.

Of increasing prominence over the last two decades has been an integrative perspective — developmental contextualism — involving a synthesis of the active organism in organicism and the active context in contextualism. This perspective, emphasizing the relation between person and context, conceives of development as involving systematic, successive, and "aptive"[1] (Gould & Vrba, 1982) changes within and across all life periods in the structure, function, and/or content of the person's mental (e.g., cognitive, emotional),

behavioral (e.g., activity level, threshold of responsivity), and interpersonal/social (e.g., approach-withdrawal, institutional affiliational) characteristics (R. M. Lerner, 1984; Lerner & Lerner, 1983).

This conception of development has direct import for the understanding of the development of psychopathology. Psychopathology is the malfunctioning of the human psychosocial system (Magnusson & Öhman, 1987). Thus, the development of psychopathology involves the emergence of unadaptive, or inadequate, characteristics in this psychosocial system. Therefore, from a developmental contextual perspective, psychopathology exists and develops when, and only when, an inadequate *relation* exists between psychological and social functioning: that is, between an individual and his or her context. Changes that do not involve this relation (or which are not systematic, successive, or aptive) are not developmental ones and, in addition, do not involve the development of psychopathology. It is a malfunctional person–context relation that defines psychopathology, therefore, and it is from the changing nature of this relation that either aptive or malaptive, and hence psychopathological, behaviors develop.

We should emphasize that this relational, developmental contextual view is compatable with those of other developmentalists studying psychopathology (e.g., Cicchetti, 1984, 1987; Magnusson, 1987; Magnusson & Öhman, 1987; Super, 1987; Wapner & Demick, 1988). To illustrate, Cicchetti (1987), writing about psychopathology during human infant development, notes that

> it is inappropriate to focus on discrete symptomatology to infer the presence of nascent or incipient infant psychopathology. Rather, disorders in infancy are best conceptualized as *relational psychopathologies*, that is, as consequences of dysfunction in the parent–child–environment system. (p. 837)

A similar stress on the relational and developmental contextual character of psychopathology is made by Super (1987), who considers "disorders of development as a class of phenomena that reveal something of the nature of our children and also of the nature of the worlds we make for them" (p. 2). Indeed, he notes that

> The settings, customs, and psychology of caretakers not only regulate the healthy emergence of human potential, they also shape the possibilities

of disorder. At every stage of the etiology, expression, course, intervention, and final outcome of developmental problems, human culture structures the experience and adjusts the odds. (Super, 1987, p. 7)

In a corresponding vein Öhman and Magnusson (1987) indicate that

any disease must be understood as resulting from a multiplicity of causal events spanning observational levels from biochemistry to sociology. Thus, any single-factor, linear causal model is unrealistic for understanding disease in general, and mental disorders in particular. Instead, multiple interacting causal factors that often change in their effect over time must be postulated. (p. 18) (See too Magnusson, 1987; Magnusson & Allen, 1983; Super & Harkness, 1982, 1986.)

Given, then, the apparent prominence of ideas pertinent to a developmental contextual perspective for understanding development across the life span and, for present purposes, the pertinence of this perspective for conceptualizing the developmental and relational bases of psychopathology, it is useful to discuss the features of developmental contextualism.

DEVELOPMENTAL CONTEXTUAL PERSPECTIVE

An interest in the context of human development has a long history in philosophy and social science (for reviews, see Dixon & Nesselroade, 1983; Kaplan, 1983). Contextualist philosophy (Pepper, 1942) was conceived of as an orientation that considered the import for human functioning of multiple, qualitatively distinct levels of existence — ranging from the individual through the sociocultural — all changing historically (Lerner et al., 1983). This philosophy began to attract increasing interest from psychologists during the late 1960s (e.g., see Bandura, 1978; Bronfenbrenner, 1977, 1979; Jenkins, 1974; Kuo, 1967; Mischel, 1977; Rosnow, 1983; Rosnow & Georgoudi, 1986; Rosnow & Rosenthal, 1984; Sarbin, 1977). One basis for this interest was the growing theoretical and empirical literature that suggested it was necessary to forgo an exclusively psychological analysis of individual development and, instead, seek explanations that emphasize the multilevel bases of human functioning *and* the connections among levels (e.g., Baltes, 1987; Bronfenbrenner, 1979; Elder, 1975; Kuo, 1967; J. V. Lerner, 1983; R. M. Lerner, 1984; Lerner &

Busch-Rossnagel, 1981; Novikoff, 1945a, 1945b; Magnusson & Allen, 1983; Tobach, 1981; Tobach & Greenberg, 1984).

Levels, in this literature, are conceived of as integrative organizations. That is,

the concept of integrative levels recognizes as equally essential for the purpose of scientific analysis both the isolation of parts of a whole and their integration into the structure of the whole. It neither reduces phenomena of a higher level to those of a lower one, as in mechanism, or describes the higher level in vague nonmaterial terms which are but substitutes for understanding, as in vitalism. Unlike other "holistic" theories, it never leaves the firm ground of material reality. . . . The concept points to the need to study the organizational interrelationships of parts and whole. (Novikoff, 1945a, p. 209)

Moreover, Tobach and Greenberg (1984) stress that

The interdependence among levels is of great significance. The dialectic nature of the relationship among levels is one in which lower levels are subsumed in higher levels so that any particular level is an integration of preceding levels. . . . In the process of integration, or fusion, *new* levels with their own characteristics result. (p. 2)

If the course of human development is the product of the processes involved in the "fusions" (or "dynamic interactions;" Lerner, 1978, 1979, 1984) among integrative levels of functioning, then the processes of development are more plastic than often previously believed (Brim & Kagan, 1980). That is, because the process of development is seen as emerging from individually distinct interactions between a changing person and his or her changing context, there exist multiple pathways (or potential person–context combinations) along which development may proceed.

To a great extent the developmental literature that suggests these ideas has been associated with the life-span view of human development (Baltes, 1987; R. M. Lerner, 1984; Lerner et al., 1983). Within this perspective, the context for development is not seen merely as a simple stimulus environment, but rather as an "ecological environment . . . conceived topologically as a nested arrangement of concentric structures, each contained within the next" (Bronfenbrenner, 1979, p. 22) and including variables from biological, psychological, physical, and sociocultural levels, all changing interdependently across history (Riegel, 1975, 1976a, 1976b). This life-span, ecological conception of development raised by developmental contextualism underscores the point made earlier regarding the relational nature of psychopathology: Behavior, either functional or malfunctional, develops as a consequence of historically and socioculturally moderated relations between people and their contexts. Thus, a temporal perspective is requisite for the understanding of psychopathology, given this historical embeddedness. As a consequence, both conceptually and methodologically, a longitudinal approach to the study of psychopathology is necessary to capture the temporality of psychopathological phenomena.

Not only must this longitudinal perspective encompass the life span, since change (history) is ceaseless, but it must be comparative as well. Comparisons must be made to nonpsychopathological developments, since both pathological and nonpathological developments are of the "same cloth," differing only in the person–context relational characteristics involved. In addition, then, comparisons must be made with other contextual conditions (e.g., proximal ones, such as family types, versus more distal ones, such as cultural mores), since such contextual conditions represent an important source of variation into the human psychosocial system (Magnusson & Öhman, 1987). Finally, the longitudinal perspective central to this set of ideas requires an age-comparative perspective, one that, as noted, involves the entire life span. From a developmental contextual perspective, one must ask what person variables (e.g., what biological attributes), in relation to what contextual variables (e.g., what family types, educational systems, or cultural standards), at what age levels (e.g., childhood, adolescence, adulthood) are associated with particular instances of pathological or nonpathological behaviors?

The longitudinal, life-span perspective associated with developmental contextualism leads to a concern with issues of the relations between evolution and ontogeny (given the idea of historical embeddedness), of life course constancy and change, of human plasticity (given the person–context relational character of development), and of the role the developing person plays in his or her own development (given the concern with the active organism and of its relation to an active context) (Baltes, 1987; Lerner, 1982; Lerner & Busch-Rossnagel, 1981; Scarr & McCartney, 1983; Tobach, 1981). These issues are linked by the idea that reciprocal relations (i.e., dynamic interactions: Lerner, 1978, 1979) between individuals and the multiple contexts within which they live characterize human development (Bronfenbrenner, 1979). Thus, all the issues raised by this perspective derive from a common appreciation of the basic role of the changing context in developmental change. It is the functional significance of this changing context that requires adoption of what Gottlieb (1970, 1983) termed a "probabilistic epigenetic" view of an organism's development.

Features of Probabilistic Epigenetic Development

Since its inception as a specialization within the discipline, developmental psychology — or, as it was initially termed, "genetic psychology" (e.g., Hall, 1904) — has been dominated by a biological model of change. Indeed, the concept of development is biological in its scientific origin (Harris, 1957; von Bertalanffy, 1933). Although the particular version of biological change that has influenced developmental psychology has been and remains Darwinian in character (White, 1968), this common heritage has nevertheless led to the formulation of quite diverse models of development (Dixon & Lerner, 1988). For instance, both the mechanistic conceptions of developmental change (e.g., Bijou, 1976; Bijou & Baer, 1961) and the organismic ones (e.g., Freud, 1949) noted earlier may be interpreted as derived from this Darwinian heritage (Dixon & Lerner, 1988).

However, despite this range of interpretations of the contribution of biology to psychological development, the organismic versions have been predominant in developmental psychology, and in fact have been termed "strong" developmental models (e.g., Reese & Overton, 1970). Thus, to the field of psychology in general, and perhaps to the scholarly community as a whole, the organismic theories of Freud (1949), Erikson (1959), and Piaget (1950) are typically held to be the classic, prototypic, or exemplary ones within developmental psychology (e.g., see Emmerich, 1968; Lerner, 1976, 1986).

These instances of organismic theory, especially those of Freud and of Erikson, have been labeled predetermined epigenetic (Gottlieb, 1983). As indicated, in this type of theory biology is seen as the prime mover of development: Intrinsic (e.g., maturational) changes are seen to essentially unfold, and although environmental or experiential variables may speed up or slow down these progressions they can do nothing to alter the sequence or quality (e.g., the structure) of these hereditarily predetermined changes (e.g., see Gesell, 1946; Hamburger, 1957).

However, another view of biological functioning exists, one that sees biological and contextual factors as reciprocally interactive; as such, developmental changes are probabilistic in respect to normative outcomes, due to variation in the timing of the biological, psychological, and social factors that provide interactive bases of ontogenetic progressions (e.g., Schneirla, 1957; Tobach, 1981). It is this probabilistic epigenetic (Gottlieb, 1983) view of development that is represented by the developmental contextual perspective and that provides the theoretical underpinning of the life-span view of human development (Lerner & Kauffman, 1985).

In essence, a probabilistic epigenetic formulation emphasizes not the intrinsically predetermined or inevitable timetables and outcomes of development; instead, such a formulation stresses that the influence of the changing context on development is to make the trajectory of development less certain with respect to the applicability of norms to the individual (Gottlieb, 1970, 1983; Tobach, 1981). Thus, such a conception emphasizes the probabilistic character of development and in so doing admits of more plasticity in development than do predeterministic conceptions. Indeed, the term probabilistic epigenesis was used by Gottlieb

> to designate the view that the behavior development of individuals within a species does not follow an invariant or inevitable course, and, more specifically, that the sequence or outcome of individual behavioral development is probable (with respect to norms) rather than certain. (Gottlieb, 1970, p. 123)

Moreover, Gottlieb explains that this probable, and not certain, character of individual development arises because

> Probabilistic epigenesis necessitates a bidirectional structure-function hypothesis. The conventional version of the structure-function hypothesis is unidirectional in the sense that structure is supposed to determine function in an essentially nonreciprocal relationship. . . . The bidirectional version of the structure–function relationship is a logical consequence of the view that the course and outcome of behavioral epigenesis is probabilistic: It entails the assumption of reciprocal effects in the relationship between structure and function whereby function (exposure to stimulation and/or movement of muscu-

loskeletal activity) can significantly modify the development of the peripheral and central structures that are involved in these events. (Gottlieb, 1970, p. 123)

This bidirectional relation between structure and function denoted by the concept of probabilistic epigenesis implies that a developmental contextual perspective promotes a very dynamic view of the nature of organism–context relations. Given the bidirectionality involved in developmental contextualism, a general assumption is that the functional significance of behavior and of any particular developmental trajectory lies neither in the organism nor in the context; rather, it is the nature of the relation, of the interaction, between person and context that establishes the meaning for aptation of any given behavior or developmental pattern. As we have noted already, for the understanding of psychopathology, this conception indicates that neither psychopathology nor nonpsychopathology are attributes of either people or contexts. Rather, it is the nature of the interaction between these two elements of the human psychosocial system that provides a given behavior with its functional significance. The developmental contextual notion of interaction is, therefore, quite an important one to consider.

Role of "Interaction"

A developmental contextual perspective captures the complexity of a multilevel context: (1) without ignoring the active role of the organism in shaping, as well as being shaped by, the context; and (2) without sacrificing commitment to useful prescriptive, universal principles of developmental change. These two foci are integrated within the contextual orientation at the level of the presumed *relation* between organismic and contextual processes. The developmental contextual conceptualization of this relation differs substantially from those of the organismic and mechanistic perspectives (Lerner, 1985). That is, a *strong* concept of organism–environment interaction (Lerner & Spanier, 1978, 1980; Overton, 1973), transaction (Sameroff, 1975), or dynamic interaction (Lerner, 1978, 1979) is associated with probabilistic epigenesis. As suggested already, this version of interaction stresses that organism and context are always embedded each in the other (Lerner et al., 1983), that the context is composed of multiple levels changing interdependently across time (i.e., historically), and that because organisms influence the context that influences them, they are efficacious in playing an active role in their own development (Lerner & Busch-Rossnagel, 1981; Tobach, 1981).

Moreover, because of the mutual embeddedness of organism and context, a given organismic attribute will have different implications for developmental outcomes in the milieu of different contextual conditions; this relationship arises because the organismic attribute is only given its functional meaning by virtue of its relation to a specific context. If the context changes significantly, as it may over time, then the same organismic attribute will have a different import for development. Embedded in one social context, a psychopathological condition may develop; yet in another contextual situation, the same organismic characteristics may result in healthy or aptive psychological development. In turn, of course, the same contextual condition will lead to alternative developments in that different organisms interact with it. To state this position in somewhat stronger terms, a given organismic attribute only has meaning for psychological development by virtue of its timing of interaction (i.e., its relation to a particular set of time-bound, contextual conditions). In turn, the import of any set of contextual conditions for psychosocial behavior and development can only be understood by specifying the context's relations to the specific, developmental features of the organisms within it. This central role for the timing of organism–context interactions in the determination of the nature and outcomes of development is, of course, the probabilistic component of probabilistic epigenesis (Gottlieb, 1970; Kuo, 1967; Scarr, 1982; Scarr & McCartney, 1983; Tobach, 1981). But, what does such probabilism mean for the ways in which individuals can, through influencing their context, produce their own development? More important, for the ultimate worth of the developmental contextual view of development and, for present purposes, for understanding the developmental character of psychopathology, we may ask what such probabilism means for the empirical study of psychopathology.

To address these issues we should reiterate that taking the probabilistic character of development seriously means focusing on the relation between organism and context and not on either element in the relation per se. The context enveloping a person is composed of, for example, a specific physical ecology and the other individually different and developing people with whom the person interacts (e.g., parents and peers). This context is as unique and changing as is the person lawfully, individually distinct as a consequence of his or her particular genotype-environment interaction history. One cannot say completely in advance what particular features of the context will exist at a specific time in a given person's life. As a consequence, it is possible only to speak probabilistically of the effects that a given person may have on his or her context, of the feedback the person is likely to receive from the context, and of the nature of the person's development that will therefore ensue.

Thus, the probabilism of development represents a formidable challenge for theory and research. To gain understanding of how people may influence their own development, and of their relations to a changing, multilevel context, we obviously need to do more than just have a conceptualization of the nature of individual characteristics or processes. In addition, we need to conceptualize and operationalize the features of the context, or of the ecology, wherein significant interactions occur for the person. Next, we must devise some means, some model, by which personological and contextual features may be integrated. Then, a last and by no means unidimensional task, is to translate all this conceptualization into methodologically sound, longitudinal research.

There is no laboratory within which all the preceding tasks have been fully accomplished. However, progress has been made in developing models with which such tasks have begun to be addressed. Data pertinent to the models derive from work in several laboratories, and in now presenting the general features of some of these models, some of this research is noted. The findings from this research underscore quite clearly the relational and comparative features of the development of psychopathology about which we have spoken.

MODELS OF PERSON–CONTEXT INTERACTION

Both life-span developmental and ecological developmental psychologists have described several intraindividual, interindividual, familial, social network, sociocultural, and historical variables presumed to be involved in the dynamic interactional processes described within developmental contextualism (e.g., Baltes, 1987; Bronfenbrenner, 1979; Featherman & Lerner, 1985; R. M. Lerner, 1984; Riegel, 1976a, 1976b; Schneirla, 1957). The resulting view of the range of the variables involved in development and of complexity of interrelations among them, is — to say the least — formidable. One depiction of this complexity, shown in Figure 2.1, represents well in our view the integrated and interdependent, that is, dynamically interactive, levels of organization first spoken of by Novikoff (1945a, 1945b), developed further by Schneirla and his collaborators (e.g., Lehrman, 1970; Tobach, 1981; Tobach & Schneirla, 1968; Schneirla, 1956, 1957), and elaborated within developmental psychology by proponents of the lifespan perspective (e.g., Baltes, 1987; Featherman, 1983, 1985; Lerner, 1976, 1984, 1986; Lerner & Kauffman, 1985).

To illustrate the empirical use in the extant developmental literature of the conception of integrative, dynamically interactive levels depicted in Figure 2.1, let us draw on two examples of pertinence to developmentalists; one involves characteristics of behavioral individuality, in regard to behavioral style or temperament, and the other involves characteristics of physical individuality, in regard to physical maturation and physical attractiveness. In regard to temperament, the child development literature contains studies examining the relation, within the child, between temperament and other characteristics of individuality, such as personality (Buss & Plomin, 1975) or cognitive status variables (such as "social referencing;" Campos, 1980–81; Feinman & Lewis, 1983). In turn, other studies examine how the child's temperamental individuality influences the parent-child (typically the mother-child relationship (Crockenberg, 1981) and/or the mother's emotional adjustment (Brazelton, Koslowski, & Main, 1974). Such studies provide data constituting "child effects" on their significant others — others that, to developmental psychologists (Belsky et al., 1984), represent a component of the child's context, here an interpersonal one. These studies comprise one portion of the bidirectional effects (here of child→parent) discussed in the child development literature (e.g., Bell, 1974; Belsky, 1984; Belsky et al., 1984; Lerner & Spanier, 1978; Lewis & Rosenblum, 1974; Scarr & McCartney, 1983).

These child→parent studies stand in contrast to those that examine how parental characteristics — such as temperament (Thomas, Chess, & Birch, 1970), demands or expectations placed on the child regarding the child's temperament (Thomas, Chess, Sillen, & Mendez, 1974), or cognitive status (e.g., stage of cognitive development; Sameroff, 1975) — influence the child; such studies are parent→child ones, and provide the other direction of effect to complement child→parent studies. Other studies in the temperament literature examine the influence of the parent's social network on the child's temperament, on the mother's characteristics, or on the parent-child relationship (e.g., Crockenberg, 1981); in turn, some studies examine how children with different temperaments "produce" different responses in their social (e.g., school) network (East, Lerner, & Lerner, 1988). Still other studies examine how child-temperament↔parent-demand relations vary in relation to their embeddedness in different social classes or communities (Thomas et al., 1974) or in different cultural settings (Super & Harkness, 1981).

Together, these temperament studies indicate that the relation between a given temperament attribute of the child (e.g., sleep arrhythmicity or high activity level) and problem behaviors or, in the extreme, psychopathology is not universal. In turn, any given feature of the context (e.g., particular family types, such as authoritarian or permissive ones) are also not linked invariably to disorders. Instead, this literature indicates that the presence of psychopathology depends on the relation between particular temperament attributes and such contextual factors as the meaning or interpretation of temperament maintained by a child's parents or teachers (Thomas & Chess, 1977), the demands or expectations regarding temperament prevalent in a given societal or cultural setting (Super & Harkness, 1981), the social support network within which the child-mother relation is embedded (Crockenberg, 1981), and the parent's pattern of embeddedness in nonfamilial social interactions (e.g., as occurs with mothers employed outside the home; Lerner & Galambos, 1985).

To illustrate the representation of the developmental contextual perspective found in Figure 2.1 in regard to characteristics of physical individuality, let us focus on a variable — menarche — that has been a central one in the study of biological-psychosocial interrelations in early adolescence (Brooks-Gunn & Peterson, 1983; Hamburg, 1974; Petersen, 1983; Ruble, 1977; Ruble & Brooks-Gunn, 1982). The adolescent developmental literature contains studies examining the relation, within-the-person, of menarche (e.g., whether it occurs early, on time, or late) and other characteristics of individuality, as for example, perceptions of self (Tobin-Richards, Boxer, & Petersen, 1983),

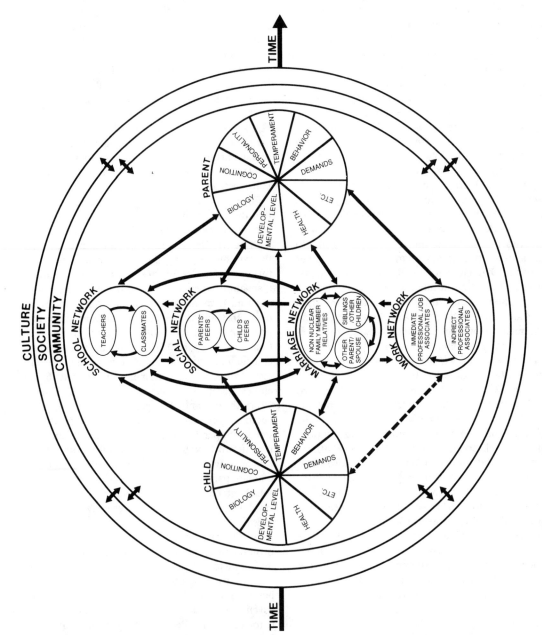

Figure 2.1. A dynamic interactional model of child and parent development (Lerner, 1986).

cognition (Hamburg, 1974; Petersen, 1983), or the experience of menstrual discomfort (Brooks-Gunn & Ruble, 1980). In turn, other studies examine how the occurrence of menarche influences a girl's relations with the significant others in her context (for example, with her parents and/or her peers) (e.g., Brooks-Gunn & Matthews, 1979; Lynch, 1981; Simmons, Blyth, & McKinney, 1983; Westney, Jenkins, & Benjamin, 1983). Such studies provide data constituting "adolescent effects" on that portion of their social context composed of significant others, and as such comprise one portion of the bidirectional effects (here an adolescent→social context one) discussed in this literature (e.g., Belsky et al., 1984; Lerner & Spanier, 1978; Petersen & Taylor, 1980).

These "adolescent→social context" studies stand in contrast to those that examine how contextual features—like parental demands regarding desired behavior in their adolescent children (e.g., Anthony, 1969; Windle et al., 1986), continuities or discontinuities in school structure (Blyth, Simmons, & Bush, 1978; Hamburg, 1974; Simmons, Blyth, Van Cleave, & Bush, 1979), or cultural beliefs regarding menstruation (Brooks-Gunn & Ruble, 1980; Ruble & Brooks-Gunn, 1979)—influence the adolescent undergoing the biopsychosocial transition of menarche. Such studies are social context→adolescent ones, and provide the other direction of effect to complement the adolescent→social context one.

Still other studies in the adolescent development literature examine how adolescent menarche ↔social context relations (e.g., in regard to adolescents and their peers) vary in relation to their embeddedness in more molar levels of the context, such as different social classes (e.g., Hamburg, 1974; Simmons, Brown, Bush, & Blyth, 1978), cultures (Hamburg, 1974; Lerner, Iwawaki, Chihara, & Sorell, 1980; Mussen & Bouterline-Young, 1964; Paige, 1983), or historical eras (Elder, 1974).

The import of these studies in regard to developmental contextualism is that an attribute of biological/physical individuality—as represented by menarche—does not exert a direct link to problematic or disordered behaviors. Rather, whether such a linkage exists depends on contextual conditions. For example, when a female adolescent undergoes a transition in social institutions (e.g., from elementary school to junior high school), at the same time she is experiencing menarche she is at enhanced risk for low self-esteem and for a diminution in academic performance (Simmons et

al., 1979, 1987). In turn, when a girl experiencing menarche is in a particular type of peer group (an athletically competitive one, as compared to an athletically noncompetitive one), she is at greater risk for eating disorders (Brooks-Gunn, 1987). Finally, when the adolescent is embedded in a culture having a negative belief system regarding the meaning of menarche, she is at greater risk for experiencing dysmenorrhea (Ruble & Brooks-Gunn, 1982).

In summary, several of the interrelations illustrated in the model in Figure 2.1 are found in the extant literature on behavioral and physical individuality. While relatively few of the studies in this literature assess both directions of relation between one component (or level) of the model and another (Bell, 1974; Lewis & Lee-Painter, 1974), the bidirectionality of relations discussed in this literature (e.g., Bell, 1974; Belsky et al., 1984; Lerner & Spanier, 1978; Lewis & Rosenblum, 1974) emerges when studies are integrated within a representation like the one presented in Figure 2.1. Furthermore, by helping to integrate extant studies of the person-context relational character of development, the model also points to other instances of such relations that are uninvestigated but that may be of potential importance.

Such use of the aforementioned model for furthering research points out other features of the model that should be stressed. It probably would not be useful or even possible to do research testing the model as a whole. Instead, this or similar representations (e.g., Baltes, 1987) of person-context relations can guide the selection of individual and ecological variables in one's research and provide parameters about the generalizability of one's findings. That is, this representation should serve as a reminder that we need to consider whether the results of a given study may be generalized beyond the particular individual and ecological variable studied herein and applied to other community, societal, cultural, and historical contexts.

To illustrate how the model of Figure 2.1 may be used as a guide for the selection of variables from the individual and contextual levels depicted (i.e., the interpersonal and physical features of the settings within which one lives), we may show how our own research is based on selected components of the model. In Figure 2.2 the "restricted" or "reduced" model used in our research on individual context relations is shown.

The studies we have conducted have focused on how the demands regarding characteristics of be-

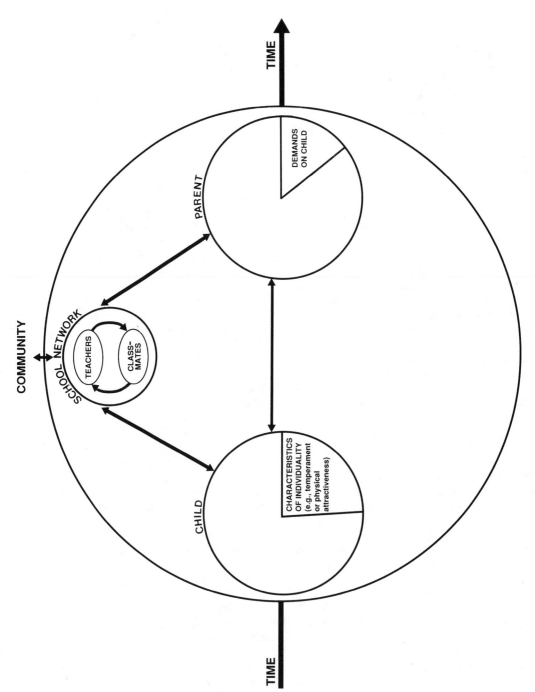

Figure 2.2. The variables and levels of analysis studied in the child temperament–social context research of Lerner and Lerner (1987).

avioral or physical individuality (e.g., temperament or physical attractiveness, respectively) held by a child's or an adolescent's parents, teachers, or peers are associated with different levels of aptation, or adjustment, among children with various repertoires of temperamental individuality or characteristics of physical attractiveness (e.g., East, Lerner, & Lerner, 1988; J. Lerner, 1983; Lerner, Lerner, & Zabski, 1985; Lerner, Delaney, Hess, Jovanovic, & von Eye, 1988; Lerner, Lerner, Jovanovic, Schwab, Talwar, Hess, & Kucher, 1988; Talwar, Nitz, & Lerner, 1988; Talwar, Schwab, & Lerner, 1989; Windle et al., 1986). The rationale for this focus derives from our interest in testing a model derived from the conception of integrated, dynamically interactive levels represented in Figure 2.1. This derived notion is termed the "goodness-of-fit" model, and we believe this model is particularly useful for understanding the relational conditions involved in the development of either psychopathological and/or nonpsychopathological behaviors. It is useful, then, to turn to a presentation of this model.

GOODNESS-OF-FIT MODEL

Although there exist several different theoretical models associated with the developmental contextual perspective, one model has received extensive attention within psychology, education, and psychiatry. This notion—the goodness-of-fit model of person–context relations—is derived from the view that the person–context interactions depicted within developmental contextualism involve "circular functions" (Schneirla, 1957). These functions are person-context relations predicated on others' reactions to a person's characteristics of individuality: As a consequence of their characteristics of physical and behavioral individuality people evoke differential reactions in their significant others; these reactions constitute feedback to people and influence their further interactions (and thus their ensuing development). The "goodness-of-fit" concept allows the valence of the feedback involved in these circular functions to be understood (Lerner & Lerner, 1983, 1987; Thomas & Chess, 1977).

It is through the establishment of such functions in ontogeny that people may be conceived of as producers of their own development (Lerner & Busch-Rossnagel, 1981). However, this circular functions idea needs to be extended. In and of itself the notion is mute regarding the specific characteristics of the feedback (for example, its

positive or negative valence) a child will receive as a consequence of its individuality. What may provide a basis of the feedback?

Just as a child brings his or her singular characteristics to a particular social setting, there are demands placed on the child by virtue of the physical and/or by the social components (i.e., by the significant others) in the setting (Lerner & Lerner, 1983). According to Super and Harkness (1981), the developing person's context is structured by three kinds of influences: the physical and social setting, culturally regulated customs involved in socialization, and the "psychology" of the caregivers or the other significant people with whom the developing person interacts. This psychology is termed an "ethnotheory" (Super & Harkness, 1980, 1981, 1988), that is, significant others' beliefs, attitudes, expectations, or values regarding the meaning or significance of particular behaviors. Together, the three types of influence comprise the *developmental niche* of a person, that is, the set (or sets) of structured demands on the developing person (Super & Harkness, 1981). It is these demands that provide the functional significance for a given characteristic of individuality; if congruent with the demands of a significant other (e.g., a parent), this characteristic should produce a positive adjustment (aptation). If that same attribute is incongruent with such demands, a negative adjustment would be expected.

To illustrate, consider the case of the child in a family context and of the psychosocial and physical climate promoted by the parents. Parents can vary in their cognitive and behavioral attributes (e.g., in regard to their child-rearing attitudes and parenting styles; Baumrind, 1971); parents can vary, too, in the physical features of the home they provide. These parent-based psychosocial and physical characteristics constitute presses for, or demands on, the child for adaptation. Simply, parent characteristics are "translated" or "transduced" into demand on the child.

The child's individuality in differentially meeting these demands provides a basis for the feedback he or she receives from the socializing environment. For example, considering the demand "domain" of attitudes, values, or expectations, teachers and parents may have relatively individual and distinct expectations about behaviors desired of their students and children, respectively. Teachers may want students who show little distractibility; since they would not want attention diverted from a lesson by the activity of children in the classroom. Parents, however, might desire their children to be moderately distractible—for example, when they require their children to move from television watching to the dinner table or to bed. Children whose behavioral individuality was either generally distractible or generally not distractible would thus differentially meet the demands of these two contexts.

Similarly, Parke (1978) has argued that the attitudes, values, and expectations for behavior held by a child's significant others represent a highly important basis for interaction. According to Parke (1978), the same behavior from a child may have a very different meaning in various settings, and this difference may reflect the demand structure of the context, a structure comprised in part of attitudes, values, and expectations. Thus, attitudes, values, or expectations about particular child behaviors—or, in the terms of Super and Harkness (1981), the ethnotheory about particular behaviors—represent one set of contextual demands to which children must adjust if they are to meet successfully the challenges present in their world. In other words, problems of adjustment to school demands or to home demands might thus develop as a consequence of a child's lack of match, or "goodness of fit," in either or both settings.

There is both laboratory and clinical evidence that supports the use of the goodness-of-fit model in understanding the bases of healthy and unhealthy developmental patterns. Let us turn to a review of this literature.

Tests of the Goodness-of-Fit Model

Much of the research literature supporting the use of the goodness-of-fit model is derived either directly from the Thomas and Chess (1977) New York Longitudinal Study (NYLS) of the functional significance of temperament, or is associated with independent research that has adopted their conceptualization of temperament. Temperament in this literature has been conceived of as behavioral style—that is, how a child does whatever it does (Thomas & Chess, 1977). For example, because all children engage in eating, sleeping, and toileting behaviors, the absence or presence of such contents of the behavior repertoire would not differentiate among them. But whether these behaviors occur with regularity (i.e., rhythmically), or with a lot of or a little intensity, might serve to differentiate among children. We consider first the contribution of the NYLS data set.

The NYLS

Within the NYLS data set, information relevant to the goodness-of-fit model exists as a consequence of the multiple samples present in the project. First, the NYLS core sample is composed of 133 white, middle-class children of professional parents. This sample, which was studied originally in 1956, is still being followed at this writing. In addition, a sample of 98 New York City Puerto Rican children of working-class parents has been followed for about 14 years. Each sample subject was studied from at least the first month of life onward. Although the distribution of temperamental attributes in the two samples was not different, the import of the attributes for psychosocial adjustment was quite disparate. Two examples may suffice to illustrate this distinction.

First to be considered is the impact of low regularity or rhythmicity of behavior, particularly in regard to sleep-wake cycles. The Puerto Rican parents studied by Thomas and Chess (1977; Thomas, Chess, Sillen, & Mendez, 1974) were very permissive. No demands in regard to rhythmicity of sleep were placed on the infant or child. Indeed, the parents allowed the child to go to sleep any time the child desired, and permitted the child to awaken any time as well. The parents molded their schedule around the children. Because parents were so accommodating, there were no problems of fit associated with an arrhythmic infant or child. Indeed, neither within the infancy period nor throughout the first five years of life did arrhythmicity predict adjustment problems. In this sample arrhythmicity remained continuous and independent of aptive implications for the child (Korn, 1978; Thomas et al., 1974).

In white, middle-class families, however, strong demands for rhythmic sleep patterns were maintained. Thus, an arrhythmic child did not fit with parental demands, and consistent with the goodness-of-fit model, arrhythmicity was a major predictor of problem behaviors both within the infancy years and across time through the first five years of life (Korn, 1978; Thomas et al., 1974).

It should be emphasized that there are at least two ways of viewing this finding. First, consistent with the idea that children influence their parents, it may be noted that sleep arrhythmicity in their children resulted in problems in the parents [(e.g., reports of stress, anxiety, anger (Chess & Thomas, 1984; Thomas et al., 1974)]. Such an effect of child temperament on the parent's own level of adjustment has been reported in other data sets wherein, for instance, infants who had high thresholds for responsiveness to social stimulation and thus were not soothed easily by their mothers evoked intense distress reactions in their mothers and a virtual cessation of maternal caregiving behaviors (Brazelton et al., 1974). Therefore, it is possible that the presence of such child effects in the NYLS sample could have altered previous parenting styles in a way that constituted feedback to the child that was associated with the development of problem behaviors in him or her.

In turn, a second interpretation of this finding arises from the fact that problem behaviors in the children were identified initially on the basis of parent reports. It may be that irrespective of any problem behavior evoked in the parent by the child and/or of any altered parent-child interactions that thereby ensued, one effect of the child on the parent was to increase the probability of the parent labeling the child's temperamental style as problematic and reporting it to the NYLS staff psychiatrist. Unfortunately, the current state of analysis of the NYLS data does not allow us to discriminate between these obviously nonmutually exclusive possibilities.

However, the data in the NYLS do allow us to indicate that the parents in the middle-class sample took steps to change their arrhythmic children's sleep patterns, and as most of these arrhythmic children were also adaptable, low rhythmicity tended to be discontinuous for most children. That the parent behaved to modify their child's arrhythmicity is also an instance of a child effect on its psychosocial context. That is, the child "produced" in his or her parents alterations in parental caregiving behaviors regarding sleep. That these "child effects" on the parental context fed back to the child and influence his or her further development is consistent with the finding that sleep arrhythmicity was discontinuous among these children.

Thus, in the middle-class sample early infant arrhythmicity tended to be a problem during this time of life but proved to be neither continuous nor predictive of later problems of adjustment. In turn, in the Puerto Rican sample, infant arrhythmicity was not a problem during this time of life but was continuous and—because in this context it was not involved in poor fit—was not associated with adjustment problems in the child in the first five years of life. Of course, this is not to say that the parents in the Puerto Rican families were not affected by their children's sleep arrhythmicity; as was the case with the parents in the middle-class families, it may be that the Puerto Rican parents

had problems of fatigue and/or suffered marital or work-related problems due to irregular sleep patterns produced in them as a consequence of their child's sleep arrhythmicity. However, the current nature of data analysis in the NYLS does not allow an investigation of this possible "child effect" on the Puerto Rican parents.

However, the data do underscore the importance of considering fit with the demands of the psychosocial context of development by indicating that arrhythmicity did begin to predict adjustment problems for the Puerto Rican children when they entered the school system. Their lack of a regular sleep pattern interfered with their obtaining sufficient sleep to perform well in school and, in addition, often caused them to be late to school (Korn, 1978; Thomas et al., 1974). Thus, before age 5 only one Puerto Rican child presented a clinical problem diagnosed as a sleep disorder. However, almost 50% of the Puerto Rican children who developed clinically identifiable problems between ages 5 and 9 were diagnosed as having sleep problems.

Another example may be given to illustrate how the differential demands existing between the two family contexts provide different presses for aptation. This example pertains to differences in the demands of the physical contexts of the families.

As noted by Thomas et al. (1974), as well as by Korn (1978), overall there was a very low incidence of behavior problems in the Puerto Rican sample children in their first 5 years of life, especially when compared to the corresponding incidence among the core sample children. However, if a problem was presented at this time among the Puerto Rican sample, it was most likely to be a problem of motor activity. In fact, across the first nine years of their lives, of those Puerto Rican children who developed clinical problems, 53% were diagnosed as exhibiting problematic motor activity. Parents complained of excessive and uncontrollable motor activity in such cases. However, in the core sample's clinical group only one child (a child with brain damage) was characterized in this way. It may be noted here that the Puerto Rican parents' reports of "excessive and uncontrollable" activity in their children does constitute, in this group, an example of a child effect on the parents. That is, a major value of the Puerto Rican parents in the NYLS was child "obedience" to authority (Korn, 1978). The type of motor activity shown by the highly active children of these parents evoked considerable distress in them, given their perception that their children's behavior was inconsistent with what would be expected of obedient children (Korn, 1978).

Of course, if the middle-class parents had seen their children's behavior as excessive and uncontrollable, it may be that—irrespective of any major salience placed on the value of child obedience—problems would have been evoked in the middle-class parents, and feedback to the child, derived from such an evocation, would have ensued. Thus, an issue remains as to why the same (high) activity level should evoke one set of appraisals among the Puerto Rican parents but another set among the middle-class parents (i.e., in the latter group no interpretation of "excessive and uncontrollable" behavior was evoked). Similarly, it may be asked why high activity level is highly associated with problem behavior in the Puerto Rican children and not in the middle-class children. The key information needed to address these issues may be related to the *physical* features of the respective groups' homes.

In the Puerto Rican sample, the families usually had several children and lived in small apartments. Even average motor activity tended to impinge on others in the setting. Moreover, and as an illustration of the embeddedness of the child-temperament-home-context relation in the broader community context (see Figures 2.1 and 2.2), it may be noted that even in the case of the children with high activity levels, the Puerto Rican parents were reluctant to let their children out of the apartment because of the actual danger of playing on the streets of East Harlem. In the core sample, however, the parents had the financial resources to provide large apartments or houses for their families. There were typically suitable play areas for the children both inside and outside the home. As a consequence, the presence of high activity levels in the homes of the core sample did not cause the problems for interaction that they did in the Puerto Rican group. Thus, as Thomas et al. (1968, 1974) emphasize, the mismatch between temperamental attribute and physical environmental demand accounted for the group difference in the import of high activity level for the development of behavioral problems in the children.

In sum, data from the NYLS are not fully consonant with the methodology required for a direct and complete test of the goodness-of-fit model. For example, measures of temperament were not directly related to measures of the context. However, in spite of such limitations, the NYLS data set provides results compatible with the goodness-of-fit model. One may conclude from the NYLS data

that it is the relation between individual and context which constitutes the basis of either a psychopathologic or a nonpsychopathologic behavior. Data independent of the NYLS, from our own laboratory, lend additional support to this conclusion.

Research from the Lerner and Lerner laboratory

Lerner, Lerner, and their students, have tested the goodness-of-fit model quite extensively, and this work has been summarized in several articles and chapters (e.g., J. V. Lerner, 1984; J. V. Lerner & R. M. Lerner, 1983; Lerner & Lerner, 1987, 1989; Lerner et al., 1986; Windle & Lerner, 1986; Windle et al., 1986). Here, then, it may be necessary to present only briefly some recently obtained findings, ones derived from the Lerner and Lerner Pennsylvania Early Adolescent Transitions Study (PEATS), a short-term longitudinal study of approximately 150 northwestern Pennsylvania early adolescents, studied from the beginning of sixth grade across the transition to junior high school and to the end of the seventh grade.

In one study derived from the PEATS, East, Lerner, and Lerner (1988) determined the overall fit between adolescents' temperament and the demands of their peers regarding desired levels of temperament. Based on the circular functions notion involved in the goodness-of-fit model, East et al. predicted that while no significant direct paths would exist between adjustment and either temperament, measured alone, or temperament-demands fit, fit would influence adolescent-peer social relations, which, in turn, would influence adjustment; in short, significant mediated paths, but insignificant direct paths, were expected. These expectations were supported. For 9 of the 12 measures of adjustment employed (involving parents' ratings of behavior problems; teachers' ratings of scholastic competence, social acceptance, athletic competence, conduct adequacy, and physical appearance; and students' self-ratings of scholastic competence, social acceptance, athletic competence, conduct adequacy, physical appearance, and self-worth), both of the two mediated paths (between adolescent-peer group fit and peer relations, and then between peer relations and adjustment) were significant; in no case, however, was a significant direct path found. Figure 2.3 presents diagrammatically one representative finding, involving the adjustment outcome of self-rated (or perceived) self-worth, from the East et al. (1988) study.

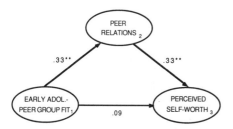

Figure 2.3. Path analysis of early adolescent-peer group fit, peer relations, and perceived self-worth. Higher scores reflect a good fit, positive peer relations, and favorable perceived self-worth.

Nitz, Lerner, Lerner, and Talwar (1989) found similar results regarding temperamental fit with parental demands and adolescent adjustment. Although at the beginning of sixth grade the number of significant relations between the adjustment measures and temperament-demands fit did not exceed the number of significant relations between temperamental alone and adjustment, at both the middle and the end of sixth grade the percentage of significant relations between fit and adjustment scores was significantly greater than the corresponding percentages involving temperament alone. Moreover, and underscoring the interconnections among the child-family relation and the other key contexts comprising the ecology of human development, Nitz et al. found virtually interchangeable results when fit scores with the peer demands were considered.

In a related study, Talwar, Nitz, and Lerner (in press) found that poor fit with parental demands (especially in regard to the attributes of mood and approach-withdrawal) at the end of sixth grade was associated in seventh grade with low teacher-related academic and social competence and negative peer relations. Corresponding relations were found in regard to fit with peer demands. Moreover, and again underscoring the importance of considering the context within which organismic characteristics are expressed, goodness-of-fit scores (between temperament and demands) were more often associated with adjustment than were temperament scores alone; this was true in regard to both peer and parent contexts at the end of sixth grade, and for the peer context after the transition to junior high school (at the beginning of seventh grade). Finally, Talwar et al. grouped the PEATS subjects into high versus low overall fit groups. Adolescents in the low-fit group in regard to peer demands received lower teacher ratings of scholastic competence, and more parent ratings

for conduct and school problems, than did the adolescents in the high-fit group in regard to peer demands. Comparable findings were found in regard to groups formed on the basis of low versus high fit with parent demands.

In a related temperament study, Talwar, Schwab, and Lerner (1989) assessed whether the links among temperament and the PEATS subjects' academic competence, as indexed by grade point average (GPA) and by standardized achievement test scores on the California Achievement Test, Form C (CAT/C), are (1) direct ones or (2) are mediated by social appraisals (by the teacher) of the adolescent's scholastic competence and by the adolescent's appraisal of his or her own scholastic competence. From a developmental contextual perspective, these latter links would be expected to be significant. In turn, however, within a personological, acontextual view of temperament-psychosocial functioning relations (Plomin & Daniels, 1984; Sheldon, 1940, 1942), only a direct link (or path) between temperament and academic competence should exist.

Talwar et al. used data from the end of the sixth grade and the end of the seventh grade to test these alternative models of the functional significance of temperament. In addition to the adolescents' self-ratings of temperament several other measures of the adolescents were used. Their grade point averages for the sixth and for the seventh grades; their total CAT/C scores for the sixth grade; teachers' ratings of the subjects' scholastic competence, on the Teacher Behavior Rating Scale (Harter, 1983); and the subject's ratings of their scholastic competence, on the Harter (1983) Self-Perception Profile were involved in these data analyses.

For the purpose of data reduction, the nine temperament variables measured on the Revised Dimensions of Temperament Survey (DOTS-R; Windle & Lerner, 1986) were first factor analyzed. Three second-order factors emerged. Factor 1 was labeled task rhythmicity, and was composed of the four DOTS-R attributes of task orientation and rhythmicity in eating, in sleeping, and in daily habits. The second factor was labeled activity, and was composed of the two DOTS-R attributes of sleep activity level and of general activity level. The third factor was labeled adaptation, and was composed of the three DOTS-R attributes of flexibility, approach behaviors, and positive mood.

Analyses subsequent to this factor analysis resulted in corresponding findings for all three of the temperament factors. For instance, the temperament factor of adaptation was correlated significantly with GPA and CAT/C scores at the end of grade 6 and with GPA at the end of grade 7. However, these correlations were not found to be the outcome of the direct influence of adaptation on academic competence. Using the path analytic procedures illustrated in Figure 2.4, Talwar et al. compared (1) the direct link between temperament and academic competence with (2) the indirect paths that included the teacher's rating of scholastic competence and the adolescent's self conception of his or her scholastic functioning. The data indicated that there were no significant paths between adaptation and either GPA or CAT/C scores. However, significant paths were found between this temperament factor, teacher ratings, self-ratings, and GPA and CAT/C scores at the end of grade 6. Corresponding findings involving GPA occurred at the end of grade 7. In respect to the task rhythmicity and the activity factors, indirect paths were also found between these factors, adolescent self-ratings, and the outcome measures of GPA and CAT/C scores. As with the adaptation factor, no direct paths were found between these latter two temperament factors and either GPA and CAT/C scores at either grade level. These findings, then, lend further support to the developmental contextual view of the nature of the relation between adolescent temperament and psychological characteristics: Links between temperament and adjustment are contingent on the character of the prevalent temperament-context relations. Positive adjustment ensues from good person-context fits; negative adjustment follows from poor fits.

Moreover, to illustrate that support for the developmental contextual, goodness-of-fit model is not limited to temperamental individuality, we may note some of the findings from the PEATS related to the functional implications of charac

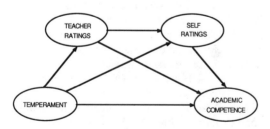

Figure 2.4. The path model linking temperament, teacher ratings, self ratings, and academic competence used in the Talwar, Schwab, and Lerner (1988) study.

teristics of physical individuality, and more specifically physical attractiveness individuality. Lerner et al. (in press) found that the circular functions component of the goodness-of-fit model was supported in regard to links between physical attractiveness (PA) and academic achievement. Based on the presence of a "what is beautiful is good" stereotype (Langlois, 1986), teachers were expected to evaluate differentially adolescents who differed on PA. These different evaluations should influence the achievements of adolescents and, as well, their self-evaluations of their academic competence; these self-perceptions should then, in turn, influence achievement. In both cases, however, it was expected that these indirect paths between PA and achievement would be significant whereas direct paths between PA and achievement would not. The results of Lerner et al. (in press) confirm these expectations in respect to the two indices of achievement noted, grade point average and the standardized achievement test scores on the CAT/C. These findings are illustrated in Figures 2.5 and 2.6, in respect to GPA and CAT/C scores, respectively.

Given this support for the developmentally contextually derived goodness-of-fit model, as well as the support found in other studies from our laboratory (e.g., see Lerner, 1984; J. Lerner & Lerner, 1983; Lerner & Lerner, 1987, 1989; Lerner et al., 1988), it is useful to make some final statements regarding the developmental contextual view of developmental bases of psychopathology.

CONCLUSIONS AND FUTURE DIRECTIONS

The concepts of person, of context, and of the relations between the two found in a probabilistic epigenetic, developmental contextual perspective are, as a set quite complex ones, ones that impose formidable challenges on those who seek to understand the developmental bases of psychopathology and of nonpsychopathologic behavior, to derive feasible research from this perspective, and to use this conception and its associated research for the design and implementation of interventions. As we have argued, this developmental contextual perspective leads to an integrated, multilevel concept of development, one in which the focus of inquiry is the organism-environment dynamic interaction. Furthermore, such an orientation places an emphasis on the potential for intraindividual change in structure and func

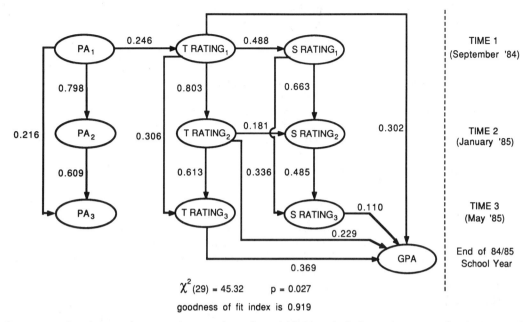

Figure 2.5. Developmental contextual perspective path model linking physical attractiveness, teachers' ratings, and self-ratings, measured at three points in time, and grade point average (all paths are significant) (Lerner et al., 1988).

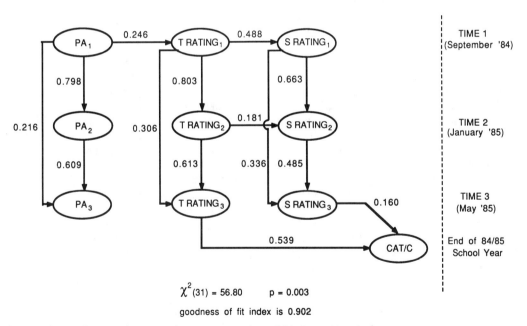

Figure 2.6. Developmental contextual perspective path model linking physical attractiveness, teachers' ratings, and self-ratings measured at three points in time, and achievement test scores (all paths are significant) (Lerner et al., 1988).

tion—for plasticity—across the life span. Moreover, this perspective requires a temporal (historical)/longitudinal and a relational/comparative orientation to research (and to intervention; Lerner & Tubman, in press).

The major challenge of this perspective is, as we have noted, the derivation and empirical testing of models reflecting the nature of dynamic, interlevel interactions across time. As we have indicated, one reasonably successful path we have taken involves the testing of the goodness-of-fit model of person–context relations. Of course, the goodness-of-fit model is not the only conception of person–context relations that may be derived from a developmental contextual orientation. There are perhaps an infinity of possible interlevel relations that may occur and a potentially similarly large array of ways to model them. Indeed, tests of other models derived from or consistent with a developmental contextual or life-span perspective also have found considerable empirical support (e.g., Baltes, 1987; Caspi & Elder, 1988; Featherman, 1985; Perlmutter, 1988).

The tests of such models will profit by triangulation of the constructs within each of the levels of analysis thought to interact dynamically within a given model. For instance, in regard to the biological/organismic-psychosocial interactions assessed within the goodness-of-fit model, biological changes could be simultaneously indexed both by more molecular (e.g., hormonal) changes, and by more molar, bodily measures; similarly contextual demands could be simultaneously appraised by assessing both attitudes/expectations about behavior held by a person's significant other and actual behavioral exchanges between a person and these others. Such triangulation would not only provide convergent and discriminant validation information. In addition, better insight would be gained about whether all modalities of functioning within a level of analysis are of similar import for the development of psychopathological or nonpsychopathological functioning in particular person-context interactions.

In sum, the relative plasticity of human development across the life span—a plasticity deriving from the dynamic interactions between organism and context that characterize human functioning—is already well documented (Baltes, 1987; Brim & Kagan, 1980; Featherman, 1983; Hetherington, Lerner, & Perlmutter, 1988; R. M. Lerner, 1984; Sorensen, Weinert, & Sherrod, 1986). Thus, a future including the sorts of directions we suggest should enrich greatly our understanding of the precise conditions promoting and constraining the development of psychopathology. Given, then, the present literature, and the promise we see for tomorrow, we believe there is reason for great optimism about the future scientific use of the developmental contextual view of the biological and social contextual bases of, on the one hand, functional, adaptive behaviors and, on the other, malfunctional psychopathological ones.

NOTE

1. Following Gould and Vrba (1982) we use the term "aptive" to describe changes that allow the organism to meet the demands of its context, instead of the more usual term "adaptive." The prefix "ad" in adaptive indicates that the changes have been shaped by natural selection to allow the developing organism to fit its environment. We do not necessarily make any inferences about the evolutionary shaping of the changes across ontogeny which we study; thus, we use the more neutral term "aptive."

REFERENCES

Anthony, J. (1969). The reaction of adults to adolescents and their behavior. In G. Caplan & S. Lebovici (Eds.), *Adolescence: Psychological perspectives* (pp. 54–78). New York: Basic Books.

Baltes, P. B. (1987). Theoretical propositions of life-span developmental psychology: On the dynamics between growth and decline. *Developmental Psychology, 23*, 611–626.

Baltes, P. B., & Baltes, M. M. (1980). Plasticity and variability in psychological aging: Methodological and theoretical issues. In G. E. Gurski (Ed.), *Determining the effects of aging on the central nervous system* (pp. 41–60). Berlin: Schering AG (Oraniendruck).

Bandura, A. (1978). The self system in reciprocal determinism. *American Psychologist, 33*, 344–358.

Baumrind, D. (1971). Current patterns of parental authority. *Developmental Psychology Monographs, 4*(1, Part 2).

Bell, R. Q. (1974). Contributions of human infants to caregiving and social interaction. In M. Lewis & L. A. Rosenblum (Eds.), *The effect of the infant on its caregiver* (pp. 1–20). New York: John Wiley & Sons.

Belsky, J. (1984). The determinants of parenting:

A process model. *Child Development, 55*, 83–96.

Belsky, J., Lerner, R., & Spanier, G. (1984). *The child in the family*. Reading, MA: Addison-Wesley.

Bijou, S. W. (1976). *Child development: The basic stage of early childhood*. Englewood Cliffs, NJ: Prentice Hall.

Bijou, S. W., & Baer, D. M. (1961). *Child development: A systematic and empirical theory* (Vol. 1). New York: Appleton-Century-Crofts.

Blyth, D. A., Simmons, R. G., & Bush, D. (1978). The transition into early adolescence: A longitudinal comparison of youth in two educational contexts. *Sociology of Education, 51*, 149–162.

Brazelton, T. B., Koslowski, B., & Main, M. (1974). The origins of reciprocity: The early mother-infant interaction. In M. Lewis & L. A. Rosenblum (Eds.), *The effect of the infant on its caregivers* (pp. 49–76). New York: John Wiley & Sons.

Brim, O. G., Jr., & Kagan, J. (Eds.). (1980). *Constancy and change in human development*. Cambridge, MA: Harvard University Press.

Bronfenbrenner, U. (1977). Toward an experimental ecology of human development. *American Psychologist, 32*, 513–531.

Bronfenbrenner, U. (1979). *The ecology of human development*. Cambridge, MA: Harvard University Press.

Brooks-Gunn, J. (1987). Pubertal processes and girls' psychological adaptation. In R. M. Lerner & T. T. Foch (Eds.), *Biological-psychosocial interactions in early adolescence: A lifespan perspective* (pp. 123–153). Hillsdale, NJ: Lawrence Erlbaum Associates.

Brooks-Gunn, J., & Matthews, W. S. (1979). *He and she: How children develop their sex role identity*. Englewood Cliffs, NJ: Prentice Hall.

Brooks-Gunn, J., & Petersen, A. C. (Eds.). (1983). *Girls at puberty: Biological and psychosocial perspectives*. New York: Plenum Press.

Brooks-Gunn, J., & Ruble, D. N. (1980). Menarche: The interaction of physiology, cultural, and social factors. In A. J. Dan, E. A. Graham, & C. P. Beecher (Eds.), *The menstrual cycle: A synthesis of interdisciplinary research* (pp. 141–159). New York: Springer.

Buss, A. H., & Plomin, R. (1975). *A temperament theory of personality development*. New York: John Wiley & Sons.

Campos, J. J. (1980–81). Human emotions: Their new importance and their role in social refer-

encing. *Annual Report for the Research and Clinical Center for Child Development*. Sapporo, Japan: Hokkaido University, Faculty of Education.

Caspi, A., & Elder, G. H., Jr. (1988). Childhood precursors of the life course: Early personality and life disorganization. In E. M. Hetherington, R. M. Lerner, & M. Perlmutter (Eds.), *Child development in life-span perspective* (pp. 115–142). Hillsdale, NJ: Lawrence Erlbaum Associates.

Chess, S., & Thomas, A. (1984). *The origins and evolution of behavior disorders: Infancy to early adult life*. New York: Brunner/Mazel.

Cicchetti, D. (1984). The emergence of developmental psychopathology. *Child Development, 55*, 1–7.

Cicchetti, D. (1987). Developmental psychopathology in infancy: Illustration from the study of maltreated youngsters. *Journal of Consulting and Clinical Psychology, 55*, 837–845.

Crockenberg, S. B. (1981). Infant irritability, mother responsiveness, and social support influences on the security of infant-mother attachment. *Child Development, 52*, 857–865.

Dixon, R. A. (1986). Contextualism and life-span developmental psychology. In R. L. Rosnow & M. Georgoudi (Eds.), *Contextualism and understanding in behavioral science* (pp. 125–144). New York: Praeger.

Dixon, R. A., & Lerner, R. M. (1988). A history of systems in developmental psychology. In M. H. Bornstein & M. E. Lamb (Eds.), *Developmental psychology* (2nd ed., pp. 3–50). Hillsdale, NJ: Lawrence Erlbaum Associates.

Dixon, R. A., & Nesselroade, J. R. (1983). Pluralism and correlational analysis in developmental psychology: Historical commonalities. In R. M. Lerner (Ed.), *Developmental psychology: Historical and philosophical perspectives* (pp. 113–145). Hillsdale, NJ: Lawrence Erlbaum Associates.

East, P. L., Lerner, R. M., & Lerner, J. V. (1988). *Early adolescent peer group fit, peer relations, and adjustment*. Unpublished manuscript.

Elder, G. H., Jr. (1974). *Children of the great depression*. Chicago: University of Chicago Press.

Elder, G. H., Jr. (1975). Age differentiation and the life courses. In A. Inkeles, J. Coleman, & N. Smelser (Eds.), *Annual review of sociology* (Vol. 1, pp. 165–190). Palo Alto, CA: Annual Reviews.

Emmerich, W. (1968). Personality development

and concepts of structure. *Child Development,* *39*, 671–690.

Erikson, E. H. (1959). Identity and the life-cycle. *Psychological Issues, 1*, 18–164.

Featherman, D. L. (1983). Life-span perspectives in social science research. In P. B. Baltes & O. G. Brim, Jr. (Eds.), *Life-span development and behavior* (Vol. 5, pp. 1–57). New York: Academic Press.

Featherman, D. L. (1985). Individual development and aging as a population process. In J. R. Nesselroade & A. von Eye (Eds.), *Individual development and social change: Explanatory analysis* (pp. 213–241). New York: Academic Press.

Featherman, D. L., & Lerner, R. M. (1985). Ontogenesis and sociogenesis: Problematics for theory about development across the lifespan. *American Sociological Review, 50*, 659–676.

Feinman, S., & Lewis, M. (1983). Social referencing at ten months: A second-order effect on infants' responses to strangers. *Child Development, 54*, 878–887.

Freud, S. (1949). *Outline of psychoanalysis.* New York: W. W. Norton.

Gesell, A. L. (1946). The ontogenesis of infant behavior. In L. Carmichael (Ed.), *Manual of child psychology* (pp. 295–331). New York: John Wiley & Sons.

Gollin, E. S. (1981). Development and plasticity. In E. S. Gollin (Ed.), *Developmental plasticity: Behavioral and biological aspects of variations in development* (pp. 231–251). New York: Academic Press.

Gottlieb, G. (1970). Conceptions of prenatal behavior. In R. Aronson, E. Tobach, D. S. Lehrman, & J. S. Rosenblatt (Eds.), *Development and evolution of behavior: Essays in memory of T. C. Schneirla* (pp. 111–137). San Francisco: Freeman.

Gottlieb, G. (1983). The psychobiological approach to developmental issues. In M. M. Haith & J. J. Campos (Eds.), *Handbook of child psychology: Infancy and developmental psychobiology* (4th ed., pp. 1–26). New York: John Wiley & Sons.

Gould, S., & Vrba, E. (1982). Exaptation: A missing term in the science of form. *Paleobiology, 8*, 4–15.

Hall, G. S. (1904). *Adolescence: Its psychology and its relations to physiology, anthropology, sociology, sex, crime, religion, and education* (Vols. 1 & 2). New York: Appleton.

Hamburg, B. (1974). Early adolescence: A specific and stressful stage of the life cycle. In G. Coelho, D. A. Hamburg, & J. E. Adams (Eds.), *Coping and adaptation* (pp. 101–125). New York: Basic Books.

Hamburger, V. (1957). The concept of development in biology. In D. B. Harris (Ed.), *The concept of development* (pp. 49–58). Minneapolis: University of Minnesota Press.

Harris, D. B. (Ed.). (1957). *The concept of development.* Minneapolis: University of Minnesota Press.

Harter, S. (1983). *Supplementary description of the self-perception profile for children: Revision of the perceived competence scale for children.* Denver: University of Denver.

Hetherington, E. M., Lerner, R. M., & Perlmutter, M. (Eds.). (1988). *Child development in life span perspective.* Hillsdale, NJ: Lawrence Erlbaum Associates.

Jenkins, J. J. (1974). Remember that old theory of memory: Well forget it. *American Psychologist, 29*, 785–795.

Kaplan, B. (1983). A trio of trails. In R. M. Lerner (Ed.), *Developmental psychology: Historical and philosophical perspectives* (pp. 185–239). Hillsdale, NJ: Lawrence Erlbaum Associates.

Kendall, P. C., Lerner, R. M., & Craighead, W. E. (1984). Human development intervention in childhood psychopathology. *Child Development, 55*, 71–82.

Korn, S. (1978, September). *Temperament, vulnerability, and behavior.* Paper presented at the Louisville Temperament Conference, Louisville, KY.

Kuo, Z. Y. (1967). *The dynamics of behavior development.* New York: Random House.

Langlois, J. H. (1986). From the eye of the beholder to behavioral reality: The development of social behaviors and social relations as a function of physical attractiveness. In C. P. Herman (Ed.), *Physical appearance, stigma, and social behavior: The Ontario Symposium on Personality and Social Policy* (pp. 23–51). Hillsdale, NJ: Lawrence Erlbaum Associates.

Lehrman, D. S. (1970). Semantic and conceptual issues in the nature-nurture problem. In L. R. Aronson, E. Tobach, D. S. Lehrman, & J. S. Rosenblatt (Eds.), *Development and evolution of behavior: Essays in memory of T. C. Schneirla* (pp. 17–52). San Francisco: W. H. Freeman.

Lerner, J. V. (1983). A "goodness of fit" model of the role of temperament in psychosocial adaptation in early adolescents. *Journal of Genetic Psychology, 143*, 149–157.

Lerner, J. V. (1984). The import of temperament for psychosocial functioning: Tests of a "goodness of fit" model. *Merrill-Palmer Quarterly, 30*, 177–188.

Lerner, J. V., & Galambos, N. L. (1985). Maternal role satisfaction, mother-child interaction, and child temperament. *Developmental Psychology, 21*, 1157–1164.

Lerner, J. V., & Lerner, R. M. (1983). Temperament and adaptation across life: Theoretical and empirical issues. In P. B. Baltes & O. G. Brim, Jr. (Eds.), *Life-span development and behavior* (Vol. 5, pp. 197–230). New York: Academic Press.

Lerner, J. V., Lerner, R. M., & Zabski, S. (1985). Temperament and elementary school children's actual and rated academic performance: A test of a "goodness of fit" model. *Journal of Child Psychology and Psychiatry, 26*, 125–136.

Lerner, R. M. (1976). *Concepts and theories of human development*. Reading, MA: Addison-Wesley.

Lerner, R. M. (1978). Nature, nurture and dynamic interactionism. *Human Development, 21*, 1–20.

Lerner, R. M. (1979). A dynamic interactional concept of individual and social relationship development. In R. Burgess & T. Huston (Eds.), *Social exchange in developing relationships* (pp. 271–305). New York: Academic Press.

Lerner, R. M. (1982). Children and adolescents as producers of their own development. *Development Review, 2*, 342–370.

Lerner, R. M. (1984). *On the nature of human plasticity*. New York: Cambridge University Press.

Lerner, R. M. (1985). Adolescent maturational change and psychosocial development: A dynamic interactional perspective. In J. Brooks-Gunn, A. C. Petersen, & D. Eichorn (Eds.), Timing of maturation and psychological adjustment. *Journal of Youth and Adolescence, 14*, 355–372.

Lerner, R. M. (1986). *Concepts and theories of human development* (2nd ed.). New York: Random House.

Lerner, R. M., & Busch-Rossnagel, N. (1981). Individuals as producers of their development: Conceptual and empirical bases. In R. M. Lerner & N. A. Busch-Rossnagel (Eds.), *Individuals as producers of their development: A*

life-span perspective (pp. 1–36). New York: Academic Press.

Lerner, R. M., Delaney, M., Hess, L. E., Jovanovic, J., & von Eye, A. (in press). Early adolescent physical attractiveness and academic competence. *Journal of Early Adolescence.*

Lerner, R. M., Hultsch, D. F., & Dixon, R. A. (1983). Contextualism and the character of developmental psychology in the 1970s. *Annals of the New York Academy of Sciences, 412*, 101–128.

Lerner, R. M., Iwawaki, S., Chihara, T., & Sorrell, G. T. (1980). Self-concept, self-esteem, and body attitudes among Japanese male and female adolescents. *Child Development, 51*, 847–855.

Lerner, R. M., & Kauffman, M. B. (1985). The concept of development in contextualism. *Developmental Review, 5*, 309–333.

Lerner, R. M., & Lerner, J. V. (1989). Organismic and social contextual bases of development: The sample case of early adolescence. In W. Damon (Ed.), *Child development today and tomorrow* (pp. 69–85). San Francisco: Jossey-Bass.

Lerner, R. M., & Lerner, J. V. (1983). Temperament-intelligence reciprocities in early childhood: A contextual model. In M. Lewis (Ed.), *Origins of intelligence: Infancy and early childhood* (2nd ed., pp. 399–421). New York: Plenum Press.

Lerner, R. M., & Lerner, J. V. (1987). Children in their contexts: A goodness of fit model. In J. B. Lancaster, J. Altmann, A. S. Rossi, & L. R. Sherrod (Eds.), *Parenting across the life span: Biosocial dimensions* (pp. 377–404). Chicago: Aldine.

Lerner, R. M., Lerner, J. V., Jovanovic, J., Schwab, J., Talwar, R., Hess, L., & Kucher, J. S. (in press). *Physical attractiveness, body type, and psychosocial functioning among early adolescents.* Unpublished manuscript.

Lerner, R. M., Lerner, J. V., Windle, M., Hooker, K., Lenerz, K., & East, P. P. (1986). Children and adolescents in their contexts: Tests of a goodness of fit model. In R. Plomin & J. Dunn (Eds.), *The study of temperament: Changes, continuities, and challenges* (pp. 337–404). Hillsdale, NJ: Lawrence Erlbaum Associates.

Lerner, R. M., & Spanier, G. B. (1978). A dynamic interactional view of child and family development. In R. M. Lerner & G. B. Spanier (Eds.), *Child influences on marital and family interaction: A life-span perspective* (pp. 1–22). New York: Academic Press.

Lerner, R. M., & Spanier, G. B. (1980). *Adolescent development: A life-span perspective.* New York: McGraw-Hill.

Lerner, R. M., & Tubman, J. (1989). Conceptual issues in studying continuity and discontinuity in personality development across life. *Journal of Personality, 57,* 343–373.

Lewis, M., & Lee-Painter, S. (1974). An interactional approach to the mother-infant dyad. In M. Lewis & L. A. Rosenblum (Eds.), *The effect of the infant on its caregivers* (pp. 21–48). New York: John Wiley & Sons.

Lewis, M., & Rosenblum, L. (Eds.). (1974). *The effect of the infant on its caregiver.* New York: John Wiley & Sons.

Liben, L. S. (1981). Individuals' contributions to their own development during childhood: A Piagetian perspective. In R. M. Lerner & N. A. Busch-Rossnagel (Eds.), *Individuals as producers of their development: A life-span perspective* (pp. 117–148). New York: Academic Press.

Lynch, M. E. (1981). *Paternal androgeny, daughters' physical maturity level, and achievement socialization in early adolescence.* Unpublished doctoral dissertation, Cornell University, Ithaca, NY.

Magnusson, D. (1987). Individual development from an interactional perspective. In D. Magnusson (Ed.), *Paths through life* (Vol. 1). Hillsdale, NJ: Lawrence Erlbaum Associates.

Magnusson, D., & Allen, V. L. (Eds.). (1983). *Human development: An interactional perspective.* New York: Academic Press.

Magnusson, D., & Öhman, A. (Eds.). (1987). *Psychopathology: An interactional perspective.* New York: Academic Press.

Meyer, J. W. (1988). The social construction of the psychology of childhood: Some contemporary processes. In E. M. Hetherington, R. M. Lerner, & M. Perlmutter (Eds.), *Child development in life-span perspective* (pp. 47–65). Hillsdale, NJ: Lawrence Erlbaum Associates.

Mischel, W. (1977). On the future of personality measurement. *American Psychologist, 32,* 246–254.

Mussen, P. H., & Bouterline-Young, H. (1964). Relationships between rate of physical maturing and personality among boys of Italian descent. *Vita Humana, 7,* 186–200.

Nagel, E. (1957). Determinism in development. In D. B. Harris (Ed.), *The concept of development* (pp. 15–24). Minneapolis: University of Minnesota Press.

Nitz, K., Lerner, R. M., Lerner, J. V., & Talwar, R. (1988). Parental and peer demands, temperament, and early adolescent adjustment. *Journal of Early Adolescence, 8,* 243–263.

Novikoff, A. B. (1945a). The concept of integrative levels of biology. *Science, 101,* 209–215.

Novikoff, A. B. (1945b). Continuity and discontinuity in evolution. *Science, 101,* 405–406.

Öhman, A., & Magnusson, D. (1987). An interactional paradigm for research on psychopathology. In D. Magnusson & A. Öhman (Eds.), *Psychopathology: An interactional perspective* (pp. 3–19). Orlando, FL: Academic Press.

Overton, W. F. (1973). On the assumptive base of the nature-nurture controversy: Additive versus interactive conceptions. *Human Development, 16,* 74–89.

Overton, W. F. (1984). World views and their influence on psychological theory and research: Kuhn-Lakatos-Lauden. In H. W. Reese (Ed.), *Advances in child development and behavior* (Vol. 18, pp. 191–225). New York: Academic Press.

Overton, W. F., & Reese, H. W. (1973). Models of development: Methodological implications. In J. R. Nesselroade & H. W. Reese (Eds.), *Life-span developmental psychology: Methodological issues* (pp. 65–86). New York: Academic Press.

Paige, K. E. (1983). A bargaining theory of menarcheal responses in preindustrial cultures. In J. Brooks-Gunn & A. C. Petersen (Eds.), *Girls at puberty* (pp. 301–322). New York: Plenum Press.

Parke, R. (1978). Parent-infant interaction: Progress, paradigms, and problems. In G. P. Sackett (Ed.), *Observing behavior: Vol. 1. Theory and implications in mental retardation* (pp. 69–95). Baltimore, MD: University Park Press.

Pepper, S. C. (1942). *World hypotheses.* Berkeley: University of California Press.

Perlmutter, M. (1988). Cognitive development in life-span perspective: From description of differences to explanation of changes. In E. M. Hetherington, R. M. Lerner, & M. Perlmutter (Eds.), *Child development in life-span perspective* (pp. 191–214). Hillsdale, NJ: Lawrence Erlbaum Associates.

Petersen, A. C. (1983). Pubertal change and cognition. In J. Brooks-Gunn & A. C. Petersen (Eds.), *Girls at puberty* (pp. 179–198). New York: Plenum Press.

Petersen, A. C., & Taylor, B. (1980). The biological approach to adolescence: Biological change and psychological adaptation. In J. Adelson (Ed.), *Handbook of adolescent psychology* (pp. 117–155). New York: John Wiley & Sons.

Piaget, J. (1950). *The psychology of intelligence.* New York: Harcourt Brace.

Plomin, R., & Daniels, D. (1984). The interaction between temperament and environment: Methodological considerations. *Merrill-Palmer Quarterly, 30*, 149–162.

Reese, H. W., & Overton, W. F. (1970). Models of development and theories of development. In L. R. Goulet & P. B. Baltes (Eds.), *Life-span developmental psychology: Research and theory* (pp. 115–145). New York: Academic Press.

Riegel, K. F. (1975). Toward a dialectical theory of development. *Human Development, 18*, 50–64.

Riegel, K. F. (1976a). The dialectics of human development. *American Psychologist, 31*, 689–700.

Riegel, K. F. (1976b). From traits and equilibrium toward developmental dialectics. In W. J. Arnold & J. K. Cole (Eds.), *Nebraska symposium on motivation, 1975* (pp. 349–408). Lincoln, NE: University of Nebraska Press.

Rosnow, R. L. (1983). Von Osten's horse, Hamlet's question, and the mechanistic view of causality: Implications for a post-crisis social psychology. *The Journal of Mind and Behavior, 4*, 319–338.

Rosnow, R., & Georgoudi, M. (Eds.). (1986). *Contextualism and understanding in behavioral research.* New York: Praeger.

Rosnow, R. L., & Rosenthal, R. (1984). *Understanding behavioral science: Research methods for research consumers.* New York: McGraw-Hill.

Ruble, D. N. (1977). Premenstrual symptoms: A reinterpretation. *Science, 197*, 291–292.

Ruble, D. N., & Brooks-Gunn, J. (1979). Menstrual symptoms: A social cognition analysis. *Journal of Behavioral Medicine, 2*, 171–194.

Ruble, D. N., & Brooks-Gunn, J. (1982). The experience of menarche. *Child Development, 53*, 1557–1566.

Sameroff, A. (1975). Transactional models in early social relations. *Human Development, 18*, 65–79.

Sarbin, T. R. (1977). Contextualism: A world view for modern psychology. In J. K. Cole & A. W. Lundfield (Eds.), *Nebraska symposium on motivation, 1976* (pp. 1–41). Lincoln, NE: University of Nebraska Press.

Scarr, S. (1982). Development is internally guided, not determined. *Contemporary Psychology, 27*, 852–853.

Scarr, S., & McCartney, K. (1983). How people make their own environments: A theory of genotype-environment effects. *Child Development, 54*, 424–435.

Schneirla, T. C. (1956). Interrelationships of the "innate" and the "acquired" in instinctive behavior. In P. P. Grassè (Ed.), *L'instinct dans le comportement des animaux et de l'homme* (pp. 387–452). Paris: Maxon et Cie.

Schneirla, T. C. (1957). The concept of development in comparative psychology. In D. B. Harris (Ed.), *The concept of development* (pp. 78–108). Minneapolis: University of Minnesota Press.

Sheldon, W. H. (1940). *The varieties of human physique.* New York: Harper.

Sheldon, W. H. (1942). *The varieties of temperament.* New York: Harper.

Simmons, R. G., Blyth, D. A., & McKinney, K. L. (1983). The social and psychological effects of puberty on white females. In J. Brooks-Gunn & A. C. Petersen (Eds.), *Girls at puberty* (pp. 229–272). New York: Plenum Press.

Simmons, R. G., Blyth, D. A., Van Cleave, E. F., & Bush, D. M. (1979). Entry into early adolescence: The impact of school structure, puberty, and early dating on self-esteem. *American Sociological Review, 44*, 948–967.

Simmons, R. G., Brown, L., Bush, D. M., & Blyth, D. A. (1978). Self-esteem and achievement of black and white early adolescents. *Social Problems, 26*, 86–96.

Simmons, R. G., Carlton-Ford, S. L., & Blyth, D. A. (1987). Predicting how a child will cope with the transition to junior high school. In R. M. Lerner & T. T. Foch (Eds.), *Biological-psychosocial interactions in early adolescence: A life-span perspective* (pp. 325–375). Hillsdale, NJ: Lawrence Erlbaum Associates.

Sorensen, B., Weinert, E., & Sherrod, L. R. (Eds.). (1986). *Human development and the life course: Multidisciplinary perspectives.* Hillsdale, NJ: Lawrence Erlbaum Associates.

Super, C. M. (1987). The role of culture in developmental disorder. In C. M. Super (Ed.), *The role of culture in developmental disorder* (pp. 2–7). San Diego, CA: Academic Press.

Super, C. M., & Harkness, S. (1980). Anthropological perspectives on child development. *New Directions for Child Development* (No. 8). San Francisco: Jossey-Bass.

Super, C. M., & Harkness, S. (1981). Figure, ground, and gestalt: The cultural context of the active individual. In R. M. Lerner & N. A. Busch-Rossnagel (Eds.), *Individuals as pro-*

ducers of their own development: A life-span perspective (pp. 69–86). New York: Academic Press.

Super, C. M., & Harkness, S. (1982). The infant's niche in rural Kenya and metropolitan America. In L. L. Adler (Ed.), *Cross-cultural research at issue* (pp. 47–56). New York: Academic Press.

Super, C. M., & Harkness, S. (1986). The developmental niche: A conceptualization at the interface of child and culture. *International Journal of Behavioral Development, 9*, 1–25.

Super, C. M., & Harkness, S. (1988). *The development niche: Culture and the expressions of human growth.* Unpublished manuscript.

Talwar, R., Nitz, K., & Lerner, R. M. (in press). Relations among early adolescent temperament, parent and peer demands, and adjustment: A test of the goodness of fit model. *Journal of Adolescence.*

Talwar, R., Nitz, K., Lerner, J. V., & Lerner, R. M. (1988, April 21–24). *Temperamental individuality, fit with parent and peer demands, and personal and social adjustment across the transition to junior high school.* Paper presented at the Fifty-ninth Annual Meeting of the Eastern Psychological Association, Buffalo, NY.

Talwar, R., Schwab, J., & Lerner, R. M. (1989). Early adolescent temperament and academic competence: Tests of "direct effects" and developmental contextual models. *Journal of Early Adolescence, 9*, 291–309.

Thomas, A., & Chess, S. (1977). *Temperament and development.* New York: Brunner/Mazel.

Thomas, A., Chess, S., & Birch, H. (1968). *Temperament and behavioral disorders in childhood.* New York: New York University Press.

Thomas, A., Chess, S., & Birch, H. G. (1968). *Temperament and behavior disorders in children.* New York: New York University Press.

Thomas, A., Chess, S., & Birch, H. G. (1970). The origin of personality. *Scientific American, 223*, 102–109.

Thomas, A., Chess, S., Sillan, J., & Mendez, O. (1974). Cross-cultural study of behavior in children with special vulnerabilities to stress. In D. F. Ricks, A. Thomas, & M. Roff (Eds.), *Life history research in psychopathology* (pp. 53–67). Minneapolis: University of Minnesota Press.

Tobach, E. (1981). Evolutionary aspects of the activity of the organism and its development. In R. M. Lerner & N. A. Busch-Rossnagel (Eds.), *Individuals as producers of their development: A life-span perspective* (pp. 37–68). New York: Academic Press.

Tobach, E., & Greenberg, G. (1984). The significance of T. C. Schneirla's contribution to the concept of levels of integration. In G. Greenberg & E. Tobach (Eds.), *Behavioral evolution and integrative levels* (pp. 1–7). Hillsdale, NJ: Lawrence Erlbaum Associates.

Tobach, E., & Schneirla, T. C. (1968). The biopsychology of social behavior of animals. In R. E. Cooke & S. Levin (Eds.), *Biologic basis of pediatric practice* (pp. 68–82). New York: McGraw-Hill.

Tobin-Richards, M. H., Boxer, A. M., & Petersen, A. C. (1983). The psychological significance of pubertal change: Sex differences in perceptions of self during early adolescence. In J. Brooks-Gunn & A. C. Petersen (Eds.), *Girls at puberty* (pp. 127–154). New York: Plenum Press.

von Bertalanffy, L. (1933). *Modern theories of development.* London: Oxford University Press.

von Bertalanffy, L. (1968). *General systems theory.* New York: George Braziller.

Wapner, S., & Demick, J. (1988, October 25–27). *Some relations between developmental and environmental psychology: An organismic-developmental systems perspective.* Paper presented at the "Visions of Development, the Environment, and Aesthetics: The Legacy of Joachim Wohlwill" conference, The Pennsylvania State University, University Park.

Westney, O. E., Jenkins, R. R., & Benjamin, C. A. (1983). Sociosexual development of preadolescents. In J. Brooks-Gunn & A. C. Petersen (Eds.), *Girls at puberty* (pp. 273–300). New York: Plenum Press.

White, S. H. (1968). The learning-maturation controversy: Hall to Hull. *Merrill-Palmer Quarterly, 14*, 187–196.

Windle, M., Hooker, K., Lernerz, K., East, P. L., Lerner, J. V., & Lerner, R. M. (1986). Temperament, perceived competence, and depression in early- and late-adolescents. *Developmental Psychology, 22*, 384–392.

Windle, M., & Lerner, R. M. (1986). Reassessing the dimensions of temperamental individuality across the life-span: The Revised Dimensions of Temperament Survey (DOTS-R). *Journal of Adolescent Research, 1*, 213–230.

MAJOR DEPRESSION

EDITORS' COMMENTS

It is only recently that the existence of depression in childhood has been recognized. Although the essential features of major depression are similar across the life span, some interesting developmental differences have been observed. Very young depressed children often have somatic complaints (stomachaches, headaches, etc.) that are less common in depressed adolescents and adults. In addition, prepubertal children often show other symptoms that decrease in frequency with age, including hallucinations, separation anxiety, and phobias. While suicidal ideation is frequent in all age groups, completed suicide is quite infrequent in prepubertal depressives. By contrast, depressed adolescents frequently evince anhedonia, hopelessness, hypersomnia, and more serious suicidal attempts, in addition to self-medication with street drugs and/or alcohol. Symptoms that have been shown to be independent of age include depressed mood, poor concentration, insomnia, and suicidal ideation.

Depressive disorders have been shown to run in families, and early onset (particularly childhood) correlates with increased familial pathology. Adoptee and twin studies suggest a genetic component to the disorder.

Biological state markers of depression in adults, including the dexamethasone suppression test and the 24-hour cortisol hypersecretion, also are seen in depressed children, which suggests continuity in the child and adult presentations of the illness. By contrast, characteristic REM sleep abnormalities found in depressed adults appear to be less consistent among depressed children.

The prevalence of major depression is relatively rare in prepubescence, the reason for which is unclear. In adolescence, the disorder becomes more common, with females outnumbering males, as is true for adult depressed populations. Follow-up data from Kovacs and colleagues indicate a very high risk rate for depressed youngsters to develop additional depressive episodes over time (within 5 years). It will be interesting to observe the risk rates for this child sample as they move into adulthood.

Anxiety symptoms and comorbid anxiety disorders are common in both depressed children and adults. Both diagnoses — anxiety disorder and depressive disorder — should be given only if there is a clear indication that the two disorders have some temporal separation (i.e., that they are discrete syndromes). Of course, major depression always must be differentiated from bipolar disorder and more minor depressive disorders (i.e., dysthymic disorder or adjustment disorder with depressed mood). Usually, careful interviewing regarding current and past symptomatology is sufficient to enable these distinctions.

Significant impairment in school/work and social relationships typically is observed regardless of the age of the depressed patient. Suicide, of course, is the most serious complication, affecting up to 15 percent of depressed patients. Although a number of risk factors empirically have been identified that appear to be linked to suicide, currently it remains extremely difficult, if not impossible, to predict who will commit suicide. Thus, the presence of suicidal ideation has become one of the main symptoms of depression that results in patients being hospitalized for both adolescents and adults.

CHAPTER 3

MAJOR DEPRESSION IN CHILDHOOD

Caroly S. Pataki
Gabrielle A. Carlson

DESCRIPTION OF THE DISORDER

Childhood depression has been a focus of increasing attention over the last few decades. Observations by parents and clinicians reveal that children of all ages are capable of clearly demonstrating "unhappiness" and "misery," but the concept of a depressive disorder, which is an enduring affective state producing functional impairment, has evolved over the last two decades. As of this writing, mood disorders in children appear to represent the same range of disorders as occur in adults, except with an earlier onset. Consequently, the primary symptoms of depressed or irritable mood, often with a concurrent diminution of ability to experience pleasure, prevail. Although the frequency of certain depressive symptoms varies with age, systematic assessment of depressive disorders in children and adolescents reveals that the essential features are the same. Moreover, if we define the presence of a *disorder* (as opposed to the syndrome or dimension of depression) by its duration and severity of impairment, it appears that depression in children is like its adult counterpart. Major depression in children has far-reach-

ing implications with respect to cognitive function, social interactions, and psychobiological indices (see review by Cantwell & Carlson, 1983). There are still many challenging aspects to making the diagnosis of a depressive disorder in childhood, particularly in view of the ongoing developmental changes in children that, in turn, influence our judgment of which behaviors are adaptive and normative at various ages. As is known to occur in adults, there are long-term sequelae of major depression in children resulting in lingering impairment in social and emotional function and continued vulnerability for relapse.

Finally, family studies demonstrate significantly increased risk of major depression in children of an affectively ill parent, with even higher risk to children with both parents affected or earlier onset of parental depression (Weissman et al., 1984; Beardslee Bemporad, Keller, & Klerman, 1983; Weissman et al., 1987).

CLINICAL PRESENTATION

Major depression is generally episodic and is most obvious when its onset is acute. In a child who is well functioning and does not have a prior history of psychopathology, the onset of a major depression may blatantly interrupt social relations, academic performance, and family life to cause marked dysfunction. On the other hand, major depression may also develop in a more prolonged and insidious fashion, leading to a gradual decline in function. In this case, it is more difficult to pinpoint the actual onset, and therefore, it is more difficult to diagnose. Furthermore, since there are many features such as poor concentration, anxiety symptoms, and conduct problems that may be components of a depressive episode or possibly of another preexisting or coexisting disorder, it is important to delineate the chronology of symptoms and the context in which they occur, to determine whether they truly represent a depressive episode. It is not uncommon, however, for a child who already has a nonaffective, underlying disorder to develop a major depressive disorder in addition. A child may also have a chronic dysthymia for a year or more, and then may go on to develop a major depressive episode. Needless to say, the concurrence of multiple syndromes and disorders makes diagnosis more complicated.

In children, especially in the very young age group, nonverbal manifestations of depression such as a persistently sad or expressionless face, or the observation that a child rarely smiles, are relevant information (Poznanski, 1982). By school age, however, there is evidence that children can be reliable verbal informants, and in fact, they are likely to be better informants than parents in describing inner experiences such as mood status, hallucinations or suicidal ideation, and other subjective feelings (Herjanic & Reich, 1982).

Dysphoric mood may be verbally described by children, sometimes as feeling sad, bored, or mad. In those children who are not articulate enough to verbalize the change in mood, it may be demonstrated by an increased sensitivity to criticism, more frequent tearfulness, and higher levels of irritability. Depressed children who are feeling unusually vulnerable to scrutiny may withdraw from peer interactions such as team sports and games that are normally pleasurable and report that these activities have become "stupid," "unfair," or "boring." Despite a distinct decrease in interest and pleasure with respect to their usual activities, very few school-aged children become anhedonic to the point of complete lack of involvement, even when they are seriously depressed. As age increases, anhedonia seems to occur more frequently and more pervasively (Carlson & Ka-

shani, 1988). It is important, thus, not to exclude the diagnosis of a major depressive episode in a child who can still enjoy certain activities.

Irritability is a phenomenon that can be expected to occur under certain circumstances in all children, but it can be a strikingly important symptom when it represents a change in a child's overall "personality" style. When children begin to exhibit behaviors such as severe temper tantrums or very poor frustration tolerance, and this is a new behavior, it may represent an irritability associated with an affective disturbance.

Aggressive behaviors and new onset of defiance such as fighting with parents or peers, and minor property destruction may also be manifestations of irritability and dysphoria in children with an onset of depression (Carlson & Cantwell, 1979). Some children, more often boys, actually present with the full syndrome of conduct disorder, including persistent physical fighting, violation of rules at home and in school, lying, and stealing, shortly after the onset of a depressive episode (Puig-Antich, 1982; Kovacs, Paulauskas, Gatsonis, & Richards, 1988). In these cases, the conduct disorder may remit with recovery of the depression, and reappear with future episodes.

New onset or marked increase in anxiety symptoms such as separation difficulties from parents, phobic symptoms regarding school, fears of the dark, preoccupation with impending doom, and increased performance anxiety are often seen in children with depression. As is commonly seen in adults, there is often a significant overlap of anxiety symptoms in children who meet the full criteria for major depression only, with those symptoms of children who have anxiety disorders, or both disorders (Hershberg, Carlson, Cantwell, & Strober, 1982). School refusal is a manifestation of distress that is often associated with depressive disorders as well as with anxiety disorders (Bernstein & Garfinkel, 1986).

Deterioration in school performance is sometimes the first phenomenon noted by a parent or a teacher marking an affective episode in a child. There may be multiple contributing factors such as poor concentration, decreased confidence, and a heightened sensitivity to being criticized or corrected. When children suddenly report that they no longer "care" about school, or that they don't "feel like doing school work anymore," in conjunction with a true decrease in achievement, an affective disturbance is one possible cause.

Vegetative symptoms are seen in children with

major depression although they seem to be less prominent than in adults. Decrease in appetite has been found to occur in one-third to one-half of depressed children and adolescents, with actual weight loss reported in less than one-third (Ryan et al., 1987; Carlson & Kashani, 1988; Mitchell, McCauley, Burke, & Moss, 1988). Initial insomnia is frequently seen in children and adolescents, while terminal insomnia and diurnal variation have been found significantly less often in children than in adults (Carlson & Strober, 1979; Mitchell et al., 1988; Baker, Dorzab, Winokur, & Cadoret, 1971). Psychomotor retardation, like anhedonia, seems to be less pervasive in children than in adults. Somatic symptoms, on the other hand, are reported very often by younger children with depression and less frequently in older children and adolescents (Carlson & Kashani, 1988).

Hopelessness, feelings of worthlessness, and negative expectations are an important part of the clinical picture of major depression in children and adolescents. Prepubertal depressed children endorse items on the hopelessness scale such as "All I can see ahead of me are bad things, not good things" (Kazdin et al., 1983). Although the expression of negative feelings is dependent on age and developmental level, school-aged children show poor self-esteem and make negative attributions about themselves. Excessive guilt is not uncommon and may be exhibited by a child who persistently worries that he or she is responsible for a negative outcome based on a behavior that took place many weeks ago. Naturally, before interpreting this as guilt, it is important to assess whether the child understands the concept of "cause and effect."

Suicidal ideation is also not uncommon in children, and may be cognitively linked to hopelessness, as is the case with adults (Kazdin et al., 1983). As one might expect, suicidal ideation increases in intensity with an increase in severity of the overall depression (Carlson & Cantwell, 1982), although completed suicide rarely occurs before the age of 10. There is a steady increase in the rate of completed suicides through puberty and adolescence (Shaffer & Fisher, 1981; Shaffer, 1985). The reasons for the relative absence of suicide in the prepubertal years remain obscure, yet children's knowledge and ability to imagine committing suicide increases with age, as does their ability to act on their fantasies (Carlson, Asarnow, & Orbach, 1987).

Psychotic symptoms are being recognized more frequently in depressed children. Hallucinations are more commonly reported by prepubertal children than by adolescents or adults, while delusions are more often reported by adolescents. Auditory hallucinations were reported by more than one-third of a sample of prepubertal major depressives, with command and persecutory hallucinations the two most common types and conversing hallucinations the least common (Chambers, Puig-Antich, Tabrizi, & Davies, 1982). In an adolescent sample, delusions were more common than in the prepubertal samples and were present in 12% (Strober, Green, & Carlson, 1981a), but they were less common than in adult samples (Baker et al., 1971). Despite the high frequency of hallucinations reported by prepubertal children, in the majority of cases, the hallucinations had little disruptive effect on the child's daily life. In view of this, it is difficult to assess whether the presence of hallucinations is indicative of more severe illness, or whether prepubertal children are simply more prone to develop them during an affective episode.

Biological indices that appear to be "state markers" of depression in adults such as cortisol nonsuppression during a dexamethasone suppression test (DST) and 24-hour cortisol hypersecretion (Greden et al., 1983) are seen in depressed children, though less reliably. The sensitivity of the DST has been found to range from 56% to 86% in prepubertal major depressives (Poznanski, Carroll, Banegas, Cook, & Grossman, 1982; Weller, Weller, Fristad, Preskorn, & Teare, 1985; Petty, Asarnow, Carlson, & Lesser, 1985), but the specificity in one study was found to be only 53% (Petty et al., 1985). Characteristic abnormalities of sleep found in depressed adults including a decreased latency of the first REM period, increased REM density, and abnormal disruption of REM periods (Kupfer, 1976; Gillin, Sitaram, & Duncan, 1979; Coble, Kupfer, Spiker, Neil, & Shaw, 1980) have been reported less consistently in depressed children. There is some evidence that in prepubertal children, the sleep abnormalities may be seen after the episode instead of during it, making them a "trait marker" (Puig-Antich, 1986).

Dysthymic disorder, which is distinguished from major depressive disorder by a longer duration, at least one year for children, is characterized by less severe symptoms and an absence of psychotic features. It appears to be related to major depression in that the majority of children who develop dysthymia are predisposed to a major depressive episode at some point in the future.

EPIDEMIOLOGY

There have been divergent reports of the epidemiology of childhood depression that may be largely explained on the basis of variability in diagnostic criteria used as well as in the instruments used to detect depression. Variation in reported incidence and prevalence of depression in different age groups, however, seems to reflect true differences in the presence of the disorder in these groups. As might be expected, the presence of some depressive symptoms in all age groups is much more common than depressive disorders (which require multiple enduring symptoms leading to functional impairment). In a study of a psychiatrically referred sample of children and adolescents, 60% were found to manifest depressive symptoms, but only 28% met DSM-III criteria for major depression (Carlson & Cantwell, 1979). When an adolescent sample of 14- to 16-year-olds in the general population was surveyed, close to 40% reported some depressive symptoms, but of those, only 4.7% met criteria for major depression, while 3.3% met criteria for dysthymic disorder (Kashani et al., 1987). When 109 preschool-aged children from community nursery schools were surveyed, 9 children, or approximately 8%, reported depressive symptoms (Kashani, Holcomb, & Orvaschel, 1986), but only one preschool child out of 350 (combining samples from two studies) met the criteria for major depression, resulting in a prevalence of 0.28% (Kashani & Ray, 1983; Kashani et al., 1986). Clearly, there are many more children of all ages with depressive symptoms than with depressive disorders.

It appears that the overall prevalence of depressive disorders rises in older age groups. There are also differences in the distribution of the depressive disorders in different age groups. Adult prevalence figures reveal that major depressive disorder is almost twice as prevalent as dysthymic disorder (Weissman & Myers, 1978), whereas in school-aged children, major depressive disorder is less frequent than dysthymic disorder (1.8% versus 2.5%; Kashani et al., 1983). This is no longer the case with adolescents, in whom major depression, as in adults, is more frequent than dysthymic disorder (4.7% versus 3.3%; Kashani et al., 1987). Prevalence figures of major depression, dysthymic disorder, and depressive symptoms can be found in Table 3.1. There is a marked association, at

least in the preschool population between depressive symptomatology and physical abuse and neglect (Kashani & Carlson, 1987).

Epidemiologic studies also show differences in the sex distribution of depressive disorders in the various age groups. Whereas in the school-aged population, reports have indicated either a higher percentage of males or little association between sex and depression (Kashani, et al., 1983), in adolescents, depressive symptomatology seems to be more frequent in females than in males (Kandel & Davies, 1982), as is the case in adults.

The utilization of accepted diagnostic criteria (DSM-III/III-R) decreases the variability in making diagnoses of major depression in children. In addition, the use of a variety of structured interviews such as the Diagnostic Interview for Children & Adolescents (DICA) (Reich, Herjanic, Welner, & Gandhy, 1982), the Diagnostic Interview Schedule for Children (DISC) (Costello, Edelbrock, Dulcan, Kalas, & Clario, 1984; Shaffer et al., 1988), and the Schedule for Affective Disorders and Schizophrenia in Children (K-SADS) (Puig-Antich & Chambers, 1978) in children and parents aids in systematically collecting the pertinent data. Numerous rating scales such as the Children's Depression Inventory (CDI) (Kovacs, 1980/81), the Children's Depression Rating Scale-Revised (Poznanski et al., 1984), and the Children's Depression Scale (Lang & Tisher, 1978) are also useful as standardized additions to a comprehensive collection of data. It is advisable to combine data from multiple sources, since discrepant information is often obtained from a child and his or her parents, with the child being a better informant on inner, subjective feelings, and the parent being more accurate regarding observable behaviors and the time frame of the symptoms (Herjanic & Reich, 1982; Kashani, Orvaschel, Burke, & Reid, 1985).

NATURAL HISTORY

Depression in children has been conceptualized in the past as a transient part of "normal" development, which should spontaneously remit with the passage of time (see review by Lefkowitz & Burton, 1978). Since longitudinal studies are now being carried out, there is clear evidence that depression in children is certainly not transient, nor is it benign (Kovacs, Feinberg, Crouse-Novak, Paulauskas, & Finkelstein, 1984). Even children whose depressive symptoms do not qualify for a diagnosis of major depression or dysthymic dis-

Table 3.1. Epidemiology of Major Depression, Dysthymic Disorder, and
Depressive Symptoms in Children and Adolescents

	PRESCHOOL	SCHOOL AGE	ADOLESCENT
MDD, community[1]	0.28%[3]	1.8%[4]	4.7%[5]
MDD, referred[2]	0.9%[6]	13%–15%[7,8]	18%–28%[9,10]
DD, community		2.5%[4]	3.3%[5]
Depressive symptoms, community	7%[11]		20%–40%[5,12,13]

[1]general population.
[2]individuals referred for psychiatric evaluation.
[3]Kashani et al., 1986; Kashani & Ray, 1983.
[4]Kashani et al., 1983.
[5]Kashani et al., 1987.
[6]Kashani & Carlson, 1987.
[7]Kashani et al., 1982.
[8]Kazdin et al., 1983.
[9]Strober et al., 1981b.
[10]Robbins et al., 1982.
[11]Kashani et al., 1986.
[12]Kaplan et al., 1984.
[13]Rutter et al., 1976.

order but who meet criteria for "adjustment disorder with depressed mood" have an average duration of symptoms for about six months, and it takes up to nine months before 90% are well. Major depressive episodes in children persist for an average of about eight months, and it takes up to two years before 92% are well. The third category of depressive illness — dysthymic disorder — has a much more chronic course with an average length of three years and up to six and a half years before 89% are recovered (Kovacs et al., 1984). Depression was found to persist for as long as 6½ years in 50% of a sample of ten adolescents (Poznanski, Krahenbuhl, & Zrull, 1976).

Among school-aged children, the onset of major depressive disorder tends to occur at an older age, often between 10½ and 11½ years old, compared to the age of onset of dysthymic disorder, which frequently occurs between 7 and 7½ years of age (Kovacs et al., 1984). One important factor that influences recovery from either depressive disorder is the age at onset, in that the earlier the age at onset, the slower the recovery, and thus the longer the illness will last (Kovacs et al., 1984).

The natural history of major depression and dysthymic disorder is interrelated in that a major depressive episode is likely to develop at some point in individuals with dysthymic disorder. In Kovacs's sample, 38% of the children with major depression had an underlying dysthymic disorder, a condition often referred to as "double depression" (Keller & Shapiro, 1982). The individuals with both dysthymic disorder and major depression represented 57% of the dysthymic group. In the school-aged sample studied, the rate of recovery from a major depression was not affected by the presence or absence of an underlying dys-

thymic disorder. The two disorders are similar in that the likelihood and prevalence of concurrent nonaffective psychiatric disorders is the same.

The probability of developing a major depressive episode within five years of a first episode of either a major depression, or dysthymic disorder, is quite high, 72% and 69%, respectively (Kovacs et al., 1984). In children with dysthymic disorder who go on to develop a major depression, 11% will do so within one year. Follow-up studies of depressed hospitalized children bear out these poor odds. Of 28 depressed inpatients age 7 to 13 years, 35% required hospitalization within the first year of discharge for depressive disorders that could not be managed with outpatient treatment, and 15% were placed outside the home within the first year of discharge (Asarnow, Golstin, Perdue, Bates, & Keller, 1988). The risk for developing a second episode of major depression seems to be highest for children who had initially experienced "double depression" (Kovacs et al., 1984). Interestingly, while most children with dysthymic disorder go on, at some point, to have a major depressive episode, the majority of children with major depression do not have an underlying dysthymic disorder. Other psychiatric disorders, such as anxiety disorders, which may coexist with either dysthymic disorder or major depression, do not appear to have an impact on the rate of subsequent major depressive episodes (Kovacs et al., 1984).

The natural history of depressive disorders in children and adolescents includes a fraction who will go on to develop bipolar disorder. There is some evidence to suggest that adolescents with an acute onset of severe depression, and who have psychosis, hypersomnia, and/or a family history of bipolar disorder, are most likely to develop a manic episode within the next four years (Strober & Carlson, 1982; Akiskal et al., 1985).

IMPAIRMENT AND COMPLICATIONS

In general, there is increasing evidence that depression in children has an impact for many years. The most direct impact is the increased risk for subsequent episodes. It is also becoming evident that children with depressive disorders experience other persistent behavioral problems as well. For example, boys with depression at age 9 years were found to exhibit persistently higher levels of antisocial behavior than depressed girls, or a nondepressed sample, at a four-year follow-up (McGee & Williams, 1988). The antisocial features were not reported in the depressed girls. Additionally over the same four-year period, a higher percentage of males than females were rated as having persistent depressive symptomatology. Females who as adolescents had endorsed the most depressive symptoms in an epidemiologic survey went on to experience more dysphoria, divorce, school attrition, unemployment, use of minor tranquilizers, and delinquency over the following decade when compared to their less depressed and nondepressed counterparts (Kandel & Davies, 1986). Adolescents with childhood onset of depressive symptoms have been found to be more impaired with regard to school achievement than have adolescents with recent onset of symptoms, implying that depression has taken a severe toll on those children by the time they reach adolescence (Carlson, 1984). In addition, adolescent onset depressives who were followed up to eight years later reported increased social adjustment problems compared to nonaffective psychiatric controls (Garber, Kris, Koch, & Lindholm, 1988). In children, at least up to age 13, the ratio of males to females with depressive disorders has been found to be as high as 4 : 1 (McGee & Williams, 1988). It is still unclear at what point in the natural history of the depressive disorders the sex ratio changes, since depressive disorders in adults are found to be more frequent in females (Boyd & Weissman, 1981).

Since the course of depression in childhood is often prolonged, one might expect the level of social impairment seen in depressed children and adolescents to be far reaching and enduring. In an assessment of prepubertal children during a major depressive episode, Puig-Antich et al. (1985) found these children to show significant impairment in their relationships with mothers and siblings, and they showed particular difficulties with peers when compared to normals and nondepressed psychiatric controls. The quality of interactions between depressed children and their mothers was characterized by sparse and superficial communication, lack of warmth, irritability, tension, and hostility. Peer relationships were severely disturbed, with depressives being less able to develop and maintain a "best" friend or even maintain a positive relationship with peers. Finally, as compared to normals or nondepressed psychiatric controls, children with major depression were teased significantly more often by peers (Puig-Antich et al., 1985).

Some aspects of these interpersonal deficits such as social withdrawal, avoidance of communication, and irritability may be expected concomitants of the depressive episode itself, and therefore, would be expected to pass with recovery. This, apparently, does not occur. When the foregoing group of prepubertal depressives was reevaluated at least four months after recovery from the affective state (Puig-Antich et al., 1985), school-related difficulties had improved, but relationships were still significantly impaired. Following recovery, the mother-child relationship was rated as somewhat improved, but communication was still markedly impaired in quality and quantity in comparison with either control group. With regard to peer and sibling relationships, there was evidence of increased frequency of contacts with friends, more of the children reported a "best friend," less shyness was reported, and there was less teasing by peers, but they still received more teasing than the control groups (Puig-Antich et al., 1985). It appears that many of the deficits that characterize social functioning in children during their episode of depression simply do not disappear when the depressive episode clears. Even the items assumed to be direct extensions of the depressive illness itself, such as decreased amount of social interaction, irritability in relationships, and hypersensitivity to teasing by peers, did not normalize with recovery. In recovered major depressives, less severe but definite social, family, and peer relationship deficits persist long after the episode. The persistence of social deficits, which have also been reported in depressed adults (Weissman, 1979), reveals the importance of treatments designed to improve social functioning, in addition to those targeting the depressive symptoms themselves.

DIFFERENTIAL DIAGNOSIS

The high prevalence of coexisting psychiatric disorders in children, along with the frequency of symptoms which overlap in multiple disorders, complicates the differential diagnosis of childhood depression. Common manifestations of depressive disorders that are also likely to occur in other disorders include anxiety features, attentional difficulties, oppositional behaviors, and conduct disordered symptoms. These features may occur as sporadic symptoms within the context of the depressive episode itself; they may present as temporally related concurrent anxiety, oppositional, or conduct disorders; or they may be components of preexisting disorders.

It appears that some symptoms of anxiety are universally seen in children with depressive disorders (Hershberg et al., 1982). Kovacs et al. (1984) found that one third of her depressed prepubertal sample also met the criteria for an anxiety disorder. In adolescents, up to one third of a depressed sample have been found to meet the criteria for an anxiety disorder as well (Ryan et al., 1987). Bernstein and Garfinkel (1986) found that in a sample of adolescent chronic school refusers, 69% of them met the criteria for a depressive disorder and 62% met the criteria for an anxiety disorder, while 50% of them fulfilled criteria for both. There is some evidence that depressed children and adolescents who exhibit concurrent anxiety disorders such as separation anxiety disorder are likely to have more severe depressions than those without the additional disorder (Mitchell et al., 1988). Thus, there is an association of anxiety symptoms with depressive disorders as well as the possible coexistence of both disorders.

It is not uncommon to find the presence of aggressive and other conduct symptoms in the context of a major depression, as well as a full conduct disorder developing along with a depressive episode. Here, too, it is possible that a child with a preexisting conduct disorder might develop a depressive disorder in addition. All these relationships between disordered conduct and depression appear to be more frequent in boys. In a sample of prepubertal depressed boys, one third also met the full criteria for a conduct disorder (Puig-Antich, 1982). In these boys, the conduct disorder developed shortly after the onset of the depressive illness and was resolved with recovery from the depression. The major depressive disorder itself was identical to that seen in boys who did not exhibit the conduct disorder. In follow-up, the children with both disorders who had relapses of major depression also had a reemergence of the conduct disorder (Puig-Antich, 1982). The boys with both disorders had a more turbulent clinical course than did the boys without the additional conduct disorder. There has been the suggestion that a connection exists between the decrease in the prevalence of male depressive symptomatology in adolescence and an increase in male antisocial behavior (Kandel & Davies, 1982), yet conduct disturbance alone is not sufficient to indicate depression.

An association between attention deficit disorder and depressive disorders has also been shown. Biederman (Biederman et al., 1987) found that 32% of children with attention deficit disorder also met criteria for major depression. In this sample, relatives of children with attention deficit disorder had higher rates of affective disorders than relatives of normals, but the rate of affective disorder in relatives did not vary depending on whether the proband child had both disorders.

In a prevalence study of DSM-III diagnoses in preadolescent children, the category with the most overlapping diagnoses was the depression/dysthymia group, in which combinations of depression or dysthymia plus attention deficit disorder and anxiety disorders and conduct or oppositional disorders were common (Anderson, Williams, McGee, & Silva, 1987).

CASE EXAMPLES

Case 1

Tim, a 10-year-old boy who was always felt to be a highly active and somewhat impulsive youngster, was socially interactive and a good student until the third grade, when he began to have some difficulty with oppositional behavior and developed a negative attitude and increasingly poor ability to concentrate. His school work suffered, and he began to argue with teachers and fight with peers. He was retained in the third grade, and although he exhibited the ability to do his work, he continued to be uncooperative, angry, and rebellious in school and at home, and his academic achievement fell below grade level.

Tim was finally promoted to the fourth grade, but he continued to feel that others treated him "unfairly," that he was continually being picked on, and that he was repeatedly being blamed for things that were not his fault. He had persistent arguments with his siblings, and even became physically abusive to his parents, and on one occasion he hit his teacher. His appetite became very poor, and he lost 15 pounds over the course of the year. Tim became more isolative over several months, electing to spend his time by himself in front of the television instead of playing with peers or siblings. When he did interact with his siblings, he was irritable and bossy. He developed insomnia and had to be nagged to take a shower and to comb his hair.

After a particularly trying week at school, Tim became more agitated, exhibiting severe temper outbursts in which he picked up several gardening tools and threatened to break windows and attempted to break the furniture. Over the next few days, he informed his family that he wished he were dead and tried to jump out of a moving car. On the day prior to admission, he picked up a hammer and swung it around, and then ran into the bathroom with a kitchen knife, locked the door, and cut his wrist superficially while screaming that he would kill himself. The police were called, and he was brought to the emergency room for immediate evaluation.

On admission, Tim appeared as a slender, pale, boy who cried for 15 minutes while he tried to bargain to go home. He remained tearful throughout the interview, although he was able to verbalize well. He admitted to suicidal ideation, which he reported to be intermittent over the last year and a half, but he denied that he would "actually do it." He admitted to hearing two male voices on several different occasions that told him that he was "worthless and might as well be dead." There was no evidence of delusions. He reported that the voices were probably right and that he hated himself for doing all those bad things that hurt his parents and sisters. He had frequent nightmares, but had trouble remembering their content. He was oriented, had age-appropriate communication skills, appeared to have a good fund of general information, and was estimated to have an IQ in the average range. His activity level was unremarkable, and there were no signs of psychomotor agitation or retardation.

During the first few days of his hospitalization, Tim no longer expressed suicidal ideation, but exhibited a depressed mood with a "chip on his shoulder." He was observed for several weeks to determine whether spontaneous improvement would occur in this milieu. During this time, he continued to feel rejected by his family and the

staff, and he felt that he was being "picked on." He was irritable and seemed to have an insatiable need for reassurance. Physical examination was unremarkable, and laboratory workup including an EEG, was negative. DST was negative. Tim was diagnosed as having a major depressive episode. When there was no improvement after several weeks in the hospital, Tim was started on a course of desipramine that was gradually titrated up to a dose of 150 mg per day. On that dose, he maintained a blood level of approximately 150 ng/dl. After two to three weeks Tim began to show some brightening of his mood and more willingness to listen to others' points of view. In spite of this, Tim continued to exhibit a marked suspiciousness that he was being "cheated out of something" and a supersensitivity to perceived criticism. He was still irritable intermittently, but he showed an increased ability to socialize and enjoy peer relations. His auditory hallucinations never emerged during his hospitalization. During the next month, his school work improved significantly. His family participated in sessions in which they agreed on ways to improve their home management of all their children. Tim was able to succeed in controlling his anger and was no longer a physical threat to himself or anybody else. Tim was excited to be discharged several weeks later, and was followed in individual and family therapy. On discharge, Tim was no longer having suicidal ideation, he was more cooperative, and his mood was no longer depressed. He still exhibited heightened sensitivity to criticism, and he sometimes reacted with a chip on his shoulder, although to a lesser degree.

Tim did relatively well for the first three months after discharge, and he then began to show increasing irritability, oppositional behavior, and an increased negative attitude. His school work remained intact, and he did not exhibit the poor appetite or the weight loss that had occurred during his previous major depressive episode. He continued in therapy, but was noncompliant with his medication, and he gradually weaned himself off medication completely. He became progressively more rebellious with his parents and began to be more and more physically threatening to his younger sisters. He was readmitted to the hospital when he became a physical threat to his siblings for an evaluation of a possible reoccurrence of major depression.

This time on admission, Tim appeared sullen and petulant, though not actually depressed. He expressed a negative attitude toward himself and his family. There was no suicidal ideation and no report of auditory hallucinations. He was initially more interactive with staff and less irritable than on his first admission. There were no vegetative symptoms, and there was no impairment in concentration or in school performance. Laboratory workup including DST was negative. Over the next several weeks, Tim quickly became involved with the milieu, but continued to be negativistic, demanding, and attention seeking. Tim did not meet the criteria on this admission for major depression, but he exhibited a persistent dysthymia and oppositional-defiant behavior. He was treated in the hospital with both individual therapy, which focused on managing his anger, and short-term family therapy with a focus on behavioral management. Tim was discharged with an improved mood, in better control of his impulses, and with a behavioral program to help him and his family to deal with his persistent negative view.

Case 2

Nina, an 11-year-old girl, was admitted to the hospital after setting a small fire in the bathroom at school. She had left a note at home saying that she "would not be back" because she was "dead." Nina had always been an excellent student and was very popular with her classmates. She had no history of medical or prior psychiatric problems and had a warm relationship with her parents and two brothers. She began to have fears of the dark, and became somewhat withdrawn shortly after the death of her maternal grandmother, with whom she was very close. Since her mother was also deeply affected by this loss, her parents decided that it would be good to get a "fresh start" somewhere else, and shortly thereafter, they decided to move to another state. As soon as Nina found out about this plan, she became adamant in her protest that she did not want to leave her old school and her friends. Her parents reassured her that their new house would be much nicer, and three months later, they moved.

For the first month after the move, Nina appeared to be making an adequate adjustment. She then began to have trouble concentrating, her grades began to drop, and she was unable to make friends. Although she had never been a shy child, she seemed to be withdrawn, which was noted by a relative who visited, and she was exquisitely sensitive, frequently becoming tearful over minor events. Over the next two months she became increasingly sullen, isolative, and irritable toward

her siblings with whom she usually played well. Nina seemed afraid to be alone, and yet did not enjoy being around her family. Her appetite diminished, and she complained of being unable to sleep. There was no weight loss noted. Nina began to leave notes around the house stating that she hated various family members and that she wished that she was dead. Although her family was concerned, they felt that this was a passing phase. They felt relieved that in spite of her new moodiness and irritability, Nina was still able to concentrate and excel in her ballet classes.

There was a history of recurrent depressions in Nina's maternal grandmother, and her mother had been treated for a depression when Nina was a toddler. Although she had not been in treatment for many years, her mother admitted to being "high strung" and irritable. Nina described her mother as short tempered, overly critical, always going through her private things, and continually expecting her to be "perfect."

Shortly before a scheduled psychiatric evaluation for Nina, her school called to report that she had set a fire and stayed in the bathroom until a teacher forced her to come out. This precipitated an emergency admission to the hospital.

On admission, Nina was noted to be an attractive girl who looked quite sad, and spoke softly and tearfully. She moved slowly and appeared to be "slowed down" in her reaction time. There was little animation in her voice, and she admitted to suicidal ideation, without a plan. She denied that she had expected to "die" in the bathroom at school and reported that she had left the note at home because she was mad at her family. She said that she had been feeling sad for at least a year, but that it became much worse at the time of her grandmother's death five months earlier. She reported feeling best when she was in an activity such as her dance class, and that she felt most sad at night. She denied hallucinations, and there was no evidence of delusions. Her motivation to do her schoolwork was poor, but her cognitive function appeared to be intact. Physical exam and laboratory exam were unremarkable except for her DST, which was positive, with a cortisol value of 6.6.

During the first few days of hospitalization, Nina was noted to have a markedly depressed mood, poor appetite, insomnia, and early morning awakening. She was observed to spend most of her unstructured time staring wistfully out of the window. She would become tearful whenever she described the events of the last few months.

During activities, however, she was able to participate, and often exhibited a much brighter affect
and good peer relationship skills.

Over the next two weeks, she interacted regularly with staff and peers. There was a noticeable
improvement in affect and mood, and she no
longer dissolved into tears during conversations
about the events leading to her hospitalization.
After three weeks in the hospital, her DST showed
a trend downward, with a blood cortisol level of
5.4. At this time, Nina was better able to verbalize
her feelings about the recent past. She expressed
her negative feelings about the move, how much
she missed her grandmother, and how angry she
was at her family for "ignoring" her feelings.
Nina's family adamantly opposed the use of antidepressant medication, and thus a conservative
course was followed. Nina remained in the hospital for another month, during which time she
continued to improve without any additional interventions. She was discharged with a substantially improved mood, without suicidal ideation
and with normalization of her ability to function
in school. The recommendation was made that
her mother receive treatment for her irritability
and labile mood, and that the family continue in
outpatient family therapy to deal with the negative family interactions as well as to monitor
Nina's affective state.

CONTINUITY AND DISCONTINUITY WITH ADULT PRESENTATION

Longitudinal study of childhood onset major
depressive disorder remains in an early stage, and
therefore, definitive understanding of its natural
history is still tentative. There are, nevertheless,
some striking trends in the manifestation of major
affective illness in young children, school-aged
children, and adolescents as well as between children (including adolescents) and adults.

The first major issue is the striking increase in
the prevalence of major depression with increasing age. As mentioned earlier (see Table 3.1),
the existence of major depression starts with a
mere 0.28% in preschool children, increases to
1.8% in school-aged children, and then drastically
increases to 4.7% in adolescence. This figure is
comparable to the 2.2% to 3.5% prevalence figures reported for adult major depression (Myers et
al., 1984). Second, the prevalence rates for males
and females switch in relative frequency from a
larger percentage of prepubertal boys to a relatively larger percentage of adolescent girls. Al-

though there are no empirical data to support any
one hypothesis, the onset of puberty and all its
ramifications must be considered in an investigation of these changes.

Aside from the differential rates of depressive
disorders, the phenomenology of major depression among different age groups also shows some
interesting trends. Symptoms that are frequently
seen in very young children but are manifested
much less often in adolescents and adults are somatic complaints such as stomachaches and headaches (Kashani & Carlson, 1987; Carlson &
Strober, 1983). Other symptoms that are often
seen in prepubertal children and decrease in frequency with age are depressed appearance, hallucinations, agitation, separation anxiety, and phobias (Ryan et al., 1987; Carlson & Kashani, 1988).
Adolescents, on the other hand, frequently manifest anhedonia, hopelessness, hypersomnia, drug
and alcohol use, and more lethal suicide attempts
(Ryan et al., 1987). Other symptoms that are more
frequently seen as age increases are diurnal mood
variation, hopelessness, delusions, and psychomotor retardation (Carlson & Kashani, 1988).
Symptoms that appear to be independent of age
are depressed mood, poor concentration, insomnia, and suicidal ideation (Carlson & Kashani, 1988). Percentages of these various symptoms in different age groups are shown in Table
3.2.

While suicidal ideation is relatively frequent in
all age groups, completed suicide is negligible before the age of 12, and it rises dramatically after
the age of 15 (Shaffer & Fisher, 1981). Developmental limitations with respect to a child's age
plays a role in that the younger children are less
realistic in suggesting "methods" of suicide
(Carlson et al., 1987). Adolescents, on the other
hand, are more knowledgeable and more realistic
about the lethality of methods. Beyond this issue,
however, it appears that even when young children
are knowledgeable on the subject of suicide, they
are less likely than adolescents to be able to
imagine circumstances in which one would actually go through with it (Carlson et al., 1987).
Overall, it appears that once development progresses to adolescence there is an increased continuity between thoughts and action (Carlson et al.,
1987). Risk factors for adolescent suicide comple-
ters include a diagnosis of bipolar disorder, comorbidity of nonaffective disorders, lack of prior
treatment, availability of firearms, and high suicidal intent (Brent et al., 1988). Additionally, correlates of the lethality of suicidal behavior include

Table 3.2. Percentage of Depressive Symptoms in Depressed Samples of Different Ages

	PRESCHOOL[1]	PREPUBERTAL[2]	ADOLESCENT[2]	ADULTS[3]
Depressed mood	100	90–95	88–92	100
Depressed appearance	89	24	16	
Anhedonia	22	66–89	74–92	77
Morning depression		15–19	14–20	46
Hopelessness		20–60	47–68	56
Low self-esteem	67	63–93	58–94	38
Fatigue	89	62–65	72–92	97
Poor concentration	56	75–80	79–82	84
Somatic complaints	100	58–77	49–78	25
Insomnia	100	60–82	64	71
Agitation	78	51–60	41–70	67
Psychomotor retardation	33	28–56	36–48	60
Anorexia	100	32–56	36–48	80
Suicidal ideation	67	51–67	49–68	63
Suicide attempts		25–39	34–39	15
Hallucinations		30	4–22	9
Delusions		4–13	4–6	16
Weight loss		18	32	61
Social withdrawal	89	78	73	
Guilt/self-blame	55	44	56	32

[1]Kashani & Carlson, 1987.
[2]Mitchell et al., 1988; Carlson & Kashani, 1988.
[3]Baker et al., 1971.

substance abuse and the availability of a lethal agent (Brent, 1987). These correlations are consistent with the age differential in suicide completion, since the development of bipolar disorder, substance abuse, and the availability of firearms are all more likely to occur in adolescence and adulthood than in childhood.

Another manifestation of affective disorder that shows a distinct increase in prevalence with adolescence is mania. Whether this means that bipolar disorders actually do not develop until puberty or that they are present in younger children but that mania is not fully expressed, this diagnosis has implications for morbidity and long-term outcome. Adolescents who go on to have a bipolar course are more likely to have had prior depressions that include delusions and psychomotor retardation (Strober & Carlson, 1982).

While there are distinctive patterns of depressive symptoms in individuals of different ages, there appears to be a significant continuity of depressive features over time. There are data to indicate that individuals with an initial depressive episode in early adolescence are at higher risk for recurrent depressions than are those whose first episode was later in adolescence (Carlson, 1984). In a sample of adolescents who endorsed depressive phenomena on a checklist at age 15 to 16

years, and were then rescreened at age 25 years, there was a remarkable degree of persistence in depressive symptoms over the nine-year period (Kandel & Davies, 1986). Depressed mood in the female adolescents was also associated with an increased incidence of psychiatric hospitalization in the females as adults, but this was not true for the males (Kandel & Davies, 1986).

The relationship between adult depressive disorders and their precursors in prepubertal children appears to be more complex. As reported by Rutter (1988) and Zeitlin (1986), in the majority of cases, major depression has its onset in adult life. When adult depression was preceded by psychopathology in childhood, the depressive symptoms manifested in childhood retained a significant consistency over time, although the actual diagnosis made in the child was often not major depression. The psychopathology in the child was found to be a conglomerate of depressive symptoms as well as other symptoms involving disturbances of behavior and conduct. A possible explanation for the lack of continuity in diagnosis given to these individuals as children and adults may be the lack of standardized assessment utilized in making a diagnosis resulting in potential omissions of an appropriate diagnosis of major depression in the child. In addition, given the high likelihood of concurrent disorders in children who meet the criteria for major depression, major depression may have been present but not diagnosed because it was overshadowed by a more blatant behavioral disturbance. The continuity of depressive phenomenology in individuals over time, along with the continuity of essential features of depression including biological features such as cortisol nonsuppression, in prepubertal and adult depressives (Puig-Antich, 1986), contribute to the evidence that depression is the same entity whether its onset is during childhood, adolescence, or adulthood.

Studies of families indicate that the children of parents with unipolar depression have significantly increased rates of major depression as compared to children of normals (13.1% vs. 0%) (Weissman et al., 1984). This risk nearly doubles when both parents have an affective disorder (Beardslee et al., 1983). Furthermore, the earlier the onset of the parental affective disorder, the higher the risk to the child of affective disorder (Weissman et al., 1987). In adults, the lifetime prevalence of major affective disorder (including schizoaffective disorder) in first-degree relatives of unipolar depressed individuals was found to be 20%, as compared to 7% in the relatives of normals (Gershon et al., 1982). The most prevalent psychiatric disorders found in relatives of severely depressed individuals and of moderately depressed individuals (all of whom met DSM-III criteria for major depression) was major depression and dysthymic disorder (Weissman et al., 1984). The continuity of depressive disorders in childhood and adulthood is further supported by the fact that first-degree relatives of both childhood and adult depressives are at increased risk for depressive disorder. Furthermore, these data imply that there may be complex factors contributing to the development of a depressive episode since the children of parents who have an earlier onset of depression appear to be more at risk for the development of the disorder than children of parents with later onset depression. It is possible that an earlier and longer exposure of biologically vulnerable children to parents who are impaired by their illness can predispose them to an earlier onset of the depression themselves.

SUMMARY

Major depressive disorder in childhood is a recognizable entity with an increasing prevalence from preschool to adolescence. It can cause severe

and long-lasting interpersonal and cognitive dysfunction in children as with adults and can contribute to continued disability in social and family relationships that may persist even after the depressive episode has resolved (Puig-Antich et al., 1985). The phenomenology of major depressive disorder appears to be affected by age and developmental level, although the essential features of the disorder seem to be the same in children of all ages and adults. For example, somatic complaints and nonverbal manifestations are very commonly seen in depressed preschool children (Kashani & Carlson, 1987), auditory hallucinations and separation anxiety are often exhibited by school-aged children, and adolescents more often show anhedonia, hypersomnia and diurnal variation (Ryan et al., 1987). There are some symptoms such as inability to concentrate, insomnia, and suicidal ideation that appear to be independent of age (Carlson & Kashani, 1988).

Although major depression at any age may have serious and long-term ramifications for the individual and the family, there is evidence to suggest that the earlier the onset of the depression, the slower the recovery, and therefore the longer the morbidity (Kovacs et al., 1984). Furthermore, once a child has experienced one episode of major depression, the probability of experiencing another episode within five years was found to be 72% (Kovacs et al., 1984).

A complicating factor in childhood major depression is the high rate of comorbidity, that is, the likelihood of major depression and an additional disorder coexisting, increasing the morbidity. Associations between major depression and attention-deficit disorder, anxiety disorders, and/or conduct disorder are common (Biederman et al., 1987; Bernstein & Garfinkel, 1986; Kovacs et al., 1984; Puig-Antich, 1982).

When adult depression has been preceded by childhood or adolescent psychopathology, a notable continuity in the specific depressive symptomatology has been described (Rutter, 1988; Zeitlin, 1986; Kandel & Davies, 1986). This consistency of depressive phenomenology over time lends support to the notion that the depression is the same entity whether it presents in childhood, in adolescence, or in adulthood.

REFERENCES

Akiskal, H. S., Downs, J., Joran, P., Watson, S., Daugherty, D., & Pruitt, D. B. (1985). Affective disorders in referred children and younger siblings of manic depressives. *Archives of General Psychiatry, 42*, 996–1004.

Anderson, J. C., Williams, S., McGee, R., & Silva, P. A. (1987). DSM-III disorders in preadolescent children: Prevalence in a large sample from the general population. *Archives of General Psychiatry, 44*, 69–76.

Asarnow, J. R., Golstin, M., Perdue, S., Bates, S., & Keller, J. (1988). Childhood onset depressive disorders: A follow-up study of rates of rehospitalization and out of home placement among child psychiatric inpatients. *Journal of Affective Disorders, 15*, 245–253.

Baker, M., Dorzab, J., Winokur, G., & Cadoret, R. (1971). Depressive disease: Classification and clinical characteristics. *Comprehensive Psychiatry, 12*, 354–365.

Beardslee, W. R., Bemporad, J., Keller, M. B., & Klerman, G. L. (1983). Children of parents with major affective disorder: A review. *American Journal of Psychiatry, 140*, 825–832.

Bernstein, G. A., & Garfinkel, B. D. (1986). School phobia: The overlap of affective and anxiety disorders. *Journal of the American Academy of Child Psychiatry, 25*, 235–241.

Biederman, J., Munir, K., Knee, D., Armentano, M., Autor, S., Waternaux, C., & Tsuang, M. (1987). High rates of affective disorders in probands with attention deficit disorder and in their relatives: A controlled family study. *American Journal of Psychiatry, 144*, 330–333.

Boyd, J. H., & Weissman, M. M. (1981). Epidemiology of affective disorders: A reexamination and future directions. *Archives of General Psychiatry, 38*, 1039–1046.

Brent, D. (1987). Correlates of medical lethality of suicide attempts in children and adolescents. *Journal of the American Academy of Child and Adolescent Psychiatry, 26*, 87–89.

Brent, D., Perper, J. A., Goldstein, C. E., Kolko, D. J., Allan, M. J., Allman, C. J., & Zelenak, J. P. (1988). Risk factors for adolescent suicide: A comparison of adolescent suicide victims with suicidal inpatients. *Archives of General Psychiatry, 45*, 581–588.

Cantwell, D. P., & Carlson, G. A. (Eds.). (1983). *Affective disorders in childhood and adolescence: An update.* New York: Spectrum.

Carlson, G. A. (1984). A comparison of early and late onset adolescent affective disorder. *Journal of Operational Psychiatry, 15*, 46–50.

Carlson, G. A., Asarnow, J. R., & Orbach, I. (1987). Developmental aspects of suicidal behavior. I. *Journal of the Academy of Child and Adolescent Psychiatry, 26*, 186–193.

Carlson, G. A., & Cantwell, D. P. (1979). A survey of depressive symptoms in child and adolescent populations. *Journal of the American Academy of Child Psychiatry, 18*, 587–599.

Carlson, G. A., & Cantwell, D. P. (1982). Suicidal behavior and depression in children and adolescents. *Journal of the American Academy of Child Psychiatry, 21*, 361–368.

Carlson, G. A., & Kashani, J. H. (1988). Phenomenology of major depressive disorder from childhood through adulthood: Analysis of three studies. *American Journal of Psychiatry, 145*, 1222–1225.

Carlson, G. A., & Strober, M. (1979). Affective disorders in adolescence. *Psychiatric Clinics of North America, 2*, 511–526.

Carlson, G. A., & Strober, M. (1983). Affective disorders in adolescence. In D. Cantwell & G. A. Carlson (Eds.), *Affective disorders in childhood and adolescence: An update.* New York: Spectrum.

Chambers, W. J., Puig-Antich, J., Tabrizi, M. A., & Davies, M. (1982). Psychotic symptoms in prepubertal major depressive disorder. *Archives of General Psychiatry, 39*, 921–927.

Coble, P. A., Kupfer, D. J., Spiker, D. G., Neil, J. F., & Shaw, D. H. (1980). EEG sleep and clinical characteristics in young primary depressives. *Sleep Research, 9*, 165–170.

Costello, A. J., Edelbrock, C., Dulcan, M. K., Kalas, R., & Clario, S. H. (1984). *Development and testing of the new NIMH diagnostic interview schedule for children in a clinic population.* Final report. Rockville, MD: Center for Epidemiologic Studies, National Institute of Mental Health.

Garber, J., Kris, M. R., Koch, M., & Lindholm, L. (1988). Recurrent depression in adolescents: A follow-up study. *Journal of the American Academy of Child and Adolescent Psychiatry, 27*, 49–54.

Gershon, E. S., Hamovit, J., Guroff, J., Dibble, E., Leckman, J. F., Sceery, W., Targun, S. D., Nurnberger, J. I., Golden, L. R., & Bunney, W. E. (1982). A family study of schizoaffective, bipolar I, bipolar II, unipolar probands and normal controls. *Archives of General Psychiatry, 39*, 1157–1173.

Gillin, J. C., Sitaram, N., & Duncan, W. C. (1979). Muscarinic supersensitivity: A possible model for the sleep disturbance of primary depression? *Psychiatry Research, 1*, 17–21.

Greden, J. F., Gardner, R., King, D., Grunhaus, L., Carroll, B. J., & Kronfol, Z. (1983). Dexamethasone suppression test in antidepressant treatment of melancholia: The process of normalization and test-retest reproducibility. *Archives of General Psychiatry, 40*, 493–500.

Herjanic, B., & Reich, W. (1982). Development of a structured interview for children: Agreement between child and parent on individual symptoms. *Journal of Abnormal Child Psychology, 10*, 307–324.

Hershberg, S. G., Carlson, G. A., Cantwell, D. P., & Strober, M. (1982). Anxiety and depressive disorders in psychiatrically disturbed children. *Journal of Clinical Psychiatry, 43*, 358–361.

Kandel, D. B., & Davies, M. (1982). Epidemiology of depressed mood in adolescents: An empirical study. *Archives of General Psychiatry, 39*, 1205–1212.

Kandel, D. B., & Davies, M. (1986). Adult sequelae of adolescent depressive symptoms. *Archives of General Psychiatry, 43*, 255–262.

Kaplan, S. L., Hong, G. K., & Weinhold, C. (1984). Epidemiology of depressive symptomatology in adolescents. *Journal of the American Academy of Child Psychiatry, 23*, 91–98.

Kashani, J. H., Cantwell, D. P., Shekim, W. O., & Reid, J. C. (1982). Major depressive disorder in children admitted to an inpatient community mental health center. *American Journal of Psychiatry, 139*, 671–672.

Kashani, J. H., & Carlson, G. A. (1987). Seriously depressed preschoolers. *American Journal of Psychiatry, 144*, 348–350.

Kashani, J. H., Carlson, G. A., Beck, N. C., Hoeper, E. W., Corcoran, C. M., McAllister, J. A., Fallahi, C., Rosenberg, T. K., & Reid, J. C. (1987). Depression, depressive symptoms, and depressed mood among a community sample of adolescents. *American Journal of Psychiatry, 144*, 931–934.

Kashani, J. H., Holcomb, W. R., & Orvaschel, H. (1986). Depression and depressive symptoms in preschool children from the general population. *American Journal of Psychiatry, 143*, 1138–1143.

Kashani, J. H., McGee, R. O., Clarkson, S. E., Anderson, J. C., Walton, L. A., Williams, S., Silva, P. A., Robins, A. J., Cytryn, L., & McKnew, D. H. (1983). Depression in a sample of 9-year-old children. *Archives of General Psychiatry, 40*, 1217–1223.

Kashani, J. H., Orvaschel, H., Burke, J. P., &

Reid, J. C. (1985). Information variance: The issue of parent-child disagreement. *Journal of the American Academy of Child Psychiatry, 24*, 437–441.

Kashani, J. H., & Ray, J. S. (1983). Depressive symptoms among preschool-age children. *Child Psychiatry and Human Development, 13*, 233–238.

Kazdin, A. E., French, N. H., Unis, A. S., Esveldt-Dawson, K., & Sherick, K. B. (1983). Hopelessness, depression and suicidal intent among psychiatrically disturbed inpatient children. *Journal of Consulting and Clinical Psychology, 51*, 504–510.

Keller, M. B., & Shapiro, R. W. (1982). "Double depression:" Superimposition of acute depressive episodes on chronic depressive disorders. *American Journal of Psychiatry, 139*, 438–442.

Kovacs, M. (1980–81). Rating scales to assess depression in school age children. *Acta Paedopsychatrica, 46*, 305–315.

Kovacs, M., Feinberg, T. C., Crouse-Novak, M. A., Paulauskas, S. L., & Finkelstein, R. (1984). Depressive disorders in childhood: I, II. *Archives of General Psychiatry, 41*, 229–237.

Kovacs, M., Paulauskas, S., Gatsonis, C., & Richards, C. (1988). Depressive disorders in childhood: III. A longitudinal study of comorbidity with and risk for conduct disorders. *Journal of Affective Disorders, 15*, 205–215.

Kupfer, D. (1976). REM latency: A psychobiologic marker for primary depressive disease. *Biological Psychiatry, 11*, 159–174.

Lang, M., & Tisher, M. (1978). *Children's depression scale.* Melbourne: Australian Council for Educational Research.

Lefkowitz, M. M., & Burton, N. (1978). Childhood depression: A critique of the concept. *Psychological Bulletin, 85*, 716–726.

McGee, R., & Williams, S. (1988). A longitudinal study of depression in nine-year-old children. *Journal of the American Academy of Child and Adolescent Psychiatry, 27*, 342–348.

Mitchell, J., McCauley, E., Burke, P. M., & Moss, S. (1988). Phenomenology of depression in children and adolescents. *Journal of the American Academy of Child and Adolescent Psychiatry, 27*, 12–20.

Myers, J. K., Weissman, M. M., Tischler, G. L., Holzer, C. E., Leaf, P. J., Orvaschel, H., Anthony, J. C., Boyd, J. H., Burke, J. D., Kramer, M., & Stoltzman, R. (1984). Six month prevalence of psychiatric disorders in three communities. *Archives of General Psychiatry, 41*, 959–967.

Petty, L. K., Asarnow, J. R., Carlson, G. A., & Lesser, L. (1985). The dexamethasone suppression test in depressed, dysthymic, and nondepressed children. *American Journal of Psychiatry, 142*, 631–633.

Poznanski, E. O. (1982). The clinical characteristics of childhood depression. In L. Grinspoon (Ed.), *The American Psychiatric Association annual review* (pp. 296–307). Washington, DC: American Psychiatric Press.

Poznanski, E. O., Carroll, B. J., Banegas, M. C., Cook, S. C., & Grossman, J. A. (1982). The dexamethasone suppression test in prepubertal depressed children. *American Journal of Psychiatry, 139*, 320–324.

Poznanski, E. O., Grossman, J. A., Buchsbaum, Y., Banegus, M., Freeman, L., & Gibbon, R. (1984). Preliminary studies of the reliability and validity of the children's depression rating scale. *Journal of the American Academy of Child Psychiatry, 23*, 191–197.

Poznanski, E. O., Krahenbuhl, J. P., & Zrull, M. (1976). Childhood depression: A longitudinal perspective. *Journal of the American Academy of Child Psychiatry, 15*, 491–501.

Puig-Antich, J. (1982). Major depression and conduct disorder in prepuberty. *Journal of the American Academy of Child Psychiatry, 21*, 118–128.

Puig-Antich, J. (1986). Psychobiological markers: Effects of age and puberty. In M. Rutter, C. E. Izard, & P. B. Read (Eds.), *Depression in young people: Developmental and clinical perspectives* (pp. 353–381). New York: The Guilford Press.

Puig-Antich, J., & Chambers, W. (1978). The schedule for affective disorders and schizophrenia for school-aged children. New York: New York State Psychiatric Institute.

Puig-Antich, J., Lukens, E., Davies, M., Brennan-Quarttrock, J., & Todak, G. (1985). Psychosocial functioning in prepubertal major depressive disorders. I, II. *Archives of General Psychiatry, 44*, 81–89.

Reich, W., Herjanic, B., Welner, Z., & Gandhy, P. R. (1982). Development of a structured psychiatric interview for children: Agreement on diagnosis comparing child and parent interview. *Journal of Abnormal Child Psychology, 10*, 325–336.

Robbins, D. R., Alessi, N. E., Cook, S. C., Poznanski, E. O., & Yanchyshyn, G. W.

(1982). The use of the Research Diagnostic Criteria (RDC) for depression in adolescent psychiatric inpatients. *Journal of the American Academy of Child Psychiatry, 21*, 251–255.

Rutter, M. (1988). Epidemiological approaches to developmental psychopathology. *Archives of General Psychiatry, 45*, 486–495.

Rutter, M., Graham, P., Chadwick, O., & Yule, W. (1976). Adolescent turmoil: Fact or fiction? *Journal of Child Psychology and Psychiatry, 17*, 35–65.

Ryan, N. D., Puig-Antich, J., Ambrosini, P., Rabinovich, H., Robinson, D., Nelson, B., Iyengar, S., & Twomey, J. (1987). The clinical picture of major depression in children and adolescents. *Archives of General Psychiatry, 44*, 854–861.

Shaffer, D. (1985). Depression, mania, and suicidal acts: In M. Rutter & L. Hersov (Eds.), *Depression in young people: Developmental and clinical perspectives* (pp. 383–396). New York: Guilford Press.

Shaffer, D., & Fisher, P. (1981). The epidemiology of suicide in children and young adolescents. *Journal of the American Academy of Child Psychiatry, 20*, 545–565.

Shaffer, D., Schwab-Stone, M. S., Fisher, P., Davies, M., Piacentini, J., & Gioia, P. (1988). *A revised version of the Diagnostic Interview Schedule for Children*. Final report. Rockville, MD: National Institute of Mental Health.

Strober, M., & Carlson, G. A. (1982). Bipolar illness in adolescents with major depression: Clinical, genetic, and psychopharmacologic predictors of bipolar illness in adolescents with major depression. A 3- to 4-year prospective follow-up investigation. *Archives of General Psychiatry, 39*, 549–555.

Strober, M., Green, J., & Carlson, G. A. (1981a). Phenomenology and subtypes of major depressive disorder in adolescents. *Journal of Affective Disorders, 3*, 281–290.

Strober, M., Green, J., & Carlson, G. A. (1981b). Reliability of psychiatric diagnosis in hospitalized adolescents. *Archives of General Psychiatry, 38*, 141–145.

Weissman, M. M. (1979). The psychological treatment of depression: Evidence for the efficacy of psychotherapy alone in comparison with and in combination with pharmacotherapy. *Archives of General Psychiatry, 36*, 1261–1269.

Weissman, M. M., Gammon, G. D., John, K., Merikangas, K. R., Warner, W. V., Prusoff,

B. A., & Sholomaskas, D. (1987). Children of depressed parents: Increased psychopathology and early onset of major depression. *Archives of General Psychiatry, 44*, 847–853.

Weissman, M. M., & Myers, J. K. (1978). Affective disorders in a US urban community: The use of the RDC in an epidemiologic survey. *Archives of General Psychiatry, 34*, 98–111.

Weissman, M. M., Prusoff, B. A., Gammon, G. D., Merikangas, K., Leckman, J. F., & Kidd, K. K. (1984). Psychopathology in the children (6–18) of depressed and normal parents. *Journal of the American Academy of Child and Adolescent Psychiatry, 23*, 78–84.

Weller, E. B., Weller, R., Fristad, M. A., Preskorn, S. H., & Teare, M. (1985). The dexamethasone suppression test in prepubertal depressed children. *Journal of Clinical Psychiatry, 46*, 511–513.

Zeitlin, H. (1986). *The natural history of psychiatric disorder in childhood*. New York: Oxford University Press.

CHAPTER 4

MAJOR DEPRESSION IN ADULTHOOD

Michael E. Thase

DESCRIPTION OF THE DISORDER

The depressive disorders are the most common psychopathologic conditions encountered in both mental health settings and general medical practice (Blacker & Clare, 1987). As classified in the revised third edition of the *Diagnostic and Statistical Manual of Mental Disorders* (American Psychiatric Association, 1987), the nonbipolar depressive disorders include major depressive disorder and its subtypes, dysthymic disorder, and depressive disorders not otherwise specified. These disorders include conditions in which mood is predominately depressed and in which individuals have never experienced an episode of mania or hypomania. Approximately 90% of the depressive disorders are nonbipolar (Keller, 1988).

Although the statement "I'm depressed" is part of everyday speech, use of the term depression should be restricted to describe conditions that fall outside of the boundary of normal experi-

ence. In practice, a clinical depression is distinguished from a normal "blue" mood by the (1) intensity, (2) duration, (3) coexistence of other clinical signs and symptoms (i.e., the core syndrome), and (4) impact on the individual's functioning (Thase, 1987). Considerable efforts over the last several decades have led to this atheoretical practice, in which diagnosis is based on delineation of an affective syndrome and exclusion of other differential diagnostic considerations.

A major depressive syndrome is defined in DSM-III-R by the presence of at least five characteristic symptoms of depression (selected from a list of nine common symptoms) that have been present for at least a two-week period and represent a change from previous functioning (APA, 1987). At least one of the symptoms must be either depressed mood or anhedonia. Further, an organic factor that is known to have initiated and maintained the disturbance cannot be identified (cf. organic affective disorder) and the mood disturbance cannot be a normal reaction to the death

Preparation of this chapter was supported, in part, by grants MH-41884 and MH-30915 from the National Institute of Mental Health. The assistance of Mrs. Lisa Stupar is gratefully acknowledged.

of a loved one (cf. uncomplicated bereavement). Psychotic features may be present, but major depression should not be diagnosed concurrently with schizophrenia.

Dysthymic disorder is defined by a chronically and persistently depressed mood (for most of the days, more days than not), with the presence of a milder depressive syndrome consisting of at least two of six common symptoms (APA, 1987). To make a diagnosis of dysthymic disorder, the depressive syndrome cannot have lifted for a period of longer than two months during the two years prior to diagnosis. Like major depression, dysthymia may not have been initiated and maintained by an organic factor, never occurred in an individual with a history of mania or hypomania, and is not superimposed on schizophrenia. The criteria for DSM-III-R major depression are summarized in Table 4.1.

Frequently, individuals with a current diagnosis of major depression will have an antecedent history of dysthymic disorder. Conversely, individuals with a current diagnosis of dysthymic disorder often will have a past history of major depressive episodes. In these cases, both diagnoses are made, resulting in a syndrome commonly known as "double depression" (Keller, 1988). Diagnostic criteria for dysthymic disorder are summarized in Table 4.2.

A residual category, depressive disorders not otherwise specified (NOS), also is included in DSM-III-R for diagnosis of mood disorders that neither meet the criteria for a specific mood disorder nor an adjustment disorder. Little is known about the patients who fall into this residual category; it will not be discussed further in this chapter.

CLINICAL PRESENTATION

The depressive disorders are noted for their heterogeneity (Nelson & Charney, 1981). Major depressive episodes may be characterized by either psychomotor retardation or agitation, detached apathy or generalized hyperarousal, anorexia or hyperphagia, and/or insomnia or hypersomnia. While there is some tendency for these varied descriptors to aggregate into prototypic subforms, which have been described as anxious-agitated and retarded-anergic depressive syndromes (Kupfer, Foster, Detre, & Himmelhoch, 1975), it is common to see patients with an admixture of symptoms.

One traditional approach to description of depression is to focus on whether the episode appears to have been precipitated by an adverse life event or has occurred without environmental provocation (Hirschfeld, 1981). The former presentation has been called "reactive" depression, with the latter often referred to as "autonomous" or "endogenous" depression (Keller, 1988). However, the validity of a situational or reactive type of depression has not been established (Hirschfeld, 1981; Keller, 1988). Thus, DSM-III-R does not include a subtype diagnosis for situational depression, although the absence of precipitating events continues to be included as a diagnostic criterion in several research classifications of endogenous depression (see Zimmerman & Spitzer, 1989). In DSM-III-R, the issue of precipitating stress is handled via multiaxial classification, with Axis-IV used for coding the nature of the stressor and its severity (American Psychiatric Association, 1987).

Another classical approach to subdividing depressive episodes is based on the nature of the presenting signs and symptoms. Depressive syndromes characterized by a pronounced disturbance neurovegetative function (including midnight and early-morning awakening, weight loss, loss of libido, anhedonia, and diurnal mood variation) have been variously described as autonomous, melancholic, or endogenous disorders (Zimmerman & Spitzer, 1989). The construct of endogenous depression implies an internal etiology and a substantial literature has documented a higher frequency of biological abnormalities in such cases, including evidence of neurochemical, neuroendocrine, and neurophysiological dysfunction (see Thase, Frank, & Kupfer, 1985). Nevertheless, broadly accepted criteria for endogenous depression have not been developed, and the construct of endogeneity is strongly confounded by differences in severity (Zimmerman & Spitzer, 1989). DSM-III-R does include criteria for the subtype diagnosis of melancholia, which is based on both neurovegetative symptoms and three life-course markers: absence of personality disturbance, history of prior depressive episodes, and past response to somatic treatment (APA, 1987). One major assumption of such subtyping is that somatic antidepressant treatment (i.e., pharmacotherapy or electroconvulsive therapy) will be more effective in endogenous syndromes than in psychological treatments (Thase, 1987). Studies employing psychotherapy response as a possible validator of clinical definitions of endogenous de-

Table 4.1. Current Criteria for a Major Depressive Episode[1]

A. At least five of the following symptoms (must include depressed mood and/or loss of interest or pleasure):[2]

    1. Depressed mood most of the day[3] (irritable mood may be substituted in children and adolescents)
    2. Markedly diminished interest or pleasure in all, or almost all, activities[3]
    3. Significant weight gain or loss (i.e., 5% change in one month) *or* decrease or increase in appetite[3]
    4. Insomnia or hypersomnia[3]
    5. Psychomotor agitation or retardation[3]
    6. Fatigue or loss of energy[3]
    7. Feelings of worthlessness or excessive guilt[3]
    8. Poor concentration or indecisiveness[3]
    9. Recurrent thoughts of death or suicidal ideation—plan, or intent

B. 1. Syndrome is not initiated or maintained by an organic factor (organic affective disorder)
    2. Syndrome is not a normal reaction to death of a loved one (uncomplicated bereavement)

C. Not reported delusions or hallucinations for as long as 2 weeks in the absence of mood-related symptoms

D. Not superimposed on another psychotic disorder (i.e., schizophrenia, schizophreniform disorder, or delusional disorder)

---

[1] Adapted from DSM-III-R (APA, 1987).
[2] Symptoms cannot be attributed to a physical condition, mood-incongruent delusions or hallucinations, incoherence, or marked loosening of associations.
[3] Symptoms must be experienced nearly every day for at least 2 weeks.

pression are necessary to resolve this issue (Simons & Thase, 1990).

Other subtypes included in DSM-III-R are the psychotic and recurrent forms of major depression. Psychotic depressions are relatively uncommon, perhaps occurring in only 5% to 10% of identified cases (Spiker et al., 1985). Depressive hallucinations and delusions usually have mood-congruent themes (such as taunting auditory hal-

lucinations and delusions of sin, guilt, disease, or nihilism). These severe and incapacitating depressive syndromes frequently are accompanied by biological dysregulation (e.g., Thase, Kupfer, & Ulrich, 1986) and have a high risk for adverse outcomes, such as recurrence, chronicity, and suicide (Thase & Kupfer, 1987). Psychotic depressions also require aggressive inpatient treatment, including the use of concomitant antipsychotic medication or electroconvulsive therapy (Thase & Kupfer, 1987).

Available evidence suggests that a majority of depressions will recur if followed for a long enough period of time (Angst, 1981; Consensus Development Panel, 1985; Keller, 1988; Zis & Goodwin, 1979). Indeed, once an individual has suffered a first recurrence of depression, the odds of experiencing a third episode approach 70% to 80% with additional risks for subsequent episodes (Angst, 1981). Thus, the subclassification of recurrent depression conveys significant prognostic information with respect to the need for preventive treatment.

Recent evidence also suggests that some forms of recurrent depression cycle in a seasonal pattern (Blehar & Rosenthal, 1989). The most common type of seasonal pattern involves recurrent depression during the fall and winter, which has been referred to as seasonal affective disorder (SAD) (Blehar & Rosenthal, 1989). Seasonal affective disorder appears to be characterized by predominantly reversed neurovegetative signs and symptoms, including hyperphagia and hypersomnia

Table 4.2. Current Criteria for Dysthymic Disorder[1]

A. Depressed mood,[2] more days than not, for at least 2 years[3]

B. At least two associated symptoms
    1. Decreased or increased appetite
    2. Insomnia or hypersomnia
    3. Low energy or fatigue
    4. Low self-esteem
    5. Poor concentration or indecisiveness
    6. Feelings of hopelessness

C. Never without mood disturbance (criterion A) for more than 2 months during a 2-year period[3]

D. No evidence of a certain major depressive episode during the first 2 years[3] of mood disturbance

E. No evidence of past mania or hypomania

F. Not superimposed on a chronic psychotic disorder (e.g., schizophrenia)

G. Syndrome is not initiated or maintained by an organic factor

---

[1] Adapted from DSM-III-R (APA, 1987).
[2] Irritable mood may be substituted in children and adolescents.
[3] Duration criterion is 1 year in children and adolescents.

(Blehar & Rosenthal, 1989). Such fall-winter depressions may be effectively treated with artificial bright light (Rosenthal, Sack, Skwerer, Jacobsen, & Wehr, 1989). There also appears to be a tendency for other forms of recurrent depression to show seasonal cycles, including depressions which respond quite well to conventional antidepressant treatment (Thase, 1989).

Reversed neurovegetative signs and symptoms appear to be more common in the depressive disorders than previously realized. Historically, reversed neurovegetative profiles have been referred to as atypical symptoms and have been linked to other presentations, including panic, anxiety, and phobic states (Himmelhoch & Thase, 1989). Whether these forms constitute truly atypical depressive disorders or are simply part of a heterogeneous spectrum of depressions remains to be established; a category for atypical depression is not included in DSM-III-R. Some evidence supports a preferential response of atypical depression to MAOIs (monoamine oxidase inhibitors) relative to tricyclic antidepressants (e.g., Liebowitz et al., 1984). Of note, categorical views of atypical depression may obscure an age-related evolution of the clinical presentation of depression (Caspar et al., 1985). Symptoms such as lethargy, hyperphagia, and hypersomnia appear to be overrepresented in teenagers (Kovacs & Gatsonis, 1989) and young adults (Caspar et al., 1985) with depression, whereas symptoms such as anorexia, agitation, and severe insomnia may be more common in older patients (Caspar et al., 1985; Himmelhoch & Thase, 1989).

The clinical heterogeneity of patients with dysthymic disorder is similarly impressive (Akiskal, 1983; Kocsis & Francis, 1987). Preliminary efforts to establish a characteristic syndromal profile for dysthymic disorder have not been particularly successful beyond specification of criteria for severity and duration (Kocsis & Francis, 1987). Efforts to establish subtypes within dysthymic disorder definition have been somewhat more successful, with several groups differentiating primary and secondary forms of dysthymia, as well as early-onset and late-onset forms (Akiskal, 1983; Klein, Taylor, Harding, & Dickstein, 1988). Early-onset dysthymia is characterized by its enduring nature, relatively poor prognosis, strongly family "loading" of affective disorder, and greater association with personality disturbance (Klein et al., 1988). Moreover, a recent study of depressed children has established the high prevalence of dysthymic disorder in a clinical sample, as well as the strong predictive risk of childhood dysthymic disorder for subsequent episode of major depression (Kovacs & Gatsonis, 1989).

Occasionally depressions may take other atypical forms. For example, depressive disorders may be characterized by strongly somatic features or conditions in which the individual flatly denies the experience of depression. In the latter case (so-called "masked" depression), anhedonia and a full affective syndrome are manifest (Thase, 1987). In such cases, diagnosis hinges on uncovering the signs and symptoms of a depressive episode, as well as detecting a past history of depression or a family history of affective disorder.

EPIDEMIOLOGY

The nonbipolar depressive disorders are the most common diagnoses given in psychiatric and medical settings. For example, among those patients seen for the first time at Western Psychiatric Institute and Clinic of the University of Pittsburgh, major depressive disorder accounts for over 30% of intakes (Mezzich, Fabrega, Coffman, & Haley, 1989). Community survey studies similarly document the ubiquity of the depressive disorders. The Epidemiologic Catchment Area (ECA) study (Regier et al., 1984) applied DSM-III criteria (APA, 1980) and standardized interview techniques to over 18,000 people. The lifetime risk for DSM-III major depressive disorder was found to range from 4.9% to 8.7% in women and 2.3% to 4.4% in men; lifetime rates for dysthymic disorder were found to range from 2% to 4% across settings (Robins et al., 1984). The one-month prevalence rate of dysthymia (3.3%) was higher than major depression (2.2%) (Regier et al., 1988).

Perhaps the strongest and most consistent epidemiologic finding relevant to the nonbipolar depressive disorders is the overrepresentation of women (Nolen-Hoeksema, 1987). Generally, studies have reported at least a twofold increase in prevalence of nonbipolar depression in women compared to men, whereas prevalence rates more closely approximate a 1 : 1 ratio in bipolar affective disorder (Nolen-Hoeksema, 1987). Attempts to account for the high rates of depression in women have included consideration of biological (e.g., Thase, Frank, & Kupfer, 1985) and psychosocial risk factors (e.g., Nolen-Hoeksema, 1987). Although women do have greater risks associated with certain gender-related biological factors (e.g., postpartum affective states, oral contraceptive use, menstrually related disorders, and increased rates of subclinical thyroid disease), even a summation of these risks probably cannot account for the larger gender difference (Thase, Frank, & Kupfer, 1985). Studies examining psychosocial risk factors point to the importance of limited social support and the burden of traditional homemaker status (Brown & Harris, 1978). Indeed, the highest rates of major depression observed in the ECA study were in women between the ages of 18 and 44 (Robins et al., 1984). Nevertheless, Angst and Dobler-Mikola (1984) have suggested that the differences in symptomatic reporting of men and women may account for this phenomenon. They found that among individuals experiencing at least two weeks of depression and social impairment, men reported an average of three associated symptoms whereas women reported an average of five associated symptoms. Thus, if gender-specific thresholds for symptomatic criteria are used for case definition, a 1 : 1 sex ratio might be achieved (Angst & Dobler-Mikola, 1984).

Mean age of onset of the first episode of depressive disorders previously has been reported to occur in the fourth or fifth decade of life for non-bipolar syndromes, about ten years later than in bipolar disorder (Angst, 1981; Perris, 1966). Results of the ECA study, as well as those of a large collaborative clinical study (Klerman et al., 1985) have documented that the mean age of onset of the first episode of nonbipolar depression appears to be decreasing with each successive generation. Although there may be alternative explanations for this phenomenon, these findings suggest that epidemiological data will reflect further increases in rates of depression in the coming years.

Marital status has an interesting and complicated epidemiologic relationship with depression. Marital separation and divorce consistently have been found to be a risk factor for depression (Boyd & Weissman, 1982). Available evidence suggests marriage may convey a protective effect for some subgroups (for example, men), while other work suggests that marriage may be a risk factor for depression in other groups (for example, younger women) (Boyd & Weissman, 1982; Brown & Harris, 1978).

Other epidemiological factors, including urban-rural status, socioeconomic status, and race, have not been consistently related to the epidemiology of nonbipolar depression (Boyd & Weissman, 1982). Indeed, earlier evidence suggesting increased rates of affective disorders in nonwhite

populations appear to have been biased by cultural differences in symptom reporting or treatment seeking behavior. In the ECA study (Robins et al., 1984), there was no difference in rates of depression in white and nonwhite samples.

NATURAL HISTORY

The episodic and remitting nature of affective disorders has served as an important variable throughout history, including their role in helping Kraepelin (1921) to distinguish affective states from dementia praecox. Several relatively arbitrary conventions will be utilized in this chapter to describe the longitudinal course of depression. The term remission will be used to describe a complete recovery from a depressive syndrome (i.e., without significant residual symptomatology). The term "treatment response" will be used to correspond to a significant reduction in the depressive symptoms (in concert with treatment) reflecting at least a 50% reduction in depressive symptoms (Thase & Kupfer, 1987). The term relapse will be used to describe the return of a full depressive syndrome within four to six months of a remission or treatment response. Finally a recurrence of depression will be used to describe the return of a full syndrome of depression after a period of at least four to six months of remission.

Controlled outpatient studies of the treatment of depression generally document an acute response rate of approximately 60% to 70% following one to three months of the initiation of treatment (Thase & Kupfer, 1987). By contrast, attention-placebo response rates generally range from 20% to 40% in outpatient studies (Thase & Kupfer, 1987). Response to inpatient treatment may be more rapid, particularly when electroconvulsive therapy is utilized (Markowitz, Brown, Sweeney, & Mann, 1987).

Among more severe cases (for example, those admitted for an initial course of inpatient treatment), remission rates after six months of treatment are approximately 65%, and only 76% after 12 months (Keller, 1988). Nevertheless, even in these more severe cases the ultimate cumulative probability of recovery still is about 90% (Keller, 1988). Less severely depressed outpatients may show approximately the same pattern of recovery when followed naturalistically (Barrett, 1984).

Patients who fail to respond to treatment include those who withdraw from therapy prematurely and those who receive a full treatment course but who do not benefit (Thase & Kupfer,

1987). Both groups may still show a significant treatment response when an alternative form of therapy is provided (Thase, in press). Serial application of several alternative treatments of depression will result in a 90% response rate within the first year of treatment (Thase, in press). Failure to respond to a series of three or four consecutively applied strategies represents an ominous prognostic sign and warrants use of the term refractory depression (Thase & Kupfer, 1987).

The most powerful predictors of response to initial treatment are the acuteness of onset, the initial severity, the absence of either dysthymia or a secondary psychiatric or comorbid medical condition, and adequacy of treatment (Bielski & Friedel, 1976; Thase & Kupfer, 1987). Secondary depressive syndromes (i.e., those major depressive episodes which are superimposed on another psychiatric disorder) appear to have the poorest rates of recovery (Keller, 1988; Winokur, Black, & Nasrallah, 1988).

Relapse following successful treatment of depression is fairly common when therapy is not provided on a continuing basis (Prien & Kupfer, 1986). In current practice, a minimum period of three to six months of continuation treatment should be routinely provided (Consensus Development Panel, 1985). A past history of dysthymic disorder is a powerful predictor of relapse. Results of one study found that approximately 40% of nonbipolar depressed patients experienced relapse or recurrence within the first year of follow-up; only 24% of patients remained well throughout a five-year study (Keller, 1988). In a study of recurrent depressive patients conducted at the University of Pittsburgh, Frank, Kupfer, and Perel (1989) found that fully 50% of their sample had relapses or recurrences within one year of follow-up when maintenance antidepressant medication was not provided. Provision of such maintenance treatment generally results in a 50% to 70% reduction in the recurrence rate (Prien, 1988). Preliminary evidence also indicates that ongoing interpersonal psychotherapy also may forestall depressive relapses and recurrence (Kupfer & Frank, 1987; Frank, Kupfer, & Perel, 1989).

Patients with recurrent forms of major depression will experience an average of approximately five to six lifetime episodes which is somewhat lower than seen in bipolar affective disorder (Angst, 1981; Perris, 1966). Episode frequency (i.e., unipolar cycle length) is a strong predictor of subsequent risk for recurrence (Prien, 1988). There are no contemporary reports describing the average length of the well interval in recurrent depression, although it is noted in the literature that the risk for recurrence of depression increases and symptom-free intervals shorten with age (Angst, 1981). A significant minority of treatment responders manifest a fluctuating and subsyndromal level of residual symptomatology (Akiskal, 1982). Such residual symptoms appear to convey an even higher risk for subsequent relapse or recurrence (Faravelli, Ambonetti, Pallanti, & Pazzagli, 1986).

Few studies have documented the natural history of dysthymic disorder. As noted by Keller (1988), the duration of dysthymic disorder may range from 2 to 20 or more years. In our Chronic Depression Clinic at the University of Pittsburgh, we have seen individuals with a history of dysthymia of over 30 years' duration (Thase, unpublished observation). Dysthymic disorder appears to respond less completely to treatment than acute depressions. Several investigators (Akiskal, 1983; Keller, 1988; Klein et al., 1988) have found that only 30% to 45% of dysthymics will experience a complete recovery during discrete one- to five-year intervals. The prognosis for recovering from a superimposed major episode of double depression is paradoxically good, although it is virtually certain that subsequent relapses will occur without recovery from the underlying dysthymia (Keller, 1988).

Only about 30% of individuals meeting criteria for a diagnosis of depression are likely to obtain care from a mental health specialist (Weissman & Klerman, 1977). Indeed, in one study only 34% of depressed patients had been treated with antidepressant medication prior to hospitalization (Keller et al., 1986). These patients were far more likely to have received antianxiety medications from their family doctors (55%) than specific treatment for depression.

The natural history of the depressive disorders presents a frustrating paradox: Depressions are quite treatable but, in a majority of cases, affected individuals either do not seek treatment or are often misdiagnosed or incorrectly treated. The net effect of this phenomenon is that a majority of those depressed persons who seek treatment do not do so until their conditions have progressed to such a point that they are more difficult to treat!

IMPAIRMENT AND COMPLICATIONS

The common impairments and complications of depression are summarized in Table 4.3. The basic functional impairments associated with an

Table 4.3. Impairments and Complications of Depressions

A. Diminished energy and interest; deconditioning and reduced pleasurable activity

B. Diminished vocational role performance
   1. Decreased efficiency
   2. Increased sick-leave time, hospitalization
   3. Long-term economic effects

C. Diminished social role performance and family dysfunction
   1. Effects on marriage
   2. Effects on children
   3. Altered communication and behavior patterns
   4. Inadvertent family reinforcement of dysfunctional behavior
   5. Exhaustion of social support matrix

D. Suicide behavior
   1. Hospitalization
   2. Injury and death

E. Personality alterations
   1. State-related exaggerations of traits
   2. Enduring changes associated with chronicity

F. Alcohol and substance abuse

episode of depression include loss of confidence, fatigue, poor concentration, and diminished libido. These common symptoms of depression often result in diminished performance in the workplace and in social role performance. The exact economic costs of such impairments cannot be calculated. At a more tangible level, a small proportion of depressed individuals (ranging from 10% to 20%) have such severe episodes that they are at least temporarily disabled from work, with approximately 5 to 10 percent of treated depressions requiring inpatient admission (Simons & Thase, 1990).

Suicide is the most compelling and devastating complication of the depressive disorders. As many as 15% of depressed patients ultimately die by suicide; it is the leading cause of death in patients with mood disorders (Clayton, 1983). Moreover, 50% to 70% of depressed patients have at least passive suicidal ideation (Nelson & Charney, 1981). During the past 25 years in the United States, suicide rates have increased by birth cohort in parallel with depression rates (Murphy & Wetzel, 1980). Although a number of clinical and epidemiologic risk factors have been linked to suicide (i.e., gender, age, past history of suicide attempts, hopelessness, chronic physical illness, and intercurrent alcohol or substance abuse; Clayton, 1983), it is impossible to accurately predict who

will commit suicide. Given such a low level of predictability of lethal behavior, suicidal ideation is one of the leading criteria for hospitalization.

Depression has substantial adverse effects on the family system. There is a high prevalence of discord in the marriages of depressed persons, as both an antecedent and a consequence of the disorder (Haas, Clarkin, & Glick, 1985). Recent research also documents a high prevalence of psychiatric morbidity in the children of depressed persons (Lee & Gotlib, 1989). Even the most harmonious family's ability to cope may become overwhelmed by the demands, needs, and behaviors of a depressed person. Thus, families may develop alternative patterns of coping during prolonged episodes of depression, including distancing from the depressed person (Haas, Clarkin, & Glick, 1985). Such behavioral changes may serve to strengthen the depressed person's perception that their family members do not care about them or, alternatively, may reinforce pathological behaviors.

Acute depressions also result in an overreporting of dependent, histrionic, and avoidant personality traits (Akiskal, Hirschfeld, & Yerevanian, 1983). When depression goes untreated for long periods of time, such personality "symptoms" of dysphoria may become more enduring (Akiskal, 1981). It is thus conceivable that untreated major depression in early life plays a major role in development of subsequent personality pathology (Akiskal, Hirschfeld, & Yerevanian, 1983).

As previously noted, depressed patients are frequently prescribed antianxiety medication (usually benzodiazepines) by primary care physicians. This practice may lead to development of a secondary sedative dependence. In a parallel fashion, some patients turn to alcohol for its sedative effects. In clinical practice, it is not uncommon for patients to conceal the history of sedative or alcohol abuse initially and only later to reveal the extent of their self-medication practice (Thase, 1987). Secondary sedative and alcohol abuse generally worsens the prognosis for treatment response and recovery (Keller, 1988; Thase & Kupfer, 1987).

DIFFERENTIAL DIAGNOSIS

Although major depressions are reliably diagnosed, a number of differential diagnoses must be considered (Table 4.4). Even when a diagnosis of a major depressive episode is fairly clearcut, a first

Table 4.4. Differential Diagnostic Considerations

CONDITION	ISSUE(S) FOR CLARIFICATION
1. Bipolar depression	Premorbid history (cyclothymic baseline, undetected past episodes of mania/hypomania), age of onset, and family history; prolonged longitudinal follow-up often necessary.
2. Adjustment disorder	Severity and persistence of depressive syndrome.
3. Uncomplicated bereavement	Presence of *severe* and *persistent* depressive features (i.e., hopelessness, suicidal ideation, psychomotor disturbance, psychotic features, and/or marked neurovegetative profile); antidepressant treatment if indicated by severity.
4. Anxiety disorders	Syndromal presentation and temporal separation of syndromes; comorbidity of conditions a reality.
5. Organic affective disorder	Thorough medical history, examination, and laboratory studies; medication history; temporal relationship of organic factor and onset of depression.
6. Primary degenerative dementia	Careful neurodiagnostic evaluation (including EEG, CT, or MRI scan and neuropsychological testing) and differentiation of depressive and dementiform clinical symptoms; empiric trial of antidepressant treatment and longitudinal follow-up helpful.
7. Schizophrenia	Premorbid state, mood-congruent versus -incongruent psychotic symptoms, and documentation of schizophreniform features (i.e., bizarre behavior, incoherence, or looseness of associations; longitudinal follow-up helpful.
8. Schizoaffective depression	Mood-incongruent symptoms, evidence of bipolarity, interepisode psychotic features, and chronicity; longitudinal follow-up helpful; presumptive antidepressant treatment similar to psychotic depression.
9. Borderline personality disorder	Persistence of depressive syndrome, including significant neurovegetative disturbance; empiric antidepressant treatment trial and longitudinal follow-up helpful; comorbidity of conditions a reality.
10. Drug and alcohol withdrawal	History of mood-and-substance-related symptoms patterns, family history of affective disorder, detoxification.

priority is to determine whether the disorder is nonbipolar or bipolar. Careful interviewing regarding age of onset and past history of more subtle past mood swings is necessary, including transient and very functional periods of mild hypomania. Additional information concerning family history of bipolar disorder also is required, since the relatives of individuals with bipolar disorder are at increased risk for both unipolar and bipolar forms of depression (Goldin & Gershon, 1988). Approximately one-half of initial episodes of bipolar disorder are depressive; thus, some "misdiagnoses" are inevitable (Thase, 1987). Moreover, approximately 5% to 10% of recurrent depressives will subsequently develop manic episodes even after three or more episodes of "unipolar" depression (Keller, 1988; Perris, 1966).

A second major differential diagnostic distinction is separation of syndromal major depression from more transient minor depressions. The principal diagnostic category for the latter condition is adjustment disorder with depressed mood (American Psychiatric Association, 1987). Given the

high likelihood that a major depressive episode is associated with some adverse life stress, there is a tendency to overdiagnose adjustment disorder in milder forms of major depression. The differentiation of major depression from uncomplicated bereavement sometimes involves rather arbitrary judgments. The frequency of partial or even full depressive syndromes following the death of a loved one is so high that the diagnosis of major depression should not be made unless the bereaved individual begins to manifest symptoms such as psychotic features, suicidal ideation, and severe neurovegetative disturbances (Clayton, 1979).

An admixture of anxiety features and depressive symptoms are present in many patients. The ability to delineate precisely between anxiety and affective syndromes is further complicated by the observations that (1) approximately 40% of individuals with obsessive/compulsive disorder or panic disorder will develop episodes of secondary depression; (2) approximately 20% to 40% of patients with fairly clear-cut major depressions will have panic, phobic, and/or obsessional symptoms; and (3) family history studies demonstrate co-aggregation of major affective disorders and anxiety disorders (Barlow, DiNardo, Vermilyea, Vermilyea, & Blanchard, 1986; Goldin & Gershon, 1988; Grunhaus, 1988). In practice, both diagnoses should be used only if it is clear that the two disorders have existed separately (APA, 1987). Therefore, in cases where there is an admixture of symptoms and no clear temporal separation of discrete syndromes, the most likely diagnosis should be given (APA, 1987). This is a somewhat moot task in clinical practice since the major antidepressant medications also are useful as treatments of panic disorder and obsessive-compulsive disorder (Thase, 1989).

A significant minority of patients with depressive syndromes subsequently will be found to have an underlying medical condition which may be responsible for the depressive disorder (Kathol, 1985). Such conditions are referred to as organic affective disorders in DSM-III-R (APA, 1987). The undetected medical syndromes underlying the affective state often is an endocrine condition, particularly hypothyroidism (Kathol, 1985). It also is important to note that a variety of medications can cause organic affective disorders, with the most common culprits being antihypertensive agents and oral contraceptives (Thase, 1987). Approximately 15% of depressed patients admitted to our tertiary care mood disorders center subsequently are found to have an organic etiology (Thase & Kupfer, 1987).

The onset of an initial episode of depression in elderly patients always should raise the suspicion of an underlying medical syndrome. A careful medical history and detailed physical evaluation with laboratory studies are essential to this differential diagnostic process. It also should be recognized that depressed mood is a common part of the prodromal phase of presenile and senile forms of primary degenerative dementia (Lazarus, Newton, Cohler, Lesser, & Schween, 1987). The cognitive impairment and motivational deficits of depression in the elderly also may cause sufficient disturbances of mentation to mimic dementia, a presentation commonly called depressive pseudodementia (Wells, 1979). Sorting out the reversible from the irreversible cognitive/affective syndromes represents one of the major differential diagnostic and treatment tasks in contemporary practice.

The differential diagnosis of schizophrenia always must be considered in younger patients with an initial episode of psychotic depression. In such cases, a family history of affective disorder can be reassuring (perhaps even falsely so), whereas a history of social withdrawal, peculiar interpersonal behavior, and presence of delusions or hallucinations independent from the affective syndrome are strongly suggestive of schizophrenia (Coryell & Zimmerman, 1987). Mood-incongruent psychotic features also convey the need for particularly close follow-up and periodic reevaluation of the diagnosis of schizophrenia. Indeed, mood-incongruent psychotic features convey some risk for poorer prognosis forms of affective disorder (Keller, 1988). The diagnosis of schizoaffective disorder remains useful as a transitional category for cases that cannot be classified as either affective or schizophrenic according to DSM-III-R criteria (American Psychiatric Association, 1987).

Younger patients with particularly unstable and chaotic life-styles often receive the diagnoses of both major depression and a personality disorder, particularly borderline personality disorder (Akiskal, 1981). Studies of patients with borderline personality disorder document a very high overlap with major depression, with rates of comorbidity of 50% to 70% (Gunderson & Elliott, 1985; Soloff, George, Nathan, & Schulz, 1987). Given the fundamental role of low self-esteem, distorted cognitions, mood lability, and suicidal behavior in the borderline syndrome, it is controversial whether a depressive disorder should be diagnosed concurrently with borderline personality disorder (Gunderson & Elliott, 1985). Alternatively, it has been suggested that many patients with borderline personality disorder may have the most severe form of early onset affective disorder, perhaps one that has been complicated by multiple traumatic life events (Akiskal, 1981). Differentiation of major depression from eating disorders is a similarly common clinical and conceptual problem (cf. Hudson, Pope, & Jonas, 1983).

A final area of importance is differential diagnosis of major depression in individuals with a history of drug or alcohol dependence. This issue is quite problematic since virtually all substances of abuse have depressive symptoms as part of their intoxication and/or withdrawal syndromes (Thase, 1987). In cases where this differential diagnosis cannot be easily made, it is entirely correct to defer a diagnosis of major depression until detoxification is complete and a several-week period of abstinence has been achieved (Schuckit, 1979). Inpatient studies document that nearly one-half of dysphoric syndromes associated with substance withdrawal spontaneously remit following such a detoxification and observation period (Schuckit, 1979). Such evaluation often needs to be conducted on an inpatient unit given the high risk of relapse and/or suicide during the detoxification period.

CASE EXAMPLE

Mr. L., a 65-year-old businessman, requested treatment for longstanding and fluctuating symptoms of depression, which had worsened during the past 6 months. Mr. L. stated that approximately 6 months earlier he had received a lucrative offer to sell his business. He had asked for some time to decide about the sale and was now approaching the end of this deadline.

Mr. L. described his mood as sad and that he had lost his ability to have fun. Mr. L. reported marked fatigue and on certain days being unable to leave his bed. Mr. L. reported profound feelings of being slowed down. His appetite was ravenous, and he had gained about 10 pounds over the past several months. He was experiencing persistent midnight and early-morning awakenings, for which he had tripled a longstanding dose of secobarbital, up to 300 mg each night. In addition, he described being quite indecisive and feeling as if his decision making capacities were virtually paralyzed. Finally, he had recently developed recurrent thoughts of death. He had contemplated taking an overdose of medication, although he had not attempted suicide.

Prior to development of a full depressive syndrome, Mr. L. described a longstanding pattern of mild depression. He reported feeling down or blue almost every day for the past ten years, with fluctuating symptoms of increased appetite, alternating insomnia and hypersomnia, and fatigue. Mr. L. also reported two previous year-long episodes of major depression (at age 44 and 55), as well as one past episode of psychiatric hospitalization at the age of 19. The first episode of depression, approximately 20 years ago, followed the death of his mother and father. The second, approximately 10 years later, occurred following a divorce from his first wife. On both occasions, Mr. L. consulted a psychoanalyst and received approximately 1 year of therapy. He reported that he had never felt quite "right" following the second episode of depression.

Mr. L.'s first episode of psychiatric illness occurred during his freshman year of college. He did not know his diagnosis but recalled being "homesick" during the winter term. He recalled being quite anxious, sleeping excessively, and contemplating death by hanging. He asked his parents' approval for withdrawal from college, which they refused to authorize. He remembered his father telling him to "be a man about it." Following his return home that spring, he began to experience a recurrent and intrusive thought that he was a homosexual. Mr. L. was hospitalized and treated with sedatives and intensive psychotherapy. During a 1-year hospitalization, his condition slowly improved, and, at discharge, he was no longer troubled by the intrusive thought.

Mr. L. reported that he never had experienced periods of time in which his mood was abnormally elated or in which he had periods of excessive energy, change in self-concept, altered spending habits, or increased libido. He denied ever experiencing hallucinations and, aside from the intrusive thought of homosexuality at age 19, showed no other evidence of delusions, obsessions, or hallucinations. He described his "usual self" in terms of being a perfectionist, with a clear need to be in control of situations, a burning desire to be successful in his business, and a certain rigidity to unexpected events or changes in plans.

Mr. L.'s medical history was remarkable for mild diabetes mellitus, coronary artery disease, and obesity. At the time of the evaluation, he was approximately 30% over ideal body weight. Mr. L.'s current medications were (1) secobarbital, prescribed 100 mg qHS (he actually was taking 300 mg qHS), and (2) Digoxin, 0.125 mg qd. Mr. L. had a complete physical examination (including EEG and CT scan) 1 month prior to this consultation that revealed a stable medical status and no evidence of thyroid disease or congestive heart failure.

Family psychiatric history was remarkable for alcohol abuse in his father and two episodes of postpartum depression in his mother. A maternal uncle had died by suicide. Both of Mr. L.'s adult children also had experienced psychiatric difficulty, with the older son seeing a psychiatrist for two courses of psychotherapy for "life problems" and the younger son receiving residential treatment as an adolescent for narcotic dependence.

Mr. L.'s developmental history was relatively uncomplicated until his psychiatric troubles in college. He described himself as socially active and athletic. He did remark, however, that he always felt inferior to his older brother. Mr. L. also described his father as distant and demanding and felt that his mother protected him when he had not measured up to his father's standards. He described a pattern in adult life of hard-driving pursuit of wealth, with no hobbies and few recreational activities. Mr. L.'s first marriage ended approximately ten years prior to this evaluation; he remarried about two years later. He stated that his current marriage was satisfactory, although he still loved his first wife.

The initial diagnostic (DSM-III) impression was

Axis I

1. Major depression, recurrent, nonpsychotic
2. Dysthymic disorder (residual to above)
3. Barbituate dependence

Axis II

1. Compulsive personality disorder

Axis III

1. Diabetes mellitus, type II
2. Coronary artery disease
3. Exogenous obesity

Axis IV

1. Planned scale of business (moderate)

Axis V

1. Highest functioning during the past year: fair

Based on this formulation, a trial of antidepressant medication was initiated with trazodone, 100 mg qHS, in concert with slow, outpatient withdrawal from the barbiturates. Mr. L. also initially was seen for weekly therapy sessions focused on resolution of a decision regarding the sale of his business and development of an increased activity level. Secobarbital was reduced by 50 mg a month down to 100 mg. Diazepam (10 mg qd) then was substituted, and withdrawn by 2-mg decrements over the next four months. During the initial course of barbiturate withdrawal, Mr. L. reported some exacerbation of insomnia and depressive complaints. These symptoms were partially successfully treated by further increases in the trazodone up to 200 mg qHS. Mr. L. was unable to tolerate higher dosages due to development of a first-degree heart block.

Mr. L. reported approximately a 60% reduction in symptoms within 3 months, with improved energy level and concentration. He reported no fur-

ther suicidal ideation and resumed his previous routine in his business. He decided not to sell his business. Over the next 6 months his condition further improved, although he did not achieve complete relief of feelings of sadness or ruminations about his business.

Mr. L. experienced a full recurrence of major depression approximately 18 months later following the sudden death of his son, despite continued treatment with trazodone 200 mg qHS. Mr. L. again withdrew from his workplace, spending progressively more time in bed. His thoughts became increasingly focused on the meaninglessness of life and his inability to handle the business without his son's assistance. Mr. L. was hospitalized and he received a course of electroconvulsive therapy (10 treatments). He showed a clear response, complicated by a transient short-term memory disturbance. Mr. L. has continued to receive follow-up outpatient treatment with trazodone and supportive psychotherapy. Residual symptoms include worries about retirement and intermittent insomnia and dysphoria. An indefinite period of maintenance treatment is planned.

CHILDHOOD AND FAMILIAL ANTECEDENTS

Childhood and familial antecedents of adult depression are summarized in Table 4.5. It should be noted that recognition of both major and minor forms of affective disorder in childhood is a relatively new development (Puig-Antich, 1980).

There is a strongly familial component to the depressive disorders. Research employing the fam-

Table 4.5. Childhood and Familial Antecedents of Nonbipolar Depression

A. Childhood onset of major depression and dysthymia

B. Family history
   1. Affective disorder
   2. Alcoholism
   3. Social learning

C. Adverse early life experience
   1. Parental loss (death and divorce)
   2. Sexual abuse (?physical abuse)
   3. Attention-deficit disorder (?genetic relationship)

D. Cognitive vulnerability
   1. Development of depressogenic schema
   2. Schema–life event interactions

E. Temperament

ily study method has documented that age of onset is a powerful correlate of family history of depression, with childhood onset predicting the heaviest burden of family pathology (see Goldin & Gershon, 1988). This observation is paralleled in studies of adults with chronic mood disorders, where an early onset of dysthymic disorder also carries the greatest burden of associated pathology (Klein et al., 1988). Indeed, as longitudinal studies of childhood-onset dysthymic disorder and major depression are continued into adulthood, these syndromes may prove to be the most important risk factor for adult affective syndromes.

A substantial body of literature documents the familial nature of depressive disorders. For example, as reviewed by Goldin and Gershon (1988), rates of affected first-degree relatives of adult unipolar depressives range from 11.0% to 18.4% (representing a two- to threefold elevation over matched control families); rates of bipolar illness also are elevated in comparison to matched controls, although the absolute number of affected relatives is substantially lower (2.0% to 3.3%); of course, familial aggregation of depressive disorders does not guarantee a genetic association, since parental affective disorder also might influence the behavior of children through mechanisms involving social learning and life stress.

A small number of studies have examined the heritability of nonbipolar depression in twins and following adoption. These studies generally indicate that (1) severe forms of depression may be inherited even when the child is raised in an adoptive household, and (2) the heritability among monozygotic twins is about double that seen in dizygotic twins (Goldin & Gershon, 1988).

A substantial amount of research has explored the relationship between various stresses encountered in childhood and subsequent risk of depression. For example, numerous studies document the relationship of early parental loss and suicide and/or depression in adult life (reviewed by Tennant, 1988). A recently emerging literature similarly points to the relationship between childhood sexual abuse and subsequent development of depression and other psychopathology (Beck & van der Kolk, 1987; Bryer, Nelson, Miller, & Krol, 1987). An association between alcoholism and sociopathy in fathers and depression in adult daughters also is well described (Winokur, 1979). Boys diagnosed as suffering from attention-deficit disorder in childhood similarly may be at increased risk for depression (Biederman et al., 1987). Although such relationships may have genetic corre-

lates, they also point to the significance of adverse developmental experiences and subsequent risk of depression.

It also is important to recognize the developmental impact of sustained dysphoria on self-concept, social confidence, and attributions. From a cognitive perspective, childhood and adolescence is a critical time for development for basic personal views (schema) of the person's self, world, and future. Beck (1976) has referred to these views as the cognitive triad and has implicated negative schema as vulnerability factors for subsequent episodes of depression. Depressed children experiencing stressful life experiences may be particularly vulnerable, since they often lack the maturity to properly test alternative explanations and shift attributions to external causes (Beck, 1976). Further, although the signs and symptoms of an episode of depression ultimately may abate, such distorted fundamental views may persist, leading to relatively rigid attitudes or maladaptive coping patterns. Thereafter, such individuals may be at high risk to reexperience depression at times of life stress centered on relevant themes (i.e., competence or romantic affection) (Hammen, Ellicott, Gitlin, & Jamison, 1989). Successful early intervention with depressive disorders during childhood may thus yield substantial benefits years later.

Other investigators have suggested that a more fundamental disturbance of temperament is the developmental precursor of depression (see, for example, Akiskal, 1983). Depressive temperaments include traits such as pessimism, dependency, and a tendency to withdraw from difficult circumstances. Retrospective interviews of depressed adults often yield descriptions of such early traits (Akiskal, Hirschfeld, & Yerevanian, 1983). Indeed, these traits also may form the basis for subsequent categorical diagnoses of personality disorder in adult life, especially after several full-blown episodes of depression. It remains to be demonstrated in prospective studies of children whether the concept of depressive temperament actually exists after accounting for cases of childhood-onset major depression and dysthymia.

Gold, Goodwin, and Chrousos (1988a, 1988b) have suggested a model that brings together the significance of adverse life experiences, genetic risk factors, and the neurobiology of stress. They propose that genetically vulnerable individuals may be at particular risk for development of prolonged and exaggerated stress responses, marked by sustained hypercortisolemia (Gold, Goodwin,

& Chrousos, 1988b). With prolonged or repeated provocation, induction to this hyperactive stress response may require progressively less amounts of stress through a neurobiological process analogous to pharmacological kindling (Post, Ballenger, Udhe, Putman, & Bunney, 1981). This interesting theory is supported by our preliminary observation that the initial episode of major depression in adults is almost always associated with stressful life events, whereas recurrent episodes are less likely to have environmental provocation (Thase, unpublished observation). Parallel studies of children experiencing initial and recurrent episodes of depression are needed.

SUMMARY

The nonbipolar forms of depression constitute a major public health problem. They are common and account for a significant amount of human suffering and excessive mortality due to suicide. It is best to view the course of depression within a broad, longitudinal perspective, drawing upon biological, psychological, and social factors. From this perspective, there is no single cause of depression, but rather there are multiple sources of potential vulnerability. Across the life span, genetic risk factors, early traumatic adverse experiences, subsequent stress in later adult life, medical illness, and changes associated with all may play a role in the initiation and maintenance of a depressive syndrome. A thorough understanding of these factors will lead to more precise assessment of depression and a greater likelihood of successful treatment.

REFERENCES

Akiskal, H. S. (1981). Subaffective disorders: Dysthymic, cyclothymic, and bipolar II disorders in the "borderline" realm. *Psychiatric Clinics of North America, 4*, 25–46.

Akiskal, H. S. (1982). Factors associated with incomplete recovery in primary depressive illness. *Journal of Clinical Psychiatry, 43*, 266–271.

Akiskal, H. S. (1983). Dysthymic disorder: Psychopathology of proposed chronic depressive subtypes. *American Journal of Psychiatry, 140*, 11–20.

Akiskal, H. S., Hirschfeld, R. M. A., & Yerevanian, B. I. (1983). The relationship of personality to affective disorders: A critical review. *Archives of General Psychiatry, 40*, 801–809.

American Psychiatric Association. (1980). *Diagnostic and statistical manual of mental disorders* (3rd ed.) (DSM-III). Washington, DC: Author.

American Psychiatric Association. (1987). *Diagnostic and statistical manual of mental disorders* (3rd ed. rev.) (DSM-III-R). Washington, DC: Author.

Angst, J. (1981). Course of affective disorders. In H. van Praag (Ed.), *Handbook of biological psychiatry: Part IV. Brain mechanisms and abnormal behavior-chemistry* (pp. 225–242). New York: Marcel Dekker.

Angst, J., & Dobler-Mikola, A. (1984). The Zurich study: III. Diagnosis of depression. *European Archives of Psychiatric and Neurological Science, 234*, 30–37.

Barlow, D. H., DiNardo, P. A., Vermilyea, B. B., Vermilyea, J., & Blanchard, E. B. (1986). Comorbidity and depression among the anxiety disorders: Issues in diagnosis and classification. *Journal of Nervous and Mental Disease, 174*, 63–72.

Barrett, J. E. (1984). Naturalistic change after 2 years in neurotic depressive disorders (RDC categories). *Comprehensive Psychiatry, 25*, 404–418.

Beck, A. T. (1976). *Cognitive therapy and the emotional disorders*. New York: International Universities Press.

Beck, J. C., & Van der Kolk, B. (1987). Reports of childhood incest and current behavior of chronically hospitalized psychotic women. *American Journal of Psychiatry, 144*, 1474–1476.

Biederman, J., Munir, K., Knee, D., Armentano, M., Autor, S., Waternaux, C., & Tsuang, M. (1987). High rate of affective disorders in probands with attention deficit disorder and in their relatives: A controlled family study. *American Journal of Psychiatry, 144*, 330–333.

Bielski, R. J., & Friedel, R. O. (1976). Prediction of tricyclic antidepressant response. *Archives of General Psychiatry, 33*, 1479–1489.

Blacker, C. V. R., & Clare, A. W. (1987). Depressive disorder in primary care. *British Journal of Psychiatry, 150*, 737–751.

Blehar, M. C., & Rosenthal, N. E. (1989). Seasonal affective disorders and phototherapy. *Archives of General Psychiatry, 46*, 469–474.

Boyd, J. H., & Weissman, M. M. (1981). Epidemiology of affective disorders: A reexamination and future directions. *Archives of General Psychiatry, 38*, 1039–1046.

Boyd, J. H., & Weissman, M. M. (1982). Epidemiology. In E. S. Paykel (Ed.), *Handbook of affective disorders* (pp. 109–125). New York: Guilford Press.

Brown, G. W., & Harris, T. (1978). *Social origins of depression: A study of psychiatric disorder in women.* London: Tavistock.

Bryer, J. B., Nelson, B. A., Miller, J. B., & Krol, P. A. (1987). Childhood sexual and physical abuse as factors in adult psychiatric illness. *American Journal of Psychiatry, 144,* 1426–1430.

Caspar, R. C., Redmond, E., Katz, M. N., Schaffer, C. B., Davis, J. M., & Koslow, S. H. (1985). Somatic symptoms in primary affective disorder: Presence and relationship to the classification of depression. *Archives of General Psychiatry, 42,* 1098–1140.

Clayton, P. J. (1979). The sequelae and non-sequelae of conjugal bereavement. *American Journal of Psychiatry, 136,* 1530–1534.

Clayton, P. J. (1983). Epidemiologic and risk factors in suicide. In L. Ginspoon (Ed.), *Psychiatry update* (Vol. II, pp. 428–434). Washington, DC: American Psychiatric Association.

Consensus Development Panel, NIMH/NIH Consensus Development Conference Statement. (1985). Mood disorders: Pharmacologic prevention of recurrences. *American Journal of Psychiatry, 142,* 469–476.

Coryell, W., & Zimmerman, M. (1987). Progress in the classification of functional psychoses. *American Journal of Psychiatry, 144,* 1471–1473.

Faravelli, C., Ambonetti, A., Pallanti, S., & Pazzagli, A. (1986). Depressive relapses and incomplete recovery from index episode. *American Journal of Psychiatry, 143,* 888–891.

Frank, E., Kupfer, D. J., & Perel, J. M. (1989). Early recurrence in unipolar depression. *Archives of General Psychiatry, 46,* 397–400.

Gold, P. W., Goodwin, F. K., & Chrousos, G. P. (1988a). Medical progress. Part 1: Clinical and biochemical manifestations of depression. *New England Journal of Medicine, 319,* 348–353.

Gold, P. W., Goodwin, F. K., & Chrousos, G. P. (1988b). Medical progress. Part 2: Clinical and biochemical manifestations of depression. *New England Journal of Medicine, 319,* 413–420.

Goldin, L. R., & Gershon, E. S. (1988). The genetic epidemiology of major depressive illness.

In A. J. Frances & R. E. Hales (Eds.), *Review of psychiatry* (Vol. 7, pp. 149–168). Washington, DC: American Psychiatric Press.

Grunhaus, L. (1988). Clinical and psychobiological characteristics of simultaneous panic disorder and major depression. *American Journal of Psychiatry, 145,* 1214–1221.

Gunderson, J. G., & Elliot, G. R. (1985). The interface between borderline personality disorder and affective disorder. *American Journal of Psychiatry, 142,* 277–288.

Haas, G., Clarkin, J. F., & Glick, I. D. (1985). Marital and family treatment of depression. In E. E. Beckham & W. R. Leber (Eds.), *Handbook of depression: Treatment, assessment, research* (pp. 151–183). Homewood, IL: Dorsey Press.

Hammen, C., Ellicott, A., Gitlin, M., & Jamison, K. R. (1989). Sociotropy/autonomy and vulnerability to specific life events in patients with unipolar depression and bipolar disorders. *Journal of Abnormal Psychology, 98,* 154–160.

Himmelhoch, J. M., & Thase, M. E. (1989). The vagaries of atypical depression. In J. E. Howells (Ed.), *Modern perspectives in the psychiatry of depression* (pp. 223–242). New York: Brunner/Mazel.

Hirschfeld, R. M. A. (1981). Situational depression: Validity of the concept. *British Journal of Psychiatry, 139,* 297–305.

Hudson, J. I., Pope, H. G., & Jonas, J. M. (1983). Phenomenologic relationship of eating disorders to major affective disorder. *Psychiatric Research, 9,* 345–354.

Kathol, R. G. (1985). Depression associated with physical disease. In E. E. Beckham & W. R. Leber (Eds.), *Handbook of depression: Treatment, assessment, research* (pp. 745–762). Homewood, IL: Dorsey Press.

Keller, M. B. (1988). Diagnostic issues and clinical course of unipolar illness. In A. J. Frances & R. E. Hales (Eds.), *Review of psychiatry* (Vol. 7, pp. 188–212). Washington, DC: American Psychiatric Press.

Keller, M. B., Lavori, P. W., Klerman, G. L., Andreasen, N. C., Endicott, J., Coryell, W., Fawcett, J., Rice, J. P., & Hirschfeld, M. A. (1986). Low levels and lack of predictors of somatotherapy and psychotherapy received by depressed patients. *Archives of General Psychiatry, 143,* 458–467.

Klein, D. N., Taylor, E. B., Harding, K., &

Dickstein, S. (1988). Double depression and episodic major depression: Demographic, clinical, familial, personality, and socioenvironmental characteristics and short-term outcome. *American Journal of Psychiatry, 145*, 1226–1231.

Klerman, G. L., Lavori, P. W., Rice, J., Reich, T., Endicott, J., Andreasen, N. C., Keller, M. B., & Hirschfeld, R. M. A. (1985). Birth-cohort trends in rates of major depressive disorder among relatives of patients with affective disorder. *Archives of General Psychiatry, 42*, 689–693.

Kocsis, J. H., & Frances, A. J. (1987). A critical discussion of DSM-III dysthymic disorder. *American Journal of Psychiatry, 144*, 1534–1542.

Kovacs, M., & Gatsonis, C. (1989). Stability and change in childhood-onset depressive disorders: Longitudinal course as a diagnostic validator. In L. N. Robins & J. E. Barrett (Eds.), *The validity of psychiatric diagnosis* (pp. 57–73). New York: Raven Press.

Kraepelin, D. (1921). *Manic-depressive insanity and paranoia*. Edinburgh: E. & S. Livingstone.

Kupfer, D. J., Foster, F. G., Detre, T. P., & Himmelhoch, J. M. (1975). Sleep EEG and motor activity as indicators in affective states. *Neuropsychobiology, 1*, 296–303.

Kupfer, D. J., & Frank, E. (1987). Relapse in recurrent unipolar depression. *American Journal of Psychiatry, 144*, 86–88.

Lazarus, L. W., Newton, N., Cohler, B., Lesser, J., & Schweon, C. (1987). Frequency and presentation of depressive symptoms in patients with primary degenerative dementia. *American Journal of Psychiatry, 144*, 41–50.

Lee, C. M., & Gotlib, I. H. (1989). Clinical status and emotional adjustment of children of depressed mothers. *American Journal of Psychiatry, 146*, 478–483.

Liebowitz, W. M., Quitkin, F. M., Stewart, J. W., McGrath, P. J., Harrison, W., Rabkin, J., Tricamo, E., Markowitz, J. S., & Klein, D. F. (1984). Phenelzine vs. imipramine in atypical depression. *Archives of General Psychiatry, 41*, 669–677.

Markowitz, J., Brown, R., Sweeney, J., & Mann, J. J. (1987). Reduced length and cost of hospital stay for major depression in patients treated with ECT. *American Journal of Psychiatry, 144*, 1025–1029.

Mezzich, J. E., Fabrega, H., Coffman, G. A., &

Haley, R. (1989). DSM-III disorders in a large sample of psychiatric patients: Frequency and specificity of diagnoses. *American Journal of Psychiatry, 146*, 212–219.

Murphy, G. E., & Wetzel, R. D. (1980). Suicide by birth cohort in the United States. *Archives of General Psychiatry, 37*, 519–523.

Nelson, J. C., & Charney, D. S. (1981). The symptoms of major depressive illness. *American Journal of Psychiatry, 138*, 1–13.

Nolen-Hoeksema, S. (1987). Sex differences in unipolar depression: Evidence and theory. *Psychological Bulletin, 101*, 259–282.

Perris, C. (1966). A study of bipolar (manic-depressive) and unipolar recurrent depressive psychoses. *Acta Psychiatrica Scandinavica, 42*(Suppl. 194), 1–188.

Post, R. M., Ballenger, J. C., Udhe, T. W., Putman, F. W., & Bunney, W. E. (1981). Kindling and drug sensitization: Implications for the progressive development of psychopathology and treatment with carbamazepine. In M. Sandler (Ed.), *The psychopharmacology of anticonvulsants* (pp. 27–53). Oxford: Oxford University Press.

Prien, R. (1988). Somatic treatment of unipolar depressive disorder. In A. J. Frances & R. E. Hales (Eds.), *Review of psychiatry* (Vol. 7, pp. 213–234). Washington, DC: American Psychiatric Press.

Prien, R. F., & Kupfer, D. J. (1986). Continuation drug therapy for major depressive episodes: How long should it be maintained? *American Journal of Psychiatry, 143*, 18–23.

Puig-Antich, J. (1980). Affective disorders in childhood: A review and perspective. In B. J. Blinder (Ed.), *Psychiatric clinics of North America* (Vol. 3, pp. 403–424). Philadelphia: W. B. Saunders.

Regier, D. A., Boyd, J. H., Burke, J. D., Rae, D. S., Myers, J. K., Kramer, M., Robins, L. N., George, L. K., Karno, M., & Locke, B. Z. (1988). One-month prevalence of mental disorders in the United States. *Archives of General Psychiatry, 45*, 977–986.

Regier, D. A., Myers, J. K., Kramer, M., Robins, L. N., Blazer, D. G., Hough, R. L., Eaton, W. W., & Locke, B. Z. (1984). The NIMH epidemiologic catchment area program. *Archives of General Psychiatry, 41*, 934–941.

Robins, L. N., Helzer, J. E., Weissman, M. M., Orvaschel, H., Burke, J. D., & Regier, D. A. (1984). Lifetime prevalence of specific psychiatric disorders in three sites. *Archives of General Psychiatry, 41*, 949-958.

Rosenthal, N. E., Sack, D. A., Skwerer, R. G., Jacobsen, F. M., & Wehr, T. A. (1989). Phototherapy for seasonal affective disorder. In N. E. Rosenthal & M. C. Blehar (Eds.), *Seasonal affective disorders and phototherapy* (pp. 273-294). New York: Guilford Press.

Schuckit, M. A. (1979). *Drug and alcohol abuse.* New York: Plenum Press.

Simons, A. D., & Thase, M. E. (1990). Mood Disorders. In M. E. Thase, M. Hersen, & B. A. Edelstein (Eds.), *Handbook of outpatient treatment*. New York: Plenum Press.

Soloff, P. H. George, A., Nathan, R. S., & Schulz, P. M. (1987). Characterizing depression in borderline patients. *Journal of Clinical Psychiatry, 48*, 155-157.

Spiker, D. G., Weiss, J. C., Dealy, R. S., Griffin, S. J., Hanin, I., Neil, J. F., Perel, J. M., Rossi, A. J., & Soloff, P. H. (1985). The pharmacological treatment of delusional depression. *American Journal of Psychiatry, 142*, 430-436.

Tennant, C. (1988). Parental loss in childhood. *Archives of General Psychiatry, 45*, 1045-1050.

Thase, M. E. (1987). Affective disorders. In R. L. Morrison & A. S. Bellack (Eds.), *Medical factors and psychological disorders* (pp. 61-91). New York: Plenum Press.

Thase, M. E. (1989). Comparison between patients with seasonal affective disorder and other recurrent forms of depression. In N. E. Rosenthal & M. Blehar (Eds.), *Seasonal affective disorders and phototherapy* (pp. 64-78). New York: Guilford Press.

Thase, M. E. (in press). Resistant depression. *Hospital and Community Psychiatry*.

Thase, M. E., Frank, E., & Kupfer, D. J. (1985). Biological processes in major depression. In E. E. Beckham & W. R. Leber (Eds.), *Handbook of depression: Treatment, assessment, research* (pp. 816-913). Homewood, IL: Dorsey Press.

Thase, M. E., & Kupfer, D. J. (1987). Characteristics of treatment of resistant depressions. In J. Zohar & R. H. Belmaker (Eds.), *Treating resistant depression* (pp. 23-45). New York: PMA Publishing.

Thase, M. E., Kupfer, D. J., & Ulrich, R. F. (1986). EEG sleep in psychotic depression. *Archives of General Psychiatry, 43*, 886-893.

Weissman, M. M., & Klerman, G. L. (1977). The chronic depressive in the community; under recognized and poorly treated. *Comprehensive Psychiatry, 18*, 523-531.

Wells, C. E. (1979). Pseudodementia. *American Journal of Psychiatry, 136*, 895.

Winokur, G. (1979). Unipolar depression: Is it divisible into autonomous subtypes? *Archives of General Psychiatry, 36*, 47-52.

Winokur, G., Black, D. W., & Nasrallah, A. (1988). Depressions secondary to other psychiatric disorders and medical illnesses. *American Journal of Psychiatry, 145*, 233-237.

Zimmerman, M., & Spitzer, R. L. (1989). Melancholia: From DSM-III to DSM-III-R. *American Journal of Psychiatry, 146*, 20-28.

Zis, A. P., & Goodwin, F. K. (1979). Major affective disorders as a recurrent illness: A critical review. *Archives of General Psychiatry, 36*, 835-839.

BIPOLAR DISORDER

EDITORS' COMMENTS

This part reflects quite well the problems in studying psychopathology in piecemeal fashion, with attention having specifically been directed to child psychopathology and adult psychopathology on an individual and independent basis. As is typical in the literature in general, much more is known about the adult manifestations of the disorder, with research lagging far behind in the understanding of the childhood version of the diagnosis. However, in recent years this situation has improved, given the increased precision of DSM-III and DSM-III-R over its predecessors and the development of structured and semistructured diagnostic interview schedules for both children and adults.

Although incidence of bipolar disorder in children younger than age 4 is rare (0.4%), it is not uncommon for adult bipolar disordered individuals to report first onset of their symptoms in adolescence. Indeed, there are several studies in the literature documenting this point, suggesting that about 33% of the patients experienced onset in adolescence or early adulthood. However, such percentages are based on retrospective reports of adults, and the need for long-term prospective studies of children and adolescents so diagnosed is apparent. This would seem to be an important undertaking, given the extant data showing the poor outcome of children and adolescents having been diagnosed as bipolar. In one study, only 10% of patients so diagnosed between ages 15 and 22 had recovered with no recurrence of symptoms, while almost half the patients had experienced a chronic course.

Another reason to examine prospectively the course of bipolar illness identified in childhood is the particular high risk the adolescent and adult bipolar patient presents for suicide. Certainly a better understanding of the course and symptomatic manifestation of the disorder over time would have ramifications for suicide preventative efforts.

In earlier childhood the diagnosis of bipolar disorder is quite difficult to make, given the diagnostic overlap with attention-deficit hyperactivity disorder (ADHD), adjustment reaction, schizophrenia, and conduct disorder. However, the most difficult differential diagnostic problem is with ADHD. When carefully examined, it is clear that manic activity is shorter lived than is hyperactivity and is not as pervasive. Also, self-esteem in the hyperactive child is poor, whereas in bipolar disorder the child has much inflated self-esteem. Finally, at the empirical level, bipolar children are less likely to respond to stimulants than to lithium — the mainstay of bipolar treatment.

On the other hand, in adulthood the differential diagnosis is easier to establish. Overlapping diagnoses in adulthood tend to be organic mental disorders, psychoactive drug abuse, some personality disorders (e.g., "borderline"), and schizophrenia and schizoaffective disorder. We might note that with improvements in the DSM, bipolar disorder is diagnosed more frequently than in the past in the United States, but still not as frequently as it is identified by our British counterparts.

For both children and adults the impact of bipolar disorder on their lives is considerable. Frequently the younger child will engage in behaviors that put him or her at physical risk necessitating hospitalization. In general, in childhood and adolescence bipolar disorder may result in impaired intellectual, social, and emotional development, especially given its chronic course. In adulthood the pervasive effects can be seen in the patient's vocational, marital, educational, and social adjustment. At times these may be extreme.

The most grave complication of bipolar disorder, both in childhood and adulthood, is suicide, especially during the course of a depressive episode. Another complication of the disorder in childhood is acting out, including alcohol and drug abuse, although such complications have received better empirical documentation in studies involving adults. In adults heavy drinking often serves to mask bipolar symptoms, with patients frequently misdiagnosed as primary alcoholics.

It is of particular importance to look at bipolar disorder from a longitudinal perspective, given its high genetic loading. Indeed, genetic counseling is warranted for the adult bipolar individual who contemplates marriage. As pointed out by Cook, Winokur, and Sobotka, although the genetic factor in bipolar disorder is considerable (offsprings of bipolars are at a particular high risk for having the disorder), a single form of genetic transmission for the disorder has not been identified. It is anticipated, however, that in the future further study of the problem via molecular genetics will clarify the issue.

CHAPTER 5

BIPOLAR DISORDER IN CHILDHOOD

Martin B. Keller
Joanne Wunder

DESCRIPTION OF THE DISORDER

Bipolar disorder is an affective (mood) disorder characterized by periods of mania, or persistent elevated mood or euphoria, that may alternate with one or more episodes of depressive disorder. Manic moods are experienced as elation or expansiveness and may be described as a "high." The mood disturbance may also be characterized by excessive irritability. Accompanying symptoms may include inflated self-esteem, grandiosity (which may be delusional), decreased need for sleep, and increased energy.

The history of bipolar disorders extends back to Kraepelin, who developed the concept of manic-depressive psychosis in the late nineteenth century. This term was used to denote a disorder in which a subject experienced periods of mania alternating with periods of depression. This concept is still in use today; however, changes in nomenclature have resulted in the term "bipolar disorder." As the term is currently used, bipolar disorder is characterized by manic episodes, with or without major depressive episodes.

The *Diagnostic and Statistical Manual of Men-*

tal Disorders (American Psychiatric Association, 1987) classifies bipolar disorder as a major affective disorder, which may be subtyped into three categories: bipolar disorder—mixed, in which symptoms of mania and depression are intermixed or alternate rapidly; bipolar disorder—manic, in which the subject is currently manic; and bipolar disorder—depressed, in which the subject is currently depressed, but has a history of one or more manic episodes.

The existence of bipolar disorder in prepubertal children has long been the subject of dispute; some investigators deny its existence, while others have presented case studies of children displaying bipolar symptoms with age of onset as young as 4 years old (Poznanski, Israel, & Grossman, 1984). Kraepelin, who developed the concept of manic-depressive disorder, reported that 0.4% of his sample of 900 manic-depressive patients had onset of the disorder before the age of 10 (Kraepelin, 1921). However, the occurrence of bipolar disorder in young children is still considered rare. Bipolar disorder in adolescence is more common, and most investigators agree that adolescent-onset bipolar disorder exists. Studies of adult bipolar patients frequently report that the first onset of the disorder occurred in adolescence or young adulthood (Baron, Risch, & Mendelwicz, 1983; Loranger & Levine, 1978; Winokur, Clayton, & Reich, 1969; Perris, 1966; Taylor & Abrams, 1981).

Because of the rarity of the disorder before puberty, this review of bipolar disorder will focus on adolescents (aged 13 to 19), unless children (younger than 13) are specified. The concept of bipolar disorder will be reviewed with an emphasis on manic episodes, since major depression has been discussed in a previous chapter. It is of interest that the nature and presentation of depressive episodes in patients with bipolar disorder appears to be identical to episodes of major depression in unipolar patients. Finally, although much of the recent literature adheres to DSM-III-R nomenclature, earlier research used the term "manic depression" to denote bipolar disorder and will be cited as originally written.

CLINICAL PRESENTATION

According to DSM-III-R, the diagnostic criteria for bipolar disorders is the same for adults and children. The essential characteristic of the disorder is a manic episode, which may be accompanied by an episode of major depression and may "cycle" from pole to pole, or be "mixed," with the subject experiencing intermixed manic and depressive symptoms or alternating between the two every few days (APA, 1987).

A manic episode is characterized by a period in which the predominant mood is elevated, expansive, euphoric, or irritable (APA, 1987). It is a mood disturbance in which the subject is more than just "up" or "in a good mood." Indeed, the mood is considered excessive by those who know the subject and interferes with functioning, which results in social or occupational impairment or hospitalization (APA, 1987).

Three of the following associated symptoms are necessary to make a diagnosis (four if the mood is only irritable):

1. Inflated self-esteem — The manic subject may feel "invincible" and may be grandiose or delusional, for instance, feeling that he or she has a special relationship with God or can run the United Nations.
2. Decreased need for sleep — The subject may be full of energy having had much less sleep than usual.

3. Pressure of speech — Engaging in fast, loud speech that cannot be interrupted is common.
4. Flight of ideas — A continuous flow of rapid speech may be evidenced, with abrupt changes of topic.
5. Distractibility — Short attention span and rapid changes in speech and activity may be present.
6. Increased activity — The subject may plan or participate in an excessive number of activities.
7. Impulsivity — The subject may have increased sociability or participate in reckless activities, such as buying sprees or reckless driving. (APA, 1987)

Lability is also associated with manic episodes, with the subject rapidly shifting to a depressed mood, with tearfulness, suicidal thoughts, and other depressive symptomatology (APA, 1987).

A child or adolescent with bipolar disorder would experience extreme mood swings in contrast to previous behavior. He or she would be overexcited, exuberant, and accident prone, due to impulsivity and inflated self-esteem that impairs the child's ability to recognize danger (*British Medical Journal*, 1979). Euphoria may be manifested as adamant denial of any illness or problems (Weinberg & Brumback, 1976; Hassanyeh & Davison, 1980). Unrestrained playfulness and noisiness may be present in children (*British Medical Journal*, 1979). The adolescent may engage in antisocial and impulsive behavior (Gammon et al., 1983; Reiss, 1985), and sexually provocative behavior may be observed in adolescent girls (Hassanyeh & Davison, 1980). Schizophrenic symptoms, such as delusions or hallucinations are often present in adolescents (Ballenger, Reus, & Post, 1982; Rogeness, Reister, & Wicoff, 1982). The manic episodes just described may also alternate with periods of major depression (described in Chapter 3) during which the child or adolescent may be tearful, refuse school, have somatic complaints, and lose interest in previously pleasurable activities.

Developmental issues cause bipolar disorders to have a different presentation in children and adolescents than in adults. This, combined with the controversy surrounding age of onset, may create diagnostic difficulties for the clinician presented with possible bipolar disorder in a young patient. Therefore, some investigators and clinicians have proposed revised or alternative criteria for childhood and adolescent bipolar disorder.

Anthony and Scott (1960), in a review of the

literature from 1898 to 1958, concluded that only 3 of the 28 cases presented in the literature met at least 5 of their 10 proposed criteria for childhood mania, which are

1. An abnormal psychiatric state similar to the adult description
2. A family history of manic-depressive disorder
3. Premorbid cyclothymia (mood swings), with increasing severity and length of mood swings
4. Recurrent or periodic mood disorder
5. Biphasic moods showing pathological swings
6. Minimal environmental influence on symptoms
7. Severe symptoms requiring hospitalization
8. Extroverted personality
9. Absence of schizophrenic symptoms
10. Diagnosis is made from evidence from current assessments, not retrospective assessments. (Anthony & Scott, 1960)

Weinberg and Brumback (1976) also developed specific criteria for childhood mania based on Feighner et al.'s (1972) criteria for adults. The criteria are very similar to those for adults, with supplemental symptoms that are relevant to children. The criteria are either

1. Euphoria, as manifested by denial of problems or inappropriate feelings of well-being, cheerfulness, giddiness, or silliness; and/or
2. Irritability or agitation, especially belligerence, destructiveness, and antisocial behavior;

plus three or more of the following symptoms:

1. Hyperactivity, intrusiveness
2. Push of speech, garrulousness
3. Flight of ideas
4. Grandiosity (may be delusional)
5. Decreased sleep and unusual sleep patterns
6. Distractibility as manifested by short attention span. (Weinberg & Brumback, 1976)

Five cases of childhood mania that fit these criteria were presented. All five children had a family history of affective disorder and depressive symptoms during the manic episode (Weinberg & Brumback, 1976).

Davis (1979) has proposed a "manic-depressive variant syndrome of childhood," an identifiable syndrome in children that is a variation of bipolar disorder seen in adults. The criteria for this syndrome include "emotional storms" (transient losses of emotional control), family history of affective disorder, hyperactivity (without grandiosity as seen in adult bipolar illness), difficulty in interpersonal relations, and absence of thought disorder. Davis (1979) proposes that when these criteria are met, lithium is usually an effective treatment.

An important aspect of the clinical presentation of bipolar disorders in children and adolescents is its association with a family history of bipolar disorder. Many clinicians feel that a positive family history is an important "flag" for diagnosing bipolar disorder in young subjects, where the diagnosis may otherwise be overlooked (Puig-Antich, 1980). Investigators have found high rates of bipolar disorder in the first- and second-degree relatives of young subjects with suspected bipolar disorder, indicating a genetic link (Akiskal et al., 1985; Rice, 1987; Taylor et al., 1981). In two of the revised criteria for bipolar disorder in children just mentioned, a positive family history is fundamental in making the diagnosis in the child. This finding has proved fruitful for determining children at risk for bipolar disorder, as well as assisting in making a diagnosis.

EPIDEMIOLOGY

Epidemiologic studies of mental disorders in children and adolescents have lagged far behind those of adults in methodologic sophistication and amount of research conducted. Studies assessing the incidence of criterion-based diagnoses in young subjects are scarce; in addition, many studies focus on one target diagnosis or group diagnoses into broad categories such as "neurosis" and "behavior disorder." Another limitation of many epidemiologic studies is that hospital samples are often used; thus, only the most severe cases of disorder are ascertained, and the general population incidence of the disorder cannot be specified.

One study (Kashani et al., 1987) overcame some of these weaknesses by applying DSM-III criteria to a school population. One-hundred and fifty adolescents aged 14 to 16 were assessed for diagnosis; so as not to overestimate the rate of disorder, a judgment of impairment (need for treatment) was required from two independent raters to make a diagnosis. Using this definition of "caseness," the authors determined that 19% of the sample received at least one diagnosis, and one subject (0.7%) in the sample was diagnosed with mania (Kashani et al., 1987).

Spicer, Hare, and Slater (1973) used information routinely obtained from every patient admitted to a National Health Service psychiatric hospital in England and Wales during 1965–1966 to determine the age incidence of affective and anxiety disorders in the population. It was found that 0.003% of the total population of 16- to 19-year-olds was hospitalized for an episode of mania. The group aged 16 to 19 comprised 4% of the total hospital admissions for mania during the study period.

Other studies of hospital admissions show variable rates of mania in adolescents. Welner, Welner, and Fishman (1979) assessed 77 adolescent inpatients and found that 12 (16%) were bipolar at admission to the hospital. Gammon et al., (1983) administered the K-SADS-E to 17 inpatients aged 13 to 18 on a psychiatric hospital's adolescent ward. Five (29%) of the patients met DSM-III criteria for bipolar I or bipolar II (hypomanic) disorder. Hudgens (1974), in a comprehensive follow-up study of 110 adolescent inpatients, found that 11 (10%) of the adolescents selected for study were diagnosed as manic. Of the total of 302 adolescent psychiatric patients admitted to the hospital during Hudgens's study period, 4% received a diagnosis of mania.

An epidemiologic study of 2,364 children discharged from child guidance clinics in Stockholm found nine cases of manic depression (0.04% of the sample) (Nylander, 1979). Friedman et al., (1982) reviewed the charts of 76 adolescents aged 13 to 19 recently discharged from a psychiatric hospital and assigned DSM-III diagnoses to each patient. They found that three adolescents (4%) received a diagnosis of bipolar disorder. Two of these subjects were currently manic, and one was currently depressed.

The studies mentioned report only on adolescents. Although they report variable rates of disorder, it may be estimated that less than 1% of the general population of adolescents suffers from bipolar disorder and 4% to 29% of adolescent psychiatric admissions may be for bipolar disorder. However, no studies exist reporting on rates of bipolar disorder in younger children. The literature does report isolated cases without indicating incidence figures. Therefore, it may be concluded that bipolar disorder in children is rare, but does occur.

Although the population incidence of bipolar disorder in young subjects has not been rigorously examined, the familial incidence of bipolar disorder has been a topic of much research in recent years. A review by Clayton (1981) concluded that approximately 50% of patients with bipolar disorder have at least one parent with bipolar disorder, and between 4% and 10% have a first-degree relative with mania.

This high rate of disorder in families of bipolar patients is especially relevant to childhood and adolescent bipolar disorders, as recent family studies have suggested that an early age of onset of bipolar disorder is associated with higher morbid risk among first-degree relatives. For example, Baron, Mendelwicz, and Klotz (1981) determined that relatives of patients with "early-onset" bipolar disorder (onset before age 40) are at a higher risk for affective disorders than were relatives of late-onset probands. Using the same age of onset cutoff, James (1977) also found a significantly higher risk of affective disorders in first-degree relatives of early-onset probands (26%), compared to late-onset (12.3%). Another study compared bipolar subjects with and without a family history of affective disorder and found that those with a positive family history were more likely to have an age of onset before age 25, compared to patients with a negative family history (Mendelwicz, Fieve, Rainer, & Fleiss, 1972). Although the age of onset cutoffs in the studies mentioned are in adulthood, the implications for children and adolescents are apparent. Further research should be conducted in this area using lower age of onset criteria to determine if the risk of bipolar disorder in relatives is linearly associated with younger age of onset.

NATURAL HISTORY

Because approximately one-third of adult probands report onset of bipolar disorder in adolescence and early adulthood (Taylor & Abrams, 1981; Winokur, Clayton, & Reich, 1969), much of what is known about the natural history of bipolar disorders in children and adolescents has been gleaned from retrospective reports of adults. Case reports of children have provided information on the course of singular occurrences of the disorder; however, precise prospective follow-ups of adolescents and children are sparse. From adult reports, we know that bipolar disorder is recurrent, with high rates of relapse and chronicity (Keller, 1987). Reports of children and adolescents have elicited similarly pessimistic findings.

Onset

The onset of bipolar disorder is often preceded by minor oscillations in mood, or mild cyclothymic mood swings (Akiskal et al., 1985; Anthony & Scott, 1960; Bowden & Sarabia, 1980; Campbell, 1955; Kraepelin, 1921). However, manic episodes typically begin suddenly, with a rapid escalation of symptoms (APA, 1987), and often develop after a clear-cut episode of depression (Carlson, 1985).

As discussed, prepubertal onset of bipolar disorder is controversial. However, case histories have been presented with onsets as young as 4 (Poznanski, Israel, & Grossman, 1984). Kraepelin (1921) reported that 0.4% of his sample of manic-depressive patients had onset of the disorder before age 10. Baron, Risch, and Mendelwicz (1983), in a study of 142 bipolar adult probands, reported that 2% were ill prior to age 15 and 11% of the probands had onsets in adolescence. Loranger and Levine (1978) reviewed the charts of 100 male and 100 female manic patients to determine age of onset using three different onset criteria: first symptom appearance, first treatment contact, and first hospitalization. They found that by age 9, 0.5% of the subjects had experienced their first symptoms and 20% of the sample had symptoms of bipolar disorder by age 19. Three percent of the subjects had been hospitalized by age 14, and 12.5% had been hospitalized by age 19 (Loranger & Levine, 1978). Thus, not only were these subjects ill at an early age, the impairment in a large number of subjects was severe enough to warrant hospitalization.

Duration of Disorder

Bipolar disorder is considered an episodic disorder, and affected individuals may experience recurrent periods of illness, alternating with periods of euthymic mood. The duration of the episodes may vary, but some investigators have found that manic episodes are shorter and more frequent in younger patients than in older patients. Paskind (1930) reported that in subjects whose "attacks" of manic depression occurred between ages 10 and 20, the median duration of the episode was 3 months, compared to 4 months for attacks occurring after age 30. Pollack (1931) studied 1,703 manic-depressive cases and determined that the average episode duration in patients under age 20

was 0.6 years. The duration of episodes lengthened with age to a maximum of 1.7 years at age 50. Of the patients whose first hospital admission was before age 20, 22% had three or more prior episodes. Similarly, Olsen's 1961 retrospective study of 28 bipolar patients with onset before age 19 found that the frequency of episodes reached a peak at age 17, gradually decreasing with time. In addition, Olsen (1961) found that episodes occurring before the age of 17 were more likely to be manic, and after time were more equally divided between mania and depression.

Outcome

Studies of the outcome of bipolar illness in children and adolescents have reported discouraging results. Landolt (1957) recontacted 60 patients 5 to 25 years after they had been discharged from a hospitalization for manic-depressive psychosis when they were between the ages of 15 and 22. She found that only 10% of these patients recovered and had no recurrence, while 45% of the subjects exhibited a chronic course. Welner, Welner, and Fishman (1979) studied 77 inpatient adolescents 8 to 10 years postdischarge and found that 12 (16%) of the inpatients received a diagnosis of bipolar disorder after chart review. Four of these patients had originally been diagnosed as unipolar, and one had been undiagnosed at intake. One of these patients displayed an episodic clinical course, and the remaining patients were chronically ill, with further hospitalizations and suicide attempts. All the bipolar patients had poor work histories, nine were considered socially disabled, and three committed suicide. The bipolar patients displayed the worst outcome of all the patients studied. Carlson, Davenport, and Jamison (1977) compared the outcome of early-onset bipolar disorder (onset before age 20) to the outcome in probands with late-onset (after 45) bipolar disorder. Although no significant differences in outcome between the two groups were found, 20% of the adolescent-onset probands were considered impaired, and 20% were considered chronically incapacitated.

In summary, bipolar disorder may have its onset at any age, although it is more common in adolescence than childhood. In younger patients, episodes are shorter, occur more frequently, and are more likely to be manic than in adult patients. Children and adolescents with bipolar disorder are at risk for chronicity and poor outcome.

IMPAIRMENT AND COMPLICATIONS

There are no published studies assessing the resultant impairment in childhood and adolescent bipolar disorders. However, the impairment resulting from bipolar disorder usually takes the form of interference in social functioning and school performance. Children and adolescents in the midst of a manic episode may be irritable, belligerent, oppositional, and even assaultative, resulting in impaired peer and family relations. Pressure of speech and delusions of grandeur may also interfere with social relations. School performance is often impaired due to difficulty concentrating and overactivity. School refusal or truancy may occur.

The bipolar child or adolescent may also place himself or herself in positions of physical risk, as inflated self-esteem may cause the individual to participate in dangerous activities (*British Medical Journal*, 1979). Episodic delinquent behavior may occur, which may result in legal problems. These difficulties are often impossible for family and teachers to manage, and the child or adolescent may be hospitalized to control behavior.

Thus, children and adolescents with bipolar disorder may face impaired social and academic functioning and hospitalization. In addition, because bipolar disorder is a recurrent and often chronic illness, these periods of disturbance may be repeated over the course of an illness and persist into adulthood. It may therefore appear that bipolar disorder developing in a child or adolescent would result in impaired intellectual, social, and emotional development (Hassanyeh & Davison, 1980; Carlson, Davenport, & Jamison, 1977) and, thus, would have more serious repercussions than adult-onset bipolar disorder. However, some studies have shown that outcome in adolescent-onset bipolar disorder is not worse than late-onset bipolar disorder (Carlson et al., 1977; McGlashan, 1988). Indeed, Carlson and Strober (1979) concluded that because episode duration is short in adolescents and children, they may avoid being developmentally impaired, and while euthymic, may be restored to their premorbid state. Another view states that because adolescence is a time of personality development, affected individuals may be able to develop ways of coping with bipolar disorder and hence evidence less impairment than if the disorder began in adulthood (McGlashan, 1988). Thus, although manic episodes may severely interfere with personality formation and the achievement of critical developmental milestones, adolescents may be able to compensate for the impaired functioning they experience during episodes. However, further work is needed in this area to assess better the developmental ramifications of early-onset bipolar disorder.

The complications and comorbidity of bipolar disorders and other disorders have not been carefully examined in children and adolescents. One complication of bipolar disorder in adulthood is substance use (APA, 1987). This relationship has not been examined in adolescents or children; however, because manic adolescents engage in more delinquent behaviors, heightened substance use may also accompany these episodes.

The most grave complication of bipolar disorder is suicide. Although two studies have reported that none of the subjects studied committed suicide during a manic episode (Robins, Gassner, Kayes, Wilkinson, & Murphy, 1959; Winokur, Clayton, & Reich, 1969), the risk of suicide is very high during depressive episodes. A review of studies of suicide in subjects with bipolar disorder reported that rates ranged from 9% to 60% (Jamison, 1986). Although these studies reported on adults, it has been determined that suicide is the second most common cause of death in Americans aged 15 to 19 (Shaw, Sheehan, & Fernandez, 1987), and it is well known that depression is the most common psychiatric disorder in children, adolescents, and adults who commit suicide (Robins et al., 1959). It must be stressed that children as well as adolescents are at risk for suicide; Rosenthal and Rosenthal (1984) reported 16 patients younger than age 5 referred to a child psychiatry clinic for suicide attempts. Thus, during the depressive phase of bipolar disorder, children and adolescents must be carefully monitored for suicidal ideation and behavior.

In summary, children and adolescents with bipolar disorder experience impaired social and academic functioning. However, it has not yet been documented that patients with early-onset bipolar disorder fare worse than those with adult-onset bipolar disorder. Of great concern is the observation that bipolar children and adolescents are at high risk for suicide during the depressive phase of the disorder.

DIFFERENTIAL DIAGNOSIS

Careful diagnosis of bipolar disorder in children and adolescents is of great importance, because the disorder has a history of misdiagnosis and is often confused with other syndromes having early onsets. Many investigators attribute the low rates of bipolar disorder in adolescents and younger children reported by epidemiologic studies to misdiagnosis or a dismissal of symptoms as transient or situational (Bowden & Sarabia, 1980; Carlson & Strober, 1979). Also, because the existence of bipolar disorder in children has been disputed, clinicians may overlook a diagnosis of bipolar disorder in favor of a diagnosis that is more "age appropriate." Children and adolescents may also be unable to recognize and/or verbalize changes in mood, creating further diagnostic difficulties (Carlson, 1985). Some investigators have also pointed to the "atypical" clinical presentation of bipolar disorder in childhood and adolescence as the reason for its misdiagnosis (Ballenger et al., 1982).

The "atypical" features of childhood and adolescent bipolar disorder are developmentally related. The psychosocial and developmental context of childhood and adolescence color the presentation of the disorder, and the expression of bipolar disorder may reflect the developmental level of the child (Carlson & Strober, 1979; Feinstein, 1982). For example, adolescents go through many periods of adjustment and may be labile or irritable; hence, some symptoms of bipolar disorder may be dismissed as "adolescent turmoil." Bipolar disorder may also be misdiagnosed in children and adolescents due to symptoms that overlap with other syndromes more common in childhood. Some of the most common differential diagnoses are the following:

Adjustment Reaction

Because adolescence is a period of adjustment, some bipolar symptoms in an adolescent may seem like expressions of "adolescent turmoil," "transient situational disturbance," or "adjustment reaction" (Gallemore & Wilson, 1972; Bowden & Sarabia, 1980; Carlson & Strober, 1979). Irritability and lability combined with school problems and delinquent behavior may be interpreted as part of the "adolescent personality," which has traditionally been characterized by rebellion and emotional turmoil.

To differentiate a normal adjustment reaction from a psychiatric disorder in an adolescent, a clinician must consider the acuteness of onset of the problem behavior, the duration and intensity of the symptoms, the child's past history, family history, and the course of the illness (Gallemore & Wilson, 1972).

Schizophrenia

Bipolar disorder is often diagnosed as schizophrenia in adolescents due to the preponderance of schizophreniform symptoms, including delusions and hallucinations, experienced by bipolar adolescents. The generally accepted ages of onset for these disorders also contribute to the misdiagnosis; schizophrenia is commonly accepted as having onset in adolescence, while the incidence of bipolar disorder in young people is more controversial.

Early writers have acknowledged that clinicians have a tendency to diagnose bipolar disorder in young patients as schizophrenia (Campbell, 1955; Kasanin, 1931). One study by Carlson and Strober (1979) exemplifies the problem of differential diagnosis. They reported on nine adolescents who met criteria for manic-depressive illness, but only one had been diagnosed correctly at hospital admission. The remaining cases received diagnoses of schizophrenia (five), adjustment reaction (two), and medical disorder (one). Of these adolescents, 56% experienced delusions, 44% paranoid grandiosity, and 33% experienced auditory hallucinations (Carlson & Strober, 1979).

In general, distinguishing the psychotic symptoms of mania from schizophrenia relies on the temporal occurrence and content of the delusional or hallucinatory references. Psychotic symptoms occurring in the absence of a mood disturbance and persisting for long periods may be indicative of schizophrenia. In addition, mood congruent delusions or hallucinations in a manic episode would be grandiose and related to inflated self-esteem; depressed delusions would center on themes of nihilism, sin, and so on (APA, 1987). Schizophrenic delusions may be more bizarre in nature, or not influenced by mood. A schizophrenic patient is also more likely to display "flat" or absent affect, while a manic patient would be exuberant, euphoric, or irritable. Premorbid adjustment may also be indicative of diagnosis; schizophrenic patients are more likely to display poor premorbid adjustment, while bipolar disorder usually appears in patients who had previously functioned well or experienced mild mood swings (Bowden & Sarabia, 1980). A family history of bipolar disorder or a history of previous mood disorder may also assist in distinguishing schizophrenia from bipolar disorder.

Hyperactivity

The manic overactivity of bipolar illness may be viewed by clinicians as a symptom of hyperactive syndrome, especially when it presents in young children. Studies have shown that a number of children diagnosed as "hyperactive" have responded to lithium rather than amphetamines, which are usually prescribed for hyperactivity. Weinberg and Brumback (1976) described a case of a "hyperactive" child whose usual hyperactivity was controlled with methylphenidate (usually prescribed for hyperactivity), but who also experienced methylphenidate resistant hyperactive periods, which responded to lithium. It must be recognized that manic overactivity is more transient and not as pervasive as in hyperactive syndrome (Bowden & Sarabia, 1980). Short attention span and distractibility are also seen in both diagnoses. However, children with hyperactivity (attention deficit disorder) show poor self-esteem, while children with bipolar disorder generally display exaggerated self-esteem (Potter, 1983). Hyperactivity also commonly appears in early childhood, while prepubertal mania is more rare (Bowden & Sarabia, 1980).

Conduct Disorder

Children and adolescents in a manic phase of bipolar disorder may be more aggressive and experience outbursts of irritability and anger that may be seen as symptoms of conduct disorder. However, the two disorders may be distinguished by the duration of the antisocial activity; bipolar disorder would manifest itself as relatively brief periods of aggressive behavior in contrast to previous behavior, while the antisocial behavior associated with conduct disorder persists over time. In addition, children and adolescents with conduct disorder often display poor self-esteem and perform antisocial acts in the context of an antisocial peer group or in response to external events. In contrast, an adolescent with bipolar disorder would display exaggerated self-esteem, would appear internally driven, and would commit antisocial acts without peer group influence (Bowden & Sarabia, 1980).

Cyclothymia

Cyclothymia is a chronic form of bipolar disorder very similar in presentation to bipolar disorder, in which periods of hypomania (episodes of elevated mood that do not cause impairment, are less severe than mania, and have no psychotic symptoms) alternate with periods of depressed mood that do not meet criteria for major depression. The mood disturbance must persist for at least one year to make the diagnosis in children or adolescents (DSM-III-R). Some investigators feel that cyclothymia is precursor of bipolar disorder (Akiskal et al., 1985; Klein, Depue, & Slater, 1985). It can be distinguished from bipolar disorder by the severity of the symptoms and the duration of the disorder. However, children and adolescents diagnosed with cyclothymia should be carefully monitored for symptom escalation so that a full-blown bipolar disorder can be detected and treated quickly.

CASE EXAMPLE

A history of bipolar disorder in a 5-year-old boy is presented in this section. As is often the case in children, the symptom picture does not conform to the classic bipolar profile. However, the subject exhibited symptomatology that meets both DSM-III-R criteria and Weinberg and Brumback's (1976) revised criteria for childhood mania.

T. F., a 5-year-old boy, was brought into a pharmacology clinic because of hyperactivity since infancy. T. F. had recently become more difficult at home, refusing school, displaying uncontrolled outbursts of rage, impulsivity, oppositional behavior, and moodiness.

History

The patient was born to parents about whom little is known. He was born at home, the mother having received no prenatal care, but was seen at the hospital on the day of his birth and was judged normal. The biological mother was noted as being emotionally unstable and was known to have a history of sexual problems. She was abused by her father, and her mother had committed suicide. The biological father was noted as being the "nervous" type and had been abused as a child. No other information is known about the biological parents. The patient was taken from his mother by the court and delivered into foster care with Mr. and Mrs. F. (hereafter referred to as the father and mother) soon after his birth. T. F. was eventually legally adopted by the F. family.

As an infant, T. F. was hyperactive and restless, was not affectionate, and refused to be held. The mother described the patient as curious and alert but destructive (e.g., regularly pulled apart toys).

At 2 years of age, after the patient broke a window by throwing a toy through it, T. F.'s mother and pediatrician arranged an evaluation at a children's hospital (cognitive functioning was found to be several months below normal, and the child evinced a significant attentional disorder). At this time, the child was described as overactive, distractible, and impulsive, with a short attention span. Medication was recommended for hyperactivity, but the parents refused. The patient began a special school program and a Fiengold diet to control hyperactivity, which had no particular effect. While in the school program, T. F. became more affectionate and began to sleep more hours. At reevaluation at age 3, it was noted that the patient had increased social relatedness and language, although he was still unable to control his behavior. Further special schooling was recommended.

Assessment

At evaluation at the psychopharmacology clinic, the mother reported that although the patient is hyperactive, he can spend hours building complicated projects with building blocks and can sit through movies. The patient was noted to display frequent tantrum behavior, screaming, flying into a rage, and removing his clothes when opposed. Socially, the patient was described as aggressive, and he occasionally started fights with boys 5 to 10 years older than he. The parents kept items in the patient's room to a bare minimum, as they often got broken. The patient's school teacher noted that although T. F. talked constantly and displayed inappropriate behavior, he could focus on structured activity and displayed normal activity levels and concentration in such situations. In addition, T. F.'s teacher noted that the patient's distraction seemed "internally generated" and that he constantly fantasized about "systems, springs, and screws." The initial diagnostic impression from the parent's report was of "atypical attention-deficit disorder."

The child psychiatrist later interviewed the patient, and impressions were of a grossly disinhibited youngster with abnormalities in thought, loose associations, and delusions of grandeur. The psychiatrist judged the patient's affect to be elevated and noted that T. F. exhibited racing thoughts, pressured speech, and disinhibited motor and verbal activity. The patient spoke of "electrical impulses in his head" and acted like a robot. A tentative diagnosis of childhood mania was made, and the patient was placed on Mellaril

10 mg h.s. to reduce psychotic symptoms. After two weeks, there was a decrease in agitation and oppositional behavior. Mellaril was increased to 25 mg in the evening and 10 mg in the morning. After six weeks on this regimen, the patient began deteriorating, displaying inappropriate laughter and agitated and oppositional behavior in school. Mellaril was increased to 75 mg/day. Eight weeks later, the patient again showed agitation and elevated mood. Follow-up three months later revealed that in school the patient displayed inappropriate physical behavior, agitation, and elevated, expansive mood. The patient was begun on lithium carbonate 150 mg b.i.d. Three weeks later, T. F. exhibited expansive mood and irritability. Lithium was increased to 300 mg b.i.d. and Mellaril was increased to 125 mg/day. The patient was maintained on this regimen for six months, at which time lithium was increased to 750 mg/day due to inappropriate behavior in school. After six months, the patient experienced breakthrough symptoms, with agitated, inappropriate outbursts of rage and oppositional behavior. Lithium was raised to 900 mg/day. The patient was maintained at this level, with lithium being increased with symptom breakthroughs.

Summary

This case example of a 5-year-old with bipolar disorder illustrates many of the diagnostic difficulties that may arise when the disorder presents in young children. T. F. was first thought to be hyperactive, due to heightened activity level and short attention span. However, T. F.'s ability to concentrate and focus on certain activities implied a more episodic hyperactivity, and the elevated mood and inappropriate laughter evidenced by the patient implied a disturbance of mood. T. F.'s oppositional behavior and rages are also a manifestation of disorder but do not meet criteria for oppositional disorder, nor does the patient display low self-esteem, as in oppositional or attention-deficit disorder. The "constant" talking and delusions are also evidence of a manic episode.

T. F. meets DSM-III-R criteria for bipolar disorder, as well as Weinberg and Brumback's (1976) revised criteria for childhood mania. T. F. displayed elevated (and irritable) mood, pressure of speech, distractibility, and increased activity. Dvoredsky and Stewart (1981) also documented a case of a 2-year-old with symptoms very similar to the case of T. F. Their patient was difficult to discipline, easily upset, active, energetic; had a short attention span; and fought with other children. By age 17, these symptoms had escalated and conformed to the classic picture of bipolar disorder: increased energy, increased libido, racing thoughts, and decreased need for sleep (Dvoredsky & Stewart, 1981). Thus, although T. F.'s case of bipolar disorder displays the atypical picture often evident in childhood, he may be at risk for developing "adult-type" bipolar disorder in later years.

CONTINUITY AND DISCONTINUITY WITH ADULT PRESENTATION

Although the controversy surrounding the existence of childhood and adolescent bipolar disorder has subsided somewhat, there is still disagreement as to the nature of the disorder and its relationship to the adult form. Some investigators have concluded that childhood and adolescent bipolar disorder is an "early onset variant" of adult bipolar disorder that differs from the adult presentation due to developmental issues (Coll & Bland, 1979; Anthony & Scott, 1960).

As noted, bipolar disorder in childhood and adolescence has "atypical" features (Ballenger, 1982) that may be developmentally related. Some of these differences are contextual; for example, parents and teachers find the bipolar child difficult to control, and school refusal and fluctuations in learning ability may occur (Bowden & Sarabia, 1980). During manic episodes, younger children tend to be predominantly irritable and labile, while adolescents and adults are more often euphoric and elated (Carlson, 1983). Depressive episodes also display developmental manifestations; younger children tend to exhibit crying spells, anxiety, and somatic complaints, while older children may develop more classic symptoms of anhedonia and retardation (Strober & Carlson, 1982).

The duration and frequency of episodes are other features of bipolar disorder that change over time. In children and adolescents, episodes are more likely to be manic than depressed, with more equal ratios developing over time (Olsen, 1961). Episodes in young patients are also shorter than in adults (Paskind, 1930; Pollack, 1931).

The most striking contrast between the adult and adolescent presentation of bipolar disorder is the preponderance of schizophreniform symptoms displayed by young patients, a finding that has been noted by several investigators (Ballenger et al., 1982; Carlson et al., 1977; McGlashan, 1988; Rosen et al., 1983). One study comparing the clinical features of episodes of mania in 9 adolescents and 12 adults found significant differences in the number who experienced psychotic symptoms. Eighty-eight percent of the adolescents had delusions during a manic episode, while only 33% of the adults did. Forty-four percent of the adolescents had ideas of reference, compared to none of the adults. Each of the adolescents studied experienced at least one schizophrenic symptom while manic; however, there was no significant difference in the number and type of manic symptoms present in both groups (Ballenger et al., 1982). Although this finding has significance for differential diagnosis, the prognostic significance of psychotic symptoms in adolescent bipolar disorder cannot be assessed. Two studies (Ballenger et al., 1982; McGlashan, 1988) noted that the psychotic symptoms in the adolescent onset patients subsided somewhat over the course of the follow-up; however, prospective follow-up, tracing the course of psychotic symptoms over time, is necessary to determine if the psychotic features of adolescent-onset bipolar disorder are truly age-specific and fade over time, or if adolescent-onset bipolar disorder is a unique entity whose features persist into adulthood.

SUMMARY

Bipolar disorder in prepubertal children has been the subject of dispute. However, it has been shown to occur in children, although rarely. The incidence of bipolar disorder in adolescence is more common, as approximately 30% of bipolar adults report onset in adolescence. The disorder is characterized by manic episodes that may be punctuated by depressive episodes. Mania in children and adolescents most often manifests itself as irritability, distractibility, and hyperactivity. The population incidence of bipolar disorder in young people is unknown due to the lack of epidemiologic studies. Bipolar disorder is a recurrent, chronic illness, and children and adolescents tend to have short, frequent episodes of mania. The disorder not only causes social and academic impairment, but the risk of suicide is high during depressive episodes. Bipolar disorder is often confused with other disorders more common in childhood, due to overlapping symptoms or accepted ages of onset. The presentation of the disorder in youngsters and adults differs due to developmental issues and the schizophrenic symptoms displayed by adolescents.

In summary, although the existence of the disorder in children and adolescents has been confirmed, much work is needed to determine the incidence of the disorder, and precise prospective follow-ups are needed to describe the phenomenology of the disorder and its relationship to the adult form of the disorder. Most important, research should focus on the question of whether the atypical features of early onset bipolar disorder persist over time, and if bipolar adolescents with schizophrenic features go on to become schizoaffective adults, or if these psychotic features are age-specific.

REFERENCES

Akiskal, H. S., Downs, J., Jordan, P., Watson, S., Daughtery, D., & Pruitt, D. B. (1985). Affective disorders in referred children and younger siblings of manic-depressives: Mode of onset and prospective course. *Archives of General Psychiatry, 42*, 996–1003.

American Psychiatric Association. (1987). *Diagnostic and statistical manual of mental disorders* (3rd ed., rev.). Washington, DC: Author.

Anthony, J., & Scott, P. (1960). Manic-depressive psychosis in childhood. *Child Psychology and Psychiatry, 1*, 53–72.

Ballenger, J. C., Reus, V. I., & Post, R. (1982). The "atypical" clinical picture of adolescent mania. *American Journal of Psychiatry, 139*(5), 602–606.

Baron, M., Mendelwicz, J., & Klotz, J. (1981). Age-of-onset and genetic transmission in affective disorders. *Acta Psychiatrica Scandinavica, 64*, 373–380.

Baron, M., Risch, N., & Mendelwicz, J. (1983). Age at onset in bipolar-related major affective illness: Clinical and genetic implications. *Journal of Psychiatric Research, 17*(1), 5–18.

Bowden, C. L., & Sarabia, F. (1980). Diagnosing manic-depressive illness in adolescents. *Comprehensive Psychiatry, 21*(4), 263–269.

British Medical Journal. (1979). Manic states in affective disorders of childhood and adolescence. *British Medical Journal, 27*, 214–215.

Campbell, J. D. (1955). Manic-depressive disease in children. *Journal of the American Medical Association, 158*(3), 154–157.

Carlson, G. A. (1983). Bipolar affective disorders in childhood and adolescence. In D. P. Cantwell & G. A. Carlson (Eds.), *Affective disorder in childhood and adolescence: An update* (pp. 60–83). New York: Spectrum.

Carlson, G. (1985). Bipolar disorder in adolescence. *Psychiatric Annals, 15*, 379–386.

Carlson, G. A., Davenport, Y. B., & Jamison, K. (1977). A comparison of outcome in adolescent- and late-onset bipolar manic-depressive illness. *American Journal of Psychiatry, 143*(8), 919–922.

Carlson, G. A., & Strober, M. (1978). Affective disorders in adolescence: Issues in misdiagnosis. *Journal of Clinical Psychiatry, 39*, 59–66.

Carlson, G. A., & Strober, M. (1979). Affective disorders in adolescence. *Psychiatric Clinics of North America, 2*(3), 511–526.

Clayton, P. J. (1981). The epidemiology of bipolar affective disorder. *Comprehensive Psychiatry, 22*(1), 31–43.

Coll, P. G., & Bland, R. (1979). Manic-depressive illness in adolescence and childhood. *Canadian Journal of Psychiatry, 24*, 255–263.

Davis, R. E. (1979). Manic-depressive variant syndrome of childhood: A preliminary report. *American Journal of Psychiatry, 136*(5), 702–706.

Dvoredsky, A. E., & Stewart, M. A. (1981). Hyperactivity followed by manic-depressive disorder: Two case reports. *Journal of Clinical Psychiatry, 42*(5), 212–214.

Feighner, J. P., Robins, E., Guze, S. B., Woodruff, R. A., Winokur, G., & Munoz, R. (1972). Diagnostic criteria for use in psychiatric research. *Archives of General Psychiatry, 26*, 57–63.

Feinstein, S. C. (1982). Manic-depressive disorder in children and adolescents (pp. 256–272). In *Adolescence.* Chicago: University of Chicago Press.

Friedman, R. C., Hurt, S. W., Clarkin, J. F., Corn, R., Aronoff, M. S., Hurt, S. W., & Murphy, M. C. (1982). DSM-III and affective psychopathology in hospitalized adolescents. *Journal of Nervous and Mental Disease, 70*(9), 511–521.

Gallemore, J. L., & Wilson, W. P. (1972). Adolescent maladjustment or affective disorder? *American Journal of Psychiatry, 129*(5), 608–612.

Gammon, G. D., John, K., Rothblum, E. D., Mullen, K., Tischler, G. L., & Weissman, M. M. (1983). Use of a structured diagnostic interview to identify bipolar disorder in adolescent inpatients: Frequency and manifestations of the disorder. *American Journal of Psychiatry, 140*(5), 543–547.

Hassanyeh, F., & Davison, K. (1980). Bipolar affective psychosis with onset before age 16 years: Report of 10 cases. *British Journal of Psychiatry, 137*, 530–539.

Hudgens, R. W. (1974). *Psychiatric disorders in adolescence.* Baltimore, MD: Williams & Wilkins.

James, N. M. (1977). Early- and late-onset bipolar affective disorder: A genetic study. *Archives of General Psychiatry, 34*, 715–717.

Jamison, K. R. (1986). Suicide and bipolar disorders. *Annals of the New York Academy of Sciences, 487*, 301–315.

Kasanin, J. (1931). The affective psychoses in children. *American Journal of Psychiatry, 10*, 897–926.

Kashani, J. H., Beck, N. C., Hoeper, E. W., Fallahi, C., Corcoran, C. M., McAllister, J. A., Rosenberg, T. K., & Reid, J. C. (1987). Psychiatric disorders in a community sample of adolescents. *American Journal of Psychiatry, 144*, 584–589.

Keller, M. B. (1987). Differential diagnosis, natural course and epidemiology of bipolar disorder. In R. E. Hales & R. J. Frances (Eds.), *Psychiatry update: The American Psychiatric Association Annual Review* (Vol. 6, pp. 10–31). Washington, DC: American Psychiatric Press.

Klein, D. N., Depue, R. A., & Slater, J. F. (1985). Cyclothymia in the adolescent offspring of parents with bipolar affective disorder. *Journal of Abnormal Psychology, 94*(2), 115–127.

Kraepelin, E. (1921). *Manic-depressive insanity and paranoia.* Edinburgh: E. & S. Livingstone.

Landolt, A. (1957). Follow-up studies on circular manic-depressive reactions occurring in the young. *Bulletin of the New York Academy of Medicine, 33*, 65–73.

Loranger, A. W., & Levine, P. M. (1978). Age at onset of bipolar affective illness. *Archives of General Psychiatry, 35*, 1345–1348.

McGlashan, T. H. (1988). Adolescent versus adult onset of mania. *American Journal of Psychiatry, 145*, 221–223.

Mendelwicz, J., Fieve, R. R., Rainer, J. D., & Fleiss, J. L. (1972). Manic-depressive illness: A comparative study of patients with and without a family history. *British Journal of Psychiatry, 120*, 523–530.

Nylander, I. (1979). A twenty-year prospective follow-up study of 2,164 cases at the child guidance clinics in Stockholm. *Acta Paediatrica Scandinavia*, (Suppl. 276), 1–45.

Olsen, T. (1961). Follow-up study of manic-depressive patients whose first attack occurred before the age of 19. *Acta Psychiatrica Scandinavica, 37*(Suppl. 162), 45–51.

Paskind, H. A. (1930). Manic-depressive psychoses as seen in private practice: Sex distribution and age incidence of first attacks. *Archives of Neurology and Psychiatry, 23*, 152–158.

Perris, C. (1966). A study of bipolar (manic-depressive) and unipolar recurrent depressive psychoses. *Acta Psychiatrica Scandinavica, 42*(Suppl. 194), I–X.

Pollack, H. M. (1931). Recurrence of attacks in manic-depressive psychoses. *American Journal of Psychiatry, 11*, 567–574.

Potter, R. L. (1983). Manic-depressive variant syndrome of childhood: Diagnostic and therapeutic considerations. *Clinical Pediatrics, 22*(7), 495–499.

Poznanski, E. O., Israel, M. C., & Grossman, J. (1984). Hypomania in a 4-year-old. *Journal of the American Academy of Child Psychiatry, 12*(1), 105–110.

Puig-Antich, J. (1980). Affective disorders in childhood: A review and perspective. *Psychiatric Clinics of North America, 3*(3), 403–424.

Reiss, A. L. (1985). Developmental manifestations in a boy with prepubertal bipolar disorder. *Journal of Clinical Psychiatry, 46*(10), 441–443.

Rice, J., Reich, T., Andreasen, N., Endicott, J., VanEerdewegh, M., Fishman, R., Hirschfeld, R. M. A., & Klerman, G. L. (1987). The familial transmission of bipolar illness. *Archives of General Psychiatry, 44*, 441–447.

Robins, E., Gassner, S., Kayes, J., Wilkinson, R. H., & Murphy, G. E. (1959). The communication of suicidal intent: A study of 134 consecutive cases of successful (completed) suicide. *American Journal of Psychiatry, 115*, 724–733.

Rogeness, G. A., Reister, A. E., & Wicoff, J. S. (1982). Unusual presentation of manic depressive disorder in adolescence. *Journal of Clinical Psychiatry, 43*(1), 37–39.

Rosen, L. N., Rosenthal, N. E., Van Dusen, P. H., Dunner, D. L., & Fieve, R. R. (1983). Age at onset and number of psychotic symptoms in bipolar I and schizoaffective disorder. *American Journal of Psychiatry, 140*, 1523–1524.

Rosenthal, P. A., & Rosenthal, S. (1984). Suicidal

behavior by pre-school children. *American Journal of Psychiatry, 141*, 520–525.

Shaw, K. R., Sheehan, K. H., & Fernandez, R. C. (1987). Suicide in children and adolescents. *Advances in Pediatrics, 34*, 313–334.

Spicer, C. C., Hare, E. H., & Slater, E. (1973). Neurotic and psychotic forms of depressive illness: Evidence from age-incidence in a national sample. *British Journal of Psychiatry, 123*, 535–541.

Strober, M., & Carlson, G. (1982). Bipolar illness in adolescents with major depression: Clinical, genetic, and psychopharmacologic predictors in a three- to four-year prospective follow-up investigation. *Archives of General Psychiatry, 39*, 549–555.

Taylor, M. A., & Abrams, R. (1981). Early- and late-onset bipolar illness. *Archives of General Psychiatry, 38*, 58–61.

Weinberg, W. A., & Brumback, R. A. (1976). Mania in childhood: Case studies and literature review. *American Journal of Diseases of Children, 130*, 380–385.

Welner, A., Welner, Z., & Fishman, R. (1979). Psychiatric adolescent inpatients: Eight- to ten-year follow-up. *Archives of General Psychiatry, 36*, 698–700.

Winokur, G., Clayton, P. J., & Reich, T. (1969). *Manic-depressive illness*. St. Louis, MO: C. V. Mosby.

CHAPTER 6

BIPOLAR DISORDER IN ADULTHOOD

Brian L. Cook
George Winokur
Jenelle Sobotka

DESCRIPTION OF THE DISORDER

Affective disorders have been classified using a variety of systems (Cook & Winokur, 1989). One widely utilized method, the Diagnostic and Statistical Manual of Mental Disorders (American Psychological Association, 1987), separates individuals with a history of manic symptoms (bipolar disorders) from those without (depressive disorders). This separation has been studied intensively, and its validation has been demonstrated through genetic studies, family studies, and biologic studies and by evaluation of illness course and treatment response. Bipolar disorders are further divided into bipolar disorder, in which at least one manic episode has been experienced, and cyclothymia in which frequent hypomanic episodes as well as depressive symptoms are seen.

The origins of the term "mania" date to Hippocrates. Clayton (1986) noted that the earliest use of the term mania referred to a mental illness with acute onset, in which a mood of merriment and/ or agitation was displayed. Aretaeus, in the first century, noted that depression and excitement alternated in the same person. Theophile Bonet in 1686 used the term "maniaco-melancholicus" to characterize a group of patients. Two centuries later, Falret's description of "circular insanity" (1854) and Baillarger's "double-form insanity" (1854) can be found (Sedler, 1983). Leonhard (1957) first proposed that bipolar and unipolar forms of affective disorder may be different and distinct illnesses.

While the definition of mania may have historically had some variability, it can be observed that clinicians have long recognized manic symptoms, and they now form the cardinal elements leading to the diagnosis of bipolar disorder. The DSM-III-R criteria for a manic episode require a distinct period of abnormal, and persistently elevated, expansive or irritable mood to make the diagnosis, plus three (four if mood is only irritable), associated symptoms that have been present to a significant degree. The associated symptoms are

This work was supported in part by the Veterans Administration.

grandiosity or inflated self-esteem, sleeplessness, excessive or pressured speech, racing thoughts, distractibility, increased goal-directed behavior, and excessive involvement in pleasurable activities with high potential for painful consequences. The mood disturbance must be of severity to cause social or occupational impairment, psychotic symptoms must be during a period of mood disturbance if they persist for over two weeks, the illness cannot be superimposed upon schizophrenia, and organic etiologies that initiated and maintained the disturbance must be ruled out.

CLINICAL PRESENTATION

Bipolar disorder refers to disturbances in mood. The clinical presentation of bipolar disorder may be that of depression, mania, mixed states, euthymia, or various degrees of residual impairment. The clinical presentation of the euthymic state in bipolar disorder refers to the remission of the mood disorder symptoms, but not necessarily to resolution of the various complications that may accompany this illness.

The presentation of the depressed phase of bipolar disorder may be indistinguishable clinically from the depressed phase of major depressive disorder. Depressed patients present with a cluster of symptoms that, as currently defined by DSM-III-R, do not specify whether affected individuals have bipolar disorder or not. Typically one sees an admixture of dysphoria, disturbance in sleep, poor interest, ideas of guilt and hopelessness, change in energy, poor concentration, poor appetite, and psychomotor slowing or agitation. Symptom clusters described as being "endogenous" or "melancholic" have been described, but they are not unique to bipolar illness despite this illness conceptually being the quintessential form of "endogenous" affective disorder. Himmelhoch, Fuchs, and Symons (1982) described patients with a depressive symptom cluster of anergia, motor retardation, volitional inhibition, frequent hypersomnia, and lack of anxiety, irritability, or agitation who respond well to monoamine oxidase inhibitors (MAOIs) that are predominantly, but not purely, bipolar. Kraepelin also recognized this general symptom profile in the depressed phase of bipolar disorder (Himmelhoch et al., 1982). Despite this reported cluster of symptoms being associated with the depressed phase of bipolar disorder, there is little other support for such distinctions in the literature.

The manic episode, as noted, represents the essential ingredient required to diagnose bipolar disorder. The manic episode is best described by Carlson and Goodwin (1973). They carefully documented the manic symptoms displayed in 20 subjects who were hospitalized through a complete manic cycle. Table 6.1 displays the frequency of some of the manic symptoms they recorded. The overlap of schizophrenic like symptoms seen (i.e., delusions and hallucinations) displays the lack of diagnostic specificity of these particular symptoms.

The timing of various manic symptoms by these predominantly untreated manics is also well illustrated by Carlson and Goodwin (1973). Figure 6.1 illustrates the progression of dysphoria, mania, and psychosis ratings for a single patient in their study. From such observations, they divided the manic episode into three stages. An initial stage is characterized by a controlled expansive mood and excessive activity in various areas (e.g., sexuality, spending, religion). The intermediate phase is notable for an admixture of dysphoria and euphoria, irritability, racing thoughts, and pressured speech. Delusional thoughts are also pronounced at this point, as well as loss of sleep. The final stage is a disorganized, frankly incoherent one. Delusions become more bizarre and are frequently mood incongruent. Disorientation is by now frequently present, and Schneiderian "first-rank" symptoms are encountered (Schneider, 1959). This final stage is frequently accompanied by catatonia (Abrams & Taylor, 1976). Treated episodes of mania generally do not pass through all phases as described, but the first two stages are very commonly seen during initiation of therapy.

EPIDEMIOLOGY

The epidemiology of psychiatric disorders has progressed through several eras. Early epidemiologic studies were concerned with identification of rates of psychiatric impairment (cases), and not specifically with diagnosable categories of psychiatric disorders. Since 1978 (Weissman & Myers, 1978), the methodology and sophistication of psychiatric epidemiology has markedly changed. The late 1970s ushered in the era of utilizing diagnostic criteria akin to those used in clinical practice to define caseness in community samples. The study by Weissman et al. (1978) set the stage for the National Institute of Mental Health Epidemiologic Catchment Area (ECA) project. Preliminary

Table 6.1. Frequency of Selected Mania Symptoms

SYMPTOMS	% PATIENTS WITH SYMPTOMS
Hyperactivity	100%
Pressured speech	100%
Grandiosity	100%
Irritability	100%
Euphoria	90%
Mood lability	90%
Hypersexuality	80%
Flight of ideas	75%
Delusions	75%
Distractibility	70%
Depression	55%
Hallucinations	40%

From: Carlson & Goodwin. (1973). The stages of mania: A longitudinal perspective. *Archives of General Psychiatry, 28,* 221–228. Copyright 1973, American Medical Association. Reprinted with permission.

data from the ECA project regarding rates of affective disorders were published by Myers et al. (1984). This study not only used diagnostic criteria, but also a structured diagnostic interview: the Diagnostic Interview Schedule (DIS). Updated age- and sex-specific prevalence rates of DSM-III affective disorders from the ECA study were reported by Weissman et al. (1988). This study presented data from all five ECA sites (New Haven, Baltimore, St. Louis, Piedmont County, Los Angeles) concerning prevalence rates for various time periods, age of onset of the disorders, and sex distribution of the affective disorders. Lifetime rates for development of bipolar disorder ranged from 0.7 per 100 to 1.6 per 100 across the five sites, with a mean of 1.2 per 100. It is interesting to note that the one-year period prevalence rates accounted for 80% of the lifetime rates, emphasizing the frequently recurring nature of this illness or, alternatively, the poor recall of episodes in the more remote past. The phenomenon of poor recall of past manic episodes is supported by experience in a 30- to 40-year follow-up study of 100 bipolar patients (Tsuang et al., 1981), where personal interviews revealed fewer past episodes of mania than did review of the patients' medical records. The mean age at onset for bipolar illness in the ECA study was 21.2 years, and was not influenced by sex. Mean sex ratio of bipolar illness (female/male) did not differ at any site, and the cross-site mean ratio was 1.2. One-year prevalence rates for the age group 18 to 44 years differed significantly from the age groups 44 to 64 or 65+, with the younger group significantly higher (1.4% versus 0.4% and 0.1%, respectively).

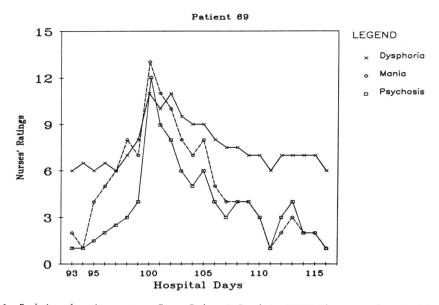

Figure 6.1. Evolution of manic symptoms. From: Carlson & Goodwin. (1973). The stages of mania: A longitudinal perspective. *Archives of General Psychiatry, 28,* 221–228. Copyright 1973, American Medical Association. Reprinted with permission.

The data from this recent study compare favorably with the other two available community surveys (Weissman et al., 1978; Angst & Dobler-Mikola, 1984), thus placing bipolar illness at about the same frequency as schizophrenia in the population.

Risk Factors

The primary known risk factor for development of bipolar disorder is that of a genetic relationship to an affected individual. The genetic evidence will be reviewed later in the familial antecedents section of this chapter. Presently, suffice it to note that such evidence derives from family studies, adoption studies, twin studies, and most recently, molecular genetic studies.

Early onset of affective disorder appears associated with a bipolar course of illness. Akiskal, Walker, Puzantian, King, Rosenthal, and Dranon (1983) reported that age of onset of depression less than 25 years was associated with a bipolar outcome over a 1 to 9-year follow-up period (mean duration to changeover was 6.4 years). In another paper looking at the changeover from unipolar to bipolar illness, Winokur and Wesner (1987) noted that multiple episodes of depression were clearly related to an eventual bipolar outcome in affective disorder. Angst, Felder, Frey, and Stassen (1978) noted that individuals with three or more past episodes of depression were particularly prone to changeover to a bipolar course of illness.

Evidence for a sex effect in bipolar illness, unlike all other forms of affective illness where females predominate, is lacking. Early information regarding social class (Faris & Dunham, 1939) indicated that bipolar illness had a distribution separate from that of schizophrenia. In that study, socially disintegrated and poor areas had high concentrations of schizophrenia, whereas bipolar illness was more concentrated in affluent areas. Diagnostic and methodologic deficiencies, particularly failure to account for social class of origin (e.g., parents), likely invalidate this classic epidemiologic finding. Recent literature may actually indicate that poor urban blacks and Hispanics have increased rates of bipolar disorder (Jones, Gray, & Parson, 1981, 1983a, 1983b) and that inpatient blacks may be underdiagnosed as having bipolar disorders (Keisling, 1981). Education levels achieved by bipolars is somewhat controversial, but the ECA findings (Myers et al., 1984) would indicate that affected individuals are more likely to be noncollege graduates. Woodruff, Robins, Winokur, and Reich (1971) had earlier reported that bipolars achieved slightly higher levels of education, but their control group consisted of nonbipolar depressed subjects. In view of the young age of onset of bipolar illness, and the disruptive nature of this disorder, it seems likely that educational achievement is impaired in this disorder.

Organic antecedents as risk factors for development of mania (Krauthammer & Klerman, 1978; Cook, Shukla, Hoff, & Aronson, 1987) have recently been receiving increased attention and will be discussed in more detail as to their affect on the natural history of bipolar illness.

NATURAL HISTORY

As noted previously, bipolar illness typically has a relatively early age of onset, with most studies pointing to a mean age of onset between 28 and 33 years of age (Coryell & Winokur, 1982). The exact percentage of bipolar individuals who begin their illness with a depression versus mania is unknown. The reason for this lack of knowledge is secondary to the fact that the prevalence of "latent" bipolars, among cohorts with histories of depression only, is inherently impossible to know. In addition to this problem, rates of manic presentation of a bipolar course of illness is confounded in the literature by a lack of consistency regarding how one counts the initial episode. For example, if the illness begins with a mild depression that shifts into a mania that requires hospitalization, is this a depressive or manic onset? Such a biphasic onset, as graphed in Figure 6.1 and as noted by Winokur, Clayton, and Reich (1969) in 51% of their 100 manic episodes, is clinically common.

Immediate Outcome

When looking at the immediate outcome of bipolar illness (and in this chapter mania in particular), one must be aware that with the availability of treatment, study of the "natural" history becomes increasing difficult, if not impossible. Pretreatment literature, however, would indicate that the natural duration of manic episodes may be 7 or 8 months (Swift, 1907; Wertham, 1928). Recovery from individual episodes of mania is the rule, with rates of such recovery dependent upon follow-up duration and definition of recovery. Keller, Lavori, Coryell, Andreasen, Endicott, Clayton, Klerman, and Hirschfeld (1986), utilizing data from the NIMH collaborative study, define recovery as having at least eight consecutive weeks with no more than two affective symptoms of mild intensity following the index episode. When using this definition, the life-table estimate of the probability of remaining ill for at least one year following an episode of pure mania was 7%, while mixed states showed 32% remaining chronic. These subjects were not treated in systematic fashion, but did receive adequate therapy. Prien, Himmelhoch, and Kuper (1988) likewise point to mixed mania as a form of bipolar illness prone to a poor acute treatment response. These studies both point out the heterogeneity of bipolar course, with index presentation being one possible predictor.

Long-term Outcome

Just as the short-term outcome is heterogeneous, so is the long-term prognosis. Few individuals, probably less than 33%, have a single episode of mania without recurrence. Episode frequency may cluster in bursts, that is, several episodes of illness followed by a quiescent period. Grof, Angst, and Haines (1974) suggested, however, that the interval between episodes of illness tended to decrease over the first five or so episodes, until the course finally stabilized with episodes every 6 to 9 months.

As one might expect of an illness with the uncertainty of recurrence, and the unpredictability of behavior during an episode, impact of the illness upon one's life may be more chronic than merely the symptoms alone. Effects upon jobs, marriage, education, and friends can be extreme. Dion, Tohen, and Anthony (1988) noted that symptomatic outcome in treated mania was superior to functional outcome. In that study, while 80% were asymptomatic or mildly symptomatic at six-month follow-up, only 44% were working, and only 20% were working at their expected level of employment.

Secondary Mania

Mania following organic antecedents has been noted via isolated case reports in the psychiatric literature for a number of years. Krauthammer et al. (1978) summarized this literature in an attempt to elucidate the concept of "secondary mania." These authors suggested that secondary mania may have a later age of onset and occur more frequently without a family history of affective disorder. Cook et al. (1987) noted a similar lack of affective disorder in first-degree relatives of bipolars whose illness began after organic insult of various causes and a later age of onset. Phenomenologically, their subjects had symptoms of irritability and assaultive behavior.

Secondary mania may have a poorer immediate prognosis. Himmelhoch and Garfinkel (1986) noted a high prevalence of lithium-resistant mixed manics (83%) to have had a significant associated neuropsychiatric factor in their past history. Black, Winokur, Bell, Nasrallah, and Hulbert (1988) also noted "complicated mania" (i.e., mania with antecedent or coexisting nonaffective psychiatric disorders or serious medical illness to have a poorer acute treatment response).

IMPAIRMENT AND COMPLICATIONS

Mortality

Excess mortality in the total psychiatric population has been documented in a number of studies. Studies looking specifically at mortality in mania, however, are more limited. Derby (1933) reported a 22.5% hospital death rate during the years 1912 to 1932 among 4,341 manics. The hospital deaths were reported, in 40% of the cases, to be due to "exhaustion." Excess mortality in bipolars compared to the general population (Petterson, 1977), and in comparison to unipolar disorder (Perris, 1966), has also been reported. Tsuang, Woolson, and Fleming (1978) noted that excess mortality was greatest in the first decade following index hospitalization.

More recent information regarding mortality in psychiatric patients comes from two large studies (Martin, Cloninger, Guze, & Clayton, 1985; Black, Warrack, & Winokur, 1985). In the Martin et al. (1985) study, mortality status was ascertained by follow-up interviews in 98.8% of 500 patients (a mean of seven years after index outpatient contact). No excess mortality was noted among patients with primary affective disorder (either unipolar or bipolar). The bipolar sample in this study was small, however, with only 17 individuals having primary bipolar affective disorder diagnoses. In this group, 1 natural death occurred during the seven-year follow-up period. It was noted that in secondary affective disorder (mostly depression antedated by alcoholism or antisocial personality), a significant excess of unnatural mortality existed. It was speculated in this study that availability of adequate treatment may have reduced the excess mortality noted in previous studies.

In the other recent mortality study, Black et al. (1985) used a record linkage methodology rather than follow-up interviews. The average "follow-up" period was 4.27 years for men and 4.20 years for women. In this study, affective disorder was not separated into bipolar and unipolar forms. Overall mortality during the first two years was significantly greater than expected, but during the entire follow-up, only mortality among women was excessive. Again, availability of effective treatment was cited as a possible explanation for reducing excessive mortality.

A study of natural and unnatural mortality in major affective disorder (Black, Winokur, & Nasrallah, 1987a) showed that excessive death from natural causes was found in women with secondary unipolar depression and bipolar depression and in manics (men and women combined) who had concurrent organic mental disorders or serious medical illness. Thus, natural-death excessive mortality in affective disorder appears due to complicating physical disorders, but unnatural-death excess is due to the primary psychiatric disorder.

Suicide

The most serious complication of bipolar disorder is suicide. Guze and Robins (1970) reported that the ultimate risk of suicide in affective disorder (not divided by polarity) is 15%, a striking 30 times that of the risk in the general population. Morrison (1982) reported that bipolar cohorts had a 7.5-fold greater risk of suicide than did patients with unipolar disorder. Martin et al. (1985), on the other hand, found no unnatural deaths among bipolars in his study, and only an increase in unnatural deaths among secondary unipolars. Black, Winokur, and Nasrallah (1987a) looked at suicide in subtypes of major affective disorder in 705 primary unipolar depressives, 302 secondary unipolar depressives, and 586 bipolars. All groups had excess risk of suicide as compared to the general population, except female bipolars. Suicides among bipolars were nearly all accounted for by male bipolars who presented for their index admission in the depressed phase. As noted earlier by Tsuang et al. (1978), suicides in this study clustered in the beginning of the follow-up period (i.e., the first two years).

Physical Morbidity

Increased cardiovascular morbidity (Weeke, 1979; Ghadirian & Engelsmann, 1985), diabetes (Lilliker, 1980), and dementia (Bratfos & Haug, 1968) have all been reported in individuals with bipolar disorder. Whether these isolated findings will remain with well-controlled studies is unknown.

Treatment Associated Morbidity

The treatment of bipolar disorder is presently dependent upon lithium as its standard. Such therapy is not without potential side effects and risks. This review cannot elucidate all such possible complications, but will rather highlight a few.

Renal complications of lithium therapy have been controversial since the early 1970s. Schou, Amdisen, and Baastrup (1971) initially suggested that polydypsia and polyuria associated with lithium use were nuisance side effects that could be regarded as harmless and fully reversible. This was disputed in 1977 in a renal biopsy study performed by Hestbech, Hansen, Amdisen, and Olsen (1977), where kidney morphologic abnormalities were associated with past lithium intoxication and polyuria. More recently, Hetmar, Brun, Clemmesen, Ladefoged, Larsen, and Rafaelsen (1987) reported renal biopsy results on 46 patients treated with lithium for an average of 8 years, versus an age-matched control group. In this study, histologic changes (scelerotic glomeruli and atrophic tubuli) were significantly correlated with multiple-dose administration of lithium as compared to once-daily dosing or in controls never exposed to lithium.

Lithium-induced hypothyroidism has been recognized since 1968 (Schou et al., 1968). If systematically evaluated, nearly all lithium-treated patients will show thyroid function abnormalities (e.g., exaggerated TSH response to intravenous TRH). The frequency of clinical thyroid abnormalities may likewise be high, with almost a third of such patients developing goiter (Lazarus, Bennie, Chalmers, & Crockett, 1981). The prevalence of lithium-treated patients requiring thyroid supplement therapy is not well elucidated, but an estimate of one-third is likely conservative.

The other major morbidities of lithium therapy fall more appropriately into either neurologic or gastrointestinal adverse reactions. Such complications include tremor, confusion, nausea, and diarrhea.

Adjunctive and/or alternative therapies for bipolar disorder are also not without adverse effects. Antipsychotic medications are frequently used, especially in the early phase of treatment. Patients with affective disorder may be predisposed to complications of such treatment, with tardive dyskinesia being a major concern in this regard (Davis, Berger, & Hollister, 1976; Mukherjee, Rosen, Caracci, & Shukla, 1986). Carbamazepine is also becoming a frequently utilized agent in this disorder. Typical anticonvulsant side effects (e.g., ataxia, diplopia, sedation), as well as rare but potentially serious hematologic side effects, may be encountered.

Social Morbidity

Bipolar disorder may be disruptive in a number of social areas of one's life. As noted previously, educational achievement may be impaired. Divorce may be more common among bipolars (Brodie & Leff, 1971) as may marital dissatisfaction (Targum, Dibble, Davenport, & Gershon, 1981). Heavy drinking and alcoholism among bipolars has long been noted, especially during manic episodes. An association between pathologic gambling and bipolar illness (McCormick, Russo, Ramirez, & Taber, 1984) has been cited. Winokur et al. (1969) present follow-up social morbidity data on 28 manics, showing that only a minority of individuals have complete and lasting social remissions, with depression frequently causing significant problems during the follow-up.

DIFFERENTIAL DIAGNOSIS

The differential diagnosis of depression is presented elsewhere in this book. This chapter will cover differential diagnosis of a manic episode. When considering this differential, it is important to remember that no individual symptom is pathognomonic for mania. Confusion regarding the diagnosis of mania may have long-term consequences, as treatment choice nearly always is affected by either making or missing this diagnosis. Similarly, the ability to advise the patient and family regarding prognosis, disability determination, and maintenance therapy are all critically dependent upon proper diagnosis. When evalu-

ating a patient presenting with psychiatric symptoms, one must develop an organized system of sequentially arriving at the most likely diagnosis. To do this efficiently, one must inquire about wide areas of psychopathology with the intention of then narrowing the differential through carefully chosen questions that point one direction or another along the differential decision tree. It is important, however, to ask broad enough questions initially, such that major areas are not overlooked. The major broad categories that need to be evaluated when assessing mania are organic mental disorders, psychoactive substance use, schizophrenia, schizoaffective disorder, and personality disorders.

Organic Mental Disorders

Manic symptoms have been noted to occur secondary to a host of chemical, physical, and metabolic insults to the central nervous system. Krauthammer et al. (1978) presented a list of medical and/or physical antecedents of mania, and this was updated by Stasiek and Zetin (1985). More recently, head trauma (Shukla, Cook, & Mukherjee, 1987) as well as nonspecific factors such as perinatal trauma, developmental delay, neuropsychologic deficits, and birth traumas (Cook et al., 1987) have been associated with the development of mania. A careful medical and psychiatric history, review of recent medications, laboratory work up with particular attention to metabolic/endocrinologic parameters, and family history are all helpful in looking for organic etiologies. The intention when elucidating organic causes is to uncover reversible abnormalities, but treatment frequently still involves standard pharmacologic measures.

Psychoactive Substance Abuse

Ingestion of various psychoactive drugs of abuse, particularly the amphetamines or similarly acting sympathomimetics, cocaine, and phencyclidine (PCP), may all give a picture characterized by euphoria, grandiosity, irritability, and recklessness. Inquiry regarding use of these substances, both of the patient and a reliable informant, should be routine, and if suspicion of such use warrants, drug screening is helpful. Manic like symptoms induced by these substances should have a relatively brief course (days to weeks) when compared to functional mania.

Schizophrenia and Schizoaffective Disorder

The classification of psychotic illness in American psychiatry has vacillated over time and highlights the differential diagnostic problems that exist between psychotic affective disorders and schizophrenia. Schizoaffective disorder has variously been classified among the schizophrenias, among affective disorders, and also as a separate category.

A problem in distinguishing between schizophrenia and mania usually involves a differential between paranoid schizophrenia, delusional (paranoid) disorder, and mania. Grandiose delusions may be seen in all three instances. If the disturbance in mood is brief in relation to the delusional beliefs, a nonbipolar diagnosis is most likely. This emphasizes the importance of gathering the longitudinal course of illness.

The differential between a bipolar depression with psychotic features and schizophrenia presents another challenge. The relevance of mood-congruence versus mood-incongruent features in depression has been reviewed by Coryell, Pfohl, and Zimmerman (1986) and Winokur, Scharfetter, and Angst (1985b). In the former study, it was noted that older depressed patients with psychotic features present with a picture more typical of severe depression. Younger subjects were also noted to display a greater familial risk for schizophrenia than the older group. The Winokur et al. study (1985b) examined the diagnostic value of assessing mood congruence in delusions and hallucinations and their relationship to the affective state. In that study, psychotic symptoms were noted to be common in unipolar depressives (48%) and bipolar depressives (42%) and were almost always seen in schizophrenics and schizoaffectives. Affective disorders showed mood-congruent symptoms more commonly, while schizophrenics evinced more mood-incongruent symptoms. A marked dissociation of affective state and psychotic symptoms was observed. Thus, though depressed, schizophrenics usually showed only mood-incongruent psychotic symptoms. Therefore, mood-incongruent symptoms may take precedence over the affective state in such a differential diagnosis. When these same patients were evaluated in a family study of transmission of psychotic symptoms (Winokur, Scharfetter, & Angst, 1985a), the schizophrenics and schizoaffectives were noted to breed true in the transmission of psychotic symptoms, but the affective disorders did not. From these studies, the importance of assessing mood congruence and family history along with longitudinal course as noted previously are again emphasized.

Personality Disorders

Affective disorders are frequently complicated or influenced by personality disorders (Akiskal, 1981; Akiskal et al., 1980; Pfohl, Stangle, & Zimmerman, 1984). Borderline and antisocial characterologic symptoms in particular overlap with various bipolar symptoms. In making the differential between bipolar disorder and personality disorder, or adding a bipolar diagnosis to a preexisting personality disorder, one should first see if the symptoms observed actually meet the full syndromal picture of a manic episode, especially the duration criteria. Next, one should consider if the symptoms represent a change in behavior, particularly an unexpected change. Finally, as in all cases, a full knowledge of lifetime functioning and family history is essential in making the correct diagnosis.

CASE EXAMPLES

Case 1

Frank is a 34-year-old male who presented for evaluation of depression. He noted marked hypersomnia, anergia, weight gain of 30 pounds, no interests, feelings of hopelessness, and irritability. He had some fleeting suicidal thoughts, but was not wishing to die and had no suicidal plan. His mood had been down persistently for about two months, and the cluster of associated symptoms had been present daily for at least six weeks. Medications at the time of evaluation included lithium, haloperidol, and amitriptyline. This patient was admitted for an inpatient evaluation, and the amitriptyline and haloperidol were discontinued.

Past Psychiatric History

This patient was first noted by his teachers in elementary school to have a behavior problem. He was overactive, disruptive, and a slow learner. He seemed distracted and was referred to school counselors by the third grade. He was treated with stimulants from third to sixth grade with no real improvement in school behavior or learning skills. He progressively became less interested in school and generally fell farther behind in his reading and math. By junior high, truancy and fighting began, but this was not accompanied by any vandalism, running away, precocious sexual behavior, or drug or alcohol abuse. By the tenth grade, this student quit high school and worked briefly driving cabs. At age 18 he enlisted in the Army, as had been his family tradition. He was discharged within three months for "failure to adapt." After leaving the military, he became very depressed and made a suicide attempt by overdose. He was treated at that time with antidepressants and seemed to improve; he returned to work as a cab driver.

At age 24, this individual was involved with a woman who wanted to end their relationship. At that time, it was reported that the patient had "changed." He was spending excessive amounts of money (primarily hers), was overtalkative, was sexually preoccupied, drank heavily, was very irritable, had grandiose beliefs about his future potential to corner the market on mass transit in a small midwestern city, and was sleeping less. His mood was described as euphoric, but he would at times become rapidly irritable and negative. When his female friend tried to leave him, he became enraged and "held her hostage." He was arrested and charged with a felony, for which he served four years in prison. During his prison term, he was first diagnosed as being bipolar and was treated with lithium. His manic symptoms remitted over the first two weeks on lithium, but he became depressed. He reports the depression was prolonged, approaching six months. No treatment other than lithium was used during this episode.

Upon release from prison at age 28, the patient continued to have both manic and depressive episodes, but most episodes of illness were mixed. He was treated with various combinations of lithium, antipsychotics, and antidepressants with little long-term benefit. He was unable to return to work upon release from prison until the time of admission for the hospitalization.

Family History

The patient's mother was treated for depression following childbirth at age 32. There was no other family history of psychiatric illness.

Medical History

Birth, developmental, and medical history were unremarkable except as noted. His physical examination was normal.

Hospital Course

This patient rather rapidly switched from depression to mania after two days off haloperidol and amitryptyline. He displayed typical manic symptoms as described during his first episode, but this time was religiously preoccupied with delusional thoughts. He felt that God had talked to him and had given him excessive strength. The lithium was discontinued, as the serum levels were well within the therapeutic limits. Carbamazepine was started, with a fair, but incomplete, remission being noted. Lithium was then restarted, and mood returned to a more euthymic state. Despite the improvement in mood, this patient remained discouraged about being able to return to work and was worried that if he did, the disability support he received would be jeopardized. A supervised living arrangement with vocational counseling was located, and the patient was discharged on lithium plus carbamazepine.

Case 2

Karen is a 54-year-old school teacher. She was brought to the hospital by her husband of 30 years with symptoms of distractibility, marked insomnia, racing and incoherent thoughts, pressured speech, euphoric mood, and reckless use of credit cards (over $400 spent one evening on unnecessary mail-order items). The symptoms had started gradually about one week prior to admission. This was only one month after maintenance therapy with lithium had been discontinued by her psychiatrist, as the patient had been doing well without symptoms for two years.

Past History

This patient had a depression at age 18 when she first went to college. This remitted after taking off classes for one semester without medications. At age 22, shortly after graduation, but before starting her first teaching job, she had a manic episode. This was treated with antipsychotics and remitted over a two-month hospital stay. At ages 36 and 38 she had depressions that required ECT. No maintenance therapy or outpatient follow-up was recorded after any of these hospitalizations. She was able to return to teaching after each of these episodes of illness. At age 45 she had her second manic episode, which required admission with symptoms similar to the ones at present. She was treated with lithium and antipsychotics and was noted to have full remission of all symptoms by discharge. She returned again to work and maintained outpatient follow-up with her mental health center. The antipsychotic was gradually tapered and discontinued over the six months following her admission. The lithium was maintained. At age 52 a mild episode of hypomanic symptoms was managed as an outpatient. This was after lithium was stopped briefly due to lapse of her prescription while on vacation.

Family History

This patient has two sons and a daughter with clear bipolar disorders. Another son and daughter are without symptoms. Family history is otherwise unknown as she was adopted.

Medical History

Lithium-induced hypothyroidism has been well-controlled by replacement therapy for two years. Physical examination was normal.

Hospital Course

Lithium was reinstituted, and symptoms began to improve within 3 to 4 days. By day 10 following admission, mood was euthymic. The patient was discharged after 12 days of hospitalization on lithium alone, with follow-up scheduled in two weeks for a repeat lithium level.

These cases illustrate, in the first example, a malignant form of illness that had a very early onset and a disabling course. The second example illustrates a good outcome, particularly since the availability of lithium maintenance for her illness.

CHILDHOOD AND FAMILIAL ANTECEDENTS

Childhood Antecedents

Childhood manifestations and premorbid personality of adult bipolar affective disorder have received limited attention. Angst and Clayton (1986), using the Freiburg Personality Inventory, found that the premorbid personality of bipolar patients did not differ from normal controls in nervousness, aggressivity, depressiveness, excitability, sociability, dominance, inhibition, frankness, extraversion, autonomic lability, neuroticism, or masculinity. There was a trend toward less stability in the premorbid personality of bipolar patients. A difference was found between the premorbid personality of unipolar and bipolar patients, with bipolars being significantly less ag-

gressive. Von Zerssen (1977) also concluded that the personality of bipolars was very similar to that of the general population. However, he primarily studied personalities of recovered bipolar patients. He did hypothesize that depending upon the number of manic or depressive episodes, bipolars should show a preponderance toward a manic or melancholic premorbid personality. In comparison to normal controls, Hirschfeld and Klerman (1979) found manics to have more obsessional premorbid personalities, while depressive patients showed more neuroticism, introversion, and obsessionality than both manic patients and normal controls.

A second way of looking for premorbid characteristics in bipolars is to follow the offspring of bipolars, as they are at higher risk to become bipolar in the future. Greenhill and Shopsin (1979) found hyperactivity, delinquent acts, and immature behavior in one third of 58 offspring of bipolar patients. Mayo, O'Connell, and O'Brien (1979) found that aggressive reactions, anxiety, and tension were significant features in children of bipolar probands. Although these children have not been followed to development of mania, it is possible that such behavior may be premorbid signs of bipolar illness that may develop later in life. There have, however, been reports (Dvoredsky & Stewart, 1981) of bipolar affective disorder occurring in adults who have a childhood history of hyperactivity or attention-deficit disorder (ADD). Whether the hyperactivity is truly a premorbid characteristic or an early misdiagnosed form of bipolar affective disorder is unknown. Misdiagnosis could easily occur since the two disease states have very similar symptoms (impulsivity, poor concentration, restlessness, learning disabilities in ADD versus physical restlessness, racing thoughts, distractibility, and mood instability in mania). Clues to diagnoses of bipolar disorder in these cases include a positive family history of affective disorder, good intellectual ability in spite of academic performance, and a good therapeutic response to lithium either in childhood or adult life (Dvoredsky & Stewart, 1981).

Familial Antecedents

The major familial contribution to bipolar disorder is likely that of genetics. Family (Winokur et al., 1969) and genetic studies (Mendlewicz & Rainer, 1977) support such a strong contribution. The present literature regarding the mechanism of genetic transmission for this disorder reveals that significant heterogeneity must exist. Conflicting results in linkage studies with X-chromosome markers for color blindness and glucose-6-phosphate dehydrogenase (G6PD) deficiency have been reported (Gershon & Bunney, 1976). Discrepancies in the various data sets that made up that X-chromosome marker literature were reviewed by Risch and Baron (1982), who concluded that the differences could be explained by genetic heterogeneity, with close linkage of G6PD and color blindness holding up. Independent replication of G6PD and color blindness linkage was just reported by Baron, Risch, Hamburger, Mandel, Kushner, Newman, Drumer, and Belmaker (1987), using a new series of pedigrees from Israel. Interestingly, within that study, linkage in non-Askenazi pedigrees was strong, while Askenazi linkage was not found, supporting the concept of genetic heterogeneity. Further support for X-linkage can be found in a report by Mendlewicz, Simon, Sevy, Charon, Brocas, Legros, and Vassart (1987), who demonstrated genetic linkage between manic depression and a different, polymorphic DNA marker on the X-chromosome (coagulation factor IX at Xq27). However, evidence has pointed to at least some cases of father-to-son transmission of bipolar illness, a situation incompatible with only X-linked transmission.

Linkage studies of chromosome 11-markers further supports genetic heterogeneity of bipolar disorder. Two such markers (c-Harvey-ras1 and the insulin gene) have been studied in different pedigrees. In an analysis of the segregation of restriction fragment length polymorphisms in an Old Order Amish pedigree, localization of a dominant gene conferring a strong predisposition to manic-depressive disorder on the tip of the short arm of chromosome 11 was demonstrated (Egeland et al., 1987). Two other studies, one using three North American pedigrees (Detera-Wadleigh et al., 1987) and the other three Icelandic pedigrees (Hodgkinson et al., 1987), showed absence of linkage being seen with the chromosome 11 markers.

While these studies cannot elucidate a single form of genetic transmission for bipolar disorder, such heterogeneity in the genetics of a disorder in medicine has been reported. Retinitis pigmentosis and the Hunter-Hurler syndrome, for example, appear in some cases to be transmitted by a gene on the X-chromosome and in some cases by an autosomal gene.

SUMMARY

Bipolar disorder is a difficult and disruptive disorder for the patient, family, and treating physician to manage. Our understanding of this disorder is increasing through research regarding its genetic etiology and treatment. The advent of lithium therapy has provided significant relief to many, if not over half of those with the disorder. Alternative treatment approaches, for example, through the use of anticonvulsants (e.g., carbamazepine, sodium valproate, or clonazepam), calcium channel blockers, and a variety of other medication may provide improved pharmacologic maintenance in poorly responsive lithium patients, or in those who develop lithium-related complications. Further work in the area of molecular genetics may also help to clarify the genetic transmission(s) of this disorder. Such an improved understanding may potentially impact upon genetic counseling, as well as development of improved treatment strategies.

REFERENCES

Abrams, R., & Taylor, M. A. (1976). Catatonia: A prospective clinical study. *Archives of General Psychiatry, 33*, 579–581.

Akiskal, H. S. (1981). Subaffective disorders: Dysthymic, cyclothymic, and bipolar II disorders in the borderline realm. *Psychiatric Clinics of North America, 4*, 25–46.

Akiskal, H. S., Rosenthal, T. L., Haykal, R. F., Lemmi, H., Rosenthal, R. H., & Scott-Strauss, A. (1980). Characterological depressions: Clinical and sleep EEG findings separating "subaffective dysthymias" from "character spectrum disorders." *Archives of General Psychiatry, 37*, 777–783.

Akiskal, H. S., Walker, P., Puzantian, V. R., King, D., Rosenthal, T. L., & Drano, M. (1983). Bipolar outcome in the course of depressive illness. Phenomenologic, familial, and pharmacologic predictors. *Journal of Affective Disorders, 5*, 115–128.

American Psychiatric Association. (1987). *Diagnostic and statistical manual of mental disorders* (3rd ed. rev.). Washington, DC: Author.

Angst, J., & Clayton, P. (1986). Premorbid personality of depressive, bipolar, and schizophrenic patients with special reference to suicidal issues. *Comprehensive Psychiatry, 27*, 511–532.

Angst, J., & Dobler-Mikola, A. (1984). The Zurich study: III. Diagnosis of depression. *European Archives of Psychiatry and Neurological Science, 234*, 13–20.

Angst, J., Felder, W., Frey, R., & Stassen, H. H. (1978). The course of affective disorders. I. Change of diagnosis of monopolar, unipolar, and bipolar illness. *Archiv fur Atrie und Nervenkrankheiten, 226*, 57–64.

Baillarger, J. (1954). De la folie à double-forme [On bipolar mania]. *Annals of Medical Psychology* (Paris), *6*, 367–391.

Baron, M., Risch, N., Hamburger, R., Mandel, B., Kushner, S., Newman, M., Drumer, D., & Belmaker, R. H. (1987). Genetic linkage between X-chromosome markers and bipolar affective disorder. *Nature, 326*, 289–292.

Black, D. W., Warrack, G., & Winokur, G. (1985). The Iowa record-linkage study: III. Excess mortality among patients with "functional" disorders. *Archives of General Psychiatry, 42*, 82–88.

Black, D. W., Winokur, G., & Nasrallah, A. (1987a). Suicide in subtypes of major affective disorder. A comparison with general population suicide mortality. *Archives of General Psychiatry, 44*, 878–880.

Black, D. W., Winokur, G., & Nasrallah, A. (1987b). Is death from natural causes still excessive in psychiatric patients? *Journal of Nervous and Mental Disease, 175*, 674–680.

Black, D. W., Winokur, G., Bell, S., Nasrallah, A., & Hulbert, J. (1988). Complicated mania: Comorbidity and immediate outcome in the treatment of mania. *Archives of General Psychiatry, 45*, 232–236.

Bratfos, O., & Haug, J. (1968). The course of manic-depressive psychosis. *Acta Psychiatrica Scandinavia, 44*, 89–112.

Brodie, H. K. H., & Leff, M. J. (1971). Bipolar depression: A comparative study of patient characteristics. *American Journal of Psychiatry, 127*, 1086–1090.

Carlson, G. A., & Goodwin, F. K. (1973). The stages of mania: A longitudinal analysis of the manic episode. *Archives of General Psychiatry, 28*, 221–228.

Clayton, P. J. (1986). Bipolar illness. In G. Winokur & P. J. Clayton (Eds.), *The medical basis of psychiatry* (pp. 39–59). Philadelphia: W. B. Saunders.

Cook, B. L., & Winokur, G. (1989). Nosology of affective disorders. *Modern perspectives in the psychiatry of the affective disorders* (pp. 117–132). New York: Brunner/Mazel.

Cook, B. L., Shukla, S., Hoff, A. L., & Aronson, T. A. (1987). Mania with associated factors. *Acta Psychiatrica Scandinavia, 76*, 674–677.

Coryell, W., & Winokur, G. (1982). Course and outcome. In E. S. Paykel (Ed.), *Handbook of affective disorders* (pp. 93–106). New York: The Guilford Press.

Coryell, W., Pfohl, B., & Zimmerman, M. (1986). Heterogeneity in psychotic depression. *Comprehensive Psychiatry, 25*, 430–438.

Davis, K. L., Berger, P. A., & Hollister, L. E. (1976). Tardive dyskinesia and depressive illness. *Psychopharmacology Communications, 2*, 508–516.

Derby, I. M. (1933). Manic depressive "exhaustion" deaths. *Psychiatric Quarterly, 7*, 435–449.

Detera-Wadleigh, S. D., Berrettini, W. H., Goldin, L. R., Boorman, D., Anderson, S., & Gershon, E. S. (1987). *Nature, 235*, 806–808.

Dion, G. L., Tohen, M., & Anthony, W. A. (1988). *Symptom and functional outcome in bipolar disorder*. Paper presented at the American Psychological Association 141st Annual Meeting, Montreal, Quebec.

Dvoredsky, A., & Stewart, M. (1981). Hyperactivity followed by manic depressive disorder: Two case reports. *Journal of Clinical Psychiatry, 42*, 212–214.

Egeland, J. A., Gerhard, D. S., Pauls, D. L., Sussex, J. N., Kidd, K. K., Allen C. R., Hostetter, A. M., & Housman, D. E. (1987). Bipolar affective disorders linked to DNA markers on chromosome 11. *Nature, 325*, 783–787.

Falret, J. P. (1854). Memoire sur la folie circulaire [Report on the circular mania]. *Bulletin of the Academy of Medicine, 19*, 382–415.

Faris, R. E. L., & Dunham, H. W. (1939). *Mental disorders in urban areas: An ecological study of schizophrenia and other psychoses*. Chicago: University of Chicago Press.

Gershon, E. S., & Bunney, W. E. (1976). The question of X-linkage in bipolar manic-depressives. *Journal of Psychiatric Research, 13*, 99–117.

Ghadirian, A. M., & Engelsmann, F. (1985). Somatic illness in manic-depressive and schizophrenic patients. *Journal of Psychosomatic Research, 29*, 281–286.

Greenhill, L. L., & Shopsin, B. (1979). Survey of mental disorders in the children of patients with affective disorder. In J. Mendlewicz & B.

Shopsin (Eds.), *Genetic aspects of affective illness* (pp. 75–93). New York: SP Medical & Scientific Books.

Grof, P., Angst, J., & Haines, T. (1974). The clinical course of depression: Practical issues. In J. Angst (Ed.), *Classification and prediction of outcome of depression* (pp. 141–148). New York: Symposia Medica Hoeschst 8, F. K. Shattauer Verlag.

Guze, S. B., & Robins, E. (1970). Suicide and primary affective disorder. *British Journal of Psychiatry, 117*, 437–438.

Hestbech, J. Hansen, H. E., Amdisen, A., & Olsen, S. (1977). Chronic renal lesions following long-term treatment of lithium. *Kidney International, 12*, 205–213.

Hetmar, O., Brun, C., Clemmesen, L., Ladefoged, J., Larsen, S., & Rafaelsen, O. J. (1987). *Journal of Psychiatric Research, 21*, 279–288.

Himmelhoch, J. M., Fuchs, C. Z., & Symons, B. J. (1982). A double blind study of tranylcypromine treatment of major anergic depression. *Journal of Nervous and Mental Disease, 170*, 628–643.

Himmelhoch, J. M., & Garfinkel, M. E. (1986). Sources of lithium resistance in mixed mania. *Psychopharmacology Bulletin, 22*, 613–620.

Hirschfeld, R., & Klerman, G. (1979). Personality attributes and affective disorders. *American Journal of Psychiatry, 136*, 67–70.

Hodgkinson, S., Sherrington, R., Gurling, H., Marchbanks, R., Reeders, S., Mallet, J., McInnis, M., Petursson, H., & Brynjolfsson, J. (1987). *Nature, 325*, 805–806.

Jones, B. E., Gray, B. A., & Parson, E. B. (1981). Manic-depressive illness among poor urban blacks. *American Journal of Psychiatry, 138*, 654–657.

Jones, B. E., Gray, B. A., & Parson, E. B. (1983a). Manic-depressive illness among poor urban Hispanics. *American Journal of Psychiatry, 138*, 654–657.

Jones, B. E., Gray, B. A., & Parson, E. B. (1983b). Manic-depressive illness among poor urban Hispanics. *American Journal of Psychiatry, 140*, 1208–1210.

Keisling, R. (1981). Underdiagnosis of manic-depressive illness in a hospital unit. *American Journal of Psychiatry, 138*, 672–673.

Keller, M. B., Lavori, P. W., Coryell, W., Andreasen, N. C., Endicott, J., Clayton, P. J., Klerman, G. L., & Hirschfeld, R. M. A. (1986). Differential outcome of pure manic, mixed/cycling, and pure depressive episodes in patients with bipolar illness. *Journal of the American Medical Association, 255*, 3138–3142.

Krauthammer, C., & Klerman, G. (1978). Secondary mania: Manic syndromes associated with antecedent physical illness or drugs. *Archives of General Psychiatry, 35*, 1333–1339.

Lazarus, J. H., John, R., Bennie, E. H., Chalmers, R. J., & Crockett, G. (1981). Lithium therapy and thyroid function: A long term study. *Psychological Medicine, 11*, 85–92.

Leonhard, D. (1957). *Aufteilung der Endogenen Psychosen* [Divisions of endogenic psychosis]. Berlin: Akademie.

Lilliker, S. L. (1980). Prevalence of diabetes in a manic-depressive population. *Comprehensive Psychiatry, 21*, 270–275.

Martin, R. L., Cloninger, C. R., Guze, S. B., & Clayton, P. J. (1985). Mortality in a follow-up of 500 psychiatric outpatients. I. Total mortality. II. Cause-specific mortality. *Archives of General Psychiatry, 42*, 47–66.

Mayo, J. A., O'Connell, R. A., & O'Brien, J. D. (1979). Families of manic-depressive patients: Effect of treatment. *American Journal of Psychiatry, 136*, 1535–1539.

McCormick, R. A., Russo, A. M., Ramirez, L. F., & Taber, J. I. (1984). Affective disorders among pathological gamblers seeking treatment. *American Journal of Psychiatry, 141*, 215–218.

Mendlewicz, J., & Rainer, J. D. (1977). Adoption study supporting genetic transmission in manic-depressive illness. *Nature, 268*, 327–329.

Mendlewicz, J., Simon, P., Sevy, S., Charon, F., Brocas, H., Legros, S., & Vassart, G. (1987). Polymorphic DNA marker on X chromosome and manic depression. *Lancet, 1*, 1230–1232.

Morrison, J. R. (1982). Suicide in a psychiatric practice population. *Journal of Clinical Psychiatry, 43*, 348–352.

Mukherjee, S., Rosen, A. M., Caracci, G., Shukla, S. (1986). Persistent tardive dyskinesia in bipolar patients. *Archives of General Psychiatry, 43*, 342–346.

Myers, J. K., Weissman, M. M., Tischler, G. L., Holzer, C. E., Leaf, P. J., Orvaschel, H., Anthony, J. C., Boyd, J. H., Burke, J. D., Kramer, M., & Stoltzman, R. (1984). Six month prevalence of psychiatric disorders in three communities: 1980 to 1982. *Archives of General Psychiatry, 41*, 959–967.

Perris, C. (1966). A study of bipolar (manic depressive) and unipolar recurrent depressive psychoses. I. Genetic investigation. *Acta Psychiatrica Scandinavia, 76*, 674–677.

Petterson, V. (1977). Manic depressive illness. *Acta Psychiatrica Scandinavia, Supplement 269.*

Pfohl, B., Stangle, D., & Zimmerman, M. (1984). The implication of DSM-III personality disorders for patients with major depression. *Journal of Affective Disorders, 7*, 309–318.

Prien, R. R., Himmelhoch, J. M., & Kupfer, D. J. (1988). Treatment of mixed mania. *Journal of Affective Disorders, 15*, 9–15.

Risch, N., & Baron, M. (1982). X-linkage and genetic heterogeneity in bipolar-related affective illness: Reanalysis of linkage data. *Annals of Human Genetics, 46*, 153–166.

Schneider, K. (1959). *Clinical psychopathology.* New York: Grune & Stratton.

Schou, M., Amdisen, A., & Baastrup, P. C. (1971). The practical management of lithium treatment. *British Journal of Psychiatry, 6*, 1–8.

Schou, M., Amdisen, A., Jensen, S. E., & Olsen, T. (1968). Occurrence of goitre during lithium therapy. *British Medical Journal, 3*, 710–713.

Sedler, M. J. (1983). Falret's discovery: The origin of the concept of bipolar affective illness. *American Journal of Psychiatry, 140*, 1127–1133.

Shukla, S., Cook, B. L., & Mukherjee, S. (1987). Mania following head trauma. *American Journal of Psychiatry, 144*, 93–96.

Stasiek, C., & Zetin, M. (1985). Organic manic disorders. *Psychosomatics, 5*, 394–402.

Swift, H. M. (1907). The prognosis of recurrent insanity of the manic depressive type. *American Journal of Insanity, 64*, 311–326.

Targum, S. D., Dibble, E. D., Davenport, Y. B., & Gershon, E. S. (1981). The family attitudes questionnaire. Patients' and spouses' views of bipolar illness. *Archives of General Psychiatry, 38*, 562–568.

Tsuang, M. T., Woolson, R. F., Winokur, G., & Crowe, R. R. (1981). Stability of psychiatric diagnosis. Schizophrenia and affective disorders followed up over a 30- to 40-year period. *Archives of General Psychiatry, 38*, 535–539.

Tsuang, M. T., Woolson, R. R., & Fleming, J. A. (1978, February). *Premature death and schizophrenia and manic depression: Effects of age, sex, socioeconomic status, diagnosis, and causes of death.* Paper presented at the American Association for the Advancement of Science, Washington, DC.

Von Zerssen, D. (1977). Premorbid personality and affective psychoses. In D. G. Burrows (Ed.), *Handbook of studies on phenomenology and aetiology of depression* (pp. 79–103). Amsterdam: Elsevier/North-Holland Biomedical Press.

Weeke, A. (1979). Causes of death in manic-depressives. In M. Schou & E. Stromgren (Ed.), *Origin, prevention and treatment of affective disorders* (pp. 289–199). London: Academic Press.

Weissman, M. M., & Myers, J. K. (1978). Affective disorders in a U.S. urban community: The use of research diagnostic criteria in an epidemiologic survey. *Archives of General Psychiatry, 35*, 1304–1311.

Weissman, M. M., Leaf, P. J., Tischler, G. L., Blazer, D. G., Karno, M., Bruce, M. L., & Florio, L. P. (1988). Affective disorders in five United States communities. *Psychological Medicine, 18*, 141–153.

Wertham, F. I. (1928). A group of benign chronic psychoses: Prolonged manic excitements. *American Journal of Psychiatry, 9*, 17–78.

Winokur, G., Clayton, P. J., & Reich, T. (1969). *Manic depressive illness.* St. Louis, MO: C. V. Mosby.

Winokur, G., Scharfetter, C., & Angst, J. (1985a). A family study of psychotic symptomatology in schizophrenia, schizoaffective disorder, unipolar depression, and bipolar disorder. *European Archives of Psychiatry and Neurological Science, 234*, 295–298.

Winokur, G., Scharfetter, C., & Angst, J. (1985b). The diagnostic value in assessing mood congruence in delusions and hallucinations and their relationship to the affective state. *European Archives of Psychiatry and Neurological Science, 234*, 299–302.

Winokur, G., & Wesner, R. (1987). From unipolar to bipolar illness: Twenty-nine who changed. *Acta Psychiatrica Scandinavia, 76*, 59–63.

Woodruff, R. A., Robins, L. N., Winokur, G., & Reich, T. (1971). Manic depressive illness and social achievement. *Acta Psychiatrica Scandinavia, 47*, 237–249.

SCHIZOPHRENIA

EDITORS' COMMENTS

Of all the disorders described in this volume, schizophrenia is probably the most devastating and disabling. The central feature of the disorder is psychotic behavior, which includes hallucinations, delusions, and/or markedly disturbed thought processes. In addition to psychotic symptoms, significant deterioration occurs with regard to social relations, employment/school functioning, and/or self-care.

There appears to be a familial factor involved in the pathogenesis of the disorder, with the children of one schizophrenic parent showing a 10% to 15% likelihood of developing the disorder and the children of two schizophrenic parents showing a 35% to 46% risk. Laboratory investigations have shown at-risk children to possess attentional and information processing deficits and, in some instances, neurological abnormalities.

Follow-back data (to childhood) suggest that maladaptive interpersonal or social functioning may be a vulnerability factor for schizophrenia. In addition to possible genetic causes, recent data indicate that familial relationships may play a role in determining which at-risk youngsters will develop the disorder.

In the childhood version of the disorder, one of the most important factors that predicts long-term outcome is age. In general, the younger the age at onset (particularly, prior to age 10), the poorer the prognosis. In adults, premorbid functioning repeatedly has been shown to be positively related to outcome. In addition, long-term outcome appears to be better for female versus male patients, at least in terms of hospitalization.

As in adult patients, the presence of affective symptomatology in childhood may indicate a better prognosis. In this regard, there has been considerable controversy regarding the differentiation between schizophrenia and schizoaffective disorder, with some investigators questioning the validity of the latter. Recent research in schizoaffective disorder led to substantial revisions in the diagnostic criteria for the illness in DSM-III-R. Future longitudinal data, using these new criteria, should help to determine the validity of the syndrome.

CHAPTER 7

SCHIZOPHRENIA IN CHILDHOOD

Israel Kolvin
T. P. Berney
Joel Yoeli

DESCRIPTION OF THE DISORDER AND CLINICAL PRESENTATION

Introduction

The traditional concept of "schizophrenia," previously employed to encompass any psychotic process that was neither manic nor depressive, led to two thrusts in childhood classification: The first was the now discredited concept of a unitary psychosis (Fish, 1977); the second was the extensive eponymous labeling of childhood syndromes regarded as psychotic (Kolvin, 1971). However, as Anthony (1958) pointed out, the latter could be regrouped to give three main syndromic groups, broadly distinguished by their age of onset. This was the springboard for the next advance, which differentiated on empirical grounds between those psychoses specific to childhood and those with adult-type phenomenology (Kolvin, 1971). These syndromic groups appear to have a bimodal age of onset (Kolvin, Ounsted, Richardson, & Garside, 1971; Makita, 1966) and include the following:

- Infantile autism (Kanner, 1943) or psychosis (Kolvin, 1971): with an onset in the early years of life. Subsequent work suggests an affiliation to a wider range of developmental disturbances, including Asperger's syndrome of autistic psychopathy (Asperger, 1944; Wing, 1981). More recent studies have suggested that these latter conditions may contribute to an autistic spectrum disorder of early childhood.

- Disintegrative psychosis: those conditions with an onset after infancy but still within the preschool years and that are characterized by widespread functional disintegration.

- Late onset psychosis or childhood schizophrenia: those conditions with an onset during the school years and characterized by primitive or more complex symptoms resembling those described in adult schizophrenia (Eggers, 1978; Green et al., 1984; Kolvin, 1971).

Later work highlighted those personality or other conditions purportedly at the margins of the psychosis and in due course has also given rise to the concept of childhood schizophrenia spectrum disorder.

Some authors have described exceptions to this main pattern, and hence one leading research group recommends that the diagnosis be based on the clinical picture rather than on the age of onset (Wing & Attwood, 1987).

Spectrum Disorders Versus Multiple Categories

In adult schizophrenia some authorities have favored a classification into multiple, complex, almost discrete subcategories, whereas other have moved toward agglomeration into the schizophrenia spectrum disorder. Can this recently fashionable concept of spectrum disorder be applied to childhood schizophrenia?

In the autistic psychoses there has been a similar dichotomy with the "splitters" in the United States (American Psychiatric Association, 1980) proposing a new class of disorders, the pervasive developmental disorders (PDD). In the United Kingdom a similar move has led Wing and her colleagues to propose their three-way split. In addition, and in contrast, there has been the delineation of the autistic spectrum disorder.

The Developmental Perspective

In this chapter we focus on the age of onset as a guide to classification, with the proviso that the diagnosis be based on the presence of the relevant clinical phenomena. This approach allows a focus on a developmental perspective that is widely endorsed in the standard schemata (International Classification of Diseases-9 [World Health Organization, 1979] and DSM-III [APA, 1980]) on both sides of the Atlantic.

This broad developmental pattern of onset is consistent with a diagnosis based on clinical phenomenology and coincides with the main categories of ICD-9 (WHO, 1979). With the advent of DSM-III (APA, 1980), it was broadly accepted because of the developmental typology suggested by Anthony (1958) and Kolvin (1971). However, it replaced the multiplicity of eponymous categories with an equal multiplicity of subcategories of disorder that are characterized by a pervasive lack of responsiveness to others, as well as by a gross and sustained impairment of social relationships. These categories are split both according to age of onset (before or after 30 months) and to whether or not there is a full syndrome or a residual state. Finally, there is a rag bag of other disorders that are difficult to classify elsewhere and that are lumped together as atypical pervasive developmental disorder. Inevitably the clinical description

of these groups overlaps, and the previous lack of clarity at the margins of the main psychotic disorders of childhood is replaced by subcategories with inadequate empirical foundations (Volkmar, 1987).

Subclassification of Autistiform Disorders

A newer clinical approach to the subclassification of preschool autistiform conditions that appears to have better empirical foundations than the DSM-III categories is provided by Wing and Gould (1979) and Wing and Attwood (1987), who describe three main groups of children—the aloof, the passive, and the active-but-odd.

The aloof are the most socially impaired, particularly in relation to their peers, and become agitated when in close proximity to others. They may approach others to obtain gratification of their basic needs, but more usually display a lack of overt affection. Both verbal and nonverbal communication may be seriously impaired. Speech is not employed as a means of social interaction. Further, even if speech has been present from infancy, there is little engagement in two-way communication in the form of cooing, babbling, or facial expression, nor are there the signs of early nonverbal communication, including social gesturing in later infancy. Associated features are poor eye contact and poverty of facial expression. In the main, children in this group have little symbolic or pretend play, or evidence of inner imagination (Wing & Gould, 1978, 1979). They are particularly prone to stereotypes, but, although these diminish with age, they tend to be replaced by more complex repetitive behaviors (Wing & Attwood, 1987). Broadly speaking, those in the aloof group have much in common with the classic picture of autism depicted in ICD-9.

The autistic features of the passive group are less marked than are those in the aloof group. The main distinction is that, although such children do not make spontaneous approaches to others, except to meet their needs, they will accept the approaches of others without protest. Their ability to imitate and copy is also less impaired (Attwood, 1984), as is their speech and verbal communication. They are the best behaved and the most easily managed; the more intelligent may cope fairly well educationally, even surviving in ordinary schools.

The active-but-odd are described as making "spontaneous approaches to others, but in peculiarly naive and one-sided fashion" (Wing & Attwood, 1987). Many of the characteristics described by the authors would tend to lead such children to be categorized as cases of Asperger's syndrome, and would include an indulgence of their circumscribed interests by talking *at* other people, together with literalness, repetitiveness, and longwindedness. One important feature is that, when older, they tend to replace their repetitive routines with more abstract but restricted interests that are "pursued so relentlessly, to the exclusion of virtually everything else, and with little grasp of the meaning or applicability to everyday life of the knowledge acquired" (Wing & Attwood, 1987).

Wisely, Wing, and Attwood (1987) do not see these as rigidly defined groups but rather as a range of abnormalities found in the spectrum of autistic disorders with the main changes over time being from the aloof into one of the other two groups. However, although the aloof group is diagnosable at an earlier age, the main characteristics of the passive and active-but-odd subgroups may not be appreciated until school age.

Disintegrative Psychosis

The onset occurs after several years of normal development and is characterized by a profound regression of general and social behavior, social interactions, and play, together with a deterioration in speech, language, and cognition. In due course, stereotypes and mannerisms may appear, giving rise to a picture reminiscent of that seen in autism. In some cases there is an evident organic basis such as encephalitis; in others there is an associated organic cortical degenerative disorder (Creak, 1963; Corbett, Harris, Taylor, & Trimble, 1977), but evidence of brain disease is not always clear-cut (Evans-Jones & Rosenbloom, 1978). In some the neurodegenerative basis becomes evident only in the course of time (Rivinus, Jamison, & Graham, 1975; Corbett et al., 1977). Thus, while there is usually the presumption of organic brain disease, in some the condition has an unknown etiology that invalidates the suggestion that it should be always classified as an organic dementia (Rutter, 1985). Rutter (1985) considers that these disorders will prove to be heterogeneous with some representing atypical forms of autism and others associated with acquired organic brain disorders. Although Rutter sees it as desirable to classify this group separately from autism, other authorities are less convinced of this (Wing & Gould, 1979).

In some there is a rapid downhill course, and in those few neurodegenerative disorders, this may progress to death. In the majority of others, after a number of months, this pattern may stabilize, leaving an overactive child with severe mental handicap, without speech, and often an autistic behavioral picture that tends to be consistent on follow-up 11 to 16 years later. Occasionally, seizures subsequently develop (Hill & Rosenbloom, 1986).

Descriptive Account of Childhood Schizophrenia

Previous work has emphasized that adult-type psychoses (mainly childhood schizophrenia) have their onset in the school years (Kolvin, Ounsted, Richardson, & Garside, 1971), being very rare in the early years and becoming less so as the child moves toward and into adolescence. This constitutes the basis of the bimodal pattern of onset already alluded to (Kolvin, Ounsted, Richardson, & Garside, 1971; Makita, 1966).

There are good reasons for suggesting that pervasive developmental disorders (or the autistic spectrum) can be distinguished from adult-type schizophrenia on phenomenological, demographic, and genetic grounds, although, inevitably, there are exceptions to this general rule (Kolvin, 1971; Petty, Ornitz, Michelman, & Zimmerman, 1984; Wing & Attwood, 1987).

Kolvin and his colleagues (Kolvin, 1971; Kolvin, Garside, & Kidd, 1971; Kolvin, Humphrey, & McNay, 1971; Kolvin, Ounsted, Humphrey, & McNay, 1971; Kolvin, Ounsted, Richardson, & Garside, 1971; Kolvin, Ounsted, & Roth, 1971) have highlighted the differences in diagnostic criteria and other features of early childhood psychoses (autism) and later-onset psychoses (childhood schizophrenia). Green et al. (1984) have taken this one stage further by replicating the main distinctions between autism and adolescent psychosis highlighted by Kolvin and his colleagues and by demonstrating that schizophrenia can be diagnosed in prepubertal children using DSM-III criteria. Other reviews point out that there is a need for a more careful examination of the symptomatology thought to be diagnostic of childhood schizophrenia together with an exploitation of possible subdivisions on symptomatological grounds and also etiology, course, and prognosis of the proposed subtypes (Beitchman, 1985).

There are few satisfactory descriptions of the

presentation and course of childhood schizophrenia. Only four studies both provide the symptom frequency and use a definition of childhood schizophrenia that would qualify for a DSM-III diagnosis (Eggers, 1978; Green et al., 1984; Kolvin, Ounsted, Humphrey, & McNay, 1971; Kydd & Werry, 1982). Together these describe 129 children whose ages range from 6 to 15 years. A number of other research reports are undermined by the lack of clear distinction between autism and schizophrenia.

Two studies (Green et al., 1984; Kolvin, Ounsted, Humphrey, & McNay, 1971) have described the type of onset as acute (12% to 20%), insidious with an acute exacerbation (21% to 33%), and insidious (45% to 66%).

Delusions occur in just over one-half of cases (Green et al., 1984; Kolvin, Ounsted, Richardson, & Garside, 1971). In the younger child they are less frequent, and there is difficulty in distinguishing fantasy from reality. Formal thought disorder, usually a disturbance of association and thought blocking, is present in over one-half of the cases. A variant, present in about one fifth, is alienation of thought, including thought deprivation, insertion, and broadcasting (Kolvin, Ounsted, Humphrey, & McNay, 1971).

Auditory hallucinations occur in 80% of older children (Eggers, 1978; Green et al., 1984; Kolvin, Ounsted, Humphrey, & McNay, 1971). Visual hallucinations, present in about half the cases, can occur with other forms of disturbance and under stress (Egdell & Kolvin, 1972; Garralda, 1984a) without predicting subsequent psychosis (Garralda, 1984b). Somatic hallucinations occur in about one third of schizophrenic children (Kolvin, Ounsted, Humphrey, & McNay, 1971) and may affect several sensory systems simultaneously (Eggers, 1978).

The most common form of affective disturbance is a constriction or blunting that is experienced by about 60% of cases; next in frequency is a sense of affective incongruity and perplexity. Depression is common in the prodrome (Kolvin, Ounsted, Humphrey, & McNay, 1971), and in nearly 10% of cases, children with depression subsequently develop schizophrenia. Motor symptoms are common, particularly as a jerky incoordination of movement, as well as mannerisms and facial grimaces (Kolvin, Ounsted, Humphrey, & McNay, 1971).

In his 16-year follow-up of prepubertal schizophrenias, Eggers (1978) found that about 46% of such children developed an affective picture. He, too, indicated that there were developmental differences. In those who developed their symptoms before the age of 10 years, the picture was an unobtrusive one with sudden, unexpected, and strange personality and behavioral changes. They included loss of contact with reality, the narrowing of interests, an indifference to the usual activities and pursuits, together with evidence of disturbed mobility, negativism, and speech disturbance. Some of these were previously affectionate children who suddenly became unkind, cold, and stubborn. Some became rather disinhibited, and some made unmotivated suicidal attempts. As the children approached 10 years of age, delusions and hallucinations became more prominent. The delusions often appeared as a rash of diffuse fears. In the prepubertal cases, delusions became more persistent, and religious and depressive themes emerged for the first time. At this age there was a greater systematization of delusional ideas, and thus, with increasing age, childhood and prepubertal psychosis began to resemble those of the adult (Eggers, 1978).

The next step therefore consists of the establishment of agreed-upon diagnostic criteria and the application of these with consistency in a disorder that manifests with protean symptomatology. Traditionally, diagnostic criteria have reflected various combinations of Schneider's (1959) approach, where there is an emphasis on the more positive delusions and hallucinations, with that of Bleuler (1950) where the emphasis is on the more negative symptoms of withdrawal, loosening of association, and blunted affect. Diagnostic agreement has been improved, but disagreement not totally resolved by the tighter definitions available in DSM-III and ICD-9 (Brockington, 1983). Such complexity is compounded in early childhood by developmental issues: for example, the very real problems of detecting relevant phenomena and distinguishing primitive variations of thinking, language, and emotional development from pathology. Thus, in the early school years there remains the allied question of how to weight immature variations of diagnostic criteria. In the original research of Kolvin and his coworkers (Kolvin, 1971; Kolvin, Garside, & Kidd, 1971; Kolvin, Humphrey, & McNay, 1971; Kolvin, Ounsted, Humphrey, & McNay, 1971; Kolvin, Ounsted, Richardson, & Garside, 1971; Kolvin, Ounsted, & Roth, 1971), there was an attempt to sharpen and limit the concept and definition of schizophrenia in school-aged children and diagnosis was achieved by using the rank criteria (Schneider, 1959).

"Borderlands" and Spectrum Disorders

The Autistic Borderlands

There is confusion regarding the classification of Asperger's syndrome, as well as of that small proportion of cases of autisticlike conditions that fall into Wing and Goulds' "passive subgroup." The latter group consists of individuals who, when adults, may present with a social impairment that resembles the social withdrawal of those schizophrenic children whose symptomatology is mainly of the negative variety (Wing & Attwood, 1987). This is less likely to be the case with those schizophrenia-type disorders that present with positive symptomatology. Wing and Attwood (1987) point out that a correct diagnosis usually can only be made from a developmental history taken from an informant who has known the psychotic person over the whole life span.

The Schizophrenia Borderland

Despite the suggestion, as a result of recent research, that these so-called first-rank symptoms are rather weak predictors (Brockington, Kendell, & Leff, 1978), other authorities have advocated widening these diagnostic criteria of Schneider (and hence the concept of schizophrenia in adulthood) to allow the inclusion of a spectrum of schizophrenic conditions (Roth & McClelland, 1979). These advocates admit that stricter definitions may give rise to greater cross-cultural agreement on diagnosis; however, broader definitions allow the heterogeneity of schizophrenia to express itself. Roth and McClelland (1979) have attempted to classify the components of a spectrum of schizophrenic disorder by delineating a gradation or ranking of disorders ranging from nuclear schizophrenia through paraphrenic or paranoid, then cycloid or episodic, then schizoaffective, then psychogenic, then toxic, and finally schizophreniform psychosis. So far this attractive concept has not been widely studied in adolescence, but an interest in examining these ideas and putting them into practice is beginning to emerge. Unfortunately, however, the all-embracing term of childhood psychosis has started to envelop unusual personalities on the margins of these psychoses, and this trend needs to be resisted unless there is strong proof of an intimate link.

Revival of the Concept of a Unitary Psychosis

Of considerable practical importance is the question of whether there is a small subgroup of autics who develop schizophrenia. Although Kolvin and his colleagues (Kolvin, 1971; Kolvin, Garside, & Kidd, 1971; Kolvin, Humphrey, & McNay, 1971; Kolvin, Ounsted, Humphrey, & McNay, 1971; Kolvin, Ounsted, Richardson, & Garside, 1971; Kolvin, Ounsted, & Roth, 1971) demonstrated that autism and adolescent schizophrenia were discontinuous, in one case in that series a clear-cut diagnostic distinction could not be achieved. More recently, Petty et al. (1984) have argued that a small subgroup of autistic children do develop schizophrenia. However, in this latter research all the autistic diagnoses were made retrospectively, and this still leaves a question mark in relation to a common subgroup. The considerable rarity of such a subgroup should prevent any attempts to resurrect the discredited single-psychosis theory.

Multiaxial Approaches

Such a behavioral classification of syndromes demands a complementary multiaxial classification (Wing & Attwood, 1987) with axes to accommodate gross etiology, on the one hand, and cognitive ability, on the other. For instance, a diversity of gross etiologies is reported in one third to one half of cases (Kolvin, Ounsted, & Roth, 1971; Wing & Gould, 1979; Rutter, 1972). Intelligence is also important, with up to 80% of autistic cases having quotients of <70 when measured on standardized tests (Kolvin, Humphrey, & McNay, 1971; Rutter & Lockyer, 1967; Wing & Gould, 1979).

EPIDEMIOLOGY

Autism

The prevalence of typical autism based on epidemiological research is approximately 4 per 10,000 (Lotter, 1967). About one half of these have a more nuclear autism that approximates to that described by Kanner with the remainder being less typical (Wing & Gould, 1979). Such epidemiological rates, even when the psychosis is narrowly defined, are far greater than the so-called administrative rates (the number in the community known to the local services). Hence the use of epidemiological rates in service planning carries the risk of overprovision. Wing and Gould (1979), from their English base, argue for a wider concept of childhood psychosis according to the quality of social contact and on these criteria 10.6 per 10,000 were aloof, 5.7 were passive, and 4.9 active-but-odd, with an overall rate of 21.2 for children under 14 years of age. Within this figure 4.9 per 10,000 were childhood autists. How many of the residual psychoses were really Asperger's syndrome? Some might consider the active-but-odd as such. Bryson, Clark, and Smith (1988) from their Canadian base, also using a broader definition of autism (Denckla, 1986), calculate a prevalence of 10 per 10,000. An association with mental retardation is reported in between 66 and 75% of children with autism (Kolvin, Humphrey, & McNay, 1971; Rutter & Lockyer, 1967). Boys outnumber girls by up to 4 to 1 (Kolvin, Ounsted, Richardson, & Garside, 1971; Lotter, 1967; Wing, 1981). The Goteborg study (Gillberg, 1984) suggests that this relationship may be nonlinear, achieving a maximum of over 5 to 1 for the middle band of the mildly mentally retarded, and decreasing to 2 to 1 both above and below this ability band.

The earlier epidemiologically based reported association with higher social class (Lotter, 1967) has had some support (Steinhausen, Gobel, Breinlinger, & Wohleben, 1983), but most major surveys have not supported this distinction (Gillberg & Schaumann, 1981; Wing, 1981). On balance it is likely that the reported association was the consequence of referral bias.

Disintegrative Psychosis

Again, clinical research suggests this to be a rare disorder (Kolvin, 1971; Makita, 1966). There have been no specific studies, but the Camberwell study of early childhood psychoses allows an estimate of prevalence (Wing & Gould, 1979). Ninety-four percent of the psychotics with an autistic picture were reported to be abnormal before the age of 3 years and the rest between 3 and 5 years (Wing, 1982).

Schizoid Personality Disorder and Asperger's Syndrome

Knowledge about the epidemiology of these two disorders is rather limited. Wolff and Chick (1980) estimated that schizoid personality disorder was present in over 3% of their child psychiatric clinic population. The wider significance of this is not clear as it needs to be reinterpreted in terms of the selectiveness of referral to their clinic; such a perspective can be achieved only by epidemiological research. What about Asperger's syndrome? The difficulties in defining and distinguishing mild autism, Asperger's syndrome, and schizoid personality have hampered the accurate estimation of prevalence. Gillberg and Gillberg (1988) suggest that Asperger's syndrome is more common than autism, is not associated with mental retardation, and has a prevalence of about 10 per 10,000. This is double the estimate of the active-but-odd subgroup derived from the Wing and Gould (1979) research.

Childhood Schizophrenia

Prevalence is age dependent, being rare in the prepubertal population. Thus, whereas the adult incidence is about 1%, fewer than 200 cases of childhood schizophrenia have been described in the world literature. Kolvin, Ounsted, Richardson, and Garside (1971), in their wide clinical search, report a rate of three quarters that of autism, which gives a rough estimate of 3 per 10,000 children. This is similar to that reported by Kramer (1978). Other estimates suggest a rate some 50 times less before the age of 15 years than after (Beitchman, 1985), which is consistent with a stress diathesis model by which few individuals within the population at risk would have a sufficient combination of biological loading and environmental stress to give rise to an early manifestation. Provided that autistic contamination is rigorously avoided, the sex ratios of adult and childhood schizophrenia reveal a remarkable similarity (Babigan, 1980; Kramer, 1978). Most studies give evidence of a male preponderance but within these the sex ratio varies widely and this is especially true of those not based on rigorous diagnostic criteria, resulting in a contamination of the index groups by autism.

NATURAL HISTORY

Autism

The clinical features vary with the stage of development. The more florid symptoms peak in the preschool years but then usually lessen during middle and later childhood; for instance, in early infancy a commonly reported characteristic is a failure to cuddle, babbling may be absent, and there may be a failure to engage in preverbal two-way social interactions with the mother. In the toddler, prominent features consist of such characteristics as profound social withdrawal and avoidance of gaze, together with language abnormalities and repetitive behaviors. Subsequently, many children continue to have difficulties in interpersonal relationships, particularly outside the home; such difficulties may arise with those adults who are not in regular contact with the child and who are unaccustomed to interpreting his or her communications or making allowance for his or her behaviors. Older autistic children may show an inability to appreciate the nuances of social relationships and have a lack of appreciation of other people's feelings. Often, the brighter autistic preadolescent and adolescent will show a desire for friendships, but the lack of social skills and empathy make this difficult. In a minority, especially in the less able autistic adolescent, there is pubertal deterioration comprising a worsening of symptomatology, a loss of developmental skills, and a change to a more gross physical appearance. Further, aggressive behavior may reemerge in some (Gillberg & Schaumann, 1981). In others, although many symptoms almost disappear, it is not uncommon for obsessional and ritualistic symptoms not only to persist, but also to expand. Finally, adulthood may bring improvement (Gillberg, 1984). Nevertheless, some of these processes can continue through to adulthood, resulting in an individual who, if the past history were to be ignored, might be thought to have Asperger's syndrome.

Although about one quarter of autistic children do moderately well, only 10% do sufficiently well to survive in an unsheltered work situation (Rutter, Greenfield, & Lockyer, 1967; Kanner, Rodriguez, & Ashenden, 1972). Three elements contribute to the limited work potential: poor cognitive development; adverse temperamental features such as inertia, inactivity, and poor concentration; and poor social skills (Lotter, 1974).

The outlook depends on the testable intelligence in the preschool years, the most able tending to show the greatest improvement, particularly on verbal skills (DeMyer et al., 1973). Closely related is the development of useful language in childhood. Other indicators are the severity of the symptomatology, the evidence of organic brain dysfunction, and the speed with which the more florid symptoms fade (Kolvin, 1985), the potential for substantial improvement usually being evident by 7 years of age (Rutter, 1967).

Childhood Schizophrenia

Any conclusion about the course of childhood schizophrenia depends on the narrowness of the diagnostic criteria; inclusion of other disorders clouds the picture. In the literature, autism is a common contaminant (Cantor et al., 1982; How-

ells & Guirguis, 1984), and so too may be the adolescent affective disorders that, particularly in their early episodes, can be mistaken for schizophrenia (Hassanyeh & Davison, 1980; Himmelhoch & Garfinkel, 1986).

Most of the reliable accounts of the course of schizophrenia concern adolescents (Masterson, 1956); few deal with a childhood onset (Eggers, 1978; Kydd & Werry, 1982). However, the themes that emerge are consistent: A younger age of onset is associated with a poor prognosis; other, possibly associated, indicators of a poor outlook are an insidious onset, a simple or hebephrenic subtype, discordant premorbid personality traits (insecure, inhibited, and shy), and low intelligence (although this is not always the case—Kydd & Werry, 1982), but the presence of affective symptomatology may indicate a better prognosis (Eggers, 1978).

There is no evidence that a range of other factors make any contribution to the prognosis, although such evidence has been sought. These factors include a high family loading of schizophrenic illness or other neuropsychiatric disorders (Eggers, 1978), the duration of episodes, the presence of precipitating triggers, a family history, and family socioeconomic status. It is surprising that factors such as a disturbed family atmosphere, the type of symptoms the child displayed, and the frequency of the psychotic episodes, have no bearing on the prognosis either (Eggers, 1978). Although most of those cases in which onset is before the age of 10 years have a poor outcome, a substantial minority of the prepubertal cases showed a favorable outcome (Eggers, 1978). Finally, in between 20% and 40% of cases the condition can be expected to remit completely, especially if the onset is after 10 years of age; this supports the notion of the prognostic significance of the age of onset. It is also helpful to note that the majority of the children achieve some form of remission; although this was complete in only 20%, a relatively good social adjustment was achieved by a further 30% (Eggers, 1978). However, a significant postpsychotic personality change was found in 26 of the 57 (46%) cases followed by Eggers (1978).

IMPAIRMENT AND COMPLICATIONS

Autism

In autism, impairments are widespread, with some relating to the more general features of autism that have already been adumbrated and others being more specific to an associated pathological entity. In this section there is a brief focus on the more general impairments outlined by Wing (1982). First and foremost, there are impairments of social interaction, with more recent research emphasizing difficulties in discriminating socioeconomic cues (Hobson, 1986) together with an impaired ability to appreciate how others think, which is based on a theory of mind (Baron-Cohen, 1989). Second, there are delays and deviances of language and communication, which include limitations in the understanding and use of gesture and also deviance in relation to eye-to-eye contact. Third, there are impairments of imaginative activities, as reflected in poor or even lack of symbolic play. These often go hand in hand with poor ability at imitation. There is often an overlay of socially bizarre and inappropriate behavior. Commonly, there are anomalies of motor control and variable anomalies of attention.

Autism is usually accompanied by intellectual impairment (Kolvin, Humphrey, & McNay, 1971; Rutter & Lockyer, 1967) and organic brain dysfunction (Kolvin, Ounsted, & Roth, 1971). As the basis of the organic pathology is so diverse, it has been postulated that there must be a common final pathway to dysfunction (Damasio & Maurer, 1978).

Epilepsy is a frequent complication, developing in about one quarter of autistic children (Deykin & MacMahon, 1979; Gillberg & Steffenberg, 1987; Rutter, 1970); the occurrence of seizures is linked to the intensity of autistic symptomatology, and about two thirds of the fits have an onset in adolescence (Deykin & MacMahon, 1979). In comparison with a normal population, these fits are substantially more frequent and of later onset—the peak being at 11 to 14 years—but it is not clear whether the association is with mental handicap or with autism.

Childhood Schizophrenia

Whereas some workers suggest a modest shift to the left in the distribution of IQ scores (Kolvin, Humphrey, & McNay, 1971), others do not support this (Eggers, 1978; Green et al., 1984). However, all studies report a deterioration from a previous level of general functioning, and, broadly, this has been true irrespective of the type of onset. The frequency of delusions and hallucinations has been described above.

The biological basis of childhood schizophrenia has not been the subject of such extensive research as has been carried out at the level of brain biochemistry, or of that at the level of the modern imaging techniques in adult schizophrenia (Crow, 1987).

Reports of organic impairment have been conflicting and often confused by the inclusion of autistic children. What is available are reports of persistent soft neurological signs, particularly hypotonia (Fish, 1984), poor fine motor coordination, and visuomotor deficits (Marcus, Hans, Lewow, Wilkinson, & Burack, 1985). These and others have been reported in a variety of studies of high-risk children (Nuechterlein, 1986). One interesting report suggested that biological impairment causes a relative inability to distinguish visual signals from background noise, but this is shared with other high-risk children (Asarnow & MacCrimmon, 1978; Nuechterlein, 1985). A related finding is that schizophrenic children fail in tasks concerning information processing (Asarnow, Tanguay, Bott, & Freeman, 1987). There is evidence to support the view that much of perceptual and attentional development in children consists of a transition toward more active control of information acquisition. This is achieved, in part, through more efficient deployment of attentional capacity (Asarnow, Sherman, & Strandberg, 1986). These last authors go on to assert that it is precisely these controlled attentional processes, which usually develop in middle childhood, that are impaired in schizophrenic children, while more automatic modes of attending remain relatively intact. To date, in contrast to the condition in adults, a search for other evidence of neurological impairment has yielded little. Nevertheless, a current popular view is that actual or presumed cerebral damage in early life contributes to the emergence of adult schizophrenia (Murray & Lewis, 1987). What evidence is there for this in childhood schizophrenia?

Unfortunately, many studies do not distinguish autism from schizophrenia, and therefore it is difficult to disentangle facts. Although not as common as in autism, presumptive brain damage/dysfunction as reflected in the complications of pregnancy and birth (PBC), neurological soft signs, or specifically abnormal EEGs are still more common than might be expected. For instance, temporal lobe discharges were reported in 12% of adolescent schizophrenics (Kolvin, Ounsted, & Roth, 1971).

DIFFERENTIAL DIAGNOSIS

Autism

Autism has been characterized by a variety of bizarre behaviors and anomalies of development, the latter being the basis of the inclusion of autism in the pervasive developmental disorder category with emphasis on the impairment of social relationships, an obsessional desire for sameness, an early onset and associated secondary features relating to communication, cognitive ability, and motor behavior (Kanner, 1943). Other criteria have proved broadly similar in terms of age of onset, self-isolating patterns of social behavior, catastrophic reactions, and repetitive behaviors (Kolvin, 1971). Rutter (1974) has pointed out that, as each of these main symptoms can occur in the absence of others, none can be regarded as specific.

A crucial issue is the differentiation of autism from other disorders of development with which there appear to be shared symptoms. Rutter and Schopler (1988) assert that the main feature distinguishing autism from these other disorders is the deviance in development rather than the delay. This pattern of deviance of social usage of language, of inner language, and socioemotional reciprocity between the child and others distinguishes autism not only from schizophrenic childhood disorders but also from other developmental disorders, particularly those associated with mental retardation. In those other disorders in which there is not this characteristic pattern of deviance but, rather, so-called "secondary autistic features," as may occur, for example, in profound deafness, the child may succeed in communicating through other modalities.

However, it is not merely these features that distinguish autism from childhood schizophrenia. A steady course is more typical of autism, while marked remissions and relapses frequently occur in childhood schizophrenia; marked intellectual retardation is a common feature of autism but less so with childhood schizophrenia; better visuo-spatial skills and poorer language skills are characteristic of autism but not of schizophrenia; there is a marked male preponderance in autism but equality of the sexes in schizophrenia; there is a higher frequency of adverse perinatal factors and organic factors in autism than in childhood schizophrenia (Kolvin, Ounsted, & Roth, 1971); there is a high genetic loading in the parents of schizophrenic children as well as in adults, but a very low loading in the parents of autists (Kolvin, Ounsted, Richardson, & Garside, 1971; Rutter, 1972). There are similar distinctions between infantile psychosis and adult-type schizophrenia, and for these reasons Rutter (1972) sees no reason for making any distinction between childhood-onset schizophrenia and adult-type schizophrenia.

There is also the issue of the relationship (and differences) between autism and specific receptive developmental language disorders (dysphasia). Although there are a number of overlapping features, such as social withdrawal and repetitive behaviors, sound empirical research has shown that children in the latter group differ from autistic children. Bartak, Rutter, and Cox (1975, 1977) have demonstrated that autism is associated with a language deficit that is more extensive in that it spans several different language modalities, including an impairment of the understanding of written language and also severe comprehension deficits. Furthermore, this language impairment involves deviance as reflected by echolalia, pronominal reversal, and metaphorical language in addition to linguistic delay.

Whereas profoundly mentally handicapped children may have some features of autism, notably they may have two-way social interactions that are appropriate for their developmental age. Thus, while their social interactions may be moderately impaired (Wing & Gould, 1979), they tend not to show the same pattern of deviance that is found in core autistic conditions.

Another question concerns extremely depriving environmental circumstances. It would be difficult to imagine how any of such deprivational experiences could give rise to the complex and specific patterns of impairments in such diverse areas as cognitive, perceptual, motor, and autonomic functioning (Wing, 1976). Rutter and Schopler (1988) point out that neither the indiscriminate friendliness of some institutionally reared children nor the insecurities of abused children (Mrazek & Mrazek, 1985; Rutter, 1981) constituted features reminiscent of autism. However, in some rare cases where children have been exposed to extreme deprivation and abuse, the picture can begin to resemble autism although the pattern of deviance is different (Skuse, 1984). Nevertheless, even here one must question how much of the picture is due to environmental adversity and how much due to constitutional influences (Rutter & Schopler, 1988).

Childhood Schizophrenia

As with the adult condition, childhood schizophrenia has to be differentiated from organic syndromes, affective disorders, and also personality disorders. Common organic conditions are the drug-induced states, such as amphetamine psychosis and temporal lobe epilepsy. Affective states are distinguished on the basis of the persistence of the dysphoria and the relationship of the hallu-cinations or delusions to the prevailing mood (Gelder, Gath, & Mayou, 1983). A common problem is that in the early stages the schizo-phrenia may be insidious and can be preceded by quite serious depression (Nissen, 1971). In all the foregoing a careful history is essential, as is an examination of the mental state together with a physical examination to exclude disorders with an organic basis.

The Borderlands of
Childhood Psychoses

It has been postulated that the phenomenon of the schizophrenia spectrum may occur in adoles-cence. Differential diagnosis of these borderland phenomena from core childhood schizophrenia can be difficult and often can be achieved only on the basis of historical accounts of the insidious changes and monitoring over time for evidence of first-rank symptoms.

Asperger's Syndrome and Schizoid
Personality Disorder in Childhood

The essential features of Asperger's syndrome are a gross lack of skills in social diplomacy, asso-ciated with a degree of naivety leading to an im-pairment of social relationships (Asperger, 1944). Additional features are male preponderance, diag-nosis after the first two years of life, the unusual use of spoken language—particularly pedantic aprosodic speech—the use of stereotyped phrases, and also abnormalities in nonverbal communica-tion. Additionally, there is a lack of affective con-tact, stereotyped movement, an obsessional at-tachment to certain toys and surroundings, and a preoccupation with rotatory movement. Finally, Asperger regarded children displaying this syn-drome as having special abilities in the areas of logic and abstraction. Such characteristics suggest a location in the "no man's land" of classification between autism, on the one hand, and schizo-phrenia, on the other (Kay & Kolvin, 1987).

A crucial question is whether there is a relation-ship between autism and the adult-derived con-cept of schizoid personality disorder. Different positions are exemplified by Wing (1981), on the one hand, and Wolff and her colleagues (Wolff & Barlow, 1979; Wolff & Chick, 1980), on the other. These have been reviewed recently by Kay and Kolvin (1987).

Wolff and Barlow (1979) attempt to highlight

similarities between the adult-derived concept of schizoid personality disorder and Asperger's syn-drome. They compare childhood schizoid person-ality with autistic and normal control children using relatively small samples matched for age, sex, and nonverbal intelligence. Reanalysis of their verbal and performance IQ data reveals that there were no significant differences between the schizoid personality and the autistic group, nor between the autistic and control group. There was, however, a significant difference between the schizoid personality disorder group and controls (Kay & Kolvin, 1987).

How do these disorders relate to each other? Wing (1981) considered schizoid personality dis-order a vague and ill-defined concept, presup-posing a relationship to schizophrenia. Asperger's syndrome shares many features with childhood autism, and (although there has been insufficient research into etiological links) it can be viewed as a mild variant of autism on the basis of sympto-matology alone (Wing, 1981). The deviance, pat-terning, and severity of features are insufficient for it to be considered as psychosis but rather as a personality variant. Furthermore, a separation of schizoid personality disorder and Asperger's syn-drome does not make sense, either on theoretical grounds or in terms of clinical patterns, and both should be classified as personality disorders of childhood, probably with each being a mild var-iant of the other (Kay & Kolvin, 1987). However, from his examination of adult data, Tantam (1988) does not seem to support this position and sees these two conditions as distinct. The answer may be that schizoid personality disorder is a het-erogeneous condition that includes cases from both of the two proposed spectra relating to au-tism and childhood schizophrenia.

Other Borderline States

Initially, this elusive concept was used to iden-tify patients who were too unstable for deep psy-chotherapy but were not obviously psychotic (Stern, 1938). Spitzer and Endicott (1979) argue that the borderline concept is not unitary and is best regarded as possessing at least two major di-mensions that are relatively independent. For in-stance, clinicians in the United States use the term "borderline" in two different ways. The first is used to describe a patient group with a disorder assumed to be genetically related to a spectrum of disorders including schizophrenia; this has been labeled "schizotypal personality" to reflect the concept of "borderline schizophrenia." Family and genetic data are suggestive of a link with schizophrenia (Kendler, 1984). Second, the term is used to describe a patient group with a "constellation of relatively enduring personality features of instability and vulnerability": This has been identified as an "unstable personality."

There are greater difficulties in applying these concepts to children and adolescents whose ego functioning and personalities are not fully developed (Kay & Kolvin, 1987). Steinberg (1983) has drawn a composite picture of the borderline personality from the American literature. It is characterized by complaints of misbehavior—particularly antisocial behavior, drug abuse, running away, and promiscuity; there may also be educational difficulties. Poor impulse control and suicidal threats are also described. Some of these children are said to be depressed and withdrawn and to show a sense of futility or enraged hostility. The overall impression is that of a child with a poorly integrated sense of self and in whom transient psychotic states may occur, although the abiding state is not one of psychosis. It is arguable that such a miscellany of behavioral and affective symptoms could equally well be encompassed within the well-known category of mixed conduct–neurotic disorder (Kay & Kolvin, 1987). Despite considerable continuity over time Stone (1984), in his review of the borderline syndromes, suggests that it is difficult to apply the concept meaningfully in adolescence.

CONTINUITY AND DISCONTINUITY WITH ADULT PRESENTATION

Autism

Although there is a lessening of the more bizarre and florid features, the impairments persist to result in an adult with an impoverished imagination and empathy (Bemporad, 1979; Rutter, 1970). Howells and Guirguis (1984) have suggested that this state is indistinguishable from chronic schizophrenia or schizotypal personality disorder (APA, 1980). There are reports of autistic children who subsequently develop schizophrenic syndromes (Petty et al., 1984; Watkins, Asarnow, & Tanguay, 1988; Nunn, Lask, & Cohen, 1986). However, this remains controversial as other research workers, such as Wing and Attwood (1987), report that they have not seen such a case and assert that there is nothing to be gained from locating these in the same category.

Asperger's Syndrome

A ten-year follow-up of 22 childhood cases of schizoid personality disorder found that the personality characteristics persisted into adulthood; in addition one of the patients became floridly schizophrenic and another was hospitalized with symptoms of simple schizophrenia (Wolff & Chick, 1980). In contrast, of Asperger's 200 cases, only 1 developed schizophrenia.

Childhood Schizophrenia

There have been few studies of the premorbid picture in childhood schizophrenia, but research into adult schizophrenia provides some clues. One strategy consists of the follow-up of children with a psychiatric disorder. From this emerges the picture of an emotionally unstable child with interpersonal difficulties leading to rejection by his or her peers and to isolation. Underlying these, and making the child particularly vulnerable, are a catalog of neurodevlopmental deficits, including poor motor functioning and visuospatial and verbal impairments, together with attention deficits (Asarnow & Goldstein, 1986). This pattern, present in about one-half of schizophrenics, although unusual does not depict the schizoid personality that might be expected from the concept of the schizophrenia spectrum (Parnas, Schulsinger, Schulsinger, Mednick, & Teasdale, 1982). However, Asarnow and Ben-Meir (1988) have shown childhood schizotypal personality disorder and schizophrenia to be similar (in contrast to depressive conditions) with regard to poor premorbid adjustment and poorer intelligence. Finally, Parnas and Schulsinger (1986) describe a continuity of formal thought disorder from childhood to adulthood, which implies that schizophrenia does not have a clear-cut onset but may develop by the gradual accretion of symptoms.

There are insufficient data to show that the very variable long-term outcome has any distinctive features or differs from that of adult-onset schizophrenia. Follow-up between 9 and 40 years later found 6 of the 57 cases described by Eggers (1978) to be in malignant defect states such as a catatonia or hebephrenia. Delusions, usually unchanged, persisted in about half of the whole population. The personality was unaffected in only 11 of the 57 patients, although, in a further 8, the changes were so slight as to be almost unnoticeable.

SUMMARY

This paper is concerned with a developmental perspective in relation to the classification and diagnosis of the psychoses and allied disorders of childhood and adolescence. It provides evidence of wide differences in psychopathology, epidemiology, natural history, impairments, and complications of autism and childhood schizophrenia and their associated spectrum disorders. The overwhelming implication is that there is little to be gained by attempts to unify these diverse clinical disorders, some of which are evidently psychotic and others merely reflecting forms of personality variations.

REFERENCES

Anthony, E. J. (1958). An experimental approach to the psychopathology of childhood autism. *British Journal of Medical Psychology, 21*, 211–225.

American Psychiatric Association (1980). *Diagnostic and statistical manual of mental disorders* (3rd ed.). Washington, DC: Author.

Asarnow, J. R., & Goldstein, M. J. (1986). Schizophrenia during adolescence and early adulthood: A developmental perspective on risk research. *Clinical Psychology Review, 6*, 211–235.

Asarnow, J. R., & Ben-Meir, S. (1988). Children with schizophrenia spectrum and depressive disorders: A comparative study of premorbid adjustment, onset pattern and severity of impairment. *Journal of Child Psychology and Psychiatry, 29*, 825–838.

Asarnow, R. F., & MacCrimmon, D. J. (1978). Residual performance deficit in chronically remitted schizophrenics: A marker of schizophrenia? *Journal of Abnormal Psychology, 87*, 267–275.

Asarnow, R. F., Sherman, T., & Strandburg, R. (1986). The search for the psychobiological substrate of childhood onset schizophrenia. *Journal of the American Academy of Child Psychiatry, 26*(5), 601–614.

Asarnow, R. F., Tanguay, P. E., Bott, L., & Freeman, B. J. (1987). Patterns of intellectual functioning in non-retarded autistic and schizophrenic children. *Journal of Child Psychology and Psychiatry, 28*, 273–280.

Asperger, H. (1944). Die "autistischen psychopathen" im kindesalter [The autistic psychopathology in childhood]. *Archiv fur Psychiatrie und Nervenkrankheiten, 117*, 76–136.

Attwood, A. (1984). *The gestures of autistic children*. Unpublished PhD thesis, University of London.

Babigan, H. M. (1980). Schizophrenia: Epidemiology. In H. I. Kaplan, A. M. Freedman, & B. J. Sadock (Eds.), *Comprehensive textbook of psychiatry*. Baltimore, MD: Williams & Wilkins.

Baron-Cohen, S. (1989). The autistic child's theory of mind: A case of specific developmental delay. *Journal of Child Psychology and Psychiatry, 30*, 285–297.

Bartak, L., Rutter, M., & Cox, A. (1975). A comparative study of infantile autism and specific developmental receptive language disorders: I. The children. *British Journal of Psychiatry, 126*, 127–145.

Bartak, L., Rutter, M., & Cox, A. (1977). A comparative study of infantile autism and specific developmental receptive language disorders: III. Discriminant function analysis. *Journal of Autism and Childhood Schizophrenia, 6*, 297–302.

Beitchman, J. H. (1985). Childhood schizophrenia. *Psychiatric Clinics of North America, 8*, 793–814.

Bemporad, J. R. (1979). Adult recollections of a formerly autistic child. *Journal of Autism and Developmental Disorders, 9*, 179–198.

Bleuler, E. (1950). *Dementia praecox or the group of schizophrenias* (J. Zinkin, trans.). New York: International University Press.

Brockington, I. (1983). *Schizophrenia: Fact and fiction*. Inaugural Lecture. Birmingham, England: University of Birmingham.

Brockington, I., Kendell, R. E., & Leff, J. P. (1978). Definitions of schizophrenia: Concordance and predictions of outcome. *Psychological Medicine, 8*, 387.

Bryson, S. E., Clark, B. S., & Smith, I. M. (1988). First report of a Canadian epidemiological study of autistic syndromes. *Journal of Child Psychology and Psychiatry, 29*, 433–446.

Cantor, S., Evans, J., Pearce, J., & Pezzot-Pearce, J. (1982). Childhood schizophrenia: Present but not accounted for. *American Journal of Psychiatry, 139*, 758–762.

Corbett, J., Harris, R., Taylor, E., & Trimble, M. (1977). Progressive disintegrative psychosis in childhood. *Journal of Child Psychology and Psychiatry, 18*, 211–219.

Creak, M. (1963). Childhood psychosis: A review of 100 cases. *British Journal of Psychiatry, 109*, 84–89.

Crow, T. J. (1987). Neurochemistry of schizophrenia in the living brain. *Transmission, 1*(2), 4–9.

Damasio, A. R., & Maurer, R. G. (1978). A neurological model for childhood autism. *Archives of Neurology, 35*, 777–786.

DeMyer, M. K., Barton, S., DeMyer, W. E., Norton, J. A., Allen, J., & Steele, R. (1973). Prognosis in autism: A follow-up study. *Journal of Autism and Childhood Schizophrenia, 3*, 199–246.

Denckla, M. B. (1986). Editorial: New diagnostic criteria for autism and related behavioral disorder—guidelines for research protocols. *Journal of the American Academy of Child Psychiatry, 25*, 221–224.

Deykin, E. Y., & MacMahon, B. (1979). The incidence of seizures among children with autistic symptoms. *American Journal of Psychiatry, 136*, 1310–1312.

Egdell, H. G., & Kolvin, I. (1972). Childhood hallucinations. *Journal of Child Psychology and Psychiatry, 13*, 279–287.

Eggers, C. (1978). Course and prognosis of childhood schizophrenia. *Journal of Autism and Childhood Schizophrenia, 8*, 21–36.

Evans-Jones, L. G., & Rosenbloom, L. (1978). Disintegrative psychosis in childhood. *Developmental Medicine and Child Neurology, 20*, 462–470.

Fish, B. (1977). Neurobiologic antecedents of schizophrenia in children. *Archives of General Psychiatry, 34*, 1297–1313.

Fish, B. (1984). Characteristics and sequelae of the neurointegrative disorder in infants at risk for schizophrenia: 1952–1982. In N. Watt, E. J. Anthony, L. C. Wynne, & J. Rolf (Eds.), *Children at risk for schizophrenia: A longitudinal perspective*. New York: Cambridge University Press.

Garralda, M. E. (1984a). Hallucinations in children with conduct and emotional disorders: I. Study of the children. *Psychological Medicine, 14*, 589–596.

Garralda, M. E. (1984b). Hallucinations in children with conduct and emotional disorders: II. A follow-up study. *Psychological Medicine, 14*, 597–604.

Gelder, M., Gath, D., & Mayou, R. (1983). *Oxford textbook of psychiatry*. Oxford: Oxford University Press.

Gillberg, C. (1984). Infantile autism and other childhood psychoses in a Swedish region: Epidemiological aspects. *Journal of Child Psychology and Psychiatry, 25*, 35–43.

Gillberg, C., & Gillberg, I. (1988, June). *The epidemiology of Asperger syndrome*. Paper presented at the First Asperger Syndrome Symposium, London.

Gillberg, C., & Schaumann, H. (1981). Infantile autism and puberty. *Journal of Autism and Developmental Disorders, 11*, 365–371.

Gillberg, C., & Steffenberg, S. (1987). Outcome and prognostic factors in infantile autism and similar conditions: A population-based study of 46 cases followed through puberty. *Journal of Autism and Developmental Disorders, 17*, 273–287.

Green, W. H., Campbell, M., Hardesty, A. S., Grega, D. M., Padron-Gayol, M., Shell, J., & Erlenmeyer-Kimling, L. (1984). A comparison of schizophrenia and autistic children. *Journal of the American Academy of Child Psychiatry, 23*, 399–409.

Hassanyeh, F., & Davison, K. (1980). Bipolar affective psychosis with onset before age 16 years: Report of 10 cases. *British Journal of Psychiatry, 37*, 530–539.

Hill, A. E., & Rosenbloom, L. (1986). Disintegrative psychosis of childhood: Teenage follow-up. *Developmental Medicine and Child Neurology, 28*, 34–40.

Himmelhoch, J. M., & Garfinkel, M. E. (1986). Sources of lithium resistance in mixed mania. *Psychopharmacological Bulletin, 22*, 613–620.

Hobson, R. P. (1986). The autistic child's appraisal of expressions of emotion: An experimental investigation. *Journal of Child Psychology and Psychiatry, 27*, 321–342.

Howells, J. G., & Guirguis, W. R. (1984). Childhood schizophrenia 20 years later. *Archives of General Psychiatry, 41*, 123–127.

Kanner, L. (1943). Autistic disturbances of affective contact. *Nervous Child, 2*, 217–250.

Kanner, L., Rodriguez, A., & Ashenden, B. (1972). How far can autistic children go in matters of social adaptation? *Journal of Autism and Childhood Schizophrenia, 2*, 9–33.

Kay, P., & Kolvin, I. (1987). Childhood psychoses and their borderlands. *British Medical Bulletin, 43*, 570–586.

Kendler, K. S. (1984). A family history study of schizophrenia-related personality disorders. *American Journal of Psychiatry, 141*, 424–427.

Kolvin, I. (1971). Studies in childhood psychoses: I. Diagnostic criteria and classification. *British Journal of Psychiatry, 118*, 381–384.

Kolvin, I. (1985). Childhood autism. In M. Craft, J. Bicknell, & S. Hollin (Eds.), *Mental handicap* (13th ed.) (pp. 147–161). London: Balliere Tindall.

Kolvin, I., Garside, R., & Kidd, J. S. H. (1971). Studies in childhood psychoses: IV. Parental personality and attitude and childhood psychoses. *British Journal of Psychiatry, 118*, 403–406.

Kolvin, I., Humphrey, M., & McNay, A. (1971). Studies in childhood psychoses: VI. Cognitive factors in childhood psychoses. *British Journal of Psychiatry, 118*, 415–419.

Kolvin, I., Ounsted, C., Humphrey, M., & McNay, A. (1971). Studies in childhood psychoses: II. The phenomenology of childhood psychoses. *British Journal of Psychiatry, 118*, 385–395.

Kolvin, I., Ounsted, C., Richardson, L. M., & Garside, R. F. (1971). Studies in childhood psychoses: III. The family and social background in childhood psychoses. *British Journal of Psychiatry, 118*, 396–402.

Kolvin, I., Ounsted, C., & Roth, M. (1971). Studies in childhood psychoses: V. Cerebral dysfunction and childhood psychosis. *British Journal of Psychiatry, 118*, 407–414.

Kramer, M. (1978). Population changes and schizophrenia, 1970–1985. In L. C. Wynne, R. L. Cromwell, & S. Matthysse (Eds.), *The nature of schizophrenia: New approaches to research and treatment*. New York: John Wiley & Sons.

Kydd, R. R., & Werry, J. S. (1982). Schizophrenia in children under 16 years. *Journal of Autism and Developmental Disorders, 12*, 343–358.

Lotter, V. (1967). Epidemiology of autistic conditions in young children: Some characteristics of the parents and children. *Social Psychiatry, 1*, 163–173.

Lotter, V. (1974). Social adjustment and placement of autistic children in Middlesex: A follow-up study. *Journal of Autism and Childhood Schizophrenia, 4*, 11–32.

Makita, K. (1966). The age of onset of childhood schizophrenia. *Folia Psychiatrica Neurologica Japonica, 20*, 111–121.

Marcus, J. Hans, S. Lewow, E., Wilkinson, L., & Burack, C. (1985). Neurological findings in the offspring of schizophrenics: Childhood assessment and 5-year follow-up. *Schizophrenia Bulletin, 11*, 85–100.

Masterson, J. C. (1956). Prognosis in adolescent disorders: Schizophrenia. *Journal of Nervous and Mental Disorder, 124*, 219–232.

Mrazek, D., & Mrazek, P. (1985). Child maltreatment. In M. Rutter & L. Hersov (Eds.), *Child and adolescent psychiatry: Modern approaches* (2nd ed.) (pp. 545–566). Oxford: Blackwell Scientific.

Murray, R. M., & Lewis, S. W. (1987). Is schizophrenia a neurodevelopmental disorder? *British Medical Journal, 295*, 681–682.

Nuechterlein, K. H. (1985). Converging evidence for vigilance deficit as a vulnerability indicator for schizophrenic disorders. In M. Alpert (Ed.), *Controversies in schizophrenia: Changes and constancies* (pp. 175–198). New York: Brunner/Mazel.

Nuechterlein, K. H. (1986). Childhood precursors of adult schizophrenia. *Journal of Child Psychology and Psychiatry, 27*, 133–144.

Nunn, K. P., Lask, B., & Cohen, M. (1986). Viruses, neurodevelopmental disorder and childhood psychosis. *Journal of Child Psychology and Psychiatry, 27*, 55–64.

Parnas, J., & Schulsinger, H. (1986). Continuity of formal thought disorder from childhood to adulthood in a high-risk sample. *Acta Psychiatrica Scandinavica, 74*, 246–251.

Parnas, J., Schulsinger, F., Schulsinger, H., Mednick, S. A., & Teasdale, T. W. (1982). Behavioural precursors of schizophrenia spectrum. A prospective study. *Archives of General Psychiatry, 39*, 658–664.

Petty, L. K., Ornitz, E. M., Michelman, J. D., & Zimmerman, E. G. (1984). Autistic children who become schizophrenic. *Archives of General Psychiatry, 41*, 29–135.

Rivinus, T. M., Jamison, D. L., & Graham, P. J. (1975). Childhood organic neurological disease presenting as a psychiatric disorder. *Archives of Disease in Childhood, 50*, 115–119.

Roth, M., & McClelland, H. (1979). Problems of diagnosis and treatment in the borderlands of schizophrenia. In J. M. Simister (Ed.), *Neuroleptics and schizophrenics* (pp. 63–81). Luton, England: Lundbeck House.

Rutter, M. (1967). Psychotic disorders in early childhood. In A. J. Coppen & A. Walk (Eds.), *Recent developments in schizophrenia* (pp. 133–151). Ashford, England, RMPA.

Rutter, M. (1970). Autistic children: Infancy to adulthood. *Seminars in Psychiatry, 2*, 435–450.

Rutter, M. (1972). Childhood schizophrenia reconsidered. *Journal of Autism and Childhood Schizophrenia, 2*, 315–317.

Rutter, M. (1974). The development of infantile autism. *Psychological Medicine, 4*, 147–163.

Rutter, M. (1981). *Maternal deprivation reassessed* (2nd ed.). Harmondsworth, England: Penguin.

Rutter, M. (1985). Infantile autism and other pervasive disorders. In M. Rutter & L. Hersov (Eds.), *Child and adolescent psychiatry: Modern approaches* (2nd ed.) (pp. 545–566). Oxford: Blackwell Scientific.

Rutter, M., Greenfield, D., & Lockyer, L. (1967). A five to fifteen year follow-up study of infantile psychosis: II. Social and behavioural outcome. *British Journal of Psychiatry, 113*, 1183–1199.

Rutter, M., & Lockyer, L. (1967). A five to fifteen year follow-up study of infantile psychosis: I. Description of the sample. *British Journal of Psychiatry, 113*, 1169–1182.

Rutter, M., & Schopler, E. (1988). Autism and pervasive developmental disorders. In M. Rutter, T. A. Hussain, & I. S. Lann (Eds.), *Assessment and diagnosis in child psychopathology* (pp. 408–434). New York: Guilford Press.

Schneider, K. (1959). *Clinical psychopathology* (M. W. Hamilton, trans.). London: Grune & Stratton.

Skuse, D. (1984). Extreme deprivation in early childhood: I. Diverse outcomes for three siblings from an extraordinary family. *Journal of Child Psychology and Psychiatry, 26*, 523–541.

Spitzer, R. L., & Endicott, J. (1979). Justification for separating schizotypal and borderline personality disorders. *Schizophrenia Bulletin, 5*, 95–104.

Stern, A. (1938). Psychoanalytic investigation and therapy in the borderline group of neuroses. *Psychoanalytic Quarterly, 7*, 467–489.

Steinberg, D. (1983). Schizoid personality and the borderline state. In D. Steinberg (Ed.), *The clinical psychiatry of adolescence: Clinical work from a social and developmental perspective*. Chichester, England: John Wiley & Sons.

Steinhausen, H.-C., Gobel, D., Breinlinger, M., & Wohleben, B. (1983, October). *A community survey of infantile autism*. Paper presented at the 30th annual meeting of the American Academy of Child Psychiatry, San Francisco.

Stone, M. H. (1984). Borderline syndromes: A consideration of sub-types and an overview, direction for research. *Psychiatric Clinics, 4*, 23.

Tantam, D. (1988). Lifelong eccentricity and social isolation: II. Asperger's syndrome or schizoid personality disorder. *British Journal of Psychiatry, 153*, 783–791.

Volkmar, F. R. (1987). Diagnostic issues in the pervasive developmental disorders. *Journal of Child Psychology and Psychiatry, 28*, 365–370.

Watkins, J. M., Asarnow, R. F., & Tanguay, P. E. (1988). Symptom development in childhood onset schizophrenia. *Journal of Child Psychology and Psychiatry, 29*, 865–878.

Wing, L. (1981). Aspergers's syndrome: A clinical account. *Psychological Medicine, 11*, 115–129.

Wing, L. (1982). Development of concepts, classification and relationship to mental retardation. In L. Wing & J. K. Wing (Eds.), *Handbook of psychiatry: Vol. 3. Psychoses of uncertain aetiology* (pp. 185–190). Cambridge: Cambridge University Press.

Wing, L., & Attwood, A. (1987). Syndromes of autism and atypical development. In D. J. Cohen & A. M. Donellan (Eds.), *Handbook of autism and pervasive developmental disorders* (pp. 3–19). New York: John Wiley & Sons.

Wing, L., & Gould, J. (1978). Systematic recording of behaviours and skills of retarded and psychotic children. *Journal of Autism and Childhood Schizophrenia, 8*, 79–97.

Wing, L., & Gould, J. (1979). Severe impairments of social interaction and associated abnormalities in children: Epidemiology and classification. *Journal of Autism and Developmental Disorders, 9*, 11–30.

Wolff, S., & Barlow, A. (1979). Schizoid personality in childhood: A comparative study of schizoid, autistic, and normal children. *Journal of Child Psychology and Psychiatry, 20*, 29–46.

Wolff, S., & Chick, J. (1980). Schizoid personality in childhood: A controlled follow-up study. *Psychological Medicine, 10*, 85–100.

World Health Organization. (1979). *International classification of diseases, injuries, and causes of death* (9th ed.). Geneva: Author.

CHAPTER 8

SCHIZOPHRENIA IN ADULTHOOD

Randall L. Morrison
Julie H. Wade

DESCRIPTION OF THE DISORDER

Schizophrenia is among the most disabling and disruptive of the mental disorders. The core symptoms of schizophrenia involve marked distortions of reality (i.e., psychotic behavior) including delusions, hallucinations, and/or disordered thought processes. Other symptoms are disturbances of attention, motor behavior, affect, and life-role functioning. However, the disorder is extremely heterogeneous; no singular symptomatology distinguishes schizophrenia from other disorders. Despite progress in the neurosciences, schizophrenia remains a clinical entity, for which individual cases are diagnosed on the basis of the presence of a minimum subset of overt behavioral symptoms from within a broad constellation of possible symptomatology. Subtypes of the disorder may exhibit different symptom clusters. Indeed, some have argued that schizophrenia may actually represent a heterogeneous collection of syndromes as opposed to a single related group of

disorders (e.g., Crow, 1985), and there even exist several conflicting diagnostic criteria for the disorder (i.e., *Diagnostic and Statistical Manual of Mental Disorders*, [American Psychiatric Association, 1987]; Research Diagnostic Criteria [Spitzer, Endicott, & Robins, 1978]; the Washington University or St. Louis criteria [Feighner et al., 1972]). A further aspect of the heterogeneity of schizophrenia is that the symptoms of schizophrenia typically vary over time and phases of the illness.

CLINICAL PRESENTATION

A DSM-III-R diagnosis of schizophrenia requires that the patient exhibit (or have exhibited during an active phase of the illness) psychotic symptoms and a deterioration of functioning in work, social, and/or self-care areas. Specific psychotic criteria are presented in Table 8.1. Additionally, continuous signs of the illness must be present for at least 6 months. During this period,

Preparation of this chapter was supported by NIMH grants MH 38636 and MH 39998.

Table 8.1. DSM-III-R Psychotic Symptom Criteria for Schizophrenia

Presence of characteristic psychotic symptoms in the active phase: either (1), (2), or (3) for at least one week (unless the symptoms are successfully treated):

(1) two of the following:

    (a) delusions
    (b) prominent hallucinations (throughout the day for several days or several times a week for several weeks, each hallucinatory experience not being limited to a few brief moments)
    (c) incoherence or marked loosening of associations
    (d) catatonic behavior
    (e) flat or grossly inappropriate affect

(2) bizarre delusions (i.e., involving a phenomenon that the person's culture would regard as totally implausible, e.g., thought broadcasting, being controlled by a dead person)

(3) prominent hallucinations [as defined in (1) (b) above] of a voice with content having no apparent relation to depression or elation, or a voice keeping up a running commentary on the person's behavior or thoughts, or two or more voices conversing with each other.

Reprinted with permission from the *Diagnostic and Statistical Manual of Mental Disorders. Third Edition, Revised.* Copyright 1987 American Psychiatric Association.

the illness must meet criteria for an active phase, in which the psychotic symptom criteria depicted in Table 8.1 are met. The course may also include a prodromal and/or residual phase (see Table 8.2). Finally, the diagnosis is to be made only when it cannot be established that an organic factor initiated and maintained the disturbance. Age of onset is typically late adolescence through early adulthood, although later onset is possible.

Variability in symptomatology is extensive, and there is no essential symptom that is invariably present. Specific subtypes of schizophrenia will be examined after a further discussion of the major symptoms.

Symptomatology

Thought Disorder

Disturbances in the thought processes of schizophrenics involve deviant thought form (i.e., the organization of ideas) and thought content. Disturbance of thought form is evidenced by verbal productions that are odd, illogical, disorganized, and potentially incomprehensible. Particular dis-

Table 8.2. DSM-III-R Prodromal or Residual Schizophrenic Symptoms

(1) Marked social isolation or withdrawal

(2) Marked impairment in role functioning as wage-earner, student, or homemaker

(3) Markedly peculiar behavior (e.g., collecting garbage, talking to self in public, hoarding food)

(4) Marked impairment in personal hygiene and grooming

(5) Blunted or inappropriate affect

(6) Digressive, vague, overelaborate, or circumstantial speech, or poverty of speech, or poverty of content of speech

(7) Odd beliefs or magical thinking, influencing behavior and inconsistent with cultural norms, e.g., superstitiousness, belief in clairvoyance, telepathy, "sixth sense," "others can feel my feelings," overvalued ideas, ideas of reference

(8) Unusual perceptual experiences, e.g., recurrent illusions, sensing the presence of a force or person not actually present

(9) Marked lack of initiative, interests, or energy

Reprinted with permission from the *Diagnostic and Statistical Manual of Mental Disorders. Third Edition, Revised.* Copyright 1987 American Psychiatric Association.

turbances of thought form that are characteristic of schizophrenia are loosening of associations, blocking, neologisms, poverty of speech, poverty of content, perseveration, echolalia, and clanging.

Delusions represent the disturbances in thought content that are most typical of schizophrenia. Delusions common to schizophrenia are those of being controlled, bizarre delusions including thought insertion, thought broadcasting, thought withdrawal, grandiose delusions, persecutory delusions, and delusions of reference. While thought disorder is among DSM-III-R criteria for schizophrenia, its presence does not differentiate between schizophrenia and other psychotic disorders (e.g., mood disorder with psychotic features) (Andreasen, 1979).

Perceptual and Attentional Disturbance

Hallucinations are common in schizophrenia. Approximately 75% of newly hospitalized schizophrenics report hallucinations (Ludwig, 1986). Auditory hallucinations in the form of voices are most prevalent and are present in nearly 90% of hallucinating patients (Ludwig, 1986). Other types of hallucinations (e.g., visual, olfactory, tactile, somatic, and gustatory) are uncommon in the absence of hallucinatory voices.

Since Bleuler's (1924) description of the lack of cognitive control associated with schizophrenia, in which he noted that schizophrenics were "incapable of holding the train of thought in the proper channels" (Bleuler, 1924, reprinted in 1976, p. 377), the contribution of primary dysfunctions in elementary cognitive processes to thought disorder and perceptual disturbances of schizophrenia has been widely considered. Studies have examined cognitive functioning of acutely psychotic schizophrenics, as well as patients in relative remission after an acute phase of the illness, and populations at risk for the development of schizophrenia. Nuechterlein and Dawson (1984) recently reviewed these findings and emphasized the relevance of processing load in the differential cognitive performance of at risk, actively ill, and postpsychotic subjects.

Deficits in vigilance tasks with high-processing loads, in forced-choice span of apprehension for large arrays, and in serial recall for items that involve active rehearsal occur across risk populations, actively symptomatic schizophrenic patients, and relatively remitted schizophrenic patients. These deficits may reflect vulnerability factors for schizophrenic disorders. . . . Cognitive deficits that have been found only during actively psychotic periods or in chronic schizophrenic patients, such as poorer recognition of briefly presented, single, familiar letters or numbers, are characterized by low demands on processing capacity. (p. 160)

However, Gjerde (1983) has emphasized that motivational, affective, and arousal disturbances may contribute to the information processing deficits of schizophrenia, in contrast to "pure" cognitive processing dysfunctions.

Controlled, effortful processes are more labile than processes that have been automaticized, and individual differences, both within and among individuals, are most likely to manifest themselves on tasks requiring effortful processing. Organismic variables (e.g., arousal, mood, and age) are therefore more likely to influence performance when the task at hand . . . has high attentional requirements than when the demand is for automatic processing. (p. 59)

The amotivational role of negative symptoms, as well as an increased prevalence of cognitive impairment in negative syndrome, has been documented.

Moreover, there has been little consideration of specific behavioral referents that may relate to particular cognitive deficits. Neale, Oltmanns, and Harvey (1985) have critiqued research regarding cognitive factors in schizophrenia, on the grounds that few studies have gone beyond the demonstration of a simple correlation between a psychological variable and schizophrenia. While it is hypothesized that cognitive dysfunction mediates impaired language production/communication in schizophrenia, the most common research strategy has been to compare a heterogeneous group of schizophrenics (without regard for subclassification in terms of communication impairment) to control samples. But as Neale et al. point out,

Within a group of schizophrenic patients, it seems reasonable that, for example, patients who experience auditory hallucinations may exhibit one form of cognitive impairment while those whose verbal conversation is difficult to follow may exhibit another. (p. 290)

Negative Symptoms

Contemporary interest in the subtyping of schizophrenic symptomatology along positive and negative dimensions was sparked by Strauss, Carpenter, and Bartko (1974). Positive symptoms consist of the manifest psychotic features of schizophrenia (i.e., Table 8.1). Negative symptoms involve a diminution of function and typically include avolition, anhedonia-asociality, flat affect, alogia, and attentional impairment (Andreasen, 1982; Andreasen & Olsen, 1982). Several investigations have shown that schizophrenic patients with prominent negative symptoms tend to be cognitively impaired and are more likely than patients with predominantly positive symptoms to have structural brain abnormalities (Andreasen & Olsen, 1982; Rieder, Donnelly, Herdt, & Waldman, 1979).

Inappropriate Affect

An additional disturbance of affect that is frequently present in schizophrenia is inappropriate affect (i.e., discordant with the content of speech or ideation).

Social/role Functioning Impairments

As noted, DSM-III-R criteria specify deterioration in social functioning as characteristic of the prodromal phase, and difficulty in interpersonal relations is almost invariably present throughout an episode (APA, 1987).

Subclassifications

DSM-III-R lists five types of schizophrenia, defined by predominant cross-sectional symptomatology (see Table 8.3). As noted, considerable recent attention has been directed toward the alternative subtyping of schizophrenic symptoms along the positive-negative symptom dimension. Carpenter, Heinrichs, and Alps (1985) recently proposed a distinction between secondary negative symptoms and deficit symptoms. Secondary negative symptoms result from factors extrinsic to schizophrenia (e.g., antipsychotic drugs, understimulating environment, dysphoric affect) or as consequential to other psychopathological dimensions of schizophrenia (e.g., positive symptoms). Deficit symptoms are negative symptoms without such causes.

EPIDEMIOLOGY

The epidemiologic study of schizophrenia has been made difficult by a number of factors. Variability in diagnostic criteria for the disorder over time, and across geographic locale, has made it difficult to compare outcome data across investigations. Given that schizophrenia is a relatively uncommon disorder, large samples are required in order to derive meaningful epidemiologic data.

Prevalence rates ranging from less than 1 per 1,000 to greater than 10 per 1,000 have been reported for schizophrenia (Helzer, 1988). The lifetime prevalence rate from the multicenter Epidemiologic Catchment Area project in the United States (Klerman, 1986) is 1% (cited in Helzer, 1988). Variability in prevalence rates across studies may reflect meaningful fluctuations across different populations. There is actually considerable stability in rates across studies that have utilized similar research methodologies in the same geographic area. For example, Ireland, and in particular its western counties, has been known for consistently exhibiting high prevalence rates of schizophrenia (e.g., Kelleher, Copeland, & Smith, 1974; Walsh, 1969). Based on such consistent differences across geographic locales, a number of investigators have concluded that there may be significant differences in prevalence among different populations (e.g., Torrey, 1987).

The epidemiologic study of incidence excludes chronic cases, and, as a result, incidence estimates probably contain greater measurement error (Helzer, 1988). Studies estimating the first use of psychiatric facilities are the best approximation to true incidence rates that are currently available (Eaton, 1986). The results of comprehensive incidence studies that have considered outpatient clinics and psychiatric wards of general hospitals, as well as mental hospitals, have indicated incidence rates from 0.11 per 1,000 in Salford, England (Hailey et al., 1974), to a high of 0.69 per 1,000 in Rochester, New York (Babigian, 1975). Reports of incidence rates for U.S. samples vary between 0.20 and 0.69 per 1,000 (Eaton, 1986).

Morbidity risk estimates have been calculated in a number of investigations. In a recent review of these data, Gottesman and Shields (1982) estimate the lifetime risk of conservatively diagnosed schizophrenia across both sexes in the general population to be approximately 1%. Morbid risk has also been estimated in cohorts with varying genetic relationship, and a positive correlation between morbid risk and degree of genetic relationship has consistently been observed. Estimated lifetime risk is approximately 2% in the uncles and aunts of schizophrenics, 4% in the parents of an identified schizophrenic patient, 8% in siblings, and increases to approximately 12% in children of a schizophrenic parent (Helzer, 1988). However, these data do not provide conclusive support for genetic transmission of the illness, as family members typically share the same environment. Thus,

Table 8.3. DSM-III-R Types of Schizophrenia

TYPE	PREDOMINANT SYMPTOMATOLOGY
Catatonic	Severe psychomotor disturbance involving stupor, negativism, rigidity, excitement, or catatonic posturing.
Disorganized	Marked thought disorder and disturbed affect (flat or inappropriate). Systematized delusions are absent.
Paranoid	Preoccupation with systematized positive symptoms (e.g., delusions, hallucinations).
Undifferentiated	Prominent psychotic symptoms which cannot be classified in any of the above types.
Residual	Absence of prominent psychotic symptoms, but at least two residual symptoms.

Adapted from the *Diagnostic and Statistical Manual of Mental Disorders. Third Edition, Revised.* (1987). American Psychiatric Association.

genetic versus environmental transmission are confounded.

Twin studies have been pursued in an attempt to resolve such confounding, by comparing monozygotic (MZ) versus dizygotic (DZ) concordance. Data from twin studies almost invariably indicate a concordance rate in MZ twins that is several times greater than that for DZ twins. In their review of epidemiologic findings, Gottesman and Shields (1982) derive estimates of concordance rates of approximately 50% for MZ pairs and 17% for DZ pairs. Increased concordance among MZ twins provides further support for genetic transmission; the 50% discordance among twins sharing the identical genome points to strong nongenetic factors. Findings of a link between cases of schizophrenia and a genetic defect on an as yet unknown gene on chromosome 5 were recently reported (Sherrington et al., 1988). However, those carrying the gene did not invariably develop the disease, but are merely susceptible to it. Further, it is not known whether the specific deficit is a sufficient cause of schizophrenia, or whether other conditions must be met before the disease develops ("Where next with psychiatric illness?", 1988).

NATURAL HISTORY

No illness has an outcome *in vacuo*, or even a natural history per se (Kendell, 1988). Outcome is invariably affected by treatment and other environmental influences. Given these considerations vis-à-vis (1) the apparent chronicity of many cases of schizophrenia, the absence of curative treatment regimens for the disorder, and the increasing use of maintenance pharmacologic and psychosocial regimens; (2) disagreement regarding whether different subtypes of the disorder may actually represent different syndromes with different outcomes; (3) evidence regarding the susceptibility of schizophrenic patients to various environmental stressors; (4) evidence regarding differential outcome for male and female patients—the course of schizophrenia becomes very difficult to specify.

Medication and Psychosocial Treatment Effects

Based on a review of findings regarding "natural" (i.e., unmedicated) course, Davis (1985) concluded that schizophrenia has a constant relapse rate of approximately 10% per month in unmedicated patients. Antipsychotic drugs appeared to reduce this rate with reported differences ranging from 2.5- to 10-fold decreases. Relapse rates for patients on neuroleptics have been shown to average approximately 40%, for both orally administered and injected medication (Falloon, Watt, & Shepperd, 1978; Hogarty, 1984; Hogarty et al., 1979; Schooler et al., 1980).

The use of psychosocial treatment combined with maintenance chemotherapy can significantly forestall schizophrenic relapse in the first year following hospital discharge. Hogarty et al. (1986) demonstrated significant effects on relapse rates of family treatment (19% relapse) and social skills training (20%), and an additive effect for the combined psychosocial treatments (0%) relative to medication-only (41%).

Differential Outcome of Schizophrenic Subtypes

Premorbid and/or preepisodic adjustment has repeatedly been shown to relate to outcome in schizophrenia—the better the premorbid functioning, the better the outcome (e.g., Strauss, Kokes, Klorman, & Sacksteder, 1977). The majority of the data relating to premorbid functioning are based on retrospective analyses. In a prospective study in which outcome data were obtained 1 year after discharge, Gaebel and Pietzcker (1987) reported that outcome was related to continuous neuroleptic treatment, initial (preepisodic) level of work adjustment, and heterosexual adjustment.

Until recently, premorbid functioning was considered a better predictor of outcome than symptomatology. However, recent data have shown a relation between symptom severity and course (e.g., Harrow, Marengo, & McDonald, 1986; Marengo & Harrow, 1987) and, in particular, findings implicate negative symptoms in poor prognosis (e.g., Kay & Lindenmayer, 1987). However, the particular symptom constellation with which a patient presents cannot be considered totally independent of other factors. For example, while negative symptoms were once considered intractible to treatment, several investigators have reported data indicating responsivity of negative syndrome patients to neuroleptics (e.g., Goldberg, 1985). Breier et al. (1987) demonstrated that negative symptoms were significantly reduced by neuroleptic treatment and that negative and positive symptoms demonstrated similar patterns of reduction and exacerbation during neuroleptic treatment and withdrawal, respectively.

Family/Environmental Stressors

Schizophrenics may be particularly susceptible to the effects of psychosocial stressors. Socioenvironmental stressors may precipitate schizophrenic episodes, and such events tend to cluster in the 2 to 3 week period immediately preceding episode onset (e.g., Day et al., 1987). One of the most significant environmental factors that can influence schizophrenic patients is expressed emotion (EE). EE represents a range of overt family attitudes toward the patient, including criticism, hostility, dissatisfaction, and overinvolvement (Brown & Rutter, 1966). A series of investigations has demonstrated that patients discharged to high-EE families relapse more rapidly (50% or higher 9-month relapse rates) than do those residing with low-EE families (approximately 15% 9-month relapse rate) (Brown, Birley, & Wing, 1972; Vaughn & Leff, 1976; Vaughn, Snyder, Jones, Freeman, & Falloon, 1984). Also, a further aspect of the treatment outcome data presented by

Hogarty et al. (1986) relates to EE. All the patients in the Hogarty et al. study were residing in high-EE families at the outset of the investigation. There were no relapses of patients from any households that changed from high to low EE during the course of the investigation.

Differential Outcome for Male and Female Patients

Long-term course appears to be better for female patients (at least in terms of hospitalization data), who show a superior response to neuroleptics and improved residential status relative to males (Seeman, 1986). While these findings may relate to social considerations (e.g., women are more likely to possess basic housekeeping skills needed for survival and also pose less threat of violence to others), the fact that women also have a later age of onset than men suggests that there may be an intrinsic difference between the sexes as well (Kendell, 1988).

IMPAIRMENT AND COMPLICATIONS

As noted, schizophrenia is an extremely debilitating disorder and, by definition, involves significant impairment in role functioning. Many schizophrenics are unable to maintain meaningfully productive lives—they often live alone in supervised residential facilities and, if able to hold a job, are most commonly involved in menial tasks. Almost as if to add insult to injury, there are significant complications that can arise from somatic treatments for schizophrenia, ranging from mild drowsiness to occasional serious and irreversible effects (Simpson, Pi, & Sramek, 1981, 1984). In general, low-potency neuroleptics (e.g., chlorpromazine, thioridizine) tend to produce more sedation, cardiovascular changes, and anticholinergic effects, such as dry mouth, blurred vision, or constipation. High-potency neuroleptics (e.g., haloperidol, fluphenazine) result in more extrapyramidal side effects, such as muscle spasm, restlessness, and Parkinsonian symptoms (see Simpson & Pi, 1987, for a more detailed discussion of neuroleptic side effects). The risks of neuroleptic drugs can be compounded when they are prescribed in combination with other medications. Tune, Strauss, Lew, Breitlinger, and Coyle (1982) found an inverse correlation between memory performance and serum anticholinergic levels among 24 outpatient schizophrenics. All the patients were symptomatically stable and were taking at least the equivalent of 200 mg per day of chlorpromazine. Fifteen of the patients were also taking anticholinergic drugs as prescribed for the management of the extrapyramidal side effects associated with neuroleptic treatment. Schmidt et al. (1987) observed a 0.77% incidence rate of toxic delirium associated with low-potency neuroleptics; the risk associated with low-potency neuroleptics and anticholinertic antidepressants combined was 1.54%.

Tardive dyskinesia (TD) is a serious, late-onset, neurologic side effect of neuroleptic treatment. It consists of spontaneous irregular (nonrhythmical) movements primarily affecting the mouth and tongue, the fingers, and the arms and legs. Constant chewing movement, facial grimacing, pouting, puffing of the lips and cheeks, tongue protrusion, and abnormal trunk movements and rocking of the pelvis can occur (Simpson, Pi, & Sramek, 1982). Typically, symptoms of TD first appear or worsen when neuroleptic dose is reduced or the medication is discontinued. Prevalence rates ranging from 0.5% to 56% have been reported (Kane & Smith, 1982). The results of a recent prospective study suggest an incidence of 24% after 7 years of cumulative neuroleptic exposure (Kane et al., 1984). In a comparison of schizophrenics with and without TD, Wegner, Catalano, Gibralter, and Kane (1985) observed that TD patients have more neurologic soft signs, are more frequently rated as poor premorbid asocials, perform more poorly on psychometric testing, and have a higher familial loading for affective disorders in first-degree relatives. Control patients (i.e., non-TD) received neuroleptics for a longer period than did TD Ss. The authors speculate that these signs may represent evidence of an increased vulnerability to TD development, and in particular, that individuals evidencing early schizoid withdrawal may be at a higher risk for TD development.

Schizophrenics have been reported to be more likely to use psychoactive substances than other psychiatric patient groups and nonpatients. A recent review concluded that schizophrenics' use of amphetamines and cocaine, cannabis, hallucinogens, inhalants, caffeine, and tobacco was significantly greater than or equal to use by psychiatric controls or nonpatients (Schneier & Siris, 1987). A number of reports have established that short-term use of moderately large doses of stimulants can induce the development of acute psychoses (e.g., Angrist & Gershon, 1970; Bell, 1973; Griffith, Oates, & Cavanaugh, 1968), and, as noted, psychostimulant-induced psychotic reactions can

present a difficult differential vis-à-vis other psychotic diagnoses. Richard, Liskow, and Perry (1985) examined recent psychostimulant use in hospitalized schizophrenics. Findings indicated that relapsing schizophrenics utilized stimulants prior to hospitalization more often than nonschizophrenic patients and that outpatient antipsychotic prophylaxis did not prevent these relapses. The authors conclude that stimulants may partially contribute to relapse.

DIFFERENTIAL DIAGNOSIS

A number of disorders can present with symptoms that are similar, or even identical, to those that comprise schizophrenia. Accurate diagnosis is critical, as it dictates treatment. The DSM-III-R (APA, 1987), and other sources (e.g., Roth, 1986), place considerable emphasis on the differentiation between schizophrenia and organic mental disorders. As noted, DSM-III-R criteria specify that an organic factor cannot be identified as relating to the initiation or maintenance of the illness in order for a diagnosis of schizophrenia to be made. Organic delusion syndromes, such as those induced by amphetamines or phencyclidine, can be cross-sectionally identical in symptomatology to schizophrenia (APA, 1987). However, the presence of persistent disorientation, memory impairment, clouding of consciousness, progressive dementia, or delirious state suggests an organic syndrome (Roth, 1986). Among the organic syndromes that must be considered in the differential diagnosis of schizophrenia is anticholinergic delirium. The possibility of cognitive toxicity resulting from the anticholinergic effects of neuroleptic medications was previously mentioned.

One of the most difficult differentials to establish is that between schizophrenia and psychotic forms of mood disorder and schizoaffective disorder (Doran, Breier, & Roy, 1986), particularly during an isolated admission based only upon a cross-sectional evaluation (Deutsch & Davis, 1983). For several decades, data have documented changing proportions in the diagnoses of schizophrenia versus affective disorders in clinical settings. For example, Baldessarini (1970) noted an inverse relation between diagnostic rates of schizophrenia versus manic-depressive and schizoaffective illness over a 24-year period. A rise in one diagnosis was associated with a corresponding fall in the other. The introduction of antipsychotic medications coincided with an increased rate of schizophrenic diagnoses and a corresponding reduction in affective illness. A parallel but opposite trend was associated with the introduction of lithium treatment for bipolar illness. In a review of findings from 18 studies, Pope and Lipinski (1978) reported that 20% to 50% of patients with manic-depressive illness have symptoms that are considered to be important in the diagnosis of schizophrenia. However, evidence to support a distinction between schizophrenia and psychotic affective disorders has been reported. Winokur, Morrison, Clancy, and Crowe (1972) and Tsuang (1978) found greater morbid risk of affective disorder in the families of affectively disordered probands than in those of schizophrenic probands, and vice versa. Certain biologic variables have also been found to differ between schizophrenia and mania (e.g., Abrams & Taylor, 1979; Buchsbaum, 1978), as have behavioral ratings of thought disorder in recent studies based on DSM-III diagnostic criteria (Solovay, Shenton, & Holzman, 1987). DSM-III-R emphasizes temporal factors in the appearance of the schizophrenic syndrome and symptoms of mood disturbance in this differential (while acknowledging that mood disturbance is common during all three phases of schizophrenia). For example,

If the total duration of all episodes of a mood syndrome are brief relative to the duration of Schizophrenia (active and residual phases), then the mood disturbance is considered an associated feature of Schizophrenia, and no additional diagnosis need be made. If the total duration of the mood disturbance is not brief, then a diagnosis of schizophrenia is not made, and Schizoaffective Disorder and Mood Disorder with Psychotic Features must be considered. (APA, 1987, p. 192)

The differentiation between schizophrenia and schizoaffective disorder has traditionally been a controversy. This has partly been the result of the fact that some investigators have questioned the validity of the schizoaffective diagnosis (e.g., Pope, Lipinski, Cohen, & Axelrod, 1980). However, new research in schizoaffective disorder has led to refinement of schizoaffective diagnostic criteria (e.g., DSM-III had no specific criteria for schizoaffective disorder). It is thought that the new criteria, used in longitudinal studies, will help to specify better the differential diagnosis of these disorders. At present, DSM-III-R criteria relate to temporal factors regarding the appearance to psychotic versus affective symptoms. This can be difficult to determine accurately, as it must often be based on the patient's report/recall.

Schizophreniform disorder is also differentiated from schizophrenia in DSM-III-R on the basis of duration of symptoms. The duration of schizophreniform disorder is less than 6 months.

Other mental disorders listed in DSM-III-R to be considered in the differential diagnosis of schizophrenia are delusional disorder, autistic disorder, obsessive-compulsive disorder, factitious disorder with psychological symptoms, and certain personality disorders, including schizotypal, borderline, schizoid, and paranoid types.

CASE EXAMPLE

Michael W. is a 26-year-old white male, the youngest of four children born to Mr. and Mrs. W. During Michael's childhood and adolescence, the family lived in a comfortable home in a residential neighborhood outside of a large city. Mr. W. is an executive for a computer firm. Mrs. W. was at home during most of Michael's childhood; she is now an administrative assistant.

Michael is described by his mother as having been a "beautiful, happy child." He entered kindergarten at age 5 and had no difficulties; his teachers found him pleasant and cooperative. In first grade Michael began to have difficulties in school, falling behind with the introduction of reading instruction. He was evaluated and referred to a reading specialist for individual and group work. After a few years of supportive reading classes in the public school, it was recommended by the school child study team that Michael transfer to a private school for students with learning disabilities. At this point another set of intellectual and psychological assessments were administered, and Michael was found to be severely dyslexic but with an above-average IQ and not evidencing any behavioral or emotional problems. In the sixth grade, as recommended, he enrolled in a private school for students with learning disabilities and was quite successful academically and socially through eleventh grade.

In the summer between eleventh and twelfth grade, Michael began to withdraw from family and friends. His mother says he "pulled away"; he was not interested in activities that he had enjoyed previously, most notably soccer, swimming, and riding his bike. He missed many days of work at his part-time summer job because he didn't get up in time, and finally he lost the job. He didn't look for another job; he spent most of his time in his room watching TV. He stopped making plans with friends, and gradually they stopped calling.

He was no longer interested in family activities, often not even coming out of his room when relatives were visiting. His parents became concerned with the change in Michael and urged him to talk with someone. He finally agreed to talk with a friend of the family, a social worker, who tried to convince him to see a psychologist, but Michael refused.

When school resumed in the fall, he attended classes — although somewhat irregularly — for the first couple of months. He did not, however, participate in the activities that he had enjoyed in previous years, nor did he make plans with friends after school. He came home and went to his room. Gradually his attendance fell off until he was not attending school at all.

Repeated efforts by his parents to get him into treatment were unsuccessful, until one night Michael came to them crying, afraid that everyone in the house was going to leave. At that point he agreed to go to the Mental Health Crisis Unit.

In an interview with the Crisis Unit psychiatrist, Michael appeared at times sad, at other times puzzled at being at the unit. His speech was at times digressive and circumstantial. He expressed some vague concerns that old women talk about him and call him names when they see him. Michael did not admit to auditory or visual hallucinations or any interference in his thinking.

The psychiatrist recommended that Michael be admitted, but Michael did not want to stay, and his parents preferred to arrange for treatment on an outpatient basis. A referral was made, and Michael followed through with outpatient treatment (psychotherapy only, no medications) for most of the following year.

No real improvement was seen. Michael continued to be withdrawn; he did not return to school or find a job. His hygiene deteriorated — he stopped shaving and showered only after repeated reminders. He began to do odd things "for laughs," like putting cigarettes in his nose and ears. He occasionally would smile for no reason and at times would mumble to himself.

Again his parents tried to get him help. He missed several appointments with his therapist. Twice his mother took him to the hospital with the hope that he would sign himself in, but each time he refused. Finally, after Michael admitted to an intake interviewer that he was considering suicide, he was hospitalized involuntarily.

During the early part of the two-month hospitalization, Michael was disorganized in his speech and behavior, and he occasionally exhibited inappropriate affect, such as laughing when he talked about conflict with his sister. He again expressed ideas that old women were calling him names and berating him. During this time he believed it had something to do with the way he smelled. He reported hearing voices almost every day for the last several months. The voices were often "garbled nonsense" with several voices talking at the same time, but sometimes he could make out a male voice, making negative remarks such as "you jerk" or commenting on what he was doing. Although he had admitted to thoughts of suicide during the intake interview, throughout his hospitalization Michael denied being depressed. He did acknowledge that the voices "really got him down" at times.

Michael responded well to neuroleptic medication. The hallucinations and delusional thinking gradually diminished over the course of hospitalization. He became more logical and clear in his speech and behavior. Upon discharge Michael was described by his mother as better than he had been for years.

Within a month of his return home, Michael found a part-time job in the stock room of a large department store. He was reliable and capable in his work, and he got along well with his coworkers. He began to look for a place of his own, and with the help of a family friend found a room to rent. He followed through with his outpatient appointments and continued on the neuroleptic medication.

After about a year, Michael began missing appointments at the mental health center. He began spending more and more time at his parents' home, strenuously resisting returning to his own place after each visit. His work attendance became erratic, and he began to express delusional thoughts about his coworkers. His parents convinced him to go to the medical health center, and when he was evaluated there, his psychiatrist recommended hospitalization. Although he was initially very much opposed to returning to the hospital, Michael finally agreed.

Michael's symptoms at admission were many of the same he had experienced the year before; in addition, Michael currently believed that a number of the people at work were trying to get him out of the job because they thought he was the devil. His medication was adjusted over the early part of his hospitalization, and Michael responded well to an increased dose of neuroleptic medication. His hospital stay was a little over a month, and he was discharged much improved.

Michael did not return to his job in the stock room, but after a few months enrolled in Graduate Equivalency Degree classes. He successfully completed the classes and passed the test during the next year. He began to look for another job but had little success. His symptoms began to worsen. The voices became more frequent and more bothersome. He walked 5 miles to his parents' house and refused to return home or even go outside because he believed that cars were emitting microwaves that had control over his thoughts. His mother convinced Michael to admit himself to the hospital and she accompanied him to the emergency room.

Two more hospitalizations have followed; presenting symptoms and treatment course have been similar. The last hospitalization was more than two years ago, and Michael has consistently followed through with outpatient treatment. He is occasionally bothered by auditory hallucinations, but reports that they are "faint" now and he is usually able to ignore them. He is working part-time as a dishwasher in a restaurant; he hopes someday to be able to learn food preparation. He still rents a room and lives fairly independently. His mother comes over one or two times a week and helps out with cleaning and laundry, and he goes to his parents' house weekly for dinner.

CHILDHOOD AND FAMILIAL ANTECEDENTS

The most prominent strategy for research on childhood antecedents of adult schizophrenic disorders has been to study subjects who are at risk for the development of schizophrenia by virtue of having a (biologic) schizophrenic parent. These individuals have a 10% to 15% risk for adult schizophrenia, while children of two schizophrenic parents have a risk of 35% to 46% (Erlenmeyer-Kimling et al., 1982). One of the most promising vulnerability indicators among children at risk for schizophrenia is attentional functioning and information processing (Nuechterlein & Dawson, 1984). The results of laboratory investigations of attention and vigilance in particular have indicated either mean differences or deficits in a disproportionately large subgroup among children born to schizophrenic parents compared to normal comparison groups (e.g., Erlenmeyer-Kimling et al., 1984; Nuechterlein, 1983; Rutschmann, Cornblatt, & Erlenmeyer-Kimling, 1986). Neurological abnormalities have also been reported among at-risk children and include prob-

lems in motor coordination and perceptual-sensory functions (e.g., Marcus, Hans, Lewow, Wilkinson, & Burack, 1985).

As noted, premorbid social functioning is one of the best predictors of outcome in schizophrenia. There are considerable "follow-back" data, derived from examining the early school records of individuals who later developed schizophrenia, suggesting that many schizophrenics exhibited maladaptive patterns of interpersonal functioning beginning in early childhood (e.g., Lewine, Watt, & Fryer, 1978; Lewine, Watt, Prentky, & Fryer, 1980; Watt, 1978). Social isolation, aggressiveness, and emotional instability have been reported as common among children of a schizophrenic parent (e.g., Janes, Worland, Weeks, & Konen, 1984; John, Mednick, & Schulsinger, 1982; Watt, Grub, & Erlenmeyer-Kimling, 1982). Beckfield (1985) observed a number of anomalies in the interpersonal role play behavior of college males hypothesized to be at risk for schizophrenia based on the presence of schizotypal personality characteristics (Chapman, Chapman, Raulin, & Edell, 1978) in comparison to controls.

Cognitive and social dysfunctions have generally been considered as independent vulnerability factors for schizophrenia (e.g., Asarnow & Goldstein, 1986). However, increasing evidence has documented the role of cognitive/information processing deficits in the interpersonal dysfunction of adult schizophrenic patients (e.g., Morrison, Bellack, & Mueser, 1988), and it is possible that neurointegrative deficits play a role in the social deficits of children at risk for schizophrenia. One particularly relevant problem in information processing of adult schizophrenic patients may involve altered patterns of lateralization of brain functions (e.g., Magaro & Chamrad, 1983a, 1983b; Morrison et al., 1988). Recently, Hallett, Quinn, and Hewitt (1986) reported defective interhemispheric integration and anomalous language lateralization in children at risk for schizophrenia in comparison to matched controls. There have not been careful longitudinal considerations of cognitive deficits in at-risk samples. However, Parnas and Schulsinger (1986) recently reported on the continuity of measures of formal thought disorder from childhood to adulthood in the high-risk sample of Mednick and Schulsinger (1965). Findings indicate significant positive correlations between childhood and adult levels of thought disorder, suggesting that at least this aspect of schizophrenic "cognitive" symptomatology develops by gradual accretion. Further study is obviously needed to evaluate carefully the possibility that persistent neurointegrative deficits play a role in the social deficits of children at risk for schizophrenia and in the persistence of these deficits into adulthood.

A number of factors have been considered as possibly potentiating individual vulnerability. There is an increased prevalence of pregnancy/birth complications among schizophrenic mothers (as well as mothers with other severe psychiatric disturbances; McNeil & Kaij, 1984), and such complications have been considered as a possible contributor to schizophrenic outcome among children born to a schizophrenic mother (Parnas et al., 1982). Mednick, Parnas, and Schulsinger (1987) found that schizophrenics are more likely than individuals with schizotypal personality disorder to have experienced a high incidence of environmental trauma in the form of perinatal birth complications and institutional care. In relation to findings that schizotypals share with schizophrenics a comparable genetic predisposition for schizophrenia (e.g., Kendler, Gruenberg, & Strauss, 1981), the authors theorize that whether such predisposed individuals actually develop schizophrenia is affected by environmental factors. Further support for this diathesis-stress theorization is provided by data on family relationships prior to the onset of psychopathology in Mednick and Schulsinger's (1965) at-risk sample (Burman, Mednick, Machon, Parnas, & Schulsinger, 1987). Results demonstrated that the family relationships of high-risk offspring who later developed schizophrenia were perceived (by family members) as less satisfactory than were the family relationships of high-risk offspring who were later diagnosed as having schizotypal personality disorder or no mental illness.

While considerable attention has been directed toward the influence of familial EE and communication patterns on the course of an established schizophrenic illness, few additional studies of family circumstances that antedate the onset of an initial active phase of schizophrenia have been reported. Doane, West, Goldstein, Rodnick, and Jones (1981) observed that high-EE familial environments were predictive of later schizophrenic spectrum outcome among a sample of disturbed but nonpsychotic adolescents. Goldstein (1985) presented data from a 15-year follow-up of this disturbed adolescent sample and again found a significant relationship between deviant parental communication styles and the lifetime prevalence of schizophrenia-spectrum disorders.

SUMMARY

Schizophrenia is a complex, heterogeneous disorder. Empirical study of schizophrenia has been made difficult by this heterogeneity, changing operational defactions, and the low prevalence of the disorder, as well as reliance on cross-sectional research in this area. Perhaps the most pressing priority for future research is longitudinal study, especially regarding the mediating role of organic pathology and the interaction of organic and environmental factors in the mediation of the expression of behavioral psychopathology by which the disorder is diagnosed.

Schizophrenia has prominent childhood antecedents. The nature of these antecedents need to be better understood. Most clearly, social dysfunction and cognitive impairment can predate by many years the onset of diagnosable psychotic symptoms. The interrelation of social and cognitive impairment, and their influence on developmental outcome, must be more comprehensively addressed.

These issues must be considered relative to the heterogeneity of schizophrenia. Different childhood and familial antecedents may precede different subtypes of the disorder. As relationships among differing subsets of symptoms are elucidated, more sophisticated interventions aimed at particular symptom groups can be developed. New developments in genetics (e.g., Sherrington et al., 1988) may lead to more precise biochemical definitions of schizophrenia and accelerate the development of more effective medications ("Where next with psychiatric illness," 1988). However, the future will undoubtedly see increasingly well-coordinated applications of new somatic therapies in conjunction with psychosocial treatment. "Whatever the degree to which schizophrenia is genetically determined, treatment for the foreseeable future will remain a matter of blending the judicious use of drugs with other treatments that enable patients to more successfully live with their disabilities in the real world" (p. 96) ("Where next," 1988).

REFERENCES

Abrams, R., & Taylor, M. A. (1979). Differential EEG patterns in affective disorder and schizophrenia. *Archives of General Psychiatry, 36,* 1355–1358.

American Psychiatric Association. (1987). *Diag-*

nostic and statistical manual of mental disorders (3rd ed. rev.). Washington, DC: Author.

Andreasen, N. C. (1979). Affective flattening and the criteria for schizophrenia. *American Journal of Psychiatry, 136*, 944–946.

Andreasen, N. C. (1982). Negative symptoms in schizophrenia. *Archives of General Psychiatry, 39*, 784–788.

Andreasen, N. C., & Olsen, S. (1982). Negative vs. positive schizophrenia: Definition and validation. *Archives of General Psychiatry, 39*, 789–794.

Angrist, B. M., & Gershon, S. (1970). The phenomenology of experimentally induced amphetamine psychosis – Preliminary observations. *Biological Psychiatry, 2*, 95–107.

Asarnow, J. R., & Goldstein, M. J. (1986). Schizophrenia during adolescence and early adulthood: A developmental perspective on risk research. *Clinical Psychology Review, 6*, 211–235.

Babigan, H. M. (1975). Schizophrenia: Epidemiology. In A. M. Freedman, H. I. Kaplan, & B. J. Sadock (Eds.), *Comprehensive textbook of psychiatry*. Baltimore, MD: Williams & Wilkins.

Baldessarini, R. J. (1970). Frequency of diagnosis of schizophrenia vs affective psychoses from 1944–1968. *American Journal of Psychiatry, 127*, 759–763.

Beckfield, D. F. (1985). Interpersonal competence among college males hypothesized to be at risk for schizophrenia. *Journal of Abnormal Psychology, 94*, 397–404.

Bell, D. S. (1973). The experimental reproduction of amphetamine psychosis. *Archives of General Psychiatry, 29*, 35–40.

Bleuler, E. (1976). *Textbook of psychiatry* (A. A. Brill, trans.). New York: Arno Press. (Original work published in 1924)

Breier, A., Wolkowitz, O. M., Doran, A. R., Roy, A., Boronow, J., Hommer, D. W., & Pickar, D. (1987). Neuroleptic responsivity of negative and positive symptoms in schizophrenia. *American Journal of Psychiatry, 144*, 1549–1555.

Brown, G. W., Birley, J. L. T., & Wing, J. K. (1972). Influence of family life on the course of schizophrenic disorders: A replication. *British Journal of Psychiatry, 121*, 241–258.

Brown, G. W., & Rutter, M. (1966). The measurement of family activities and relationships: A methodological study. *Human Relations, 19*, 241–263.

Buchsbaum, M. S. (1978). The average evoked response technique in differentiation of bipolar, unipolar, and schizophrenic disorders. In H. S. Akiskal & W. L. Webb (Eds.), *Psychiatric diagnosis: Explorations of biological predictors* (Chap. 22). New York: Spectrum.

Burman, B., Mednick, S. A., Machon, R. A., Parnas, J., & Schulsinger, F. (1987). Children at high risk for schizophrenia: Parent and offspring perceptions of family relationships. *Journal of Abnormal Psychology, 96*, 364–366.

Carpenter, W. T., Heinrichs, D. W., & Alphs, L. D. (1985). Treatment of negative symptoms. *Schizophrenia Bulletin, 11*, 440–452.

Chapman, L. J., Chapman, J. P., Raulin, M. L., & Edell, W. S. (1978). Schizotype and thought disorder as a high risk approach to schizophrenia. In G. Serban (Ed.), *Cognitive defects in the development of mental illness* (pp. 351–360). New York: Brunner/Mazel.

Crow, T. J. (1985). The two-syndrome concept: Origins and current status. *Schizophrenia Bulletin, 11*, 471–486.

Davis, J. M. (1985). Maintenance therapy and the natural course of schizophrenia. *Journal of Clinical Psychiatry, 46*, 18–21.

Day, R., Nielson, J. A., Korten, A., Ernberg, G., Dube, K. C., Gerhart, J., Jablensky, A., Leon, C., Marsella, A., Olatawura, M., Sartorius, N., Stromgren, E., Takahashi, R., Wig, N., & Wynne, L. C. (1987). Stressful life events preceding the acute onset of schizophrenia: A cross-national study from the World Health Organization. *Culture, Medicine, and Psychiatry, 11*, 123–205.

Deutsch, S. I., & Davis, K. L. (1983). Schizophrenia: A review of diagnostic and biological issues. *Hospital and Community Psychiatry, 34*, 313–322.

Doane, J., West, K., Goldstein, M., Rodnick, E., & Jones, J. (1981). Parental communication deviance and affective style: Predictors of subsequent schizophrenia spectrum disorders in vulnerable adolescents. *Archives of General Psychiatry, 38*, 679–685.

Doran, A. R., Breier, A., & Roy, A. (1986). Differential diagnosis and diagnostic systems in schizophrenia. *The Psychiatric Clinics of North America, 9*, 17–34.

Eaton, W. W. (1986). The epidemiology of schizophrenia. In G. D. Burrows, T. R. Norman, & G. Rubinstein (Eds.), *Handbook of studies on schizophrenia: Part I. Epidemiology, aetiology and clinical features* (pp. 11–34). New York: Elsevier.

Erlenmeyer-Kimling, L., Cornblatt, B., Friedman, D., Marcuse, Y., Rutschmann, J., Simmens, S., & Devi, S. (1982). Neurological, electrophysiological and attentional deviations in children at risk for schizophrenia. In F. A. Henn & H. A. Nasrallah (Eds.), *Schizophrenia as a brain disease* (pp. 61–98). New York: Oxford University Press.

Erlenmeyer-Kimling, L., Marcuse, Y., Cornblatt, B., Friedman, D., Rainer, J. D., & Rutschmann, J. (1984). In N. F. Watt, E. J. Anthony, L. C. Wynne, & J. Rolf (Eds.), *Children at risk for schizophrenia: A longitudinal perspective.* New York: Cambridge University Press.

Falloon, I., Watt, D. C., & Shepperd, M. (1978). A comparative controlled trial of pimozide and fluphenazine decanoate in the continuation therapy of schizophrenia. *Psychological Medicine, 8,* 59–70.

Feighner, J. P., Robins, E., Guze, S. B., Woodruff, R. A., Winokur, G., & Munoz, R. (1972). Diagnostic criteria for use in psychiatric research. *Archives of General Psychiatry, 26,* 57–63.

Gaebel, W., & Pietzcker, A. (1987). Prospective study of course of illness in schizophrenia. *Schizophrenia Bulletin, 13,* 307–316.

Gjerde, P. F. (1983). Attentional capacity dysfunction and arousal in schizophrenia. *Psychological Bulletin, 93,* 57–72.

Goldberg, S. C. (1985). Negative and deficit symptoms in schizophrenia do respond to neuroleptics. *Schizophrenia Bulletin, 11,* 453–456.

Goldstein, M. J. (1985). Family factors that antedate the onset of schizophrenia and related disorders: The results of a fifteen year prospective longitudinal study. *Acta Psychiatrica Scandinavica, 71,* 7–18.

Gottesman, I. I., & Shields, J. (1982). *Schizophrenia: The epigenetic puzzle.* New York: Cambridge University Press.

Griffith, J. D., Oates, J., & Cavanaugh, J. (1968). Paranoid episodes induced by drugs. *Journal of the American Medical Association, 205,* 39–46.

Hailey, A. M., Hurry, L. J., Powell, M., Shannon, B., Wing, J. K., Wing, L. (Camberwell), Fryers, T., Newton, P., Sousa, R., & Woolff, K. (Salford) (1974). *Psychiatric services in Camberwell and Salford: Statistics from the Camberwell and Salford Registers, 1964–1973.* London: MRC Social Psychiatric Unit.

Hallett, S., Quinn, D., & Hewitt, J. (1986). Defective interhemispheric integration and anomalous language lateralization in children at risk for schizophrenia. *Journal of Nervous and Mental Disease, 174,* 418–427.

Harrow, M., Marengo, J., & McDonald, C. (1986). The early course of schizophrenic thought disorder. *Schizophrenia Bulletin, 12,* 208–224.

Helzer, J. E. (1988). Schizophrenia: Epidemiology. In R. Michels, J. O. Cavenar, Jr., A. M. Cooper, S. B. Guze, L. L. Judd, G. L. Klerman, & A. J. Solnit (Eds.), *Psychiatry.* New York: J. B. Lippincott.

Hogarty, G. E. (1984). Depot neuroleptics: The relevance of psycho-social factors. *Journal of Clinical Psychiatry, 45,* 36–42.

Hogarty, G. E., Anderson, C. M., Reiss, D. J., Kornblith, S. J., Greenwald, D. P., Javna, C. D., Madonia, M. J., & Environmental/Personal Indicators in the Course of Schizophrenia Research Group. (1986). Family psychoeducation, social skills training, and maintenance chemotherapy in the aftercare treatment of schizophrenia. *Archives of General Psychiatry, 43,* 633–642.

Hogarty, G. E., Schooler, N. R., Ulrich, R. F., Mussare, F., Herron, E., & Ferro, P. (1979). Fluphenazine and social therapy in the aftercare of schizophrenic patients: Relapse analyses of a two-year controlled study of fluphenazine decanoate and fluphenazine hydrochloride. *Archives of General Psychiatry, 36,* 1283–1294.

Janes, C. L., Worland, J., Weeks, D. G., & Konen, P. M. (1984). Interrelationships among possible predictors of schizophrenia. In N. F. Watt, E. J. Anthony, L. C. Wynne, & J. E. Rolf (Eds.), *Children at risk for schizophrenia: A longitudinal perspective* (pp. 160–166). New York: Cambridge University Press.

John, R. S., Mednick, S. A., & Schulsinger, F. (1982). Teacher reports as a predictor of schizophrenia and borderline schizophrenia: A Bayesian decision analysis. *Journal of Abnormal Psychology, 91,* 399–413.

Kane, J. M., & Smith, J. M. (1982). Tardive dyskinesia: Prevalence and risk factors. *Archives of General Psychiatry, 39,* 473–481.

Kane, J. M., Woerner, M., Weinhold, P., Wegner, J., Kinon, B., & Borenstein, M. (1984). Incidence of tardive dyskinesia: Five-year data from a prospective study. *Psychopharmacological Bulletin, 20,* 39–40.

Kay, S. R., & Lindenmayer, J. P. (1987). Outcome predictors in acute schizophrenia. Prospective significance of background and clinical dimensions. *The Journal of Nervous and Mental Disease, 175,* 152–160.

Kelleher, M. J., Copeland, J. R., & Smith, A. J. (1974). High first admission rates for schizophrenia in the west of Ireland. *Psychological Medicine, 4,* 460–462.

Kendell, R. E. (1988). Schizophrenia: Clinical features. In R. Michels, J. O. Cavenar, Jr., A. M. Cooper, S. B. Guze, L. L. Judd, G. L. Klerman, & A. J. Solnit (Eds.), *Psychiatry.* New York: J. B. Lippincott.

Kendler, K. S., Gruenberg, A. M., & Strauss, J. S. (1981). An independent analysis of the Copenhagen sample of the Danish Adoption Study of Schizophrenia. *Archives of General Psychiatry, 38,* 982–984.

Klerman, G. L. (1986). The National Institute of Mental Health — Epidemiologic Catchment Area (NIMH-ECA) program: Background, preliminary findings, and implications. *Journal of Social-Psychiatry, 21,* 159–166.

Lewine, R. R. J., Watt, N. F., & Fryer, J. H. (1978). A study of childhood social competence, adult premorbid competence, and psychiatric outcome in three schizophrenic subtypes. *Journal of Abnormal Psychology, 87,* 271–294.

Lewine, R. R. J., Watt, N. F., Prentky, R., & Fryer, J. H. (1980). Childhood social competence in functionally disordered psychiatric patients and in normals. *Journal of Abnormal Psychology, 89,* 132–138.

Ludwig, A. M. (1986). *Principles of clinical psychiatry.* New York: The Free Press.

Magaro, P. A., & Chamrad, D. L. (1983a). Information processing and lateralization in schizophrenia. *Biological Psychiatry, 18,* 29–44.

Magaro, P. A., & Chamrad, D. L. (1983b). Hemispheric preference of paranoid and nonparanoid schizophrenics. *Biological Psychiatry, 18,* 1269–1285.

Marcus, J., Hans, S., Lewow, E., Wilkinson, L., & Burack, C. (1985). Neurological findings in the offspring of schizophrenics: Childhood assessment and 5-year follow-up. *Schizophrenia Bulletin, 11,* 85–100.

Marengo, J. T., & Harrow, M. (1987). Schizophrenic thought disorder at follow-up: A persistent or episodic course? *Archives of General Psychiatry, 44,* 651–659.

Mednick, S. A., Parnas, J., & Schulsinger, F. (1987). The Copenhagen High-Risk Project, 1962–86. *Schizophrenia Bulletin, 13,* 485–495.

Mednick, S. A., & Schulsinger, F. (1965). A longitudinal study of children with a high-risk for schizophrenia: A preliminary report. In S. Vandenberg (Ed.), *Methods and goals in human behavior genetics* (pp. 401–429). New York: Academic Press.

McNeil, T. F., & Kaij, L. (1984). Offspring of women with nonorganic psychoses. In N. F. Watt, E. J. Anthony, L. C. Wynne, & J. E. Rolf (Eds.), *Children at risk for schizophrenia: A longitudinal perspective* (pp. 465–481). New York: Cambridge University Press.

Morrison, R. L., Bellack, A. S., & Mueser, K. T. (1988). Facial affect recognition deficits and schizophrenia. *Schizophrenia Bulletin, 14,* 67–83.

Neale, J. M., Oltmanns, T. F., & Harvey, P. D. (1985). The need to relate cognitive deficits to specific behavioral referents of schizophrenia. *Schizophrenia Bulletin, 11,* 286–291.

Nuechterlein, K. H. (1983). Signal detection in vigilance tasks and behavioral attributes among offspring of schizophrenic mothers and among hyperactive children. *Journal of Abnormal Psychiatry, 92,* 4–28.

Nuechterlein, K. H., & Dawson, M. E. (1984). Information processing and attentional functioning in the developmental course of schizophrenic disorders. *Schizophrenia Bulletin, 10,* 160–202.

Parnas, J., & Schulsinger, H. (1986). Continuity of formal thought disorder from childhood to adulthood in a high-risk sample. *Acta Psychiatrica Scandinavica, 74,* 246–251.

Parnas, J., Schulsinger, F., Teasdale, T. W., Schulsinger, H., Feldman, P. M., & Mednick, S. A. (1982). Perinatal complications and clinical outcome within the schizophrenia spectrum. *British Journal of Psychiatry, 140,* 416–420.

Pope, H. G., & Lipinski, J. F. (1978). Diagnosis in schizophrenia and manic-depressive illness: A reassessment of the specificity of "schizophrenic" symptoms in the light of current research. *Archives of General Psychiatry, 35,* 811–828.

Pope, H. G., Lipinski, J. F., Cohen, B. M., & Axelrod, D. T. (1980). "Schizoaffective disorder": An invalid diagnosis? A comparison of schizoaffective disorder, schizophrenia, and affective disorder. *American Journal of Psychiatry, 137,* 921–927.

Richard, M. L., Liskow, B. I., & Perry, P. J. (1985). Recent psychostimulant use in hospitalized schizophrenics. *Journal of Clinical Psychiatry, 46,* 79–83.

Rieder, R. O., Donnelly, E. F., Herdt, J. R., & Waldman, I. N. (1979). Sulcal prominence in young chronic schizophrenic patients: CT scan findings associated with impairment on neuropsychological tests. *Psychiatry Research, 1*, 1–8.

Roth, M. (1986). Diagnosis and prognosis of schizophrenia. In G. D. Burrows, T. R. Norman, & G. Rubinstein (Eds.), *Handbook of studies on schizophrenia: Part 1. Epidemiology, aetiology and clinical features.* New York: Elsevier.

Rutschmann, J., Cornblatt, B., & Erlenmeyer-Kimling, L. (1986). Sustained attention in children at risk for schizophrenia: Findings with two visual continuous performance tests in a new sample. *Journal of Abnormal Child Psychology, 14*, 365–385.

Schmidt, L. G., Grohmann, R., Strauss, A., Spiess-Kiefer, C., Lindmeier, D., & Muller-Oerlinghausen, B. (1987). Epidemiology of toxic delirium due to psychotropic drugs in psychiatric hospitals. *Comprehensive Psychiatry, 28*, 242–249.

Schneier, F. R., & Siris, S. G. (1987). A review of psychoactive substance use and abuse in schizophrenia. Patterns of drug choice. *The Journal of Nervous and Mental Disease, 175*, 641–652.

Schooler, N. R., Levine, J., Severe, J. B., Brauzer, B., DiMascio, A., Klerman, G. L., & Tuason, V. B. (1980). Prevention of relapse in schizophrenia: An evaluation of fluphenazine decanoate. *Archives of General Psychiatry, 37*, 16–24.

Seeman, M. V. (1986). Current outcome in schizophrenia: Women vs men. *Acta Psychiatrica Scandinavica, 73*, 609–617.

Sherrington, R., Brynjolfsson, J., Petursson, H., Potter, M., Dudleston, K., Barraclough, B., Wasmuth, J., Dobbs, M., & Gurling, H. (1988). Localization of a susceptibility locus for schizophrenia on chromosome 5. *Nature, 336*, 164–167.

Simpson, G. M., & Pi, E. H. (1987). Issues in pharmacological treatment. In R. L. Morrison & A. S. Bellack (Eds.), *Medical factors and psychological disorders: A handbook for psychologists* (pp. 19–40). New York: Plenum Press.

Simpson, G. M., Pi, E. H., & Sramek, J. J. (1981). Adverse effects of antipsychotic agents. *Drugs, 21*, 138–151.

Simpson, G. M., Pi, E. H., & Sramek, J. J. (1982). Management of tardive dyskinesia: Current update. *Drugs, 23*, 381–383.

Simpson, G. M., Pi, E. H., & Sramek, J. J. (1984).

Neuroleptics and antipsychotics. In M. N. G. Dukes (Ed.), *Meyler's side effects of drugs* (10th ed.). Amsterdam: Elsevier Science Publishing.

Solovay, M. R., Shenton, M. E., & Holzman, P. S. (1987). Comparative studies of thought disorders. *Archives of General Psychiatry, 44*, 13–20.

Spitzer, R. L., Endicott, J., & Robins, E. (1978). *Research Diagnostic Criteria (RDC) for a selected group of functional disorders* (3rd ed.). New York: Biometrics Research, New York State Psychiatric Institute.

Strauss, J. S., Carpenter, W. T., Jr., & Bartko, J. J. (1974). The diagnosis and understanding of schizophrenia: III. Speculations on the processes that underlie schizophrenic symptoms and signs. *Schizophrenia Bulletin, 11*, 61–69.

Strauss, J. S., Kokes, R. F., Klorman, R., & Sacksteder, J. L. (1977). Premorbid adjustment in schizophrenia: Concepts, measures, and implications: I. The concept of premorbid adjustment. *Schizophrenia Bulletin, 3*, 182–185.

Torrey, E. F. (1987). Prevalence studies in schizophrenia. *British Journal of Psychiatry, 150*, 598–608.

Tsuang, M. T. (1978). Familial subtyping of schizophrenia and affective disorder. In R. Spitzer & D. Klein (Eds.), *Critical issues in psychiatric diagnosis* (pp. 203–211). New York: Raven Press.

Tune, L. E., Strauss, M. E., Lew, M. F., Breitlinger, E., & Coyle, J. T. (1982). Serum levels of anticholinergic drugs and impaired recent memory in chronic schizophrenic patients. *American Journal of Psychiatry, 139*, 1460–1462.

Vaughn, C. E., & Leff, J. P. (1976). The influence of family and social factors on the course of psychiatric illness: A comparison of schizophrenic and depressed neurotic patients. *British Journal of Psychiatry, 129*, 125–137.

Vaughn, C. E., Snyder, K. S., Jones, S., Freeman, W. B., & Falloon, I. R. H. (1984). Family factors in schizophrenic relapse: Replication in California of British research on expressed emotion. *Archives of General Psychiatry, 41*, 1169–1177.

Walsh, D. (1969). Mental illness in Dublin—First admissions. *British Journal of Psychiatry, 115*, 449–456.

Watt, C. G. (1978). Patterns of childhood social development in adult schizophrenics. *Archives of General Psychiatry, 35*, 160–170.

Watt, N. F., Grubb, T. W., & Erlenmayer-Kimling, L. (1982). Social emotional, and intellectual behavior at school among children at high risk for schizophrenia. *Journal of Consulting and Clinical Psychology, 50*, 171–181.

Wegner, J. T., Catalano, F., Gibralter, J., & Kane, J. M. (1985). Schizophrenics with tardive dyskinesia. *Archives of General Psychiatry, 42*, 860–865.

Where next with psychiatric illness? (1988, November). *Nature, 336*, 95–96.

Winokur, G., Morrison, J., Clancy, J., & Crowe R. (1972). The Iowa 500. *Archives of General Psychiatry, 27*, 462–464.

SEPARATION ANXIETY DISORDER AND AGORAPHOBIA

EDITORS' COMMENTS

Although it is a theoretically compelling argument that separation anxiety in childhood and disruptions in personal relationships are antecedents to agoraphobia in adulthood, the extant literature provides at best minimal confirmation of this link, and that primarily for females. Despite the fact that there is some evidence that agoraphobia and panic attacks may be preceded by life stressors, the longitudinal link from childhood to adulthood has not been established. Unfortunately, studies tend to be of a retrospective nature, and the obviously needed long-term investigations considering the possible developmental features of agoraphobia simply have not been carried out.

In further considering the possible relationship of separation anxiety disorder and agoraphobia, Ollendick and Huntzinger have identified four types of studies that have examined the issues. The first concerns the efficacy of tricyclic drugs with school phobic children. The second deals with family concordance for separation anxiety and agoraphobia. The third looks at the histories of agoraphobics, with special emphasis on separation anxiety in childhood. And the fourth details the outcome of children who have received separation anxiety diagnoses.

Although there is some evidence showing that tricyclic medication (specifically imipramine) is effective in the treatment of separation anxiety in children and agoraphobia in adults, the point is well taken by Ollendick and Huntzinger that in both such children and adults, about half also evinced depressive symptomatology. It is not clear, then, whether the effect of the drug was with respect to the depressive or anxious features of the patients. Thus, the link may be more in terms of affective disorder and the efficacy of imipramine rather than with anxiety. Furthermore, even if there were additional studies showing comparable efficacy in separation anxiety disordered children and adult agoraphobics, such demonstration would only represent indirect evidence of continuity. Imipramine has been shown to be effective for a wide range of childhood and adult disorders, and thus, positive treatment response for these two different disorders does not necessarily mean that they are related.

As for the family concordance studies conducted to date, there is minimal evidence confirming increased incidence of separation anxiety disorder in children of adult agoraphobics. Conversely, if there were a direct link between separation anxiety disorder and agoraphobia, one would expect that parents of children would evince an exceptionally high rate of agoraphobia. Data adduced at this point indicate a high rate of anxiety disorders in the parents of children with separation anxiety but not agoraphobia in particular (only 5% in one study).

Early history of separation anxiety in adult agoraphobics would represent strong evidence of a link between childhood and adult psychopathology. However, all the studies conducted have been of a retrospective nature and, unfortunately, with diagnoses (with the exception of one study) not determined on the basis of DSM-III criteria.

The fourth type of study that examines the long-term outcome of separation anxiety disordered children, through young adulthood and adulthood, simply has not been carried out. Such a study, of course, would represent a massive undertaking, requiring many years to complete and huge expenditures of staff time and money, but it certainly would yield much more conclusive evidence than currently is available.

When making the differential diagnosis of separation anxiety disorder in children, the possible overlaps are with avoidant disorder, overanxious disorder, and simple phobia. Anxiety is a central feature in all the anxiety disorders, but in separation anxiety disorder, the focus on anxiety is situation specific. This is similar to simple phobia, but in simple phobia the diagnosis is made if avoidance involves anything other than being alone, away from home, or social embarrassment.

Complicating the diagnostic appraisal is the fact that many children suffering from separation anxiety disorder are also school phobic. Indeed, some investigators have argued for a separate diagnostic entity of school phobia, since separation anxiety is not the only etiological factor in that disorder. Yet an additional problem in making the differential diagnosis is the difficulty of separating anxiety disorder from depression. In this instance it becomes important to differentiate which is the primary diagnosis, because the treatment implications may differ.

Differential diagnosis of agoraphobia in adulthood is not terribly difficult, given the central feature of spontaneous panic attacks and marked behavioral avoidance. However, there is overlap with other psychiatric conditions, such as aspects of obsessive-compulsive disorder, certain social phobias, and generalized anxiety disorder. In addition, some medical disorders (vestibular, cerebral traumas, colitis, esophageal spasms, focal neurological symptoms) may lead the patient to develop a restrictive, agoraphobic life-style, due to embarrassment. Finally, ingestion of drugs (e.g., cocaine, marijuana) may precipitate panic attacks similar to those noted in agoraphobia. However, careful clinical assessment of medical complications usually results in a correct diagnostic appraisal.

In children and adults diagnosed as separation anxiety disordered and agoraphobic, respectively, the impact on their lives can be considerable. In the more extreme forms of the child and adult disorders, their lives often are circumscribed and fraught with anxiety and negative anticipation. Whereas the agoraphobic may become homebound, the child with separation anxiety is likely to suffer from school phobia and other fears about leaving home, such as dealing with neighborhood children. It is understandable why links between the child and adult disorders have been posited, given some of the obvious descriptive similarities. However, in the absence of careful empirical study on a prospective basis, these will remain as unconfirmed, albeit shrewd, notions.

CHAPTER 9

SEPARATION ANXIETY DISORDER IN CHILDHOOD

Thomas H. Ollendick
Rose M. Huntzinger

DESCRIPTION OF THE DISORDER

Although significant effort has been directed toward the description, assessment, and treatment of anxiety disorders in adults, anxiety disorders in children have not, until recently, received comparable attention. Historically, this absence of systematic research with children has resulted from a lack of consensus on how to classify childhood disorders, the unavailability of reliable assessment devices, and the belief by numerous psychopathologists that childhood disorders should be conceptualized merely as downward extensions of adult problems (Achenbach, 1974). However, in recent years, a series of advances occurred that has resulted in the burgeoning of research in this area: (1) the specification of particular disorders and criteria for children and adolescents in the third edition of the *Diagnostic and Statistical Manual of Mental Disorders* and its recent revision (American Psychiatric Association, 1980, 1987), (2) the development of symptom-oriented interview schedules (e.g., the Anxiety Disorders Inventory for Children: Silverman & Nelles, 1988) and reliable self-report instruments (e.g., the Fear Survey Schedule for Children — Revised: Ollendick, 1983), and (3) the acknowledgment of important developmental issues in child psychopathology (Sroufe & Rutter, 1984).

The primary purpose of the present chapter is to provide an overview of one of the recently specified childhood problems — separation anxiety disorder (SAD). Issues related to its description, epidemiology, and differential diagnosis will be presented, and its relationship to panic disorder with agoraphobia in adulthood will be explored.

Unfortunately, an examination of the literature reveals that separation anxiety has been conceptualized historically in ways other than as a specific childhood disorder. For example, the term "separation anxiety" has been used as a developmental concept denoting an adaptive and appropriate response in infants (i.e., "normal" fear). It also has been used as a label reflecting general pathological reactions to separation in older children. To add further to the confusion, "separation anxiety" has been used interchangeably with the term "school phobia." To understand separation anxiety as a disorder, it is necessary first to review these alternative definitions and to introduce the theoretical issues that have contributed to the complexity of the problem.

According to Gittelman and Klein (1985), separation anxiety is one aspect of a complex behavioral system in which a child becomes attached and bonded to a significant other. As such attachment develops, infants begin to avoid strangers and seek comfort and protection from their primary attachment figure, usually the mother. Simultaneously, they begin to display apprehension in the face of anticipated separations from this primary figure and distress in the event of actual separation. In this context, separation anxiety refers to infant protest at the mother's departure, distress caused by her absence, and anxiety about her anticipated absence (Bowlby, 1973). The term also includes a number of behaviors, such as crying, clinging, and searching, which are emitted to prevent separation or restore contact. Thus, separation anxiety can be viewed as a universal developmental phenomenon that is observed after the age of 6 to 8 months and persists in varying degrees until 2 to 3 years of age (Ainsworth, Blehar, Waters, & Wall, 1978).

Bowlby (1973) notes that infants who have experienced sensitive, responsive, and available mothering quickly develop a sense of security and trust and are less likely to become upset by subsequent separations. On the other hand, infants who have experienced a relationship with an unpredictable, unavailable, unresponsive, or rejecting mother are more insecure, prone to more intense upset at separation, and/or experience chronic anxiety about the attachment figure. This suggests that distress reactions to separation that are evident in early development might persist or reemerge later. Indeed, Gittelman and Klein (1985) have indicated that overt behavioral distress and misery during anticipated or real separation from a primary attachment figure and mental preoccupations and worries concerning harm befalling the attachment figure have been observed clinically in some children and adolescents. The term "separation anxiety" has been used to label these reactions in older children.

Complicating matters has been the relationship between separation anxiety and school phobia. The term "school phobia" was introduced in the clinical literature in 1941 by Johnson and her colleagues (Johnson, Falstein, Szurek, & Svendsen, 1941). The label was used to denote a syndrome of childhood characterized by marked anxiety about attending school and absenteeism. It was thought that fear of leaving the mother or home rather

than fear of school per se precipitated the syndrome. Early psychodynamic accounts contributed to this conclusion.

Specifically, school-phobic children were said to be obsessed by thoughts of harm or death to their mothers, which could be alleviated only by finding ways to return or stay home from school. Mothers, in turn, were thought to support the children's fears unconsciously by viewing school as impersonal and unpleasant, and communicating a wish for the children to remain at home. Thus, fear of school represented a form of displacement of anxiety from its real source (separation from mother) to a more palatable source (the school) and was thought to be produced by an unresolved mother-child dependency relationship (Yates, 1970).

Estes, Haylett, and Johnson (1956) later applied the term "separation anxiety" to this school-related problem. It was argued that this label would reflect more accurately the focus of pathology from the psychodynamic perspective. As a result, the terms "school phobia" and "separation anxiety" were used synonymously. From another theoretical perspective, however, such equivalence need not be assumed. For example, from a behavioral point of view, children may be viewed as having a phobic reaction to some aspect of the school environment itself (Ollendick & Mayer, 1984). In this instance, school phobia and separation anxiety may be viewed as distinct problems and not necessarily interrelated.

Recently, it has been suggested that school phobia and separation anxiety should be regarded as clinical entities in their own right. Further, there has been a call for the development of agreed-upon criteria for diagnosis and treatment that does not prejudge etiology (Ollendick & Mayer, 1984). For example, Berg, Nichols, and Pritchard (1969) have recommended that school phobia be specified objectively as involving severe difficulties attending school, which often results in prolonged absences, severe emotional upset when faced with prospects of going to school (e.g., excessive fearfulness, temper outburst, or complaints of feeling ill), staying at home from school with the knowledge of parents, and absence of antisocial characteristics (e.g., stealing, lying, or destructiveness). Using these criteria, it can be seen that school phobia need not be associated with separation anxiety. Indeed, school phobia can result from a multitude of causes, only one of which might be separation anxiety.

To summarize, separation anxiety has a number

of definitions and theoretical underpinnings in the professional clinical literature. The term has been used as a developmental construct, a pathological syndrome, a synonym for school phobia, and a distinct clinical disorder. It is the intent in the remainder of this chapter to focus on a discussion of separation anxiety disorder as a clinical disorder.

There is somewhat more formal agreement regarding separation anxiety as a clinical entity. The DSM-III and its revision have identified a separation anxiety disorder in which the essential feature is excessive anxiety concerning separation from a major attachment figure and/or the home. Nine descriptive symptoms (three of which must be met to receive a diagnosis) are enumerated in this classification schema, and efforts have been made to avoid statements regarding etiology. The criteria for separation anxiety disorder are presented in Table 9.1 (APA, 1987).

These formal characteristics represent the best description of the disorder available at this time, but they are not without controversy. Some problems are immediately evident. For example, SAD is characterized by excessive distress upon separation from major attachment figures. The disorder is said to emerge before the individual is 18 years of age, and the reaction must be beyond that expected for the child's developmental level. This latter requirement implies that at some age the essential features of the disorder might be considered "normal." Yet, as we have noted, for most children separation anxiety as a developmental phenomenon is usually mild, transient, and of little particular concern. Moreover, the diagnostic manuals do not specify how clinicians and researchers should make decisions regarding "excessiveness beyond developmental expectations." Although we might suppose that this phrase means beyond that time at which normal children display "separation anxiety" (i.e., 2 to 3 years of age), this is not at all clear. For instance, should a 4-year-old who displays problems in separation be diagnosed as SAD? The only guideline provided by DSM-III-R is that the "age at onset may be as early as preschool age; by definition, it is before the age 18" (APA, 1987, p. 59). Greater clarification on these issues would be helpful.

Still another problem involves the nature of the nine symptoms presented in Table 9.1. Interestingly, among these nine criteria, there appears to be an inherent or rational grouping of the symptoms. For example, the first, second, and sixth criteria seem to emphasize subjective worries or

internal, subjective factors. The seventh criterion focuses on somatic complaints, while the remaining criteria reflect overt behaviors, particularly distress, reluctance, or avoidance in specific separation situations. Since only three of these symptoms must be met to receive a diagnosis, it is apparent that many combinations of symptoms are possible. Thus, a diagnosis of SAD might be made when criteria from only one symptom-type are present (e.g., just "subjective" or just "behavioral"), or when all the symptoms are different in nature. This, in turn, suggests that SAD might be a heterogeneous phenomenon, with different patterns of symptomatology. Thus, although specific criteria are provided, the clinical picture may vary considerably. It is to this issue that we now turn our attention.

CLINICAL PRESENTATION

The essential feature of SAD is excessive anxiety when faced with separation from persons to whom the child is attached. Such anxiety can be manifested in a number of ways. These children frequently have exaggerated and unrealistic worries that they will be separated from major attachment figures (e.g., harm will come to their parent or themselves, their parents will leave and never return). As such, they may express persistent reluctance or refusal to sleep alone or go to school in order to remain with major attachment figures. In fact, such children often avoid being left alone at home and complain of physical distress on school days (e.g., stomachaches, nausea, headaches). Such excessive anxiety, which may reach panic proportions, is evident even when the child merely considers or anticipates separation. Additionally, social withdrawal, depression, or problems concentrating may result when these children are not with major attachment figures. These disturbances may occur in children as young as preschool age and are equally common in both sexes. The duration of the difficulties must be at least two weeks in order to warrant a DSM-III-R diagnosis of SAD. The magnitude of the disorder can range from relatively mild (e.g., the child expresses some anxiety and reluctance to separate from parents but can function adequately in novel situations) to quite severe (e.g., the child panics at the very thought of separation from parents and refuses to attend school or to remain at home alone).

Children who present with SAD may also report a host of fears, including animals, monsters,

Table 9.1. Diagnostic Criteria for Separation Anxiety Disorder

(A) Excessive anxiety concerning separation from those to whom the child is attached, as evidenced by at least three of the following:

　　1.　Unrealistic and persistent worry about possible harm befalling major attachment figures or fear that they will leave and not return

　　2.　Unrealistic and persistent worry that an untoward calamitous event will separate the child from a major attachment figure (e.g., the child will be lost, kidnapped, killed, or be the victim or an accident)

　　3.　Persistent reluctance or refusal to go to school in order to stay with major attachment figures or at home

　　4.　Persistent reluctance or refusal to go to sleep without being near a major attachment figure or to go to sleep away from home

　　5.　Persistent avoidance of being alone, including "clinging" to and "shadowing" major attachment figures

　　6.　Repeated nightmares involving the theme of separation

　　7.　Complaints of physical symptoms (e.g., headaches, stomachaches, nausea, or vomiting, on many school days or on other occasions when anticipating separation from major attachment figures)

　　8.　Recurrent signs or complaints of excessive distress in anticipation of separation from home or major attachment figures (e.g., temper tantrums or crying, pleading with parents not to leave)

　　9.　Recurrent signs of complaints of excessive distress when separated from home or major attachment figures (e.g., wants to return home, needs to call parents when they are absent or when child is away from home)

B.　Duration of disturbance of at least two weeks.

C.　Onset before the age of 18.

D.　Occurrence not exclusively during the course of a pervasive developmental disorder, schizophrenia, or any other psychotic disorder.

Reprinted with permission from the *Diagnostic and Statistical Manual of Mental Disorders. Third Edition, Revised.* Copyright 1987 American Psychiatric Association.

and situations that are perceived as dangerous to the welfare of themselves (i.e., bodily injury fear) or their caregivers. Consequently, they frequently fear muggers, burglars, kidnappers, car accidents, or plane travel. Concern about death and dying may be evident, as are sleep problems. These children often have difficulty going to sleep and may insist that someone stay with them until they fall asleep. Frequently, parents indicate a host of nighttime problems, including reports of scary monsters, trips to the bathroom, and refusal to go to bed. At times, parents wake up to find their child in their bed or asleep outside their door. Nightmares are common.

To date, only one study has examined the distribution of the nine symptoms of SAD in a clinical population. Francis, Last, and Strauss (1987) divided 45 children with SAD into groups according to gender and chronological age (5 to 8 years representing a young group, 9 to 12 years a middle group, and 13 to 16 years an adolescent group). The nine symptoms of the disorder were treated as dichotomous variables, which were judged to be either present to a clinically significant degree or absent.

While the percentage of males and females meeting each diagnostic criterion did not differ

significantly, a number of age-related differences were found. For example, the most prevalent symptom varied across the three age groups: "worry about harm befalling an attachment figure" for young children (85%), "excessive distress upon separation" for the middle group (79%), and "physical complaints on school days" for adolescents (100%).

The most frequently coexisting symptoms also were somewhat different for each age group. A pattern of worries about harm befalling the attachment figure and school refusal was identified in young children. Symptoms indicating excessive distress upon separation and associated feelings of sadness and withdrawal when separated were found among the middle children. Adolescents were more likely to present with both physical complaints and school refusal.

Because this is only a single, cross-sectional study, the implications of the Francis, Last, and Strauss work must be viewed with caution. However, the initial evidence suggests that different patterns of symptoms might exist in SAD, and that these patterns appear to change with age. Anecdotally, we have observed similar patterns in our clinical work; school refusal appears more evident in our younger and older clients, with depressed moods and social withdrawal more evident in our middle age-group clients.

EPIDEMIOLOGY

A number of researchers have asserted that it is quite common for children to display multiple mild fears and anxieties (e.g., Jersild & Homes, 1935; Lapouse & Monk, 1959; Agras, Sylvester, & Oliveau, 1969; Werry & Quay, 1971; Richman, Stevenson, & Graham, 1975; Earls, 1980; Abe & Masui, 1981). For example, in the now classic epidemiological study by Lapouse and Monk (1959), 43% of a randomly selected sample of children between the ages of 6 and 12 were found to evince seven or more fears and worries, as reported by their mothers. In a subsequent study (Abe & Masui, 1981), 11- to 12-year-old boys and girls completed a self-report questionnaire that evaluated physiological symptoms, physical and social fears, and worries. Up to 43% of the sample expressed some fears, while another 33% endorsed numerous worries. More recently, Ollendick and his colleagues have reported similar findings, with boys and girls of differing ages and living in different countries (Ollendick, 1983; Ollendick, Matson, & Helsel, 1985; Ollendick, King, & Frary, 1989).

Excessive fears and phobias in children, on the other hand, are viewed as problematic and indicative of more severe psychopathology. Marks (1969) originally characterized excessive fears and phobias as being out of proportion to the demands of the situation, not easily explained or reasoned away, beyond voluntary control, and as leading to avoidance of the feared situation. Miller, Barrett, and Hampe (1974) further refined this description to include the criteria that such fears and phobias persist over an extended period of time, are unadaptive, and are not age- or stage-specific. Thus, while mild fears may be adaptive, appropriate, and transitory responses to threat, excessive fears and phobias are inappropriate, unrealistic, and persistent. Available evidence suggests that excessive fears and phobias are less common than "normal" fears, but that they are present in 3% to 8% of the child population (Graziano, Mooney, Huber, & Ignasiak, 1979; Ollendick, 1979).

This distinction between "normal" and "excessive" fears has important implications for the present discussion of separation anxiety disorder. When conceptualized as a disorder, it constitutes a clinical entity with its own diagnostic criteria, associated features, and course. Unfortunately, prevalence studies of SAD in the normal population have not yet been undertaken. However, several studies have examined the prevalence of school phobia. (We recognize that there will be a margin of error involved in reviewing these studies, since all school-phobic youngsters are not diagnosed as SAD).

The prevalence of school phobia depends to a large extent on the explicit criteria used to define it. By using the criteria of Berg et al. (1969), the incidence of school phobia is generally considered small but nonetheless significant. Kennedy (1965) has estimated the incidence of school phobia to be 1.7% of school-aged children, while Kahn and Nursten (1962) estimated it to be between 5% and 8%. However, the accuracy of these estimates is unknown due to unclear or nonexacting definitions of school phobia. Nonetheless, Eisenberg (1958) had reported that children with school phobia were being referred for psychiatric services with increasing frequency. In a survey of admissions to his clinic, the incidence was noted to have risen from 3 cases per 1,000 to 17 cases per 1,000 over an 8-year period. These rates appear to be supported by other workers, who have reported that the incidence rate of school phobia for psychiatrically referred youngsters has increased and ranges from about 1% (Chazan, 1962) to 3.8% (Smith, 1970).

Even though school phobia does not occur frequently in the general population and accounts for only 1% to 4% of psychiatric referrals, its clinical significance is affirmed by its frequent representation in the professional literature. In this regard, Graziano and DeGiovanni (1979) reviewed behavioral studies on all childhood fears published since 1924. Somewhat surprisingly, they found that 86% of these case studies addressed school phobia. Clearly, school phobia is of clinical interest.

While boys outnumber girls for most types of child behavior disorders (Ollendick & Hersen, 1983; Quay & Werry, 1979; Ross, 1980), school phobia tends to be equally common in both sexes (e.g., Berg et al., 1969; Johnson, 1979; Kennedy, 1965). The phobia most often originates during the elementary school years and has an acute onset. Occasionally, however, it does occur during the secondary years; if so, it is typically accompanied by associated difficulties centering on family conflict and, possibly, truancy. Generally, school phobia is thought to occur most frequently between 5 and 6 and 10 and 11 years of age.

Finally, while it might be expected that school phobia would appear more often in children of lower intellectual ability or those who show "learning disabilities," this has not been found to be so. In fact, children of high, intermediate, and low intelligence have been found to be equally represented, although any one study may report disproportionate frequencies. Similarly, so-called "learning-disabled" children are not disproportionately represented. As noted by Davids (1973), "it is not the child who is destined to school failure who seems to acquire school phobia, but rather the child who is sufficiently intelligent to do good work but who is unable to do so because of the unbearable anxiety engendered by the school setting" (p. 139).

In summary, school phobia occurs in a small portion of the general population; yet, it is disproportionately represented in psychiatric referrals for fear-related difficulties. It appears to occur primarily in younger children and to be evident in both boys and girls. Children of varying levels of intelligence and diverse levels of academic achievement are equally represented. Just how representative these findings are for SAD is currently unknown.

Only one clinical study (Last, Hersen, Kazdin, Finkelstein, & Strauss, 1987) provides some evidence of the prevalence of SAD in a clinical setting. Over an 18-month period, 91 children between the ages of 5 and 18 referred to a child and adolescent anxiety disorders clinic were evaluated for the co-occurrence of anxiety problems. A reliable, semistructured psychiatric interview (Interview Schedule for Children [Kovacs, 1978]) was used to assign diagnoses.

Overall, a majority (76%) of the total sample met criteria for either SAD alone, overanxious disorder alone (OAD, a childhood disorder in which anxiety is generalized to a variety of situations), or both SAD and OAD. Interestingly, the number of children within each of these three categories was distributed rather evenly. Twenty-four percent of the total sample received a diagnosis of just SAD, whereas 23% received a diagnosis of SAD plus OAD, suggesting that this disorder occurs frequently among clinically referred anxious children. These referral rates for SAD in specialized clinics approximate those obtained with school phobia. However, we must quickly remind the reader that SAD and school phobia are distinct disorders and that they need not necessarily occur together (Last, Francis, Hersen, Kazdin, & Strauss, 1987; Ollendick & Mayer, 1984).

NATURAL HISTORY

Although DSM-III-R asserts that there are times of exacerbation and remission "over a period of several years" (APA, 1987, p. 60), there are little or no empirical data to affirm this assertion. As far as we know, there are no studies that have tracked the natural course of this disorder when left untreated. As a result, we know little about what happens to these children over time. One distinct possibility is that such children simply "outgrow" the disorder and develop into healthy functioning adolescents and adults. This possibility seems less probable, however, based on long-term follow-up studies of children treated for school phobia or school refusal (at least some of whom might now be diagnosed as SAD). As we shall see later, a significant proportion of these children continue to display problems into adulthood. Obviously, this is an area in need of concerted research attention.

IMPAIRMENT AND COMPLICATIONS

Last and her research group have also examined the age, sex, race, and socioeconomic status of the children referred to their clinic. A number of significant differences have been found among the three previously mentioned anxiety categories in terms of demographic characteristics (Last, Hersen, Kazdin, Finkelstein, & Strauss, 1987). In particular, the SAD and combined groups were found to be younger than the OAD group, with the SAD group containing the highest percentage of children under the age of 13. The SAD and combined groups tended to have more girls than boys, while the OAD group had equal numbers of each sex. Based on the Hollingshead Four-Factor Index, families of SAD children received significantly lower socioeconomic ratings than did OAD families, and virtually all the children across the three categories were white.

A similar pattern of demographic characteristics was found in a second study by Last, Francis, Hersen, Kazdin, and Strauss (1987). Children with SAD were compared to a group of children who manifested a phobic disorder of school. Those with SAD consisted of young, prepubertal females from lower socioeconomic levels. Most school-phobic children, on the other hand, were postpubertal adolescent males whose families received middle to upper socioeconomic ratings. Thus, it appears that the typical clinically referred child with SAD is a young white girl, under the age of 13, from a lower-class family, at least at this clinic.

A consistent finding among clinical samples of children is that many of the specific disorders coexist; that is, it often is possible to assign more than one diagnosis to a single case. In addition to the descriptive data, these studies provide some interesting evidence regarding the presence of other anxiety disorders with SAD. For example, in the first study reported earlier (Last, Hersen, Kazdin, Finkelstein, & Strauss, 1987), it was found that a significant number (23%) of the clinically referred sample of anxious children received diagnoses of both SAD and OAD. As noted by the researchers, this combined group was slightly older than the SAD group but was significantly younger than the OAD children, thus raising the possibility that SAD may be a risk factor for OAD. It also is noteworthy that among the young children with SAD, only a single case out of 22 met the criteria for any other anxiety disorder (i.e., an avoidant disorder diagnosis). On the other hand, problems such as simple phobia and panic disorder were identified in over half of the older OAD children. This disparity in concurrent diagnosis suggests that SAD in young children may be a relatively circumscribed anxiety problem.

Finally, since a number of investigations have indicated that adults with anxiety disorders often present with a coexisting affective disorder (e.g., Barlow, 1985), the comorbidity between SAD and affective disorders in children has been examined. In the investigations conducted by Last and her colleagues, one-third of the children with SAD also received a diagnosis of major depression. This finding was not significantly different, however, from the rate of affective disorders among children with OAD alone, both SAD and OAD, or school phobia.

To summarize, it appears that SAD is a common diagnosis among children referred for anxiety problems. The expression of the disorder, both in terms of the most prevalent symptom and the patterns of coexisting symptoms, appears to vary with age. As for descriptive characteristics, children with SAD as compared to some other anxiety disorder tend to be white, prepubertal females from lower socioeconomic levels. While an additional diagnosis of OAD seems to occur frequently with SAD, other anxiety disorders have not been found to coexist with it. Finally, as has been indicated in the adult literature, a significant percentage of children with SAD manifest a con-current affective disorder, usually major depression.

It is essential to note that these findings are limited in their generalizability. First, the data were obtained from only two studies, all completed by the same research group. Second, as observed by these investigators themselves, the analyses of the characteristics, symptom expression, and co-morbidity of SAD were completed on clinical referrals to an outpatient anxiety clinic. It is necessary, therefore, to obtain information from other samples. For example, it would be useful to examine the presence of SAD in the general population of referred children, many of whom are referred for other forms of psychopathology.

It also would be useful to assess the frequency and intensity of separation anxiety symptoms in a normative sample of children (Francis et al., 1987). As noted, the presence of only three clinically significant symptoms is required for a diagnosis of SAD. However, it is not known whether the symptoms occur "normally" in the general, nonreferred population of children. If most young children display a comparable number of symptoms, it might be necessary to modify the requirements for diagnosis.

In addition to the generalizability concern, many other issues remain regarding the nature of SAD. For example, the preliminary finding that there are coexisting SAD symptom patterns that differ across age groups (Francis et al., in press) suggests that there may be subtypes of SAD, perhaps related to development or maturation. A more sophisticated examination of the heterogeneity of the disorder (e.g., employing factor-analytic techniques), and the use of longitudinal rather than cross-sectional designs seem warranted.

DIFFERENTIAL DIAGNOSIS

In our clinical experience, the most difficult diagnostic decisions are related to differentiating separation anxiety disorder from the other anxiety disorders of childhood or adolescence and the anxiety disorders in adulthood. Briefly, DSM-III-R recognizes three distinct types of anxiety disorders of childhood: separation anxiety disorder, avoidant disorder, and overanxious disorder. While anxiety is the predominant clinical feature of each, the focus of anxiety is said to be situation-specific in separation anxiety and avoidant disorders, but generalized to various situations in the overanxious disorder. In addition, DSM-III-R recognizes phobic disorders in which anxiety is also the predominant feature. According to DSM-III-R, the essential features of phobic disorders are the same in children and adults; thus, no special subcategories for children are provided.

Phobic Disorders

The essential feature of phobic disorders is irrational and persistent fear of a specific object or situation coupled with the overwhelming desire to avoid contact with the phobic stimulus. Generally, the individual recognizes that the fear is excessive given the actual threat of the object or situation. The avoidance behavior can be quite disruptive and distressing to the individual, as it may interfere with social functioning. Phobic disorders are divided into three types: agoraphobia (see Chapter 10), social phobia (see Chapter 11), and simple phobia (see Chapter 13). According to DSM-III-R, the age of onset of agoraphobia typically is not until the late teens or early twenties. The phobias most likely to occur in childhood are social phobias and simple phobias. With social phobias, the persistent fear and avoidance behavior revolve around situations in which the individual is exposed to the scrutiny of others and fears he or she may behave in a humiliating or embarrassing manner. Examples of social phobias include fear of public speaking, eating in public places, or using public lavatories. This disorder often emerges in late childhood or early adolescence (Francis & Ollendick, in press).

A diagnosis of simple phobia is made when the persistent irrational fear and avoidance behavior is of something other than being alone, being away from home, or embarrassment in social situations. Instead, the phobic stimuli in simple phobias include such stimuli as animals, closed spaces, or heights. While the age of onset of most phobias varies, animal phobias are said to begin nearly always in childhood (Ollendick & Francis, 1988).

Avoidant Disorder

The essential features of the avoidant disorder are persistent and excessive avoidance of contact with strangers sufficiently severe to disrupt social functioning, coupled with an expressed desire for social acceptance. Such children tend to have satisfactory interpersonal relationships with family members but not with their peers. They tend to be shy, timid, and easily embarrassed and may feel isolated and depressed. As such, these children avoid interacting with their peers even though they seem interested in forming social relationships. In order to warrant a DSM-III-R diagnosis of avoidant disorder, such problems must be evident for at least six months. Presently, no information is available on the sex ratio of the disorder.

Overanxious Disorder

The essential feature of the overanxious disorder (see Chapter 17) is excessive worrying that is not situation-specific but rather is generalized to a variety of situations and not related to any recent identifiable stress. These children often worry about the future and are preoccupied with the appropriateness of their own past behavior. They are overly concerned with what others may think of their behavior and are in need of constant reassurance. Such children also complain of physical distress (e.g., dizziness, shortness of breath, headaches) and are self-conscious and embarrassed easily. As such, they present persistent anxiety and/or an inability to relax. Given the numerous somatic complaints of these children, they often undergo unnecessary medical evaluations. At present, there is no information concerning the age of onset of this disorder, but generally it is equally common in males and females (Last, Hersen, Kazdin, Finkelstein, & Strauss, 1987). These difficulties must be apparent for at least six months in order to warrant a DSM-III-R diagnosis of overanxious disorder.

As was evident in our earlier section on impairment and complications, the differential diagnosis of SAD is not an easy task. There is considerable comorbidity among the anxiety and affective disorders of childhood, just as there is in adulthood. Nonetheless, it is clear that SAD can be diagnosed reliably, especially when using highly structured diagnostic interview schedules (Silverman & Nelles, 1988).

CASE EXAMPLE

Lacy, an 8-year old, white female, in the third grade of a local elementary school, was brought to our clinic by her parents for a psychological evaluation. Presenting complaints centered on three problematic areas: (1) Lacy's concern that her mother might be injured and possibly die, (2) nighttime problems characterized by refusal to go to and sleep in her own bed, and (3) statements from Lacy that "Maybe I just don't belong on this earth." These problems were reported to have begun approximately seven months prior to her first appointment. At that time, Lacy's mother had back surgery. The surgery occurred in early July, with Lacy's fears about her mother's health preceding surgery by about three weeks. These worries continued to mount over the summer months but did not reach a point where they kept Lacy homebound or continually at her mother's side. In fact, she was able to attend a church summer camp (first week in August) and spend the night with friends periodically throughout the remainder of the summer. The worries were expressed primarily through excessive questions about mother's health, statements about her own health, and seeking reassurance from her mother (and occasionally her father) that it was okay for her to be away from home.

With the beginning of the third grade, her problems began to worsen, as she expressed continual concern about "being away from mother all day." Lacy reported that she was afraid something might happen to her mother and that no one would be there to help her. Lacy's father worked an early-morning shift (6:00 a.m. to 2:00 p.m.) and her only sister (Tammy, age 19) worked during the day as well (8:00 a.m. to 3:00 p.m.). Due to travel requirements, her father left home about 5:00 a.m. and returned about 3:30 p.m. Her sister left home for work about 7:15 a.m., whereas Lacy left for school at 7:45 a.m. Lacy was the last member of her family to leave the home. Her mother, due to complications with the back surgery, remained at home and was temporarily unemployed. Prior to surgery, she worked as a receptionist at a local medical clinic.

Lacy never became school avoidant, possibly because both parents insisted that she go to school each day. The parents did report, however, that she frequently complained of headaches and stomachaches on school days and that, on at least four occasions, she had been allowed to stay home from school due to reported illness. Throughout this time period, she continued to excel in school (A's and B's) and to have several friends. Teachers reported her to be well-liked, a class leader, hard-working, and a good student.

Around the third week of the school term, she began to express increasing concern about sleeping in her own bedroom (her bedroom was upstairs, across the hall from her sister's; her parents' bedroom was downstairs on the first floor). She complained about having nightmares and being frightened by "zombies" who came into her room.

Over the course of the next three months, the nightmare problems increased to the point where she was either sleeping in her parents' room or outside their door. In addition, she exhibited a number of avoidant behaviors, including arguing about bedtime, refusing to go to bed, getting out of bed, calling out once in bed, and making numerous requests (e.g., drink of water, go to the bathroom). Also, she became more "clinging" to her mother, wanting to be near her after school until bedtime. Further, she stopped spending weekend nights at her friends and did not invite any of her friends to stay with her. She continued to go to school, however, and did well academically. Her mother started back to work on a part-time basis at this time.

About four weeks before her first appointment (February), Lacy began to make disparaging statements about herself and seemed to be "sad and unhappy." At this time, her father reported first hearing the statement, "Maybe I just don't belong on this earth." Both parents reported similar depressive statements over the ensuing weeks. Although they felt that Lacy would "outgrow" her worries about her mother's health and the nighttime fears, they were greatly concerned by her verbal statements and sullen appearance. Referral was made at that time, upon recommendation of the family physician.

During the initial interview, conducted with her parents present, Lacy appeared more anxious than depressed. She fidgeted in her chair, clasped and unclasped her hands, swung her feet, bit her lips, and stammered as she spoke. She reported being "very afraid" that her mother "might get sick again," even though at this time her mother had returned to work on a part-time basis. She wondered aloud, "Who will take care of her . . . Daddy is always at work and Sissy is at work too, you know." Regarding her nighttime fears, she indicated that the zombies were real ("I really saw them! They were real!") and that they might kill her. She stated further that a boy had told her that "nightmares can cause you to be frightened to death." Presumably, linking this thought with her overarching concerns about her mother's well-being, she was convinced that she would die and "no one would be there to help Mommy." As for her depressive and suicidal-like thoughts, she stated in a rather straightforward way, "I can't be happy . . . I used to be . . . but not now . . . even my friends don't like me now."

Based on this initial interview and the reported chronology of events, it was hypothesized that

Lacy's primary problem centered on separation anxiety. She had exaggerated and unrealistic worries that harm would come to her mother and/or herself and that she would be separated from her mother. She complained of physical distress upon leaving for school, was reluctant to have friends over or to stay with friends, and refused to sleep alone. Further, social withdrawal and depression were evident. In brief, she showed signs of the nine major criteria for SAD.

During the second session, the Anxiety Disorders Inventory for Children (Silverman & Nelles, 1988) was administered. It confirmed the impression of SAD, as well as accompanying major depression. Other anxiety disorders, such as avoidant disorder and overanxious disorders, were ruled out by the presence of good friendships at school and on weekends, and the specific focus of the separation anxiety concerns. She did have additional phobias, but these all seemed related to nighttime fears and being left alone.

Results of psychometric assessment supported this picture (see Table 9.2). Lacy completed the Revised Children's Manifest Anxiety Scale (Reynolds & Richmond, 1979), the Fear Survey Schedule for Children—Revised (Ollendick, 1983), and the Children's Depression Inventory (Kovacs, 1978). On the RCMAS, she received a score of 18, well above the mean for her age. Among her endorsements were "Often I feel sick in my stomach," "I have bad dreams," "I wake up scared some of the time," "I worry when I go to bed at night," and "It is hard for me to get to sleep at night." Similarly, she scored above age and gender norms on the FSSC-R. She obtained a total score of 168 and endorsed 26 fears ("a lot"). Among the specific fears were "Ghosts or spooky things," "getting lost in a strange place," "a burglar breaking into our house," "the sight of blood,"

"cemeteries," "nightmares," "going to bed in the dark," "being alone," "dark places," and "having my parents argue." Similarly, on the CDI, she obtained an elevated score of 16; again, this score was well above the average for her age and gender. Items such as "I am sad many times," "I do not like myself," "I have trouble sleeping every night," and "I think about killing myself, but would not do it" were endorsed. Importantly, she also reported that "I have fun in many things," "I have fun at school many times," and "I have plenty of friends." Finally, on the Revised Behavior Problem Checklist (Quay & Peterson, 1983), both parents rated her high on the anxiety-withdrawal factor (scores of 15 and 12). Other factor scores, except the one for motor excess, were within normal limits. Clearly, these self-report and other report instruments confirmed the overall picture of Lacy as having separation anxiety to a significant degree.

Based on our assessment, we decided to address her nighttime fears directly. This decision was based on the relationship of these fears to the separation problems and our previous experience that children generally respond favorably to the available treatment procedures for nighttime fears. A procedure based on the work of Graziano and Mooney (1980, 1982) was used. Initially, relaxation training and self-instruction training were implemented over six sessions. Response to these procedures was slow and only partially effective. Lacy continued to report considerable "state" anxiety about sleeping in her own bed and to average only two nights a week sleeping in her own room throughout this phase of treatment. Accordingly, a reinforcement component was added. Within three weeks, Lacy was sleeping in her own bed seven nights a week and reporting much less anxiety. Nightmares desisted and she started, once again, to have friends spend the night with her. In addition, four weekly sessions served to bolster these effects. A total of 13 weekly treatment sessions was conducted. Follow-up sessions at one month and six months posttreatment were provided to monitor these gains and to conduct posttreatment assessment. Significant reductions in anxiety (8), fear (134), and depression (9) were noted (see Table 9.1). Further, although both mother and father continued to view Lacy as somewhat anxious (anxiety-withdrawal scores of 8 and 7, respectively), her scores were significantly below those reported at pretreatment. Finally, at follow-up, she was sleeping in her own bed seven nights a week, reporting no nightmares, no longer

Table 9.2. Lacy's Pretreatment and Posttreatment Scores

MEASURE	PRE	POST
Revised Children's Manifest Anxiety Scale	18	8
Fear Survey Schedule for Children—Revised		
Total score	168	134
Severe fears	26	16
Children's Depression Inventory	16	9
Revised Behavior Problem Checklist		
Anxiety-withdrawal (mother)	15	8
Anxiety-withdrawal (father)	12	7

expressing concern about her mother's or her own well-being, and expressing positive statements about herself. Throughout treatment, her father and sister continued to work their regular schedules; as previously noted, her mother worked on a part-time basis as well.

Overall, this case nicely illustrates the complexity of SAD, as well as its assessment and treatment. Multimodal assessment was undertaken, and treatment, based on this assessment, was implemented. Follow-up of a more extended duration is currently underway.

CONTINUITY AND DISCONTINUITY WITH ADULT PRESENTATION

As mentioned in the introduction to this chapter, the notion of continuity of psychopathology from childhood to adulthood is a source of considerable controversy in the field of clinical child psychology. Nowhere is this issue more prominent than with SAD. Thus, in this section we will review this controversy by presenting the evidence for such a relationship.

Contemporary psychiatric and psychological literature often contains the hypothesis that adult agoraphobia and panic disorder are related closely to childhood anxiety (Casat, 1988; Gittelman & Klein, 1985; Thyer, Neese, Cameron, & Curtis, 1985; Thyer, Neese, Curtis, & Cameron, 1986; Thyer & Sowers-Hoag, 1988). Indeed, the DSM-III and its revision explicitly state that SAD may predispose individuals to these adult anxiety disorders. This assertion seems to have originated in psychodynamic and developmental theory.

From the psychodynamic perspective, Greenson (1959) characterized agoraphobic persons as those who have been separated from a love object. Subsequently, they suffer the loss of their own internal object and ego functions, resulting in panic. Rhead (1969) also suggested that agoraphobia occurs because individuals fail to achieve "separation individuation" out of their original symbiotic ties with their mothers.

Bowlby (1973), on the other hand, proposed that agoraphobic persons are sensitized to "overattachment" because actual separation or threats of abandonment by caretakers during development disrupt normal mother-infant bonding. Like Bowlby, Klein (1981) viewed the panic and dependent behavior of agoraphobia as a maladaptive outbreak of "separation anxiety," an innate biological mechanism that controls attachment behavior between a mother and child.

Unfortunately, there has been more theoretical speculation regarding the relationship between childhood anxiety disorders and adult anxiety disorders than empirical evidence. Not surprisingly, the diagnostic manuals have been criticized for violating their own rule of remaining atheoretical.

Research examining the relationship between SAD and adult panic disorder or agoraphobia has been of four types: (1) response of children with school phobia to tricyclic medications, (2) family concordance for separation anxiety and agoraphobia, (3) history of childhood separation anxiety in agoraphobic or panic disordered adults, and (4) outcome of children with separation anxiety.

Separation Anxiety and Tricyclic Medications

The positive effect of imipramine in adult agoraphobia and panic disorders is reasonably well established (Gittelman & Klein, 1984; Gittelman & Klein, 1985). It has been proposed that if separation anxiety and these adult disorders represent variants of the same pathology, a similar response to medications should be evident in children with SAD.

Only a few placebo-controlled studies of tricyclic antidepressant medications in children have been reported (Gittelman-Klein & Klein, 1973, 1980; Berney et al., 1981). In the typical study, children with school phobia are administered either imipramine or placebo. Children's self-reports of "feeling better," number of physical complaints on school days, and responses to separation as reported by mothers are assessed over a period of time. Gittelman-Klein and Klein (1973, 1980) reported significant improvement for the imipramine group: 90% of the drug-treated children reported feeling much better, compared with 24% of those on placebo. Further, 81% were attending school regularly compared with 47% for the placebo group. Berney et al. (1981), however, found no differences between clomipramine treatment and a placebo in a 12-week trial.

Gittelman and Klein (1985) have dismissed the failed trial, arguing that the dosage levels of clomipramine were too low in the Berney et al. study (the dose range was 40–70 mg/day, a level earlier reported by Gittelman and Klein to be ineffective). Thus, on the basis of one reasonably well-controlled study, Gittelman and Klein tentatively concluded that the response of separation-anxious children to imipramine treatment was similar to that of agoraphobic adults. The implication of this conclusion is that children improve for the same reasons adults do and that the effect of the drug is on the underlying nature of the anxiety disorders. Consequently, it is assumed that continuity exists between SAD and agoraphobia.

However, this research can be criticized on a number of grounds, including the assumption that school phobia is equivalent to SAD (Gittelman and Klein do acknowledge that all school phobics do *not* necessarily have separation anxiety) and the less than rigorous methods used to assess improvement (self-report, parent report). Of greater significance is the overlooked finding that as many as one-half of both children and adults with anxiety disorders simultaneously manifest major depression (e.g., Last, Strauss, & Francis, 1987). Response to the medication by children and adults, therefore, could have more to do with the effects of imipramine on depressive symptoms than with the fact that the children and adults each qualified for an anxiety disorder. Certainly, investigations controlling for presence of depressive symptoms with SAD and agoraphobia should be undertaken before firm conclusions can be drawn from this line of research.

Family Concordance

Another group of studies has examined the extent of family concordance for separation anxiety and agoraphobia or panic disorder. Two types of findings might be expected in family concordance research. First, if there is a relationship between childhood separation anxiety and adult agoraphobia, an increase of the childhood condition should be present in children of agoraphobic parents (Gittelman & Klein, 1985). To date, three investigations have provided marginal support for this hypothesis.

Berg (1976), for example, used an extensive questionnaire to inquire about the presence of school refusal and difficulties with separation in the children of a nationwide sample of British agoraphobic women. The overall incidence of school phobia in these children (who ranged in age from 7 to 15 years) was 7% (boys 5%, girls 9%). Interestingly, more of the school-phobic youngsters were of secondary school age than primary school age, with the highest incidence at age 12. Unfortunately, the significance of these findings in comparison to the general population cannot be determined because neither a group of normal women and their children nor a group of psychiatric comparison women and their children was included. Furthermore, school phobia was assumed to have been present when mothers answered "yes" to the question: "Has the child ever completely refused to go to school for longer than one or two days since starting Junior School at 7?" Quite obviously, an exacting definition of school phobia was not used.

The second study provided a somewhat more sophisticated evaluation of this hypothesis. Weissman, Leckman, Merikangas, Gammon, and Prusoff (1984) assessed the presence of a number of DSM-III diagnoses, including SAD in 6- to 18-year-old children of depressed (major depression) and normal adults. The depressed adults were diagnosed using a structured diagnostic interview and placed into one of four distinct clinical groups: with agoraphobia, with panic disorder, with generalized anxiety disorder, and without any anxiety disorder at any time in their adult life. Information on the children was obtained from medical records, parents, and other relative reports if they were available during an interview. Children were not interviewed directly, and a "best estimate" diagnosis was made. It was reported that SAD occurred in 37% of the children whose parents had depression *and* panic, 11% of the children whose parents had depression and agoraphobia, 6% of the children whose parents had depression and generalized anxiety disorder, and 0% of the children whose parents were pure depressives or had no disorders.

The two major limitations of this study are that the adults were diagnosed as having both depression *and* an anxiety disorder and that a direct evaluation of the children was not obtained. Adult patients with anxiety disorders alone were not included; thus, a clear relationship between SAD and agoraphobia and panic disorder, though suggested, was not established. Further, we are uncertain of the bias of parents and relatives in providing evidence for the "best estimate" diagnoses.

Recently, Turner, Beidel, and Costello (1987) reported on 16 children who were the offspring of a parent with an anxiety disorder (agoraphobia or obsessive-compulsive disorder), 14 who were the offspring of a parent with dysthymic disorder, and 13 who were the offspring of a parent with no identified psychiatric disorder. All parents were diagnosed with a structured psychiatric interview (Anxiety Disorders Interview Schedule [DiNardo, O'Brien, Barlow, Waddell, & Blanchard, 1983]), as were the children (Child Assessment Schedule [Hodges, McKnew, Cytryn, Stern, & Kline,

1982]). Seven of the 16 offspring (44%) of anxiety disorder patients met diagnostic criteria for a psychiatric disorder: separation anxiety (4), overanxious disorder (2), and dysthymic disorder (1). In comparison, 3 of the 14 offspring (21%) of dysthymic disorders met diagnostic criteria: separation anxiety (1), overanxious disorder (1), and social phobia (1). Only one of the normal-parent offspring (9%) met diagnostic criteria (overanxious disorder). Quite obviously, the children of anxiety disordered patients were at increased risk for having an anxiety disorder themselves. These children were more than seven times as likely to be diagnosed with an anxiety disorder than were the offspring of normal parents and twice as likely than the offspring of dysthymic patients.

A second finding that might be expected in family concordance research is that parents of children with SAD should display greater frequency of panic disorder or agoraphobia than parents of other children. Again, only a few studies have examined this possibility specifically.

Berg, Butler, and Pritchard (1974) assessed the rates of psychiatric illness in mothers of school-phobic adolescents and a comparison group of nonschool-phobic psychiatric patients. The overall incidence of psychiatric disorder in parents was 22%; however, the rates did not differ between the two comparison groups.

Last and her colleagues examined lifetime rates of psychiatric illness in mothers of control children and children with a variety of anxiety disorders. One study (Last, Francis, Hersen, Kazdin, & Strauss, 1987) determined the rates of anxiety and affective disorders for mothers of children with school phobia versus SAD, while a second study (Last, Hersen, Kazdin, Francis, & Grubb, 1987) examined the presence of similar disorders in the mothers of children with SAD alone, OAD alone, and SAD plus OAD. All subjects were interviewed independently and diagnoses were based on DSM-III criteria.

The majority of the mothers in each of the anxiety groups had a lifetime history of at least one anxiety disorder: separation anxiety mothers (68%), overanxious disorder mothers (86%), and the combined group (94%). In contrast, control group mothers had a 40% rate. Within the separation anxious group, the most common adult disorder was generalized anxiety disorder (47%) followed by simple phobia (16%), panic disorder (5%), and agoraphobia (5%). Thus, even though the lifetime rates were unusually high, panic disorder and agoraphobia were not represented as

much as DSM-III-R and the continuity hypothesis would suggest.

Taken together, the family concordance studies do not provide strong support for the relationship between SAD and adult agoraphobia or panic disorder. The early research did not assess SAD per se in children, and in one instance, the adult anxiety diagnoses were confounded by the presence of major depression. When a relationship was found between SAD and adult anxiety disorders, the specific type of adult disorder was not the one specified by the DSM-III.

Early History of Separation Anxiety

Separation anxiety should be a more common feature in the early histories of adults with panic or agoraphobic disorders than in those of other patients (Gittelman & Klein, 1985). Analyses of the psychiatric histories of adults with these disorders constitute the most frequently used method for assessing continuity.

Results have been mixed. In an original study by Klein (1964), half of a small sample of agoraphobic inpatients reported marked separation anxiety in childhood. Importantly, this developmental pattern apparently was specific to this patient group and was not found in patients diagnosed with schizophrenia, affective, or character disorders.

Gittelman and Klein (1985) compared adult patients with agoraphobia or simple phobia. Clinical assessments of childhood and adolescent separation anxiety were made by a senior psychologist during the course of the diagnostic process. Results indicated that female agoraphobics had experienced significantly more separation anxiety as youngsters than patients with simple phobia.

A number of other studies have failed to identify separation anxiety as a unique historical feature of either agoraphobia or panic disorder. For example, Berg, Butler, and Pritchard (1974) assessed the presence of school phobia (i.e., school refusal) in a large group of agoraphobics and in a smaller comparison group of "neurotics." About one fourth of each group evidenced a history of school refusal. It was concluded, therefore, that separation anxiety is related to subsequent neuroticism, but not specifically to agoraphobia.

Raskin, Peeke, Dickman, and Pinskee (1982) obtained the developmental and psychiatric histories of small samples of subjects with either panic disorder or generalized anxiety disorder. No significant differences were found between these groups with regard to the incidence of early physical separations from parents or the presence of SAD (determined if subjects reported DSM-III criteria as present in childhood).

Finally, Thyer and his colleagues assessed the historical presence of separation anxiety in a sample of agoraphobics (Thyer et al., 1985) and a sample of patients with panic disorder (Thyer et al., 1986). In each case, simple phobics served as a comparison group. All patients completed a brief questionnaire consisting of 14 items about childhood and adolescent separation experiences. The items were drawn from a review of the literature on the developmental precursors of agoraphobia and panic disorder. Subjects rated each question on a five-point scale, with higher scores indicating presence of the anxiety factor to a greater extent. Agoraphobics and simple phobics did not differ on their mean ratings for any of the items. Subjects with panic disorder differed from phobics on only two items.

Overall, six studies have examined the presence of SAD in the developmental and psychiatric histories of adults with agoraphobia or panic disorder. All these investigations have been retrospective in nature, and only one (Raskin et al., 1982) has actually assessed the presence of SAD as defined by the DSM-III. Although far from conclusive, the majority of these studies suggest that separation anxiety disorder is not a selective precursor to either agoraphobia or panic disorder.

Outcome Studies

In a final type of research, it is suggested that if SAD is a predisposing factor for agoraphobia and panic disorder, children with that disorder will be at greater risk for agoraphobia and panic disorder in adulthood. Unfortunately, there are no controlled studies that have analyzed this specific relationship. Only one uncontrolled study by Berg, Butler, and Hall (1976) has provided any data.

In this study, 100 children hospitalized for school phobia were reexamined approximately three years after discharge. A third of the sample had improved substantially or completely. Another third had improved appreciably but were bothered by other neurotic symptoms such as depression. About half were either unable to return to school or had marked attendance difficulties when they did so. Five percent of the children had developed persistent and marked agoraphobic symptoms. How unusual this latter finding is from what might be expected in a nonreferred

school-phobic sample or in the general population of children is unknown.

To summarize, the research to date suggests that the statement in DSM-III specifying SAD as a predisposing factor for agoraphobia and panic disorder is premature. As outlined in the foregoing sections, there is a paucity of empirical evidence documenting such a relationship. Two overriding problems limit the conclusions that can be drawn from these studies. First, it is important to note that much of the research in this area has not examined the continuity of SAD per se. Many of the studies were conducted prior to the development of the DSM-III criteria, when separation anxiety was viewed as synonymous with school phobia. As noted earlier, the two may be distinct problems.

There also has been an absence of controlled, prospective longitudinal studies. This seems to be a function of the only recent specification of SAD—not enough time has elapsed for children to have been identified with the disorder and followed into adulthood. Therefore, it is somewhat unfair to dismiss entirely the notion of continuity between childhood and adult anxiety disorders based on the data available at this time.

However, considering the nature of DSM-III, it is surprising that a relationship between these disorders was proposed in the first place. The diagnostic and statistical manuals constitute a categorical classification system. Specific symptoms occurring together comprise the disorders, and each disorder is a discrete entity. Importantly, the symptoms within one disorder are expected to correlate with each other, but not with the symptoms of the other disorders. Thus, an inherent discontinuity exists between disorders in this system. It appears unjustified to expect that any disorder would specifically precede another.

A direct comparison of the criteria for SAD and agoraphobia or panic disorder as listed in the diagnostic manuals reveals that they are not the same. Consequently, trying to establish SAD as a precursor for the adult disorders is like trying to place a round peg into a square hole—it might fit, but not neatly.

Instead of examining the continuity of *disorders* from childhood to adulthood, some researchers have suggested that it would be more useful to follow generalized patterns of problem behavior. For example, Achenbach and Edelbrock (1989) have identified a number of configurations of normal and pathological responding in children using sophisticated multivariate statistical procedures. One broad-based group of problems that has emerged repeatedly is comprised of fearfulness, anxiety, withdrawal, unhappiness, and somatic complaints. Although there are difficulties associated with this method in terms of deciding what and how to gather and analyze data, it seems possible that behavioral patterns like this noted internalizing factor could be identified and examined consistently from childhood through adulthood. The early results of Berg et al. (1974) and those reported more recently by Turner et al. (1987) support such a conclusion.

SUMMARY

The general purpose of this chapter has been to examine the current status of separation anxiety disorder. Issues related to definition, current diagnosis, prevalence, demographic characteristics, and co-morbidity have been presented. The explicit assertion that SAD is a predisposing factor for adult agoraphobia and panic disorder also has been evaluated. It should be apparent that more research is needed, especially to determine the presence of SAD symptoms within the general population and to establish the prevalence of the disorder in nonreferred clinical samples. Further, a clear distinction between school phobia and SAD is warranted. Although similarities exist, these are distinct disorders. In regard to the issue of continuity, there is also a fundamental need for prospective, longitudinal studies in which standardized assessment procedures are used to specify either the disorders or the behavioral patterns purported to manifest from childhood through adulthood. Certainly, clearer characterization of SAD will have important implications both in terms of determining the etiology of the disorder and developing effective forms of intervention.

REFERENCES

Abe, K., & Masui, T. (1981). Age-sex trends of phobic and anxiety symptoms. *British Journal of Psychiatry, 138,* 297–302.

Achenbach, T. M. (1974). *Developmental psychopathology.* New York: The Ronald Press.

Achenbach, T. M., & Edelbrock, C. (1989). Diagnostic, taxonomic, and assessment issues in child psychopathology. In T. H. Ollendick & M. Hersen (Eds.), *Handbook of child psychopathology* (2nd ed.). New York: Plenum Press.

Agras, S., Sylvester, D., & Oliveau, D. (1969). The epidemiology of common fears and phobias. *Comprehensive Psychiatry, 10,* 151–156.

Ainsworth, M. D. S., Blehar, M., Waters, E., & Wall, S. (1978). *Patterns of attachment.* Hillsdale, NJ: Lawrence Erlbaum Associates.

American Psychiatric Association. (1980). *Diagnostic and statistical manual of mental disorders* (3rd ed.). Washington, DC: Author.

American Psychiatric Association. (1987). *Diagnostic and statistical manual of mental disorders* (3rd ed. rev.). Washington, DC: Author.

Barlow, D. H. (1985). The dimensions of anxiety disorders. In A. H. Tuma & J. D. Maser (Eds.), *Anxiety and anxiety disorders.* Hillsdale, NJ: Lawrence Erlbaum Associates.

Berg, I. (1976). School phobia in the children of agoraphobic women. *British Journal of Psychiatry, 128,* 86–89.

Berg, I., Butler, A., & Hall, G. (1976). The outcome of adolescent school phobia. *British Journal of Psychiatry, 128,* 80–85.

Berg, I., Butler, A., & Pritchard, J. (1974). Psychiatric illness in the mothers of school-phobic adolescents. *British Journal of Psychiatry, 125,* 466–467.

Berg, I., Nichols, K., & Pritchard, C. (1969). School phobia—its classification and relationship to dependency. *Journal of Child Psychology and Psychiatry, 10,* 123–141.

Berney, T., Kolvin, I., Bhate, S. R., Garside, R. F., Jeans, J., Kay, B., & Scarth, L. (1981). School phobia: A therapeutic trial with clomipramine and short-term outcome. *British Journal of Psychiatry, 138,* 110–118.

Bowlby, J. (1973). *Attachment and loss: Vol. 2. Separation.* New York: Basic Books.

Casat, C. D. (1988). Childhood anxiety disorders: A review of the possible relationship to adult panic disorder and agoraphobia. *Journal of Anxiety Disorders, 2,* 51–60.

Chazan, M. (1962). School phobia. *British Journal of Educational Psychology, 32,* 200–217.

Davids, A. (Ed.). (1973). *Issues in abnormal child psychology.* Monterey, CA: Brooks/Cole.

DiNardo, P. A., O'Brien, G. T., Barlow, D. H., Waddell, M. T., & Blanchard, E. B. (1983). Reliability of DSM-III anxiety disorder categories using a new structured interview. *Archives of General Psychiatry, 40,* 1070–1075.

Earls, F. (1980). The prevalence of behavior problems in three-year-old children. A cross-cultural replication. *Archives of General Psychiatry, 37,* 1153–1157.

Eisenberg, L. (1958). School phobia: A study in the communication of anxiety. *American Journal of Psychiatry, 114*, 712–718.

Estes, H. R., Haylett, C. H., & Johnson, A. M. (1956). Separation anxiety. *American Journal of Orthopsychiatry, 10*, 682–695.

Francis, G., Last, C. G., & Strauss, C. C. (1987). Expression of separation anxiety disorder: The roles of age and gender. *Child Psychiatry and Human Development, 18*, 82–89.

Francis, G., & Ollendick, T. H. (in press). Behavioral treatment of social anxiety. In E. L. Feindler & G. R. Kalfus (Eds.), *Casebook in adolescent behavior therapy*. New York: Springer.

Gittelman, R. (1986). *Anxiety disorders of childhood*. New York: the Guilford Press.

Gittelman, R., & Klein, D. (1985). Childhood separation anxiety and adult agoraphobia. In A. H. Tuma & J. D. Maser (Eds.), *Anxiety and anxiety disorders*. Hillsdale, NJ: Lawrence Erlbaum Associates.

Gittelman, R., & Klein, D. (1984). Relationship between separation anxiety and panic and agoraphobic disorders. *Psychopathology, 17*, 56–65.

Gittelman-Klein, R., & Klein, D. (1980). Separation anxiety in school refusal and its treatment with drugs. In L. Hersov & I. Berg (Eds.), *Out of school*. London: John Wiley & Sons.

Gittelman-Klein, R., & Klein, D. F. (1973). School phobia: Diagnostic considerations in the light of imipramine effects. *Journal of Nervous and Mental Disease, 156*, 199–215.

Graziano, A. M., & DeGiovanni, I. S. (1979). The clinical significance of childhood phobias: A note on the proportion of child-clinical referrals for the treatment of children's fears. *Behaviour Research and Therapy, 17*, 161–162.

Graziano, A. M., & Mooney, K. C. (1980). Family self-control instruction for children's nighttime fear reduction. *Journal of Consulting and Clinical Psychology, 48*, 206–213.

Graziano, A. M., & Mooney, K. C. (1982). Behavioral treatment of "night-fears" in children: Maintenance of improvement at 2- to 3-year follow-up. *Journal of Consulting and Clinical Psychology, 50*, 598–599.

Graziano, A. M., Mooney, K. C., Huber, C., & Ignasiak, D. (1979). Behavioral treatment of children's fears: A review. *Psychological Bulletin, 86*, 804–830.

Greenson, R. (1959). Phobia, anxiety, and depression. *Journal of the American Psychoanalytic Association, 7*, 663–674.

Hodges, K., McKnew, D., Cytryn, L., Stern, K., & Kline, J. (1982). The Child Assessment Schedule (CAS) Diagnostic Interview: A report on reliability and validity. *Journal of the American Academy of Child Psychiatry, 21*, 468–473.

Jersild, A. T., & Holmes, F. B. (1935). Children's fears. *Child Development Monographs*, No. 20.

Johnson, A. M., Falstein, E. I., Szurek, S. A., & Svendson, M. (1941). School phobia. *American Journal of Orthopsychiatry, 11*, 702–711.

Johnson, S. B. (1979). Children's fears in the classroom setting. *School Psychology Digest, 8*, 382–396.

Kahn, J. H., & Nursten, S. P. (1962). School refusal: A comprehensive review of school phobia and other failures of school attendance. *American Journal of Orthopsychiatry, 32*, 707–718.

Kennedy, W. A. (1965). School phobia: Rapid treatment of fifty cases. *Journal of Abnormal Psychology, 70*, 285–289.

Klein, D. F. (1964). Delineation of two drug-responsive anxiety syndromes. *Psychopharmacologia, 3*, 397–408.

Klein, D. F. (1981). Anxiety reconceptualized. In D. G. Klein & J. Rabkin (Eds.), *Anxiety: New research and changing concepts*. New York: Raven Press.

Kovacs, M. (1978). *The Interview Schedule for Children (ISC): Inter-rater and parent–child agreement*. Unpublished manuscript, University of Pittsburgh.

Lapouse, R., & Monk, M. A. (1959). Fears and worries in a representative sample of children. *American Journal of Orthopsychiatry, 29*, 223–248.

Last, C. G., Francis, G., Hersen, M., Kazdin, A. E., & Strauss, C. C. (1987). Separation anxiety and school phobia: A comparison using DSM-II criteria. *American Journal of Psychiatry, 144*, 653–657.

Last, C. G., Hersen, M., Kazdin, A. E., Finkelstein, R., & Strauss, C. C. (1987). Comparison of DSM-III separation anxiety and overanxious disorders: Demographic characteristics and patterns of comorbidity. *Journal of the American Academy of Child and Adolescent Psychiatry, 26*, 527–531.

Last, C. G., Hersen, M., Kazdin, A. E., Francis, G., & Grubb, H. J. (1987). Psychiatric illness in the mothers of anxious children. *American Journal of Psychiatry, 144*, 1580–1583.

Last, C. G., Strauss, C. C., & Francis, G. (1987). Comorbidity among childhood anxiety disorders. *Journal of Nervous and Mental Disease, 175*, 726–730.

Marks, I. M. (1969). *Fears and phobias.* New York: Academic Press.

Miller, L. C., Barrett, C. C., & Hampe, E. (1974). Phobias of childhood in a pre-scientific era. In A. Davids (Ed.), *Child personality and psychopathology: Current topics.* New York: John Wiley & Sons.

Ollendick, T. H. (1979). Fear reduction techniques with children. In M. Hersen, R. M. Eisler, & P. M. Miller (Eds.), *Progress in behavior modification.* New York: Academic Press.

Ollendick, T. H. (1983). Reliability and validity of the revised Fear Survey Schedule for Children (FSSC-R). *Behaviour Research and Therapy, 21*, 685–692.

Ollendick, T. H., & Francis, G. (1988). Behavioral assessment and treatment of childhood phobias. *Behavior Modification, 12*, 165–204.

Ollendick, T. H., & Hersen, M. (1983). An historical introduction to child psychopathology. In T. H. Ollendick & M. Hersen (Eds.), *Handbook of child psychopathology.* New York: Plenum Press.

Ollendick, T. H., King, N. R., & Frary, R. P. (1989). Fears in children and adolescents in Australia and the United States. *Behaviour Research and Therapy, 27*, 19–26.

Ollendick, T. H., Matson, J. L., & Helsel, W. J. (1985). Fears in children and adolescents. *Behaviour Research and Therapy, 23*, 465–467.

Ollendick, T. H., & Mayer, J. A. (1984). School phobia. In S. M. Turner (Ed.), *Behavioral treatment of anxiety disorders.* New York: Plenum Press.

Quay, H. C., & Peterson, D. R. (1983). *Manual for the Revised Behavior Problem Checklist.* Unpublished manuscript.

Quay, H. C., & Werry, J. S. (Eds.). (1979). *Psychopathological disorders of childhood* (2nd ed.). New York: John Wiley & Sons.

Raskin, M., Peeke, H. U. S., Dickman, W., & Pinskee, H. (1982). Panic and generalized anxiety disorders: Developmental antecedents and precipitants. *Archives of General Psychiatry, 39*, 687–689.

Reynolds, C. R., & Richmond, B. O. (1979). Factor structure and content validity of "What I Think and Feel:" The Revised Children's Manifest Anxiety Scale. *Journal of Personality Assessment, 43*, 281–283.

Rhead, C. (1969). The role of pregenital fixations in agoraphobia. *Journal of the American Psychoanalytic Association, 17*, 484–861.

Richman, N., Stevenson, J. E., & Graham, P. J. (1975). Prevalence of behavior problems in three-year-old children: An epidemiologic study in a London borough. *Journal of Child Psychology and Psychiatry, 16*, 277–287.

Ross, A. O. (1980). *Psychological disorders of children: A behavioral approach to theory, research, and therapy.* New York: McGraw-Hill.

Silverman, W. K., & Nelles, W. B. (1988). A new semistructured interview to assess childhood anxiety disorders. *Journal of the American Academy of Child and Adolescent Psychiatry, 27*, 772–778.

Smith, S. L. (1970). School refusal with anxiety: A review of sixty-three cases. *Canadian Psychiatric Association Journal, 15*, 257–264.

Sroufe, L. A., & Rutter, M. (1984). The domain of developmental psychopathology. *Child Development, 55*, 17–29.

Thyer, B. A., Neese, R. M., Cameron, O. G., & Curtis, G. C. (1985). Agoraphobia: A test of the separation anxiety hypothesis. *Behaviour Research and Therapy, 23*, 75–78.

Thyer, B. A., Neese, R. M., Curtis, G. C., & Cameron, O. G. (1986). Panic disorder: A test of the separation anxiety hypothesis. *Behaviour Research and Therapy, 24*, 209–211.

Thyer, B. A., & Sowers-Hoag, K. M. (1988). Behavior therapy for separation anxiety disorder. *Behavior Modification, 12*, 205–233.

Turner, S. M., Beidel, D. C., & Costello, A. (1987). Psychopathology in the offspring of anxiety disorders patients. *Journal of Child Clinical Psychology, 55*, 229–235.

Weissman, M. M., Leckman, J. F., Merikangas, K. R., Gammon, S. D., & Prusoff, B. A. (1984). Depression and anxiety disorders in parents and children. *Archives of General Psychiatry, 41*, 845–852.

Werry, J. S., & Quay, J. C. (1971). The prevalence of behavior symptoms in younger elementary school children. *American Journal of Orthopsychiatry, 41*, 136–143.

Yates, A. J. (1970). *Behavior therapy.* New York: John Wiley & Sons.

CHAPTER 10

AGORAPHOBIA IN ADULTHOOD

Bruce A. Thyer

*Then comes my fit again: I had else been perfect,
Whole as the marble, founded as the rock, As
broad and general as the casing air: But now I am
cabin'd cribb'd, confined, Bound in to saucy
doubts and fears"*

Shakespeare, *Macbeth*

DESCRIPTION OF THE DISORDER

In the past two decades there have been remarkable scientific and clinical advances relating to the disorder known as agoraphobia. What was formerly a poorly understood condition, resistant to treatment, and of unknown etiology has emerged as one of the most extensively researched psychiatric syndromes. There is now a considerable empirical literature concerning the epidemiology, natural course, and etiology of agoraphobia, and the condition is now known to respond favorably to a number of psychosocial and pharmacological therapies. Literally hundreds of articles in the psychological, social work, and psychiatric literatures have recently appeared related to agoraphobia, as have numerous articles in the popular press and several national television programs. Dozens of self-help groups have been formed to help agoraphobic sufferers and their families; three professional journals have been established (*Journal of Anxiety Disorders*; *Phobia Practice and Research*; *Anxiety Research: An International Journal*). And in 1980, the Phobia Society of America was formed, consisting of current and former phobics, their families, and mental health professionals active in the treatment of anxiety, many of whom have expertise in the care of agoraphobics. The Yellow Pages of most major cities commonly contain advertisements for specialized anxiety disorder clinics for agoraphobics and other persons with phobias. Clearly, agoraphobia has moved to the forefront of public attention and professional care. These developments have occurred for good reasons, and the remainder of this chapter will review these developments, with a focus upon the empirical clinical research literature pertinent to agoraphobia in adulthood.

Like most shorthand labels, the convenience of the term "agoraphobia" is obtained by sacrificing accuracy. "Agoraphobia" was coined in 1871 by Carl Otto Westphal, a German psychiatrist, to describe individuals who fear open and public places (Knapp, 1988; Knapp & Schumacher, 1988). The prefix *agora* is derived from the Greek word for "open public place," and *phobia* from *Phobos*, a terrifying attendant to Ares, the god of war. Thus, from the earliest beginnings of professional attention to the constellation of behaviors known as agoraphobia, it has been assumed that these individuals' primary problem is a severe and incapacitating fear of certain pervasive external stimuli, such as public places. Such fears purportedly may lead agoraphobic sufferers to become virtually housebound.

CLINICAL PRESENTATION

The agoraphobic is *not* usually completely housebound, contrary to stereotyped views of the disorder. What is crucial to the diagnosis of the condition known as agoraphobia with panic disorder is the individual experiencing one or more phenomena labeled "panic attacks": sudden, apparently unprovoked episodes of severe terrifying anxiety that appear without warning: one of the most frightening experiences a human being may undergo. Panic attacks are defined as being accompanied by at least four or more of the following symptoms: "shortness of breath, dizziness, palpitations or tachycardia, trembling, sweating, choking, abdominal distress, depersonalization or derealization, numbness, flushing or chills, chest discomfort, fear of dying, fear of going crazy or of doing something uncontrolled" (American Psychiatric Association, 1987, p. 238). Panic-like states involving less than four of these symptoms are labeled as "limited symptom attacks." In addition, true panic attacks are not known to be the result of actual or anticipated exposure to phobic stimuli. Severe anxiety associated with such conditions is more properly labeled as "phobic anxiety" or "anticipatory anxiety." Preliminary self-report studies do suggest that the panic attack experiences undergone by agoraphobics and phobic anxiety experienced by simple phobics are distinct phenomena (Thyer & Himle, 1987).

Virtually all agoraphobics do experience the onset of panic attacks prior to developing agoraphobic avoidance behaviors (Mendel & Klein, 1969), and most attribute agoraphobia to their prior experience of panic attacks (Thyer & Himle, 1985). Such centrality of panic attacks is now recognized in the third edition, revised, of the *Diagnostic and Statistical Manual of Mental Disorders* (APA, 1987). In the DSM-III, the chapter on anx-

iety disorders contained the categories of panic disorder and of agoraphobia with panic attacks (APA, 1980). The revision of the DSM-III has panic disorder, but now includes panic disorder with agoraphobia. The diagnosis of agoraphobia without history of panic disorder is rarely found among clinic patients (Thyer, Parrish, Curtis, Nesse, & Cameron, 1985), and it is unclear if such a condition exists at all. Accordingly, for the purposes of this chapter, the term "agoraphobia" is used to refer to the DSM-III-R diagnosis of "panic disorder with agoraphobia."

The current diagnostic criteria for panic disorder with agoraphobia are displayed in Table 10.1 and are reasonably clear.

EPIDEMIOLOGY

The recent national survey on psychiatric epidemiology conducted by the National Institute of Mental Health has thus far reported results obtained from three catchment areas: New Haven, CT; Baltimore, MD; and St. Louis, MO. A probability sampling procedure was used to obtain respondents who agreed to undergo a structured diagnostic interview schedule administered by trained interviewers. The six-month prevalence rates of agoraphobia for the three communities is 2.8%, 5.8%, and 2.7%, respectively. The corresponding prevalence rates for panic disorder were 0.4%, 0.8%, and 0.6% (Myers et al., 1984). These figures may have changed slightly with the adoption of the revised DSM-III criteria in 1987, but probably not to any appreciable extent. In his more comprehensive review, Reich (1986) estimates that the prevalence of agoraphobia is 6% and that of panic disorder is 3%. Women outnumber men with respect to agoraphobia by a factor of about 2 to 1; the corresponding figure for panic disorder is somewhat less, about 1.5 to 2.0 to 1 (Reich, 1986; Bourdon et al., 1988). In sum, these are relatively common disorders and are among the most prevalent of the psychiatric illnesses (Myers et al., 1984).

NATURAL HISTORY

The average age of onset of clinic patients diagnosed as suffering from agoraphobia with panic attacks (now called panic disorder with agoraphobia) is approximately 26 years; that for panic disorder is also about 26 years (Thyer, Parrish, Curtis, Nesse, & Cameron, 1985). Similar figures for agoraphobia (27.7 years, on average)

Table 10.1.   Diagnostic Criteria for Panic Disorder with Agoraphobia

A. Meets the criteria for Panic Disorder.

B. Agoraphobia: Fear of being in places or situations from which escape might be difficult (or embarrassing) or in which help might not be available in the event of a panic attack. (Include cases in which persistent avoidance behavior originated during an active phase of Panic Disorder, even if the person does not attribute the avoidance behavior to fear of having a panic attack.) As a result of this fear, the person either restricts travel or needs a companion when away from home, or else endures agoraphobic situations despite intense anxiety. Common agoraphobic situations include being outside the home alone, being in a crowd or standing in a line, being on a bridge, and traveling in a bus, train, or car.

Specify current severity of agoraphobia avoidance:

Mild: Some avoidance (or endurance with distress), but relatively normal life-style, e.g., travels unaccompanied when necessary, such as to work or to shop; otherwise avoids traveling alone.

Moderate: Avoidance results in constricted life-style, e.g., the person is able to leave the house alone, but not to go more than a few miles unaccompanied.

Severe: Avoidance results in being nearly or completely housebound or unable to leave the house unaccompanied.

In Partial Remission: No current agoraphobic avoidance, but some agoraphobic avoidance during the past six months.

In Full Remission: No current agoraphobic avoidance and none during the past six months.

Specify current severity of panic attacks:

Mild: During the past month, either all attacks have been limited symptom attacks (i.e., fewer than four symptoms) or there has been no more than one panic attack.

Moderate: During the past month attacks have been intermediate between "mild" and "severe."

Severe: During the past month, there have been at least eight panic attacks.

In Partial Remission: The condition has been intermediate between "In Full Remission" and "Mild."

In Full Remission: During the past six months there have been no panic or limited symptom attacks.

Reprinted with permission from the *Diagnostic and Statistical Manual of Mental Disorders. Third Edition, Revised.* Copyright 1987 American Psychiatric Association.

were recently determined by Öst (1987). The typical progression of the syndrome follows something along the following lines: An otherwise normal, reasonably intelligent individual, man or woman (although women present for professional counselling more frequently), without any history of prior disturbance, has an unexpected panic attack that peaks within a minute or two and then gradually subsides over the next five to ten minutes, but may last for an hour or so. This initial panic leaves the victim shaken but otherwise unharmed, although considerably perplexed over what happened.

If panics continue to occur, it is common for the individual to begin avoiding places and circumstances where such panics previously happened. Over months of random panics, phobic avoidance becomes overlaid by anticipatory anxiety; the panic sufferer begins avoiding places where "if a panic attack did occur," escape might be difficult or embarrassing, or assistance unavailable. For example, if an initial panic occurs while driving (flying, shopping, etc.), the person may begin restricting his or her driving, avoiding expressways, long bridges, tunnels, or other roads where it would not be possible to halt quickly and safely. For similar reasons, long lines, such as those found at the bank or in grocery stores, become phobic circumstances, since, if a panic did happen, the victim could not quickly flee. Thus, over time, a wide variety of apparently unrelated phobic stimuli may come to dominate the individual's life. In fact, these individuals may not recognize that their multiple fears are being driven by anticipation of panic episodes. Since these random panic attacks themselves may fluctuate widely in frequency and severity, the associated agoraphobic avoidance may wax and wane correspondingly. On one day the person may feel comfortable going shopping and yet the next day refuse to do so. This is not only confusing to the agoraphobic, but quite frustrating for family members who cannot predict their relative's abilities.

In the early stages of the disorder individuals so afflicted may seek medical attention and "doctor shop," vainly seeking the one expert consultant who can diagnose and effectively treat them. It is common for such patients to see a succession of cardiologists, neurologists, internists, allergists, and the like. Vast sums of money may be expended, numbers of medications consumed, and diagnostic tests endured, in these often fruitless efforts.

IMPAIRMENT AND COMPLICATIONS

In extreme cases, the agoraphobic may well remain housebound for many years. Perman (1966) describes one such case: "Ms. C. was unmarried, aged 46, and had a 14-year-old daughter. She had a seventh grade education and had been on public assistance for eight years. Ms. C. led a relatively solitary existence and for years saw little of her relatives. She left her apartment only to shop for groceries. She admitted that in order to leave the house, she had to prepare herself well in advance, which required considerable energy. After she moved to the [housing] project, an attempt to sit on an outside bench stimulated considerable anxiety. Many hypochondriacal symptoms would be prominent at such times . . . [her] travel phobia had kept her from attending a hospital clinic to investigate her various somatic complaints. It was obvious that she would need considerable support and would have to be accompanied whenever such appointments were to be kept or when shopping . . . " (pp. 611–612). Fortunately, such severe cases are the exception rather than the rule.

The abuse of alcohol or other sedative drugs is common among agoraphobics (Thyer et al., 1986; Thyer, McNeece, & Miller, 1987), as is the use of tobacco (Himle, Thyer, & Fischer, 1988). Such abuse should be carefully assessed at intake and may require professional attention prior to therapies directed toward panic attacks or agoraphobic avoidance.

Marital dysfunction and family problems may be common, as spouses and family members adapt to their significant other's limitations. Fortunately, it is often the case that as the panic attacks and agoraphobia are alleviated with professional care, marital and family dysfunction spontaneously improve without special attention. If such problems persist over time or appear to impair the course of therapy (as in the case of an extremely jealous husband who sabotages his wife's treatment efforts), marital or family therapy may well be indicated prior to or concurrent with therapy for the anxiety disorder.

DIFFERENTIAL DIAGNOSIS

Although patients suffering from panic disorder or agoraphobia with panic attacks often present with myriad signs and symptoms, the differential diagnosis of these conditions is usually not difficult. Many psychiatric or medical disorders may shape patients into displaying the phobiclike avoidance and dependent behaviors associated with agoraphobia. Likewise, numerous medical conditions may be accompanied by "paniclike" experiences secondary to the underlying organic condition. The diagnostic alternatives to either panic disorder with agoraphobia, or of panic disorder alone, may be roughly grouped into two major categories: *psychiatric disorders* or *medical disorders*.

Psychiatric Disorders

The polyphobic behaviors associated with agoraphobia may be secondary to a number of psychiatric conditions apart from the presumptive core disorders of either agoraphobia or panic disorder. For example, some obsessive compulsives with fears of ubiquitous stimuli, such as germs or chemical contamination, may become virtually housebound, topographically similar to the stereotypical agoraphobic, but lacking the central feature of spontaneous panic attacks driving the development of agoraphobia. The same factors may cause patients with certain forms of simple or social phobia, again related to pervasive stimuli (loud noises, heterosocial fears, insects, or small animals) to likewise resemble agoraphobia. A case history describing a dog phobic with agoraphobiclike behaviors may be found in Thyer (1981). Particularly severe cases of posttraumatic stress disorder may also present with withdrawal to the home environment. Patients with generalized anxiety disorder rarely develop agoraphobiclike restrictions.

Some other psychiatric conditions not directly related to the anxiety disorders may mimic selected features of agoraphobia. For example, some individuals with schizophrenia of the paranoid type or patients with delusional disorder, persecutory type, may develop pronounced interpersonal withdrawal secondary to their psychotic processes. Some cases of patients with severe depressive disorders avoid circumstances they find overly stressful, which may also resemble selected features of agoraphobia.

In all these differential diagnoses, it is relatively

easy to elicit the patient's history of spontaneous panic attacks. Their absence, of course, precludes the diagnosis of panic disorder with agoraphobia. If the avoidance behaviors are deemed secondary to a primary disorder (social phobia, schizophrenia, etc.), then agoraphobia is precluded as a diagnosis. This would also apply to patients who meet the criteria for one or more of the Axis-II so-called personality diagnoses that may be characterized by extreme reclusiveness or social withdrawal (paranoid personality disorder, schizoid personality disorder, schizotypal personality disorder, antisocial personality disorder, avoidant personality disorder, etc.).

Medical Disorders

A number of medical disorders, particularly those with symptoms of an unpredictably painful, embarrassing, or spasmodic nature may cause their sufferers to develop agoraphobic-like restrictions. Examples described in an earlier report (Thyer, Himle, Curtis, Cameron, & Nesse, 1985) include epilepsy and spastic colitis. Other examples that may be found in the literature include vestibular disorders (Jacob, Moller, Turner, & Wall, 1985; Hallam & Stephens, 1985), esophageal spasms (Schuster, 1983; Clouse & Lustman, 1983), focal neurological symptoms (Coyle & Sterman, 1986), cerebral tumors (Dietch, 1984), and mitral valve prolapse (Crowe, 1985). Undoubtedly, the actual number of such medical disorders that may mimic panic attacks or otherwise promote pronounced phobic avoidance is much larger. In such cases the diagnosis of agoraphobia is precluded by the primary organic disorder.

Ingestion of certain drugs may cause panic-like symptomatology that can lead the way to pronounced phobic avoidance similar to that seen in agoraphobia, but the effects are usually transient (e.g., caffeine, nicotine, hallucinogens). Some exceptions appear to be the apparent actual precipitation of a course of free-running panic attacks following use of some drugs. Among those reported in the literature are cocaine (Aronson & Craig, 1986) and marijuana (Moran, 1986). In such cases panic disorder with agoraphobia or panic disorder alone *would* be the primary Axis-I diagnosis, regardless of the nature of the purported precipitants.

A number of endocrine disorders may cause symptoms similar to those of panic disorder. Examples include Cushing syndrome, hyperthyroidism, hypoglycemia, pheochromocytoma, and various pituitary disorders. Such differential diagnoses may be supported or ruled out by the relevant diagnostic tests, such as the glucose tolerance test in the case of suspected hypoglycemia or plasma catecholamine levels in presumptive pheochromocytoma (see Lindemann, Zitrin, & Klein, 1984; Carlson, 1986, for further illustrations).

To complicate the assessment and treatment process, however, it should be noted that just as organic dysfunctions may mimic panic disorder, panic disorder by itself may be masked in the form of apparently organic problems. Lydiard, Laraia, Howell, and Ballenger (1986) describe five cases of patients with panic attacks and irritable bowel syndrome (IBS), whose IBS cleared up following effective treatment of the panic attacks. These authors concluded that some patients with functional gastrointestinal problems may have a primary case of panic disorder.

Similarly, following the course of chronic agoraphobia or panic disorder, some patients may develop secondary psychological disorders as a consequence of the experience of pathological anxiety. Neenan, Felkner, and Reich (1986) describe two patients who developed schizoid, paranoid, and schizotypal traits following years of panic disorder. Clearly, the temporal order of the appearance of both psychological and organic disorders is a crucial variable in the process of arriving at a differential diagnosis. Additional information on the differential diagnosis of panic disorder or agoraphobia may be found in Cameron (1985).

CASE EXAMPLE

The case example that follows was solicited from the membership of Agoraphobics in Motion, an agoraphobia self-help group located in the Detroit area. The writer and patient, Susan (a pseudonym), is atypical, in that her panic attacks seem to have had such an early onset. Unfortunately, the misery and grief her condition caused are all too common. I am most grateful for her willingness to share her story.

"My name is Susan and I am a recovering agoraphobic. Perhaps it is necessary to understand a little of my background and struggle to know the success that only recently I have achieved. At the age of 6 I began school as a shy, withdrawn child who fought back tears and fear in my parents' absence. Fortunately, I had a wonderful teacher, who held me and loved me and gave much support to me. I also remember her telling my parents how I must come out of my shell. Unfortunately, she died halfway into the school year the evening of a parent-teachers' meeting.

"Three years later my own father kissed his wife and six children goodbye as he left to work the midnight shift. He never returned. He too, like my teacher, died very suddenly. It was then I learned, but did not quite understand, that a person one loved could be out of this life forever in the blink of an eye.

"A year or so after these tragic events I began experiencing something I had never known before in my young life. I attended a parochial school that was very rigid in nature. One exchanged classrooms silently and in single file. One went to church every day, and one *never* disobeyed one's teacher. One day I needed to use the bathroom very badly. I asked the teacher for permission and was refused. Classes exchanged and I asked the next teacher and was refused again. I was in terrible discomfort but would never question the authority of a teacher. It was time for church attendance and I was still not allowed restroom privileges. During the service I fainted and was reprimanded for not eating breakfast as I should. Being an insecure youngster, I said nothing and took the blame.

"It was at this time at the age of 11 that I began having my first panic attacks. Although I knew what they felt like, I did not know what they were. Each day in church I would experience the classic horrifying symptoms and often fled the building. It also began to carry over into the classroom. Soon I would wake in the morning not feeling well, *making* myself not feel well, and was given permission to stay home. 'Ahhh, safety,' I thought. However, after this pattern continued, the doctor insisted I needed a tonsillectomy. Even after the surgery my absenteeism continued, and I finally confided in my mother the way I would feel in church and the classroom. She focused on the symptoms of distorted vision and promptly took me to an eye surgeon. I was scheduled for surgery quickly thereafter for a right eye correction. While medicated at the hospital I was told maybe this was the time to have surgery for both eyes. In my groggy state I went along with what the doctor advised. I awoke frightened with bandaged eyes and spent a few days in a state of blindness.

"These experiences taught me only one important lesson. That lesson was to be quiet about my feelings because the consequences were terrifying and of no help. For many years afterward I suffered in silence. I am not asking for pity but understanding. I had no understanding of my condition. I began to believe I was possibly crazy and certainly abnormal. No one else knew I felt this way; I was a freak of nature. I had no choice but to persist in my uncomfortable life-style. I sat through graduation commencement exercises seized with panic. I heard nothing at the podium. I enjoyed no part of this rite into adulthood. Even at my wedding I experienced panic. Total embarrassment was felt at the altar, as the priest had to offer me water or a chair in front of not only my friends and relatives but my new ones through marriage. I had panic on the flight to a gloriously planned honeymoon. The events that most found joyous were trying and torturous for me. For me this was hell on earth, but why was I being punished?

"Unexplainably, there were times in my life when the anxiety was not there; but those were shortlived. After my baby's birth, I reached the lowest point in my life. I won't describe my symptoms, but because of them my world became smaller than ever. I stopped shopping. I sold my car and stopped driving. I could not walk five houses down my own block. And so I became reclusive and gave all my time to caring for my baby. But babies do not stay babies. Soon there was nursery school to think about. How was I going to get her there! The thought of the five-block drive caused a panic in itself. These times strained my marriage, my friendships, and my finances. It was time as an adult to consult a physician myself.

"After an electrocardiogram, a thyroid panel, and complete blood workup, ironically the blood sugar test came back extremely high. The doctor believed me to be diabetic and I was thrilled! At last I could really explain and have a reason for these symptoms. The glucose tolerance test proved otherwise, however, and the doctor could not explain the initial blood results. He gave me tranquilizers, which made me feel only a little bit better but a whole lot sleepier. I happened to change doctors so that my drives to my appointments would not be as far. He examined me, spoke with me, and asked if I had ever heard of agoraphobia. He explained a little and gave me literature from a local support group that might help, the group called Agoraphobics in Motion . . . [Susan goes on to describe her recovery over the next year and a half]."

It is unclear what role the deaths of Susan's teacher and father may have played in the etiology of her panics and subsequent agoraphobia. Parental deaths do *not* seem to be selectively associated with agoraphobia or panic disorder when such patients are examined as a group (Thyer, in press; Thyer, Himle, & Fischer, 1988; Thyer, Himle, & Miller-Gogoleski, 1989); however, it is certainly possible that for some individual patients, factors such as parental loss are etiologically salient.

CHILDHOOD AND FAMILIAL ANTECEDENTS

The only predisposing factors for panic disorder or agoraphobia found in the DSM-III-R is the contention that "Separation Anxiety Disorder in childhood and sudden loss of social supports or disruption of important interpersonal relationships apparently predispose to the development of this disorder" (American Psychiatric Association, 1987, p. 237). The research on which this statement is based suffers from a number of methodological flaws, and its strongest advocates have recently admitted that their latest data only support the separation anxiety hypothesis for female patients, not male ones (Gittleman & Klein, 1985). A number of studies quite simply have failed to support this separation anxiety hypothesis (Thyer, Nesse, Cameron, & Curtis, 1985; Thyer, Nesse, Curtis, & Cameron, 1986; Thyer, Himle, & Fischer, 1988; Thyer, Himle, & Miller-Gogoleski, 1988), so the hypothesis that adult-onset panics or agoraphobia represent a variant of childhood separation anxiety disorder should be given little credence. In fact, a recent review by Nelles and Barlow (1988) suggests that the phenomenon of spontaneous panic attacks is an extremely rare occurrence among children.

There is some modest evidence that onset of agoraphobia/panic attacks may be associated with the experience of nonspecific life stress (e.g., Last, Barlow, & O'Brien, 1984; Nelles & Barlow, 1988). At present, however, there is insufficient evidence to conclude that there is an entity called an "agoraphobic personality," or that certain patterns of familial or marital behavior lead to the development of agoraphobia, despite the persistent non-data-based speculations of some theorists in this regard (e.g., Rohrbaugh & Shean, 1987). The lack of adequately controlled longitudinal studies on these developmental aspects of agoraphobia

suggests that this would be a fertile area for further research. Certainly, these issues are not settled.

It should be noted that the disorders of agoraphobia and panic disorder do seem to run in families, especially among female members (reviewed in Marks, 1987). Although the evidence to date is suggestive of a genetic mode of transmission, the role of familial modeling or sex role stereotyping remain to be excluded in accounting for these results.

By and large, the evidence with respect to specific childhood and familial antecedents is negative. The conclusion reached by Prince and Putnam over 75 years ago (1912) has not appreciably changed: Agoraphobia occurs "in people of all types and characteristics, amongst the normally self-reliant as well as amongst the timid" (Marks, 1987, p. 349).

SUMMARY

This chapter has reviewed the empirical clinical research literature concerning the condition called agoraphobia. Several case vignettes were used to illustrate the phenomenology of the disorder. It is clear that virtually all instances of agoraphobia are secondary to the individual experiencing a series of apparently spontaneous panic attacks. Such persons usually become fearful, first of places where panic attacks occurred in the past, then with passage of time and recurrent episodes of unexpected panic; they develop phobic avoidance to places and circumstances where, if a panic were to occur, escape would be difficult, help unavailable, or embarrassment likely. Circumscribed phobias of certain places related to these factors (e.g., expressway driving, elevators, airplanes, public gatherings, long lines, barbershops, or hairdressers) may be superseded by far more pervasive fears that may come to dominate the individual's life and result in an increasingly housebound existence.

Several important areas have not been addressed, for example, the issue of effectively treating the agoraphobic. Texts devoted to treatment per se are plentiful. Among them are Marks (1987), Barlow and Cerny (1988), Turner (1984), and Thyer (1987). Also not addressed was the issue of the cause of panic attacks, the driving force producing agoraphobia. Marks (1987) provides the best review of this area as well. Suffice it to say that panic attacks are slowly being uncovered as an explicable phenomenon, amenable to scientific inquiry, and the focus of a considerable amount of exciting research. The most promising leads seem to suggest that panic attacks are related to hyperventilatory processes and that treatment programs incorporating elements of exposure therapy and breathing training can reduce both phobic avoidance *and* apparently spontaneous panic attacks (Barlow & Cerny, 1988).

REFERENCES

American Psychiatric Association. (1980). *Diagnostic and statistical manual of mental disorders* (3rd ed.). Washington, DC: Author.

American Psychiatric Association. (1987). *Diagnostic and statistical manual of mental disorders* (3rd ed. rev.). Washington, DC: Author.

Aronson, T. A., & Craig, T. J. (1986). Cocaine precipitation of panic disorder. *American Journal of Psychiatry, 143*, 643–645.

Barlow, D. H., & Cerny, J. A. (1988). *Psychological treatment of panic*. New York: The Guilford Press.

Bourdon, K. H., Boyd, J. H., Rae, D. S., Burns, B. J., Thompson, J. W., & Locke, B. Z. (1988). Gender differences in phobias: Results of the ECA community survey. *Journal of Anxiety Disorders, 2*, 227–241.

Cameron, O. G. (1985). The differential diagnosis of anxiety. In G. C. Curtis, B. A. Thyer, & J. M. Rainey (Eds.), *Psychiatric clinics of North America: Anxiety disorders* (pp. 3–23). Philadelphia: W. B. Saunders.

Carlson, R. J. (1986). Longitudinal observations of two cases of organic anxiety syndrome. *Psychosomatics, 27*, 529–531.

Clouse, R. E., & Lustman, P. J. (1983). Psychiatric illness and contraction abnormalities of the esophagus. *The New England Journal of Medicine, 309*, 1337–1342.

Coyle, P. K., & Sterman, A. B. (1986). Focal neurologic symptoms in panic attacks. *American Journal of Psychiatry, 143*, 648–649.

Crowe, R. R. (1985). Mitral valve prolapse and panic disorder. In G. C. Curtis, B. A. Thyer, & J. M. Rainey (Eds.), *Psychiatric clinics of North America: Anxiety disorders* (pp. 63–71). Philadelphia: W. B. Saunders.

Dietch, J. T. (1984). Cerebral tumor presenting with panic attacks. *Psychosomatics, 25*, 861–863.

Gittelman, R., & Klein, D. F. (1985). Childhood separation anxiety and adult agoraphobia. In A. H. Tuma & J. Maser (Eds.), *Anxiety and the anxiety disorders* (pp. 389–402). Hillsdale, NJ: Lawrence Erlbaum Associates.

Hallam, R. S., & Stephens, S. D. G. (1985). Vestibular disorders and emotional distress. *Journal of Psychosomatic Research, 29*, 407–413.

Himle, J., Thyer, B. A., & Fischer, D. (1988). Prevalence of smoking among anxious outpatients. *Phobia Practice and Research Journal, 1*, 25–31.

Jacob, R. G., Moller, M. B., Turner, S. M., & Wall, C. (1985). Otoneurological examination in panic disorder and agoraphobia with panic attacks: A pilot study. *American Journal of Psychiatry, 142*, 715–720.

Knapp, T. J. (1988). Carl Otto Westphal and agoraphobia: A case history in medical discovery. *Phobia Practice and Research Journal, 1*, 5–12.

Knapp, T. J., & Schumacher, M. T. (1988). *Westphal's "Die Agoraphobie."* Lanham, MD: University Press of America.

Last, C. G., Barlow, D. H., & O'Brien, G. T. (1984). Precipitants of agoraphobia: Role of stressful life events. *Psychological Reports, 54*, 567–570.

Lindemann, C. G., Zitrin, C. M., & Klein, D. F. (1984). Thyroid dysfunction in phobic patients. *Psychosomatics, 25*, 603–606.

Lydiard, R. B., Laraia, M. T., Howell, E. F., & Ballenger, J. C. (1986). Can panic disorder present as irritable bowel syndrome? *Journal of Clinical Psychiatry, 47*, 470–473.

Marks, I. M. (1987). *Fears, phobias, and rituals*. New York: Oxford University Press.

Mendel, J., & Klein, D. F. (1969). Anxiety attacks and subsequent agoraphobia. *Comprehensive Psychiatry, 10*, 190–195.

Moran, C. (1986). Depersonalization and agoraphobia associated with marijuana use. *British Journal of Medical Psychology, 59*, 187–196.

Myers, J. K., Weissman, M. M., Tischler, G. L., Holzer, C. E., Leaf, P. J., Orvachel, H., Anthony, J. C., Boyd, J. H., Burke, D., Kramer, M., & Stoltzman, R. (1984). Six-month prevalence of psychiatric disorders in three communities. *Archives of General Psychiatry, 41*, 959–967.

Neenan, P., Felkner, J., & Reich, J. (1986). Schizoid personality traits developing secondary to panic disorder. *Journal of Nervous and Mental Disease, 174*, 483.

Nelles, W. B., & Barlow, D. H. (1988). Do children panic? *Clinical Psychology Review, 8*, 359–372.

Öst, L.-G. (1987). Age at onset in different phobias. *Journal of Abnormal Psychology, 96,* 233–229.

Perman, J. M. (1966). Phobia as a determinant of single-room occupancy. *American Journal of Psychiatry, 123,* 609–613.

Prince, M., & Putnam, J. J. (1912). Clinical study of a case of phobia: A symposium. *Journal of Abnormal and Social Psychology, 7,* 259–303.

Reich, J. (1986). The epidemiology of anxiety. *Journal of Nervous and Mental Disease, 174,* 129–136.

Rohrbaugh, M., & Shean, G. D. (1987). Anxiety disorders: An interactional view of agoraphobia. *Journal of Psychotherapy and the Family, 3,* 65–85.

Schuster, M. M. (1983). Esophageal spasm and psychiatric disorder. *New England Journal of Medicine, 309,* 1382–1383.

Thyer, B. A. (1981). Prolonged in-vivo exposure therapy with a 70-year-old woman. *Journal of Behavior Therapy and Experimental Psychiatry, 12,* 69–71.

Thyer, B. A. (1987). *Treating anxiety disorders: A guide for human service professionals.* Newbury Park, CA: Sage.

Thyer, B. A. (in press). Childhood separation anxiety disorder and adult-onset agoraphobia: A review of the evidence. In C. G. Last (Ed.), *Anxiety across the lifespan: A developmental perspective on anxiety and the anxiety disorders.* New York: Springer.

Thyer, B. A., & Himle, J. (1985). Temporal relationship between panic attack onset and phobic avoidance in agoraphobia. *Behaviour Research and Therapy, 23,* 607–608.

Thyer, B. A., & Himle, J. (1987). Phobic anxiety and panic anxiety: How do they differ? *Journal of Anxiety Disorders, 1,* 59–67.

Thyer, B. A., Himle, J., Curtis, G. C., Cameron, O. G., & Nesse, R. M. (1985). A comparison of panic disorder and agoraphobia with panic attacks. *Comprehensive Psychiatry, 26,* 208–214.

Thyer, B. A., Himle, J., & Fischer, D. (1988). Is parental death a selective precursor to either panic disorder or agoraphobia? A test of the separation anxiety hypothesis. *Journal of Anxiety Disorders, 2,* 333–338.

Thyer, B. A., Himle, J., & Miller-Gogoleski, M. A. (1989). The relationship of parental death to panic disorder: A community-based replication. *Phobia Practice and Research Journal, 2,* 29–36.

Thyer, B. A., McNeece, C. A., & Miller, M. A. (1987). Alcohol abuse among agoraphobics: A community-based replication. *Alcoholism Treatment Quarterly, 4,* 61–67.

Thyer, B. A., Nesse, R. M., Cameron, O. G., & Curtis, G. C. (1985). Agoraphobia; A test of the separation anxiety hypothesis. *Behaviour Research and Therapy, 23,* 75–78.

Thyer, B. A., Nesse, R. M., Curtis, G. C., & Cameron, O. G. (1986). Panic disorder: A test of the separation anxiety hypothesis. *Behaviour Research and Therapy, 24,* 209–211.

Thyer, B. A., Parrish, R. T., Himle, J., Cameron, O. G., Curtis, G. C., & Nesse, R. M. (1986). Alcohol abuse among clinically anxious patients. *Behaviour Research and Therapy, 24,* 357–359.

Thyer, B. A., Parrish, R. T., Curtis, G. C., Nesse, R. M., & Cameron, O. G. (1985). Ages of onset of DSM-III anxiety disorders. *Comprehensive Psychiatry, 26,* 113–122.

Turner, S. M. (Ed.). (1984). *Behavioral theories and treatment of anxiety.* New York: Plenum Press.

SOCIAL PHOBIA

EDITORS' COMMENTS

Among all the anxiety disorders, social phobia appears to have received the least attention, both from clinicians and researchers in the field. This "neglect" is even more serious when one examines the literature on social phobia in children and adolescents.

The lack of attention to social phobia in general may be due to the unfounded assumption that it is a mild disorder with relatively little accompanying impairment, simply representing, in essence, a variation of normal social discomfort or apprehension. In children, phobias usually are thought to be transitory, developmental phenomena, which may, in part, account for the scarcity of investigations conducted on the childhood form of the disorder.

However, it is clear upon further study that social phobia may be severely incapacitating for both afflicted adults and youngsters. In addition to limiting interpersonal relationships, social phobia can result in school avoidance in children and substantial employment difficulties (and absenteeism) in adults.

Most social phobias appear to begin in adolescence, about the same time that problems with social embarrassment appear in normal adolescents. Interestingly, in both child and adult populations, epidemiological data suggest that the disorder is more prevalent in females. However, as Schneier and Liebowitz note in Chapter 12, the prevalence of primary social phobia in women may be overestimated by including individuals who have the disorder secondary to another anxiety disorder, such as panic disorder.

Public speaking appears to be one of the most common social phobias among both children and adults. Generalized social phobia – where most social situations cause discomfort and are avoided – while less common may be more impairing, resulting in substantial, extensive avoidance. However, it should be emphasized that severe, specific social phobias may result in comparable levels of phobic avoidance, depending on the nature of the phobic situation.

Data from family studies indicate that social phobia may run in families, and twin studies, comparing monozygotic and dizygotic pairs, suggest a genetic contribution to the disorder. Additional interesting data that speak to the constitutional nature of social phobia have been provided by Kagan in his follow-up of "shy" 2-year-old children. While the children became socially avoidant 7-year-olds, it remains to be determined whether they will become socially phobic adolescents. Further prospective data on this issue are awaited with interest.

CHAPTER 11

SOCIAL PHOBIA IN CHILDHOOD

Greta Francis

DESCRIPTION OF THE DISORDER

The essential feature of social phobia is persistent and intense fear of situations in which the person is exposed to the scrutiny of others. According to the *Diagnostic and Statistical Manual of Mental Disorders* (American Psychiatric Association, 1987), the diagnostic criteria for social phobia are (1) a persistent fear of one or more situations in which the person is exposed to the scrutiny of others and fears that he or she may do something or act in a way that will be humiliating or embarrassing; (2) the fear is unrelated to any other Axis-I or Axis-III disorder, for example, the fear is not of having a panic attack; (3) exposure to the phobic situation almost invariably provokes an immediate anxiety response; (4) the phobic situation is avoided or endured with intense anxiety; (5) the avoidance behavior interferes significantly with occupational (e.g., school) or social functioning, or the person exhibits marked distress about having the fear (e.g., the child indicates that he or she is troubled by the fact that he or she is

fearful); and (6) the person recognizes that the fear is excessive or unreasonable.

CLINICAL PRESENTATION

A number of different types of social phobias have been identified. Common social phobias include fears of public speaking, using public bathrooms, eating or drinking in public, dressing in the presence of others, blushing, and writing in front of others. In addition, the DSM-III-R states that social phobia may present as generalized social anxiety regarding saying or doing something foolish whenever in social situations, coupled with subsequent avoidance of such situations. No data are available currently describing the relative prevalence of these types of social phobias in children and adolescents.

Children with social phobia are likely to evidence anxiety-related problems in school. They may fear speaking in front of the class, eating in the cafeteria, or changing clothes for gym class. Common avoidance behaviors include frequent trips to the school nurse or to the office during the school day. With careful questioning of the child, parent, and/or teacher, it often is possible to identify a pattern in which the avoidant behaviors occur during times at which the child would be exposed to the social phobic stimuli. For example, a child may consistently refuse school on gym days or request to go to the nurse's office when he or she knows it is his or her turn to give a speech in school. Outside of school, these children may be extremely reluctant to order in a restaurant or speak to a store clerk. They may attempt to enlist siblings, parents, or friends to speak for them.

Youngsters with the more generalized type of social phobia likely will evidence more pervasive avoidance than will those with circumscribed phobias. That is, while the child with an intense fear of changing in front of others may avoid gym class or take excessive care to undress privately, the child with generalized social anxiety likely will restrict a variety of social activities. He or she may avoid a number of potentially social situations such as shopping, parties, and school. In the extreme, such children may withdraw almost entirely from their peer group. A youngster with generalized social anxiety will be described in the Case Example.

EPIDEMIOLOGY

There is very little information currently available regarding the prevalence of social phobia in children and adolescents. Anderson, Williams, McGee, & Silva (1987) investigated the prevalence of social phobia in a community sample of 11-year-old children in New Zealand. Their diagnosis of social phobia was made on the basis of DSM-III criteria using child interviews and parent and teacher questionnaires. Using their least stringent method, in which the diagnostic criteria were reported by only one source, the rate of social phobia was 0.9%. However, using a more conservative method in which diagnostic criteria were confirmed by at least one other source, no children received a diagnosis of social phobia. Evidently, childhood social phobia is rare in the general population.

Last, Strauss, and Francis (1987) recently examined the rate of social phobia in a clinic-referred sample of anxiety-disordered youngsters. They found that approximately 15% of children who presented with anxiety disorder diagnoses received a primary diagnosis of social phobia involving school avoidance. Moreover, using a larger sample, Strauss and Francis (1989) reported that almost 9% of youngsters in an anxiety-disordered

clinic sample received a diagnosis of social phobia unrelated to school avoidance.

A fairly consistent finding across community samples of children and adolescents is that females report more fears and worries than do males (e.g., Anderson et al., 1987; Lapouse & Monk, 1959). The only study of DSM-III phobic disorders in a community sample of children was conducted by Anderson et al. (1987). These authors reported a sex ratio of 0.2 : 1.0 (M : F) for social phobia. Similarly, Strauss and Francis (1989) found that females more commonly received a DSM-III diagnosis of social phobia than did males in their anxiety-disordered outpatient sample.

NATURAL HISTORY

Numerous studies of subclinical fears demonstrate changes in the number and types of fears over the course of childhood and adolescence (Graziano, DeGiovanni, & Garcia, 1979). In their review of the literature, Graziano et al. (1979) found an age-related increase in social and school fears. Similarly, the typical age of onset for social phobia has been placed at late childhood or early adolescence (e.g., Marks, 1970). As such, the usual age of onset for social phobia coincides with the time at which problems with social embarrassment appear to develop in normal adolescents (Aimes, Gelder, & Shaw, 1983). Virtually nothing is known about the natural course of social phobias that develop in youngsters.

Since social phobia can be related to school avoidance (Francis, Strauss, & Last, 1987), and data are available regarding the prognosis of school avoidance, the course of school avoidance will be discussed briefly. Follow-up data have suggested that anxiety-based school refusal in children is related to later adjustment problems (e.g., Coolidge, Brodie, & Feeney, 1964; Waldron, 1976). In particular, Berg and colleagues (Berg, Butler, & Hall, 1976; Berg & Jackson, 1985) have studied the long-term prognosis of large numbers of school phobic adolescents originally treated by inpatient hospitalization. Three years postdischarge, one third showed a remission of symptoms, one third showed little improvement, and one third showed additional anxiety problems. In addition, one half of the total sample continued to evidence significant school avoidance. Moreover, Berg and Jackson's (1985) ten-year postdischarge follow-up study of 168 school refusers revealed that almost 50% required further psychiatric treatment. Although no information is available as to the extent of social phobia in these samples of anxiety-disordered school refusers, it is clear that anxiety problems that lead to school refusal are associated with a poor prognosis.

IMPAIRMENT AND COMPLICATIONS

The extent of impairment for children and adolescents with social phobia can vary widely. Those children who present with relatively circumscribed social phobias may seldom be incapacitated, but rather inconvenienced. For instance, it may be inconvenient for a child to avoid using a public bathroom or to refuse to eat or drink in restaurants. Youngsters with generalized social phobias likely will avoid a large variety of social situations and thus evidence pervasive disruption in their functioning. For example, the child may avoid most situations in which he or she must interact with other people because of fear of saying or doing something foolish. This can lead to marked constriction of normal activities.

A significant potential problem for social phobic youngsters is school refusal. Francis, Strauss, and Last (1987) found that almost one-half of their clinic sample of phobic school refusers received a diagnosis of social phobia. Clearly, school refusal is a serious and difficult problem to treat. Youngsters who avoid school miss out on important normative and developmental opportunities for academic and social-emotional growth.

Strauss and Francis (1989) described the relationship between childhood phobias and depression. In their outpatient clinic sample, they found that children with social phobias reported more depressive symptoms than did children with simple phobias. That is, using the Children's Depression Inventory (Kovacs, 1980–81), social phobic youngsters received a mean score of 14.3 compared with a mean score of 9.9 obtained by simple phobic youngsters. However, although the groups differed, neither endorsed clinically significant depression ratings. No published data currently are available regarding the relationship between social phobia and major depression and/or dysthymic disorder in children.

Although a large body of research indicates that multiple mild fears are common in children (e.g., Jersild & Holmes, 1935; Lapouse & Monk, 1959), preliminary data suggest that clinic-referred social phobic children do not present with multiple phobias. Strauss and Francis (1989) found that 67% of social phobics in their sample received no additional phobia diagnoses. However, socially phobic children frequently may have nonphobic anxiety problems, as evidenced by a rate of 67% of the earlier-mentioned sample presenting with comorbid overanxious disorder.

DIFFERENTIAL DIAGNOSIS

In children and adolescents, social phobia first needs to be distinguished from normal fears of social embarrassment that commonly are experienced by this age group. Many youngsters experience nervousness when faced with the scrutiny of others. For example, a child may express anxiety about having to give a speech in school or having to play a musical instrument in front of his or her classmates. Typically, some anticipatory anxiety is present that dissipates as the child becomes involved in the task. However, persistent anxiety and avoidance do not characterize nonphobic anxiety. Moreover, nonphobic anxiety is not related to the perception that the fear is excessive or unreasonable compared to same-age peers.

Another distinction is between social and simple phobias. This distinction has to do with the nature of the phobic stimuli. A diagnosis of simple phobia is made when the phobic situations are not related to fear of humiliation, embarrassment, or the scrutiny of others.

Social phobia also must be differentiated from overanxious disorder. While social phobia, by definition, involves avoidance or an intense wish to avoid, overanxious disorder does not necessarily involve avoidance. The overanxious child is likely to show discomfort, as opposed to avoidance, in a variety of social and nonsocial situations. In addition, overanxious children evidence other symptoms not typically seen in phobic children, such as somatic complaints, generalized tension, and excessive need for reassurance. The differential diagnosis may become difficult when faced with the distinction between generalized social phobia and overanxious disorder, since both may involve pervasive social discomfort.

Avoidant disorder may be confused with social phobia. The hallmark of avoidant disorder is distress and avoidance related to social situations with unfamiliar people. When anxiety is limited to social interactions with strangers, social phobia should not be diagnosed.

Finally, children with nonanxiety disorders such as schizophrenia or major depression may evidence avoidance of social interactions. In these cases, avoidance is not due primarily to intense anxiety, and, thus, social phobia should not be diagnosed.

CASE EXAMPLE

Rebecca was a 16-year-old, black female in the ninth grade who was evaluated at an outpatient psychiatric clinic that specialized in the assessment and treatment of children and adolescents with anxiety disorders. Her presenting complaint was a long-standing problem with school attendance. This problem was reported to have begun during sixth grade, when Rebecca showed some mild reluctance to attend school. No other precipitating events were identified. During seventh grade, Rebecca missed 40 days of school by the end of the first grading period. Both seventh and eighth grades were repeated due to lack of sufficient attendance. She was promoted to ninth grade on the basis of her age; however, at the time of her evaluation, Rebecca had attended only two days during the first four months of school. Prior to sixth grade, Rebecca attended school regularly and without reluctance, reportedly enjoyed school, and received above-average grades.

Rebecca lived with her mother and 15-year-old sister. Her mother was a 35-year-old, single parent who worked as a secretary. Rebecca's parents never married, and she had no contact with her biological father. Family psychiatric history was significant for social phobia (public speaking) as well as major depression.

A social history revealed that Rebecca had only one current peer relationship. Although she maintained some contact with a boyfriend, she rarely went out in public with him. Given the length of time Rebecca had been out of school, she had no contact with many of her peers. As such, the majority of her social contacts were with family members. She was described by her mother as sensitive, reticent, and uncomfortable around people.

Rebecca had a history of prior psychiatric contact, including both inpatient and outpatient treatment. Unfortunately, these various therapeutic interventions were unsuccessful in returning Rebecca to school. In fact, since Rebecca had not returned to school, her mother eventually was required to go to court and was fined.

Rebecca and her mother were interviewed by a clinical child psychologist using a version of the Schedule for Affective Disorders and Schizophrenia for School-Aged Children (K-SADS [Puig-Antich & Chambers, 1982]) modified by Last (1986) for use with anxiety-disordered populations. At first, Rebecca pretended to go to school, and it was not until three months into seventh grade that her mother became aware of the excessive absenteeism. However, once the absenteeism was discovered, Rebecca began to avoid school openly. She reported feeling sick and worried in the mornings before school and, thus, unable to attend. Although Rebecca was noncompliant about attending school, she did not exhibit acting-out behavior or pervasive problems with noncompliance. When she was not at school, Rebecca remained at home. In fact, she spent the majority of her time at home. At those times that mother did insist that she attend school, Rebecca became upset, tearful, and shaky, and appeared to be nervous. At the time of this evaluation, mother had given up trying to get Rebecca to attend school and simply allowed her to remain at home.

In addition, mother reported that Rebecca had difficulty in situations other than school. She stated that Rebecca was hesitant to enter social situations, worried in advance about many social situations, and subsequently avoided them. For example, she would become extremely upset at the thought of having to speak or eat in front of other people and would avoid going to stores or restaurants. Generally, Rebecca would not enter social situations even if accompanied by family members. On those rare occasions that Rebecca did enter social situations, she spent an excessive amount of time preparing and required almost constant reassurance that her appearance and behavior were appropriate. She appeared to be extremely anxious before, during, and after entering social situations.

Rebecca was interviewed alone upon completion of her mother's interview. She acknowledged that school attendance had been a major problem for her over the past four years. Rebecca stated that she felt uncomfortable and nervous when in school. She described feeling extremely self-conscious about having to speak in class, eat in the cafeteria, and dress for gym. Moreover, Rebecca felt unable to tolerate the crowded classrooms, and was fearful of doing or saying "something stupid" in front of the other kids. She also reported feeling very nervous when in a variety of social situations outside of school, such as crowded places, stores, and waiting in lines. Rebecca described feeling embarrassed whenever she was around groups of people because she felt as though she was being scrutinized and evaluated negatively. She was tense much of the time and worried frequently about what others thought of her appearance and behavior.

Rebecca denied experiencing panic attacks; rather, she reported avoiding situations out of fear of making a mistake or feeling embarrassed. In addition, she denied separation fears such as worry about herself or her mother, difficulty being away from her mother, and separation-related sleep difficulties. Symptoms of other anxiety disorders, depression, mania, psychosis, attention deficit, and/or conduct disorders were denied by both Rebecca and her mother.

Rebecca's school social worker was contacted by phone, with both Rebecca's and her mother's permission, and was asked to provide information about Rebecca. The social worker reported that school personnel were very frustrated. They had made numerous attempts to help Rebecca get back to school, none of which were successful. As Rebecca had missed so much school, alternate placement options were discussed. The social worker's recommendation was for a Graduate Equivalency Degree study program; however, she was very skeptical of Rebecca's ability and willingness to comply.

It appeared as though Rebecca was described best as suffering from pervasive social anxiety and avoidance consistent with a diagnosis of social phobia, generalized type. The goal of Rebecca's outpatient treatment was to decrease her anxiety about, and avoidance of, social situations. Although return to school was a high priority, it appeared as though Rebecca first would need to experience success in confronting less anxiety-provoking social situations. A program of graduated in vivo exposure to anxiety-provoking situations was used. Treatment consisted of nine one-hour sessions over the course of a three-month period.

Rebecca made rapid progress using graduated exposure. Given her age and the intensity of her anxiety, an alternate educational placement was obtained that involved smaller groups of peers. Rebecca tolerated the new academic setting well and quickly was able to tolerate larger social situations. In fact, by the sixth session, Rebecca was able to attend a party with a dozen peers and have an enjoyable time. Although she did report some anticipatory anxiety about attending the party, Rebecca excitedly described the event as "a lot of fun." She described feeling more confident about her ability to enter social situations without fear of embarrassing herself. Rebecca noted that once her anxiety decreased and she started paying more attention to those around her, she realized that nobody seemed to be scrutinizing her behavior.

By the end of treatment she was able to approach most social situations with only minimal anxiety. In those situations in which her anxiety level remained somewhat high (e.g., walking in a crowded park alone), she no longer exhibited avoidance behavior. Rebecca was able to see clearly that exposure to anxiety-provoking situations led to decreased anxiety. In addition, by the end of treatment Rebecca had completed a GED study program, passed the GED, and enrolled in a local community college. Not only was she exposed to large groups of people while attending classes at the community college, Rebecca also was required to ride the bus for transportation to and from the campus. She frequently went out with her boyfriend and family members and reported feeling very satisfied with the outcome of treatment. A phone call to Rebecca two months after treatment ended found her to have maintained her treatment gains with a continued decrease in social anxiety. The reader is referred to Francis and Ollendick (in press) for additional details of this case.

CONTINUITY AND DISCONTINUITY WITH ADULT PRESENTATION

Given the lack of clinical and research data regarding social phobia in childhood, it is not surprising that virtually nothing is known about the comparison between child and adult presentations of the disorder. Clinical experience suggests that there is some continuity in terms of the common types of social phobias. For example, fear of public speaking is seen in children and adults. Moreover, social phobias can lead to significant impairment regardless of age. Socially phobic children who avoid school and socially phobic adults who avoid their jobs are likely to be impaired seriously. To understand continuity and discontinuity in the clinical course of social phobia through the life span, prospective empirical information is sorely needed.

SUMMARY

Adult social phobia recently has been referred to as a "neglected" anxiety disorder (Liebowitz, Gorman, Fyer, & Klein, 1985). If social phobia has been neglected in the adult literature, it has been almost completely ignored in the child literature. Although childhood anxiety disorders have received increased clinical and research attention of late, a paucity of information exists regarding childhood social phobia. As such, this chapter will end with a summary of questions rather than answers.

- What is the relationship between childhood social anxiety in normal populations and childhood social phobia in clinic populations?
- What happens to social phobic children as they enter adolescence and adulthood?
- What is the relationship between social phobia and anxiety-based school refusal?
- Is treatment effective in modifying social phobias in youngsters?
- Are the treatment approaches that have been used for childhood *simple* phobias effective for the treatment of *social* phobias?

With time and a concerted effort by clinicians and researchers, these and other questions can be answered.

REFERENCES

Aimes, P. L., Gelder, M. G., & Shaw, P. M. (1983). Social phobia: A comparative clinical study. *British Journal of Psychiatry, 142*, 174–179.

American Psychiatric Association. (1987). *Diagnostic and statistical manual of mental disorders* (3rd ed. rev.). Washington, DC: Author.

Anderson, J. C., Williams, S., McGee, R., & Silva, P. A. (1987). DSM-III disorders in preadolescent children. *Archives of General Psychiatry, 44*, 69–76.

Berg, I., Butler, A., & Hall, J. (1976). The outcome of adolescent school phobia. *British Journal of Psychiatry, 128*, 80–85.

Berg, I., & Jackson, A. (1985). Teenage school refusers grow up: A follow-up study of 168 subjects, ten years on average after inpatient treatment. *British Journal of Psychiatry, 147*, 366–370.

Coolidge, J., Brodie, R., & Feeney, B. (1964). A ten-year follow-up study of sixty-six school-phobic children. *American Journal of Orthopsychiatry, 34*, 675–684.

Francis, G., & Ollendick, T. H. (in press). Behavioral treatment of social anxiety. Chapter to appear in E. L. Feindler & G. R. Kalfus (Eds.), *Casebook in adolescent behavior therapy*. New York: Springer.

Francis, G., Strauss, C. C., & Last, C. G. (1987). *Social anxiety in school phobic adolescents*. Paper presented at the annual meeting of the Association for the Advancement of Behavior Therapy, Boston.

Graziano, A., DeGiovanni, I. S., & Garcia, K. (1979). Behavioral treatment of children's fears: A review. *Psychological Bulletin, 86*, 804–830.

Jersild, A. T., & Holmes, F. B. (1935). Methods of overcoming children's fears. *Journal of Psychology, 1*, 75–104.

Kovacs, M. (1980–81). Rating scales to assess depression in school-aged children. *Acta Paedopsychiatry, 46*, 437–457.

Lapouse, R., & Monk, M. A. (1959). Fears and worries in a representative sample of children. *American Journal of Orthopsychiatry, 29*, 803–818.

Last, C. G. (1986). *Modification of the K-SADS for use with anxiety-disordered populations*. University of Pittsburgh School of Medicine. Unpublished manuscript.

Last, C. G., Strauss, C. C., & Francis, G. (1987). Comorbidity among childhood anxiety disorders. *Journal of Nervous and Mental Disease, 175*, 726–730.

Liebowitz, M. R., Gorman, J. M., Fyer, A. J., & Klein, D. F. (1985). Social phobia: Review of a neglected anxiety disorder. *Archives of General Psychiatry, 42*, 729–736.

Marks, I. M. (1970). Classification of phobic disorders. *British Journal of Psychiatry, 116*, 377–386.

Puig-Antich, J., & Chambers, W. (1982). *Schedule for affective disorders and schizophrenia for school-age children* (6–16 years) — Kiddie-SADS. New York: New York State Psychiatric Institute.

Strauss, C. C., & Francis, G. (1989). Phobic disorders. In C. G. Last & M. Hersen (Eds.), *Handbook of child psychiatric diagnosis*. New York: John Wiley & Sons.

Waldron, S. (1976). The significance of childhood neurosis for adult mental health: A follow-up study. *American Journal of Psychiatry, 133*, 532–538.

CHAPTER 12

SOCIAL PHOBIA IN ADULTHOOD

Franklin R. Schneier
Michael R. Liebowitz

DESCRIPTION OF THE DISORDER

The adult with social phobia experiences recurrent episodes of significant anxiety in one or more social situations. Symptoms of autonomic discharge, such as trembling, sweating, and blushing, often accompany the fear. The sufferer fears embarrassment or humiliation in these situations, and either actively avoids them or endures them with dread, resulting in social and/or occupational impairment.

In its milder forms, social phobia may be limited to a single situation, such as public speaking. For example, an otherwise well-adjusted business executive may find it difficult to give presentations at meetings and is therefore limited in his career. At the other end of the social phobic spectrum, social anxiety may intrude into virtually every aspect of life. Walking into a classroom may become an awkward experience of public scrutiny, and such situations as talking to colleagues or supervisors, asking someone for a date, or attending a party may become intolerable, leaving the social phobic socially and occupationally disabled.

Historically, the term social phobia (*phobie du situations sociales*) was introduced by Janet (1903, 1909) to describe patients who feared public speaking, performing at the piano, and writing while being observed. In 1926, Freud (1961) explicated his theory of anxiety, which grouped all phobias as psychological symptoms produced by ego defenses externalizing unacceptable instinctual drives. Behaviorists similarly grouped phobias as learned avoidance behavior. The pooling of all phobias, and its implicit etiological uniformity, was accepted by the American Psychiatric Association in the first two versions of the *Diagnostic and Statistical Manual of Mental Disorders* (1952, 1968).

Marks and Gelder (1966) took another approach to classification, by dividing phobias into agoraphobia, social phobia, and simple or specific phobias. They noted that social phobia had an earlier age of onset than agoraphobia, a finding supported by subsequent studies (Marks, 1970; Amies, Gelder, & Shaw, 1983). The concept of social phobia as a separate disorder was incorporated into DSM-III (1980) and into the current criteria for social phobia in DSM-III-R (1988). Current DSM-III-R criteria include:

1. A persistent fear of one or more situations (the social phobic situations) in which the person is exposed to possible scrutiny by others and fears that he or she may do something or act in a way that will be humiliating or embarrassing.
2. If an Axis-II or another Axis-I disorder is present, the fear in (1) is unrelated to it, for example, the fear is not of having a panic attack (panic disorder), stuttering (stuttering), trembling (Parkinson's disease), or exhibiting abnormal eating behavior (anorexia nervosa or bulimia nervosa).
3. During some phase of the disturbance, exposure to the specific phobic stimulus (or stimuli) almost invariably provokes an immediate anxiety response.
4. The phobic situation(s) is avoided or is endured with intense anxiety.
5. The avoidant behavior interferes with occupational functioning or with usual social activities or relationships with others, or there is marked distress about having the fear.
6. The person recognizes that his or her fear is excessive or unreasonable.

Additionally, DSM-III-R permits social phobia to be subtyped as "generalized" if anxiety occurs in most social situations. Individuals with generalized social phobia suffer anxiety when talking to strangers, acquaintances, colleagues, or authority figures. They may avoid work or seek jobs with limited interpersonal demands, remain with their family of origin or live alone, and avoid dating, marriage, or friendships. Many also meet DSM-III-R criteria for avoidant personality. (Previously, in DSM-III, but not in DSM-III-R, a diagnosis of avoidant personality disorder excluded social phobia, by definition. Thus DSM-III social phobia may be considered roughly equivalent to the DSM-III-R concept of the nongeneralized, or discrete subtype of social phobia.) Most generalized social phobics also have fears of specific performance situations, such as public speaking. In the nongeneralized, or discrete, form of social phobia, social fears are commonly limited to performance anxiety or anxiety related to discrete public acts, such as using a pen, eating utensil, drinking cup, or urinal in front of others.

These subtypes have received tentative validation from several evaluations that have found differential psychophysiological responses to social stressors and to various treatments. In a double-blind controlled study in our clinic (Liebowitz et al., 1988), 42 generalized social phobics responded significantly better to phenelzine than to atenolol or placebo. A smaller group of patients with discrete performance anxiety showed a nonsignificant superior response to atenolol over phenelzine and placebo. Heimberg (1986) found that public speaking phobics responded better than did generalized social phobics to a treatment including simulated exposures, cognitive restructuring, and homework assignments. A recent comparison of these groups found generalized social phobics to appear more anxious and perform more poorly in an individualized behavioral test, to differ in their responses to cognitive assessment tasks, and to differ in their patterns of heart rate acceleration during behavioral tests (Heimberg, unpublished data).

CLINICAL PRESENTATION

Social phobia has received relatively little attention from clinicians in comparison to other anxiety diagnoses, such as panic disorder. Because of the very nature of their dysfunction, social phobics may be reticent about seeking out professional help. Clinician and patient may downplay social phobics' symptoms as a variant of normal social anxiety, or treatment may focus on complications like alcoholism or depression.

Characterizations of social phobia in clinical populations have yielded a rather consistent description of the syndrome, especially within subtypes. Marks (1970) initially reported on a sample of social phobics who were 50% male, had a mean age of onset of 19 years, and sought treatment at a mean age of 27 years. Several groups have reported a mean age of onset between 16 and 19 years and a predominance of males in clinical samples (Amies et al., 1983; Liebowitz, unpublished data; Solyom, Ledwidge, & Solyom, 1986; Turner, Beidel, Dancu, & Keys, 1986). Reports of a higher prevalence in the middle and upper classes may reflect differential access to treatment programs.

Turner et al. (1986) reported that social fears most commonly experienced by DSM-III social phobics (i.e., excluding avoidant personality disorder subjects) included formal speaking (81%), informal speaking (76%), eating in public (33%), writing in public (19%), taking tests (9.5%), and drinking in public (4.8%). Over 90% of the social phobics reported more than one type of feared situation and most subjects reported marked avoidance of their feared situations. While DSM-III-R loosely defines the generalized subtype of social phobia as having anxiety in "most social situations," the distinction between subtypes requires further clarification based on empirical study.

In a study of cognitive aspects of social phobia, (Heimberg, Hope, Doge, & Becker, 1988), subjects with generalized or specific subtypes were observed while role playing in feared social situations. The groups did not differ in their reported anxiety or self-evaluation of performance. Observers, however, rated the generalized social phobics as more anxious and less skillful. The generalized social phobics assessed their poor performance more objectively than did the specific social phobics, who underestimated the skill of their performances. Specific social phobics may also respond better to cognitive therapy than do generalized social phobics (Heimberg, 1986).

Somatic symptoms most commonly reported by DSM-III social phobics in their phobic situations include palpitations (79%), trembling (75%), sweating (74%), tense muscles (64%), sinking feeling in stomach (63%), dry mouth (61%), feeling hot/cold (57%), and blushing (51%) (Amies et al., 1983). The presence of prominent symptoms of autonomic nervous system activation have led to study of physiological differences in social phobics.

Early studies by Lader et al. (1967) suggested that patients with social phobic complaints had more resting spontaneous galvanic skin fluctuations and habituated more slowly following auditory stimuli than did simple phobics or normals. This work has not been replicated in more rigorously defined social phobics. Studies comparing cardiovascular function (Beidel, Turner, & Dancu, 1985; Turner et al., 1986) of social phobics to normals have reported small but significant differences in elevations in heart rate and systolic blood pressure during social interaction and public speaking. Beidel et al. (1985) also reported that heart rate and systolic blood pressure returned to normal more slowly during a social stressor in anxious subjects compared to controls. In a comparison of social phobia subgroups (Heimberg et al., 1988), public speaking phobics showed greater and more prolonged heart rate increases during role-played public speaking than generalized social phobics showed during role-played social interactions.

In a study of stressful public speaking by nor-

mals, plasma epinephrine levels briefly increased by two to three times baseline levels (Dimsdale & Moss, 1974). This suggested that social phobia might be caused by either an exaggeration of catecholamine production under social stress or by increased sensitivity to normal catecholamine elevation during stress. Such a hypothesis has been supported by evidence that acute treatment with beta-adrenergic blocking drugs alleviates performance anxiety in normal subjects (Desai, Taylor-Davies, & Barnett, 1983; Liden & Gottfries, 1974) and may relieve social phobia, particularly the specific form (Liebowitz et al., 1988). In a more direct test of the theory, 11 patients with DSM-III social phobia were infused intravenously with epinephrine over 60 minutes. Although their mean plasma epinephrine level increased from 113 pg/ml to 928 pg/ml, only one of the patients experienced observable anxiety. Increase in plasma epinephrine level alone appears insufficient to explain social anxiety (Papp et al., 1988).

In another study of catecholamine function (A. Levin, unpublished data), 23 DSM-III social phobics and 14 normal controls gave a speech in the laboratory. Heart rate and blood chemistry were directly monitored. Although patients reported significantly more subjective complaints and demonstrated more anxious behaviors than controls, there were no differences in heart rate or plasma epinephrine, norepinephrine, or cortisol. To the extent that peripheral autonomic arousal contributes to social anxiety, social phobics appear to suffer from an exaggerated awareness rather than an increased amount of such arousal. In the only double-blind study to date, generalized social phobics did not appear to benefit from treatment with atenolol, a beta blocker with primarily peripheral activity. They did, however, respond to treatment with the monoamine oxidase inhibitor phenelzine, which presumably modifies the response to social situations by a central nervous system mechanism (Liebowitz et al., 1988).

Cognitive dysfunction in social phobia has been emphasized by other researchers (Heimberg & Barlow, 1987). In stressful situations, social phobics tend to focus their thoughts toward "task-irrelevant" stimuli, such as negative expectancies, perceived lack of control, and public consequences of poor performance and away from the task at hand. This leads to a cycle of poor performance and worsening expectations for social situations. This theory suggests that exposure therapy should be coupled with social skills training and/

or cognitive restructuring to enhance the individual's ability to focus on thoughts relevant to the social task.

Further work is required to determine the psychological and physiological bases of social phobia. It also remains to be established whether the generalized and discrete subtypes represent separate disorders or differing levels of severity on a continuum. The finding of a differential response to specific modalities of psychotherapy and pharmacotherapy in the two subtypes may be clinically important, but requires further study.

EPIDEMIOLOGY

A recent epidemiological study of two urban populations found six-month prevalences of DSM-III social phobia from 0.9% to 1.7% for men and 1.5% to 2.6% for women (Myers et al., 1984). The prevalence of primary social phobia may have been overestimated among women by including subjects whose social anxiety was secondary to another disorder, such as panic disorder. Prevalence figures for social phobia also approximate its incidence, because the disorder tends to run a very chronic course.

Another community survey (Pollard & Henderson, 1988) measured the prevalence of four specific social fears — public speaking, writing in public, eating in public, and using public restrooms. While the combined prevalence rate of these fears was quite high, greater than 20%, the prevalence fell to 2% when the additional social phobia criterion of impairment was added. Many people with subsyndromal social phobia may be able to avoid their feared social situations without substantial negative consequences. One study of first-year students at a British college estimated that 3% to 10% of the students manifested typical social phobic symptoms (Bryant & Trower, 1974).

In studies of clinical populations, Marks (1970) found that 8% of a phobic population had social phobia, while 60% had agoraphobia. Other investigators, however, have noted that the ratio of social phobics to agoraphobics increased after the investigators' interest in social phobia became known (Amies et al., 1983). Among outpatients applying for treatment to one American anxiety and phobia center, 8 of 60 (13.3%) were found to have DSM-III social phobia, which equaled the proportion with panic disorder and was exceeded only by agoraphobia (DiNardo, O'Brien, Barlow, Waddell, & Blanchard, 1983). The prevalence of the generalized subtype of social phobia has not

been established, but appears to be less common than discrete social phobia.

The only available study (Ndtei & Vadher, 1984) of social unease across cultural groups showed no differences across 593 patients in nine cultural groups admitted to a London hospital. In a Japanese outpatient clinic population, social phobia represented 12% of DSM-III anxiety disorder diagnoses. Male social phobics outnumbered females by nearly 2 to 1, and the mean age of onset was 22.6 years, the earliest of any anxiety disorder (Takahashi et al., 1987). This demographic profile is quite similar to that noted in Western populations; however, cultural differences may alter the expression of social phobia. Korean and Japanese investigators have included in their conception of the disorder patients with the fear of making others uncomfortable and thus harming others by such social "defects" as body odor or direct eye contact (Si, 1985).

NATURAL HISTORY

The natural history of social phobia in adulthood has been established largely by retrospective report and clinical impression. In one study (Amies et al., 1983), the mean duration of illness for patients presenting with social phobia was 12 years. Most often the onset of the disorder occurs in late adolescence, although some patients recall having the disorder as early as the preschool years. The onset may be insidious, or characterized by a specific embarrassing or traumatic event. Many patients report no evidence of shyness prior to the onset of social phobia in adolescence. Once symptoms of the disorder are established, the course is usually chronic, with some waxing and waning of severity, but periods of remission are not commonly reported by clinical populations. The nature of social phobia in the geriatric age group has not been studied, to our knowledge.

IMPAIRMENT AND COMPLICATIONS

The morbidity of social phobia ranges from mild dysfunction to extreme social, academic, and occupational impairment, with more severe dysfunction especially in the generalized subtype. In one unselected series of 11 patients meeting DSM-III-R social phobia criteria in our clinic, 2 were unable to work, 2 had dropped out of school, 4 had abused alcohol, 1 had abused tranquilizers, 6 were blocked from work advancement, and 5 avoided almost all social interaction outside their immediate family. Five of the 11 had either past or present secondary major depression. Turner et al. (1986) reported that 85% of DSM-III social phobics felt impaired in academic or school functioning, 92% felt their occupational performance was significantly impaired, 69% felt their general social functioning was impaired, and half of the unmarried social phobics felt that their heterosocial functioning was limited.

A past or present history of depression was found in one-third of another series of social phobic patients (Munjack & Moss, 1981). Amies et al. (1983) found depressive symptoms in one half of social phobics in a large sample. They also found that 14% of their social phobics had a history of "parasuicidal acts," exceeding the 2% rate among agoraphobics.

Social phobia is also frequently accompanied by alcohol abuse. In a study of alcoholic inpatients, 16 (21%) had a history of social phobia by Research Diagnostic Criteria (RDC) (Spitzer, Endicott, & Robins, 1978), the highest rate of any anxiety disorder in this population (Chambless, Cherney, Caputo, & Rheinstein, 1987). The anxiety disorder preceded substance abuse in 80% of the patients. Other studies of alcoholic populations (Mullaney & Trippett, 1979; Smail, Stockwell, Canter, & Hodgson, 1984) have reported rates of social phobic symptoms as high as 39% during the subjects' last drinking period and 56% during an alcoholism-related hospitalization, respectively.

Similarly, high rates of alcoholism have been found among social phobic patient populations. Thyer, Parrish, Himle, Cameron, Curtis, and Nesse (1986) screened 156 DSM-III diagnosed anxiety disorder patients for alcoholism, finding a 36% rate of alcoholism among social phobics, a higher prevalence than for any other anxiety disorder. In a population of 98 DSM-III-R social phobics without current alcoholism, 16 (16%) had a past history of alcoholism by RDC criteria (Schneier, Martin, Liebowitz, Gorman, & Fyer, 1989). Among the dual-diagnosis patients, the social phobia tended to be severe, and it had an onset before alcoholism in 15 of the 16 patients, most of whom reported using alcohol to self-medicate social phobic symptoms. It is not uncommon for social phobics to drink to the point of intoxication prior to attending a social event. Turner et al. (1986) reported that approximately one half of 21 DSM-III social phobics they studied used alcohol intentionally prior to attending a social event and one half used anxiolytic drugs to relieve anxiety.

DIFFERENTIAL DIAGNOSIS

The characteristic symptoms of social phobia must be distinguished from other forms of anxiety and social avoidance that are present in many mental disorders, including agoraphobia and panic disorder, simple phobias, obsessive-compulsive disorder, depressive disorders, substance abuse disorders, psychoses, and personality disorders.

Panic Disorder and Agoraphobia

The key distinctions between social phobics and individuals with panic disorder with agoraphobia lie in the nature of their phobic situations and the motivation for their avoidance. Unlike social phobics, agoraphobics often avoid nonsocial situations where it would be difficult to get help in the event of a panic attack, such as closed spaces or traveling alone. Agoraphobics prefer to be accompanied and usually seek people out when having an anxiety attack, whereas social phobics actively avoid people to prevent an anxiety attack. When agoraphobics do avoid social situations, their fear of humiliation is not general, but it is instead limited to the circumstances of having a panic attack. Agoraphobics are also more likely to give a history of unexpected or spontaneous anxiety attacks.

Physical symptoms of severe episodic anxiety occur in both panic disorder with agoraphobia and social phobia, but the patterns of symptoms are not the same. Amies et al. (1983) found that social phobics report more blushing and muscle twitching than do agoraphobics and less limb weakness, breathing difficulty, dizziness or faintness, actual fainting, and buzzing or ringing in the ears. Agoraphobics also experienced more frequent and severe depersonalization and derealization.

These findings were confirmed by Cameron, Thyer, Nesse, and Curtis (1986), who compared symptom profiles on the Acute Panic Inventory by diagnosis among 316 patients with anxiety disorders. In comparison to panic disorder patients, social phobics scored significantly lower on most symptoms, including feeling faint, fear of dying, palpitations, breathing changes, dizziness, confusion, derealization, depersonalization, difficulty concentrating, and nausea. Social phobics scored higher on sweating and difficulty speaking. Another study (Munjack, Brown, & McDowell, 1987) demonstrated that social phobic patients reported fewer somatic symptoms than did nonagoraphobic panic disorder patients, as measured by the SCL-90R somatization subscale. Social phobics also score higher on measures of interpersonal sensitivity than do panic disorder patients (Munjack et al., 1987) and lower on measures of extraversion than do agoraphobics (Amies et al., 1983). These differences in symptom profiles of panic disorder and agoraphobia versus social phobia may reflect differences in pathophysiology of the syndromes.

Biological challenge studies have also differentiated social phobia from panic disorder and agoraphobia. Sodium lactate infusion induces panic attacks in most panic disorder patients, but fails to induce panic in most social phobics. When patients meeting DSM-III criteria for agoraphobia with panic attacks or social phobia were challenged with 0.5 M racemic sodium lactate administered intravenously over 20 minutes, 4 (44%) of 9 agoraphobics panicked, in contrast to 1 (7%) of 15 social phobics, a significant difference (Liebowitz et al., 1985).

Another method of provoking panic attacks is the inhalation of carbon dioxide. Inhalation of 5% carbon dioxide for 20 minutes in a canopy system induced panic in 12 of 31 panic disorder patients, but in none of 8 social phobics (Gorman et al., 1988). Studies using higher concentrations of carbon dioxide have yielded mixed results. While Rapee, Mattick, and Murrell (1986) found that a single inhalation of 50% carbon dioxide led to significantly less anxiety in social phobics than in panic disorder patients, preliminary results in our clinic suggest that 35% carbon dioxide provokes panic at a similar rate in both groups.

There are also well-established demographic differences between social phobia and panic disorder with agoraphobia. While these group differences are not specific enough to determine the diagnosis of an individual, they support the distinction between the disorders. In Marks's (1970) series, social phobics were 50% male, had an average age of onset of 19 years, and sought treatment at a mean age of 27 years. Agoraphobics were less likely to be male (25%), had a later mean age of onset (24 years), and sought treatment at a later age (32 years). These differences were confirmed by Amies et al. (1983), who also reported that social phobics came from a higher social class. Persson and Nordlund (1985) also reported that social phobics belonged to a higher social class, had higher education and higher verbal intelligence, and had an earlier onset of illness,

based upon a comparison of 31 social phobic and 73 agoraphobic subjects. Another recent comparison (Solyom et al., 1986) agreed that social phobics were younger, more likely to be male, and better educated than were agoraphobics.

While social phobia and panic disorder have been established as distinct syndromes, it is also clear that they often co-occur. Solyom et al. (1986) found that 55% of DSM-III agoraphobics suffered from clinically significant social phobias (though rated at lower intensity than their agoraphobia) and 30% of DSM-III social phobics suffered from clinically significant agoraphobia (though rated at lower intensity than their social phobia). Family studies and prospective long-term studies may help to clarify its relationship to agoraphobia.

Simple Phobias

The simple phobias, including specific animal phobias (e.g., birds, cats, insects) and situational phobias (e.g., heights, darkness, thunderstorms, blood injury), are similar in form to the specific fears of social phobics (public speaking, writing, eating, or drinking), but also differ in several ways besides the content of the phobias. Marks (1970) noted that social phobics showed a later age of onset, higher overt anxiety levels, and higher Maudsley neuroticism scores than did animal phobics. Solyom et al. (1986) confirmed the findings of a significantly later age of onset and higher neuroticism scores for social phobics, in comparison to simple phobics. They also found that social phobics had significantly lower Maudsley extraversion scores and were more likely to report occupational or school difficulties as precipitants for the onset of their illness. Simple phobics were significantly more likely to report fright, generally involving an incident with the phobic object, as precipitating their illness. Another comparison of social and simple phobics (Thyer, Parrish, Curtis, Nesse, & Cameron, 1985) found no difference in ages of onset for these disorders.

There may also be physiological differences in the anxiety responses of simple and social phobics. Lader, Gelder, and Marks (1967) found social phobics to have more spontaneous fluctuations in galvanic skin response than did animal phobics. Weerts and Lang (1978) reported that students fearful of spiders react with greater affect and greater change in heart rate to fear-relevant scenes than did students fearful of public speaking. Simple phobics, unlike social phobics, have not been reported to respond to medication treatments.

Obsessive Compulsive Disorder

Individuals with obsessive compulsive disorder will sometimes fear and avoid social situations that are involved in their obsessional thoughts or compulsive rituals. For example, a person with obsessions about contamination might feel anxious sitting on a public bench. Another, who practices excessive checking, might avoid social situations where this behavior might be revealed. In both situations the anxiety or avoidance is secondary to obsessive compulsive symptomatology. Conversely, social phobics may have repetitive thoughts of being embarrassed, but these thoughts, unlike obsessions, are not ego-dystonic to the individual, and they are limited to fears of social humiliation or criticism.

Depression

The social withdrawal commonly seen in depressive disorders is usually associated with a lack of interest in or anticipatory pleasure for the company of others, rather than a fear of scrutiny. In contrast, social phobics have a desire to socialize freely. They believe social activity would be enjoyable if only their anxiety could be reduced.

Sometimes the distinction between these disorders is less clear. Social phobia is often complicated by secondary depression, which may exacerbate underlying social anxiety. Sensitivity to criticism or rejection is characteristic of both social phobia and "atypical" depression. Some patients experience phasic social phobia while depressed and can subsequently become chronically avoidant.

Substance Abuse

Social phobia and alcohol abuse occur in the same individuals to a far greater extent than chance association (see Impairment and Complications). It is clear that for some social phobics, alcohol abuse develops out of an effort to blunt social anxiety with heavy alcohol consumption (Schneier et al., 1989). For these patients, treatment of the underlying social phobia in conjunction with alcoholism treatment may diminish the urge to drink and improve treatment results. On the other hand, alcoholism and alcohol withdrawal states can lead to episodic social anxiety, which will not respond to any treatment but abstinence. The relationship of other substance abuse to social phobia is less well documented, but may parallel the situation with alcohol abuse. Establishing the temporal relationship of disorders in patients with dual diagnoses can be crucial to treatment selection.

Psychoses

Patients with psychotic disorders may be socially avoidant, but they are distinguished from social phobia by the presence of delusions and/or hallucinations that may support the avoidance. Panic anxiety or fears of humiliation leading to social avoidance are not diagnosed as social phobia when they occur in the context of schizophrenia, schizophreniform disorder, or brief reactive psychoses. This should be studied further, however, because both cognitive/behavioral and drug therapies for social phobia may have some utility in socially avoidant schizophrenics on concurrent antipsychotic medication.

Personality Disorders

Avoidant personality disorder, which is characterized in DSM-III-R by a chronic pattern of difficulty in relating comfortably to others, with social withdrawal and a fear of rejection and humiliation, appears to overlap social phobia significantly, particularly the generalized subtype. In DSM-III-R, as opposed to DSM-III, both diagnoses may be given concurrently. The current definition of avoidant personality disorder, however, extends beyond the realm of social phobia by describing a more general fear of nonsocial novelty that is said to be common in the disorder. The validity of this definition remains to be empirically determined. Most studies to date comparing social phobia to avoidant personality disorder have used DSM-III diagnoses, and in current terminology, they really compare the equivalents of specific and generalized subtypes of social phobia.

Greenberg and Stravynski (1983) have argued that generalized social phobia should be reclassified as avoidant personality disorder because of its chronic pervasive nature, and the diagnosis of social phobia should be limited to patients with discrete social fears. More empirical information on the characteristics of these syndromes needs to be collected before a definitive classification is determined.

In schizoid, schizotypal, and paranoid personality disorder, individuals may prefer to avoid social situations due to a mistrust of others or a lack of interest in forming relationships with others. In contrast, social phobics do not generally mistrust or dislike other people. Instead of lacking interest, they desire to make social contact, but are blocked by fear that they will act inappropriately and cause their own embarrassment or humiliation.

CASE EXAMPLES

Case 1

E. F. is the youngest of three sons, raised in a middle-class Catholic family. He describes his childhood and development as unremarkable, except for shyness. He recalls that this did not bother him much because most of his free time was spent in sports activity or activities of "doing" rather than talking with his friends. It did affect his performance in school, where he was a "back-of-the-classroom" kid and a below-average student. Although E. F. remembers being shy and generally more nervous than other children, he denies significant impairment during childhood. He did not avoid speaking in class or attending friends' parties.

E. F. began to fear humiliation and embarrassment at age 15. He remembers realizing there were many more social expectations placed on him. No longer did his friends simply play sports, they began to "hang out" and talk. He felt awkward and tongue-tied in these situations. He felt particularly embarrassed talking to girls, and began to fear scrutiny and humiliation when walking through large groups of people. Casual social contact would cause him to feel self-conscious, twitch, sweat, and experience palpitations.

In school, he avoided English classes where he would have to speak and preferred mechanics class, where he could work alone. When walking through the high school cafeteria, he felt as though all eyes were upon him. By the middle of his senior year, he had completed all courses necessary for graduation except seven credits of English, and when he had to give a speech in front of his class, he fled the room and never returned to school again. His father offered him a construction job and E. F. dropped out of school.

Shortly after the onset of severe social anxiety,

E. F. had begun to drink alcohol almost every evening to help him talk more comfortably in social situations. Soon he was drinking more than a six-pack of beer a night and was occasionally using cocaine to counteract the sedation from alcohol. The alcohol use led to frequent blackouts, hangovers, fights, and family discord.

At age 20, E. F. developed a satisfying relationship with a girlfriend who was also extremely shy. Her shyness made him feel less scrutinized when he was with her. He was able to stop his alcohol and drug abuse and enjoyed his work.

When E. F. decided to apply for a job as a bus mechanic, he was told he would first have to serve as a bus driver. He spent two years in "torture. Everyone in the bus could see me. I felt like everyone was looking at me all the time." He called in sick a few times per month due to fear of being embarrassed in front of passengers, despite realizing that this was absurd.

During this time E. F. became demoralized, with trouble falling asleep, low energy, and occasional thoughts that being dead would relieve him of fears of scrutiny and low self-esteem. His mood continued to be generally low, with occasional improvement until the time of his presentation to our clinic at age 24. At that time he continued to feel scrutinized when walking past his coworkers, and worked the evening shift to minimize social contact. He avoided friends' parties and public speaking. E. F. had managed to get his high school equivalency diploma by taking a written test. At the initial evaluation interview for our clinic, E. F. donned dark glasses, which he wore constantly to help him feel less observable. He had been in psychotherapy for several months in a neighborhood mental health clinic without benefit.

E. F. was diagnosed as having social phobia, generalized subtype, and dysthymic disorder. He entered a medication treatment study and was randomly assigned to the beta blocker atenolol 100 mg/day, which he took for 8 weeks without benefit. Subsequently, on the monoamine oxidase inhibitor phenelzine 60 mg/day he began to feel significantly better after 3 weeks, and his anxiety symptoms virtually disappeared. However, he developed decreased libido, weight gain, and urinary hesitancy, and the phenelzine was discontinued. E. F.'s social phobic symptoms then recurred, and he resumed phenelzine. Despite recurrent partial anorgasmia, he chose to continue the phenelzine, which allowed him to be much more comfortable in social situations and to work more effectively.

Case 2

R. T. was the second of six children born to a wealthy family. When she was 2 her family moved and she was separated from the nanny who was her primary caretaker. This move apparently went smoothly. She recalls her father as being forceful and critical, whereas her mother was gentle and accepting, but always acquiesced to R. T.'s father.

R. T. developed normally and recalls crying on the first day of kindergarten but adapting to it afterward. At age 6 she first developed intense fear of embarrassment while speaking in front of children at school. She always considered the fear to be irrational and did not avoid public speaking, but endured it with discomfort. R. T. functioned without difficulty in other social situations. She had several good friends and was a top student. Within her family she was considered headstrong and demanding.

At age 15, her social phobic symptoms worsened. When speaking in front of the class she would blush and sweat and feel extremely humiliated and scrutinized, fearing others would notice her anxiety. She began to go out of her way to avoid public speaking. Two years later she developed severe anxiety while actually being criticized by her boyfriend's family over the dinner table. Thereafter she began to avoid eating in front of others when possible, fearing she would embarrass herself by dropping food and becoming anxious. She had frequent episodes of trembling, rapid heart rate, sweating, lightheadedness, and derealization, occurring exclusively in performance situations. R. T. also began to avoid drinking and writing in public. Her self-esteem was chronically low, but she never developed major depression and maintained an active social and work schedule.

In her early twenties R. T.'s anxiety problem improved partially as she received counseling and repaired old rifts with her parents. When she entered a public service job that required some public speaking, however, her anxiety symptoms returned in full force. Despite the anxiety, she would usually force herself to speak, grabbing the podium to prevent her hands from shaking uncontrollably. Outside of her phobic situations she continued to function well, maintaining friendships, marrying and becoming a mother, and doing well at work.

R. T.'s symptoms would wax and wane depending on the performance demands placed upon her. When she got a promotion, at age 35, that required additional public speaking, she presented to our clinic to participate in a study of medication treatment. She was diagnosed as having the discrete subtype of social phobia. She was randomly assigned to phenelzine, and her anxiety symptoms resolved completely during the 6-month duration of treatment. She experienced side effects of postural hypotension and drowsiness. Upon discontinuing the medication, R. T.'s symptoms recurred but were less severe. She began psychodynamic psychotherapy, which helped her functioning in relationships, but didn't affect her performance anxiety. One and one-half years later she returned to request medication treatment and is currently doing well taking Atenolol 50 mg only on days when she must do public speaking or attend a business lunch.

CHILDHOOD AND FAMILIAL ANTECEDENTS

Social phobia is a disorder that commonly begins in childhood and continues through adulthood with relatively little change in its characteristics. Often patients report a history of childhood shyness prior to the onset of more severe anxiety and avoidance. The onset of social phobia may be insidious or may coincide with increased social stress from developmental experiences, such as performance demands in school or adolescence and new expectations for developing intimacy.

Sometimes social phobia appears to be conditioned by a traumatic event, such as temporarily disfiguring surgery or an actual humiliating experience. Öst and Hugdahl (1981) mailed a questionnaire on the origin of phobias to 34 social phobic outpatients. Of the 31 who replied, 18 (58%) cited conditioning by their own experience, 4 (13%) cited vicarious experiences, 1 (3%) cited instruction or information from others, and 8 (26%) could not recall the origins of their phobias. The importance of conditioning as a factor in social phobia is unclear. Unlike laboratory conditioned avoidance behavior, social phobias are not extinguished by repeated contrary experiences.

Social anxiety may have an inheritable component. Torgersen (1979) compared social fears among 95 monozygotic and dizygotic twin pairs chosen for the most part on an unselected basis from a Norwegian twin registry. The monozygotic twins were significantly more concordant for such social phobic features as discomfort when eating with strangers or when being watched working, writing, or trembling, suggesting a genetic contribution to social fears. One family study (Reich & Yates, 1988) found that the prevalence of DSM-III social phobia in relatives of social phobics (6.6%) was significantly higher than the prevalence of social phobia in relatives of panic disorder patients (0.4%). Although this finding is consistent with a genetic distinction between the disorders, it could also be due to social familial factors.

Further evidence for a constitutional basis for social avoidance is suggested by studies of young children. Kagan, Reznick, and Snidman (1988) recently reported that 2-year-olds, selected because they were extremely shy, quiet, and restrained in a variety of unfamiliar contexts became 7-year-olds who were quiet, cautious, and socially avoidant with peers and adults. The behavioral differences in this cohort were associated with greater sympathetic reactivity than in uninhibited children, especially larger cardiac accelerations to cognitive activity and to a postural change from sitting to standing. It remains uncertain whether these avoidant children will become social phobic adolescents, but further prospective study would be quite interesting.

Other studies have retrospectively examined potential childhood and familial factors in social phobic patients. Greenberg and Stravynski (1985) reported that among 46 outpatients with severe social anxiety and avoidance, 26 (56%) were either only children or first born, including 22 (63%) of 35 males. They raised the speculation that the absence of an older sibling as a social role model is an etiological factor in the development of social dysfunction. The validity of this finding is unclear in the absence of a control group.

Psychodynamic theories of "phobic character" postulate parental rejection and deprecation as an etiological factor. Several controlled studies have compared how adult social phobics, agoraphobics, simple phobics, and normal controls retrospectively rate their parents' child rearing practices and attitudes. As a group, social phobics perceived their parents to have been less caring, more rejecting, and overprotective as compared with normal controls (Arrindell, Emmelkamp, Monsma, & Brilman, 1983; Parker, 1979). No comparisons were carried out among the phobic groups, so the specificity of these findings for social phobia is uncertain. These studies also suffer from the deficiencies inherent in retrospective assessment.

The traditional psychoanalytic view that phobias represent the transformation of internal anxiety into external fear through displacement, and that the specific content of a phobia has symbolic meaning, is also theoretically applicable to social phobia. This has not yet, however, been subject to systematic controlled investigation.

Nichols (1974) has cataloged a variety of other psychological and somatic traits observed in a social phobic sample. These include low self-evaluation, an unrealistic tendency to experience others as critical or disapproving, rigid concepts of appropriate social behavior, negative fantasy-producing anticipatory anxiety, an increased awareness and fear of scrutiny by others, a fear of social situations from which it is difficult to leave unobtrusively, an exaggerated awareness of minimal somatic symptoms such as blushing or feeling faint, a tendency to overreact with greater anxiety to the somatic symptoms of anxiety, and an exaggerated fear of others noticing that one is anxious. It is unclear, however, which among these or other factors are causal, which are consequences of, and which are not even specifically related to social phobia. Other postulated acquired causes of social phobia are social skills deficits and faulty cognitions.

SUMMARY

Social phobia is a chronic disorder, with onset typically in adolescence, characterized by fear of embarrassment in social situations, and subsequent avoidance of those situations. In feared situations, sufferers often experience symptoms of autonomic nervous system arousal, such as sweating, trembling, and palpitations. The disorder occurs in a wide spectrum of severity, from fears limited to a specific situation, such as eating in public, to severe anxiety and avoidance of almost all social settings. Social and occupational morbidity can be devastating. Social phobia is commonly complicated by depression and alcohol abuse.

Major uncertainties still exist regarding the definition, prevalence, etiology, pathophysiology, and treatment of social phobia, as this disorder has received little study until only recently. It is currently being studied from biological, psychological, and development perspectives, and the disorder offers a valuable testing ground for integrating these approaches.

REFERENCES

American Psychiatric Association. (1987). *Diagnostic and statistical manual of mental disorders* (3rd ed. rev.). Washington, DC: Author.
American Psychiatric Association. (1980). *Diag-

nostic and statistical manual of mental disorders (3rd ed.). Washington, DC: Author.

American Psychiatric Association. (1968). *Diagnostic and statistical manual of mental disorders* (2nd ed.). Washington, DC: Author.

American Psychiatric Association. (1952). *Diagnostic and statistical manual of mental disorders* (1st ed.). Washington, DC: Author.

Amies, P. L., Gelder, M. G., & Shaw, P. M. (1983). Social phobia: A comparative clinical study. *British Journal of Psychiatry, 142*, 174–179.

Arrindell, W. A., Emmelkamp, P. M. G., Monsma, A., & Brilman, E. (1983). The role of perceived parental rearing practices in the aetiology of phobic disorders: A controlled study. *British Journal of Psychiatry, 143*, 183–187.

Beidel, D. C., Turner, S. M., & Dancu, C. V. (1985). Physiological, cognitive, and behavioral aspects of social anxiety. *Behaviour Research and Therapy, 23*, 109–117.

Bryant, B., & Trower, P. E. (1974). Social difficulty in a student sample. *British Journal of Educational Psychology, 44*, 13–21.

Cameron, P. G., Thyer, B. A., Nesse, R. M., & Curtis, G. C. (1986). Symptom profiles of patients with DSM-III anxiety disorders. *American Journal of Psychiatry, 143*, 1132–1137.

Chambless, D. L., Cherney, J., Caputo, G. C., & Rheinstein, B. J. G. (1987). Anxiety disorders and alcoholism: A study with inpatient alcoholics. *Journal of Anxiety Disorders, 1*, 29–40.

Desai, N., Taylor-Davies, A., & Barnett, D. B. (1983). The effects of diazepam and oxprenolol on short term memory in individuals of high and low state anxiety. *British Journal of Clinical Pharmacology, 15*, 197–202.

Dimsdale, J. E., & Moss, J. (1974). Short-term catecholamine response to psychological stress. *Psychosomatic Medicine, 42*, 493–497.

DiNardo, P. A., O'Brien, G. T., Barlow, D. H., Waddell, M. T., & Blanchard, E. B. (1983). Reliability of DSM-III anxiety disorder categories using a new structured interview. *Archives of General Psychiatry, 40*, 1070–1074.

Freud, S. (1961). Inhibitions, symptoms and anxiety. In J. Strachey (Ed.), *The standard edition of the complete works of Sigmund Freud* (Vol. 20). London: Hogarth Press.

Gorman, J. M., Fyer, M. R., Goetz, R., Askanazi, J., Liebowitz, M. R., Fyer, A. J., Kinney, J., & Klein, D. F. (1988). Ventilatory physiology of patients with panic disorder. *Archives of General Psychiatry, 45*, 31–42.

Greenberg, D., & Stravynski, A. (1985). Patients who complain of social dysfunction as their main problem: 1. Clinical and demographic features. *Canadian Journal of Psychiatry, 30*, 206–211.

Greenberg, D., & Stravynski, A. (1983). Social phobia. *British Journal of Psychiatry, 143*, 526.

Heimberg, R. G. (1986). *Predicting the outcome of cognitive-behavioral treatment of social phobia*. Paper presented at the annual meeting of the Society for Psychotherapy Research, Wellesley, MA.

Heimberg, R. G., & Barlow, D. H. (1988). Psychosocial treatments for social phobia. *Psychosomatics, 29*, 27–37.

Heimberg, R. G., Hope, D. A., Dodge, C. S., & Becker, R. E. (in press). DSM-III-R subtypes of social phobia: Comparison of generalized social phobics and public speaking phobics. *Journal of Nervous and Mental Disease*.

Janet, P. (1909). *Les nevroses* [The neuroses]. Paris: Flammarion.

Janet, P. (1903). *Les obsessions et la psychasténie* [Obsessions and neurasthenia]. Paris: F. Alcan.

Kagan, J., Reznick, J. S., & Snidman, N. (1988). Biological bases of childhood shyness. *Science, 240*, 167–171.

Lader, M., Gelder, M., & Marks, I. (1967). Palmar skin-conductance measures as predictors of response to desensitization. *Journal of Psychosomatic Research, 11*, 283–290.

Liden, S., & Gottfries, C. G. (1974). Beta blocking agents in treatment of catecholamine-induced symptoms in musicians. *Lancet, 2*, 529.

Liebowitz, M. R., Fyer, A. J., Gorman, J. M., Dillon, D., Davies, S. O., Stein, J. M., Cohen, B., & Klein, D. F. (1985). Specificity of lactate infusions in social phobia vs. panic disorders. *American Journal of Psychiatry, 142*, 947–949.

Liebowitz, M. R., Gorman, J. M., Fyer, A. J., Campeas, R., Levin, A. P., Sandberg, D., Hollander, E., Papp, L., & Goetz, D. (1988). Pharmacotherapy of social phobia: A placebo controlled comparison of phenelzine and atenolol. *Journal of Clinical Psychiatry, 49*, 252–257.

Marks, I. M. (1970). The classification of phobic disorders. *British Journal of Psychiatry, 116*, 377–386.

Marks, I. M., & Gelder, M. G. (1966). Different ages of onset in varieties of phobia. *American Journal of Psychiatry, 123*, 218–221.

Mullaney, J. A., & Trippett, C. J. (1979). Alcohol dependence and phobias: Clinical description

and relevance. *British Journal of Psychiatry,*
135, 563–573.

Munjack, D. J., & Moss, H. B. (1981). Affective
disorder and alcoholism in families of agoraphobics. *Archives of General Psychiatry, 38*,
869–871.

Munjack, D. J., Brown, R. A., & McDowell, D.
E. (1987). Comparison of social anxiety in patients with social phobia and panic disorder.
Journal of Nervous and Mental Disease, 175,
49–51.

Myers, J. K., Weissman, M. M., Tischler, G. L.,
Holzer, C. E., Leaf, P. J., Orvaschel, H., Anthony, J. C., Boyd, J. H., Burke, J. D., Kramer, M., & Stoltzman, R. (1984). Six-month
prevalence of psychiatric disorders in three
communities: 1980–1982. *Archives of General
Psychiatry, 41*, 959–967.

Ndetei, D. M., & Vadher, A. (1984). Patterns of
anxiety in a cross cultural hospital population.
Acta Psychiatrica Scandinavia, 70, 69–71.

Nichols, K. A. (1974). Severe social anxiety. *British Journal of Medical Psychology, 47*, 301–
306.

Öst, L., & Hugdahl, K. (1981). Acquisition of
phobias and anxiety response patterns in clinical patients. *Behaviour Research and Therapy,
19*, 439–447.

Papp, L. A., Liebowitz, M. R., Klein, D. F., Fyer,
A. J., Cohen, B., & Gorman, J. M. (1988).
Epinephrine infusions in patients with social
phobia. *American Journal of Psychiatry, 145*,
733–736.

Parker, G. (1979). Reported parental characteristics of agoraphobics and social phobics. *British Journal of Psychiatry, 135*, 555–560.

Persson, G., & Nordlund, C. L. (1985). Agoraphobics and social phobics: Differences in
background factors, syndrome profiles and
therapeutic response. *Acta Psychiatrica Scandinavica, 71*, 148–159.

Pollard, C. A., & Henderson, J. G. (1988). Four
types of social phobia in a community sample.
Journal of Nervous and Mental Disease, 176,
440–445.

Rapee, R., Mattick, R., & Murrell, E. (1986).
Cognitive mediation in the affective component of spontaneous panic attacks. *Journal of
Behavioral Therapy and Experimental Psychiatry, 17*, 245–273.

Reich, J., & Yates, W. (1988). Family history of
psychiatric disorders in social phobia. *Comprehensive Psychiatry, 29*, 72–75.

Schneier, F. R., Martin, L. Y., Liebowitz, M. R.,
Gorman, J. M., & Fyer, A. J. (1989). Alcohol
abuse in social phobia. *Journal of Anxiety Disorders, 3*, 15–23.

Si Hyung Lee. (1985). *On social phobia*. Seoul
National University, Seoul, Korea.

Smail, P., Stockwell, T., Canter, S., & Hodgson,
R. (1984). Alcohol dependence and phobic
anxiety states: I. A prevalence study. *British
Journal of Psychiatry, 144*, 53–57.

Solyom, L., Ledwidge, B., & Solyom, C. (1986).
Delineating social phobia. *British Journal of
Psychiatry, 149*, 464–470.

Spitzer, R. L., Endicott, J., & Robins, E. (1978).
Research diagnostic criteria: Rationale and reliability. *Archives of General Psychiatry, 35*,
773–782.

Takahashi, S., Nakamura, M., Iida, H., Iritani,
S., Fujii, M., Yamashita, Y., & Yoichi, I.
(1987). Prevalence of panic disorder and other
subtypes of anxiety disorder and their background. *The Japanese Journal of Psychiatry
and Neurology, 41*, 9–18.

Thyer, B. A., Parrish, R. T., Curtis, G. C., Nesse,
R. M., & Cameron, O. G. (1985). Ages of onset of DSM-III anxiety disorders. *Comprehensive Psychiatry, 26*, 113–122.

Thyer, B. A., Parrish, R. T., Himle, J., Cameron,
O. G., Curtis, G. C., & Nesse, R. M. (1986).
Alcohol abuse among clinically anxious patients. *Behaviour Research and Therapy, 24*,
357–359.

Torgersen, S. (1979). The nature and origin of
common phobic fears. *British Journal of Psychiatry, 134*, 343–351.

Turner, S. M., Beidel, D. C., Dancu, C. V., &
Keys, D. J. (1986). Psychopathology of social
phobia and comparison to avoidant personality disorder. *Journal of Abnormal Psychology,
95*, 389–394.

Weerts, T. C., & Lang, P. J. (1978). Psychophysiology of fear imagery: Differences between focal phobia and social performance anxiety.
*Journal of Consulting and Clinical Psychol-
ogy, 46*, 1157–1159.

SIMPLE PHOBIA

EDITORS' COMMENTS

Despite the obvious similarity between phobia in childhood and its counterpart in adulthood, there are some major differences as well. To begin with, clinical phobias in childhood are relatively rare and represent a small proportion of cases that are referred to clinicians for outpatient treatment. Indeed, in childhood, simple phobia must be carefully differentiated from fear, which is common and often age appropriate but generally transient in character. When phobia is diagnosed in accordance with DSM-III-R criteria, children, by direct contrast to adults, usually are unable to comprehend or admit that their phobic response is "out of proportion to the demands of the situation."

When examining the somewhat sparse research literature on childhood phobia, the reviewer must keep in mind that studies have appeared over several decades, conducted with varying methodologies, assessment strategies, and nosological criteria. In some instances fear and the more pervasive and pathological phobia have received no differentiation. Thus, interstudy comparisons are speculative at best, yielding few definitive conclusions. In the adult literature, on the other hand, the status of the art is a bit more secure, and considerably more data have been adduced over the years.

With respect to differential diagnosis, we should underscore that the same guidelines in DSM-III-R are applicable both to children and adults. For children, however, problems in making the correct diagnosis involve differentiating phobia from fear, separation anxiety disorder, and posttraumatic stress disorder. With some similarity, in adulthood there may be, at times, some overlap with panic disorder, agoraphobia, social phobia, and the phobic elements in obsessive-compulsive disorder.

As for an analysis of the comparative effects of impairment at the childhood and adult levels, the empirical literature for children is sparse. However, clinically, difficulties with school work, concentration, peer relations, and a variety of somatic symptoms have been reported. In adulthood, the more severe phobics will have their life circumscribed to the extent that considerable energy and time are expended to avoid the phobic stimulus, thus disrupting the sufferer's life and that of his or her family. However, the vast majority of adult phobics who are not that disturbed never seek treatment, or successfully circumvent the dreaded object (e.g., a height phobic scrupulously avoiding bridges and tall buildings).

The study of the natural history of fears and phobia has considerable implications for tracing possible links between childhood fears and phobias and their adult manifestations. First, as already noted most childhood fears dissipate as the child develops. Second, most animal phobias of middle childhood do not continue past adolescence. Third, a small subset of phobias that begins in childhood (such as blood and injury and dentistry) will persist throughout development and into adulthood. In some instances the phobia has been preceded by a traumatic incident. Reasons for such continuity are suggested by Silverman and Welles in terms of a "genetically determined, extreme autonomic response." In general, the later the phobia develops in childhood, the greater the likelihood that it will persist into adulthood.

To avoid further speculation in this area, it is clear that long-term prospective studies, with identified child phobics who meet clear-cut diagnostic criteria, are very much needed. Otherwise, the relationship between childhood and adult phobic response will remain unclear.

CHAPTER 13

SIMPLE PHOBIA IN CHILDHOOD

Wendy K. Silverman
Wendy B. Nelles

DESCRIPTION OF THE DISORDER

In the *Diagnostic and Statistical Manual of Mental Disorders* (American Psychiatric Association, 1987) no distinction is made in either the classification of or criteria for simple phobia among children and adults. Simple phobias are persistent and focal fears restricted to specific objects or situations, such as animals, heights, thunder, darkness, travel, blood or tissue injury, and closed spaces. Phobias are distinguished from fears (an appropriate response to frightening stimuli) on the basis of the former's "persistence, maladaptiveness, and magnitude" (e.g., Barrios, Hartmann, & Shigetomi, 1981; Graziano & De-Giovanni, 1979; Marks, 1969; Miller, Barret, & Hampe, 1974; Morris & Kratochwill, 1983). As first described by Marks (1969), and elaborated upon by Miller, Barret, and Hampe (1974), a phobia is a special form of fear that:

1. Is out of proportion to the demands of the situation.
2. Cannot be explained or reasoned away.
3. Is beyond voluntary control.

4. Leads to avoidance of the feared situation.
5. Persists over an extended period of time.
6. Is unadaptive.
7. Is not age- or stage-specific.

This description of phobia has been adopted by most investigators and theorists working in the area (e.g., Barrios et al., 1981; Morris & Kratochwill, 1983; Ollendick, 1979).

Although these criteria are applicable with both children and adults, there is one important difference. Unlike adults, children, because of their level of cognitive development, may not be aware that their fear (or phobia) is "out of proportion to the demands of the situation" (criterion 1).

CLINICAL PRESENTATION

We have evaluated and treated a large number of children who present with simple phobia at our Child and Adolescent Fear and Anxiety Treatment Program within the Center for Stress and Anxiety Disorders in Albany, New York. Our clinical experience with these children, the reports of others (e.g., Miller, Barret, & Hampe, 1974; Poznanski,

1973; Rachman & Costello, 1961), and DSM-III-R provide the basis for information contained in this and the following sections.

Consistent with DSM-III-R's description of simple phobia, we have found that children with this disorder, when exposed to the phobic stimulus, experience an immediate anxiety response. This response may vary in terms of the nature and complexity of the threatening stimulus, the nature and extent of the response modalities affected (the subjective/cognitive, the physiological, and/or the motoric/behavioral), and whether the phobia is self-contained or associated with other problem behaviors (Schwartz & Johnson, 1981).

The child phobics we have seen typically describe feelings of "panic" or extreme tension upon exposure to the phobic object or event. Some adolescents have even described feelings of imminent death to us. Feelings of losing control have also been reported. Childhood phobias have an obsessional quality; the children ruminate about the phobia and cannot completely free their thoughts from it. Consequently, many of the youngsters report that concentrating on school work or engaging in recreational or play activities is difficult, if not impossible, for them.

Although obtaining information from children about how their "body feels" when exposed to the phobic stimulus requires careful questioning, and is often difficult for children to report, we have found that using our structured interview, the Anxiety Disorders Interview Schedule for Children (ADIS-C: Silverman & Nelles, 1988), children can provide us with this information. Thus, some of the physiological changes that children have told us that they experience include sweating, difficulty breathing, "their heart beats faster than usual," "feeling like they were going to throw up," "butterflies in the stomach," and so forth. Rachman and Costello (1961) described a 7-year-old child, who, when confronted by a bee, would become "white, sweaty, cold, and trembly, and his legs were like 'jelly.'" Physiological changes such as these may occur either when youngsters are exposed to the phobic stimulus or when they are merely thinking about a future encounter with the stimulus. In severe cases, parents have told us that it almost appears as though their child has gone into "shock" when exposed to the phobic stimulus (e.g., the skin is pale, perspiration occurs, the child is weak, and the pulse is quite rapid).

Behavioral responses displayed by phobic children include screams, cries, and pleas for assistance, as well as for escape. Gross motor re-

sponses such as exaggerated flight responses also appear. Finally, anticipatory anxiety, leading to behavioral avoidance of the phobic stimulus, is a prevalent feature of all phobic children. For example, a child with a phobia of injections would avoid going to the doctor, out of fear of getting a shot; a child with a phobia of cats would avoid going outdoors, out of fear of confronting stray cats.

EPIDEMIOLOGY

Epidemiological data on simple phobia is quite sparse; most of the reports involve childhood fears rather than phobias. This section will review results of both types of studies as well as several more recent reports that examine phobias, specifically. It is important to keep several issues in mind that have influenced these results. First as mentioned, much of the work has focused on childhood fears, both "normal" and excessive. Detailed analysis of whether excessive fears constitute phobias is unreported in most of the studies. Depending largely on the years in which they were conducted, the studies employ different classification systems and definitions of phobia. Last, one should consider the methods of assessment when interpreting the results. Methods range from a single self-report questionnaire to multiple measures that include both interview and questionnaire data from parents, teachers, and children. Given our knowledge of possible discrepancy across assessment measures and informants, it is important to consider the information source when evaluating the findings.

Fears

Early studies of fears demonstrated that most children have mild to moderate fears and that multiple fears are not uncommon. Jersild and Holmes (1935) found that children aged 2 to 6 had an average of 4.6 fears; Hagman (1932), using a comparable sample, reported 2.7 fears per child. Both studies utilized parental reports, exclusively. Lapouse and Monk (1959), in a series of studies, summarized data on children's fears (ages 6 to 12) as reported by mothers, from 482 randomly selected households. Almost half the children (43%) were found to have 7 or more fears. Mothers reported significantly more fears for girls (50%) than for boys (36%); black mothers reported significantly more fears for their children (63%) than did white mothers (44%). In addition, the authors found a nonsignificant trend for younger children (ages 6 to 8) and lower–socioeconomic-status (SES) children to have more fears than older, higher-SES children. (This contrasts with Angelino, Dollins, & Mech's [1956] report of a greater number of fears among higher-SES children, ages 9 to 18 years old, as reported directly by the children.) The Lapouse and Monk (1959) results should be cautiously interpreted, however; when the incidence of fear was directly acquired from an additional sample of 193 children, it was found that mothers underreported their children's fear by 41%.

In a series of studies, Croake and Knox (1973) examined fears of adolescents, and third and sixth grade children, utilizing a questionnaire designed specifically for the study. Adolescent girls reported a greater number of fears (29.9) than boys (22.5); lower-SES adolescents reported a greater number of fears (26.8) than did higher-SES adolescents (22.4). These differences were not found among the younger children. Interestingly, political fears (i.e., war) were mentioned most frequently; the most intense fears were related to natural phenomena.

Estimated fear prevalences among three studies examining overall behavior problems yield data from three different countries. Richman, Stevenson, and Graham (1975) surveyed behavior problems of 705 3-year-old children in London. According to both child and parental reports, girls had significantly more (17.2%) moderate-severe fears than did boys (8.0%), with a total population percentage prevalence of 12.8%. In Denmark, Kastrup (1976) found that among 175 children aged 5 to 6 years, fear prevalence for boys (3%) was less than that for girls (5%). Earls (1980), in a study conducted in the United States, examined the prevalence of behavior problems in 100 3-year-old children. He found the prevalence of severe worries and fear to be 7.5% for boys and 8.6% for girls (8.0% total) for worries, and 3.7% for boys and 25.5% for girls (14.0% total) for fears.

In a more recent study, Ollendick, Matson, and Helsel (1985) examined the prevalence and intensity of fear in children ages 7 to 18 years old. The children were administered the Revised Fear Survey Schedule for Children (FSSC-R), which is widely used to measure fear in clinical and research settings. Consistent with the previously reviewed studies, girls exhibited greater fear prevalence (mean of 16.14 fears) than boys (mean of 8.28 fears), and greater fear intensity on 73 out of the 80 Fear Survey Schedule items. No differences

emerged in quantity and patterns of fear across the age range.

The conclusions drawn from these studies on children's fears are that they are quite common among children of all ages, with girls exhibiting a greater number of fears than boys; the role of age and socioeconomic status is inconclusive.

Excessive Fears/Phobias

Miller, Barret, and Hampe (1974) reported the incidence of intense fears or phobias in a sample of 249 children age 7 to 12. Parents rated their children's fears at three intensity levels: no fear, normal/expected fear, and unrealistic/excessive fear. The prevalence of intense fear was found in only 5% of the children sampled.

Several other authors investigated the prevalence of phobic children who were referred to therapists for treatment. Graham (1964) reported that only 4% of an overall sample of referred children was phobic. Rutter, Tizard, and Whitmore (1970) found the prevalence to be about 7% of a population of 1,000 10- and 11-year-olds on the Isle of Wright. Graziano and DeGiovanni (1979) found that 7.1% of 547 child referrals were found to be highly fearful or phobic (ages were not given in this study).

Ryle, Pond, and Hamilton (1965), in a comprehensive study of 159 school-aged children, used a combination of child interview, parental reports, and school reports to examine fear prevalence at several levels of intensity. The authors noted that 3% of the boys and 0% of the girls had extreme, incapacitating fear, and 6% of the boys and 8% of the girls had fears that were less extreme (but that might cause them to flee). Ryle et al.'s (1965) use of multiple informants undoubtedly yielded greater accuracy than did previous studies where only one class of respondents was utilized.

Agras, Sylvester, and Oliveau (1969) also employed data from multiple respondents (using test questionnaires, observation, and intensive interviews) to examine the prevalence of fears and phobias in a sample of 325 children and adults. Data were not presented separately for children and adults in this study, however. The prevalence for phobic behavior was 7.7%; phobias were reported as mildly disabling in 74.7% of the cases and severely disabling in 0.2% of cases.

Finally, Anderson, Williams, McGee, and Silva (1987), in the only study that investigated disorders using DSM-III (APA, 1980) criteria, examined the prevalence of DSM-III disorders in 792 children aged 11 years old (from the general population in New Zealand). Information from multiple informants (child interview, parent questionnaire, teacher questionnaire, and behavioral history) revealed the prevalence of simple phobia to be 2.4% of the sample. Included were 7 males and 12 females identified as simple phobic.

The aforementioned studies reveal that, unlike fears, simple phobias are found in a small sample of children and constitute a relatively small fraction of cases referred for treatment. Epidemiological data on specific childhood phobias have yet to be reported.

NATURAL HISTORY

Natural history data, like epidemiological findings, are clustered into fear and excessive fear/phobia categories. Again, several issues must be considered when comparing results across studies. Methods of diagnosing "phobia" or "excessive fear" vary greatly, as do the methods used for assessment (i.e., multiple versus single respondents, questionnaire versus interview). More directly relevant to the issue of natural history is the fact that the follow-up period involved in each study varies widely. Consequently, the results obtained should be interpreted cautiously.

Fears

Results are mixed regarding the stability of childhood fears. Several studies have documented a general decline in both the percentage of child reports of one or more specific fears (Graziano et al., 1979; MacFarlane, Allen, & Hozik, 1954) and number of fears reported from young childhood to adolescence (Angelino & Shedd, 1953; MacFarlane et al., 1954). For instance, Hagman (1932) found that, in a sample of preschool children, 6% of the fears disappeared within 1 week, 54% had vanished in 3 months, and 100% had disappeared within 3 years. Slater (1939) reported that 2- and 3-year-old children exhibited fearful behavior that almost completely vanished after 4 weeks, and Cummings (1946) reported on the transitory nature of fear in children aged 2 to 7. Similarly, Jersild and Holmes (1935) followed a sample of 15 2- to 5-year-olds (observed by their parents on two occasions over a 1-year period) and concluded that fears were indeed transitory over this period.

Bauer (1976) found that children's self-reported fears change with development (specifically, between 4 and 12 years of age). That is, the majority

of young children's fears reflect the imaginary realm. With increasing age (into adolescence) and cognitive sophistication, children's fears become more realistic, reflecting bodily injury and physical danger, loss, natural hazards, and concern about school achievement and social relationships (Angelino et al., 1956; Miller et al., 1974).

These results suggest that while certain fears may be transitory, other fears may replace them depending upon the child's level of cognitive sophistication and perceptions of reality. Particular fears, according to Eme and Schmidt (1978), may in fact be more stable once the child reaches a particular age. Specifically, these investigators examined the stability of fears over a 1-year period in a sample of 27 fourth grade children. Fears were evaluated through individual interviews with the children, and then coded according to the categories described by Jersild and Holmes (1935). The authors concluded that both the number and types of fears remained quite stable, in that 83% of the children's initial fears were expressed one year later. Fear of bodily harm, disaster, and animals were noted most frequently, with girls showing more stability than boys.

Recently, Silverman and Nelles (1989) examined the stability (one-year) of childhood fears in children 8 to 11 years old, based upon mothers' ratings of child fearfulness on the Fear Survey Schedule for Children—Revised (FSSC-R) (Ollendick, 1983). The results revealed that mothers' ratings of their child's fears were relatively stable over a 1-year period, in terms of their intensity and frequency. However, from year 1 to year 2, there was only 10% overlap in the ten specific objects or situations that mothers rated as eliciting the most fear in the child. Only one item, "a burglar breaking into our house," was reported during both year 1 and year 2. All other items reported during the two time periods were different. The original ten items appeared to be primarily in the area of bodily injury and harm, whereas the second list contained primarily evaluative fears.

Excessive Fears/Phobias

As mentioned earlier, there are few data on the natural history of childhood phobia. However, in an important longitudinal study, Agras, Chapin, and Oliveau (1972) followed a sample of 10 phobic children and 20 phobic adults over a five-year period and found that 100% of the children (under age 20) were improved, while only 43% of the adults were improved. In a reinterpretation of the data, Ollendick (1979) pointed out that while all children had improved, only 40% were symptom-free: 60% of the children still had phobias of sufficient intensity to be rated directly between "no disability" and "maximum disability." This suggests that for a sample of children phobias do indeed persist.

Hampe, Noble, Miller, and Barrett (1973) followed 62 children 1 and 2 years after treatment for phobia. This study utilized parent and clinician ratings of phobia and behavior checklists. The authors found a gradual decrease in phobic behavior over the 2-year period; younger children (6 to 10 years) showed rapidly diminished phobic behavior, whereas older children (11 to 15 years) showed a less marked reduction of phobic behavior. At two years posttreatment, 80% of the entire sample (both treated and untreated) was symptom-free, while 7% still had severe phobias. This suggests that even with treatment, phobias tend to persist in a small sample of affected children, although most phobias will disappear even without treatment.

Two retrospective studies further suggest that for some individuals, certain types of phobias that develop in childhood persist into adulthood. Abe (1972) studied the course of phobic and nervous symptoms in mothers of children who were invited for routine medical checkups.

> The childhood data of these mothers on phobic and nervous symptoms were obtained from their respective mothers, i.e., the paternal and maternal grandmothers of the children. The mothers (of the children) also responded to questions as to whether they were currently experiencing these symptoms as adults.

Among 86 mothers who reported having a marked fear of thunder, animals, or injections between 6 and 15 years of age, 30 still reported having a phobia for one of these things at the interview. The same object of fear was reported in 18 cases and was different in 12 cases. Abe (1972) also reported that those women who displayed phobia for any of the foregoing objects during childhood were significantly more likely to show phobia for one of these objects in adulthood than those who did not.

Solyom, Beck, Solyom, and Hugel (1974), in an investigation into the etiology of "phobic neurosis" (i.e., agoraphobia and specific phobias), reported that of the individuals with specific phobias ($n = 13$), the majority (57%) had experienced their phobias since childhood.

In summary, it appears that mild fears and phobias are common, transient developmental phenomena that tend to disappear with time. More excessive fears and phobias are significantly less common, but a subset of these phobias tends to persist from childhood into adulthood.

IMPAIRMENT AND COMPLICATIONS

Based upon the children whom we have seen at the clinic, we have found that the more severe the child's phobia, the greater the impairment and complications. In extreme cases, the child becomes housebound, as a way to avoid a possible encounter with the phobic object or event. Since the child's contact with the outside is minimal, his or her peer relations suffer as well. Attending school may also be difficult, as the child fears that he or she may confront the phobic stimulus on the way. Consequently, the child's school work may deteriorate, not to mention that difficulties with concentration that the child experiences also interfere with his or her school work. It is not unusual for phobic children to also develop a wide range of somatic complaints (headaches, gastrointestinal problems, etc.), perhaps as a consequence of their constant worrying about and preoccupation with the phobic stimulus.

Interestingly, however, when we examine the behavior problems associated with simple phobia in childhood, as measured by the Child Behavior Checklist (CBCL), no consistent patterns emerge across children (Silverman & Nelles, 1988). Perhaps patterns would emerge if this issue were examined separately for boys versus girls, and for younger children versus older children. Upon accumulating a larger N, we will further explore this issue.

Like the epidemiology and natural history literature, the literature on the impairment and complications of clinic samples of phobic children (i.e., children receiving DSM-III/DSM-III-R diagnoses of simple phobia) is sparse. Thus, as in our previous sections, we examine separately the literature on children with fears versus children with excessive fears and phobia.

Fears

Lapouse and Monk (1959) examined the relationship between "fears and worries" and other forms of psychopathological behaviors in children 6 to 12 years of age (49% boys, 51% girls). The mothers were interviewed in areas that covered the child's adjustment (interpersonal, social, intellectual, and general) as well as on the children's fears, worries, and other symptomatology (bedwetting, thumbsucking, nail-biting, etc.). Behaviors described were evaluated in terms of their presence or absence, frequency, and intensity.

According to Lapouse and Monk (1959), no significant correlation was found between fears and worries and other problematic behaviors. Nor did a relationship emerge when the authors examined separately the children with ten or more fears and these children's combined scores (based upon totaling the seven "tension phenomena," which included nail-biting, grinding teeth, thumbsucking, biting or sucking clothing, picking nose, picking sores, chewing lips or tongue *plus* bed-wetting, having nightmares, stuttering, losing one's temper, and exhibiting tics). Furthermore, when a subsample of children was directly interviewed, no significant relationship emerged between the youngsters' reports about their fears and worries and other pathologic behaviors, thereby corroborating the results obtained with the mothers. Overall, the Lapouse and Monk (1959) study strongly suggests that excessive fears in children are not necessarily related to other behavioral impairment and complications, although, as Graziano, DeGiovanni, and Garcia (1979) note, perhaps a relationship would have emerged if intensity rather than frequency of fears was used.

In contrast to the Lapouse and Monk results, several investigators have found a relationship between fears and behavior problems (overdependence, mood swings, poor appetites, temper tantrums, etc.) in samples of 3-year-old children (Earls, 1980; MacFarlane, Allen, & Hozik, 1954; Richman, Stevenson, & Graham, 1975; Stevenson & Richman, 1978).

Excessive Fears/Phobias

Based upon a chart review of 28 children (4½ to 12 years old) from an outpatient psychiatric clinic, Poznanski (1973) reported that children with excessive fears displayed significantly increased dependent behavior, especially the more immature forms of dependency behaviors, compared with a control group from the same outpatient psychiatric population. A relationship between bedsharing and excessive fears was also noted, with more of the fearful children occasionally or consistently sleeping with their parents, relative to the control sample.

In the only study that we are aware of that focused specifically on phobic children, Miller, Barrett, Hampe, and Noble (1972) compared 67 child phobics (some of whom were school phobics) with a matched sample of children drawn from the general population, with regard to ratings on the Louisville Behavior Checklist (LBC), the School Behavior Checklist (SBC), and the Louisville Fear Survey Schedule (LFSS). On the LBC, phobic children differed significantly (i.e., more undesirable) from their "normal" counterparts on a large number of variables (aggression, hyperactivity, antisocial behavior, social withdrawal, sensitivity, fear, academic disability, immaturity, normal irritability, rare deviance, and prosocial behavior). Phobic children also displayed lower need achievement, more anxiety, and greater academic disability and were less extraverted on the SBC. These children also reported more fears on the LFSS.

Overall, it is difficult to make firm conclusions with respect to the impairment and complications of clinically phobic children, due to methodological differences in the studies cited. These include the different samples studied (e.g., outpatients of a psychiatric clinic versus a community sample), the different ages of the child samples (e.g., 3-year-olds versus 6- to 12-year-olds), the different procedures used to assess the children's fears (e.g., a list and rank technique versus direct interviews with the parent), and the different countries where the studies were conducted (e.g., the United States versus Great Britain). Finally, and most important, as mentioned earlier, it is not definitive that the children in these studies with excessive "fears and worries" were indeed suffering from simple phobia. Our research and the work of others, it is hoped, will help to clarify the nature and the extent of impairment and complications of phobic children.

DIFFERENTIAL DIAGNOSIS

DSM-III-R provides some guidelines to assist in the differential diagnosis of simple phobia. These guidelines are applicable to both children and adults. First, by definition, it is important to ensure that the circumscribed feared stimulus is not a fear of having a panic attack or a fear of humiliation or embarrassment in social situations. The former would be diagnosed as panic disorder (which is rarely seen in young children; see Nelles & Barlow, 1988, for further discussion of this point), while the latter would be diagnosed as social phobia. Second, the phobic stimulus must be unrelated to the content of the obsessions of obsessive-compulsive disorder. Although, like obsessions, phobias have a repetitive and ruminative quality, obsessions typically involve repetitive thoughts of violence, dirt, or contamination. Thus, in an obsessive-compulsive child who displays washing rituals, fear of dirt would not be a separate simple phobia. On the other hand, if the child also has an excessive and/or irrational fear of heights, then simple phobia of heights would be an additional diagnosis. This is particularly true if the fear of heights has a different time of onset and/or has nothing to do with feelings of contamination, which, as mentioned, is a crucial component of most obsessive-compulsive syndromes (e.g., Barlow, DiNardo, Vermilyea, Vermilyea, & Blanchard, 1986).

A third important distinction that is important to make is that between simple phobia and posttraumatic stress disorder (PTSD). Just as the phobic stimulus in simple phobia must be unrelated to the content of the obsessions of obsessive-compulsive disorder, it must also be unrelated to the trauma of PTSD. For example, in a child with a previous history of abuse who now displays phobic avoidance of stimuli associated with the trauma (e.g., dark-haired, mustached men), fear of dark-haired, mustached men would not be a separate simple phobia. In addition, simple phobias do *not* involve the extreme trauma at the onset and the more generalized distress observed in PTSD. PTSD typically involves an additional, broader nonphobic disturbance that is usually absent in a simple phobia.

A final important distinction concerns the differential diagnosis between simple phobia and "school phobia." Children refuse to go to school for a variety of reasons (Burke & Silverman, 1987; Last & Francis, 1988; Kessler, 1972). Although phobias of school may be "simple" (e.g., a youngster with an excessive or irrational fear of the ringing of the school bell), school phobias may also result from anxieties related to separation, social evaluation, fear of failure, fear of teachers, and so on. Thus, when assessing a school refuser, it is necessary to determine the particular reasons for that individual's avoidance. For example, can the child attend school when accompanied by his or her parent? If the child can, then separation anxiety disorder might be the appropriate diagnosis. If the youngster cannot, then the problem is probably not separation. Rather, he or she may be suffering from either a simple or a social phobia. Determining which of these two phobias is primary would be the important next step.

Francis, Strauss, and Last (1987) recently reported data that may further assist in the differential diagnosis of "simple" school refusers versus "social" school refusers. Based upon an evaluation of 25 adolescent school refusers who were classified into either one of these two groups (1) simple phobics or (2) social phobics—Francis et al. (1987) found that the social phobics were significantly more likely to evidence a concurrent anxiety disorder than were simple phobics (85% versus 30%). These results suggest that adolescent simple phobics who avoid school tend to be less psychologically impaired than do adolescent social phobics who avoid school. The extent to which this is also true for younger school refusers warrants investigations.

CASE EXAMPLE

Natalie is a 10-year-old Caucasian female referred to our Child and Adolescent Fear and Anxiety Treatment Program at the Center for Stress and Anxiety Disorders because of her increasing fear of strange dogs. To obtain a comprehensive picture of the problem, and because child and parent reports of symptomatology are frequently discordant, we assessed both the child and parents, separately. Furthermore, we obtained information from Natalie's teacher at school to acquire a picture of her behavior in a different situation, other than her home.

Assessment

Both Natalie and her parents were assessed with several standard questionnaires, in addition to our Anxiety Disorders Interview Schedule for Children (Silverman & Nelles, 1988), the child and parent versions, respectively. The interviews assess for all possible child and adult anxiety disorders. The interviews also permit the clinician to rule out alternative diagnoses such as affective disorders and to provide quantifiable data concerning anxiety symptomatology, etiology, course, and a functional analysis of the disorder.

When asked to describe her problem, Natalie reported that she was "afraid of dogs" and rated her fear as a "4" on our 0 ("no fear/never avoids") to 4 ("very severe fear/always avoids") severity scale. When asked what she thought about when in a situation with a dog, Natalie replied, "I think of what might happen — it might bite, or jump, or circle around you. I have to go into the house." Natalie reported her phobia to have started 2 years ago, when two dogs had jumped on her while she crossed the street to go to a friend's house.

Upon encountering a dog, Natalie reported that her heart beats very fast, she cries and screams, and runs away. Natalie also expressed frustration with the fact that she could not understand why she was so afraid of dogs, while other children her age were not. She was also quite upset that previous attempts on her part to control her fear "did not work" and that she had no control over the fear. On the child self-report measures, the data indicated that Natalie was not depressed (as measured by the Child Depression Inventory), that her manifest and trait anxiety was relatively low (as measured by the Revised Children's Manifest Anxiety Scale and the State-Trait Anxiety Inventory for Children), but that her anxiety level during the assessment session, that is, state anxiety, was mild to moderate. She reported a high number of specific fears on the FSSC-R.

The interview with Natalie's parents resulted in a more complete picture of Natalie's phobic behavior, as well as her overall functioning across multiple situations. When Natalie's parents were asked why they had sought treatment for their daughter at this time, they reported that their daughter's fear of dogs, although existing for the past year and one half to 2 years, was now increasingly interfering with desired activities. Specifically, Natalie was now afraid to go outside alone, was avoiding going to friends' and relatives' homes if they owned a dog, and would not go to her grandparent's home because she feared their neighborhood dogs. Natalie also would not get out of the car in their town, even if no dogs were in sight.

When the parents were asked if they could recall a specific event that appeared to precipitate their daughter's fear, Natalie's parents described several events that occurred within a short period of time from one another. While camping, the family's own dog, while tied on a rope, was attacked by a dog that had broken loose from its owner. Uncharacteristically, Natalie's father reacted quite fearfully while Natalie witnessed the whole event. Second, their neighbors had purchased two rather large dogs, which Natalie's family had to pass each day to get from their house to the main road. Although these dogs were fenced in, they jumped up when people passed by them. Natalie had en-

countered these dogs several times, and had reportedly "panicked" when they jumped up and barked at her. Since so many dogs were around Natalie, her parents believed that their daughter felt "smothered," and therefore, watched constantly for dogs, even if dogs were obviously not around (e.g., in a shopping mall parking lot).

When asked what they have done to try to alleviate Natalie's phobia, the parents reported first "brushing it off," hoping that the behavior would disappear by itself. They also reported that they tried supporting and reinforcing Natalie's "brave" attempts at facing her fear (albeit unsuccessfully), and they encouraged her to face dogs with the parents acting as models. As these efforts were unsuccessful, the parents became increasingly frustrated, and began insisting that Natalie behave "reasonably," scolding her when her fearful behavior appeared to be unwarranted (such as when there were no dogs around).

Aside from the phobic behavior, Natalie functioned quite well in all other areas. Her school performance was reported as being exceptional (which was corroborated by reports from her teacher), and she had many friends both in school and out. Questionnaires completed by her parents indicated no excessive anxiety, depression, or adjustment difficulties. Natalie's parents did not report any coexisting anxiety or other disorders when interviewed.

Overall, Natalie and her parents reported consistent information regarding the history of the phobic behavior and the series of events that appeared to lead up to the phobic reaction. The importance of gathering information from multiple sources is highlighted by this case. Although background information was similar when obtained by the parent and child, Natalie provided the subjective reports of fear, while her parents reported their response to the fearful behavior. Both have important treatment implications, as they provide information on the actual behavior and responses that have helped to both decrease and maintain the phobic behavior.

Treatment

Our treatment requires both child and parent participation; both child and parent responses to the child's fear behaviors are monitored and modified accordingly. Therefore, self-monitoring, conducted by the child, is done throughout treatment to identify consistencies in phobic behavior, to identify controlling variables (i.e., secondary gains from parental response to phobic behavior), and to monitor progress throughout treatment. In this way, the integrity of our treatment can be continually assessed, and treatment can be modified as needed. A multicomponent treatment program was employed that included exposure (both in vivo and imaginal), relaxation, cognitive coping procedures, contingency management, and participant modeling.

After thoroughly explaining the nature of a phobic reaction (in behavioral, cognitive, and physiological terms), Natalie was taught both relaxation and cognitive coping procedures. Once learned, she was instructed to employ these coping skills in graded exposure tasks based upon an individually derived fear hierarchy (see Table 13.1); exposures (both in vivo and imaginal) were conducted both in-session and at home with the parents. The combination of in-session and homework practice is done with the intent of both maintenance and generalization of treatment effects. Throughout these exposure sessions—both the in-sessions and homework practices—the therapist and parents, respectively, modeled calm, coping behavior toward the feared stimulus in Natalie's presence.

During the active treatment phase (3 months), Natalie was able to learn all the coping skills and was able to progress through the exposure sessions with both the therapist and parents. At the end of the 3 months, Natalie's self-monitoring data revealed that the number of phobic situations that she was avoiding decreased substantially. However, the intensity of her fear, upon confronting a dog, remained quite high. Weekly parental reports were consistent with her self-monitoring data. A similar pattern of results was obtained at the 6-month follow-up. This pattern of results illustrates an example of disynchrony in fear responses. That is, patterns of responding across the three modes (i.e., self-report, behavioral, and physiological) may vary, either before or after treatment. In Natalie's case, she displayed decreases in her avoidance of dogs at the end of treatment, but high self-reports of fear toward dogs remained.

CONTINUITY AND DISCONTINUITY WITH ADULT PRESENTATION

Child and adult phobias are similar in most respects, as indicated in earlier sections of this chapter (clinical presentation, differential diagnoses, etc.), but there are several important differences that should be noted. First, in the introductory section, we indicated that all defining features of phobia listed are applicable to both children and adults. However, we indicated that an important exception to this is the first feature, namely, that a phobia must be "out of proportion to the demands of the situation."

Unlike adults, children frequently have difficulty in grasping the irrational nature of their phobia. Adult thunder/lightning phobics, for example, are likely to acknowledge that the probability of being struck by lightning is low, and hence, constantly staying indoors, even when there is just a slight "thunderstorm warning," is irrational (but they "cannot help it"). The foregoing reasoning is not always easy for youngsters to follow, however. Children believe that they just may get struck by lightning. Further, it seems reasonable to them to stay indoors constantly to avoid the possibility of getting struck, even if the chances of this occurring are very low.

Further, young children who are still at a rather concrete level of cognitive development may not always comprehend, unlike adults and older children, the distinction between a phobic stimulus that is "imaginary" versus one that is "real." For example, an adult who is now afraid of going swimming in the ocean subsequent to seeing the movie *Jaws* is likely to admit that such avoidance behavior is irrational, that the shark in *Jaws* was "not real," and that the chances of actually encountering such a shark in the ocean is low. Try convincing the young child that the shark in *Jaws* was "make-believe"! Moreover, as in our earlier example with the thunder/lightning phobic, even if the youngster does understand that the shark was "not real," it is extremely difficult to help the child to understand that such avoidance behavior

Table 13.1. Natalie's Fear Hierarchy, in Descending Order

Stuffed dog
Dog commercials
Her dog
Petting her dog
TV shows about dogs
Dog fighting with person on TV
Dog on a leash
Nonbarking (quiet) dog
Dog far away
Barking (sound only)
Barking, and seeing dog
Loose dog
Dog nearby
Dog jumping, barking, licking Natalie

on his or her part is irrational, given the low probability of actually encountering such a shark in the water.

A further difference between child and adult phobias are the types of phobias that tend to develop at these different points in development, their etiology, and their course. In most cases, adults who present with simple phobia report that their phobias developed at all different ages, including adulthood. For example, Thyer, Parish, Curtis, Nesse, and Cameron (1985) reported the mean age of onset of 152 adult simple phobics to be 16.1 years of age, with a range of 3 to 67 years. (Forty-seven percent of the sample reported onset of symptoms in preteen years, while 23% reported symptom onset as teenagers.) However, there are certain phobias that clearly tend to start in early childhood or before adolescence and that continue into adulthood. Marks and Gelder (1968) examined the age of onset in different varieties of phobia and found that specific animal phobics ($n = 18$) experienced symptom onset in childhood, mostly by age 5. This is consistent with the findings of other investigators (e.g., Hugdahl & Öst, 1985; Liddell & Lyons, 1978; McNally & Steketee, 1985; Öst, 1986), although their reports of mean onset of animal phobias tend to be a bit later — between ages 8 and 10. We should also note that most animal phobias do *not* persist past puberty; yet, there is this small proportion that does persist. The reasons for such persistence are unknown.

In addition to animal phobias, other simple phobias that tend to develop in childhood and continue into adulthood are phobias of blood and injury (mean onset of 7 years: Öst, Sterner, & Lindahl, 1984), phobias of height (mean onset of 12 years: Williams & Kleifield, 1985), and phobias of dentistry (mean onset of 12 years: Hugdahl & Öst, 1985). As we noted in our Natural History section, the results obtained by Agras et al. (1972) suggested that childhood phobias are more likely to dissipate over time than are adult phobias (100% child phobics improved versus 43% adult phobics improved). However, we also indicated in this section that for a sample of children, phobias do continue. It appears that it is the small subset of the phobias just listed that persist.

It is unclear why the phobias listed show greater continuity between children and adults than do other phobias. However, both blood and dentistry phobias (which are frequently associated with fears of blood and injury) possibly originate in a genetically determined, extreme autonomic response: a response that is present from an early age and that continues throughout development (Marks, 1987). Further, it appears that some selective learning occurs, in that young children appear prepared to acquire intense fears of these stimuli (i.e., animals, blood and injury, and heights, with little or no cause). In contrast, when these phobias do develop (rarely) in adulthood, they usually were precipitated by some traumatic experience (e.g., a dog bite) (Friedman, 1966).

To obtain a better understanding of the continuity and discontinuity of simple phobia, prospective, longitudinal studies that involve samples of clinically phobic children, not merely fearful children, are needed. Moreover, these children must be followed long-term, into adulthood, not just for a brief period of time (such as 5 years in the Agras et al., 1972, study or 1 and 2 years as in the Hampe et al., 1973, study, reviewed in the Natural History section).

SUMMARY

In this chapter we described simple phobia of childhood. We indicated the major ways in which phobias differ from "normal" fears and highlighted one important difference between child and adult phobics. Unlike adults, children may not be aware that their fear (or phobia) is "out of proportion to the demands of the situation." We also indicated that although fears are common among children at all ages, simple phobias are found in only a small sample of children and constitute a small fraction of cases referred for psychological or psychiatric treatment. Our review of the natural history literature suggested that mild fears and phobias are transient, developmental phenomena that dissipate over time. On the other hand, there appears to be a subset of excessive fears and phobias that persist from childhood into adulthood.

Due to the methodological limitations of the studies conducted that have been concerned with the impairment and complications of phobic children, drawing any firm conclusions with regard to this issue is difficult. Our own clinical experience has not revealed any consistent patterns with respect to the behavior problems of these children. On the other hand, in the one study that did focus specifically upon a clinic sample (Miller et al., 1972), the phobic children did exhibit more impaired behavior than a matched control group.

We next discussed the major issues that pertain to the differential diagnosis of simple phobia of children. Specific issues discussed were differentiating between simple phobia and obsessive-compulsive disorder, simple phobia and posttraumatic stress disorder, and simple phobia and what is frequently referred to in the literature as "school phobia."

The case of Natalie, a dog phobic seen at our clinic, revealed just how incapacitating a simple phobia in a child can be. The case further highlighted the value of obtaining information from multiple sources (i.e., parent, child, and teacher) to obtain a comprehensive picture of the problem, as well as the issue of disynchrony in fear responses.

Although in most respects child simple phobics who present for treatment are similar to adult simple phobics, there are several important differences. These differences were discussed in the final section of this chapter. Specifically, child phobics, unlike adult phobics, frequently do not comprehend the irrational nature of their phobia. Further, certain phobias (e.g., animals, heights, thunder and lightning, and dentistry) are more likely to first appear in childhood, and a small subset of these persist into adulthood, for reasons that are yet unknown. Finally, whereas children appear prepared to acquire intense fears of these stimuli, when these phobias do develop in adulthood, albeit rarely, they usually are precipitated by some traumatic event.

REFERENCES

Abe, K. (1972). Phobias and nervous symptoms in childhood and maturity: Persistence and associations. *British Journal of Psychiatry, 120,* 275–283.

Agras, S., Chapin, H. N., & Oliveau, D. C. (1972). The natural history of phobia: Cause & prognosis. *Archives of General Psychiatry, 26,* 315–317.

Agras, S., Sylvester, D., & Oliveau, D. (1969). The epidemiology of common fears and phobia. *Comprehensive Psychiatry, 10*(2), 151–156.

American Psychiatric Association. (1980). *Diagnostic and statistical manual of mental disorders* (3rd ed.). Washington, DC: Author.

American Psychiatric Association. (1987). *Diagnostic and statistical manual of mental disorders* (3rd ed. rev.). Washington, DC: Author.

Anderson, J. C., Williams, D., McGee, R., & Silva, P. A. (1987). DSM III disorders in preadolescent children: Prevalence in a large sample from the general population. *Archives of General Psychiatry, 44,* 69–76.

Angelino, H., Dollins, J., & Mech, E. V. (1956). Trends in the "fears & worries" of school children as related to socio-economic status and age. *Journal of Genetic Psychology, 89,* 263–276.

Angelino, H., & Shedd, C. (1953). Shifts in the content of fears & worries relative to chronological age. *Proceedings of the Oklahoma Academy of Science, 34,* 180–186.

Barlow, D. H., DiNardo, P. A., Vermilyea, B. B., Vermilyea, J. A., & Blanchard, E. B. (1986). Co-morbidity and depression among the anxiety disorders: Issues in classification and diagnosis. *Journal of Nervous and Mental Disease, 174,* 63–72.

Barrios, B. A., Hartmann, D. P., & Shigetomi, C. (1981). Fears and anxieties in children. In G. J. Mash & L. G. Terdal (Eds.), *Behavioral assessment of childhood disorders* (pp. 259–304). New York: The Guilford Press.

Bauer, D. H. (1976). An exploratory study of developmental changes in children's fears. *Journal of Child Psychology & Psychiatry, 17,* 69–74.

Burke, A. E., & Silverman, W. K. (1987). Prescribed treatment for school refusal. *Clinical Psychology Review, 7,* 353–362.

Croake, J., & Knox, F. (1973). The changing nature of children's fears. *Child Study Journal, 3,* 91–105.

Cummings, J. D. (1946). A follow-up study of emotional symptoms in school children. *British Journal of Educational Psychology, 16,* 163–177.

Earls, F. (1980). Prevalence of behavior problems in 3-year-old children. *Archives of General Psychiatry, 37,* 1153–1157.

Eme, R., & Schmidt, D. (1978). The stability of children's fears. *Child Development, 49,* 1277–1279.

Francis, G., Strauss, C. C., & Last, C. G. (1987). *Social anxiety in school phobic adolescents.* Paper presented at the Annual Meeting of the Association for Advancement of Behavior Therapy, Boston.

Friedman, D. (1966). Treatment of a case of dog phobia in a deaf mute by behavior therapy. *Behaviour Research and Therapy, 4,* 141.

Graham, P. (1964). Psychiatric disorder in the young adolescent: A follow-up study. *Proceedings of the Royal Society of Medicine, 66,* 1226–1229.

Graziano, A. M., & DeGiovanni, I. S. (1979). The clinical significance of childhood phobias: A note on the proportion of child-clinical referrals for the treatment of children's fears. *Behaviour Research and Therapy, 17*, 108–102.

Graziano, A. M., DeGiovanni, I. S., & Garcia, K. (1979). Behavioral treatment of children's fears: A review. *Psychological Bulletin, 86*, 804–830.

Hagman, E. (1932). A study of fears of children of pre-school age. *Journal of Experimental Education, 1*, 110–130.

Hampe, E., Noble, M., Miller, L. C., & Barrett, C. L. (1973). Phobic children are at two years post-treatment. *Journal of Abnormal Psychology, 82*, 446–453.

Hugdahl, K., & Öst, L. G. (1985). Subjective physiological and cognitive symptoms in six different clinical phobias. *Personality and Individual Differences, 6*, 175–188.

Jersild, A., & Holmes, F. (1935). Children's fears. *Child Development Monographs*, No. 20. New York: Columbia University Press.

Kastrup, M. (1976). Psychic disorders among pre-school children in a geographically delimited area of Arhus county, Denmark. *Acta Psychiatrica Scandinavica, 54*, 29–42.

Kessler, J. W. (1972). Neurosis in childhood. In B. B. Wolman (Ed.), *Manual of child psychopathology*. New York: McGraw-Hill.

Lapouse, R., & Monk, M. (1959). Fears and worries in a representative sample of children. *American Journal of Orthopsychiatry, 29*, 803–818.

Last, C. G., & Francis, G. (1988). School phobia. In B. B. Lahey & A. E. Kazdin (Eds.), *Advances in clinical child psychology* (Vol. 11, pp. 193–222). New York: Plenum Press.

Liddell, A., & Lyons, M. (1978). Thunderstorm phobias. *Behaviour Research and Therapy, 16*, 306–308.

MacFarlane, J. W., Allen, L., & Hozik, M. P. (1954). *A developmental study of the behavior problems of normal children between twenty-one months and fourteen years*. Berkeley: University of California Press.

Marks, I. M. (1969). *Fears and phobias*. New York: Academic Press.

Marks, I. M. (1987). *Fears, phobias, and rituals*. New York: Oxford University Press.

Marks, I. M., & Gelder, M. G. (1968). Different ages of onset in varieties of phobia. *American Journal of Psychiatry, 123*, 218–221.

McNally, R. J., & Steketee, G. S. (1985). The etiology & maintenance of severe animal pho-

bias. *Behaviour Research and Therapy, 23*, 431–435.

Miller, L. C., Barrett, C. L., & Hampe, E. (1974). Phobias of childhood in a prescientific era. In A. Davids (Ed.), *Child personality and psychopathology: Current topics*. New York: John Wiley & Sons.

Miller, L. C., Barret, C. L., Hampe, E., & Noble, H. (1972). Factor structure of childhood fears. *Journal of Consulting and Clinical Psychology, 39*, 204–208.

Morris, R. J., & Kratochwill, T. R. (1983). *Treating children's fears and phobias: A behavioral approach*. Elmsford, NY: Pergamon Press.

Nelles, W. B., & Barlow, D. H. (1988). Do children panic? *Clinical Psychology Review, 8*, 359–372.

Ollendick, T. H. (1979). Fear reduction techniques with children. In M. Hersen, R. M. Eisler, & P. M. Miller (Eds.), *Progress in behavior modification* (Vol. 8). New York: Academic Press.

Ollendick, T. H. (1983). Reliability and validity of the revised fear survey schedule for children (FSSC-R). *Behaviour Research and Therapy, 21*, 395–399.

Ollendick, T. H., Matson, J., & Helsel, V. (1985). Fears in children and adolescents: Normative data. *Behaviour Research and Therapy, 23*, 465–467.

Öst, L., Sterner, U., & Lindahl, I.-L. (1984). Physiological responses in blood phobics. *Behaviour Research and Therapy, 22*, 109–117.

Öst, L. G. (1986). Age at onset in different phobias. *Journal of Abnormal Psychology, 96*, 223–229.

Poznanski, E. O. (1973). Children with excessive fears. *American Journal of Orthopsychiatry, 43*, 428–438.

Rachman, A., & Costello, C. G. (1961). The aetiology and treatment of childhood phobias: A review. *American Journal of Psychiatry, 118*, 97–105.

Richman, N., Stevenson, J., & Graham, P. (1975). Prevalence of behavior problems in 3-year-old children: An epidemiological study in a London borough. *Journal of Child Psychology and Psychiatry, 16*, 277–287.

Rutter, M., Tizard, J., & Whitmore, K. (Eds.). (1970). *Education, health and behavior*. New York: John Wiley & Sons.

Ryle, A., Pond, D. A., & Hamilton, M. (1965). The prevalence and patterns of psychological disturbance in children of primary age. *Jour-*

nal of Child Psychology and Psychiatry, 6, 101–113.

Schwartz, S., & Johnson, J. M. (1981). Psychopathology of childhood: A clinical-experimental approach. New York: Pergamon Press.

Silverman, W. K. (1987). Childhood anxiety disorders: Diagnostic issues, empirical support and future research. Journal of Child and Adolescent Psychotherapy, 4, 121–126.

Silverman, W. K., & Nelles, W. B. (1988). Behavior problems of phobic children. Unpublished manuscript.

Silverman, W. K., & Nelles, W. B. (1989a). The Anxiety Disorders Interview Schedule for Children. Journal of the American Academy of Child and Adolescent Psychiatry, 27, 772–778.

Silverman, W. K., & Nelles, W. B. (1989b). The stability of mothers' ratings of child fearfulness. Journal of Anxiety Disorders, 3, 1–5.

Slater, E. (1939). Responses to a nursery school situations of 40 children. Society for Research in Child Development, 11(4).

Solyom, L., Beck, P., Solyom, C., & Hugel, R. (1974). Some etiological factors in phobic neurosis. Canadian Psychiatric Association, 19, 69–77.

Stevenson, J., & Richman, N. (1978). Behavior, language, and development in three-year-old children. Journal of Autism and Childhood Schizophrenia, 8, 299–313.

Thyer, B. A., Parrish, R. T., Curtis, E. C., Nesse, R. M., & Cameron, O. G. (1985). Ages of onset of DSM-III anxiety disorders. Comprehensive Psychiatry, 26, 113–122.

Williams, S. L., & Kleifield, E. (1985). Transfer of behavioral change across phobias in multiple phobic clients. Behavior Modification, 9, 22–31.

CHAPTER 14

SIMPLE PHOBIA IN ADULTHOOD

F. Dudley McGlynn
Daniel W. McNeil

DESCRIPTION OF THE DISORDER

The term "simple phobia" refers to a large but clinically rare category of specific anxiety disorders characterized by a "persistent, irrational fear of, and compelling desire to avoid an object or situation" (American Psychiatric Association, 1980). The most common simple phobias seen clinically involve heights, confinement, and animals. If formal nosological rules are relaxed, then fears involving transportation, violent weather, and medically related phenomena are among the most common. In principle, virtually any object or situation can become a cue stimulus for phobic behaviors.

Clinicians must deal with one or more of three classes of events. First, there is anxiety behavior sometimes close to the order of panic when the phobic person confronts the relevant stimulus. Second, there is skillful and steadfast avoidance of the relevant stimulus. Third, there is episodic anxiety behavior even when the stimulus is not present. In behavioral terms, simple phobia is characterized by private/cognitive fear behaviors and/or physiological fear behaviors and/or mo-toric fear behaviors that are under the direct or indirect (i.e., generalized, mediated) stimulus control of some objective stimulus configuration.

CLINICAL PRESENTATION

Stimulus Control

The single descriptive feature that sets simple phobic patients most clearly apart from other anxiety-disordered patients is the relatively narrow and often objective stimulus control over their anxious responding. Objective stimulus control is seen, for example, when the sight of a dog cues headlong flight or when viewing a dog on television cues cardiopulmonary changes and ruminations. Stimulus control often is a property of abstract "themes" (Wolpe, 1973) that serve to bind objectively different stimuli into functionally unified phobia clusters. Wolpe (1973), for example, showed how 14 different phobias were reducible to 4. According to modern cognitive psychology (e.g., Anderson, 1985), these fear clusters are associated in memory to form higher-order "schemas."

Response Properties

It is convenient to describe phobic behaviors as patterns of private/cognitive, physiological, and overt behavioral responses (Lang, 1978). The private/cognitive behaviors that occur on confrontation with a phobia cue stimulus are attenuated forms of those characteristic of panic (e.g., terror, loss of control, impending doom). According to cognitive psychology, confrontation with the phobia cue stimulus activates a schema that contributes to the panic by facilitating catastrophic information processing and inhibiting the processing of information that might be benign or reassuring (e.g., Beck, Emery, & Greenburg, 1985). When the cue stimulus is not present, these behaviors occur in lesser forms (e.g., uneasiness, worry, vigilance).

Only a few studies have investigated systematically the private/cognitive themes of different anxiety disorders (e.g., Hibbert, 1984; Rappee, 1985). Beck and his colleagues have argued repeatedly and plausibly that exaggerated estimates of danger typify the phobic person's thinking. Beck (1976) described the cognitive underpinnings of exaggerated danger: overestimates of the probability and adversity of a phobic encounter and underestimates of one's own and others' ability or willingness to cope effectively.

A great deal of attention has been devoted to the psychophysiology of anxiety. Two principles articulated by Lacey (1950, 1967) served to guide our early thinking. "Stimulus-response specificity" means that a phobic patient's pattern of physiological responding will vary according to the stimulus but will be stable for a specific stimulus. "Individual response stereotypy" means that when persons are compared their physiological activity will be different, both in terms of the patterning of various response system components and in terms of the response system that dominates the pattern. Engel (1960) demonstrated early on that stimulus-response specificity and individual response stereotypy operate intraindividually. That demonstration set the stage for the argument that multiple-event psychophysiological recording is necessary to describe anxiety adequately. More recently, workers in the field of behavior therapy have begun to express doubts about the reliability (Arena, Blanchard, Andrasik, Cotch, & Myers, 1983) and clinical relevance of psychophysiological information. Suffice it to say here that most simple phobics will show some pattern of physiological change upon confronting a phobia cue stimulus. The pattern will reflect numerous and complex biological inputs that include the metabolic support of ensuing cognitive and motor behavior as well as sympathetic activation (heightened alpha-adrenergic action). The pattern can include changed cardiac function (Taylor et al., 1986), increased blood flow to the skeletal muscles (Gelder & Mathews, 1968; Mathews & Lader, 1971), increased blood pressure (Kelly & Martin, 1969), increased respiration rate (Lande, 1981), and elevated levels and fluctuations in electrodermal flow (Lader & Wing, 1964, 1966).

The motor behaviors seen in simple phobia also can vary dramatically. They can range from headlong flight to "freezing" and can include diverse performance-quality decrements. Frequently, phobic behavior blends into obsessive-compulsive displays — as when the germ or contaminant phobic develops toward obsessive-compulsive checking or washing.

The nature of the connections between behaviors occurring in the three response domains is a matter of historic and contemporary controversy. There is agreement that low and usually nonsignificant correlations across the three domains are the rule (Lang, 1971, 1977; Lick & Katkin, 1976; Rachman & Hodgson, 1974). Whether these low correlations reflect the actual organization of anxiety behavior (Lang, Rice, & Sternbach, 1972) or the inadequate quality of our methodology (Schwartz, 1978) remains at issue. Seemingly, reification of the anxiety construct lies close to the heart of these debates.

EPIDEMIOLOGY

Little is known about the prevalence of simple phobia in the general population. There are several reasons for this state of affairs. First, many epidemiological studies did not separate phobias from other so-called psychoneuroses. Second, those epidemiological studies that did separate out phobias often did not distinguish between simple phobia and other phobia categories. Third, the criteria for defining phobia have been diverse, thus precluding a cumulative set of findings. Fourth, data derived from clinical samples are erroneous because simple phobics usually do not seek treatment for that problem. Fifth, there appear to be low interrater reliabilities for simple phobia even in relatively well-done studies.

Some of these problems have been overcome in the National Institute of Mental Health Epidemiological Catchment Area (ECA) program (Regier et al., 1984). The ECA effort has provided relatively good data on both 6-month (Myers et al., 1984) and lifetime (Robins et al., 1984) prevalence of simple phobia, defined in terms of DSM-III criteria.

Myers et al. (1984) described the preceding 6-month prevalence of psychiatric disorders as judged by structured interviews in three community sites: New Haven, Baltimore, and St. Louis. Rates of simple phobia in New Haven were 3.2% for men and 6.0% for women. Rates for simple phobia in Baltimore were 7.3% for men and 15.7% for women. In St. Louis the rates were 2.3% and 6.5% for men and women, respectively. The reliably higher rates of simple phobia among women were portrayed as accurate. While it was statistically significant, the disproportionate rate of simple phobia in Baltimore was portrayed as reflecting procedural differences.

Robins et al. (1984) described the lifetime prevalence of psychiatric disorders, including simple phobias, at the same three sites. The lifetime prevalence of phobia per se was 7.8% in New Haven, 23.3% in Baltimore, and 9.4% in St. Louis. In New Haven, simple phobia was found in 8.5% of females and 3.8% of males. In Baltimore, simple phobia was found in 25.9% of females and 14.5% of males. In St. Louis, simple phobia was found in 9.4% of females and 4.0% of males. Procedural and personnel differences were again cited as contributors to the disproportionate rates of phobia and simple phobia at the Baltimore site. The differing rates for females and males again were described as accurate. In addition, the authors noted that lifetime prevalence is a good measure in the case of simple phobia, because there is ordinarily an early onset and there should, therefore, be a flat lifetime prevalence. This observation was borne out by the age-category data from all three sites. For example, the rates of simple phobia for Baltimore were 21.0%, 21.1%, 21.5%, and 18.1% for four age groupings collapsed over all other variables.

The Robins et al. (1984) work produced race and education differences in simple phobia incidence. Lifetime prevalence rates were higher for blacks than for nonblacks in Baltimore (27.6% vs. 17.4%) and in St. Louis (11.1% vs. 5.9%) but were not different in New Haven. College graduates in New Haven had a 3.8% lifetime incidence of simple phobia, while others had 7.2%. In Baltimore, college graduates produced a lifetime incidence of 12.8%, while others showed an incidence of 21.4%.

Even though the studies above appear to be the best to date, seasoned workers in the anxiety field probably will believe that the figures are inflated and almost certainly will discount the figures from Baltimore. Reich (1986) reviewed the epidemiological literature, including the work just described, and concluded that 2.5% of U.S. residents display lifetime prevalence of simple phobia. Interestingly, rates for phobia seem to differ dramatically in different nations and cultures. Phobic persons seemingly are difficult to find at all in Nigeria (Odejide, 1976), Botswana (Ben-Tovin, 1985), and India (Verghese & Beig, 1974). The reasons for the differing incidence rates of phobia across cultures are not clear. For example, Nandi et al. (1980) found a 2.7% prevalence rate of phobic disorder in a westernized Indian city, but Robins et al. (1984) found no influence of rural-urban factors on incidence rates for simple phobia in the ECA program study.

NATURAL HISTORY

The natural history of those behaviors we label as simple phobia will entail one or more of three classes of etiological events that combine with cognitive elaborations to yield persistent escape/avoidance of the phobia cue stimulus. One class of etiological events involves direct aversive experience with the later-to-be-feared circumstance. Early on there was a narrow Pavlovian interpretation of this etiology (Watson & Morgan, 1917), in which the phobia cue stimulus preceded in time the onset of a painful unconditional response. For example, the sight of a growling dog is followed by a painful bite, rendering the sight of a growling dog into a conditional stimulus for the somatovisceral responses that accompany sudden, acute leg pain. Later on, the obvious narrowness of an orthodox Pavlovian view prompted several revisions aimed at preserving a direct learning, if not conditioning, interpretation of phobia etiology. Eysenck (1968, 1976), for example, argued that there are many circumstances other than painful ones that can serve as unconditional stimuli for fear (e.g., withdrawal of reinforcement, conflict). He argued also that backward conditioning occurs. No doubt some simple phobias are acquired as a direct consequence of aversive experiences.

Öst and Hugdahl (1981), for example, found direct learning histories in 68.6% of claustrophobics, 47.5% of animal phobics, and 68.6% of dental phobics. However, direct aversive experiences are clearly absent from the histories of many phobic persons. Kleinknecht (1982), for example, reported that none of his spider phobic patients reported direct traumatic encounters with spiders.

A second class of etiological events involves vicarious aversive experience with the later-to-be-feared circumstance. Laboratory support for vicarious fear acquisition is unambiguous. Berger (1962), for example, conditioned electrodermal responses to a buzzer by instructing subjects to observe a model exhibit buzzer-occasioned pain behavior. Self-report data likewise support vicarious fear acquisition. Hekmat (1987), for example, reported that 30.36% of animal phobics pointed to aversive motion picture scenes involving animals as etiologically significant.

A third class of etiological events involves simple information acquisition and instructions. There is venerable support for the view that instructions alone can produce anxious responding. Cook and Harris (1937) demonstrated increased electrodermal flow and numbers of SCRs in response to a cue after subjects were simply informed that the cue would be followed by a shock (see also Grings, 1965).

Rachman (1977) popularized the view that direct experience, vicarious experience, and information/instructions comprise the "three pathways" through which phobic responding develops. Rachman (1977) and others also have proposed that the pathway through which a phobia develops influences the fine grain of the phobic display. Phobic anxiety with important cognitive features, for example, develops out of experience with information and instructions. Phobic anxiety with strong somatovisceral components, in turn, develops out of direct aversive encounters. However, available data do not support this view (Öst & Hugdahl, 1981). Furthermore, Staats (1972, 1975, 1980) and others have argued persuasively that, as phobic behaviors develop, cognitive/semantic factors play a fundamental role above and beyond the initial circumstances of acquisition. Demonstrations that very negative self-instructions are correlated with psychophysiological events (Russell & Brandsma, 1974) and with walkway avoidance (Eifert & Schermelleh, 1985) offer support for a semantic elaboration view (see also Evans & Weiss, 1978; Hekmat, 1987).

IMPAIRMENT AND COMPLICATIONS

The adaptive impairments that coexist with phobic behavior are best identified by studying the circumstances of clinical presentation. The great majority of simple phobics do not seek treatment for the problem. Rather, they develop life-styles that minimize the likelihood and/or expected likelihood of encounters with the objects of their fears. When persons who display simple phobias do seek treatment, it is often because they anticipate that circumstances will force one or more confrontations with a dreaded cue stimulus. For example, a long-time animal phobic treated by McGlynn some years ago sought help several weeks before having to perform required dissections in a required biology class, entreaties and protestations to the professor having been to no avail. Phobic patients often seek treatment also because their life-styles have become too confined, too disruptive to their families, or critically devoid of reinforcing activities. Dengrove (1972), for example, reported a patient whose fear of dogs was so restricting that she appeared to be agoraphobic. Cameron (1963) described a patient whose avoidance of heights forced her to give up work as a well-paid executive secretary and become a poorly paid salesperson on the ground floor of a department store. Some phobic patients seek treatment to attenuate the chronic fear behaviors (e.g., tenseness, ruminations, nightmares) that plague them even when they have succeeded in developing life-styles that minimize outright confrontations with phobia-related objects and events. No small number of persons seek treatment shortly after they have learned that effective treatment is conveniently available.

DIFFERENTIAL DIAGNOSIS

We have not distinguished ourselves as taxonomists with regard to the universe of anxiety behaviors. Our first taxonomic efforts were mired in the psychodynamic view of etiology. For example, even when experimental anxiety was not reported by the patient, anxiety reduction was said to be the primary gain from behaving neurotically. With DSM-III there came the results of an effort to rid the nosology of theoretical overtones (by using overlapping empirical features of behavior to form conjunctive diagnostic categories). The effort was compromised from the outset by the plain fact that behavior cannot be described in a theoretically neutral way. With DSM-III-R we have come full circle; theory is once again an explicit determinant of diagnosis. "Panic" is now the theoretically regnant concept; the role of panic attacks in the development and maintenance of the phobia more or less determines the differential diagnosis. Indeed, the DSM-III-R classification of anxiety disorders "can be usefully seen as a taxonomy of the contexts in which the anxiety attacks occur" (Lipschitz, 1988, p. 43).

A critique of the use of panic in DSM-III-R is well beyond the scope of this chapter. It is interesting to point out, however, that when it is painted with a broad brush, the picture of panic-mediated phobia is much like that of the psychodynamics' and very much like that of the dual-process fear mediation theory of avoidance (Mowrer, 1939, 1947; Miller, 1951). The latter theory has not served us impressively in accommodating experimental results (Delprato & McGlynn, 1984), even though we have had 50 years to work with it and our data were gathered under controlled observational conditions. It is interesting to point out, also, that empirical comparisons of phobic anxiety and panic have produced differences that are more impressive than are the similarities (e.g., Thyer & Himle, 1987).

The contemporary professional environment constrains us to use DSM-III-R, and clinically it can be useful in thinking about patients early on. It provides rules for assigning multiple diagnoses concurrently, and thus it accords well with what we actually find ourselves doing when we treat patients with multiple problems.

Differential diagnosis begins by ruling out panic disorder, agoraphobia, and social phobia. These decisions are not always simple. Apparent agoraphobia, for example, can result from a simple phobia in which the cue stimulus is widely and necessarily encountered (e.g., Dengrove, 1972). Simple dental phobia, for another example, can result from social phobic concerns.

Having chosen a diagnosis of simple phobia, it remains to fit that diagnosis into the system of concurrent diagnoses via the DSM-III-R rules. Usually, the rules produce reasonable diagnostic decisions. For example, a patient with a diagnosis of posttraumatic stress disorder can receive a diagnosis of simple phobia if the cue stimuli are unrelated to the trauma. Similarly, a patient with a diagnosis of obsessive-compulsive disorder can also receive a diagnosis of simple phobia, provided that the phobia cue stimuli are not functionally related to the obsessive-compulsive behavior, as in contamination fears. Sometimes the rules produce unreasonable diagnostic decisions. For example, a patient whose specific phobia presumably evolved out of spontaneous panic would now receive a diagnosis of panic disorder even though the presenting complaint is peripherally cued fear and/or geographic avoidance.

Within the category of simple phobias, a case can be made for differential diagnosis of animal phobias and blood-injury phobias. The strongest case can be made for blood injury phobias because the events often are different than are those in most simple phobias, for example, bradycardia, falling blood pressure, and fainting (Öst, Sterner, & Lindahl, 1984). Clearly, support for the special natures of animal phobias and blood-injury phobias is no less persuasive than is support for the panic-mediation view that (currently) dominates the rest of the taxonomy.

Notwithstanding the practical need for a system such as DSM-III-R, the fact remains that it affords poor guidance for our specific clinical efforts. Better guidance in the case of simple phobias comes from the concepts and procedures of classical behavior therapy (McGlynn & Cornell, 1985; Wolpe, 1973) and those subsets of cognitive behavior therapy that comport well with modern cognitive psychology (e.g., Beck, Emery, & Greenberg, 1985). The basic things we need to know to describe simple phobic behavior are as follows: (1) the exact cue stimulus or stimuli; (2) the exact features, dimensions, or meanings of the cue stimulus that influence anxiety behaviors; (3) the nature and patterning of the individuals' anxiety behaviors as described in three-channel terms; and (4) the reciprocal interfaces that exist between patterned anxiety behaviors and the ever-changing environmental context.

CASE EXAMPLE

Description

Michael is a 48-year-old white male. He is married, has a college degree plus some graduate credit, and is employed in the field of journalism. Multiple simple phobias are present. Phobias about dental and medical procedures prompted Michael to seek help. Other phobias include confinement, water, heights, and small animals (i.e., bats, snakes). Michael also fears the possibility of being homosexual, and, at various points in his life, he has had problems with depression.

Michael's presenting phobias involve diagnostic and therapeutic contacts with health care professionals. Phobic behaviors have occurred with dentists, physicians, and a chiropractor. Novel and/or unexpected events during dental/medical procedures are particularly aversive. For example, Michael displayed syncope when, for the first time, his dentist wore a mask. Seemingly, the mask served to prompt schematic thinking that, somehow, the upcoming procedure was extraordinary. The use of professional dental and medical jargon during procedures disturbs Michael as well. Indeed, it is disturbing when health professionals speak to him at all during their work.

Michael delays or avoids scheduling necessary medical procedures. Dental visits are infrequent; he reports having to "shame" himself into making dental appointments. Michael regards his dental/medical phobias as "self-defeating" and "contrary to reason, logic, and good health."

Although Michael reports only mild aversion to blood, his physiological response to medical/dental contexts is characteristic of blood-injury phobia. Throughout his life he has fainted when undergoing even simple dental and medical procedures. Prior to syncope, he experiences intense fear. No pathological organic process has been identified that is related to the syncope. Hence, Michael's principal anxiety disorders might best be conceptualized as blood-injury-illness phobias (Thyer, Himle, & Curtis, 1985).

Michael's fears about dental and medical procedures have been present since childhood. Medical fears have continued virtually unabated throughout his life. For a brief period of time the dental fear was somewhat ameliorated by a dentist who used nitrous oxide and who reportedly had a good chairside manner. When this dentist moved his practice, Michael's dental fears returned to their normal high intensity.

Differential diagnoses include panic disorder, agoraphobia without history of panic disorder, and social phobia. While Michael does manifest fear of panic proportions, it is tied to specific environmental circumstances and is not known to have been acquired via "panic mediation." Similarly, there is an agoraphobic schema that is related to fear intensity that involves difficulty of escape. Nevertheless, the cue stimuli involve procedures being performed on Michael, so simple phobia was determined to be the principal diagnosis.

Michael also manifests social fears, such as general anxiety about negative social evaluation and specific anxiety about one-to-one conversations. The social fears are clearly contributory to Michael's simple phobias, as is shown by the aversion to conversation during medical/dental procedures.

Michael was self-referred to a university-affiliated psychological service center. He had sought individual psychological treatment for his fears six years previously, but only remained in therapy for two sessions at that time. There also was a course of individual divorce adjustment counseling after his first marriage ended. Michael has also been in therapy with his second (and current) wife in two separate series of sessions for marital problems.

Natural History

The environmental context in which Michael spent childhood and adolescence provided many opportunities to develop phobic behavior. Michael is the youngest of five siblings, including two brothers and two sisters. The oldest sibling is 18 years Michael's senior; the youngest is 9 years his senior. When Michael was 6 months old, his father died of complications secondary to appendicitis; complications that had not been diagnosed early enough to prevent his death. When Michael was 5 years old, one of his brothers died of ulcerative colitis; again there had been difficulty in diagnosing his condition. The other brother left home within a year after that time. While relating the events surrounding the deaths of his father and brother, Michael did not mention the diagnostic difficulties as etiologic factors in his own fears. Nonetheless, familial experiences with poor diagnostic practices probably were important in Michael's dental/medical phobias.

In addition to losing a husband and a son, Michael's mother lost her own mother and a sister within a 5-year period. She became extremely cautious about the well-being of her offspring, and she was "panicky" whenever any of her children were ill. Michael's mother did not remarry after the death of her husband. According to Michael, she was afraid that a new husband would not treat her children well.

Michael had a special and positive status in the family. He was an unplanned child and clearly was the "baby" of the family. After the father's death, Michael's presence was viewed as "wonderful" because he could "take the place . . . of dad." The mother was very protective. For example, she urged him to avoid playing sports with male peers because they "played too rough."

The mother's cautiousness was particularly pronounced in situations involving water or high places, both of which still cause Michael discomfort. Despite four attempts to learn to swim, Michael still is a nonswimmer. The mother also never learned to swim, although apparently all four of Michael's siblings became swimmers. (Unlike Michael, his siblings are not significantly troubled with phobias.) The special protectiveness of Michael by his mother, particularly at and beyond age 6, encouraged avoidance behavior at a critical time and precluded the possibility of corrective exposure. Michael described his mother's cautiousness, and the overall environmental context in his childhood home, as the "birthplace of a lot of my fears."

Direct Aversive Experience

Shortly after the death of one brother and the departure of the other to World War II, Michael had a tonsillectomy at age 6. He remembers having been forcefully held down by medical personnel prior to administration of a general anesthetic. There were bruises on his arms due to his struggling. The mother heard him crying out from some distance away. This experience probably contributed to his phobias and, possibly, to the syncope behavior.

Vicarious Aversive Experience

When Michael was 9 years of age, a child in his neighborhood contracted diphtheria. A group of children from the neighborhood, including Michael, went with one of the fathers to a clinic for inoculations. (Michael's mother did not go to the clinic.) Michael was one of the first to receive an injection. Later, while watching others receive inoculations he fainted. At that point, Michael reports that a "pattern" of fear associated with medical procedures had been established. In his first dental visit, which occurred approximately two years later, he became faint while in the dental chair.

Information and Instruction

At about age 9, Michael was bitten by a dog while selling magazine subscriptions door to door. While he acknowledged that the event "scared the dickens out of me," he continued working and only later reported the bite to his mother when he returned home. The mother telephoned the dog owner to check on rabies and then called a physician for advice. Michael recalled that, as he was listening to the conversations, "all this concern being expressed . . . kind of threw me into a panic." He fainted as his mother was talking to the physician over the telephone. This event is one of Michael's first recollections of fear as a significant factor in his life. It is interesting that Michael has never been phobic or even particularly fearful of dogs.

Around age 14, one of Michael's sisters contracted the mumps. There was concern expressed at home since Michael had not yet had the mumps. A visit to a physician was arranged, and it included Michael receiving an injection. Michael reports that, at that time, he had some concern about his future reproductive functioning if he became ill with the mumps. On the same day, but after the medical visit, Michael got a haircut and became panicked while in the barber's chair. He feared an acute episode of sickness from the mumps while in the chair. Even though haircuts do not cause Michael much current concern, the influence of information at that time set the stage for schematic thinking that was part of the phobic display in the barbershop.

Concluding Comments on the Case

Michael's adult phobic behavior has clear antecedents in childhood fear behavior. The link between his mother's cautiousness and fears and his own phobias is clear as well. The influence of specific environmental events can be seen here. However, these specific experiences are best viewed as participants in a continuous process of development that involves other diverse life experiences and additional factors (e.g., the biology of the organism). Behavior ontogeny is rarely simple. For example, despite a childhood that included strong familial fear of storms and "pandemonium in the household" when storms threatened, Michael is nonplussed by violent weather.

CHILDHOOD AND FAMILIAL ANTECEDENTS

It is not likely that adult phobias are related directly to the fears of very early childhood. Children 2 to 6 years of age display three to five fears on average (Jersild & Holmes, 1935), but the number of extreme fears is very small, and, in general, the fears of very young children disappear with age.

It is likely that many adult phobias are related directly to the fears of later childhood and adolescence. Survey data suggest that fears are stable from age 6 to at least adolescence (Ollendick, Matson, & Helsel, 1985). In addition, factor analytic studies of fears from this same group reveal several themes in common with adult phobias (e.g., fears of animals and medical fears).

The genesis of many adult phobias during adolescence and young adulthood is argued by the age-of-onset data reported in various surveys. Sheehan, Sheehan, and Michiello (1981) found a mean reported age of onset of 19.6 years for simple phobia. Thyer et al. (1985) found that 70% of simple phobias reported having developed the phobia before age 20.

Data reported by Öst (1986) suggest that simple phobias in adults can be traced to events throughout the midchildhood to young adult years. He studied the reported age of onset in 370 phobic patients and found the following mean ages: animal phobia (age 7), blood phobia (age 9), dental phobia (age 12), and claustrophobia (age 20).

Clearly, there are familial influences on fears during childhood and, ultimately, on fears during adulthood. Positive correlations have been found routinely between the fears of children and their mothers. In addition, covariations between children's and mothers' fears have been observed in the context of treatment outcome studies (for a review, see Barrios & Hartman, 1987).

Sibling fears also have been found to be correlated with the fears of young children. And, again, covariation between the fears of siblings has been observed in the context of treatment outcome work (e.g., Ghose, Giddon, Shiere, & Fogels, 1969; Hawley, McCorkle, Witteman, & Van Ostenberg, 1974).

The influence of mothers' and siblings' fears on the fears of children is probably greater among younger than among older children (cf. Klorman et al., 1979). Familial influences might be relatively stronger also among children from lower socioeconomic strata.

Of course, connections between adult simple phobias and childhood (and familial) antecedents need not be based entirely on childhood fears. Genetic factors could function as antecedents in the development of phobias. Torgersen (1979), for example, studied phobic fears among 50 monozygotic twin pairs and 49 dizygotic (but same-sex) twin pairs. The MZ twin partners were more similar than were the DZ twin partners with respect to both the strength of phobic fears and the cue stimuli for phobic fears.

Similarly, "personality traits" (psychometric factors) could function as antecedents in the development of phobias. Gray (1988), for example, has argued that, "We do not all run an equal risk of developing symptoms of anxiety. With the exception of simple animal phobias . . . such symptoms are predominately observed in individuals who score high on neuroticism and introversion in tests . . . " (p. 31).

It is well to remember, however, that results from genetic experiments always are open to environment as well as genetic explanations. It is well to consider also that nearly all the empirical literature on "personality" is derived from checkmarks made next to lists of declarative sentences and that the commonplace use of personality in anxiety theory reifies the quantitative results of those checkmarks.

One way to avoid both competing genetic versus environmental explanations and reification of personality constructs is to adopt a thorough-going development perspective. Such a perspective can be articulated so as to avoid genetic versus environment explanations by rejecting the concept of explanation per se, along with the nineteenth-century traditions of reductionism, mechanism, and causality with which the concept of explanation is associated (see, especially, Delprato, 1987). Reification of all constructs can be avoided by assiduously taking care to use a thorough-going action language (Delprato & McGlynn, 1984; Schafer, 1976). Behavioral systems methodology (e.g., Ray & Delprato, 1988) provides a contemporary model of how we can proceed scientifically in ways that are compatible with this sort of thinking.

SUMMARY

The behaviors that prompt us to diagnose a person as "having simple phobia(s)" are (1) high-amplitude anxiety responses upon confrontation with phobia cue stimuli, (2) skillful and steadfast avoidance of the phobia cue stimuli, and (3) episodic anxiety behavior when phobia cue stimuli are not present. Simple phobic behavior differs from other phobic and anxiety behavior mainly in terms of its relatively narrow stimulus control. Simple phobic behavior can be usefully construed in three response channel terms. Cognitive behaving during environmental transactions that include phobia cues includes schematic thinking that exaggerates estimates of variables related to the likelihood of harm. Physiological behaviors are, concurrently, idiosyncratic and sometimes fractionated. Overt behavior-in-the-world ranges from headlong flight to freezing and includes diverse performance decrements. Adequate methodology has not been brought to bear on the idiographic problem of describing how the three response channels are empirically related (nor has adequate justification been provided for a single-construct model of the problem).

A lifetime prevalence rate for simple phobia can be reasonably estimated as between 2.5% and 8% in the United States. Higher prevalence rates occur among females, African-Americans, and persons not graduated from college than among males, non-African-Americans, and college graduates. There appear to be dramatic differences in the prevalence of simple phobias across cultures.

Phobic behaviors develop out of direct aversive experiences, vicarious aversive experiences, and the acquisition of information or misinformation via other avenues. Soon after the initial ontogenetic events, schematic thinking becomes influential.

The impairments associated with simple phobic behavior are rarely sufficient to prompt help seeking. Usually they take the form of excessive restrictions and familial disruptions. Sometimes there is ruminative thinking, nightmare behavior, and the like.

We have not distinguished ourselves as taxonomists vis-à-vis "the anxiety disorders." DSM-III-R permits multiple concurrent diagnoses, and that is beneficial. The DSM-III-R taxonomy is influenced heavily by a panic mediation "theory" of behavioral ontogeny, and that is probably not beneficial in the long run. Simple animal phobias and blood-injury phobias probably deserve differential diagnosis from other simple phobias.

Many adult phobias are related directly to the fears of later childhood and adolescence. Mothers' and siblings' fears, in turn, influence the development of fears during this period. Genetic factors might participate also in the ontogeny of phobic behavior but genetic explanations of behavior always are pitted against plausible alternatives. It is worthwhile to pursue a thorough-going, action-oriented developmental perspective that bypasses many problems on the order of nature versus nurture by rejecting the mechanistic version of explanation.

REFERENCES

American Psychiatric Association. (1980). *Diagnostic and statistical manual of mental disorders* (3rd ed.). Washington, DC: Author.

American Psychiatric Association. (1987). *Diagnostic and statistical manual of mental disorders* (3rd ed. rev.). Washington, DC: Author.

Anderson, J. R. (1985). *Cognitive psychology and its implications* (2nd ed.). New York: W. H. Freeman.

Arena, J. G., Blanchard, E. B., Andrasik, F., Cotch, P. A., & Myers, P. E. (1983). Reliability of psychophysiological assessment. *Behaviour Research and Therapy, 21*, 447–460.

Barlow, D. H. (1988). *Anxiety and its disorders: The nature and treatment of anxiety and panic.* New York: Guilford Press.

Barrios, B. A., & Hartmann, D. P. (1987). Fears and anxieties. In E. J. Mash & L. G. Terdal (Eds.), *Behavioral assessment of childhood disorders* (pp. 196–262). New York: Guilford Press.

Beck, A. T. (1976). *Cognitive therapy and the emotional disorders.* New York: International Universities Press.

Beck, A. T., Emery, G., & Greenberg, R. L. (1985). *Anxiety disorders and phobias: A cognitive perspective.* New York: Basic Books.

Ben-Tovin, D. I. (1985). DSM-III in Botswana: A field trial in a developing country. *American Journal of Psychiatry, 142*, 342–345.

Berger, S. M. (1962). Conditioning through vicarious instigation. *Psychological Review, 69*, 450–466.

Cameron, N. (1963). *Personality development and psychopathology: A dynamic approach.* Boston: Houghton Mifflin.

Cook, S. W., & Harris, R. E. (1937). The verbal conditioning of the galvanic skin reflex. *Journal of Experimental Psychology, 21*, 202–210.

Delprato, D. J. (1987). Developmental interactionism: An integrative framework for behavior therapy. *Advances in Behaviour Research and Therapy, 9*, 173–205.

Delprato, D. J., & McGlynn, F. D. (1984). Behavioral theories of anxiety disorders. In S. M. Turner (Ed.), *Behavioral theories and treatment of anxiety disorders* (pp. 1–49). New York: Plunum Press.

Dengrove, E. (1972). Practical behavioral diagnosis. In A. A. Lazarus (Ed.), *Clinical behavior therapy* (pp. 73–86). New York: Brunner/Mazel.

Eifert, G. H., & Schermelleh, K. (1985). Language conditioning, emotional instructions, and cognitions in conditioned responses to fear-relevant and fear-irrelevant stimuli. *Journal of Behavior Therapy and Experimental Psychiatry, 16*, 101–109.

Engel, B. T. (1960). Stimulus-response and individual response specificity. *Archives of General Psychiatry, 2*, 305–313.

Evans, I. M., & Weiss, A. R. (1978). Process studies in language conditioning. II: The role of semantic, negative, emotional responses. *Journal of Behavior Therapy and Experimental Psychiatry, 9*, 121–124.

Eysenck, H. J. (1968). A theory of the incubation of anxiety/fear responses. *Behaviour Research and Therapy, 6*, 309–321.

Eysenck, H. J. (1976). The learning theory model of neurosis – A new approach. *Behaviour Research and Therapy, 14*, 251–267.

Gelder, M. G., & Mathews, A. M. (1968). Forearm blood flow and phobic anxiety. *British Journal of Psychiatry, 114*, 1371–1376.

Ghose, J. L., Giddon, D. B., Shiere, F. R., & Fogels, H. R. (1969). Evaluation of sibling support. *Journal of Dentistry for Children, 36*, 35–40.

Gray, J. A. (1988). The neuropsychological basis of anxiety. In C. G. Last & M. Hersen (Eds.), *Handbook of anxiety disorders* (pp. 10–37). Elmsford, NY: Pergamon Press.

Grings, W. W. (1965). Verbal-perceptual factors in the conditioning of autonomic responses. In W. F. Prokasy (Ed.), *Classical conditioning: A symposium*. New York: Appleton-Century-Crofts.

Hawley, B. P., McCorkle, A. D., Witteman, J. K., & Van Ostenberg, P. (1974). The first dental visit for children from low socioeconomic families. *Journal of Dentistry for Children, 41*, 376–381.

Hekmat, H. (1987). Origins and development of human fear reactions. *Journal of Anxiety Disorders, 1*, 197–218.

Hibbert, G. A. (1984). Ideational components of anxiety: Their origin and content. *British Journal of Psychiatry, 144*, 618–624.

Jersild, A., & Holmes, F. (1935). Children's fears. *Child Development Monographs* (No. 20). New York: Columbia University Press.

Kelly, D., & Martin, I. (1969). Autonomic reactivity, eyelid conditioning, and their relationship to neuroticism and extraversion. *Behaviour Research and Therapy, 7*, 233–244.

Kleinknecht, R. A. (1982). The origins and remission of fear in a group of tarantula enthusiasts. *Behaviour Research and Therapy, 20*, 437–443.

Klorman, R., Michael, R., Hilpert, P. L., & Sveen, O. B. (1979). A further assessment of predictors of child behavior in dental treatment. *Journal of Dental Research, 58*, 2338–2343.

Lacey, B. C. (1950). Individual differences in somatic response patterns. *Journal of Comparative and Physiological Psychology, 43*, 338–350.

Lacey, J. L. (1967). Somatic response patterning and stress: Some revisions on activation therapy. In M. H. Appley & R. Trumbull (Eds.), *Psychological stress: Issues in research* (pp. 14–37). New York: Appleton-Century-Crofts.

Lader, M. H., & Wing, L. (1964). Habituation of the psycho-galvanic reflex in patients with anxiety states and in normal subjects. *Journal of Neurology, Neurosurgery and Psychiatry, 27*, 210–218.

Lader, M. H., & Wing, L. (1966). *Physiological measures, sedative drugs and morbid anxiety*. London: Oxford University Press.

Lande, S. D. (1981). Physiological and subjective meaning of anxiety during flooding. *Behaviour Research and Therapy, 18*, 162–163.

Lang, P. J. (1971). The application of psychophysiological methods to the study of psychotherapy and behavior modification. In A. E. Bergin & S. L. Garfield (Eds.), *Handbook of psychotherapy and behavior change: An empirical analysis* (pp. 75–125). New York: John Wiley & Sons.

Lang, P. J. (1977). The psychophysiology of anxiety. In J. D. Cone & R. P. Hawkins (Eds.), *Psychiatric diagnosis: Exploration of biological criteria* (pp. 178–195). New York: Spectrum.

Lang, P. J. (1978). Anxiety: Toward a psychophysiological definition. In H. S. Akiskal & W. L. Webb (Eds.), *Psychiatric diagnosis: Exploration of biological predictions* (pp. 365–389). New York: Spectrum.

Lang, P. J., Rice, D. G., & Sternbach, R. A. (1972). The psychophysiology of emotion. In N. S. Greenfield & R. A. Sternbach (Eds.), *Handbook of psychophysiology* (pp. 623–643). New York: Holt, Rinehart and Winston.

Lick, J. R., & Katkin, E. S. (1976). Assessment of anxiety and fear. In M. Hersen & A. Bellack (Eds.), *Behavioral assessment: A practical handbook* (pp. 175–206). Elmsford, NY: Pergamon Press.

Lipschitz, A. (1988). Diagnosis and classification of anxiety disorders. In C. G. Last & M. Hersen (Eds.), *Handbook of anxiety disorders* (pp. 41–65). Elmsford, NY: Pergamon Press.

Mathews, A. M., & Lader, M. H. (1971). An evaluation of forearm blood flow as a physiological measure. *Psychophysiology, 8,* 509–524.

McGlynn, F. D., & Cornell, C. E. (1985). Simple phobia. In M. Hersen & A. S. Bellack (Eds.), *Handbook of clinical behavior therapy with adults* (pp. 23–48). New York: Plenum Press.

Miller, N. E. (1951). Learnable drives and rewards. In S. S. Stevens (Ed.), *Handbook of experimental psychology* (pp. 435–472). New York: John Wiley & Sons.

Mowrer, O. H. (1939). A stimulus-response analysis of anxiety and its role as a reinforcing agent. *Psychological Review, 46,* 553–565.

Mowrer, O. H. (1947). On the dual nature of learning — A reinterpretation of "conditioning" and "problem solving." *Harvard Educational Review, 17,* 102–148.

Myers, J. K., Weissman, M. M., Tischler, G. L., Holzer, C. E. III, Leaf, P. J., Orvaschel, H., Anthony, J. C., Boyd, J. H., Burke, J. D., Kramer, M., & Stoltzman, R. (1984). Six-month prevalence of psychiatric disorders in three communities. *Archives of General Psychiatry, 41,* 959–967.

Nandi, D. N., Das, N. N., Chaudrey, A., Banerjee, G., Dalta, P., Ghosh, A., & Boral, G. C. (1980). Mental morbidity in urban life — an epidemiological study. *Indian Journal of Psychiatry, 22,* 324–330.

Odejide, A. O. (1976). A psychiatric service in a Nigerian hospital. *African Journal of Psychiatry, 3,* 97–102.

Ollendick, T. H., Matson, J. L., & Helsel, W. J. (1985). Fears in children and adolescence: Normative data. *Behaviour Research and Therapy, 23,* 465–467.

Öst, L. G. (1986). *Age at onset in different phobia.* Unpublished manuscript.

Öst, L. G., & Hugdahl, K. (1981). Acquisition of phobias and anxiety response patterns in clinical patients. *Behaviour Research and Therapy, 19,* 439–447.

Öst, L. G., Sterner, U., & Lindahl, I. L. (1984). Physiological responses in blood phobics. *Behaviour Research and Therapy, 22,* 109–117.

Rachman, S. (1977). The conditioning theory of fear acquisition: A critical examination. *Behaviour Research and Therapy, 15,* 375–387.

Rachman, S., & Hodgson, R. I. (1974). Synchrony and desynchrony in fear and avoidance. *Behaviour Research and Therapy, 12,* 311–318.

Rappee, R. M. (1985). Distinctions between panic disorder and generalization anxiety disorder: Clinical presentation. *Australian and New Zealand Journal of Psychiatry, 19,* 227–232.

Ray, R. D., & Delprato, D. J. (1989). Behavioral systems analysis: Methodological strategies and tactics. *Behavioral Science, 34,* 81–127.

Ray, R. D., & Delprato, D. J. (in press). Systems methodology: Investigating continuity and organization in developmental interactions. In S. H. Cohen and H. W. Reese (Eds.), *Life-span development psychology: Methodological innovations.* Hillsdale, NJ: Lawrence Erlbaum Associates.

Regier, D. A., Myers, J. K., Kramer, M., Robins, L. N., Blazer, D. G., Hough, R. L., Eaton, W. W., & Locke, B. Z. (1984). The NIMH epidemiologic catchment area program: Historical context, major objectives, and study population characteristics. *Archives of General Psychiatry, 41,* 934–941.

Reich, J. (1986). The epidemiology of anxiety. *Journal of Nervous and Mental Disease, 174,* 129–136.

Robins, L. N., Helzer, J. E., Weissman, M. M., Orvaschel, H., Gruenberg, E., Burke, J. D., & Regier, D. A. (1984). Lifetime prevalence of specific psychiatric disorders in three sites. *Archives of General Psychiatry, 41,* 949–958.

Russell, P. T., & Brandsma, J. M. (1974). A theoretical and empirical integration of the rational-emotive and classical conditioning theories. *Journal of Consulting and Clinical Psychology, 42,* 389–397.

Schwartz, G. E. (1978). Psychobiological foundations of psychotherapy and behavior change. In S. L. Garfield & A. E. Bergin (Eds.), *Handbook of psychotherapy and behavior change: An empirical analysis* (pp. 63–99). New York: John Wiley & Sons.

Schafer, R. (1976). *A new action language for psychoanalysis.* New Haven, CT: Yale University Press.

Sheehan, D. V., Sheehan, K. E., & Michiello, W. E. (1981). Age of onset of phobic disorders: A reevaluation. *Comprehensive Psychiatry, 22,* 544–553.

Staats, A. W. (1972). Language behavior therapy: A derivative of social behaviorism. *Behavior Therapy, 3,* 165–192.

Staats, A. W. (1975). *Social behaviorism.* Homewood, IL: Dorsey Press.

Staats, A. W. (1980). "Behavioral interaction" and "interactional psychology" theories of personality: Similarities, differences, and the need for unification. *British Journal of Psychiatry, 71*, 205–220.

Taylor, C. B., Sheikh, J., Agras, S., Roth, W. T., Margraf, J., Ehlers, A., Maddock, R. J., & Gossard, D. (1986). Ambulatory heart rate changes in patients with panic attacks. *American Journal of Psychiatry, 143*, 478–482.

Thyer, B. A., & Himle, J. (1987). Phobic anxiety and panic anxiety: How do they differ? *Journal of Anxiety Disorders, 1*, 59–67.

Thyer, B. A., Himle, J., & Curtis, G. C. (1987). Blood-injury-illness phobia: A review. *Journal of Clinical Psychology, 41*, 451–459.

Thyer, B. A., Parrish, R. T., Curtis, G. C., Neese, R. M., & Cameron, O. G. (1985). Age of onset of DSM-III anxiety disorders. *Comprehensive Psychiatry, 26*, 113–122.

Torgersen, S. (1979). The nature and origin of common fears. *British Journal of Psychiatry, 134*, 343–351.

Verghese, A., & Beig, A. (1974). Neurosis in Vellore Town—An epidemiological study. *Indian Journal of Psychiatry, 16*, 1–8.

Watson, J. B., & Morgan, J. J. B. (1917). Emotional reactions and psychological experimentation. *American Journal of Psychology, 28*, 163–174.

Wolpe, J. (1973). *The practice of behavior therapy*. Elmsford, NY: Pergamon Press.

OBSESSIVE COMPULSIVE DISORDER

EDITORS' COMMENTS

While nearly one half of adults with obsessive compulsive disorder (OCD) developed the illness in childhood or adolescence, the childhood form of the disorder has received considerably less attention than the adult manifestation. The largest sample of OCD youngsters studied to date is the NIMH cohort discussed in depth by Swedo and Rapaport in Chapter 15. Interestingly, the childhood presentation appears to be remarkably similar to the adult presentation of the disorder with respect to symptoms, comorbidity, and prognosis. More specifically, washing and checking rituals are most common, multiple compulsions are usual, obsessions without compulsions are relatively rare, associated depression is often present, and prognosis typically is poor.

By contrast, childhood OCD differs from adult OCD in its sex distribution. Females are overrepresented in the adult form of the disorder, whereas males are overrepresented in the childhood form of the disorder. Also of note is the lack of compulsive personality traits in OCD children and adolescents, as contrasted to OCD adults.

The data on familial aggregation of OCD are variable but in general not terribly impressive. For example, the presence of OCD symptoms in the parents of OCD patients has ranged from 0 to 8%. In addition, examination of the children of OCD parents similarly has failed to show significant aggregation for the disorder. However, by contrast, the data from the NIMH childhood cohort showed that 25% of the probands had a first-degree relative with OCD, although the specific symptom patterns (i.e., washing rituals versus checking rituals) were not congruent within families.

Data from twin studies, used to examine possible genetic transmission of the disorder, also are variable. As Emmelkamp points out in Chapter 16, earlier studies showed a higher frequency of OCD in monozygotic versus dizygotic cases, but the representativeness of these studies was questionable. New data, with representative samples, should help to shed light on this issue.

In both the childhood and adult form of OCD, impairment can be considerable. The disorder frequently interferes with social relationships and school/work performance, and is associated with high levels of subjective distress. The patients also are at risk for depressive episodes and the accompanying impairment associated with that condition.

Differential diagnosis usually is not too difficult for the experienced clinician, in both the childhood and adult forms of OCD. The major disorders that need to be differentiated from OCD are psychotic depression, schizophrenia, anorexia/bulimia, Tourette's syndrome, and phobias. Phobias may be the most difficult to differentiate, particularly in an anxiety disorder clinic setting, because fear and avoidance behavior usually are present in both types of disorders. However, discerning the content of the fear often can be helpful, as well as whether symptoms persist when the patient is not exposed to the feared circumstances.

CHAPTER 15

OBSESSIVE COMPULSIVE DISORDER IN CHILDHOOD

Susan E. Swedo
Judith L. Rapoport

DESCRIPTION OF THE DISORDER

Childhood-onset obsessive compulsive disorder (OCD) is remarkably similar to that seen in adults; indeed, one third (Black, 1974) to one half (Pitres & Regis, 1902) of adult OCD cases have onset by age 15. The children present with overwhelming compulsive rituals, such as washing or checking, and/or painful, repetitive obsessive thoughts. To meet the criteria set by the *Diagnostic and Statistical Manual of Mental Disorders* (American Psychiatric Association, 1987), obsessions or compulsions must be present; the obsessions or compulsions must be a significant source of distress to the individual or interfere with social or role functioning; and the obsessions and/or compulsions cannot be due to another mental disorder, such as Tourette's disorder, schizophrenia, major depression, or organic mental disorder, although OCD can be diagnosed concomitantly with these disorders.

Obsessions are defined as recurrent, persistent ideas, thoughts, images, or impulses that are egodystonic, and attempts are made to ignore or suppress them. Compulsions are repetitive and seem-

ingly purposeful behaviors that are performed according to certain rules in a stereotyped fashion and that are regarded as undesirable. The ritual is performed with a sense of subjective compulsion and, initially at least, resistance is attempted (APA, 1987).

Janet (1903) first described childhood-onset OCD in his report of a 5-year-old child with typical symptoms. Later, Kanner (1962) stressed the social isolation, premorbid constricted personalities, and familial overinvolvement in his review of the German literature. He also noted the children's efforts to "reason things out" in an attempt to deal with their illness. Berman (1942) described four cases with symptom profiles identical to those found in adults, while Anna Freud (1965) focused on the difference between adult and childhood cases; that is, the OC symptoms in children are usually isolated and not part of an obsessive personality.

Despert (1955) was the first to present a large sample of childhood-onset OCD patients in her review of 401 consecutive pediatric psychiatric cases. Her description of the 68 OCD patients reminds us that the children may "hide" their OCD while requesting treatment for other symptoms, such as anxiety or depression, and that the children are painfully aware of the abnormality of their obsessive symptoms. Adams (1973) described 49 clinical cases and noted the lack of punitive toilet training or precipitating events, the male preponderance, and early age of onset. Hollingsworth, Tanguey, Grossman, and Pabst (1980) confirmed the male predominance in childhood and noted the chronicity of the OC symptoms and the frequent association of medical problems.

CLINICAL PRESENTATION

The National Institute of Mental Health (NIMH) sample of over 70 children with severe primary obsessive compulsive disorder is the largest prospective study to date. Many earlier clinical observations have been replicated. Very early onset (below age 4) has been confirmed by family informants, although the children report that they hide their OC symptoms for as long as possible. Initially, the child may disguise his handwashing rituals as more frequent voiding, or he might "schedule" the ritualization for times when he is alone. The children report that they had been performing rituals for 6 months or more before their parents became aware of the problem. Schoolteachers, peers, and grandparents frequently remain unaware of the problem until it is totally incapacitating.

Parents are frustrated and confused by the "willfulness" of the obsessions and compulsions. The patient controls it while at school or with friends, but he "has" to ritualize at home. Why? The children explain that they spend tremendous amounts of energy resisting the compulsions in public and need to "let go" when they get home. Eventually, the illness progresses in severity to the point where any control is impossible.

The mental health professional may also be frustrated by the patient's secrecy. Even when confronted with parental reports of hours spent in the bathroom showering and washing his or her hands, the child denies it. Knowledge of the symptom pattern and reassurance about the commonality of the problem may allow the patient to reveal the nature and extent of the ritualization. Obsessive thoughts are even more carefully guarded; occasionally, the thought content dictates secrecy. The patient realizes that the obsessions are out of his or her control and fears that he or she is "crazy." Young children respond to the

analogy between obsessive thoughts and "hiccups of the brain," while older children can be drawn out by asking them to become detectives or reporters of the OCD.

Many obsessive thoughts fall into one of three categories:

1. Fear of harm, illness, or death
2. Fear of doing wrong or having done wrong
3. Fear of contamination

Unusual obsessions include fear of vomiting, fear of "dumb people," and "tunes in my head." Young boys frequently have number obsessions, that is, fear of "bad" numbers, "safe" numbers, or repetitions. At adolescence, religious scrupulosity, an excessive concern about doing right/being religious, becomes common. The children become obsessed about having only good thoughts and worry about "going to Hell" for stray bad thoughts.

Washing/cleaning rituals are the most commonly seen compulsions in childhood OCD. The most frequently reported compulsion is handwashing, either extremely frequent (50 to 100 times/day) or excessively thorough. Other compulsions include checking rituals, repeating rituals, counting rituals, ritualized symmetry, hoarding, and obsessive slowness (rare in children).

A complete discussion of childhood OC symptoms can be found in *Obsessive Compulsive Disorder in Children and Adolescents* (Rapoport, 1989) and in *The Boy Who Couldn't Stop Washing* (Rapoport, 1988).

EPIDEMIOLOGY

Most estimates about the prevalence of childhood OCD have been made from its incidence in child psychiatric clinics. Berman (1942) found six cases of obsessive compulsive neurosis out of more than 3,000 pediatric cases admitted to the Bellevue Hospital and the Bradley Home in a 5-year period, a prevalence of 0.2%. A retrospective chart review of 405 children seen at the UCLA Neuropsychiatric Institute yielded 5 cases of OCD, representing 1.2% of its child psychiatric cases (Judd, 1965). More recently, Hollingsworth and colleagues (1980) found 17 OCD cases in a review of more than 8,000 records from the same center, a prevalence of 0.2% of child psychiatric cases.

The first study of OCD in a nonclinic population came from the Isle of Wight study and yielded no "pure" cases of OCD. The prevalence of "mixed obsessional/anxiety disorders" in this unselected population of over 2,000 10- and 11-year-olds in England was 0.3% (Rutter, Tizard, & Whitmore, 1970).

Flament et al. (1988) have recently reported the results of a large epidemiologic study of OCD in adolescence that was part of a broader two-stage investigation of eating, depressive, and anxiety symptoms in high school students (Whitaker, Davies, Shaffer, Walsh, & Kalikow, 1985). The target population consisted of the entire ninth to twelfth grade enrollment (5,596 students) in a semirural, middle-class, predominantly white county. In the first stage, students completed a questionnaire that included the 20-item survey form of the Leyton Obsessional Inventory—Child Version (LOI-CV) (Berg, Whitaker, Davies, Flament, & Rapoport, 1988). In the second stage, clinicians conducted blinded semistructured interviews of selected students (those scoring above the LOI-CV cutoff and controls); 80% of this sample were interviewed (Flament et al., 1988).

Eighteen current cases of OCD were found among the 356 adolescents interviewed in stage II. This represents 0.35% of the population surveyed. Two additional subjects had histories of past episodes of OCD. From these data, Flament et al. (1988) estimated a minimum point-prevalence rate of 0.35% in the adolescent population, and a minimum figure of 0.40% for the lifetime prevalence rate in adolescents. When the sample was weighted to reflect the sampling design, the prevalences were 1.0 (±0.5%) and 1.9 (±0.7%) (Flament et al., 1988).

The ritual patterns and content of the obsessions were quite similar for these nonreferred community cases and the NIMH sample. The most common rituals were washing and cleaning rituals, compulsive checking, and straightening. The obsessions included fear of contamination and fear of hurting self and/or familiar persons. Most subjects had multiple obsessions and/or compulsions. Associated diagnoses, such as depression, dysthymia, bulimia, overanxious disorder, phobic disorder, and panic attack, were found in the majority of patients (Flament et al., 1988).

A 2-year follow-up study of the OCD cases and age- and sex-matched controls has recently been completed demonstrating adequate reliability of the diagnosis and poor outcome for this nonreferred population (Berg et al., 1989).

NATURAL HISTORY

Follow-up studies of adult patients have stressed the relative "purity" of outcome of uncomplicated cases of OCD, with depression being the most common factor (Lo, 1967; Goodwin et al., 1969; Welner, Reich, & Robins, 1976). These studies show that the disorder is chronic, with at least half the patients remaining either unchanged or with moderate disability.

Berman (1942) reported on six clear-cut child cases from two different institutions and found that while prognosis is good for a single episode, the long-term follow-up is less favorable. Warren (1965) followed 15 children and adolescents who had been hospitalized at ages 12 to 17 and were seen 6 to 10 years later; he found half doing poorly and only 2 completely recovered. Hollingsworth et al. (1980) identified 17 cases from a retrospective chart review of inpatient and outpatient records and interviewed 10 of these 1½ to 14 years later. Seven of these 10 still had obsessive compulsive symptoms.

The ongoing childhood-onset OCD studies at the NIMH provided the subjects for the first prospective study of the clinical prognosis of childhood OCD (Flament et al., 1989). Twenty-five of 27 consecutive OCD cases and 23 of 29 matched controls were seen in follow-up. The most striking finding is the continued psychopathology for the patient sample and the mixed diagnostic picture. Only 7 (28%) were considered OC symptom-free. Of the 17 patients (68%) who still qualified for the diagnosis of OCD, only 5 (20%) had OCD as their only diagnosis. The remaining 12 had 1 or more additional diagnoses, most commonly depressive disorder (recurrent, unipolar depression) and/or anxiety disorder, including generalized anxiety, social phobia, and separation anxiety. One patient was diagnosed as having atypical psychosis; he was the only patient for whom the diagnosis had been questioned initially because of the lack of ego-dystonicity and his severely defective communication patterns about his straightening rituals.

Of the eight patients no longer meeting criteria for obsessive compulsive disorder, only three were considered well. The other five all suffered from some disorder: one had separation anxiety, one unipolar depression, one atypical psychosis (discussed earlier), and two both depression and an anxiety disorder (phobic and panic disorder, respectively). Thus, 13 patients (48%) had current or past depressive episodes, and 11 (40%) had an anxiety disorder.

Outcome was surprisingly poor for all the patients. Severity at baseline, results of neurological examinations, outcome on neuropsychological testing, or family history of depression, OCD, or anxiety disorder did not predict outcome. The most striking fact to emerge was that an initial good response to clomipramine therapy did not convey any prognostic benefit. Some of the nonresponders had done extremely well, while some former good responders had continued OC symptoms that were no longer controlled by the drug, and/or they developed other disorders (Flament et al., 1989).

Reports from adult patients with childhood-onset OCD support many aspects of this follow-up study. Depressive or anxiety episodes are common during late adolescence, and the OC symptoms fluctuate, with waxing and waning severity over time. In some patients, it is more episodic, with periods of total remission interspersed between bouts of full-blown illness.

Both adolescents and adults report that their symptom patterns change slowly over time. Many patients report counting or washing rituals during their early childhood years, but these symptoms frequently fade gradually and are replaced by checking or repeating rituals. While the majority of children are "washers," most adults with OCD are "checkers."

IMPAIRMENT AND COMPLICATIONS

Although the surprisingly high prevalence of OCD in the community sample contrasted with the low incidence in psychiatric clinic populations suggests that most OC cases remain "subclinical," that is, not under psychiatric care, the disorder can be quite disabling. Severely affected individuals can spend 8 to 12 hours per day ritualizing, while others have become completely catatonic in response to their tormenting obsessions.

OCD is associated with several disorders, including depression, phobias and anxiety disorders, schizophrenia, Tourette's syndrome, simple motor tics, speech and learning disorders, and compulsive personality disorder. Table 15.1 summarizes the associated psychopathology in a sample of 70 children and adolescents with severe primary obsessive compulsive disorder seen in the NIMH. As Tourette's syndrome, mental retardation, psychosis, and eating disorders are excluded from the NIMH study sample, they are not represented.

Only 26% (18 patients) had OCD as their only diagnosis, although in several cases the secondary diagnosis was mild. Depression, either past or current, and anxiety disorder were most common, occurring in 35% and 40% of the group, respectively. For about half the cases, the anxiety or affective disorder predated OCD, while for the rest it appeared that these symptoms were reactive. The children report that they are so disgusted by their enforced ritualization, so plagued by their tormenting obsessions, or so ashamed of their "craziness" that life seems too painful and hopeless to continue. The risk of attempted and completed suicide is increased for OCD patients. In the follow-up study, over 10% percent of the patients had made a life-threatening suicide attempt.

Minor motor tics were noted in 20% of the NIMH study patients, occurring more often in acute cases, in males, and in younger patients. In some cases, touching rituals were used to disguise an involuntary tic. It is unknown how the pattern and severity of OC symptoms differ between Tourette's cases and primary OCD cases, but it is suspected that the compulsions of Tourette's are less severe and less frequently involve washing (D. Pauls, personal communication, 1988).

Compulsive personality disorder appears to be less common in children than in adults. Follow-up interviews with the OCD cases in the adolescent epidemiologic study suggest that some adolescents "develop" compulsive personality traits in an effort to control their OCD (Berg et al., 1989). For example, one young woman reported that she was extremely neat and organized in order not to have to begin her straightening ritual; and a 20-year-old man reported that he was so preoccupied with his obsessions that he couldn't "let go" and have fun.

DIFFERENTIAL DIAGNOSIS

Symptom complexes often overlap; children are imprecise historians and dynamic issues or associated conditions may obscure the primary symptomatology and make the diagnosis of OCD difficult. The major disorders that must be differentiated from OCD include psychotic depression, anorexia/bulimia, autism, schizophrenia, Tourette's syndrome, and severe phobias and anxiety disorders. Psychotic depression is exceedingly rare in childhood, and the psychotic thoughts would tend to be ego-syntonic and thereby distinguishable from OCD; temporal sequencing can provide additional help as the depression precedes the psychosis but usually appears secondary to the OCD.

The anorexic patient's consuming concern with

Table 15.1. Associated Psychopathology at First Admission for 70 Children and Adolescents With Severe Primary Obsessive-Compulsive Disorder

Associated Diagnosis	MALES (N = 47) N	FEMALES (N = 23) N	TOTAL (N = 70) N (%)*
Axis-I			
No other diagnosis	12	6	18 (26%)
Major depression			
Current	12	6	17 (26%)
Past	4	2	6 (9%)
Adjustment disorder with depressed mood	6	3	9 (13%)
Separation anxiety disorder	1	4	5 (7%)
Overanxious disorder	4	7	11 (16%)
Simple phobia	8	4	12 (17%)
Alcohol abuse	2	1	3 (4%)
Substance abuse	1	0	1 (1%)
Conduct disorder	3	2	5 (7%)
Attention-deficit disorder	7	0	7 (10%)
Oppositional disorder	6	2	8 (11%)
Enuresis	2	1	3 (4%)
Encopresis	1	1	2 (3%)
Axis-II			
Compulsive personality	7	1	8 (11%)
Specific developmental disability	12	5	17 (24%)

*Multiple diagnoses given, total exceeds 70.

caloric intake, exercise, and food bears a striking resemblance to the OCD patient's obsessions. However, the anorexic patient denies any ego dystonicity, and in fact, denies that there is any problem. The bulimic patient may recognize that her binging and purging are abnormal and fears she will be unable to stop eating voluntarily, just as the obsessive patient recognizes the futility of his compulsions but must perform them. These overlapping symptom features, the increased incidence of a history of anorexia in adult obsessive compulsive disorder patients (Kasvikis et al., 1986), and the recent report of clomipramine's efficacy for anorexia (Crisp, Lacey, & Crutchfield, 1987) suggest a strong relationship between these disorders that invites further investigation. At present, differentiation depends upon the primary symptom complex.

The rituals of the obsessive compulsive child can appear somewhat similar to the stereotypies of autism, as both disorders result in prolonged, repetitive ritualized behaviors. Stereotypies tend to be simpler than OCD rituals and are not ego-dystonic. Other features typical of autism, such as mental retardation, speech defects, and severely impaired interpersonal relationships, are not seen in OCD.

Insel and Akiskal (1986) have addressed the problem of differentiating psychosis from obsessive compulsive disorder. They suggest that the two disorders can coexist. In addition, they speculate that OCD patients can exhibit a transient reactive affective or paranoid psychosis. Differentiation depends on careful history taking, including insight of the source of the obsessive thoughts, the ego-dystonicity, and the recognition of the obsession or compulsion's irrationality. Prolonged observation may be necessary in some cases to allow the disease process to declare itself.

As previously discussed, the differentiation between OCD and Tourette's syndrome is difficult. In OCD the primary symptoms are obsessive thoughts and/or complex ritualistic compulsions, while in Tourette's, it is multiple, rapid, stereotypic, and involuntary muscular and/or verbal tics. Both diseases have a fluctuating course and some voluntary control. The associated diagnoses differ, as OCD is associated with depression and anxiety disorders while Tourette's is associated with coprolalia, copropraxia, echolalia, echopraxia, and palilalia. Simple motor tics are seen in 15% to 20% of OCD patients and obsessions and compulsions in 10% (Shapiro, Shapiro, & Sweet, 1978) to 68% (Nee, Polinsky, & Ebert, 1982) of

Tourette's patients. The relationship between these two disorders is intriguing.

Phobias may become so severe as to be hard to distinguish from OCD. The anxiety generated by obsessions and by the phobics' feared objects is indistinguishable. The content of the obsessions and the phobias may differ, however. Phobias involve things such as fear of flying or fear of heights, while obsessions center on fear of contamination or fear of harm. One diagnostic clue is provided by the fact that phobics are usually symptom-free when not in confrontation with the feared object, while distance does not offer the OCD patient any relief.

CASE EXAMPLES

Case 1

Case 1 is a 14-year-old white male who, since age 6, has had a series of obsessive thoughts concerning harm to self or others. His symptoms began gradually. Initially, he was obsessed with thoughts of destructive tornados. Around that time, he had seen the beginning of *The Wizard of Oz* and was frightened by seeing Dorothy swept away from her home and family by the twister. This obsession was manifest in checking rituals. He would go to the window and check that the sky was clear or repeatedly ask his mother if there was a tornado warning in effect. He struggled to master this obsession by dedicated study of meteorology, and at age 7 could correctly identify clouds as cirrus or cumulus, and could read radar weather maps on television.

Over the next few years, his obsession shifted to concern about power lines and electrocution. Now, instead of studying meteorology, he concentrated on current, resistance, electrical accidents, and safety. His checking rituals revolved around electrical outlets and light switches, batteries, and power lines. Initially, he spent hours riding his bike along the base of a high-tension power line near his home to "check that the posts were strong enough" and later had to avoid all power lines and developed a lengthy circuitous route to school that detoured all visible power lines and transformers. When he got home, he would spend hours flipping light switches until he felt sure they were off and running his hand over the outlet plates to make sure everything was really unplugged.

Concomitant with these obsessions, the patient suffered from a generalized fear of harm coming to himself or his family. This required extensive "protective" ritualization to keep his family safe and to protect himself. Particularly at times of separating, such as bedtime, leaving for school, or his parents leaving for work, the patient would be compelled to repeat actions perfectly or to check repetitively. When asked how many times he would have to repeat an action, he replied, "It depends. The number isn't always the same, I just have to do it *right*." When asked how he knew when it was right, he said, "I don't *know*, it just *feels* right."

As the patient entered puberty, his obsessional content shifted from fear of harm coming to his family to concern about dying. He felt that he was dying or was about to die. He feared poisoning from germs and chemicals. In response to the concern about germs, he began to compulsively wash his hands, refused to eat any chips if someone else had their hand in the bag first, and drank lots of water to flush the poisons from his body. After hearing of Rock Hudson's death from AIDS, he became obsessed with AIDS and was convinced that he would acquire it through his mouth. He began spitting in an effort to cleanse his mouth and would spit every 15 to 20 seconds.

He also felt compelled to check the house for dangerous chemicals as well as to vacuum the house daily to remove "toxic dust." Despite these cleaning and washing compulsions, his personal appearance was slovenly and dirty. He never tied his shoelaces as they had touched the ground and were contaminated; if he tied them, then his hands would be "dirty" and he would have to wash until they were "clean" again.

A. was also plagued by recurrent obsessions of pins or needles sticking through him. If he saw a sewing needle, straight pin, or safety pin, he would have an obsessive thought that the needle would penetrate his hand or foot and he would die. Initially, the intensity of this image suggested a psychotic delusion, but the patient was very disturbed by this obsession, knew that it was "just a thought and couldn't really happen," and acknowledged that "it's irrational and silly. I know a pin couldn't really kill me, but I get these thoughts about them."

He also began to have obsessive thoughts about intentionally hurting himself. He was clearly able to separate the thoughts from suicidal ideation, but was concerned that he could sit on his shirttail and strangle himself or take too big a bite of food and choke. The patient found these obsessions especially distressing and became quite depressed in response. Suppose he weren't careful enough and he actually did kill himself? Killing himself would be wrong and he would go to Hell. To be careful enough, he had to minimize his activity so he could do everything perfectly and avoid all danger. As his secondary depression deepened, he occasionally had volitional thoughts of suicide, proving he was evil. At this point, his "fear of harming himself" obsessions continued and were joined by depressive guilt and ruminations.

A. was treated with clomipramine, in a double-blind comparison with desipramine, and had a dramatic response. He reported that initially his resistance against the obsessive thoughts strengthened, so that he was able to push them away for short periods of time. He explained that it was "like the irrational part of my brain finally listened to the rest of my brain screaming 'shut up!'." His resistance against his checking and washing rituals also increased to the point where he was spending only one to two hours per day, instead of 8 to 10 hours, ritualizing. After a month on clomipramine, he noted a diminution in the intensity of the obsessions and compulsions as well. By eight weeks he was virtually symptom-free.

Case 2

B. is a 16-year-old girl whose symptoms began abruptly, shortly after the onset of menses. She called herself a "prisoner of my own mind." Her obsessions centered on fear of harm to her parents. She was plagued by recurrent thoughts of her mother dying in a car accident, her father being killed by an intruder, or both her parents dying of burns received in a house fire. Always a light sleeper, she began to get up in the night to check. She spent hours checking that the doors were locked, that the coffee pot was unplugged, and that the family dog was safely ensconced in the garage. Interestingly, despite her obsessions about fire, she did not check that the smoke detector functioned, an excellent example of the irrationality of this superficially rational, purposeful disorder.

B. involved all her family members in her rituals, and like many families, they participated. Her mother made a checklist that B. carried to school with her. Both parents had to check the 24 items on the list and sign that they had done so. When the patient would start obsessing about her home or parents while in school, she would look at the checklist. If that were not completely reassuring, she would leave the classroom to call her mother and seek verbal affirmation. At night, she

frequently woke her father and he would check with her. He never complained, but laughingly acknowledged that he was a bit tired since he had been up with B. six times the night before! The patient's younger sister was also involved because of confrontations over the electric curling iron. B. insisted that her sister used the iron "just to torment me. She never unplugs it, and leaves it laying on the bathroom counter." Her sister maintained that even when she did unplug it, B. would repetitively touch it to see if it were warm.

CONTINUITY AND DISCONTINUITY WITH ADULT PRESENTATION

The overinvolvement of the family in the childhood cases is one of the differences between childhood and adult OCD. The others are the sex distribution (males outnumber females) and lack of compulsive personality traits. In general, however, OCD is nearly identical between children and adults in its symptoms, associated diagnoses, and prognosis.

Childhood onset occurs between 5 and 8 years of age or during early adolescence. In the NIMH patient sample, the mean age at onset was 10.19 years, with 24% of the patients having early onset (less than 7 years of age) and 45% of the patients having their onset in adolescence. Males typically begin earlier than females.

The male : female ratio in the NIMH sample changes with increasing age; males predominate in early onset (13 males : 0 females) and increasing numbers of females (13 males : 10 females) presenting in adolescence. Early onset patients may represent a different disease, since the disparity in sex distribution is so striking, and there is an increased incidence of familial OCD in young children, with fathers of sons most frequently affected (Lenane et al., 1988). The mean age at onset for the children with a positive parental history is slightly less than for those without OCD symptoms (10.1 years vs. 12.4 years).

Although 25% of the NIMH probands had a first-degree relative with OCD, there was no support for familiality of symptom pattern. For example, a father might have had checking compulsions, while the child presented with washing compulsions; in another case, the child counted and the mother had had contamination fears. Recently, we studied 15-year-old monozygotic twin boys who have different symptoms. One had only washing rituals (without obsessive thoughts), while the other had pure obsessions of religious scrupulousity. Both responded well to drug treatment, and we believe them to have the same disorder, suggesting that although the disorder may be genetically based, the symptom selection is not.

Two- to five-year follow-up of the first 27 NIMH study subjects suggests that the associated depression and anxiety continues despite progression of the OC symptom pattern. In addition to the expected cooccurrence of affective and anxiety disorder, developmental disability (reading or language delay) occurred in one fourth of the sample and simple motor tics in 30%. The motor tics were more prominent on initial presentation, with less than 10% still having tics at two- to five-year follow-up. Tics are not frequently seen in adult OCD patients.

It appears that fewer children than adults with OCD have associated compulsive personality disorder (CPD), although the lack of standardized diagnosis of CPD makes this conjectural. In both the epidemiological and the clinical studies, however, CPD was uncommon in children and adolescents, making this finding unlikely to be an artifact of referral bias.

Black (1974) summarized the available literature for adults with OCD, finding moderate to marked obsessional traits in 71% of 383 patients and no premorbid traits in 29% of 451 patients, noting that criteria for obsessional traits vary widely between papers. Between 16% and 36% of OCD patients had no premorbid obsessional traits, while 55% of control patients did. More recently, Rasmussen and Tsuang (1984) found this same percentage (55%, or 24/44) of adult OCD patients to have premorbid compulsive personality traits. Studies using structured personality measures have not found a predominance of compulsive personality disorder in OC adult subjects while other personality disorders did occur with greater frequency (Black, Yates, Nowyes, Pfohl, & Reich, 1988).

Preliminary findings from a follow-up study of the community-based sample (Berg et al., 1989) suggest that some children with early onset OCD (without premorbid CPD) appear to "form" compulsive personality traits as part of an adaptive coping pattern. If, for example, a child initially had felt compelled to write the number 7 perfectly, he describes now being "deliberately" slow, careful, and rigid in an effort to "get it right the first time" and "beat the compulsion!" Systematic data are being collected on the development of compulsive personality disorder in relationship to OCD in childhood.

SUMMARY

The clinical presentation of OCD in children and adults is strikingly similar. The content of the obsessions and the patterns of the compulsive rituals overlap completely between the two groups. Both age groups report similar anxiety accompanying the compulsion. Not only is resistance described similarly by adults and children, but the description is almost identical between individuals. It appears that OCD is a remarkably continuous disorder with virtually identical presentation in children and adults.

REFERENCES

Adams, P. L. (1973). *Obsessive children*. New York: Penguin Books.

American Psychiatric Association. (1987). *Diagnostic and statistical manual of mental disorders* (3rd ed. rev.). Washington, DC: Author.

Berg, C. Z., Whitaker, A., Davies, M., Flament, M. F., & Rapoport, J. L. (1988). The survey form of the Leyton Obsessional Inventory—Child Version: Norms from an epidemiological study. *Journal of the American Academy of Child and Adolescent Psychiatry, 27*(6), 759–763.

Berg, C. Z., Rapoport, J. L., Whitaker, A., Davies, M., Leonard, H., Swedo, S. E., Braimen, S., & Lenane, M. (1989). Childhood obsessive compulsive disorder: A two-year prospective follow-up of a community sample. *Journal of the American Academy of Child and Adolescent Psychiatry, 28*(4), 528–533.

Berman, L. (1942). Obsessive-compulsive neurosis in children. *Journal of Nervous and Mental Disease, 95*, 26–39.

Black, A. (1974). The natural history of obsessional neurosis. In H. R. Beech (Ed.), *Obsessional states* (pp. 19–54). London: Methuen.

Black, D., Yates, W., Noyes, R., Pfohl, B., Reich, J. (1988, May 12). *Personality disorder in obsessive compulsives*. Poster presentation at 137th meeting of the American Psychiatric Association, Montreal.

Crisp, A. H., Lacey, J. H., & Crutchfield, M. (1987). Clomipramine and "Drive" in people with anorexia nervosa: An in-patient study. *British Journal of Psychiatry, 150*, 355–358.

Despert, L. (1955). Differential diagnosis between obsessive-compulsive neurosis and schizophrenia in children. In P. H. Hoch & J. Zubin

(Ed.), *Psychopathology of childhood*. New York: Grune & Stratton.

Flament, M. F., Whitaker, A., Rapoport, J. L., Davies, M., Berg, C. Z., Kalikow, K., Sceery, W., & Shaffer, D. (1988). Obsessive compulsive disorder in adolescence: An epidemiological study. *Journal of the American Academy of Child and Adolescent Psychiatry, 27*, 764–771.

Flament, M. F., Koby, E., Rapoport, J. L., Berg, C. J., Zahn, T., Cox, C., Denckla, M., & Lenane, M. (1989). Childhood obsessive compulsive disorder: A prospective follow-up study. *Journal of Child Psychology and Psychiatry*.

Freud, A. (1965). *Normality and pathology in childhood*. New York: International University Press.

Goodwin, D. W., Guze, S., & Robins, E. (1969). Follow-up studies in obsessional neurosis. *Archives of General Psychiatry, 20*, 182–187.

Hollingsworth, C., Tanguey, P., Grossman, L., & Pabst, P. (1980). Long-term outcome of obsessive compulsive disorder in children. *Journal of the American Academy of Child Psychiatry, 19*, 134–144.

Janet, P. (1903). *Les obsessions et la psychiatrie* (Vol. 1.) [Obsessions and psychiatry]. Paris: Felix Alan.

Judd, L. (1965). Obsessive compulsive neurosis in children. *Archives of General Psychiatry, 12*, 136–143.

Insel, T. R., & Akiskal, H. S. (1986). Obsessive compulsive disorder with psychotic features: A phenomenologic analysis. *American Journal of Psychiatry, 143*, 1527–1533.

Kanner, L. (1962). *Child psychiatry* (3rd ed.). Springfield, IL: Charles C Thomas.

Kasvikis, Y. G., Tsakiris, F., & Marks, I. M. (1986). Women with obsessive compulsive disorder frequently report a past history of anorexia nervosa. *International Journal of Eating Disorders, 5*, 1069–1075.

Lenane, M., Swedo, S., Leonard, H., Cheslow, D., Rapoport, J. L., & Pauls, D. (1988, May 10). *Obsessive compulsive disorder in first degree relatives of obsessive compulsive disorder children*. Talk given at the 137th meeting of the American Psychiatric Association, Montreal, Canada.

Lo, W. (1967). A follow-up study of obsessional neurosis in Hong Kong Chinese. *British Journal of Psychiatry, 113*, 823–832.

Nee, L., Polinsky, R. J., & Ebert, M. H. (1982). Tourette syndrome: Clinical and family studies. In A. J. Friedhoff & T. N. Chase (Eds.), *Gilles de la Tourette syndrome* (pp. 291–295). New York: Raven Press.

Pitres, A., & Regis, E. (1902). *Les obsessions et les impulsions* [Obsessions and impulses]. Paris: Doin.

Rapoport, J. L. (Ed.). (1989). Obsessive compulsive disorder in children and adolescents. Washington, DC: American Psychiatric Association.

Rapoport, J. L. (1988). *The boy who couldn't stop washing*. New York: E. P. Dutton.

Rasmussen, S. A., & Tsuang, M. T. (1984). The epidemiology of obsessive compulsive disorder. *Journal of Clinical Psychiatry, 45*, 450–457.

Rutter, M., Tizard, J., & Whitmore, K. (1970). *Education, health and behavior*. London: Longmans.

Shapiro, A. K., Shapiro, E. S., & Sweet, R. D. (1978). *Gilles de la Tourette syndrome*. New York: Raven Press.

Warren, W. (1965). A study of adolescent psychiatric inpatients and the outcome six or more years later. *Journal of Child Psychology and Psychiatry, 6*, 141–160.

Welner, A., Reich, T., & Robins, L. (1976). Obsessive compulsive neurosis: Record follow-up and family studies: I. Inpatient record study. *Comprehensive Psychiatry, 17*, 527–539.

Whitaker, A., Davies, M., Shaffer, D., Johnson, J., Abrams, S., Walsh, B. T., Kalikow, K. (1989). The struggle to be thin: A survey of anorexic and bulimic symptoms in a non-referred adolescent population. *Psychological Medicine, 19*(1), 143–163.

CHAPTER 16

OBSESSIVE COMPULSIVE DISORDER IN ADULTHOOD

Paul M. G. Emmelkamp

DESCRIPTION OF THE DISORDER

Compulsive rituals and obsessive thoughts (ruminations) are usually distinguished, although most obsessional patients have obsessions as well as compulsions. According to the *Diagnostic and Statistical Manual of Mental Disorders* (American Psychiatric Association, 1987) obsessions are recurrent and persistent ideas, thoughts, impulses, or images that are experienced as intrusive and senseless (e.g., thoughts about harming others). Attempts are made to ignore or suppress such thoughts or impulses or to neutralize them with some other thought or action. The most common obsessions are repetitive thoughts of harming others (e.g., killing one's child), contamination, and doubt (e.g., repeatedly wondering whether one has not made a serious failure).

Compulsions are defined in DSM-III-R as repetitive, purposeful, and intentional behaviors that are performed in response to an obsession, or according to certain rules or in a stereotyped fashion; the behavior is designed to neutralize or to prevent discomfort or some dreaded event or situation, and the person recognizes that his or her be-

havior is excessive or unreasonable. The most common compulsions involve handwashing, cleaning, counting, checking, and touching. When a person's obsessions or compulsions cause marked distress, are time consuming (take more than an hour or day), or significantly interfere with the person's normal routine, occupational functioning, or usual social activities or relationship with others, the person qualifies for the DSM-III-R diagnosis of obsessive compulsive disorder.

CLINICAL PRESENTATION

There are now a number of studies reporting on the phenomenology of obsessive compulsive disorders. The form and content of obsessions and compulsions appear to be strikingly similar in England (Rachman & Hodgson, 1980; Stern & Cobb, 1978), Scotland (Dowson, 1977), Germany (Zaworka & Hand, 1980), the United States (Welner, Reich, Robins, Fishman, & van Doren, 1976), Canada (Roy, 1979), and India (Akhtar, Wig, Verma, Pershod, & Verma, 1975).

About 80% of obsessional patients have obsessions as well as compulsions. A minority suffer from obsessions only. Pure rituals without accompanying obsessive thoughts are rare. Usually obsessions precede the rituals, but sometimes the obsessive thoughts follow the performance of rituals, especially with obsessional doubting. The most common obsessional thoughts consist of fears of dirt and contamination. Harming obsessions are reported by about one quarter of the patients. Table 16.1 shows that the distribution of obsessional themes in England (Rachman & Hodgson, 1980) and India (Akhtar et al., 1975) are essentially similar.

Factor analyses of obsessional questionnaires revealed several interpretable factors, which varied from study to study. However, all studies found two independent factors: "cleaning" and "checking" (see Emmelkamp, 1982; Kraaykamp, Emmelkamp, & Van den Hout, 1989). Cleaning compulsions are usually associated with contamination fears. Patients fear that they may become contaminated and therefore clean their house, themselves, and children. Whenever such a patient touches anything that might be contaminated (e.g., doorknobs, other people, food), they have to wash their hands and arms, often for many minutes, or take a bath. With some patients, thoughts by themselves may provoke washing and cleaning rituals. Checking rituals may involve checking whether doors and windows are closed, and whether the gas is turned off. Whenever they leave their house a number of checkers will go back numerous times to see if everything is all right. Checking may also occur in other situations, for example, driving back to see if an accident has happened, going back to the office to see if anyone is locked up in a cupboard, and so forth.

There is a considerable overlap. Ritualizers often have obsessions as well. Further, checkers often have washing compulsions, and vice versa. Women preponderate among cleaners, and men

more often have compulsive checking (Hoekstra, Visser, & Emmelkamp, 1989).

Patients with obsessions and compulsions usually try to avoid the situations that evoke obsessive thoughts and compulsions. With passive avoidance the individual avoids stimuli, situations, and so on, that might provoke anxiety and discomfort. Active avoidance refers to the motor component of obsessive compulsive behavior—for example, checking and cleaning. The difference between both types of avoidance may be illustrated by a clinical example. Dianne is an obsessive compulsive patient who fears being contaminated by germs and dust. She avoids going outdoors in order to prevent contamination. For the same reason windows are always kept closed. The avoidance of any contamination by staying at home and keeping the windows closed can be classified as passive avoidance. When objects from the outside are brought into Dianne's home (e.g., newspaper, food), she cleans these for a long time. Touching any of these objects evokes excessive hand washing. The washing and cleaning are examples of active avoidance. Active avoidance (rituals) serves to reduce anxiety as was shown in a number of laboratory studies (reviewed by Emmelkamp, 1982).

Neutralizing thoughts often have the same function as ritualizing. Obsessional patients often engage in neutralizing thoughts to undo the possible harmful effects of their obsessions. For example, one of our patients with the blasphemous obsession "God is mad" had to think positive thoughts ("I remain Catholic") each time the obsession occurred, which led to relief of anxiety provoked by the blasphemous thought.

Patients with harming obsessions may avoid sharp objects (knives), strings, poisonous matters, or being alone with children, thus preventing themselves from killing someone. A few of these patients are more concerned about harming themselves rather than others.

Avoidance behavior engaged in by obsessive compulsive patients is clearly related to the type of disorder. Checkers will avoid all kinds of situations that may trigger their rituals; that is, they may avoid being alone, driving, using matches, and being the last one going to bed. Similarly, patients with washing rituals will go to great lengths to prevent contamination. When obsessions and compulsions are related to death, patients usually avoid all kinds of situations that may evoke thoughts about death, such as reading newspapers (the obituaries), watching television,

Table 16.1. Distribution of Obsessional Themes in Different Cultures

CONTENT OF OBSESSION	AKHTAR ET AL.	RACHMAN & HODGSON
Dirt/disease contamination	59%	55%
Aggression/harm	25%	19%
Impersonal/orderliness	23%	35%
Religion	10%	10%
Sex	5%	13%

or going to a cemetery. The rituals (active avoidance) in such cases are often very subtle and may consist of touching specific objects, mentioning particular numbers or proverbs, or repeating again and again whatever one was occupied with.

Less common types of obsessive compulsive disorder are compulsive buying and hoarding. Compulsive buyers have the urge to buy all kinds of objects, that they don't need at all and often don't use at all, "because they are so cheap." Patients who suffer from hoarding compulsions may have cupboards full of 10-year-old cash slips, old notes, hundreds of pairs of shoes, underwear, and clothes that in extreme cases may fill whole rooms. None of these things will ever be used, but the patient is afraid to throw them away in case they might come in handy. Compulsive hoarding is a severe variant of doubting.

Counting is another variant of obsessive compulsive behavior that accompanies checking and washing, but for some patients counting is often the essential feature of their disorder. Patients have to repeat their actions a certain number of times, for example, four times. When they are interrupted during their ritual or become uncertain whether they have done it right, they might multiply and repeat the action 16 times. Other numbers (e.g., 3 or 7) may be danger signals, and in this example the patient has to avoid performing the rituals 3 or 7 times. The performance of the ritual can often not be explained according to common logic. One of my patients had to wash her hands 25 times each time she felt contaminated. When asked why she was able to stop after 25 times she frankly replied, "You don't expect me to go on forever?"

For a few patients orderliness is the main problem. Such patients have to arrange objects again and again in a particular way. For example, books, gramophone discs, clothes, furniture, cutlery, and crockery may have to be arranged in a particular manner. In extreme cases, patients may spend the whole day in arranging such objects in the correct way. Finally, a few patients suffer from obsessional slowness. Such patients spend an unusually long time in performing routine actions, such as dressing and undressing.

EPIDEMIOLOGY

Although in earlier years obsessive compulsive disorder was thought a rare condition and its prevalence in the general population was rated at 0.05% (Emmelkamp, 1982), more recent community surveys have shown that obsessive compulsive disorder exists in a larger proportion of the adult general population, but only a minor proportion of those who are affected ever consult health services. The major community surveys into the prevalence of obsessive compulsive disorder are summarized in Table 16.2.

In the Epidemiologic Catchment Area program on the prevalence of specific psychiatric disorders, interviews were held with nearly 17,000 persons from large general population samples in four metropolitan areas, New Haven, Baltimore, St. Louis, and Los Angeles, and in five contiguous counties in the Piedmont of North Carolina whose residents were nearly equally distributed between urban and rural counties. The lifetime prevalence of a disorder is stated as the proportion of persons in a representative sample of the population who had ever experienced that disorder up to the date of assessment. The lifetime prevalence of obsessive compulsive disorders was 2.6% for New Haven, 3.0% for Baltimore, 1.9% for St. Louis, and 2.1% for Los Angeles (Robins et al., 1984; Karno et al., 1987). Nearly similar figures for lifetime prevalence of obsessive compulsive disorder were reported from Germany (2.0%, Wittchen, 1988), Finland (2.5%, Vaisänen, 1975), Canada (3.0%, Bland, Orn, & Newman, 1988a), and Uganda (2.4%, Orley & Wing, 1979). Taking the data from all the community surveys together the mean lifetime prevalence appears to be 2.6%.

Myers et al. (1984), Blazer et al. (1985), and Burnam et al. (1987) focused on the prevalence rates for the 6-month period immediately preceding the interview in the Epidemiologic Catchment Area program. The 6-month prevalence for obsessive compulsive disorder was 1.5% for New Haven, 2.1% for Baltimore, 1.3% for St. Louis, 0.7% for Los Angeles, and 2.2% for Piedmont. Nearly similar figures for the 6-month prevalence of obsessive compulsive disorder were found in Germany (1.8%, Wittchen, 1988) and Canada (1.6%, Bland, Newman, & Orn, 1988b). Taking the data from these studies together the pooled 6-month prevalence rate appears to be 1.6%.

In most of the community surveys obsessive compulsive disorder was more dominant among women than among men. The female preponderance of obsessive compulsive disorder in adults is striking because in children with obsessive compulsive disorder boys predominated (Turns, 1985). This might suggest that there is a lack of continuity between obsessive compulsive disorder as presented in children and adults. Further, the 6-month prevalence of obsessive compulsive dis-

Table 16.2. Prevalence of Obsessive-Compulsive Disorder

| | | PREVALENCE | | |
	SAMPLE (N)	LIFETIME	6-MONTH	SITE
Vaisänen (1975)	991	2.5%	—	Finland
Orley & Wing (1979)	206	2.4%	—	Uganda
Robins et al. (1984)	3,058	2.6%	1.5%	New Haven, CT, USA
Meyers et al. (1984)	3,481	3.0%	2.1%	Baltimore, MD, USA
Burnam et al. (1987)	3,004	1.9%	1.3%	St. Louis, MO, USA
Karno et al. (1987)	3,125	2.1%	0.7%	Los Angeles, CA, USA
Blazer et al. (1985)	3,912	—	2.2%	Piedmont
Wittchen (1988)	2,158	2.0%	1.8%	Germany
Bland et al. (1988a,b)	3,258	3.0%	1.6%	Canada

order in Piedmont was higher among the rural population (2.7%) than among an urban population (1.5%), but this difference was not significant (Blazer et al., 1985) and not found in the St. Louis area (Robins et al., 1984). Further, no differences in the prevalence of obsessive compulsive disorder were found between Mexican-Americans and non-Hispanic whites in the Los Angeles study (Burnam et al., 1987).

Bland, Newman, and Orn (1988c) investigated lifetime prevalence and 6-month prevalence of psychiatric disorders among elderly (age >65). They found a lower 6-month prevalence for most psychiatric disorders in elderly household residents than in other age groups, a notable exception being obsessive compulsive disorders that remained quite stable across time (1.5%). In institutional samples the rate of obsessive compulsive disorder was particularly high among female elderly (4.7%). Because obsessive compulsive disorder seldom starts after age 40 (see the following data), these figures might indicate that this condition is a chronic disorder.

The relatively high prevalence of obsessive compulsive disorder among the general population is not mirrored in the figures of obsessive compulsive patients seen in mental health institutions. Among psychiatric patients obsessive compulsive disorder as primary diagnosis is rare. The occurrence of obsessive compulsives among outpatients was estimated from 0.6% (Lo, 1967) to 2% (Pollitt, 1960). Among inpatients obsessive compulsive disorder was diagnosed 0.1% (Lo, 1967), 0.5% (Coryell, 1981), 0.9% (Ingram, 1961), 2.5% (Kringlen, 1965), and 4% (Pollitt, 1960). The last

three authors, however, were less restrictive in their diagnosis, and depressed cases with obsessive compulsive symptoms were included as well. Presumably, many obsessive compulsive patients avoid psychological help. A substantial number of obsessive compulsives seek professional consultation only when pressed by relatives.

NATURAL HISTORY

Although information on the age of onset of psychiatric disorders might be of importance, there are often problems in fixing the exact age of onset since such information has to be gathered retrospectively. Bland, Newman, and Orn (1988c) provided data with respect to onset age of obsessive compulsive disorder in their community survey. Obsessive compulsive disorder show most cases with first symptoms at about 20 years. Onset after age 50 does not occur. No differences in onset age was found between males and females. Black (1974) and Yaryura-Tobias and Neziroglu (1983) reviewed earlier clinical studies of onset age in obsessive compulsive disorder and found a mean onset age in the early twenties. Onset age before age 10 or after age 40 was rare. In a clinical sample the mean age of onset was found to be 25.6 (Thyer, Parrish, Curtis, Nesse, & Cameron, 1985). Noshirvani, Kasvikis, Tsakiris, Basoglu, and Marks (1988) reported a mean onset age of 22 years in 307 obsessive compulsives, the bulk of them (over 90%) starting from age 10 to 40. In their series mean onset age of males was younger than that of females.

IMPAIRMENT AND COMPLICATIONS

Many obsessional patients are concurrently depressed or have had previously one or more depressed episodes. In most cases the depression is secondary to the obsessive compulsive disorder. Given the severity of the disorder, it is not surprising that many obsessive compulsive patients become depressed. Yaryura-Tobias and Neziroglu (1983) found among 100 obsessive compulsive patients that 94% of them were also depressed. Similarly, Goodwin, Guze, and Robins (1969) found secondary depression very often associated with obsessive compulsive disorder. Indirect evidence for the notion that depression is secondary to the obsessive compulsive disorder comes from behavior therapy studies. Depressed mood usually improves as a result of successful behavioral treatment for the obsessive compulsive disorder (Emmelkamp, 1982; Visser, Hoekstra, & Emmelkamp, 1989). Depression is most often of the neurotic, reactive type; psychotic depression is seldom reported in obsessive compulsive disorder.

Given the association between depression and obsessive compulsive disorder, one would expect a relatively high rate of suicide and suicide attempts among obsessive compulsive patients, but this is not the case. In a large community survey (n = 3,258), Dijck, Bland, Newman, and Orn (1988) studied the relationship between various psychiatric disorders and attempted suicide. The suicide risk ratio was calculated by dividing the lifetime prevalence rate of the disorder in suicide attempters by the rate in nonattempters. The greatest relative suicide risks were associated with schizophrenia (23.1), mania (21.0), major depressive episode (8.0), and obsessive compulsive disorder (5.9). Since persons in this survey could have overlapping diagnoses, it is unclear how high the risk is for obsessive compulsive patients who are not also depressed. Only three clinical studies (one on depressed and the other on obsessional patients) provide data with respect to suicide risk. In a clinical study on patients with depressive psychoses, Gittelson (1966) found that depressed patients with obsessions were 6.5 times less likely to attempt suicide than those with obsessions who were not depressed. Thus, obsessions seemed to have a protective function with respect to suicide in these depressed patients. Rosenberg (1968) found a reduced suicide risk among obsessive compulsives in comparison with "anxious neurotics." Similarly, Templer (1972) found a reduced risk of suicide among depressed obsessional patients in comparison with other depressives.

Many obsessive compulsive patients have problems in social relationships, although it is difficult to establish whether such problems are the result of the disorder or were already present before the disorder developed. Obsessive compulsive patients have been found to be socially anxious (Steketee, Grayson, & Foa, 1987) and fear criticism (Thyer, Curtis, & Fechner, 1984), and to be more hostile than controls (Millar, 1983; Emmelkamp, de Haan, & Hoogduin, in press).

The frequency of personality disorders among obsessive compulsives is high. In a number of studies (Joffe, Swinson, & Regan, 1988; Rasmussen & Tsuang, 1986; Jenike, Baer, & Minichiello, 1986), a wide range of personality disorders were found, most patients having mixed personality disorder with avoidant, dependent, and passive-aggressive features. In one study (Jenike et al., 1986), one third of the patients also had a schizotypal personality disorder, but this was lower in the other studies.

The celibacy rate among obsessive compulsive patients is high (Black, 1974; Roy, 1979; Steketee et al., 1981; Welner et al., 1976). Few data are available with respect to the quality of the marital relationship. Emmelkamp et al. (in press) found the marriages of obsessive compulsives less satisfactory than those of control couples, but again it is unclear whether the marital dissatisfaction is either result or cause of the obsessive compulsive disorder; the exact relationship between these problems will vary from couple to couple. Contrary to system theoretically oriented views (Hafner, 1982), the partners of obsessive compulsive patients were found to be essentially normal people (Emmelkamp et al., in press). There was no evidence that the partners of obsessive compulsive patients were psychologically disturbed themselves.

The unemployment rate among obsessive compulsive patients is relatively high. In a community survey by Bland, Stebelsky, Orn, and Newman (1988), the prevalence rate of obsessive compulsive disorder among employed persons was lower than among unemployed. Steketee et al. (1987) compared obsessive compulsive patients with patients with other anxiety disorders and found many more anxious patients (68.3%) to be employed than obsessive compulsives (30.7%).

DIFFERENTIAL DIAGNOSIS

The diagnosis of obsessive compulsive disorder usually provides little problems for experienced clinicians (Barlow, 1985). In a few cases the distinction between various anxiety disorder categories can be difficult. For example, obsessive cleaners who avoid going outside, crowded areas, and traveling by public transport out of fear of contamination may be confused with agoraphobics who avoid the same type of situations. However, in the case of agoraphobia such situations are usually avoided because the person is afraid of having a panic attack or panic symptoms such as becoming dizzy, falling, or having palpitations rather than out of fear of contamination. In a few obsessive compulsives agoraphobic fears are also present.

In depressed persons obsessive thoughts (brooding) are quite common but these usually disappear when the depression is over. Such cases should not be diagnosed as obsessive compulsive disorder. A difficult but important clinical distinction has to be made in cases of suicidal thoughts. A number of obsessive compulsives have obsessions containing suicidal thoughts but will never act on them. However, in depressed patients such thoughts may require immediate clinical action. A crucial issue for the differential diagnosis is whether such thoughts are ego-syntonic or ego-dystonic. In the latter case the person does not intend to commit suicide, although he usually is quite afraid that he might do so. When the suicidal thoughts are ego-syntonic, the person may really want to put an end to her life, although she may currently be too depressed to actually commit suicide.

The diagnosis obsessive compulsive disorder is not made when the obsessions and compulsions occur exclusively during a psychotic episode. Hallucinations and delusions need to be differentiated from obsessions. The main diagnostic question here is whether the person recognizes that his thoughts are unreasonable. However, in cases with overvalued ideas this differentiation is not always easy to make. Such overvalued ideas can be quite bizarre. If the person even after considerable discussion cannot acknowledge the possibility that the beliefs may be unfounded, the diagnosis of schizophrenia may be considered.

Persons who are preoccupied with some imagined defect in appearance (e.g., shape of nose, facial flaws) and have obsessive thoughts about their appearance are diagnosed as having body dysmorphic disorder rather than obsessive compulsive disorder. Similarly, obsessive thoughts centered on the unfounded belief of having a serious disease are diagnosed as hypochondriasis instead of obsessive compulsive disorder. Finally, when obsessive thoughts are the result of a very traumatic experience (e.g., rape, car accident, bombing, natural disasters) and in addition the person persistently avoids stimuli associated with the trauma and shows persistent symptoms of increased arousal, the diagnosis of posttraumatic stress disorder should be considered.

Although eating disorders can be considered to be compulsive, these are not diagnosed as such. However, a small number of obsessive compulsive females do also qualify for the diagnosis eating disorder (e.g., anorexia nervosa) or have suffered from an eating disorder in the past.

When patients have tics (motor or vocal), these are diagnosed as tic disorder. Tics are differentiated from compulsions in that they are involuntary, whereas compulsions are intentional behaviors. It should be noted, however, that a substantial number of patients with Gilles de la Tourette's syndrome, which is characterized by multiple motor and one or more vocal tics, have prominent obsessive compulsive symptoms (Pauls et al., 1986).

CASE EXAMPLES

The variety in the clinical picture is illustrated in the following examples.

David (age 27) has been suffering from blasphemous obsessions since he was 8 years old. Before being referred to us, he had been psychopharmacologically treated for a psychosis; nevertheless his obsessional complaints remained. His obsessions are "God be cursed," "God is bastard," "God is crazy," "Fucking God," "I piss on you," and so on. These thoughts were often expressed in German instead of in Dutch to make them less terrifying. He was trying to neutralize these thoughts by kneeling in random places at home about 20 times a day, asking God for forgiveness by praying out loud, moaning, shaking his head, turning to the left, stepping one step backward, not walking on the lines, and other similar methods. In addition he suffered from obsessional ruminations such as "Am I praying to God or to the devil?" "Am I allowed to look at a beautiful woman, or not?" "Am I allowed to eat cream butter?" "Do I love my wife?" "Am I allowed to buy a car?" "Am I allowed to buy a video?" He also attempted to neutralize these particular thoughts. After having married his wife (his first girlfriend), he had also been suffering from harming obsessions.

David was raised by his parents in a repressive Calvinistic way. From the age of 8 he had been insecure about what is right or wrong because the Bible did not present clear guidelines. The patient was emotionally unable to reconcile his own feelings of anger toward his parents with the commandments he heard every day. The first compulsive thought he remembers was "My parents are cursed." To undo these thoughts he added the word "not," so that he used this word about five or six times. This resulted in "My parents are not not not not not cursed."

The doubting obsessions originated from the time he got married. His mother disagreed with his choice, which put him into serious trouble. His harming obsessions arose from that time as well and pertained to killing his parents-in-law and his wife. Interestingly, in contrast with other patients, this patient did not experience aggravating obsessions during a period of depression.

Janet (age 32) has been suffering from obsessions from the time she got married. She feared that her husband was enjoying pornographic magazines and masturbated when she was not at home, and also that he could watch other nude women (e.g., in the swimming pool or on television). Furthermore, she was frequently seized by the obsession of being raped in the street by a group of boys. The patient became anxious when seeing large breasts or women wearing provocative clothes, even when her husband was not around. For this reason she was anxious in places such as a swimming pool, cinema, and the street. She also experienced anxiety for magazines and television programs on account of possible occurrence of nudity. These situations were avoided by her husband (because of his wife's pressure) and herself. She was often depressed, suffered from bulimia nervosa, and was dissatisfied with the sexual relationship with her husband. They had sex once a week, which, in the patient's opinion, was not enough.

John, a 32-year-old single man, had a house of his own but lived with his parents as a consequence of his insecurity. His main complaint was a compulsion to write down all kinds of thoughts, because he was afraid of forgetting the things he had seen, felt, and experienced. He was very perfectionistic. Seven years ago he started writing compulsively without any apparent reason. What began with keeping a diary developed into continuously written reports of his feelings and thoughts. The idea of losing track of things made him very anxious, and by writing them down the tension abated temporarily. He jotted down his feelings and thoughts on scraps of paper which he kept in boxes. He felt he must write down things like age, bodily sensations, titles of books, memories, and so on. He avoided reading newspapers because he felt compelled to reread and write things down continuously. This daily routine took up hours. Furthermore, he suffered from checking (gas, lights, doors) and orderliness. Everything was kept in the same place, nothing was thrown away (hoarding). Apart from his parents he had no social contacts.

Mrs. D. (age 52) developed her compulsions at an older age. Although she had always been very tidy it was not until four years ago when her compulsive cleansing set in after a hospital admission on account of a endometritis. It was about the same time that her dog died of cancer. From that time on she became very anxious for everything connected with disease and possible contamination. This anxiety engendered avoidance of all kinds of situations in which she might become contaminated, among which were shopping areas, crowded stores, and contact with people. She wore a shawl whenever she went shopping to avoid contamination. Should she meet anyone who coughed or was looking dirty, she immediately put aside her shopping, went home, and took a shower; this she did about four times a day. Her laundry was meticulously treated. Nothing should be touched when hanging out her clothes. Underwear especially presented problems. They must be protected and were therefore hung behind other clothing. She nearly always washed them several times and took them upstairs one by one. If anyone observed her in this activity she would perform the whole ritual all over again. She did not allow herself to touch the seat of her underwear with her feet. Her feet were thoroughly cleaned several times and were protected by special shoes. In case that particular part of her underwear was touched, it would immediately be washed over and over again. Panties, jeans, and pajama trousers were never worn. The floor also gave cause for anxiety. Nothing should touch the ground (e.g., blankets, ironing, towels) or it had to be washed at once. She frequently washed her hands while cooking dinner, and all food (bread, meat, oranges, etc.) was cleaned. Going to the toilet also posed its problems. First, all doors leading to the toilet were opened and then she walked to the toilet holding her hands in front of herself "like a surgeon" as she called it. The door of the toilet always remained agape and toilet paper was used in excessive quantities in a particular fashion. She never went to the toilet in other places. Apart from the symptoms already mentioned, the patient suffered from compulsive checking of the gas, the light switches, the stove, and her car. When leaving home she had to return at least 10 times to check everything over and over again. She also constantly checked her knitting for fear of having dropped a stitch. She badgered the life out of her spouse (who had to reassure her repeatedly) to ask whether he had broken anything, whether he was not dirty, and whether he had checked the house.

Diane was a depressed 23-year-old teacher who was obsessed by being a lesbian and who had to check all sorts of things. The complaints started three years earlier after she had been accosted by a "lesbian" woman. They did not have sexual relations, but she feared being a lesbian herself because she liked the attention the other women paid to her. She thought this discovery to be horrific and became afraid of accidentally telling it to others. After this episode various rituals emerged, such as checking magazines, books, and school notes for fear of having written about other people being homosexuals. In addition she repeatedly checked the cupboard in school because she might have locked pupils inside. At home she checked the gas (for fear of fire), the tap, and the toilet (for fear of flooding), and doors and windows (for fear of burglary). Finally, she had to make notes on everything she had done during the day to make sure she had checked everything.

Gail was a 33-year-old married woman who had two children. Up to 6 months before treatment she had worked as a nurse. She was referred for help because of fear of contamination and related compulsive cleaning and washing rituals. Only recently (since about 1½ years) she considered these compulsive behaviors problematic, although they had existed for quite some time. When the complaints started, the patient had been subjected to

great stress. She pointed to the causative role of the increasingly heavy responsibility in her job: she found it hard to cope with the dying of young children on the ward where she was employed. From this time on she developed a fear of being contaminated by a cancer virus that was supposed to reside in the hospital. Objects were avoided that had been in contact directly or (later on) indirectly with the hospital and particularly with her own ward. In case it was impossible to avoid these situations, she washed herself intensively after such a contact had taken place. Before this period she reported that she had never suffered from fear of contamination nor could she mention any special event that started the pattern of fear and compulsion. The amount of contaminated objects increased rapidly as did the number and intensity of the performed cleaning rituals. The number of "contaminated places" in their house became so plentiful that the family had to move some months prior to treatment. In their new house the number of similar places gradually increased. She considered the clinic where she worked to be thoroughly contaminated, and this contamination was thought to spread via shoes, hair, hands, and paper and the like. The patient was rather ambivalent regarding the irrationality of these thoughts: On the one hand, she admitted that such things could not be true; on the other hand, she rationalized her fears. In the period of the referral she had rearranged all objects in her house according to the supposed degree of contamination with the virus. She avoided bodily contact with a great many objects she considered contaminated, and if she failed to do so she washed her hands after such contact. The frequency of washing her hands had increased to several hundred times a day according to the patient and her husband. The patient also imposed all kinds of irrational rules of conduct upon her family members, such as not touching doorknobs; while washing the laundry she performed extensive cleaning rituals.

Paul was 36 years old, married, and the father of two children. He was very motivated and compliant. He appeared to be an unassertive, insecure, and anxious person, and his thoughts were confused. He had to express himself very carefully and every now and then told the therapist that he had to say something. He constantly asked for reassurance. His main complaint was the obsession to offend the dead, which predominantly occurred while uncertain in making decisions, that is, during most parts of the day. In addition he suffered from mild compulsive checking and doing things in a special way, for example, turning the tap of the shower. At the age of 16 Paul was shy with girls. He had had sexual fantasies about a girl who had later died, which had a great impact on him. This event (it was said that the girl had committed suicide) and his guilt feelings about his sexual fantasies might have caused his obsessions concerning "I am offending a dead person" or "I am having sexual intercourse with a dead person." The latter thought could be related to any action and decision. Furthermore, he examined his mind to determine whether he might have had wrong thoughts that should be sorted out and corrected.

CHILDHOOD AND FAMILIAL ANTECEDENTS

Scarcely anything is known on the adult outcome of obsessive compulsive disorder in childhood, since systematic follow-up studies have not been carried out. It seems that obsessive compulsive disorder only rarely begins in childhood.

In this section a variety of issues will be dealt with on the link between childhood and adult life with regard to obsessive compulsive disorder. The first is why obsessive compulsive disorder usually begins after puberty without identifiable behavioral precursors in childhood. The second question is how to tell which obsessive compulsive disorders in childhood will persist into adult life and the mechanisms underlying this continuity. The third issue is whether obsessive personality in childhood is a precursor of obsessive compulsive disorder in adulthood. The final issue concerns the role of deficiencies in loving family relationships as vulnerability factors.

As we have seen, the onset of most obsessive compulsive disorders is at about 20 years; onset before puberty does occur but is rare. Obsessive compulsive disorder often develops in a stressful period (Emmelkamp, 1982; McKean, Roa, & Mann, 1984). Stress can be related to having to live on one's own, taking job responsibilities, marriage, child bearing, rearing children, household responsibilities, and so on. Such responsibilities usually start after puberty. Other precipitants of obsessive compulsive disorder such as death of a close relative and uncertainty about sexual issues are not necessarily restricted to after puberty. Hoekstra, Visser, and Emmelkamp (1989) found that the predominant phenomenon of a given obsessional patient depends primarily on the area

for which the patient is responsible. In our culture most women are responsible for running the household (i.e., cleaning). In line with this Hoekstra et al. (1989) found a washing compulsion much more typical for women than for men. In contrast, checking was more typical for males.

Although the continuities in emotional disorders over time are quite modest, obsessional symptoms appear to be an exception. Zeitlin (1983, cited in Rutter, 1984) found that obsessional symptomatology showed a surprising degree of consistency over the years. However, the persistence of obsessions as symptoms was found to be substantially greater than the persistence of obsessive compulsive disorder as a diagnosis.

We do not know whether obsessive compulsive disorders that arise de novo in adult life differ meaningfully from those with an onset in childhood but persist into adult life. The question of which obsessive compulsive disorders will continue into adult life can at present only be answered retrospectively. A further limitation is that we have only information on obsessive compulsives who come to mental health agencies. We have no idea how many persons who had obsessive compulsive symptoms in childhood improved in time, or still have an obsessive compulsive disorder but do not seek treatment (see the section on epidemiology). Given the severe constraints of such retrospective reporting the clinical evidence indicates that persistence of obsessive compulsive disorder is most likely if the obsessive compulsive symptoms manifest themselves in early childhood, if the obsessive compulsive symptoms are severe, if peer relationships are poor, and, presumably most important, if there is a lack of parental affection and/or there is parental discord.

The linkage between child and adult obsessive compulsive disorder might reflect a common genetic origin or the continuing influence of adverse environmental features (e.g., lack of care and parental rejection). The evidence with respect to a genetic contribution to obsessive compulsive disorder was reviewed by McGriffin and Reich (1984) and Torgersen (1988). Although a small number of relatives of obsessive compulsive patients were found to have obsessive compulsive symptoms themselves, that does not necessarily imply a common genetic factor but simply may reflect common rearing experiences. The twin studies are more informative with respect to a genetic contribution. Both monozygotic (MZ) and dizygotic (DZ) twins are more or less exposed to similar environmental factors when they are growing up

in the same family. Although older studies found
a higher frequency of MZ cases compared to DZ
cases, these studies were far from representative.
The information from more recent studies is still
quite insufficient to draw conclusions with respect
to the contribution of genetic factors. It should be
noted that the incidence of obsessive compulsive
symptoms in the parents of obsessional patients is
far from impressive, ranging from 0% to 8%
(Insel, Hoover, & Murphy, 1983; Rachman &
Hodgson, 1980; Rapoport et al., 1981. Rachman
and Hodgson (1980) reviewing earlier studies in
this area found that most studies failed to show an
increased incidence of obsessional patients among
the children of obsessive compulsive patients.
However, a significant number of children were
found to have other psychological difficulties.

Another issue is whether an obsessional personality in childhood is related to obsessive compulsive disorder in adulthood. According to psychoanalytic notions, obsessive compulsive patients
should have a premorbid obsessional personality
in childhood. Black (1974) found that 71% of obsessional patients had marked or moderate premorbid obsessive traits. Kringlen (1965) compared
the premorbid personality traits of obsessional
patients with those of nonobsessional control patients. Seventy-two percent of the obsessional patients and 53% of the control patients were rated
to have premorbid obsessional traits. Similar figures were reported by McKean et al. (1984). Interestingly, the latter study found that patients with
an obsessional personality experienced significantly
fewer life events in the period before the onset of
the obsessive compulsive disorder than those
without such traits. This suggests that persons
who already have an obsessional personality in
childhood develop obsessive compulsive symptoms without experiencing an excess of stressful
life events before the onset of the disorder. Findings from studies by Kringlen (1965) and Rachman and Hodgson (1980) suggest that a premorbid obsessional personality may also be
associated with the development of *other* disorders. Taken together, these data indicate that there
is a strong relationship between premorbid obsessional personality trait and the development of
obsessive compulsive disorder. However, the data
of Kringlen (1965) and Rachman and Hodgson's
(1980) nonobsessional control patients bring the
clinical significance of this finding into a different
perspective. Moreover, the finding that in a small
but substantial number of patients obsessive compulsive disorder develops without any evidence of

an obsessional personality in childhood shows
that there is no one-to-one relationship.

Hoehn-Saric and Barksdale (1983) hypothesized that in a limited number of adult obsessive
compulsives the obsessive compulsive symptoms
were attempts to control acting-out impulses. In a
number of their obsessive compulsives, they
found indeed a history of socially undesirable
acting-out from adolescence. Acting-out was defined as frequent argumentativeness, explosive-
ness, sexual excesses, sprees of excessive drinking
and spending, and other behavior that was under
poor self-control. This subgroup of obsessive
compulsive patients who exhibited high levels of
impulsiveness suffered more disturbances during
childhood than a comparable group of nonim-
pulsive obsessive compulsive patients. These
childhood behaviors were associated with disorders labeled as "minimal brain dysfunction" or
"attentional deficit disorder."

Rachman (1976) postulated that differences in
ritualistic behavior arise from differences in
rearing practices. According to this theory checking rituals are most likely to arise from families
where the parents set high standards and are
overly critical. Checking compulsions can therefore be identified with active avoidance behavior
to avoid errors, motivated by fear of criticism or
guilt. On the other hand cleaning rituals will
emerge in families where the parents are overly
controlling and overly protective.

Steketee, Grayson, and Foa (1985) found that
checkers more often perceived their mothers as
meticulous and demanding than washers did. The
latter results gave some support for Rachman's
theory but were not totally confirmative and are
hard to interpret, since a nonvalidated questionnaire has been used to measure the parental
rearing practices. In a study by Hoekstra et al.
(1989), Rachman's theory was tested on a large
sample ($n = 122$) of obsessive compulsives using
a validated questionnaire to assess rearing practices. According to Rachman's theory, it was hypothesized that patients with checking rituals will
rate higher on "rejection" than patients with
washing rituals, whereas washers will rate higher
on "overprotection" than will checkers. All patients were expected to rate their rearing higher on
"rejection" and "overprotection" and lower on
"emotional warmth" than normals. These analyses revealed significant differences between the
pooled patient group and the normal controls on
the factors "rejection" and "emotional warmth."
Compared to normals, "overprotection" was rated

higher for both parents by washers and nonritualizing obsessionals and lower for fathers by checkers. Between washers and checkers significant differences were found on the factors "overprotective father" and "rejecting mother." These findings partially support Rachman's theory: Washers reported a more overprotective father than checkers did. On the other hand, they also judged their mothers as more rejecting than checkers, which is in contradiction with this theory. Thus, insufficient empirical evidence has been found to support a rearing practice specificity in the etiology of compulsive rituals.

The main results of this study, that obsessive compulsive patients perceive their rearings as far more negative than normals, suggest that such parental rearing practices are related to the development of obsessive compulsive disorder in their children. It should be noted, however, that these same parental characteristics have also been found to be associated with other forms of psychopathology in the child: phobias and social anxiety (Arrindell, Emmelkamp, Monsma, & Brilam, 1983), drug addiction (Emmelkamp & Heeres, 1988), Type A behavior (Emmelkamp & Karsdorp, 1987), and depression (Gerlsma, Emmelkamp, & Arrindell, in press). It may be that such negative parental rearing practices may make children vulnerable to psychopathology in general rather than to one or a few specific forms of psychopathology. In that case, it would be necessary to search for other factors in addition to the negative parental rearing practices that eventually determine the specific form of psychopathology.

SUMMARY

The form and content of obsessions and compulsions appear to be strikingly similar in a number of countries all around the world. Most patients have obsessions as well as compulsions. The two forms of compulsions that are most often seen are "cleaning" and "checking." Obsessive compulsive disorder is a less rare condition than once thought. In community surveys the mean lifetime prevalence is estimated to be 2.6%; the mean 6-month prevalence appears to be 1.6%.

Few of the obsessive compulsive individuals in the community seek help from professionals and often only under pressure of relatives. Obsessive compulsive disorder is more dominant among females than among males. Obsessive compulsive disorder is a chronic condition as evidenced in the high prevalence rate among elderly. Onset of obsessive compulsive disorder is usually in the early twenties. In very few patients the disorder starts before puberty or after 40 years of age.

Impairment associated with obsessive compulsive disorder is considerable. Most cases have secondary depression that often improves after successful treatment of the obsessive compulsive disorder. Obsessive compulsive disorder is not associated with an increased risk for suicide. Many obsessionals have problems in social relationships, are socially anxious, fear criticism, and are hostile. If they marry, the quality of the marriage is worse than in control couples. The disorder is often associated with unemployment.

The disorder usually develops in stressful periods. The evidence in favor of a genetic contribution is at present insufficient to draw valid conclusions. Nearly two thirds of obsessive compulsive patients have a premorbid obsessional personality. The parental rearing practices and emotional climate when the child is growing up may be important vulnerability factors for mental disorders in general and obsessive compulsive disorder in particular.

REFERENCES

Akhtar, S., Wig, N. H., Kerma, V. K., Pershod, D., & Kerma, S. K. (1975). A phenomenological analysis of symptoms in obsessive-compulsive neuroses. *British Journal of Psychiatry, 127,* 342–348.

American Psychiatric Association. (1987). Diagnostic and statistical manual of mental disorders (3rd ed. rev.). Washington, DC: Author.

Arrindell, W. A., Emmelkamp, P. M. G., Brilman, E., & Monsma, A. (1983). The role of perceived parental rearing practices in the aetiology of phobic disorders. *British Journal of Psychiatry, 143,* 183–187.

Barlow, D. H. (1985). The dimensions of anxiety disorders. In A. H. Tuma & J. D. Maser (Eds.), *Anxiety and the anxiety disorders.* Hillsdale, NJ: Lawrence Erlbaum Associates.

Black, A. (1974). The natural history of obsessional neurosis. In H. R. Beech (Ed.), *Obsessional states.* London: Metheun.

Bland, R. C., Orn, H., & Newman, S. C. (1988a). Lifetime prevalence of psychiatric disorders in Edmonton. *Acta Psychiatrica Scandinavica, 77*(Suppl. 338), 24–32.

Bland, R. C., Newman, S. C., & Orn, H. (1988b). Period prevalence of psychiatric disorders in

Edmonton. *Acta Psychiatrica Scandinavica, 77*(Suppl. 338), 33–42.

Bland, R. C., Newman, S. C., & Orn, H. (1988c). Age of onset of psychiatric disorders. *Acta Psychiatrica Scandinavica, 77*(Suppl. 338), 43–49.

Bland, R. C., Stebelsky, G., Orn, H., & Newman, S. C. (1988). Psychiatric disorders and unemployment in Edmonton. *Acta Psychiatrica Scandinavica, 77*(Suppl. 338), 72–80.

Blazer, D., George, L. K., Landerman, R., Pennybacker, M., Melville, M. L., Woodburry, M., Manton, K. G., Jordan, K., & Locke, B. (1985). Psychiatric disorder: A rural/urban comparison. *Archives of General Psychiatry, 42*, 651–656.

Burnam, M. A., Hough, R. L., Escabar, J. I., Karno, M., Timbers, D. M., Telles, C. A., & Locke, B. Z. (1987). Six month prevalence of specific psychiatric disorders among Mexican Americans and non-Hispanic whites in Los Angeles. *Archives of General Psychiatry, 44*, 687–694.

Coryell, W. (1981). Obsessive-compulsive disorder and primary unipolar depression: Comparison of background, family history, course and mortality. *Journal of Nervous and Mental Disease, 169*, 220–224.

Dijck, R. J., Bland, R. C., Newman, S. C., & Orn, H. (1988). Suicide attempts and psychiatric disorders in Edmonton. *Acta Psychiatrica Scandinavica, 77*(Suppl. 339), 64–71.

Dowson, J. H. (1977). The phenomenology of obsessive-compulsive neurosis. *British Journal of Psychiatry, 132*, 233–239.

Emmelkamp, P. M. G. (1982). *Phobic and obsessive-compulsive disorder: Theory, research & practice.* New York: Plenum Press.

Emmelkamp, P. M. G., & Heeres, H. (1988). Drug addiction and parental rearing style: A controlled study. *International Journal of the Addictions, 23*, 207–216.

Emmelkamp, P. M. G., de Haan, E., & Hoogduin, C. A. L. (in press). The quality of the marital relationship of obsessive compulsives and personality of their partners. *British Journal of Psychiatry.*

Emmelkamp, P. M. G., & Karsdorp, E. P. (1987). The effects of parental rearing style on the development of Type A pattern. *European Journal of Personality, 1*, 223–230.

Gerlsma, C., Emmelkamp, P. M. G., & Arrindell, W. A. (in press). Parental rearing style and affective disorders. *Clinical Psychology Review.*

Gittleson, N. L. (1966). The phenomenology of obsessions in depressive psychosis. *British Journal of Psychiatry, 112*, 261–000.

Goodwin, D. W., Guze, S. B., & Robins, E. (1969). Follow-up studies in obsessional neurosis. *Archives of General Psychiatry, 20*, 182–187.

Hafner, R. J. (1982). Marital interaction in persisting obsessive compulsive disorders. *Australian and New Zealand Journal of Psychiatry, 16*, 171–178.

Hoehn-Saric, R., & Barksdale, V. C. (1983). Impulsiveness in obsessive compulsive patients. *British Journal of Psychiatry, 143*, 177–182.

Hoekstra, R. J., Visser, S., & Emmelkamp, P. M. G. (1989). A social learning formulation of the etiology of obsessive compulsive disorders. In P. M. G. Emmelkamp, W. T. A. M. Everaerd, F. Kraaimaat, & M. van Son (Eds.), *Annual series of European research in behavior therapy: Vol. IV: Fresh perspectives on anxiety disorders.* Amsterdam: Swets.

Ingram, I. M. (1961). Obsessional illness in mental hospital patients. *Journal of Mental Science, 107*, 382–402.

Insel, T. R., Hoover, C., & Murphy, D. L. (1983). Parents of patients with obsessive compulsive disorder. *Psychological Medicine, 13*, 807–811.

Jenike, M. A., Baer, L., & Minichiello, W. E. (1986). Concomitant obsessive compulsive disorder and schizotypal personality disorder. *American Journal of Psychiatry, 143*, 530–532.

Joffe, R. T., Swinson, R. P., & Refan, J. J. (1988). Personality features of obsessive compulsive disorder. *American Journal of Psychiatry, 145*, 1127–1129.

Karno, M., Hough, R. L., Burnam, A., Escobar, J. I., Timbers, D. M., Santana, F., & Boyd, J. H. (1987). Lifetime prevalence of specific psychiatric disorders among Mexican Americans and non-Hispanic whites in Los Angeles. *Archives of General Psychiatry, 44*, 695–701.

Kraaykamp, H. J. M., Emmelkamp, P. M. G., & Van den Hout, M. A. (1990). *The Maudsley Obsessional-Compulsive Inventory: Reliability and validity. Unpublished manuscript*, University of Granigen.

Kringlen, E. (1965). Obsessional neurotics: A long-term follow-up. *British Journal of Psychiatry, 111*, 709–722.

Lo, W. H. (1967). A follow-up study of obsessional neurotics in Hong Kong Chinese. *British Journal of Psychiatry, 113*, 823–832.

McGriffin, R., & Reich, R. (1984). Psychopathology and genetics. In H. E. Adams & P. B. Suther (Eds.), *Comprehensive handbook of psychopathology*. New York: Plenum Press.

McKean, J., Roa, B., & Mann, A. (1984). Life events and personality traits in obsessive compulsive neurosis. *British Journal of Psychiatry, 144*, 185–189.

Millar, D. G. (1983). Hostile emotion and obsessional neurosis. *Psychological Medicine, 13*, 813–819.

Myers, K., Weissman, M., Tischler, L., Holzer, E., Leaf, J., Orvaschel, H., Anthony, C., Boyd, H., Burke, D., Kramer, M., & Stolzman, R. (1984). Six-month prevalence of psychiatric disorders in three communities: 1980–1982. *Archives of General Psychiatry, 41*, 959–967.

Noshirvani, H. F., Kasvikis, Y. G., Tsakiris, F., Basoglu, M., & Marks, I. M. (1988). *Demographic characteristics of 280 cases of obsessive-compulsive disorder*. Unpublished manuscript, University of London.

Orley, J., & Wing, J. K. (1979). Psychiatric disorders in two African villages. *Archives of General Psychiatry, 36*, 513–520.

Pauls, D. L., Towbin, K. E., Leckman, J. F., Zahner, G. E., & Cohen, D. J. (1986). Gilles de la Tourette's syndrome and obsessive compulsive disorder: Evidence supporting a genetic relationship. *Archives of General Psychiatry, 43*, 1180–1182.

Pollitt, J. (1960). Natural history studies in mental illness: A discussion based on a pilot study of obsessional states. *Journal of Mental Science, 106*, 93–113.

Rachman, S. (1976). Obsessional-compulsive checking. *Behaviour Research Therapy, 14*, 264–277.

Rachman, S., & Hodgson, R. J. (1980). *Obsessions and compulsions*. Englewood Cliffs, NJ: Prentice Hall.

Rapoport, J., Elkins, R., & Langer, D. (1981). Childhood obsessive-compulsive disorder. *American Journal of Psychiatry, 138*, 1545–1554.

Rasmussen, S. A., & Tsuang, M. T. (1986). Clinical characteristics and family history in DSM-III obsessive-compulsive disorder. *American Journal of Psychiatry, 143*, 317–322.

Robins, L. N., Helzer, J. F., Weissman, M. M., Overaschel, H., Gruenberg, F., Burke, J. D., & Regier, D. A. (1984). Life-time prevalence of specific psychiatric disorders in three sites. *Archives of General Psychiatry, 41*, 949–958.

Rosenberg, C. M. (1968). Obsessive neurosis. *Australian and New Zealand Journal of Psychiatry, 2*, 33–38.

Roy, A. (1979). Obsessive-compulsive neurosis: Phenomenology, outcome and a comparison with hysterical neurosis. *Compulsive Psychiatry, 20*, 528–531.

Rutter, M. (1984). Psychopathology and development: I. Childhood antecedents of adult psychiatric disorder. *Australian and New Zealand Journal of Psychiatry, 18*, 225–234.

Steketee, G., Grayson, J. B., & Foa, E. B. (1987). A comparison of characteristics of obsessive compulsive disorder and other anxiety disorders. *Journal of Anxiety Disorders, 1*, 325–335.

Steketee, G. S., Grayson, J. B., & Foa, J. B. (1985). Obsessive-compulsive disorder: Differences between washers and checkers. *Behaviour Research and Therapy, 23*, 197–201.

Stern, R. S., & Cobb, J. P. (1978). Phenomenology of obsessive compulsive neurosis. *British Journal of Psychiatry, 132*, 233–239.

Templer, D. I. (1972). The obsessive-compulsive neurosis: Review of research findings. *Comprehensive Psychiatry, 13*, 375–383.

Thyer, B. A., Curtis, G. C., & Fechner, S. L. (1984). Fear of criticism is not specific to obsessive compulsive disorder. *Behaviour Research and Therapy, 22*, 77–80.

Thyer, B. A., Parrish, R. T., Curtis, G. C., Nesse, R. M., & Cameron, G. G. (1985). Age of onset of DSM-III anxiety disorders. *Comprehensive Psychiatry*, 113–122.

Torgerson, S. (1988). Genetics. In C. G. Last & M. Hersen (Eds.), *Handbook of anxiety disorders*. Elmsford, NY: Pergamon Press.

Turns, D. M. (1985). Epidemiology of phobic and obsessive compulsive disorders among adults. *American Journal of Psychiatry, 39*, 360–370.

Vaisänen, E. (1975). Psychiatric disorders in Finland. In T. Anderson, C. Astrup, & A. Forsdahl (Eds.), Social, somatic and psychiatric studies of geographically defined populations. *Acta Psychiatrica Scandinavica, 69*(Suppl. 263), 22–33.

Visser, S., Hoekstra, R. J., & Emmelkamp, P. M. G. (1990). Follow-up study on behavioural treatment of obsessive compulsive disorder. In I. Fiegenbaum, I. Florin, A. Ehlers, & J. Margraf (Eds.), *Perspectives in Clinical Psychology*. New York: Springer.

Welner, A., Reich, T., Robins, E., Fishman, R., & Van Doren, T. (1976). Obsessive compulsive neurosis. *Comprehensive Psychiatry, 20*, 528–531.

Wittchen, H. U. (1988). Natural course and spontaneous remissions of untreated anxiety disorders. In I. Hand & H. U. Wittchen (Eds.), *Panic and phobias* (Vol. 2). New York: Springer.

Yaryura-Tobias, J. A., & Neziroglu, F. A. (1983). *Obsessive compulsive disorders*. New York: Marcel Dekker.

Zaworka, W., & Hand, I. (1980). Phänomenologie (Dimensionalität) der Zwangssymptomatik [Phenomenon (dimensions) of compulsive symptoms]. *Archiv für Psychiatrie und Nervenkrankheiten, 228*, 257–273.

Zeitlin, H. (1983). *The natural history of psychiatric disorder in childhood*. MP Theses, University of London.

OVERANXIOUS DISORDER AND GENERALIZED ANXIETY DISORDER

EDITORS' COMMENTS

Upon first examination, overanxious disorder in children and generalized anxiety disorder in adults have much in common as diagnostic entities. Both have a short nosological history under their current rubrics, but the respective diagnostic pictures portrayed have received other labels in the past. Therefore, as currently constituted research data for both categories are relatively sparse. Clinically, however, it is clear that these diagnostic categories have contemporary value, given that for both children and adults the diagnoses are frequently made in reliable fashion in the outpatient setting.

A further similarity between overanxious disorder in children and generalized anxiety disorder in adults is that excessive anxiety and unrealistic worrying are hallmarks of the categories. In children over 11 years of age, an additional concern frequently expressed is having performed poorly in some school, peer, or family interaction. Also, there tend to be physical complaints about the legs, back, stomach, or head. Similarly, in generalized anxiety disorder in adulthood anxious rumination is accompanied by autonomic symptoms and hypervigilance.

Given the similarity to generalized anxiety in adulthood and the chronicity of overanxious disorder in children, it has been hypothesized that the childhood disorder is the precursor to the adult version. However, as for so many of the other diagnostic categories evaluated in this book, the necessary prospective longitudinal studies simply have not been carried out. Indeed, the etiology of generalized anxiety disorder at this point in time is not well understood, especially because the results of genetic and family studies tend to be contradictory. Furthermore, in instances where overanxious disorder in childhood abates and years later there is appearance of generalized anxiety disorder in adulthood, what is the precipitating event? Are there specific stressors that elicit the adult version of the disorder? What is the role of affective disorder, if any, in the child and adult diagnoses? What are the most promising treatments for overanxious disorder in children and generalized anxiety disorder in adults?

Although the chapters by Strauss and Hoehn-Saric and McLeod raise some tantalizing hypotheses to address these questions, the necessary meticulous research still needs to be carried out. Perhaps this pair of chapters will stimulate clinical researchers to carry out the long range investigations that will permit answers to the etiological and treatment questions that have been raised.

CHAPTER 17

OVERANXIOUS DISORDER IN CHILDHOOD

Cyd C. Strauss

DESCRIPTION OF THE DISORDER

The *Diagnostic and Statistical Manual* (American Psychiatric Association, 1987) presents three subtypes of anxiety disorders that occur primarily in childhood and adolescence: separation anxiety, overanxious, and avoidant disorders. Accumulating empirical evidence has demonstrated that both separation anxiety disorder and overanxious disorder are common psychiatric problems in clinic samples, can be reliably diagnosed using structured clinical interviews, and are associated with significant impairment (Last, Hersen, Kazdin, Finkelstein, & Strauss, 1987; Strauss, Last, Hersen, & Kazdin, 1988; Strauss, Lahey, Frick, Frame, & Hynd, 1988). The present chapter will focus on the recent findings of studies examining overanxious disorder in childhood and adolescence, as well as clinical observations of overanxious children and adolescents evaluated in the Child and Adolescent Anxiety Disorder Clinic at Western Psychiatric Institute and Clinic over a four-year period.

Overanxious disorder in childhood and adolescence is characterized by pervasive anxiety or worry that is not focused on a specific situation or object. The DSM-III-R presents seven specific criteria that define this disorder: (1) excessive or unrealistic worry about future events, (2) excessive or unrealistic concern about the appropriateness of past behavior, (3) overconcern about competence in one or more areas (e.g., academic, social, athletic), (4) somatic complaints, such as headaches or stomachaches, for which no physical basis can be established, (5) excessive need for reassurance in a variety of areas, (6) marked self-consciousness, and (7) marked feelings of tension or inability to relax. Children must demonstrate frequent occurrence of a minimum of four of these criteria over a period of at least six months in order to receive a diagnosis of overanxious disorder. In addition, the diagnoses of overanxious disorder can be made if the individual is 18 years or older and he or she cannot meet criteria for generalized anxiety disorder. Finally, overanxious disorder cannot be diagnosed when it occurs exclusively during the course of a pervasive developmental disorder, schizophrenia, or any other psychotic disorder. These defining feature of overanxious disorder presented in DSM-III-R are essentially the same as those contained in DSM-III (APA, 1980) for this diagnostic category.

CLINICAL PRESENTATION

The hallmark of overanxious disorder appears to be excessive or unrealistic worrying about future events, which has been shown to be present in greater than 95% of a clinic sample of children diagnosed with overanxious disorder (Strauss, Lease, Last, & Francis, 1988). Overanxious children and adolescents report a variety of future worries, including worries about upcoming tests; social activities; what teachers will say to him or her; what will happen when they get older; family problems; what will happen the next day, next week, or next month; and so on. The rate of worries about future events that is considered clinically significant ranges from several times per week to almost constant worrying.

The second diagnostic criterion, preoccupation about past behavior, typically involves rumination about having done or said the wrong thing at school, with peers, or during interactions with family members. For example, overanxious children and adolescents describe frequent worries about having given the wrong answer at school, having performed poorly on a test, having made another child angry, minor critical comments made toward the child, and having made an error in gym class. As with worries about future events, worries about the appropriateness of past behavior are viewed as clinically meaningful if they occur three times per week or more. Strauss, Lease, Last, and Francis (1988) found that older children (over 11 years of age) diagnosed with overanxious disorder were significantly more likely than were younger children (under 12 years of age) to demonstrate this symptom. In particular, 90% of older overanxious disorder children reported excessive or unrealistic worries about past behavior, whereas 62% of younger children reported problems with past worries.

In terms of overconcern about the child's competence in a variety of areas, children with overanxious disorder tend to worry excessively about minor mistakes made academically, socially, or athletically. In this regard, overanxious children often are described by parents as "perfectionistic" about their school work, appearance, abilities in sports, or how they act in social situations. Again, these concerns are expressed at least several times each week by the overanxious child.

Physical complaints primarily consist of stomachaches or headaches, but may also include complaints about leg aches, back aches, and so on. Upon inquiry, it is learned that there is no clear pattern in the occurrence of these somatic complaints, such that they can occur at any time of the day and any day of the week. It is important to establish that somatic complaints do not occur only in separation situations, thus fulfilling a criterion for separation anxiety disorder and not overanxious disorder. These physical complaints usually have been evaluated medically prior to the child's arrival at an outpatient clinic, and no physical basis for the complaints has been uncovered. Children with overanxious disorder complain of aches and pains a minimum of once per week.

The fifth diagnostic criterion, marked self-consciousness, includes extreme discomfort when called on in class, when the center of attention in groups of people, and when discussed in front of others. Overanxious children may blush easily, as evidence of their embarrassment. Self-consciousness is not limited to a single situation in which the child is exposed to possible scrutiny by others (e.g., public speaking), and instead occurs in many social situations. The overanxious child usually experiences this symptom a minimum of three times per week and in response to most situations in which he or she is evaluated by others.

Parents and teachers find themselves constantly having to reassure their overanxious disordered children and adolescents about worries and concerns. Overanxious disordered children will elicit such reassurance from others by frequently asking if what they are doing is okay, asking for confirmation of choices that they make, and/or by making disparaging remarks about themselves in hopes that others will deny their claims. Typically, others have to repeat reassurances multiple times before the overanxious disordered child's anxiety diminishes. Both parents and children report that such reassurance is very important to the child and occurs approximately three times per week or more. Many parents report the need for constant reassurance about a variety of worries.

Finally, marked tension and difficulty relaxing is demonstrated by frequent nervous mannerisms (e.g., nail-biting, hair twirling, knuckle cracking), an exaggerated startle response, pacing, and/or general feelings of being "up tight." This symptom occurs a minimum of one time per week to be considered clinically significant.

Although not a diagnostic criterion, overanxious children often display subtle avoidance behaviors in a variety of situations that provoke their anxiety and worries. For example, overanxious disordered children may avoid raising their hands in class to avoid becoming the center of attention. They also may make frequent excuses so that they are not required to participate in gym activities, or they may decline invitations to parties or other social gatherings in which they might become the center of attention or have their behavior scrutinized by others. In more severe cases, overanxious youngsters may fail to complete classroom assignments, and ultimately refuse school attendance, due to an overconcern about academic competence and perfectionism.

General clinical impressions also indicate that overanxious disorder is associated with hypermaturity, such that the child often is described as a "little adult." For instance, overanxious disordered youngsters may be more comfortable in the company of adults, tend to discuss adult topics, and often are observed to use a mature linguistic style in conversation. They also frequently are described as "eager to please" and seek out the approval of others. Thus, overanxious disordered children typically are model students in school, often are liked by adults, but may be overlooked by their peers. It is not uncommon for overanxious disordered children to have one or two close friends, and otherwise not to be very active socially.

EPIDEMIOLOGY

Very little empirical research has been devoted to the study of the epidemiology of overanxious disorder in childhood and adolescence. In particular, there has been only one investigation that has examined the epidemiology of overanxious disorder in childhood in the general population (Anderson, Williams, McGee, & Silva, 1987). Two additional studies reported on the prevalence and sociodemographic characteristics of clinic samples of children and adolescents diagnosed with overanxious disorder (Last, Hersen, Kazdin, Finkelstein, & Strauss, 1987; Last, Strauss, & Francis, 1987).

In the first study, Anderson et al. (1987) evaluated prevalence of a range of DSM-III (APA, 1980) disorders in 792 11-year-old prepubertal children from the general population in New Zealand. DSM-III diagnoses were based on information obtained from structured child interviews and standardized parent and teacher questionnaires. The overall prevalence of overanxious disorder found in this study was 2.9%. Findings re-

vealed that boys were diagnosed with overanxious disorder more commonly than girls in this sample, with a sex ratio of 1.7 : 1.

In one study of clinic children, it was observed that those meeting diagnostic criteria for overanxious disorder were referred at a high rate for evaluation and treatment to an outpatient clinic for children and adolescents with anxiety disorders (Last, Hersen, Kazdin, Finkelstein, & Strauss, 1987). In a sample of 91 anxiety-disordered children between the ages of 5 and 18 years who were evaluated over an 18-month period, a total of 47 children (52%) met DSM-III criteria for overanxious disorder. The rate of overanxious disorder was comparable to the rate of separation anxiety disorder, both of which were the most common anxiety disorder diagnoses in this sample.

Three groups of children subsequently were compared in terms of sociodemographic characteristics in the Last, Hersen, Kazdin, Finkelstein, and Strauss (1987) study: children with overanxious disorder (OAD, $n = 26$; 29%), children with separation anxiety disorder (SAD, $n = 22$; 24%), and children with both overanxious disorder and separation anxiety disorder (OAD + SAD, $n = 21$; 23%). Findings revealed that equal numbers of boys and girls in the OAD group were referred for clinical services, whereas both SAD and OAD + SAD groups contained more girls than boys (% female = 76 and 64, respectively). These differences in sex ratio were not statistically significant, however.

On the other hand, the groups differed significantly with regard to age at intake. OAD + SAD and SAD children were significantly younger at intake than OAD children, with OAD + SAD and SAD groups not showing age differences at intake. The mean ages at intake were 13.4 years for OAD children, 9.6 years for OAD + SAD children, and 9.1 years for SAD children. It was also observed that a significantly higher percentage of children in the OAD (69%) group were adolescents (i.e., over 12 years old) than the SAD (9%) and OAD + SAD (29%) groups.

In terms of racial composition, almost all children in the three groups were Caucasian. Specifically, 100% of the OAD, 95% of the OAD + SAD, and 86% of the SAD groups were Caucasian. No statistical differences were found among the groups on this demographic variable.

Finally, the socioeconomic status of the three groups was examined. Families of OAD children were observed to be of significantly higher socioeconomic status than were SAD and OAD +

SAD families. Indeed, 43% of children in the OAD group were from upper or middle-upper social-status families, compared to 25% of OAD + SAD families and 13% of SAD families with these social strata ratings. No differences in social class emerged between the OAD + SAD and SAD groups.

In the second clinic study, the prevalence of overanxious disorder as a "primary diagnosis" (i.e., the disorder causing the greatest impairment in functioning and targeted first for intervention), was evaluated (Last, Strauss, & Francis, 1987). Findings indicated that overanxious disorder was designated as the primary diagnosis in 15% of 73 consecutive admissions to an outpatient clinic for anxiety disordered children and adolescents. Overanxious disorder was the second most common primary diagnosis in this anxiety disorder sample (separation anxiety was the most common primary diagnosis). Sociodemographic characteristics of children with primary overanxious disorder diagnoses were presented, although these findings were tentative due to the small n (11) of this group. Children with primary diagnoses of overanxious disorder had a mean age of 10.8, were approximately equally likely to be male or female, were primarily Caucasian, and were more likely to be from middle- to upper-social-status families. These results closely resembled findings from the Last, Hersen, Kazdin, Finkelstein, and Strauss (1987) study that generally examined children with overanxious disordered diagnoses (but not only those with overanxious disorder as the primary diagnosis).

In sum, the available data indicate that overanxious disorder is moderately prevalent in the general population of preadolescent children and constitutes a common reason for referral for clinical services. Overanxious disordered clinic children tend to be from upper and upper-middle socioeconomic families, are equally likely to be male or female, and primarily are Caucasian. Epidemiological studies in the general population clearly are needed, however, to determine if the available data are representative of overanxious children of different ages who have not been referred for clinical services.

NATURAL HISTORY

Overanxious disorder appears to be a chronic disorder in childhood and adolescence. The mean age of onset reported in our clinic children with overanxious disorder is 8.98 years, with a range in age of onset extending from 2.5 years through 16.17 years. Clinic children with overanxious disorder on average are referred for outpatient services 4½ years following onset of overanxious symptoms, with parents frequently commenting that the child has "always been a worrier." Overanxious disorder does not seem to remit spontaneously, although severity of symptoms may fluctuate in response to environmental stressors and developmental milestones. For instance, overanxious disordered children and adolescents often report an alleviation of symptoms during the summer months when academic and social demands are absent or reduced. The long-term prognosis for overanxious disorder is unknown at the present time, but clinical impressions suggest that this disorder persists without intervention. Overanxious disordered children and adolescents are considered at particular risk for the later development of generalized anxiety disorder in adulthood, although follow-up data for overanxious disorder are lacking.

The only data currently available on the change of overanxious disorder over the course of development are presented in a cross-sectional study of clinic children and adolescents of different ages (Strauss, Lease, Last, & Francis, 1988). In this investigation, younger (ages 5 to 11) and older (ages 12 to 19) children with overanxious disorder were compared in the rates of the diagnosis in the two age groups, sociodemographic characteristics, symptom expression, association with other forms of maladjustment, and levels of self-reported anxiety and depression. The prevalence of overanxious disorder diagnoses and sociodemographic characteristics were not found to differ in the two age groups. Results also showed that younger and older children did not differ in the rates of most individual criteria for the disorder, but older overanxious disordered children were more likely to report presence of excessive or unreasonable worries about the appropriateness of past behavior than younger children. In addition, older children demonstrated a higher total number of overanxious disordered symptoms, with 66% of older children and 35% of younger children exhibiting six or seven diagnostic criteria for the disorder.

Younger and older overanxious disordered children also were dissimilar in their rates of specific coexisting disorders. In particular, older overanxious children were more likely to show evidence of a concurrent major depression or simple phobia, whereas younger children more often displayed simultaneous attention-deficit or separation anxiety disorders. Finally, older overanxious disordered children consistently reported higher levels of state and trait anxiety and depression on self-report instruments.

Overall, these findings suggest that presentation of overanxious disorder may indeed change over the course of childhood and adolescence. Older overanxious disordered children appear to demonstrate greater impairment, including more symptoms of the disorder, higher levels of self-reported anxiety and depression, and a greater likelihood of a coexisting major depression. Of course, longitudinal studies are needed to clarify the development of overanxious disorder over time.

Clinical impressions of changes that occur with age in the manifestation of overanxious disorder also suggest that adolescents display more severe symptomatology. As adolescents, worrying appears to be more frequent, and obsessional worrying may persist for longer durations. Recent clinic data demonstrate that older overanxious disordered children are more likely to develop social phobias. Included are intense fear of scrutiny or humiliation in situations such as public speaking, dressing in front of others in gym, eating in front of others, or blushing (Last, Strauss, & Ron, 1990). Furthermore, adolescents with overanxious disorder may be more likely to develop a generalized social phobia, in which they show substantial discomfort in most social situations. Clinical observations also suggest that adolescents with overanxious disorder may be at higher risk to develop anxiety and avoidance associated with school attendance.

IMPAIRMENT AND COMPLICATIONS

Children with overanxious disorder show a range of impairment, with some overanxious youngsters reporting no additional complications other than worrying and anxiety, whereas other overanxious children may describe serious concurrent problems such as major depression and substance abuse. Children with *mild* overanxious disorder may report difficulty falling asleep at night due to excessive worrying that may occur at bedtime, problems interacting with large groups of peers due to self-consciousness, and/or mild interference with academic performance because of overconcern about performance during tests. On the other hand, mildly overanxious children may be described as functioning well in most areas despite their excessive worrying. For instance, overanxious children often are very conscientious

about school work and may devote considerable time and energy to achieve high marks. In fact, it is not uncommon for overanxious children to be overachievers. Although overanxious children may not be exceptionally popular among peers, they may have one or two close friends with whom they frequently interact at home and at school. Thus, children with less severe overanxious symptoms may demonstrate few associated problems, despite the fact that their rates of worrying and tension are considered excessive and problematic.

Youngsters with *severe* overanxious symptoms, in contrast, are likely to have serious forms of impairment. In particular, overanxious disorder may be accompanied by major depression and suicidal ideation. Last and her colleagues (Last, Hersen, Kazdin, Finkelstein, & Strauss, 1987) have shown that approximately one third of overanxious disordered children and adolescents simultaneously meet diagnostic criteria for major depression. Research has further demonstrated an association between child and adolescent reports of overanxious disorder and their reports of greater severity of suicidal ideation (Brent et al., 1986). Overanxious youngsters report use of drugs or alcohol in efforts to alleviate anxiety symptomatology.

In addition, serious impairment may be demonstrated in specific areas of functioning. Severe problems with overanxious disorder may be accompanied by serious interference with academic performance. Anxiety about performance may be so intense that overanxious youngsters may be unable to complete assignments for fear of failure. As the overanxious youngster procrastinates due to fear of poor performance, he or she may fall behind in school work, and grades may decline so that he or she begins to avoid school attendance. Severe overanxious symptoms also may seriously impair social relationships, such that overanxious children or adolescents may avoid most social contacts for fear of negative evaluation or rejection by peers. Overanxious youngsters show high rates of anxiety about school attendance and school refusal that appear to be related to these academic and social concerns, with a prevalence of school phobia of 38% observed in one sample of 35 children meeting DSM-III-R criteria for overanxious disorder (Last, Strauss, & Ron, 1990).

Finally, as noted, the degree of impairment associated with overanxious disorder has been shown to vary with age (Strauss, Lease, Last, & Francis, 1988). Younger overanxious children tend to report fewer symptoms and describe themselves as less anxious and depressed on self-report measures than do older overanxious youngsters. More-over, older overanxious children demonstrate more severe forms of maladjustment, including coex-isting major depression.

DIFFERENTIAL DIAGNOSIS

Overanxious disorder needs to be differentiated from normal worrying that is not excessive or un-reasonable. Children and adolescents ordinarily worry about tests, academic performance gener-ally, athletic performance, family conflict, their appearance, and other concerns. The frequency and duration of worries, however, is considerably reduced in children who are not overanxious. It is not uncommon for children and adolescents to report occasional worries (e.g., one time each week) that last for only brief periods (e.g., 5 to 10 minutes). It is also important to distinguish fre-quent and enduring worrying that is reasonable in specific circumstances (e.g., worries about im-pending major surgery of a family member, fre-quent conflict between parents, failing grades at school, actual rejection by most peers at school) from unreasonable and excessive worrying. Wor-rying and tension that are sufficiently severe to warrant a diagnosis of overanxious disorder typi-cally are described by children and adolescents as causing them considerable concern and to be ex-cessive relative to their peers.

A distinction between overanxious disorder and social phobias also needs to be made in childhood and adolescence. As discussed in DSM-III and DSM-III-R, social phobias tend to involve a cir-cumscribed stimulus that the individual fears and avoids, and people generally have only one social phobia. Children diagnosed with overanxious dis-order may also show excessive discomfort asso-ciated with situations involving possible scrutiny by others, but they do not necessarily display spe-cific anxiety and avoidance behavior; instead, they tend to have a pervasive discomfort asso-ciated with multiple situations in which their behavior may be evaluated (e.g., school perfor-mance, social interactions with peers, perfor-mance in gym). Moreover, in overanxious dis-order, worrying and tension are not related only to social situations. Finally, children and adolescents with overanxious disorder demonstrate additional symptoms that are not present in youngsters with social phobias, such as an excessive need for reas-surance about a variety of worries, somatic com-plaints, and marked feelings of generalized ten-sion or an inability to relax.

Overanxious disorder also must be distin-guished from simple phobias, in which the child or adolescent shows a persistent fear of a circum-scribed object or situation (other than situations involving possible scrutiny by others and situa-tions related to agoraphobia). The youngster with a simple phobia may report excessive worrying and marked tension, but these are focused on stimuli associated with the phobic object or situa-tion. In contrast, overanxious disordered children and adolescents have multiple fears and worries, and anxiety is not restricted to a single stimulus or situation as in simple phobia. As with social pho-bia, children with a simple phobia do not show the whole constellation of symptoms associated with overanxious disorder.

In separation anxiety disorder, anxiety and wor-ries are focused exclusively on situations involving separation. In some cases of separation anxiety disorder the anxiety is so extensive that children report worries in multiple circumstances, but care-ful assessment will uncover that such anxiety is consistently related to separation. Children with overanxious disorder and those with separation anxiety disorder may similarly report frequent so-matic complaints; however, children with overanx-ious disorder do not only demonstrate these symptoms on school mornings and prior to sepa-ration from attachment figures, as with separation anxiety disorder.

Children with attention-deficit hyperactivity disorder sometimes appear nervous and jittery and may be described by parents as "worriers." Upon further inquiry, however, it becomes ap-parent that parents are mislabeling overactivity and excessive talking or inquisitiveness in children with attention-deficit hyperactivity disorder as nervousness and expression of worries. Children with attention-deficit hyperactivity disorder often ask many questions about upcoming events, but rarely demonstrate concern or worry about these future activities. Similarly, motor excess is almost constant and is not related to nervousness or anx-iety. Additional symptoms of overanxious dis-order also are absent in children with attention-deficit hyperactivity disorder, such as overconcern about competence, marked self-consciousness, and an excessive need for reassurance about wor-ries.

Children and adolescents younger than 18 years of age who meet the diagnostic criteria for over-anxious disorder are not given the diagnosis of generalized anxiety disorder. On the other hand, if the individual is 18 years or older and meets diagnostic criteria for both disorders, he or she must be diagnosed with generalized anxiety disorder. It should be noted that although there is overlap between the childhood category of overanxious disorder and the adult diagnosis of generalized anxiety disorder, the symptoms of autonomic hyperactivity and vigilance/scanning required for the diagnosis of generalized anxiety disorder (e.g., shortness of breath, palpitations, sweating, dry mouth, dizziness, difficulty concentrating, and frequent urination) are not necessarily present in children diagnosed with overanxious disorder. In fact, many youngsters with overanxious disorder deny the presence of these symptoms.

Finally, the diagnosis of adjustment disorder with anxious mood is assigned when anxiety and worrying occur following a psychosocial stressor and lasts less than six months. Although symptoms of overanxious disorder may intensify following stressful events, children with overanxious disorder met diagnostic criteria for the disorder prior to the event as well or demonstrate symptoms for a period lasting longer than 6 months.

CASE EXAMPLE

Robin is a 15-year-old girl who was referred for an evaluation in the Child and Adolescent Anxiety Disorder Clinic at Western Psychiatric Institute and Clinic in Pittsburgh, Pennsylvania. She was referred for clinical services by her school principal and counselor due to problems with school attendance and excessive worrying. Robin attends the tenth grade at a parochial school. She resides with both natural parents and her two brothers in an urban setting.

Robin was described as a "worrier" and as "perfectionistic" since age 4. Symptoms of anxiety worsened when Robin entered the fifth grade, at which time she showed evidence of excessive worrying, an overconcern about her competence in a variety of areas, and generalized tension. During her fifth grade year, Robin constantly worried about her academic performance, her social behavior, and her appearance. Her anxiety about academic performance reportedly was related to her own and others' expectations that she would excel in school work, due to exceptional abilities demonstrated on individually administered IQ tests and standardized achievement tests. In particular, Robin demonstrated anxiety concerning writing assignments. She showed a repeated pattern of failing to complete writing assignments and then refusing school attendance, due to her

not having finished such assignments. Because of these problems with anxiety, the child was placed in a parochial school in the sixth grade in efforts to reduce pressure placed on her by particular teachers in her public school. Despite this intervention, worrying, anxiety, and avoidance of situations associated with an expectation for success persisted into the tenth grade, at which time a referral was initiated by school personnel.

In addition to excessive worrying and anxiety associated with school performance, Robin was described as having been overly sensitive socially and as having had problematic peer relationships since the fifth grade. She reportedly had been neglected by peers, in that they tended not to include her in social activities both at school and after school. She had few friends and generally had difficulty relating to same-aged peers.

At the time of referral, Robin continued to demonstrate excessive worries about upcoming events, including tests, homework assignments, social interactions, and teachers' responses to her. She also frequently ruminated for extended periods of time about incidents that already had occurred, such as answers she gave in class, her social behavior with her peers, and remarks made to her about her behavior in class by teachers. Robin continued to be overly concerned and perfectionistic about her performance during academic tasks, athletic activities, and social interactions. In addition, she reportedly was extremely self-conscious, in that she became easily embarrassed when she spoke during class, refused to participate in activities that required that she assume a leadership role, blushed easily, and was very anxious and uncomfortable when she was the center of attention in groups with other adolescents. Finally, Robin generally was tense and had difficulty relaxing. These overanxious symptoms ultimately led to her failure to complete school assignments and intermittent absenteeism at school. At the time of referral, Robin had missed approximately 21 days during her first three months of tenth grade.

Assessment of Robin's difficulties was conducted using a semistructured diagnostic interview schedule. Robin and her parents individually were administered an updated version of the Schedule for Affective Disorders and Schizophrenia for School-Age Children (K-SADS [Puig-Antich & Ryan, 1986]). The K-SADS was modified to include questions about symptoms included in the 1986 draft version of the DSM-III-R for anxiety disorders occurring in childhood and adulthood, as well as mood disorders, attention-deficit hyperactivity disorder, conduct disorder, oppositional disorder, and psychotic symptomatology. The diagnostic criteria for overanxious disorder in the draft version are essentially the same as those presented in the final DSM-III-R, as is true for the other psychiatric diagnoses assessed using the modified K-SADS. Responses provided by both Robin and her parents indicated that she met diagnostic criteria for overanxious disorder, as well as a social phobia of school. Robin also demonstrated some affective symptoms, but these were not sufficiently severe to warrant a mood disorder diagnosis. Specifically, Robin showed evidence of depressed mood, negative self-image, fatigue, difficulty concentrating, and loss of appetite that appeared to be secondary to excessive worrying and school refusal.

In addition to information derived from interviews, Robin completed self-report measures that assessed anxiety and depression. These included the State-Trait Anxiety Inventory for Children (STAIC [Spielberger, 1973]), the Revised Fear Survey Schedule for Children (FSSC-R [Ollendick, 1983]), the Children's Depression Inventory (CDI [Kovacs, 1978]), and the Loneliness Scale (LS [Asher, Hymel, & Renshaw, 1984]). Robin's responses on these self-report questionnaires were consistent with information obtained during administration of the semistructured interviews. In particular, she reported high levels of state (score of 28) and trait (score of 42) anxiety on the STAIC. Her total FSSC-R score (157) was substantially higher than the mean (143) obtained for a normative sample (Ollendick, Matson, & Helsel, 1985). It was noteworthy that Robin reported excessive fearfulness on the fear of failure and criticism factor of this measure.

In addition, Robin's responses on questionnaires supported descriptions from interviews suggesting that she had concurrent problems with mild depression and impaired social relationships. Her score of 17 on the CDI revealed a mild level of depression. She also reported high levels of loneliness and dissatisfaction with peer relations on the LS (score of 55).

Finally, teachers' perceptions of Robin's classroom behavior were obtained using the Revised Behavior Problem Checklist (Quay & Peterson, 1983). The teachers' ratings on this checklist indicated that Robin similarly demonstrated anxious-withdrawn behavior in the school setting, but that she did not otherwise show problematic behavior in the classroom. Teachers also evaluated Robin's

social adjustment by providing ratings on a scale assessing peer popularity and social status. The teachers indicated that Robin was neither well liked nor actively disliked among peers. That is, teachers estimated that Robin was socially neglected by her peers, which was consistent with descriptions given by the adolescent and her parents.

Treatment for Robin's overanxious disorder and associated problems consisted of a behavior therapy approach including multiple components: relaxation training, cognitive behavior therapy, and exposure. This treatment package was selected based on procedures that have been implemented successfully to reduce adult forms of generalized anxiety, since virtually no published reports have been presented in the literature describing effective behavioral treatments for children or adolescents with overanxious disorder. Similar therapy methods previously have been used successfully to treat specific childhood fears and phobias. This treatment approach was aimed at reducing the physiological, cognitive, and behavioral aspects of overanxious anxiety disorder.

Initially, Robin was trained in deep muscle relaxation (Jacobsen, 1938), using a modified technique devised for children and adolescents by Ollendick and Cerny (1981). She practiced each set of muscle groups at home twice daily on a regular basis and quickly became skillful at achieving a relaxed state. Instruction in relaxation was completed after six treatment sessions.

While learning relaxation techniques, Robin gradually began to resume school attendance. Her return to school was facilitated by a graduated in vivo exposure program, in which Robin attempted to go to school for increasingly long periods, at a pace that she helped to determine. For example, as her first step, Robin chose to get dressed for school, to drive to school with her mother, and to enter the front door of the school by herself. Once Robin was able to complete this step with little or no anxiety, she progressed to the next step in the treatment hierarchy. Using this procedure, Robin successfully returned to school full time over the course of 12 weeks.

However, once Robin began attending classes, her worrying about school work, peers, and teachers escalated. To reduce her maladaptive thoughts, a cognitive restructuring procedure was implemented that followed Beck and Emery's (1985) cognitive therapy approach for anxious adults. First, a cognitive model of anxiety was described to Robin (i.e., it was explained that her anxiety resulted from automatic, exaggerated thinking). Cognitive treatment was aimed at substituting more rational, logical thoughts for faulty thinking. A Socratic method of asking questions to lead Robin to identify irrational thoughts and to replace them with more appropriate thoughts was used.

Finally, social skills training was employed to help Robin deal more effectively with peers. Instruction, role playing, and positive feedback were used to teach Robin initiation skills, assertiveness, and conversation skills. She demonstrated improvements in social skills during her weekly treatment sessions and reported use of these social behaviors in the school setting as well.

This treatment package resulted in substantial improvements in Robin's functioning in terms of her completion of school assignments, school attendance, rate of worrying, social acceptance, and feelings of anxiety and depression. At termination of treatment after 7 months, Robin attended school on a daily basis, completed school assignments on time, had several friends at school, and was active in numerous extracurricular activities sponsored at her school. She reportedly worried about future and past behaviors only occasionally. Her tendency to be perfectionistic had reduced substantially, although she continued to show evidence of high expectations intermittently. However, Robin quickly identified her overly high expectations and attempted to adopt more appropriate and realistic expectations. At the end of treatment, Robin no longer met diagnostic criteria for overanxious disorder or any other psychiatric disorder. Therefore, our treatment package was associated with significant improvements in Robin's adjustment; unfortunately, it cannot be determined which of the treatment components were necessary in achieving these gains. Further research evaluating the utility of this therapy approach with other overanxious youngsters and determining the effectiveness of each of these treatment components for overanxious disorder clearly is needed.

CONTINUITY AND DISCONTINUITY WITH ADULT PRESENTATION

The long-term outcome associated with overanxious disorder is unknown at present. It has been speculated that overanxious disorder in childhood and adolescence continues into adulthood as generalized anxiety disorder, although no data are yet available to support this claim. None-theless, the resemblance of the features of these two disorders (e.g., excessive worrying, generalized tension) and the clinical support for the chronicity of overanxious disorder in childhood together suggest that overanxious disorder in childhood indeed may extend into adulthood as generalized anxiety disorder. Unfortunately, no follow-up studies of overanxious disorder have yet been completed nor have follow-back studies been conducted to evaluate the presence of overanxious disorder in the childhood histories of adults with generalized anxiety disorder. Long-term studies, as well as follow-up studies, that are presently underway (e.g., Last, Hersen, & Kazdin, 1990), will help to uncover the continuity of these two disorders.

SUMMARY

Researchers have only recently begun to examine the occurrence and phenomenology of overanxious disorder in childhood and adolescence. Initial evidence suggests that overanxious disorder is moderately prevalent in preadolescent children in the general population. It constitutes one of the two most common anxiety diagnoses leading to referral to an outpatient clinic for children with anxiety disorders. Overanxious disorder is equally prevalent among males and females in clinic samples and is as likely to occur prior to the onset of adolescence as following adolescence. This childhood anxiety disorder is more commonly found in families of upper-middle and upper socioeconomic status.

Overanxious disorder appears to be a chronic condition in childhood and adolescence. It does not appear to remit spontaneously, with overanxious children on the average referred to an outpatient clinic for treatment services 4½ years following onset of the disorder. However, no follow-up data have yet appeared in the literature to allow a proper evaluation of the course of this disorder.

Overanxious disorder has been shown to be associated with coexisting problems with separation anxiety, simple phobias, attention-deficit disorder, major depression, and elevated rates of severe suicidal ideation. Approximately one half of youngsters referred for clinical services show serious symptoms and impairment, with older children tending to demonstrate more marked impairment.

No empirical research has yet examined treatment for this disorder, although a case study has been presented in this chapter that outlines clinical impressions of the most effective intervention for overanxious disorder to date. Additional study of this childhood anxiety disorder is clearly needed to understand further its epidemiology, associated characteristics, prognosis, and effective treatments.

REFERENCES

American Psychiatric Association. (1980). *Diagnostic and statistical manual of mental disorders* (3rd ed.). Washington, DC: Author.

American Psychiatric Association. (1987). *Diagnostic and statistical manual of mental disorders* (3rd ed. rev.). Washington, DC: Author.

Anderson, J. C., Williams, S., McGee, R., & Silva, P. A. (1987). DSM-III disorders in preadolescent children. *Archives of General Psychiatry, 44*, 69–76.

Asher, S. R., Hymel, S., & Renshaw, P. D. (1984). Loneliness in children. *Child Development, 55*, 1456–1464.

Beck, A. T., & Emery, G. (1985). *Anxiety disorders and phobias: A cognitive perspective*. New York: Basic Books.

Brent, D. A., Kalas, R., Edelbrock, C., Costello, A. J., Dulcan, M. K., & Conover, N. (1986). Psychopathology and its relationship to suicidal ideation in childhood and adolescence. *Journal of the American Academy of Child Psychiatry, 25*, 666–673.

Jacobsen, F. (1938). *Progressive relaxation*. Chicago: University of Chicago Press.

Kovacs, M. (1978). *Children's Depression Inventory (CDI)*. Unpublished manuscript, University of Pittsburgh School of Medicine.

Last, C. G., Hersen, M., & Kazdin, A. E. (1988). [A follow-up study of anxiety-disordered children and adolescents]. Unpublished data.

Last, C. G., Hersen, M., Kazdin, A. E., Finkelstein, R., & Strauss, C. C. (1987). Comparison of DSM-III separation anxiety and overanxious disorders: Demographic characteristics and patterns of comorbidity. *Journal of the American Academy of Child Psychiatry, 26*, 527–531.

Last, C. G., Strauss, C. C., & Francis, G. (1987). Comorbidity among childhood anxiety disorders. *Journal of Nervous and Mental Disease, 175*, 726–730.

Last, C. G., Strauss, C. C., & Ron, D. (1990). An empirical examination of overanxious disorder in children and adolescents: Toward DSM-IV. Manuscript in preparation.

Ollendick, T. H. (1983). Reliability and validity of the Revised Fear Survey Schedule for Children (FSSC-R). *Behavior Research and Therapy, 21*, 685–692.

Ollendick, T. H., & Cerny, J. A. (1981). *Clinical Behavior Therapy with Children*. New York: Plenum Press.

Ollendick, T. H., Matson, J. L., & Helsel, W. J. (1985). Fears in children and adolescents: Normative data. *Behavior Research and Therapy, 4*, 465–467.

Puig-Antich, J., & Ryan, N. D. (1986). *Schedule for Affective Disorders and Schizophrenia forSchool-Age Children (6-18 Years), Kiddie SADS — Present Episode (K-SADS-P)* (4th working draft). Unpublished manuscript.

Quay, H. C., & Peterson, D. R. (1983). *Revised Behavior Problem Checklist*. Coral Gables, FL: University of Miami Press.

Spielberger, C. D. (1973). *Manual for the State-Trait Inventory for Children (STAIC)*. Palo Alto, CA: Consulting Psychologists Press.

Strauss, C. C., Lahey, B. B., Frick, P., Frame, C. L., & Hynd, G. W. (1988). Peer social status of children with anxiety disorders. *Journal of Consulting and Clinical Psychology, 56*, 137–141.

Strauss, C. C., Last, C. G., Hersen, M., & Kazdin, A. E. (1988). Association between anxiety and depression in children and adolescents with anxiety disorders. *Journal of Abnormal Child Psychology, 15*, 57–68.

Strauss, C. C., Lease, C. A., Last, C. G., & Francis, G. (1988). Overanxious disorder: An examination of developmental differences. *Journal of Abnormal Child Psychology, 16*, 433–443.

CHAPTER 18

GENERALIZED ANXIETY DISORDER IN ADULTHOOD

Rudolf Hoehn-Saric
Daniel R. McLeod

DESCRIPTION OF THE DISORDER

During the 1960s, Klein and his colleagues (Klein, 1981) observed that some anxiety patients experienced paroxysmal attacks of anxiety, while others suffered from persistent anxiety without sudden anxiety attacks. Klein (1981) stated that the former type of patient responded favorably to antidepressant medications, while the latter type did better on benzodiazepines. Based on these observations, the *Diagnostic and Statistical Manual of Mental Disorders* (American Psychiatric Association, 1980) divided the diagnostic category of anxiety neurosis into "panic disorder" and "generalized anxiety disorder" (GAD). In the subsequent edition of the manual, the DSM-III-R (APA, 1987), the essential feature of generalized anxiety disorder is the presence of unrealistic or excessive anxiety and worry (apprehensive expectation) about two or more life circumstances. Such worrying must persist for about 6 months or longer, bothering the person more often than not during this time. When the patient is anxious, many signs of motor tension, autonomic hyperactivity, increased vigilance, and scanning must be present.

DSM-III-R revised the definition of GAD found in DSM-III by placing greater emphasis on apprehensive expectation. It further requires anxiety symptoms to be present for at least 6 months rather than just 1. In addition, DSM-III-R permits the diagnosis of GAD to be made in the presence of another psychiatric disorder, provided that the focus of anxiety and worry is unrelated to that disorder. For example, the worry should not center on having panic attacks, as seen in panic disorder, or being humiliated in public, as seen in social phobias. The diagnosis of GAD also cannot be made if the anxiety is a part of other disorders frequently associated with increased anxiety, such as mood disorders, psychotic disorders, or specific organic conditions (e.g., hyperthyroidism or caffeine intoxication).

CLINICAL PRESENTATION

It is advantageous to view anxiety as a multidimensional phenomenon consisting of psychic symptoms, hypervigilance, somatic symptoms, and behavioral manifestations. Several studies have shown that psychic and cognitive anxiety, expressed as apprehensive expectations, and somatic symptoms are separate, albeit interacting, entities (Buss, 1962; Schwartz, Davidson, & Coleman, 1978).

Psychic Symptoms

The psychic symptoms of GAD can be divided into affective and cognitive symptoms. Affective symptoms range from feelings of increased tension to profound fear. The predominant cognitive symptom of GAD is the tendency to worry constantly. Such apprehension may be internalized, manifesting itself as insecurity with respect to one's own ability and performance, or externalized into expectations of disaster that may strike oneself or important persons in one's life. The importance of psychic symptoms as central characteristics of GAD has been emphasized by Barlow, Blanchard, Vermilyea, Vermilyea, and DiNardo (1986), and psychic symptoms have been made central criteria for GAD in DSM-III-R. Clinical studies have shown that psychic symptoms respond better to the antidepressant imipramine than to the benzodiazepine aprazolam (Hoehn-Saric, McLeod, & Zimmerli, 1988a). Buspirone also may have a stronger effect on psychic than on somatic symptoms (Rickels et al., 1982).

Hypervigilance

Hypervigilance usually accompanies GAD, but is not necessarily a constant symptom. Patients feel hyperalert, startle easily, and often have difficulties sleeping. Difficulties falling asleep are more frequently reported, but many patients complain of waking up during the night, particularly around 3:00 or 4:00 in the morning. Hypervigilance can be seen in EEG tracings. Anxiety patients characteristically have a low output in the alpha-band, poor alpha organization, and increased beta frequencies (Koella, 1981).

The presence of hyperarousal is also suggested in sleep recordings obtained from GAD patients. Reynolds, Shaw, Newton, Coble, and Kupfer (1983) compared sleep patterns of anxious patients with those of depressed patients and found impairment of sleep continuity and reduction of delta sleep in both groups. However, patients with GAD differed from depressed patients by exhibiting greatly reduced stage one sleep and REM percentage, whereas patients with primary depression exhibited a shorter REM latency. Based on REM sleep latency and REM percent, the authors were

able to classify correctly 86.7% of their patients. Similar results were reported by Papadimitriou, Linkowski, Kerkhofs, Kempenaers, and Mendlewicz (1988), who were able to differentiate GAD patients from patients with primary depression by means of sleep records, even when depression coexisted with GAD. Akiskal (personal communication) noticed that patients with GAD adapted less well to laboratory sleep during the first night of recordings than patients with other diagnoses, suggesting that even nonthreatening situations may cause hyperarousal in these patients. In contrast to psychic symptoms, which respond better to tricyclic antidepressants, feelings of hyperalertness and insomnia are more successfully treated with benzodiazepines (Hoehn-Saric et al., 1988a).

Somatic Symptoms

Somatic symptoms occurring in anxiety disorders can be subdivided into muscular and autonomic symptoms. Increased muscular tension results in a feeling of achiness, fatigue, tension, headaches, and, in severe cases, tremor. Autonomic symptoms may be predominantly sympathetic, consisting of palpitations and increased perspiration, or parasympathetic, consisting of butterflies in the stomach, nausea, and, in severe cases, vomiting, loose bowels, and increased urinary frequency. Sympathetic and parasympathetic symptoms usually coexist, but differ among individuals in relative frequency and severity. In some patients somatic symptoms occur secondary to hyperventilation, which induces feelings of tightness in the chest, palpitations, air hunger, paresthesia, and dizziness. Appetite and sex drive can either be increased or decreased. Some people find overeating or an orgasm tension releasing; others lose interest in food and sex when under great pressure. In contrast to depression, such changes are usually transitory and tension related.

On physiological measures, increased muscular tension is the most consistent finding in anxiety disorders, including GAD. However, not all muscle groups respond equally to anxiety. At rest, forehead muscles are usually more tense than are other muscle groups (Malmo, 1957), but, being tense, they are less responsive to stressors than other muscle groups (Balshan, 1962; Hoehn-Saric, McLeod, & Zimmerli, 1988b). The muscle response depends also on the patient's psychopathology and the particulars of the situation. For instance, Malmo, Smith, and Kohlmeyer (1956) reported that discussion of hostile conflicts was associated with increased forearm muscle tension, whereas discussion of sexual conflicts was associated with increased leg muscle tension in the same patient.

In contrast to increased muscle tension, autonomic hyperactivity is not a consistent finding in GAD patients. Several studies have found no differences between GAD patients and nonanxious controls in autonomic measures, such as heart rate, skin conductance, and respiration during baseline conditions (Hoehn-Saric & Masek, 1981; Hoehn-Saric et al., 1988b; Malmo, 1957). These results support reports of other investigators who failed to find differences in catecholamine (Mathew, Ho, Francis, Taylor, & Weinman, 1982) or cortisol levels (Rosenbaum et al., 1983) between normal volunteers and patients with GAD. We found that GAD patients responded in a manner comparable to that of controls on cardiovascular measures and respiration, but not on skin conductance measures, during laboratory induced psychological stress. Skin conductance, however, was less reactive during stress in the GAD group (Hoehn-Saric et al., 1988b). These findings suggest a sympathetic inhibition rather than hyperarousal in GAD patients. Autonomic inhibition has been found in anxious or poorly adjusted patients in a number of studies. Lader and Wing (1964) found that normals exhibited a larger galvanic skin conductance response and habituated faster than patients with anxiety states, and Kelly (1980) reported greater increases in forearm blood flow under mental stress for normals than for anxiety patients. These findings are consistent with reports by Forsman (1980) and Frankenhaeuser (1983), who found that persons with stable personalities had stronger catecholamine responses to stressors than did persons who were poorly adjusted or had higher levels of neuroticism. After termination of stress, catecholamines returned to previous levels more rapidly in the well-adjusted persons. The catecholamine response in persons with poorer adjustment was initially weak, but was slower in returning to baseline levels. Thus, well-adjusted persons exhibited a more flexible response to stress than did those with poor adjustment or heightened anxiety. We have elsewhere referred to this phenomenon as autonomic flexibility (Hoehn-Saric & McLeod, 1988).

Central nervous system (CNS) measures support an inhibitory, rather than excitatory, autonomic response in GAD patients. Grillon and Buchsbaum (1987) examined the EEG topography of responses to visual stimuli in patients with GAD and found that these patients showed less alpha response than nonanxious controls. Gur et al. (1988) examined regional cerebral blood flow in normal volunteers and found that lower levels of anxiety increased, but higher levels of anxiety decreased cerebral blood flow. Mathew and Wilson (1988) found no differences in cerebral blood flow between GAD patients and controls when subjects were exposed to CO_2 inhalation; however, those with higher levels of anxiety showed a weaker blood flow response. Thus, it appears that increased levels of anxiety in GAD patients, as well as in the general population, lead to an inhibition rather than excitation of various CNS, as well as peripheral autonomic nervous system, manifestations. The mechanism for this inhibitory response is not clear. Various explanations have been offered, ranging from heightened physiological baseline activity, which permits only small additional changes (Kelly, 1980) to diminished attention to external stimuli due to competing internal interference (Grillon & Buchsbaum, 1987). However, none of these interpretations can explain all study results. At present, the only conclusion that can be drawn is that increased levels of arousal, which manifest themselves in various subjective symptoms and increased muscle tension, also lead to secondary inhibition in the CNS and other body systems. However, various autonomic systems function independently from each other, and an inhibitory response in one system may not necessarily correspond to comparable responses in other systems.

Excessive respiratory activity leading to hyperventilation occurs in some patients with GAD. However, induced hyperventilation appears to be less symptom provoking in GAD than in panic disorder patients. Rapee (1986) reported that only 25% of GAD patients who underwent induced hyperventilation described symptoms resembling those of anxiety, in contrast to the 80% of panic disorder patients who underwent the same procedure.

The relationship between self-reports of somatic manifestations of anxiety and actual physiological changes is complex, and correlations between these sets of measures are poor. In our laboratory, we have demonstrated that patients with GAD are capable of detecting the direction, but not the degree, of physiological change under stress (McLeod, Hoehn-Saric, & Stefan, 1986). To what extent the severity of somatic symptoms depends on actual physiological activity levels and magnitude of change and to what degree it represents a hypersensitivity to somatic manifestations, which nonanxious persons generally ignore, remains unknown. Experimental evidence supports both reaction patterns, but the degree to which they contribute to the perception of bodily states may vary from case to case.

Not every anxious patient experiences all, or even the same, types of somatic symptoms. We have found that some patients complain predominantly of cardiopulmonary symptoms and an increased tendency to perspire, while other patients with comparable levels of psychic anxiety suffer mostly from muscular symptoms. Still other patients experience predominantly gastrointestinal and urinary symptoms (Weiner, 1985). Irritable bowel syndrome in particular is frequently associated with generalized anxiety (Lolas & Heerlein, 1986; Richter, Obrecht, Bradley, Young, & Anderson, 1986). Certain somatic response patterns may be constitutionally determined. For instance, blood pressure and heart activity response (Manuck, Giordani, McQuaid, & Garrity, 1981; Williams et al., 1982), as well as cortisol output in response to psychological stress (Williams et al., 1982), were found to be higher in persons with family histories of hypertension than in controls, even if the subjects were normotensive at the time of the examination.

Hormonal levels in GAD patients differ little from those found in normals. This has been demonstrated for catecholamines (Mathew et al., 1982), cortisol (Rosenbaum et al., 1983), and thyroid hormone levels (Munjack & Palmer, 1988). In several studies, however, the dexamethasone suppression test has resulted in nonsuppression of cortisol blood levels in 27% (Schweizer, Swenson, Winokur, Rickels, & Maislin, 1986; Tiller, Biddle, Maguire, & Davis, 1988) to 38.4% (Avery et al., 1985) of the examined GAD patients. The reason for the high levels of nonsuppression is unknown. They appear to be unrelated to coexisting depression (Schweizer et al., 1986). In one study, nonsuppressors were found to have low dexamethasone plasma levels (Tiller et al., 1988). Interestingly, the response normalizes in nonsuppressors after successful nondrug treatment (Tiller et al., 1988). Since high levels of stress increase the rate of nonsuppression, it is possible that the large number of nonsuppressors in GAD is related to the experience of stress rather than depression (Baumgartner, Graf, & Kuten, 1985). Platelet [³H] imipramine binding, which is frequently depressed in unipolar depression, was not altered

from the norm in GAD patients (Schneider, Munjack, Severson, & Palmer, 1987). Tribulin, a substance found in urine that inhibits benzodiazepine receptor binding and monoaminoxidaze activity, has been reported to be elevated in GAD patients. Its values remained high even after reduction of anxiety following behavior therapy (Clow, Glover, Sandler, & Tiller, 1988). The significance of this finding, however, remains unknown. As was the case with hyperarousal, somatic symptoms in GAD patients respond better to benzodiazepines than to imipramine (Hoehn-Saric et al., 1988a).

Behavioral Manifestations

The behavioral manifestations of GAD depend on the intensity of the anxiety, the type of stress, the available coping mechanisms, and personality factors. Low levels of anxiety can be hidden from other people. When patients become highly anxious, however, their faces become flushed or pale, they may exhibit tremor, and their hands might feel sweaty or cold. Their interactions with other people may show various levels of disorganization.

A person's overall reaction to GAD is modified by personality traits. For example, an outgoing Type A personality may try to cope with anxiety in an aggressive manner, while a passive and avoidant personality would perhaps tend to go into hiding. A person with obsessive personality traits may become overconscientious when facing stressors, while a person with hysterical traits may exhibit anxiety in a dramatic manner.

EPIDEMIOLOGY

The exact prevalence of GAD is difficult to establish because diagnostic criteria, as well as the presenting symptoms, are more ambiguous than are those of other anxiety disorders (for discussion see Validity of the GAD Diagnosis that follows). Moreover, the population selection and survey instrumentation differ considerably from study to study. A community survey of 511 patients in New Haven, using the Schedule for Affective Disorder and Schizophrenia (SADS) and Research Diagnostic Criteria (RDC), found a 1-month prevalence of 2.5/100 (Weissman, Myers, & Hardig, 1978). The National Survey of Psychotropic Drug Use, which screened 3,161 individuals, using the Symptom Check-List-90 (SCL-90), reported a 1-year prevalence of 6.26/100 (Uhlenhuth, Balter, Mellinger, Cisin, & Clinthorne, 1983). The Zürich study, which limited itself to a population of 19- and 20-year-old males, and also used the SCL-90, reported a 1-year prevalence of 5.2/100 (Angst & Dobler-Mikola, 1985). In these surveys, GAD occurred, respectively, 6.25, 6.4, and 1.7 times more frequently than panic disorder.

The National Institute of Mental Health Epidemiologic Catchment Area Study has not yet published results on the prevalence of GAD, but information was obtained for a subsample of 3,481 adults from the Baltimore area surveyed by the Diagnostic Interview Schedule (DIS) and the General Hospital Questionnaire (GHQ). Eight hundred and ten subjects who rated positive on the questionnaires were, in addition, interviewed by psychiatrists. This study reported a 1-month prevalence of 2.3/100 GAD patients (Romanoski & Nestadt, personal communication), which is comparable to the values obtained in the New Haven study (Weissman et al., 1978). In another study, a survey of 1,242 patients seen in a medical clinic showed a prevalence of 4.6% for GAD, which was 3.3 times more frequent than panic disorder (von Korf et al., 1987). In certain subgroups of patients, GAD is particularly high. This is the case in patients with irritable bowel syndrome, a condition that shows a significantly higher prevalence of GAD than, for example, duodenal ulcer (Lolas & Heerlein, 1986) or esophageal spasms (Richter et al., 1986).

Chronic pain patients, particularly female patients, showed a high prevalence of GAD even when no financial compensation was involved (Fishbain, Goldberg, Labbe, Steele, & Rosomoff, 1988). Homosexuals with HIV infection had an understandably high rate of GAD (39.9%), but in many of them GAD preceded the onset of the AIDS epidemic (Atkinson et al., 1988). Reviewing several studies, Weissman and Merikangas (1986) concluded that "there is some agreement that generalized anxiety disorder is the most common and panic disorder the least common of the anxiety disorders."

NATURAL HISTORY

The average age of onset for GAD is 21 years, with a range of 16 to 26 years (Thyer, Parrish, Curtis, Nesse, & Cameron, 1985). Many patients report that they have been anxious "all of their lives" which suggests that their anxiety may be a personality trait. Anderson, Noyes, and Crowe (1984) found that stressful events preceded the onset of GAD in approximately half of the examined 18 patients. One third of the patients thought of themselves as "nervous" before the anxiety problems developed. GAD tends to have a prolonged course (Anderson et al., 1984; Barlow et al., 1986) during which symptoms tend to fluctuate in severity. The severity of the disorder often depends on the degree and number of perceived external stressors (Ilfeld, 1979). Anxious patients acquire phobic reactions faster than do nonanxious persons and desensitize more slowly when the stressor is removed (Öhman, Fredrikson, & Hugdahl, 1978). Therefore, patients with increased anxiety are prone to avoidance behavior that can take on phobic proportions. Phobic reactions in GAD patients, however, are usually less intense than in patients with simple phobias or agoraphobia. Constant worrying, which is a characteristic of GAD, may approach obsessive ruminative proportions. Since patients with chronic anxiety frequently become demoralized, they are prone to transitory depression as well. Finally, chronic anxiety predisposes certain people to substance abuse.

Patients with GAD tend to have increased numbers of physician visits and hospitalizations, but whether they experience excessive numbers of physical diseases in comparison to the general population is not known (Appenheimer & Noyes, 1987). However, in contrast to panic disorder (Coryell, Noyes, & Clancy, 1982), the mortality of GAD patients is not elevated (Murphy et al., 1987). In general, younger patients with a mild form of the disorder have the best prognosis, while older patients, those with poor social support, and those with severe physical diseases, appear to have the worst prognosis (Appenheimer & Noyes, 1987). The overall prognosis also depends on the diagnostic criteria. Breslau and Davis (1985a) found that when they applied the stricter criteria of DSM-III-R rather than DSM-III for the diagnosis of GAD, patients showed greater severity of the illness.

IMPAIRMENT AND COMPLICATIONS

In comparison to panic disorder the overall impairment in GAD is usually milder, but more chronic. The tendency to become overly conscientious or disorganized when exposed to comparatively mild stress may impair performance. Insomnia induces chronic fatigue. Mild levels of depression are frequently present in GAD, and many patients report one or more episodes of more severe secondary depression during the course of the illness (Anderson et al., 1984). According to the patient's personality, GAD may accentuate certain traits, such as obsessive, hostile, or avoidance traits. Some patients, particularly men, tend to self-medicate themselves with drugs and alcohol.

DIFFERENTIAL DIAGNOSIS

Before discussing the differential diagnosis of GAD, it is necessary to examine the validity of GAD as a diagnostic category. Soon after introduction of GAD as a distinct diagnostic entity (APA, 1980), concerns were raised about its validity (Breier, Charney, & Heninger, 1985; DiNardo, O'Brien, Barlow, Waddell, & Blanchard, 1983). Questions have been raised as to what degree GAD can be distinguished from normal anxiety, other anxiety disorders, and major depression.

Phenomenologically, GAD is closer to normal anxiety than other anxiety disorders (DiNardo et al., 1983) and differs from normal anxiety in degree rather than quality. Therefore, the dividing line between normal anxiety and GAD is arbitrary. Moreover, GAD lacks specific distinguishing symptoms, such as panic attacks, obsessive thoughts, or compulsive checking rituals. Therefore, the diagnosis is made predominantly on phenomenological, rather than on more easily defined behavioral, criteria. In addition, symptoms, such as phobias, obsessions, and compulsions, or depression, which are readily incorporated as secondary symptoms in other anxiety disorders, may or may not be accepted in the diagnosis of GAD, depending on the degree to which they are regarded as independent of generalized anxiety. Thus, the diagnosis of GAD depends, to a large extent, on the clinical judgment of the assessor.

It is not surprising that GAD has proved to be a less reliable diagnostic entity than other anxiety disorders. DiNardo et al. (1983), using the Anxiety Disorders Interview Schedule, found that interviewers were less likely to agree on the diagnosis of GAD than on that of other anxiety disorders. However, the number of patients was small, and the diagnostic reliability of major depression was also low. Semler et al. (1987) used the NIMH Diagnostic Interview Schedule (DIS) on 60 psychiatric inpatients with various diagnoses, of which only a few actually carried the diagnosis of an anxiety disorder, and found acceptable agreement

for all diagnostic categories, except for dysthymic disorder and GAD. A group that used the Newcastle Anxiety Depression Index (Davidson et al., 1986) reported that, among the examined diagnostic categories, GAD received the least validation. On the other hand, Riskind, Beck, Berchick, Brown, and Steer (1987) employed the Structured Clinical Interview for DSM-III (SCID) and found 86% agreement among raters for the diagnosis of GAD. They concluded that the SCID can be employed reliably to differentiate major depression from GAD. A comparison of outpatients with GAD and primary major depression or dysthymic disorder, using the Beck Depression Inventory, also differentiated the two conditions, primarily on items of sadness and loss of libido (Steer, Beck, Riskind, & Brown, 1986). Thus, the reliability of the diagnosis of GAD depends at least in part on the diagnostic instrument.

The diagnosis of GAD is further complicated by the fact that it may be a prodromal condition, since many patients who experience GAD later go on to develop panic disorder (Cloninger, Martin, Clayton, & Guze, 1981; Garvey, Cook, & Noyes, 1988), social phobia (Tyrer, 1986), or obsessive-compulsive disorder (Hoehn-Saric & Barksdale, 1983). GAD may also be a residual condition since patients who have suffered from panic disorder in the past may continue to experience high levels of anxiety (Katon, Vitaliano, Anderson, Jones, & Russo, 1987). GAD also coexists in the majority of patients with other anxiety disorders, such as panic disorder, obsessive-compulsive disorder, or posttraumatic stress disorder (Barlow, 1985). Thus, GAD might be a prodromal, incomplete coexisting, or residual manifestation of another anxiety disorder. On the other hand, many patients with GAD never develop an additional anxiety disorder, indicating that a subgroup of patients fulfills the criteria for an independent disorder.

It is well known that the symptoms of anxiety and depression overlap. Most anxiety scales contain items that describe depressive symptoms, while depression scales contain anxiety symptoms (Riskind, Beck, Brown, & Steer, 1987). Hoehn-Saric (1983) and Lipman (1982) found that anxiety levels in nonpsychotic patients were equally prevalent in anxious and depressed patients. The clinical diagnosis of depression was made when the depressive symptoms exceeded those of anxiety. Breslau and Davis (1985b), who examined 357 mothers using the DIS, found that 31% of those diagnosed as suffering from GAD also carried a secondary diagnosis of major depressive disorder, and 85% of those with major depressive disorder carried a secondary diagnosis of GAD. Davidson et al. (1986) also found many GAD patients with depression.

Attempts at differentiating between GAD and depression, which is also a heterogeneous disorder, are further complicated by the limited reliability (DiNardo et al., 1983; Semler et al., 1987) and questionable validity of survey instruments (Anthony et al., 1985). In the Baltimore study the comparisons between diagnoses obtained by the DIS and a subsequent psychiatric examination showed marked discrepancies (Anthony et al., 1985). Moreover, while the DIS data classify a set of depressive symptoms operationally as "major depressive disorder" (Breslau & Davis, 1985a, b), clinical assessments tend to describe the depression in etiological terms, such as "secondary" (i.e., a reaction to pathological anxiety) (Anderson et al., 1984). Breslau and Davis (1985b) state that "accounts of GAD symptoms in association with major depressive disorders are no more than a manifestation of psychological distress or demoralization experienced by persons with severe psychiatric illness." This assumes, of course, that depression is the primary disorder, which includes, among other manifestations, GAD-like symptoms. However, the same could also be said for symptoms of depression secondary to demoralization due to prolonged anxiety that, being more severe than uncomplicated GAD, has a greater impact on the patient and his or her environment (Breslau, Davis, & Prabucki, 1987).

British psychiatry side-stepped this dilemma by categorizing patients who exhibit marked symptoms of anxiety and depression as being in the mixed "anxiety depressive group" (Tyrer, 1984). Roth, Mountjoy, and Caetano (1982) stated that "the depression and anxiety syndromes are distinct, but related phenomena separated by a limited area of diagnostic uncertainty," and "the clean, sharp line of distinction implied by DSM-III does not exist." Further research into etiological, pathological, and biological markers, for instance, sleep patterns (Papadimitriou et al., 1988; Reynolds et al., 1983), may clarify the position of GAD within the family of anxiety and depressive disorders.

Symptoms of GAD occur in many psychiatric, as well as medical, conditions. Prior to assigning the diagnosis of GAD, one must rule out anxiety as a symptom of another disorder or illness. GAD differs from panic disorder by the absence of par-oxysmal anxiety attacks. Hoehn-Saric (1981, 1982) and Anderson et al. (1984) found that the two populations differed in the severity of somatic symptoms, with panic disorder patients complaining more of cardiopulmonary symptoms and GAD patients complaining more of muscular and gastrointestinal symptoms. Rapee (1985) found that panic disorder is characterized by a sudden onset of somatic symptoms that are accompanied by thoughts of death or physical or mental illness, whereas GAD is characterized by a gradual onset of somatic symptoms that are recognized as being the result of anxiety. Rapee (1986) also found that panic disordered patients have a higher resting heart rate and lower resting PCO_2 than do GAD patients, indicating that panic disordered patients have a greater tendency to hyperventilate. This was confirmed by the finding that panic disordered patients associate manifestations of hyperventilation with anxiety symptoms more frequently than do GAD patients. Patients with panic disorder and GAD also seem to differ in sleep patterns. In one study, panic disordered patients tended to experience more delta sleep, and GAD patients less delta sleep, than normal volunteers (Hauri, Ravaris, & Friedman, 1986).

A good mental status examination separates GAD from incipient schizophrenic illness or from agitated depression. Generalized anxiety disorder usually begins at an early age; a person who has a first wave of anxiety in his or her forties or fifties is more likely to develop an agitated depression than a primary anxiety disorder (Marks, 1987). Central nervous system changes, particularly those associated with delirium, can also produce anxiety symptoms. Various endocrine system disorders, particularly thyroid disturbance, can mimic GAD. A good physical examination and appropriate laboratory tests can clarify this issue. Occasionally, patients who present themselves with complaints of persistent anxiety fail to mention abuse of stimulants, alcohol, or sedative medications. Stimulants can act to trigger anxiety, while alcohol and sedatives induce anxiety during withdrawal periods. A history obtained from relatives or a drug screen can verify the diagnosis (Hoehn-Saric & McLeod, 1985).

The differentation of anxiety and depression has been discussed. The distinction can be difficult, particularly in patients who exhibit similar levels of anxiety and depression. However, in anxiety disorders, symptoms of anxiety are persistent, whereas depression is short-lived and usually occurs as a reaction to some event. On the other hand, in a depressive disorder, symptoms of depression are pervasive and anxiety occurs more intermittently.

CASE EXAMPLES

Case 1

Ms. W. was a 25-year-old, single, white woman who had been feeling tense since her teens. In school she felt self-conscious because she was tall and thin, tended to have sweaty palms, and perspired when tense. At the age of 15, she developed spastic colon, for which her family physician prescribed chlordiazepoxide. She continued to be shy and tended to worry excessively during college and later at her job as a computer assistant. At the age of 23, she developed palpitations, breathing difficulties, sweaty palms, increased muscular tension, tension headaches, butterflies in the stomach, nausea, abdominal cramps in the right lower quadrant, and frequent loose bowel movements. She had difficulty falling asleep, frequently awakening from sleep after 2 or 3 hours with dreams of failure. Her condition was present almost continuously in a mild form, but became worse when she was under interpersonal stress or had financial worries. The exacerbation of her symptoms during the last year was attributed to adjustment problems with her boyfriend.

Her medical history was positive for spastic colon. She also had increased premenstrual tension lasting for approximately 1 to 2 days. She did not smoke or drink alcohol and rarely drank caffeine-containing beverages.

The patient's history was positive for chronic anxiety in her mother. Her early childhood and school adjustment were satisfactory until high school, when she became self-conscious about her height (i.e., she eventually reached 6 feet). In general, she was a shy child. After she finished high school, she started to work for the government as a computer assistant. She performed adequately at work, but found it boring. Therefore, she attended evening classes with the intention of eventually becoming a drug counselor. She dated infrequently, but had serious involvements with two men.

Ms. W. presents a fairly typical case of chronic GAD. She grew up with an anxious and tense mother. As a child, she was shy but had no overt symptoms until she felt increased social pressure in school. Subsequently, she continued to have a variety of psychological and physical symptoms that were generally mild, but worsened whenever she was under even the slightest degree of stress. In treatment, she was given psychotherapy and was placed on a benzodiazepine. The medication was gradually decreased as she improved. She became more relaxed, had fewer physical symptoms, and eventually learned to cope more effectively with stressful situations. She continued to be somewhat symptomatic, however, and needed medication from time to time when under stress.

Case 2

Mr. B. was a 44-year-old, married, white, college-educated sales manager who had been tense throughout most of his life, but had become decidedly more tense during the last 15 years, especially over the last 8 months. He complained that he felt constantly tense, had increased muscular tension, particularly in the neck, which led to headaches, and he tended to awaken in the middle of the night worrying about work and business. He also experienced butterflies in the stomach, but had no palpitations, increased perspiration, or symptoms of hyperventilation. His habits were rather perfectionistic. His general health was good. He did not smoke, drank alcohol socially, and had one cup of coffee per day. He noticed during vacations that his symptoms, particularly the headaches, while still present, decreased markedly.

The patient's father was described as having been a constant worrier. He was loud and argumentative, and the patient never felt close to him. The patient's mother was more easygoing. The patient's early childhood was uneventful, and his academic performance was good, but his social adjustment was only fair, because he tended to be a loner who had few close friends. After college, he fulfilled his military obligations and subsequently began to work for a large corporation where he steadily advanced. He married a woman whom he had known since high school and had a daughter who now attends college. The patient's relationship with his wife is good, except for some tension brought on by his excessive preoccupation with work and work performance.

The patient appears to be a driven perfectionist who places high demands on himself and his coworkers. When frustrated at work, he tends to lose self-control and have temper tantrums.

The patient's acute symptoms responded to a benzodiazepine which was given regularly at first and later on an as-needed basis. He did very well with a cognitive behaviorally oriented psychotherapy, and his ability to tolerate frustration improved. The medication alleviated his headaches and permitted him to sleep better.

Like Ms. W. in Case 1, this patient's disorder represents chronic GAD. Symptoms consisted predominantly of excessive worrying, hypervigilance, and increased muscular tension leading to tension headaches. He had a Type A personality and converted his anxieties into high work performance and large demands on his coworkers. Therapy permitted him to see his life in more balanced terms. At work he continued to perform satisfactorily, but with less anxiety.

Case 3

Ms. F. was a 40-year-old, single, white, salesperson who had been rather tense all of her life. As a child, she was shy and anxious and avoided unpleasant situations whenever possible. After high school, she began to work for a department store as a salesperson. She remained at this job until she was laid off, shortly before coming to the clinic. The patient's father died when she was 12 years old, leaving the family in financial difficulties. Her mother was described as an anxious and overprotective person. The patient never married and continued to live with her mother. In high school she made a few friends, with whom she spent her vacations. When these friends eventually married or left town, the patient did not replace them with new friends. Her life became increasingly more centered on work and home. After losing her job, she became almost housebound, being afraid of going to job interviews or traveling in the downtown area. This fear, however, was not as severe as that seen in panic disorder. When sufficiently motivated, she was quite capable of taking a bus and reaching her destination with moderate but tolerable levels of anxiety, consisting of feelings of tension, tightness in the throat, increased perspiration, and, occasionally, rapid heart rate.

Like Mr. B., this patient suffered from chronic GAD. However, having an avoidant personality, she generally escaped high levels of tension by means of social withdrawal. For most of her life, she had remained on the same job. When such security was taken away, she was unable to replace it with new social contacts or work opportunities.

Therapy consisted of dealing with her psychological problems. Little progress was made until she ran out of her unemployment benefits. Only when financial necessities outweighed her tendency to avoid unpleasantness did she choose to look for another job. Eventually, she found a sales job that, after a period of heightened anxiety, permitted her to continue to live the restricted life she had lived before losing her previous position.

CHILDHOOD AND FAMILIAL ANTECEDENTS

Torgersen (1983), who examined monozygotic and same-sex dizygotic twins, found that in GAD, unlike panic disorder, genetic factors were not apparent. In a family study, Cloninger et al. (1981) found an excess of anxiety neurosis in families of patients with panic disorder, but not in those with anxiety disorder without panic attacks. On the other hand, Noyes, Clarkson, Crowe, Yates, and McChesney (1987) reported that the frequency of GAD was higher among first-degree relatives of probands with GAD than among the relatives of control subjects, but it was not higher among relatives of probands with panic disorder. Relatives of probands with GAD who had the same disorder had a mild, stress-related illness. The authors concluded that their results confirmed the separation between GAD and panic disorder, but challenged the distinction between generalized anxiety and adjustment disorder. Among relatives of probands with GAD, 30.1% were found to have an anxiety disorder, of which 19.5% had GAD. These results suggest that relatives of patients with GAD have an increased vulnerability to stressors and respond to them with GAD-like symptoms. However, many such responses are transitory, which gives them the appearance of being adjustment disorders. Such mild responses can easily be missed in surveys.

Thomas and Chess (1984) noted that various personality traits, including a tendency toward anxiety, were already present in young infants. This suggests a constitutional predisposition toward anxiety disorders. A variety of environmental stressors occurring during childhood, especially high levels of anxiety in the mother (Windheuser, 1977), or the death of a parent (Torgersen, 1986), as well as stressors occurring in later life, such as disturbances of interpersonal relationships (Blazer, Hughes, & George, 1987; Ilfeld, 1979), have been related to the emergence, and possibly the maintenance, of anxiety. However, no conclusive studies have been presented. In Torgersen's study (1986) the incidence of the death of a parent did not reach significant levels. Raskind, Peeke, Dickman, and Pinsker (1982) found no difference in separation anxiety among persons who developed GAD or panic disorder. Hoehn-Saric (1981) found that GAD patients rated themselves no higher than nonanxious persons on the Childhood Behavior Disturbance Scale, a scale that measures disturbances in development, learning, attention, hyperactivity, and interpersonal relationships before the age of 14.

The question of whether chronic anxiety can be precipitated in adults with healthy personalities remains unanswered. Extreme conditions, such as internment in a concentration camp, leave permanent scars (Levan & Abramson, 1984), but the etiological importance of less stressful events on long-term anxiety remains controversial (Lader, 1983). Precipitating factors are frequently responsible for the development of a transitory anxiety disorder or the exacerbation of GAD.

SUMMARY

Generalized anxiety disorder, as defined by DSM-III and DSM-III-R, remains the most controversial of the anxiety disorders. The essential features of GAD are the presence of excessive anxiety and worrying (apprehensive expectation), lasting for at least 6 months. Such worrying is accompanied by hypervigilance and muscular as well as autonomic symptoms. Clinical observations suggest that GAD is a disorder in its own right. However, GAD-like symptoms often accompany other anxiety disorders or depression and may occur as a prodrome or residual of another anxiety disorder. Phenomenologically, GAD is closer to normal anxiety than other disorders. Thus, no sharp differentiation exists between the two conditions. Equally undefined is the border between GAD with depression and a depressive disorder with heightened levels of anxiety. In spite of frequent somatic complaints, autonomic and neuroendocrine measures in GAD patients are generally within normal limits and may actually show an inhibited response to mental challenges. Only muscle tension appears to be regularly elevated, although the tension levels of different muscle groups may vary from one situation to the other.

Next to simple phobia, GAD is the most prevalent of the anxiety disorders. The disorder has an early onset, starting usually in the late teens or early twenties. The course tends to be chronic with fluctuations. Fatigue, secondary depression, and substance abuse can complicate the picture. Overt behavior induced by anxiety depends to a large degree on personality traits. It may lead to over-conscientiousness or to histrionic outbursts, and may lead to aggressive attempts to cope with anxiety-provoking situations or to fearful withdrawal.

The etiology of GAD is poorly understood. The results of genetic and family studies are contradictory. Traumatic experiences during early development may be of etiological importance, while stressors occurring in later life may play a contributory role. Further research is needed to obtain a better understanding of the etiology of GAD and to clarify its position in the family of anxiety disorders.

REFERENCES

American Psychiatric Association. (1980). *Diagnostic and statistical manual of mental disorders* (3rd ed.). Washington, DC: Author.

American Psychiatric Association. (1987). *Diagnostic and statistical manual of mental disorders* (3rd ed. rev.). Washington, DC: Author.

Anderson, D. J., Noyes, R., & Crowe, R. R. (1984). A comparison of panic disorder and generalized anxiety disorder. *American Journal of Psychiatry, 141*, 572–575.

Angst, J., & Dobler-Mikola, A. (1985). The Zürich Study: V. Anxiety and phobia in young adults. *European Archives of Psychiatry and Neurological Sciences, 235*, 171–178.

Anthony, J. C., Folstein, M., Romanoski, A. J., von Korf, M. R., Nestadt, G. R., Chahal, R., Merchant, A., Brown, H., Shapiro, S., Kramer, M., & Gruenberg, E. M. (1985). Comparison of the lay diagnostic interview schedule and a standardized psychiatric diagnosis. *Archives of General Psychiatry, 42*, 667–675.

Appenheimer, T., & Noyes, R., Jr. (1987). Generalized anxiety disorder. *Primary Care, 14*, 635–647.

Atkinson, J. H., Grant, I., Kennedy, C. J., Richman, D. D., Spector, S. A., & McCutchan, J. A. (1988). Prevalence of psychiatric disorders among men infected with human immunodeficiency virus. *Archives of General Psychiatry, 45*, 859–864.

Avery, D. H., Osgood, T. B., Ishiki, D. M., Wilson, L. G., Kenny, M., & Dunner, D. L. (1985). DST in psychiatric outpatients with generalized anxiety disorder, panic disorder, or primary affective disorder. *American Journal of Psychiatry, 142*, 844–848.

Balshan, I. D. (1962). Muscle tension and personality in women. *Archives of General Psychiatry, 7*, 436–448.

Blazer, D., Hughes, D., & George, L. K. (1987). Stressful life events and the onset of generalized anxiety syndrome. *American Journal of Psychiatry, 144*, 1178–1183.

Barlow, D. H. (1985). The dimensions of anxiety disorders. In A. H. Tuma & J. Maser (Eds.), *Anxiety and the anxiety disorders* (pp. 479–500). Hillsdale, NJ: Lawrence Erlbaum Associates.

Barlow, D. H., Blanchard, E. B., Vermilyea, J. A., Vermilyea, B. B., & DiNardo, P. A. (1986). Generalized anxiety and generalized anxiety disorder: Description and reconceptualization. *American Journal of Psychiatry, 143*, 40–44.

Breier, A., Charney, D. S., & Heninger, G. R. (1985). The diagnostic validity of anxiety disorders and their relationship to depressive illness. *American Journal of Psychiatry, 142*, 787–797.

Breslau, N., & Davis, G. C. (1985a). DSM-III generalized anxiety disorder: An empirical investigation of more stringent criteria. *Psychiatry Research, 14*, 231–238.

Breslau, N., & Davis, G. C. (1985b). Further evidence on the doubtful validity of generalized anxiety disorder. *Psychiatry Research, 16*, 177–179.

Breslau, N., Davis, G. C., & Prabucki, K. (1987). Searching for evidence on the validity of generalized anxiety disorder: Psychopathology in children of anxious mothers. *Psychiatry Research, 20*, 285–297.

Baumgartner, A., Graf, K. J., & Kuten, I. (1985). The dexamethasone suppression test in depression, in schizophrenia, and during experimental stress. *Biological Psychiatry, 20*, 675–679.

Buss, A. H. (1962). Two anxiety factors in psychiatric patients. *Journal of Abnormal and Social Psychology, 65*, 426–427.

Cloninger, C. R., Martin, R. L., Clayton, P., & Guze, S. B., (1982). A blind follow-up and family study of anxiety neurosis: Preliminary analysis of the St. Louis 500. In D. F. Klein & J. G. Rabkin (Eds.), *Anxiety: New research and changing concepts* (pp. 137–154). New York: Raven Press.

Clow, A., Glover, V., Sandler, M., & Tiller, J. (1988). Increased urinary tribulin output in generalized anxiety disorder. *Psychopharmacology, 95*, 378–380.

Coryell, W., Noyes, R., & Clancy, J. (1982). Excess mortality in panic disorders. *Archives of General Psychiatry, 39*, 701–703.

Davidson, J., Pelton, S., Krishnan, K. R. R., McLeod, M., Raft, D., Miller, R. D., & Allf, B. (1986). The assessment of the Newcastle Anxiety Depression Index. *Acta Psychiatrica Scandinavica, 73*, 533–543.

DiNardo, P. A., O'Brien, G. T., Barlow, D. H., Waddell, M. T., & Blanchard, E. B. (1983). Reliability of DSM-III anxiety disorder categories using a new structured interview. *Archives of General Psychiatry, 40*, 1070–1074.

Fishbain, D. A., Goldberg, M., Labbe, L., Steel, R., & Rosomoff, H. (1988). Compensation and non-compensation chronic pain patients compared for DSM-III operational diagnosis. *Pain, 32*, 197–206.

Forsman, L. (1980). Habitual catecholamine excretion and its relation to habitual distress. *Biological Psychology, 11*, 83–97.

Frankenhaeuser, M. (1983). The sympathetic-adrenal and pituitary-adrenal response to challenge: Comparison between the sexes. In T. M. Dembroski, T. H. Schmidt, & G. Blümchen (Eds.), *Biobehavioral basis of coronary heart disease* (pp. 91–105). Basel: S. Karger.

Garvey, M. J., Cook, B., & Noyes, R., Jr. (1988). The occurrence of a prodrome of generalized anxiety in panic disorder. *Comprehensive Psychiatry, 29*, 445–449.

Grillon, C., & Buchsbaum, M. S. (1987). EEG topography of response to visual stimuli in generalized anxiety disorder. *Electroencephalography and Clinical Neurophysiology, 66*, 337–348.

Gur, R. C., Gur, R. E., Skolnick, B. E., Resnick, S. M., Silver, F. L., Chawluk, J., Muenz, L., Obrist, W. D., & Reivich, M. (1988). Effect of task difficulty on regional blood flow: Relationship with anxiety and performance. *Psychophysiology, 25*, 392–399.

Hauri, P. J., Ravaris, C. L., & Friedman, M. J. (1986, April). *Sleep laboratory evaluations and double-blind medication trials in patients with panic disorder*. Paper presented at the Panic Disorder Biological Research Workshop (sponsored by The Upjohn Company, Kalamazoo, Michigan), Washington, DC.

Hoehn-Saric, R. (1981). Characteristics of chronic anxiety patients. In D. F. Klein & J. G. Rabkin (Eds.), *Anxiety: New research and changing concepts* (pp. 399–409). New York: Raven Press.

Hoehn-Saric, R. (1982). Comparison of generalized anxiety disorder with panic disorder patients. *Psychopharmacology Bulletin, 18,* 104–108.

Hoehn-Saric, R. (1983). Affective profiles of chronically anxious patients. *Hillside Journal of Clinical Psychiatry, 5,* 43–56.

Hoehn-Saric, R., & Barksdale, V. C. (1983). Impulsiveness in obsessive-compulsive patients. *British Journal of Psychiatry, 143,* 177–182.

Hoehn-Saric, R., & Masek, B. J. (1981). Effects of naloxone in normals and chronically anxious patients. *Biological Psychiatry, 16,* 1041–1050.

Hoehn-Saric, R., & McLeod, D. R. (1985). Generalized anxiety disorder. *Psychiatric Clinics of North America, 8*(1), 73–88.

Hoehn-Saric, R., & McLeod, D. R. (1988). The peripheral sympathetic nervous system: Its role in normal and pathological anxiety. *Psychiatric Clinics of North America, 11*(2), 375–386.

Hoehn-Saric, R., McLeod, D. R., & Zimmerli, W. D. (1988a). Differential effects of alprazolam and imipramine in generalized anxiety disorder: Somatic versus psychic symptoms. *Journal of Clinical Psychiatry, 49,* 293–301.

Hoehn-Saric, R., McLeod, D. R., & Zimmerli, W. D. (1988b, May 7–13). *Subjective and somatic manifestations of anxiety in obsessive-compulsive and generalized anxiety disorder.* Paper presented at the 141st Annual Meeting of the American Psychiatric Association, Montreal.

Ilfeld, F. W. J. (1979). Persons at high risk for symptoms of anxiety. In B. Brown (Ed.), *Clinical anxiety/tension in primary medicine.* Princeton, NJ: Excerpta Medica.

Katon, W., Vitaliano, P. P., Anderson, K., Jones, M., & Russo, J. (1987). Panic disorder: Residual symptoms after the acute attacks abate. *Comprehensive Psychiatry, 28,* 151–158.

Kelly, D. (1980). *Anxiety and emotions.* Springfield, IL: Charles C Thomas.

Klein, D. F. (1981). Anxiety reconceptualized. In D. F. Klein & J. G. Rabkin (Eds.), *Anxiety: New research and changing concepts* (pp. 235–263). New York: Raven Press.

Koella, W. P. (1981). Electroencephalographic signs of anxiety. *Progress in Neuro-Psychopharmacology and Biological Psychiatry, 5,* 187–192.

Lader, M. H. (1983). Behavior and anxiety: Physiologic mechanisms. *Journal of Clinical Psychiatry, 44*(Sec. 2), 5–11.

Lader, M. H., & Wing, L. (1964). Habituation of the psychogalvanic reflex in patients with anxiety states and in normal subjects. *Journal of Neurology, Neurosurgery and Psychiatry, 27,* 216–218.

Levan, I., & Abramson, J. H. (1984). Emotional distress among concentration camp survivors: A community study in Jerusalem. *Psychological Medicine, 14,* 215–218.

Lipman, R. S. (1982). Differentiating anxiety and depression in anxiety disorders: Use of rating scales. *Psychopharmacology Bulletin, 18,* 69–77.

Lolas, F., & Heerlein, A. (1986). Content category analysis of affective expression in irritable bowel, duodenal ulcer and anxiety disorder patients. *Psychopathology, 19,* 309–316.

Malmo, R. B. (1957). Anxiety and behavioral arousal. *Psychological Review, 64,* 276–287.

Malmo, R. B., Smith, A. A., & Kohlmeyer, W. A. (1956). Motor manifestations of conflict in interview: A case study. *Journal of Abnormal and Social Psychology, 52,* 268–271.

Manuck, S. B., Giordani, B., McQuaid, K. J., & Garrity, S. J. (1981). Behaviorally-induced cardiovascular reactivity among sons of reported hypertensive and normotensive parents. *Journal of Psychosomatic Research, 25,* 261–269.

Marks, I. M. (1986). *Fears, phobias and rituals.* New York: Oxford University Press.

Mathew, R. J., Ho, B. T., Francis, D. J., Taylor, D. L., & Weinman, M. L. (1982). Catecholamines and anxiety. *Acta Psychiatrica Scandinavica, 65,* 142–147.

Mathew, R. J., & Wilson, W. H. (1988). Cerebral blood flow changes induced by CO_2 in anxiety. *Psychiatry Research, 23,* 285–294.

McLeod, D. R., Hoehn-Saric, R., & Stefan, R. L. (1986). Somatic symptoms of anxiety: Comparison of self-reports and physiological measures. *Biological Psychiatry, 21,* 301–310.

Munjack, D. J., & Palmer, R. (1988). Thyroid hormones in panic disorder, panic disorder with agoraphobia, and generalized anxiety disorder. *Journal of Clinical Psychiatry, 49,* 229–231.

Murphy, J. M., Monson, R. R., Olivier, D. C., Sobol, A. M., & Leighton, A. H. (1987). Affective disorders and mortality. *Archives of General Psychiatry, 44,* 473–480.

Noyes, R., Jr., Clarkson, C., Crowe, R. R., Yates, W. R., & McChesney, C. M. (1987). A family study of generalized anxiety disorder. *American Journal of Psychiatry, 144,* 1019–1024.

Öhman, A., Fredrikson, M., & Hugdahl, K.

(1978). Towards an experimental model of simple phobic reactions. *Behavioural Analysis and Modification, 2*, 97–114.

Papadimitriou, G. N., Linkowski, P., Kerkhofs, M., Kempenaers, C., & Mendlewicz, J. (1988). Sleep EEG recordings in generalized anxiety disorder with significant depression. *Journal of Affective Disorders, 15*, 113–118.

Rapee, R. M. (1985). Distinction between panic disorder and generalized anxiety disorder: Clinical presentation. *Australian and New Zealand Journal of Psychiatry, 19*, 227–232.

Rapee, R. M. (1986). Differential response to hyperventilation in panic disorder and generalized anxiety disorder. *Journal of Abnormal Psychology, 95*, 24–28.

Raskin, M., Peeke, H. V. S., Dickman, W., & Pinsker, H. (1982). Panic and generalized anxiety disorder: Developmental antecedents and precipitants. *Archives of General Psychiatry, 39*, 687–689.

Reynolds, C. F., Shaw, D. H., Newton, T. F., Coble, P. A., & Kupfer, D. J. (1983). EEG sleep in outpatients with generalized anxiety: A preliminary comparison with depressed outpatients. *Psychiatry Research, 8*, 81–89.

Richter, J. E., Obrecht, F., Bradley, L. A., Young, L. D., & Anderson, K. O. (1986). Psychological comparison of patients with nutcracker esophagus and irritable bowel syndrome. *Digestive Diseases and Sciences, 31*, 131–138.

Rickels, K., Weisman, K., Norstad, N., Singer, M., Stoltz, D., Brown, A., & Danton, J. (1982). Buspirone and diazepam in anxiety: A controlled study. *Journal of Clinical Psychiatry, 43*(Sec. 2), 81–86.

Riskind, J. H., Beck, A. T., Brown, G., & Steer, R. A. (1987). Taking the measure of anxiety and depression. *Journal of Nervous and Mental Disease, 175*, 476–479.

Riskind, J. H., Beck, A. T., Berchick, R. J., Brown, G., & Steer, R. A. (1987). Reliability of DSM-III diagnoses for major depression and generalized anxiety disorders using the Structured Clinical Interview for DSM-III. *Archives of General Psychiatry, 44*, 817–820.

Rosenbaum, A. H., Schatzberg, A. F., Jost, F. A., Cross, P. D., Wells, L. A., Nai-Siang, J., & Maruta, T. (1983). Urinary free cortisol levels in anxiety. *Psychosomatics, 24*, 835–837.

Roth, M., Mountjoy, C. Q., & Caetano, D. (1982). Further investigations into the relationship between depressive disorders and anxiety states. *Pharmacopsychiatry, 15*, 135–141.

Schneider, L. S., Munjack, D., Severson, J. A., & Palmer, R. (1987). Platelet [3H] imipramine binding in generalized anxiety disorder, panic disorder, and agoraphobia with panic attacks. *Biological Psychiatry, 22*, 59–66.

Schwartz, G. E., Davidson, F. J., & Coleman, D. J. (1978). Patterning of cognitive and somatic processes in the self-regulation of anxiety: Effects of medication versus exercise. *Psychosomatic Medicine, 40*, 321–328.

Schweizer, E. E., Swenson, C. M., Winokur, A., Rickels, K., & Maislin, G. (1986). The dexamethasone suppression test in generalized anxiety disorder. *British Journal of Psychiatry, 149*, 320–322.

Semler, G., Wittchen, H. U., Joschke, K., Zaudig, M., von Geiso, T., Kaiser, S., von Cranach, M., & Pfister, M. (1987). Test–retest reliability of a standardized psychiatric interview (DIS/CIDI). *European Archives of Psychiatry and Neurologic Sciences, 236*, 214–222.

Steer, R. A., Beck, A. R., Riskind, J. H., & Brown, G. (1986). Differentiation of depressive disorders from generalized anxiety by the Beck Depression Inventory. *Journal of Clinical Psychology, 42*, 475–478.

Thomas, A., & Chess, S. (1984). Genesis and evolution of behavioral disorders: From infancy to early adult life. *American Journal of Psychiatry, 141*, 1–9.

Thyer, B. A., Parrish, R. T., Curtis, G. C., Nesse, R. M., & Cameron, O. G. (1985). Ages of onset of DSM-III anxiety disorders. *Comprehensive Psychiatry, 26*, 113–122.

Tiller, J. W. G., Biddle, N., Maguire, K. P., & Davies, B. M. (1988). The dexamethasone suppression test and plasma dexamethasone in generalized anxiety disorder. *Biological Psychiatry, 23*, 261–270.

Torgersen, S. (1983). Genetic factors in anxiety disorders. *Archives of General Psychiatry, 40*, 1085–1089.

Torgersen, S. (1986). Childhood and family characteristics in panic and generalized anxiety disorders. *American Journal of Psychiatry, 143*, 630–632.

Tyrer, P. (1984). Classification of anxiety. *British Journal of Psychiatry, 144*, 78–83.

Tyrer, P. (1986). Classification of anxiety disorders: A critique of DSM-III. *Journal of Affective Disorders, 11*, 99–104.

Uhlenhuth, E. D., Balter, M. B., Mellinger, G. D., Cisin, I. H., & Clinthorne, J. (1983). Symptom checklist syndromes in the general population: Correlations with psychotherapeutic drug use. *Archives of General Psychiatry, 40*, 1167–1173.

von Korf, M., Shapiro, S., Burke, J. D., Teitelbaum, M., Skinner, E. A., German, P., Turner, R. W., Klein, L., & Burns, B. (1987). Anxiety and depression in a primary care clinic. *Archives of General Psychiatry, 44*, 152–156.

Weissman, M. M., & Merikangas, K. R. (1986). The epidemiology of anxiety and panic disorders: An update. *Journal of Clinical Psychiatry, 47*(Suppl.), 11–17.

Weissman, M. M., Myers, J. K., & Hardig, P. S. (1978). Psychiatric disorders in a U.S. urban community. *American Journal of Psychiatry, 135*, 459–462.

Weiner, H. (1985). The psychobiology and physiology of anxiety and fear. In A. H. Tuma & J. Maser (Eds.), *Anxiety and anxiety disorders* (pp. 333–354). New York: Raven Press.

Williams, R. B., Jr., Lane, D., Kuhn, C. M., Melosh, W., White, A. D., & Schanberg, S. M. (1982). Type A behavior and elevated physiological and neuroendocrine responses to cognitive tasks. *Science, 218*, 483–485.

Windheuser, H. J. (1977). Anxious mothers as models for coping with anxiety. *Behavioural Analysis and Modification, 2*, 39–58.

POST-TRAUMATIC STRESS DISORDER

EDITORS' COMMENTS

Combat-related stress reactions have been documented in the clinical literature for decades. With the publication of DSM-III in 1980, these reactions were given acknowledgment in the diagnostic system under the heading of "post-traumatic stress disorder" (PTSD). In addition to combat-related reactions, other extremely traumatic life events — such as natural disasters, personal injury, and so on — outside the realm of usual human experience were considered as possible precipitants for this type of stress reaction.

Given the recency of the inclusion of PTSD in the DSM system, it is only during the past decade that research findings have appeared in the literature. Most of these reports have focused on adult populations, although in the past few years, a few papers have examined the disorder in children. It appears that the core characteristics of PTSD — reexperiencing the trauma, psychic numbing, and increased arousal — occur for both affected children and adults. However, young children may additionally show regressive behavior as well. Such regressive behavior may include separation or stranger anxiety, use of transitional objects, and enuresis/encopresis. In addition, unlike their adult counterparts, children who have experienced a traumatic event usually do not exhibit denial or repression of the trauma, and generally do not report "flashbacks" (although they do report intrusive memories). As Eth speculates in Chapter 19, these cognitive differences between children and adults with PTSD may reflect neuropsychological dissimilarities between the two age groups that have as yet been undefined.

Given the nature of the disorder, one might predict that PTSD has less of a genetic component involved in its pathogenesis. However, as Keane, Litz, and Blake note in Chapter 20, it is possible that certain individuals inherit a psychological vulnerability, through a positive family psychiatric history, that increases the risk of developing PTSD under objectively less stress. Apparently, to date, only one study has been published that has examined the prevalence of psychiatric illness in the families of PTSD patients. While two thirds of the PTSD sample had family histories that were positive for psychopathology, this rate was no higher (and in fact was lower) than rates obtained in depressed (79%) and generalized anxiety disordered (93%) samples.

In diagnosing PTSD, the main difficulty for the clinician may be in overlooking the significance of the psychosocial stressor, thereby misconstruing the symptoms that present as multiple other Axis-I disorders rather than a cohesive syndrome. Alternatively, the diagnosis can be inappropriately given if a particularly sensitive or vulnerable individual develops PTSD-like symptoms following a stressful, but not catastrophic, event (e.g., a minor car accident where no injuries have occurred). It is these considerations that may make PTSD a more difficult diagnosis to establish compared to other anxiety disorders.

CHAPTER 19

POST-TRAUMATIC STRESS DISORDER IN CHILDHOOD

Spencer Eth

DESCRIPTION OF THE DISORDER

The term post-traumatic stress disorder (PTSD) was introduced into the psychiatric nomenclature with the publication of the *Diagnostic and Statistical Manual of Mental Disorders* in 1980 (American Psychiatric Association). However, syndromes that today would be recognized as PTSD have been described in the medical literature for at least a century (Eth, Randolph, & Brown, 1988). In particular, traumatic neurosis, shellshock, combat fatigue, survivor syndrome, gross stress reaction, fright hysteria, stress response syndrome, and rape trauma syndrome all bear strong resemblance to PTSD evoked by various specific stressors.

Children are certainly not immune to the pathogenic impact of traumatic events, although, curiously, they have until recently received scant attention in the published reports of these many syndromes. With very few exceptions children were either omitted entirely or characterized through secondhand accounts from parents and teachers. Lacey's brief clinical paper on the 1966 Aberfan mining disaster (1972), Newman's fo-

rensic derived material on the 1972 Buffalo Creek dam flood (1976), and especially Terr's study of the 1976 Chowchilla school bus kidnapping (1979) laid the foundation for our present understanding of PTSD in children. The emergence of the field of child psychotraumatology (Eth & Pynoos, 1985) is reflected by the first appearance of specific references to children in the section on PTSD in the revision of DSM-III (APA, 1987).

CLINICAL PRESENTATION

PTSD refers to the cluster of symptoms that typically arises after an extremely disturbing event. Although the DSM-III-R avoids etiological assumptions, for PTSD there is the clear implication that the psychosocial stressor, which must be outside the range of usual human experience, would be markedly distressing to almost anyone and actually precipitates the initial intense fear, terror, and helplessness. Traumatic events usually involve a serious life threat, often in the form of a natural or human-induced disaster, accident, or violent crime. The person experiencing psychic trauma may be the direct victim or an eyewitness to the tragic occurrence.

The hallmarks of PTSD are the core symptoms of reexperiencing the trauma, psychic numbing, and increased arousal. The traumatic event is repeatedly reexperienced in several different ways. The person is commonly plagued by recurrent, intrusive, and markedly dysphoric memories and dreams of the trauma. Of equivalent diagnostic significance for younger children is traumatic play, which reenacts elements of the event in a repetitive, stereotyped, and joyless fashion. In unusual instances reexperiencing may be associated with dissociative states, flashbacks, or hallucinatory reliving of the trauma. These phenomena are rare in children, though some suggest that juvenile dissociation as a response to severe physical abuse may signal a predisposition to multiple personality disorder (Kluft, 1985). However, children are susceptible to distress when exposed to events that symbolize or resemble an aspect of the trauma or on the anniversary of its occurrence.

Psychic numbing refers to a group of related symptoms that range from an isolated inability to remember an important feature of the trauma (psychogenic amnesia) to a pervasive erosion of interest in life, that in very young children may present as a regressive loss of acquired skills such as expressive language. Psychic numbing may also be manifested by constricted affect, interpersonal detachment, and pessimism about the future. Another way to minimize the pain of reexperiencing is by persistent avoidance of reminders of the trauma. Suppression of thoughts and feelings as well as attempts to avoid activities or situations reminiscent of the traumatic event are common, though usually unsuccessful efforts to control the subjective distress intrinsic to the disorder.

The final cluster of symptoms that permit the diagnosis of PTSD are the indicators of pathologic psychophysiologic arousal. Irritability, hypervigilance, exaggerated startle reactions, and poor concentration are readily observable and contribute to the visual appearance of nervousness. Not surprisingly, anxious trauma victims have difficulty falling asleep and staying asleep, which compounds their underlying arousal disturbance. These symptoms, unlike the subjective complaints of reexperiencing and numbing, can be elicited by audiovisual stimuli and measured in the laboratory, and thus provide an objective method of validating the disorder and monitoring its response to treatment (Keane, Wolfe, & Taylor, 1987).

EPIDEMIOLOGY

There is no direct information on the prevalence, sex ratio, or familial pattern of PTSD (APA, 1987). However, studies of the psychological effects of disasters and other traumatic events have provided some data on the susceptibility of certain populations to PTSD. The generalizability of these studies is limited by essential differences in the nature of the psychosocial stressor and in the techniques used to measure symptomatology (Green, 1982). "There is no generally agreed on, obviously fundamental taxonomy" of disasters (Kinston & Rosser, 1974). Traumatic events vary along several dimensions, including origin, speed of onset, social preparedness, duration, scope of impact, proportion affected, degree of life threat and suffering, and the potential for reoccurrence. DSM-III-R's statement that the disorder is apparently more severe and longer lasting when the stressor is of human design reaches but one of the many salient variables (APA, 1987). Data collection factors that influence our notions of morbidity involve decisions about subject sampling, choice of interview protocol and rating instrument, and the time interval at follow-up.

In a recent survey of 281 Midwest college students, 80% endorsed having experienced a "highly stressful" event (Segal & Figley, 1988). Most of the incidents involved the unexpected death of a loved one or being hospitalized for serious illness or injury. However, 6% had been abused or assaulted. Perhaps as many as 10% of this high-functioning sample fulfilled the PTSD criterion of a markedly distressing episode outside the usual range of human activity. It is not reported whether any respondents were suffering from post-traumatic symptoms. Terr's (1983) study of a group of "normal" children also provides data on the prevalence of traumatic events and symptoms in a nonclinical population. Of the 25 public school students interviewed, 5 conveyed the psychiatric impression of psychic trauma. Each gave a history of a frightening incident and evidenced characteristic post-traumatic findings. Thus, the cumulative exposure to major psychosocial stressors is considerable and is associated with a significant prevalence of residual post-traumatic symptomatology in a nonclinical sample of children.

Other studies have examined the incidence of psychopathology in a population facing a known stressful event. Milgram and Milgram (1976) found that anxiety ratings in sixth grade Israeli children increased after the 1973 Yom Kippur War.

Massachusetts preschoolers were evaluated before and after a 1978 blizzard and flood. Aggressive conduct and anxiety scores were higher postdisaster and persisted for at least 5 months (Burke, Borus, Burns, Millstein, & Beasley, 1982). Fifth graders from the same town were asked to write stories that were interpreted as revealing emotional distress for as long as 10 months afterward (Burke, Moccia, Borus, & Burns, 1986).

McFarlane conducted a longitudinal study of a large number of school-aged children exposed to a devastating 1983 Australian bushfire. These children were compared to a control group on the Rutter parent and teacher questionnaires administered at 2, 8, and 26 months after the fire. McFarlane, Policansky, and Irwin demonstrated that significant morbidity arose more than 2 months after the disaster and did not diminish over the following 2 years (1987). The children from the burned area had twice the expected rate of emotional and behavioral symptoms. Further, even the mildly affected children appeared to be educationally disadvantaged. The clear implication is that early intervention is imperative, since spontaneous remission of symptoms is uncommon and the long-term impact on achievement can be severe. Another article in this series reports that a major contribution to the children's outcome is the ongoing reactions of their mothers. Post-traumatic phenomena in the parents, overprotective parenting, maternal separation, and changed family function were powerful determinants of emotional and behavioral symptoms in the children (McFarlane, 1987). This finding recalls the World War II observation that children "measure the danger that threatens them chiefly by the reactions of those about them, especially of their trusted parents and teachers" (Papanek, 1942).

The most important work in epidemiology was performed by Pynoos and colleagues (1987) following a fatal sniper attack on the playground of a Los Angeles elementary school in 1984. These investigators responded within days of the event by directly interviewing 159 children exposed in varying degrees to this isolated episode of life-threatening violence. The data, derived from a PTSD reaction index, showed a clear dose-effect relationship. The mean score for the children under fire was twice as great as for those who were already walking home and four times that of the children who were not in school on the day of the shooting. At least 80% of the severely exposed children described the immediate onset of a full range of posttraumatic symptoms, regardless of age, sex, or ethnicity. The children who were not in direct danger rarely demonstrated acute PTSD unless other situational risk factors were also present. Feelings of guilt and knowledge of the deceased victim were both correlated with higher reaction index scores.

Other studies also document extremely high prevalence rates of PTSD following particularly intense stressors. Each of the 23 Chowchilla children abducted in their school bus kidnapping, who were interviewed before the publication of DSM-III, demonstrated unequivocal post-traumatic phenomena (Terr, 1981). Frederick (1986) found that all 15 preadolescent and adolescent boys sexually molested by male mental health professionals fulfilled criteria for PTSD based on their responses to a reaction index. Similarly, out of 10 preschool children who were sexually abused in day care, all received the clinical diagnosis of PTSD (Kiser et al., 1988). In a heterogeneous group of 31 children sexually abused by relatives or strangers, 15 (48.4%) met the full DSM-III-R criteria for PTSD while 25 (80.6%) exhibited one or more symptoms of reexperiencing behavior (McLeer, Deblinger, Atkins, Foa, & Ralphe, 1988). Pynoos and Nader (1988) examined 10 children who were eyewitnesses to the rapes of their mothers. Each of these children were suffering from moderate or severe PTSD. This finding is consistent with the author's research, in which PTSD was ubiquitous in a sample of children present during a parent's homicide (Eth & Pynoos, 1985).

NATURAL HISTORY

The natural history of disaster-related PTSD has been described as consisting of a sequence of psychological reactions. In the initial "threat" phase there is commonly denial of the increasing danger that may serve as an adaptation to chronic environmental stress, such as living comfortably in an earthquake zone. The "impact" phase marks the sudden breakdown of any feeling of person invincibility along with an overwhelming appreciation of the extent of the threat. This relatively brief period is characterized by very intense, possibly fluctuating, affects. Persons may appear stunned, dazed, terrified, unresponsive, or even elated. Children in this traumatic state of regression and helplessness may present as exhibiting disorganized thoughts and behavior, ranging from numbness to frenzy and autonomic dysfunction (Solnit & Kris, 1967). Because of its brevity, the impact phase has not been studied contemporaneously, and the child's later accounts are surely influenced by retrospective elaboration, distortion, and especially suppression.

"Recoil" refers to the return of psychic equilibrium, with its hallmarks of awareness and recall. As the individual struggles to cope, symptoms of dependency, hyperactivity, and irrationality may persist. Over the ensuing days the trauma victim regains considerable personality stability and social function. Some individuals, however, remain in distress during this "aftermath" phase and are troubled by fears, anxiety, sadness, and separation anxiety in young children. These dysphoric and disabling symptoms crystallize into the recognizable pattern of PTSD.

I wish to propose an alternative conceptualization for the natural history of PTSD (see Figure 19.1). This stress/vulnerability model is derived from one offered for schizophrenia (Nuechterlein & Dawson, 1984). The model is activated by the experience of a psychosocial stressor of sufficient magnitude to trigger a symptomatic response. The susceptibility of a particular child to psychic trauma depends on several factors, including genetic, constitutional, and personality makeup; life history; developmental stage; state of mind; and the content and intensity of the event. These factors determine the degree of competence of the child's stimulus barrier, coping abilities, and autonomic regulation. When the child is exposed to an event that causes helplessness in the face of anxiety, danger, and arousal, it can be inferred that these functions have been overwhelmed. The resulting transient intermediate state is that brief, critical interval that validates the experience of psychictrauma and heralds the onset of PTSD with its characteristic constellation of signs and symptoms.

IMPAIRMENT AND COMPLICATIONS

It may hold heuristic value to consider separately the immediate, early, and late effects of childhood PTSD. This perspective will draw heavily on the elegant studies performed by Terr on the kidnapped children of Chowchilla (1979, 1981, 1983). The recently traumatized child generally appears as frightened and unable to adapt to new people and situations. The presence of visual, and perhaps auditory, misperceptions and hallucinations in the child's account reflects the traumatic disruption of reality testing. Time sense may also be compromised, with distortions in time duration and misordering the sequence of events commonly observed. Over the course of days and weeks, the traumatized child's fears generalize to both trauma-related and mundane items. In severe instances the child may develop panic symptoms when confronted with an object or situation that is linked with the trauma. Under these circumstances the associated anticipatory anxiety may result in the child's refusing to separate from a parent or leave the home. Such a child may also qualify for the diagnoses of phobia, panic disorder, or panic disorder with agoraphobia. In a case where the child's anxiety has infiltrated into all daily activities, the additional diagnosis of overanxious disorder may be appropriate.

Post-traumatic dreams constitute a group of typical early effects. Some children report repetitive dreams of the traumatic event that may resemble the intrusive, painful memories of the awake state. Others experience modified dreams or nightmares based on the event. Clinicians must be alert to two uniquely post-traumatic dream forms that can be deeply troubling to the child. In one, the child dreams about his or her own premature death, while in the second, the dream is felt to be predictive of the future or prophetic, much as the conscious child may search for omens. Traumatized children very commonly exhibit post-traumatic play that is stereotyped and joyless. This play may act out an element of the trauma, occasionally in a dangerous way involving weapons or accident-prone behavior. Unaffected children may participate in the play sequence, being assigned roles by the traumatized child. The author interviewed a 10-year-old boy who witnessed a youngster's suicide. Upon returning to school, the boy gathered all his classmates around to watch his reenactment of the suicide (Eth, Pynoos, & Carlson, 1984).

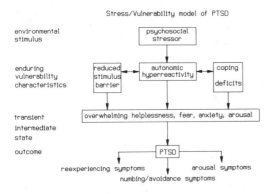

Figure   19.1.   Stress/vulnerability model of PTSD.

Many of the long-term effects of childhood trauma include continuing elaborations and extensions of the earlier findings of the fears and repetitive phenomena. Further, children may, for the first time report pessimistic thoughts about their own lives and futures. Memories of the traumatic occurrence may lose some affect and clarity in their retelling. However, children with chronic PTSD do remain anxious, fearful, and avoidant. As they grow older, these youngsters may become increasingly ashamed by their helplessness at the time of their trauma and often are bothered by a lingering conviction of guilt for not having done more. Prominent personality alterations have been noted, and there is concern that these may reflect permanent changes in character. Prolonged variations in mood may complicate the recovery of traumatized children. McLeer et al. (1988) has found that 58% of sexually abused children score as depressed on the children's depression inventory. Molestation victims may also have persistent problems with trust and with sexual dysfunction.

When the traumatic event causes the death of a parent, the child must contend with grief as well as trauma. It is widely accepted that children can demonstrate a range of mourning responses, whose expression is shaped by the child's developmental phase, personality, and culture. Grief-stricken children may feel sad, lonely, angry, guilty, and tired as they struggle to face the reality of their loss. If that child has also been traumatized, as when he or she witnesses a parent's violent death, then the natural grieving process will be disrupted by the intrusion of traumatic symptoms. For example, painful images of a murdered parent will contaminate memories of previous, happier interactions and interfere with reminiscing. Reunion fantasies may serve both to recapture the lost parent and to reverse the traumatic mode of death. For certain children, depressed affect combines with the desire to join the deceased to produce frank suicidal ideation. For other children pathological mourning can contribute to the clinical picture of a major depressive episode.

DIFFERENTIAL DIAGNOSIS

The principal difficulty in establishing a definitive diagnosis of PTSD is overlooking or devaluating the pathogenic significance of the psychosocial stressor, while misconstruing the nonspecific symptoms of the disorder. The longer the duration of time since the traumatic event, the more likely the chronic sequela will be attributed to another condition. Imagine an adolescent complaining of failing school, aggressive behavior, marijuana use, bad dreams, and feeling "weird." At first glance, this adolescent may be presenting with delinquency, substance abuse, or an identity disturbance. Only through careful questioning would the relevant history of a psychic trauma be elicited, permitting the reframing of his symptoms as manifestations of PTSD. For some children, PTSD may be complicated by comorbid conditions, including overanxious disorder, panic disorder, phobia, and depression. In cases of brutal physical and sexual abuse, children may respond by dissociation or depersonalization, which itself would be listed as a possible supplemental diagnosis. Eventually, a few such patients have developed multiple personality disorder, which becomes the primary focus of therapeutic attention (Kluft, 1985).

Substance abuse is prevalent in modern society, and as the example illustrates, seems to be present in even greater frequency among adolescent patients with PTSD. Some of these teenagers have preexisting alcohol and drug abuse, while others begin to drink and use drugs in an effort to relieve dysphoric symptoms. Similarly, emerging personality disorders are often seen in adolescence, but appear to be overrepresented in the population of patients with PTSD. If this impression is valid, it may be that certain character traits predispose or promote the experience of psychic trauma by lowering resilience to stress. An alternative hypothesis is that the syndrome of PTSD disrupts character formation, facilitating the development of personality disorders. Regardless of the nature of the interaction, the dual presence of PTSD and substance abuse and/or personality disorder complicates and exacerbates the symptomatology of these syndromes.

Just as the diagnosis of PTSD may be missed, the condition may also be attributed in error. Technically, the diagnosis requires the occurrence of an event outside the range of usual human experience that would be markedly distressing to almost anyone. If a particularly sensitive child develops symptoms following a stressful but not catastrophic event, then a diagnosis of an adjustment disorder or an anxiety disorder not otherwise specified would have to be made. It is axiomatic that attention must be paid to the possibility that the patient's complaints and history are not genuine. Factitious PTSD has been described for adults who are stimulating or exaggerating their symptoms to maximize financial reward. Such motivation is unlikely in childhood, although reports of false allegations of sexual abuse raises the suspicion that an analogous dynamic may be operating (Eth, 1988).

CASE EXAMPLE

Nine-year-old Ted was eager to enroll in a 3-week computer summer camp held on the campus of a local college. The program was directed by Bob Smith, a successful middle-aged computer consultant. Ted's mother and stepfather agreed, and Ted left for his first experience living away from home.

Early the third morning at camp, Ted was alone in his dormitory room. Bob entered the room and called Ted over to him. Bob grabbed Ted and whispered in his ear, "You're an excellent student, and you deserve the best." Bob starting hugging, kissing, and rubbing against Ted and warned, "If you tell anybody, you will go to jail." While Ted sat on his bed crying, he noticed that his pants were wet. A few days later Ted was in the bathroom after showering. Bob walked in, pulled off Ted's towel and with one arm behind Ted's back began hugging and kissing him on the face and lips. Ted tried to scream, but Bob squeezed tightly and threatened, "Don't shout or this will happen again and I'll kill your parents." Ted was scared by the painful way he was held, and he had the thought that Bob might try to murder him.

One night during the second week of camp Bob slipped into Ted's room and crawled into bed with him. Bob hugged and kissed Ted, whispering "I like you and I'd like to be your father." Bob then pulled Ted's pajama bottoms down and proceeded to perform fellatio on the frightened child. Having finished, Bob pulled up Ted's pajamas and silently crept out of the room. Ted was very afraid and embarrassed. Assuming that he was the only boy affected, Ted decided not to tell anyone what had happened to him. The next day several boys ran away from camp. That afternoon the police arrived to release the children to their parents.

Ted did not confide to his mother what had happened to him because he felt "scared" for his parents' safety. After a few days Ted was interviewed by a police detective, at which time he first admitted details of the sexual abuse. However, Ted was too humiliated and frightened to disclose all three incidents, and did not mention the act of oral copulation. Ted later was called upon to testify at Bob Smith's preliminary hearing and subsequent trial. Ted recalls his court appearances as painful: "It hurts when they make it seem like you lie. Bob was sitting there staring at me." Bob Smith was convicted the following summer and was sentenced to eight years in state prison.

Ted began to have nightmares while at the computer camp. These anxiety dreams featured Bob chasing Ted down a hallway, holding him, and trying to chain or knife him. The nightmares increased in frequency and intensity over the next few months, despite Bob's arrest. In addition, Ted became fearful of being alone in his own bedroom or in the family bathroom. He would become so terrified that he could not sleep and would be forced to seek refuge every night in bed with his older sister. His fears generalized to the point where Ted was "afraid of everything" and demanded to stay at home to protect himself from "getting held up or shot."

Ten months after the molestation, Ted's mother sought psychotherapy for the family. Ted, who had received no previous psychiatric treatment, was seen approximately twice weekly by a psychologist, while other family members were seen together once a week. After 4 months of therapy, Ted revealed for the first time to his therapist all the details of the molestation, including the episode of oral copulation. Bob was, by then, free on bail pending appeal. Despite his complete disclosure, Ted became increasingly anxious, depressed, and obsessed with "all the bad things that happened to me." He expressed thoughts of cutting his wrists, and actually put a kitchen knife to his wrists, "but I was afraid of the pain." Ted's therapist, concerned about his deteriorating course and the threat of suicide, referred Ted to a psychiatrist, who admitted him to the hospital 11 months after the molestation.

Mental status examination at the time of hospitalization revealed an agitated, frightened youngster with cold, moist palms and tremulous lips and extremities. He was fully oriented to person, place, time, and situation and showed no difficulty with recent or remote memory. He admitted to fears of being harmed by strangers or by Bob. He was terrified at being alone, especially in the bathroom or at night. He also complained of being sad and tearful, and requested help for "being mixed up by what I've been through." Physical examination was essentially normal.

Ted is the second child born to his natural parents, his sister having been born 5 years earlier. Ted's mother recalls having received medications for premature labor. Delivery was, however, induced at term. Ted's infancy was complicated by a milk allergy, but his developmental milestones were all within normal limits. Ted's childhood was apparently unremarkable until a series of tragic events disrupted the family. When Ted was 5 years old, his father committed suicide by carbon monoxide poisoning in his car parked in the driveway. Ted was home and was exposed to the associated commotion. When Ted became suicidal after the molestation, he wondered whether he was going "to end up like my dad."

About 1 month after his father's suicide, a man broke into the home and attempted to rape Ted's mother at knifepoint. Ted witnessed this attack; the man was later apprehended and prosecuted. Later the same year, Ted and his mother were involved in a car accident resulting in injuries to both of them. Ted sustained a serious tongue laceration and was hospitalized for a day. Following these family crises Ted's mother was forced to sell their house because of severe financial difficulties. The family received no psychiatric assistance at that time. The mother noted that Ted was very protective of her, especially because she had developed a seizure disorder since the automobile accident.

Ted repeated kindergarten to catch up in size and age to his classmates. While in second grade a learning disability was identified. The public school arranged for a reading specialist to work with Ted for about a year, and he has since done well. Ted enjoys school and receives good grades for his academics and behavior. He is quite popular with his peers and teachers and makes a consistent effort to please.

Ted's mother remarried when Ted was 6 years old. Ted's stepfather was divorced with two sons a few years older than Ted. His children spend every other weekend in the home. Ted's parents work for the federal government and are homeowners in the suburbs of a large city. Prior to the molestation, the family reported being quite happy together. Since then, Ted's symptoms have worsened despite the family's efforts to reassure him of their love and his safety.

While in the hospital Ted received psychological testing. His full-scale IQ on the WISC-R was 97, though there was a significant discrepancy between verbal and performance scores. On projective tests he saw himself as having little control over external circumstances, leaving him feeling overwhelmed and powerless. He described a boy playing happily, when "all of a sudden he tripped and fell." It was interpreted that his anxiety and depression were associated with a preoccupation with the molestation. On Card IV of Rorschach he began by describing a "small castle surrounded by dark trees" and followed with a "monster with his large tongue out." Elsewhere, there were suggestions of strong aggressive impulses underlying his more passive exterior. Overall Ted was found to be a very depressed, fearful child whose experience of sexual abuse left him feeling overwhelmed, powerless, and suicidal.

Ted's initial response to psychiatric hospitalization was positive. Nursing notes indicated that he experienced no sleeping or behavior problems and that he tended to be "cooperative, pleasant, and active" on the ward. However, his therapist found him to be anxious and depressed and to delineate enumerable phobic situations, including fears of being alone, harmed and murdered, and fears of his parents being kidnapped. Further, while on pass all his symptoms rapidly resurged. In the hospital Ted received the following forms of therapy: daily psychotherapy, twice weekly art therapy, weekly movement therapy, occupational therapy, multiple family group therapy, and special educational services.

Over the next several months Ted's participation in therapy deepened, and his improvement extended to all settings. Treatment focused on his fears and on the depressive themes of guilt and low self-esteem. As Ted's suicidality diminished he was transferred to the open unit, and the time spent on pass out of the hospital increased. Ted was finally discharged after 6 months. At that time his therapist noted that Ted's presenting symptoms had been greatly alleviated or eradicated.

Ted was examined 3 years after his traumatic molestation. At age 12 Ted presented as a thin, casually dressed prepubertal male. Ted was appropriate and responsive in the interview situation. He seemed to have no difficulty separating from his mother and appeared comfortable and alert throughout the session. Ted's speech was clear and coherent, and he answered all questions with minimal hesitation. Cognition was judged to be at age level, with good memory function. Ted's concentration was excellent, and he demonstrated no evidence of disordered thinking or of psychotic symptomatology.

Ted's thought content was marked by intrusive, dysphoric recollections of the molestation experiences. Consistent with these memories, anxiety was the predominant affect, and his mood was depressed. When Ted described what had happened to him, he became tearful and subdued.

Ted endorsed a history of all the DSM-III diagnostic criteria for post-traumatic stress disorder, including (1) reexperiencing of the trauma with recurrent memories and dreams; (2) psychic numbing with diminished interest in school, feelings of detachment from others, and constricted affect ("zoned out"); and (3) related symptoms of sleep disturbance, avoidant behavior, and guilt. In addition, prior to his hospitalization Ted's depression had worsened, perhaps severely enough to qualify as a major depressive episode with active suicidal ideation.

Since discharge from the hospital Ted's depressive symptoms have resolved, and his post-traumatic stress disorder is in remission. He attends sixth grade at the local public school and receives B's and C's on his report card. He states that he might feel sad from time to time, as for instance when he knew that he had to speak about the incident, and he occasionally experiences fears or bad dreams. These intermittent symptoms do not currently interfere with his daily functioning. Ted tries not to think about what had happened and hopes it "won't make a difference" in his life. He would like some day to become a police officer and have a family.

Ted is a 12-year-old boy who is in the process of recovering from a severe episode of post-traumatic stress disorder. He was in his usual state of mental health prior to his experience of several incidents of sexual abuse perpetrated by a camp director, who has since been convicted in criminal court. Ted developed symptoms of nightmares, painful memories, fears, and intense sadness almost immediately. Significant premorbid factors, especially his father's suicide and the attempted rape of his mother, contributed to the severity of Ted's distress, but were not the proximate cause. His deteriorating course and the emergence of active suicidal ideation, in the context of psychotherapy, appropriately prompted psychiatric hospitalization. Although Ted's post-traumatic stress disorder is now in remission, he may be predisposed to the future emergence of anxiety, depression, and post-traumatic stress disorder.

CONTINUITY AND DISCONTINUITY WITH ADULT PRESENTATION

Until now the features of PTSD common to children of all ages have been emphasized. In general, children respond to psychic trauma with changes in cognition, affect, interpersonal relations, impulse control, behavior, and vegetative function. There are, however, important differences in phenomenology according to the developmental phase of the child. For the purpose of charting these phase-specific differences, the developmental period will be divided into preschool age, school age, and adolescence (Eth & Pynoos, 1985b).

The capacity to encode and retrieve a verbal memory of a traumatic experience begins for most persons between 30 and 36 months (Terr, 1988). Prior to that time infants may react to psychic trauma, but the ensuing symptoms are nonspecific, and confirmation of their etiology is doubtful (Terr, 1985). The 3-year-old will demonstrate changes in personality, play, and fears that reflect the traumatic event. Verbal recollections are usually spotty, with single, brief traumas more easily recalled. These memories may be embellished and reworked as the child grows older. Condensations with subsequent upsetting incidents and with later, developmentally meaningful symbols are common.

Preschoolers are particularly helpless when confronted by great danger and may require the most assistance to recover their equilibrium. In the face of fear from an external threat, they feel defenseless, being hardly able to image how to manage the traumatic situation. Young children may choose to escape or remain, to look or turn away, to stay awake or try to sleep, but these are all the limited choices of a passive observer, not of an active participant. Children under 4 years of age are notably dependent and will readily respond to parental anxiety with an intensification of their own distress. Occasionally, older preschool children will imagine superhero powers protecting them from attack or will fantasize aid from an older sibling or relative.

More than any other age group, preschool children can initially appear as withdrawn, subdued, or even mute. Glover (1942) described a girl, who, during a London air raid, sat in place for several days and would not spontaneously talk, eat, or play. Many children maintain a stance of silent aloofness, refusing to speak of the traumatic occurrence. This should not be mistaken for amnesia, since the child may, after some delay, choose to reveal the details of the incident to a loved one. Bergen (1958) wrote of a girl who witnessed the aftermath of her mother's fatal stabbing, but told not a soul until a session with her analyst many months later.

Preschool children typically engage in reenactments and play around traumatic themes. Bergen's patient carefully painted her hands red and pretended to stab herself with the paintbrush. A 3¹/₂-year-old boy was observed in treatment replaying an attack by a wild animal (Maclean, 1977). Disregarding other details, these young children focus on the central action of the traumatic encounter. The author interviewed a 3-year-old boy who repeatedly acted out the phrase: "Daddy squished Mommy's neck." This core memory became reified in an endless, burdened play sequence that failed to relieve his anxiety or reverse the tragic outcome of his mother's death.

Young children are prone to regression in the wake of a traumatic experience. Anxious attachment behavior, intensified separation and stranger anxiety, and a return to the use of transitional objects are emblematic of the early response of the traumatized preschooler. Whining, moaning, crying, and throwing tantrums are also frequently seen. Elizur and Kaffman (1982) have characterized this cluster of symptoms as an "overanxious-dependent" reaction. An example was the little girl who was still sleeping each night in her mother's bed 2 years after the Buffalo Creek flood (Newman, 1976). Other regressive behaviors include lapses in toilet training, self-stimulation, and the loss of previously attained skills.

Several accounts of traumatized preschoolers have commented on the incidence of nightmares and sleep disturbances in this age group. The author has been impressed with the frequency of stage four sleep disorders, such as somnambulism, sleep talking, night terrors, and restlessness. Other noteworthy symptoms documented in the literature include aggressive conduct, anxiety, fears, and avoidance behavior.

The school-aged child exhibits a wider range of cognitive, behavioral, and emotional responses to psychic trauma. In the cognitive domain, school-children often display the features of cognitive constriction seen in adults. This dullness, obtuseness, and functional impairment of intelligence are most apparent in the corresponding decline in school performance. The child's decreasing ability to concentrate in class may derive from the distracting intrusion of traumatic memories, from an inhibition of spontaneous thought consistent with an evolving cognitive style of forgetting, or from the interference of anxious and depressed affects on mental processes.

School-aged children are no longer bound to the passive role of spectator, but can become participants in the traumatic event, if only in fantasy. In fact, imagined plans of action may reflect the magical invulnerability of this older age group and frequently involve fantasies of rescuing those injured in the traumatic occurrence. Waelder (1967) wrote of a 7-year-old boy who stood frozen as his father was gored by a stag. Although he had been a terrified witness at the time, in his later play he became the hero who kills the stag and saves his desperate father. These children may also devise inner plans of action extending after the traumatic event. Youngsters who have seen a parent murdered may fantasize extracting revenge by themselves, without the assistance of police, courts, or prisons. After learning that his parent's killer had been apprehended, an 8-year-old challenged his friends: "Let's get some bats and play baseball with his head!" These fantasies may also serve to relieve the child's guilt over not having done more during the trauma.

Some latency age children spend considerable time discussing the fine details of the traumatic event. By so doing, the child may be temporarily defended from feelings of anxiety and fear. This obsessional ploy can become a form of fixation to the trauma when it leads to unemotional, journalistic accounts that imply a failure of trauma mastery. The reverse is also possible, where the child remains in a perpetual state of arousal, as if to prepare for imminent danger. The terms pseudophobia (Krystal, 1978) and traumatophobia (Rado, 1942) also refer to a dread of the recurrence of the traumatic experience of its associations. This hypervigilance may permit the child to replace memories of the past trauma with self-initiated fantasies of future threat. A 7-year-old, who witnessed his father murdered by a stranger, emphasized his current fear of personal harm to the exclusion of all reference to the actual violence his family had suffered.

School-aged children display a diversity of behavioral alterations in the aftermath of trauma. Parents and teachers complain that children afflicted with PTSD seem both different and inconsistent, often becoming irritable, rude, and provocative. As a consequence peer relationships can suffer, especially if the child turns inhibited, aggressive, or unpredictable. Children themselves may be aware of these changes and may react with a loss of self-esteem and self-confidence. Traumatic play is more elaborate and sophisticated in the older child. As these children are better able to communicate with words, they depend less on actions to recreate the traumatic situations. School-aged children may also involve their friends in redramatizations and trauma-related games, as, for example, the "tornado games" alluded to by Bloch and colleagues (1956).

Schoolchildren can undergo an intense perceptual experience during a trauma. Depending on the nature of the event, any or all sensory modalities may be activated. In addition, the child may notice the concomitant autonomic arousal. Children in this age group are particularly susceptible to the development of psychosomatic symptoms, such as stomach pains, headaches, and other bodily complaints. Following a disaster at school, visits to the school nurse multiply without a corresponding increase in organic illness. Krystal (1978) attributed the incidence of these symptoms to a post-traumatic resomatization of affect. Others believe that the children may be identifying with victims of real physical injury. The author favors the hypothesis that the latency age child's greater awareness of and investment in body image increases the likelihood of linking anxious affect and intrusive memories associated with the trauma to autonomic perceptions in a recurring way.

The manifestations of PTSD during adolescence begin to resemble the adult syndrome. In fact, a not uncommon response to adolescent trauma is the precipitation of a precocious entrance into childhood or a premature closure of identity formation. The feelings of anger, shame, and betrayal can erode the traumatized teenager's position in the social group and propel an anxious search for a new community. A group of veterans who served as adolescents in Vietnam were found years later to exhibit chronic PTSD compounded by drug abuse, rage, and despair. Their profound disillusionment and moral stagnation raises a concern that these young adults are languishing in a state of perpetual, pathological adolescence (Jackson, 1982).

The traumatized adolescent frequently embarks upon a period of acting-out behavior characterized by truancy, sexual indiscretion, substance abuse, and delinquency. These adolescents adopt a rebellious attitude that is seemingly impervious to intervention by authority figures. Because of their access to automobiles and weapons, the combination of poor impulse control, bad judgment, and reenactment behavior can be life-threatening. A few adolescents have subsequently explained that their use of illicit drugs was a way to relieve the dysphoria arising from the traumatic event. They may also be engaging in self-destructive activities in order to expiate guilt.

Adolescents are capable of anticipating how the trauma will personally affect their future lives. Unlike their younger counterparts, they no longer envision themselves as invulnerable. Rather, they are quite sensitive to their imperfections and to the stigmatization that may result from a traumatic event. Some teenagers vow never to marry or have children in order to spare their offspring what they have endured. Anniversary reactions to the trauma may prompt a reaffirmation of their conviction not to tempt fate. In the extreme case of adolescent Holocaust survivors, chronic identity diffusion, interpersonal difficulties, and poor work values attest to the potentially devastating consequence of trauma during this developmental phase (Koenig, 1964).

Over the course of the developmental period, the phenomenology of childhood PTSD comes to resemble that of adulthood. However, there remain salient differences that may reflect fundamental, but as yet undefined, neuropsychological dissimilarities between adults and children. Unlike adults who have experienced a traumatic event, children do not commonly exhibit denial and repression of the trauma. Although it may be emotionally difficult for children to describe the details of the incident, they retain clear, accessible memories. Amnesia for single episode traumas is of yet unreported in childhood and may be safely assumed to be extremely rare. In fact vivid, specific childhood recollections of these events may be held with unusual clarity for many years (Eth & Pynoos, 1985). In addition to failing to demonstrate denial or amnesia for discrete traumatic events, youngsters as a rule do not complain of "flashbacks." They do experience intrusive, dysphoric memories, but these lack the sudden, striking effect of what adults characterize as a true "flashback." However, children exhibit the symptom of traumatic play that is unknown in adults. The behavioral performance of reenactments exemplifies the syndrome of PTSD in young children. There is some preliminary evidence that repeated acts of severe physical and sexual abuse during childhood may be associated with a defensive reliance on dissociation and a propensity for the formation of multiple personality disorder (Kluft, 1985). If this impression is confirmed, then this type of psychic trauma may be uniquely pathologic to the developing organism.

SUMMARY

Symptoms of reexperiencing, avoidance, and arousal have always been a fact of life for children experiencing an overwhelming event. Not until 1980 was this syndrome formally identified as PTSD, and not until 1987 were child-specific examples included in the official diagnostic manual. It is now possible for all mental health professionals to recognize that this disorder is a common response in children exposed to the variety of traumas endemic to modern society. Primary prevention of PTSD would require the eradication of violence and disasters, and is not possible. Because the syndrome will cause prolonged distress and disability for the child, early diagnosis is critical. Fortunately, its many signs and symptoms can be reliably elicited in clinical interviews of children, parents, and teachers. And although treatment has not been addressed in this chapter, it is important to note that effective therapeutic interventions are readily available. Childhood PTSD has truly come of age.

REFERENCES

American Psychiatric Association. (1980). *Diagnostic and statistical manual of mental disorders* (3rd ed.). Washington, DC: Author.

American Psychiatric Association. (1987). *Diagnostic and statistical manual of mental disorders* (3rd ed. rev.). Washington, DC: Author.

Bergen, M. (1958). Effect of severe trauma on a 4-year-old child. *Psychoanalytic Study of the Child, 13*, 407–429.

Bloch, D. A., Silber, E., & Perry, S. E. (1956). Some factors in the emotional reaction of children to disaster. *American Journal of Psychiatry, 113*, 416–422.

Burke, J. D., Borus, J. F., Burns, B. J., Millstein, K. H., & Beasley, M. C. (1982). Changes in children's behavior after a natural disaster. *American Journal of Psychiatry, 94*, 107–113.

Burke, J. D., Moccia, P., Borus, J. F., & Burns, B. J. (1986). Emotional distress in fifth-grade children ten months after a natural disaster. *Journal of the American Academy of Child Psychiatry, 25*, 536–541.

Elizur, E., & Kaffman, M. (1982). Children's bereavement reactions following death of the father: II. *Journal of the American Academy of Child Psychiatry, 21*, 474–480.

Eth, S. (1988). The child victim as witness in sexual abuse proceedings. *Psychiatry, 51*, 221–232.

Eth, S., & Pynoos, R. S. (Eds.). (1985a). *Post-traumatic stress disorder in children*. Washington, DC: American Psychiatric Press.

Eth, S., & Pynoos, R. S. (1985b). Developmental perspective on psychic trauma in childhood. In C. Figley (Ed.), *Trauma and its wake* (pp. 36–52). New York: Brunner/Mazel.

Eth, S., & Pynoos, R. S. (1985). Psychiatric interventions with children traumatized by violence. In D. H. Schetky & E. P. Benedek (Eds.), *Emerging issues in child psychiatry and the law* (pp. 285–309). New York: Brunner/Mazel.

Eth, S., Pynoos, R. S., & Carlson, G. A. (1984). An unusual case of self-inflicted death in childhood. *Suicide and Life-Threatening Behavior, 14*, 157–165.

Eth, S., Randolph, E. T., & Brown, J. A. (1988). Post-traumatic stress disorder. In J. G. Howells (Ed.), *Modern perspectives in the psychiatry of the neuroses* (pp. 210–234). New York: Brunner/Mazel.

Frederick, C. J. (1986). Post-traumatic stress disorder and child molestation. In A. Burgess & C. Hartman (Eds.), *Sexual exploitation of clients by mental health professionals* (pp. 133–151). New York: Praeger.

Glover, E. (1942). Notes on the psychological effects of war conditions on the civilian population. *International Journal of Psychoanalysis, 23*, 17–37.

Green, B. L. (1982). Assessing levels of psychological impairment following disaster. *Journal of Nervous and Mental Disease, 170*, 544–552.

Jackson, H. C. (1982). Moral nihilism: Developmental arrest as a sequela to combat stress. *Adolescent Psychiatry, 10*, 228–242.

Keane, T. M., Wolfe, J., & Taylor, K. J. (1987). Post-traumatic stress disorder: Evidence for diagnostic validity and methods of psychological assessment. *Journal of Clinical Psychology, 43*, 32–43.

Kinston, W., & Rosser, R. (1974). Disaster: Effects on mental and physical state. *Journal of Psychosomatic Research, 18*, 437–456.

Kiser, L. J., Ackerman, B. J., Brown, E., Edwards, N. B., McCalgan, E., Pugh, R., & Pruitt, D. B. (1983). Post-traumatic stress disorder in young children: A reaction to purported sexual abuse. *Journal of the American Academy of Child and Adolescent Psychiatry, 27*, 645–649.

Kluft, R. P. (1985). *Childhood antecedents of multiple personality*. Washington, DC: American Psychiatric Press.

Koenig, W. K. (1964). Chronic or persisting identity diffusion. *American Journal of Psychiatry, 113*, 416–422.

Krystal, H. (1978). Trauma and affects. *Psychoanalytic Study of the Child, 22*, 81–116.

Lacey, G. (1972). Observations on Aberfan. *Journal of Psychosomatic Research, 16*, 257–260.

Maclean, G. (1977). Psychic trauma and traumatic neurosis. *Canadian Psychiatric Association Journal, 22*, 71–76.

McFarlane, A. C. (1987). Post-traumatic phenomena in a longitudinal study of children following a natural disaster. *Journal of the American Academy of Child and Adolescent Psychiatry, 26*, 760–764.

McFarlane, A. C., Policansky, S. K., & Irwin, C. (1987). A longitudinal study of the psychological morbidity in children due to a natural disaster. *Psychological Medicine, 17*, 727–738.

McLeer, S. V., Deblinger, E., Atkins, M. S., Foa, E. B., & Ralphe, D. L. (1988). Post-traumatic stress disorder in sexually abused children. *Journal of the American Academy of Child and Adolescent Psychiatry, 27*, 650–654.

Milgram, R. M., & Milgram, N. A. (1976). The effects of the Yom Kippur War on anxiety level in Israeli children. *Journal of Psychology, 94*, 107–113.

Newman, C. J. (1976). Children of disaster: Clinical observations at Buffalo Creek. *American Journal of Psychiatry, 133*, 306–312.

Neuchterlein, K. H., & Dawson, M. E. (1984). A heuristic vulnerability model of schizophrenic episodes. *Schizophrenia Bulletin, 10*, 300–313.

Papanek, E. (1942). My experiences with fugitive children in Europe. *Nervous Child, 2*, 301–307.

Pynoos, R. S., Frederick, C., Nader, K., Arroyo, W., Steinberg, A., Eth, S., Nunez, F., & Fairbanks, L. (1987). Life threat and posttraumatic stress in schoolage children. *Archives of General Psychiatry, 44*, 1057, 1063.

Pynoos, R. S., & Nader, K. (1988). Children who witness the sexual assaults of their mothers. *Journal of the American Academy of Child and Adolescent Psychiatry, 27*, 567–572.

Rado, S. (1942). Psychodynamics and treatment of traumatic war neurosis (traumatophobia). *Psychosomatic Medicine, 4*, 362–368.

Segal, A. S., & Figley, C. R. (1988). Stressful events. *Hospital and Community Psychiatry, 39*, 998.

Solnit, A. J., & Kris, M. (1967). Trauma and infantile experience. In S. S. Furst (Ed.), *Psychic trauma* (pp. 179–220). New York: Basic Books.

Terr, L. (1979). Children of Chowchilla: A study of psychic trauma. *Psychoanalytic Study of the Child, 34*, 547–623.

Terr, L. (1981). Psychic trauma in children: Observations following the Chowchilla schoolbus kidnapping. *American Journal of Psychiatry, 138*, 14–19.

Terr, L. C. (1983). Life attitudes, dreams, and psychic trauma in a group of "normal" children. *Journal of the American Academy of Child Psychiatry, 22*, 221–230.

Terr, L. C. (1985). The baby as a witness. In D. H. Schetky & E. P. Benedek (Eds.), *Emerging issues in child psychiatry and the law* (pp. 313–323). New York: Brunner/Mazel.

Terr, L. C. (1988). What happens to early memories of trauma? *Journal of the American Academy of Child and Adolescent Psychiatry, 27*, 96–104.

Waelder, R. (1967). Trauma and the variety of extraordinary challenges. In S. S. Furst (Ed.), *Psychic trauma* (pp. 221–234). New York: Basic Books.

CHAPTER 20

POST-TRAUMATIC STRESS DISORDER IN ADULTHOOD

Terence M. Keane
Brett T. Litz
Dudley David Blake

DESCRIPTION OF THE DISORDER

When individuals are exposed to extremely stressful life events, a certain portion of them develops the constellation of symptoms now known as post-traumatic stress disorder (PTSD). For some, the disorder is immediately present and the symptoms are intense and disturbing; for others, there is a gradual exacerbation of symptoms over months and years giving the appearance of a delay in onset; for others still, as in the case of incest, the effects of the traumatic events may not be apparent immediately, but surface only when new information regarding the meaning of this event becomes clear to the individual.

The first type of PTSD is referred to as acute, while the last two types are generally viewed as chronic PTSD due to the length of time since the onset of traumatic event. Acute PTSD is most readily seen in individuals who have been in some form of community or personal disaster and where crisis intervention teams are readily available and are provided by community resources. Floods, tornados, fires, train crashes, and airplane accidents are all examples of extreme stress-

ors that stimulate the provision of large-scale community resources, including mental health resources to the survivors and their families. Here, individuals will be observed who display a range of emotional responses to the event, including those syndromes called PTSD. Rape and crime victims are also good examples of people who may have acute PTSD and who seek mental health services.

Chronic PTSD is by far the most common form of PTSD seen by clinicians in clinics, hospitals, and practices. Typically, the symptoms of PTSD have gradually worsened for these individuals, yielding over time significant emotional, vocational, and interpersonal impairment. Survivors of sexual abuse, war, political imprisonment and torture, assault, moving vehicle accidents, and other life-threatening events are individuals who are at risk for developing PTSD.

As will be explained in detail in the next section, PTSD is characterized by a host of reliving experiences that can preoccupy the person with florid details of the traumatic event. Nightmares, intrusive images, ruminative thoughts and feelings, and intensely frightening hallucinations known as flashbacks are examples of these reliving experiences. PTSD is also accompanied by social withdrawal, avoidance behavior, and numbing of emotional reactance, all of which serve to isolate the individual and impair social support systems. Symptoms of increased arousal, indicative of the imbalance between physiological activation and inhibition, complete the diagnostic criteria for PTSD. Difficulties with sleep, concentration impairment, physiological hyperreactivity to cues of the traumatic event, hypervigilance, and startle responses are additional symptoms of arousal that are associated with PTSD. Yet, it is widely recognized that the diagnostic criteria for PTSD and the clinical presentation of patients with PTSD are not always mirror images of one another (Keane, Wolfe, & Taylor, 1987).

CLINICAL PRESENTATION

PTSD is a clinical syndrome that is influenced by pretrauma, trauma, and posttrauma factors. The formally recognized signs and symptoms postulated to comprise PTSD were described in the previous section. However, the presenting symptoms of individuals with PTSD can differ in some important ways. At the outset it is important to understand the context in which to frame an individual's presenting problems. This context is most succinctly described in the *Diagnostic and Statistical Manual of Mental Disorders*:

> The person experienced an event that is outside the range of usual human experience and that would be markedly distressing to almost anyone, e.g., serious threat to one's life or physical integrity; serious threat or harm to one's children, spouse, or other close relatives and friends; sudden destruction of one's home or community; or seeing another person who has recently been or is being, seriously injured or killed as a result of an accident or physical violence. (American Psychiatric Association, 1987, p. 250)

As a rule, the traumatic event gives meaning to the signs and symptoms that are subsequently noted by the practitioner.

Although there are data showing the considerable role of the pre- and posttrauma factors in the development of PTSD, the most conclusive evidence points to the preeminence of trauma factors for explaining the greatest development of PTSD symptomatology (e.g., Foy, Carroll, & Donahoe, 1987; Foy, Resnick, Sipprelle, & Carroll, 1987; Foy, Sipprelle, Rueger, & Carroll, 1984; Frye &

Stockton, 1982; Gallers, Foy, Donahoe, & Goldfarb, 1988). Generally, one can expect greater symptomatology in individuals who experience greater trauma, be it threat to life or loss of significant others and objects (Foy et al., 1984; Green, Lindy, & Grace, 1985; Wilson, Smith, & Johnson, 1985). However, the magnitude of the stressor is not the only variable important in the presentation of PTSD. For example, Wilson et al. (1985) propose ten additional dimensions of stressor events (based on factors empirically identified by Gleser, Green, & Winget, 1981) that are likely to influence the presence and severity of PTSD. These dimensions are (1) degree of life threat; (2) degree of bereavement; (3) speed of onset (of traumatic event); (4) duration of trauma; (5) degree of displacement in home community; (6) potential for recurrence (of trauma); (7) degree of exposure to death, dying, and destruction; (8) degree of moral conflict inherent in traumatic situation; (9) role of person in trauma; and (10) proportion of community affected by the trauma.

For nearly all the dimensions, greater disturbance can be expected the more that dimension applies or is true. For example, the greater the degree of exposure to life-threatening situations, the more PTSD symptomatology the clinician can expect to observe. Similarly, the longer the trauma or stressor lasts, the greater the likelihood of symptomatology. The more moral conflict engendered by the trauma, the more pervasive and intense will be the disturbance. Some of the dimensions can also yield qualitative changes in the symptoms experienced. For example, the passive victim and the active participant are apt to experience phenomenologically different disorders. If the individual experiences the trauma with a community of friends and family (e.g., flood) versus alone (e.g., rape), he or she may show less distress and sharing the trauma experience(s) may produce an altogether different symptom picture, for example, displays of grief or outrage over the misfortune experienced by loved ones, or enhanced feelings of commonality with the other survivors. Thus, the 10 dimensions provide a useful template by which to view the effects of extreme stressors.

PTSD is a heterogeneous disorder that varies considerably in clinical presentation. Nevertheless, there does appear to be a symptom complex that is consistent across many variations of the disorder. First, increased anxiety symptoms, as shown in hyperarousal, hypervigilance, startle, sleep disturbance, memory and concentration problems, and irritability and anger outbursts, are characteristic of PTSD (APA, 1987; Ellis, 1983; Fairbank, Keane, & Malloy, 1983; Lindemann, 1944). These symptoms can be assessed while observing the client, interviewing him or her about recent symptoms, or by utilizing psychological tests (e.g., Minnesota Multiphasic Personality Inventory [Hathaway & McKinley, 1967]; Symptom Checklist – 90 – R [Derogatis, 1983]; State-Trait Anxiety Inventory [Spielberger, Gorsuch, & Lushene, 1970]). Individuals with PTSD also seem to exhibit anxiety in heightened physiological reactivity and high basal level of central nervous system (CNS) activity (Blanchard, Kolb, Pallmeyer, & Gerardi, 1982; Malloy, Fairbank, & Keane, 1983). These symptoms can be measured using psychophysiological assessments to determine both arousal level and sympathetic reactivity. Recent research has demonstrated that PTSD veterans can be discriminated from controls on the basis of heart rate responsivity to combat cues.

Perhaps the hallmark of PTSD is the individual's recurrent and intrusive recollections of the traumatizing event (APA, 1987; Fairbank et al., 1983; Wilkinson, 1983). This phenomenon is most evident in the well-publicized flashbacks of some Vietnam veterans. Here, the individual has a dissociative, hallucinatorylike experience in which he or she suddenly feels and acts as if he or she is again undergoing the traumatic event. More typically, reexperiencing is manifested in the form of repeated and unwanted memories of the event(s) despite, and perhaps because of, the individual's active attempts at suppressing such memories. Clinically, this symptom is usually spontaneously reported, for example, "I can't get 'the Nam' out of my mind" or "I keep seeing the rapist's face."

The clinician can learn a great deal about the presence and severity of PTSD symptoms when he or she asks about sleep disturbance (Leopold & Dillon, 1963; Titchener & Kapp, 1976; Wilkinson, 1983). Sleep disturbances that are likely to be reported include avoidance of sleep, decreased total sleep time, increased midsleep awakenings and nightmares, and early-morning awakening.

Another response to trauma frequently seen at the clinical level is a feeling of hopelessness and helplessness (APA, 1987; Ellis, 1983; Silverman, 1986). The individual with PTSD may have a profound sense that external forces govern his or her fate (Foa, Steketee, & Olasov Rothbaum, 1989). In many cases, such as when the individual was a victim (e.g., natural disasters, rape) rather than an active participant (e.g., war atrocities), this belief can be linked to the uncontrollability and unpredictability of the trauma itself. Seligman's model of learned helplessness (Seligman, 1974; Seligman & Garber, 1980) may have particular relevance to this aspect of post-traumatic stress (Foa et al., 1989). This model and supporting data hold that animals exposed to unpredictable and inescapable shock become helpless and passive and exhibit this helplessness across many new dimensions of and contexts for behavior. Research with human subjects that has replicated these learned helplessness laboratory data has been utilized to conceptualize the development of PTSD (Van der Kolk, Boyd, Krystal, & Greenburg, 1984; Wilson et al., 1985).

Relatedly, depression is commonly seen at the clinical level (Ellis, 1983; Silverman, 1986; Titchener & Kapp, 1976), sometimes masking PTSD symptoms. This finding is consistent with the learned helplessness and the hopelessness aspects of PTSD. However, in addition to these aspects, the entire spectrum of depressive disorder may be present. In particular, guilt and shame are frequently seen at the clinical level in individuals with PTSD. For these persons, guilt for surviving when others did not, and for acts of commission or omission, can be a prominent aspect of the individual's presentation. Moral guilt and conflict may also play a role, for example in cases where the individual derives some pleasure from an act that he or she generally finds repulsive, possibly feelings of closeness in an incestuous relationship, or feelings of power during combat. Not uncommonly, guilt or perceived culpability can be a hidden aspect of the disorder, sometimes overshadowed by other affective states (e.g., anger). Clinicians can observe the full range of vegetative signs of depression, including appetite disturbance, anhedonia, and suicidal ideation. Thus, it is important to recognize that depressive symptoms may be a consequence of exposure to trauma so that both the depression and the PTSD can be treated.

Constricted affect is also seen in individuals with PTSD (Fairbank et al., 1983; Leopold & Dillon, 1963; Wilkinson, 1983). This symptom may initially develop as an adapting response to the overwhelming physiological reactions to the stressful event. For example, after witnessing a loved one perish in a car accident, emotional numbing may provide an affective buffer for an individual until he or she can adequately address the loss; however, when this buffer persists or generalizes to other relationships, it no longer serves a useful function and perhaps prevents the individual from having experiences that might help him or her to recompensate following the loss (e.g., by engaging in intimacy with shared emotional processing). Combat veterans who lost compatriots during wartime are particularly prone to display these characteristics. In combat, emotional involvement with others was severely punished by the deaths of the persons with whom relationships had been established. The soldiers learned, and often overlearned, to avoid emotional pain by not forming relationships and by maintaining interpersonal distance from others. Victims of rape may show emotional detachment of a somewhat different type. With the cues of their trauma (i.e., those related to physical closeness and coitus) having obvious counterparts in accepted heterosexual intimacy, expressions of these latter behaviors may be inhibited as a result of their association with the trauma. Attempts by others, particularly males, to comfort the victim may elicit anxiety, fear, and emotional withdrawal (Ellis, 1983).

In light of the intensity of the symptoms experienced by the individual with PTSD, it is not surprising that alcohol and drug abuse are seen concurrently with this disorder (cf. Keane, Gerardi, Lyons, & Wolfe, 1988). Indeed, substance abuse is often the presenting problem that brings traumatized patients to treatment. Individuals with PTSD may self-medicate their symptoms to dampen the anxiety components of the disorder and also to enhance sleep. Unfortunately, the long-term effects of alcohol use can actually exacerbate sleep problems and contribute to increased irritability, arousal, concentration impairment, depression, and often excessive PTSD symptoms. Furthermore, recurrence of PTSD symptoms may increase the individual's use of alcohol and other substances, since this pattern becomes associated with at least short-term amelioration of symptoms.

For many persons, the symptoms of PTSD persist or become more intense over time, even years after the traumatizing incident occurred (Archibald & Tuddenham, 1965; Black & Keane, 1982; Dobbs & Wilson, 1960; Eaton, Sigal, & Weinfeld, 1982; Gleser, Green, & Winget, 1981; Leopold & Dillon, 1963). Sometimes, patients first seek treatment for trauma 5, 10, or even 40 years after the event itself. Furthermore, the durability of symptoms across time is one feature that distinguishes PTSD from similar-appearing disorders, such as adjustment disorder, which is considered to have an outer limit of 6 months. Frequently, current stressors such as those originating from marital distress, car accidents, deaths of loved ones, and so on, are associated with the appearance of "dormant" PTSD symptomatology, often years or decades after the inciting trauma (Horowitz, 1976). In fact, the PTSD individual's help-seeking behavior is frequently an attempt to resolve a current crisis or stressor.

In summary, if practitioners astutely interview patients, they can discover the existence of extremely stressful life events that may in part have motivated psychopathology. This discovery provides a meaningful template by which to view the patient and his or her symptoms. At times patients do not relate current disturbance to the traumatic event, and this may become a focus of therapy. In still other patients, access to the memories of traumatic events is impeded and psychogenic amnesia occurs. This retrieval failure (most typically of the most intense components of a memory) may be overcome over the course of therapy when cues are presented and discussed by the therapist and patients.

EPIDEMIOLOGY

Accurate estimates of the prevalence of PTSD in specific populations (e.g., rape victims) and in the general population are important to determine the nature and scope of the disorder as well as to form hypotheses about factors responsible for its development. Epidemiological research is also important for social policymakers to use in basing their decisions for the distribution of resources for prevention and treatment of PTSD. Unfortunately, until recently, little sound epidemiological data had been collected regarding the prevalence or incidence of PTSD.

However, there have been several pioneering efforts at determining the presence of more general psychological adjustment problems stemming from traumatic experiences. These studies have contributed to our understanding of the psychological impact of various trauma (e.g., in combat veterans [Egendorf et al., 1981], in victims of disasters [Green et al., 1983], and rape victims [Kilpatrick et al., 1979]), and in some cases have been helpful in establishing the criteria for the diagnosis of PTSD. These early studies also enabled the field of PTSD research to become more methodologically rigorous.

Recent studies of the prevalence of PTSD in the general population indicate that the disorder poses a substantial mental health problem. Helzer,

Robins, and McEvoy (1987) were the first to report data about the prevalence of PTSD in both the general population and in specific cohorts and subgroups. They based their estimates on a nationwide sample of nonhelp-seeking men and women who took part in a broader epidemiological study that investigated the prevalence of DSM-III (APA, 1980) psychiatric disorders (Epidemiological Catchment Area Survey [Helzer et al., 1987]). Utilizing the Diagnostic Interview Schedule (DIS [Robins, Helzer, Croughan, & Ratcliff, 1981]), these researchers found a 1% prevalence rate for PTSD in the general population. Their data suggest that PTSD is about as prevalent as schizophrenia. PTSD is a unique psychological disorder to study in that etiology is part of the diagnostic criteria; that is, the traumatic stressors responsible for the development of the disorder are specified during diagnosis. Thus the prevalence of PTSD can be delineated into specific categories of traumatic events. The following is a review of several epidemiological studies that measured PTSD in various traumatized populations.

Combat-Related PTSD

Combat was the most common traumatic experience reported for men while physical assault (including rape) was the most common trauma reported by women in Helzer et al.'s (1987) general epidemiological study. Based on a very small sample of Vietnam combat veterans ($N = 43$), Helzer et al. (1987) found a prevalence rate of 3.5% for nonwounded and 20% for wounded male veterans for an overall rate of about 12%. Unfortunately, as discussed by Keane and Penk (1988) in their critique of the Helzer et al. (1987) study, the DIS is not a sensitive measure of PTSD, and it is quite likely that the Helzer et al. (1987) data underestimated the prevalence of PTSD.

A second study that investigated the prevalence of PTSD specifically in Vietnam combat veterans was conducted by the Centers for Disease Control (CDC, 1988). Administering the DIS to a random sample of Vietnam and Vietnam-era veterans, these investigators found that 15% of combat veterans had PTSD in their lifetime and 2.2% had PTSD within the month of their examination.

In the most comprehensive epidemiological evaluation of PTSD in combat veterans to date, the National Vietnam Veterans Readjustment Study (NVVRS [Kulka et al., 1988]) studied a large representative nationwide probability sample

of veterans. These investigators diagnosed PTSD using multiple measures, including the Mississippi Scale for Combat-Related PTSD (Keane, Caddell, & Taylor, 1988), the Structured Clinical Interview for DSM-III-R (Spitzer & Williams, 1985), and the PTSD subscale of the MMPI (Keane, Malloy, & Fairbank, 1984). In addition, Kulka et al. (1988) measured the extent of combat exposure in Vietnam veterans to determine the relationship between extent of the stressor (combat) and the development of PTSD.

Based on their data, Kulka et al. (1988) estimated that approximately 479,000 of the 3.14 million men (15%) and 600 of the 7,100 women (8.5%) who served in the Vietnam conflict are currently troubled by PTSD. Lifetime estimates of PTSD indicated that 30.9% of the men and 26.9% of the women developed PTSD secondary to their experiences in the war. Consistent with other studies of combat-related PTSD, the level of combat-related stressors correlated with the probability of having PTSD (cf. Foy et al., 1987). Thus, if a combat veteran had sustained injuries or experienced other forms of intensive exposure to combat stressors he was roughly four times as likely to have developed PTSD in his lifetime. Women veterans who were exposed to high levels of war zone stress (e.g., exposure to wounded or dead soldiers) were seven times more likely to have PTSD.

Crime-Related PTSD

Victimization by criminal violence or threat of violence can produce immediate physical and psychological stress responses in the form of anxiety (Kilpatrick, Resick, & Veronen, 1981), depression and helplessness (Atkeson, Calhoun, Resick, & Ellis, 1982), and sleep disturbance (Nadelson, Notman, Zackson, & Gornick, 1982). It appears that these acute but often debilitating reactions abate in the majority of victims of crime between days and months after the trauma (Kilpatrick, Veronen, & Resick, 1979; Steketee & Foa, 1987). Recent research has shown, however, that for a surprising number of victims, PTSD and related symptomatology interfere with functioning in a lasting manner, particularly when individuals are exposed to more violent crimes (Kilpatrick, Saunders, Veronen, Best, & Von, 1987). In addition, Kilpatrick et al. (1985) found that both environmental and personality variable predicted long-term recovery from criminal victimization experiences (e.g., a prior history of victimization, coping skills, social support, severity, intensity and context of the stressor, perceived threat; see also Steketee & Foa, 1987).

In the most thorough study to date investigating the prevalence of PTSD in a broad range of women who reported criminal victimization experiences, Kilpatrick et al. (1987) utilized a community sample and based their estimates on self-reported crime and DIS-based interviews. These researchers found a 27.8% overall lifetime prevalence of PTSD for all crimes and a current prevalence rate of PTSD of 7.5%. The following are the current (and lifetime) prevalence rates for different types of crime: completed rape, 16.5% (57.1%); attempted rape, 5.9% (15.7%); completed molestation, 8.3% (33.3%); aggravated assault, 10.5% (36.8%); robbery, 9.2% (18.2%); and burglary, 6.8% (28.2%). Interestingly, many of the PTSD symptoms assessed in Kilpatrick et al.'s (1987) study were present between 15 to 25 years posttrauma. These data closely parallel data from current studies of PTSD in Vietnam combat veterans and affirm the general prevalence of PTSD in contemporary American society.

Man-Made Disaster-Related PTSD

It appears that as societies become more technologically sophisticated major man-made disasters are more likely to occur. Surprisingly little is known about the short- and long-term psychological sequelae of exposure to man-made disasters, and even less is known about the prevalence of man-made disaster-related PTSD. Several recent man-made disasters have, however, provided clinical investigators with natural laboratories for quasi-experimental research on the lingering psychological aftereffects of exposure to technological stressors. Most notable have been the studies of the effects of the Three Mile Island (TMI) nuclear power plant disaster on the surrounding community (Baum, Gatchel, & Shaeffer, 1983; Bromet, Schulberg, & Dunn, 1982; Davidson & Baum, 1986; Schaeffer & Baum, 1984; Smith & Fisher, 1981), and the Beverly Hills Supper Club fire's effects on victims and relatives of survivors (Green, Grace, Lindy, Titchener, & Lindy, 1983). Unfortunately, there is a dearth of data about the psychological morbidity and treatment needs of victims of most other modern man-made catastrophes (e.g., Chernoble, Bhopal, Love Canal, plane crashes, use of chemical weapons).

Wilkinson (1983) was the first to attempt to determine the presence of PTSD following the Hyatt Regency skywalk collapse in 1981. Utilizing a nonrandomized sample of victims and rescue workers Wilkinson determined through a semistructured interview administered 5 months after the disaster that the acute effects of such a man-made disaster could indeed be characterized as PTSD in many cases. He found that 88% of the men and women who were present during the skywalk collapse reported experiencing repeated disturbing intrusive thoughts about the incident, 52% reported sleep disturbances, 52% nightmares of the incident, 45% stated that they startled easily, 45% reported anhedonia, 40% avoided reminders of the event, and 37% reported feeling more anxious when reminded of the disaster. Unfortunately, Wilkinson did not report on the actual percentage of victims or rescue workers who met the diagnostic criteria for the disorder.

Other man-made disasters are less immediate and brutal yet certainly act as threats that tax individuals' coping resources. These are the silent insidious calamities of environmental contamination (e.g., nuclear radiation leaks, toxic waste, asbestos). The disaster at the TMI nuclear power plant (March 1979) epitomizes this type of man-made stressor.

The psychological effects of the TMI accident on the surrounding community has been studied extensively by Bromet and also by Baum and his colleagues (Baum, Gatchel, & Schaeffer, 1983; Davidson & Baum, 1986; Bromet, Schulberg, & Dunn, 1982). They have suggested that the symptom picture of individuals exposed to life-threatening environmental contamination, like the TMI nuclear power plant's release of radioactivity into the air, can be characterized as a chronic, prolonged, and milder form of PTSD. Using group data, Baum and his colleagues have found that individuals living in a radius of 5 miles from the TMI disaster, when compared to matched controls subjects living 80 miles from the TMI plant, reported more intrusive and worrisome thoughts about the disaster, depression, anxiety, greater attempts to avoid thoughts of the disaster and its effects as well as reminders of the incident, and increases in secondary measures of hyperarousal (greater resting heart rate and blood pressure, and blood levels of catecholomines). These symptoms were reported nearly 5 years after the incident, indicating that such events can adversely affect the mental health status of individuals for a protracted period.

Natural Disaster-Related PTSD

Sudden, unexpected, and overwhelming natural disasters (e.g., floods, tornados, earthquakes, fires) pose a serious problem for individuals and communities that tax resources on various levels (economic, physical, and mental health; Adams & Adams, 1984; Frederick, 1980; Gleser, Green, & Winget, 1981; Lifton & Olson, 1976; Logue, Mellick, & Struening, 1981; Ollendick & Hoffman, 1982). As would be expected given the scope of the destructive power of natural disasters there are data that suggest that PTSD can occur in both acute (Madakasira & O'Brien, 1987) and chronic manifestations (Shore, Tatum, & Vollmer, 1986).

In the only study of its kind, Shore et al. (1986) assessed the psychological impact of the Mount St. Helens disaster utilizing the DIS. These researchers found that among the 1,025 individuals studied, those who had the most exposure to the disaster were more likely to develop one of three psychiatric disorders—generalized anxiety disorder (GAD), depression, and PTSD—with an aggregated prevalence rate of 30% for men and 40% for women during the year of the disaster. The prevalence of PTSD was 2% overall (0.7% for men and 3.3% for women). Interestingly, GAD and depression were likely to abate within 1 to 2 years postdisaster, yet many of the PTSD cases still met diagnostic criteria for the disorder 3 years later.

NATURAL HISTORY

The course of PTSD is presently not well defined and is a scientific question that needs to be addressed. To date, there have not been any longitudinal studies conducted on patients with PTSD. The epidemiology studies that have provided us with estimates of prevalence in various populations are not able to provide information on the natural history of PTSD. Clearly, more information is needed in this area.

From the perspective of experienced clinicians, it might be useful to note that a perspective that is growing in acceptance is that PTSD is an eminently treatable disorder using psychological methods (e.g., Keane, Fairbank, Caddell, & Zimering, 1989), but for many PTSD patients the disorder is episodic or phasic. Viewing PTSD as a phasic disorder provides an explanation for the frequently observed phenomenon of patients seeking treatment for their PTSD symptoms (i.e., an increase in nightmares or intrusive thoughts)

when there is an increase in stressors in their lives. Examples of this would be those patients having an exacerbation of their PTSD symptomatology following the loss of a job or an intimate personal relationship. This formulation of PTSD is similar to other disorders where a diathesis and stress model is used to predict the development of psychopathology and extends this model to explain relapse and recidivism.

A separate, but equally important, issue to discuss is the development of varying symptom pictures in individuals exposed to similar highly stressful events. For those people exposed to sexual assault or to military experience, for example, there is a range of disorders that can develop. PTSD is just one of these. Substance abuse, generalized anxiety disorder, and depression can also occur with some frequency. Yet even within the PTSD category there are considerable differences in the clinical manifestations of the disorder. Keane (1989) has described a subtype of PTSD patients who primarily exhibit the positive symptoms of PTSD (i.e., nightmares, intrusive thoughts, physiological reactivity to trauma cues) and distinguished these people from PTSD patients who display more negative symptoms (i.e., numbing, avoidance, constricted emotion) of the disorder. Although this distinction between positive and negative presentations has been conceptualized as possible subtypes of the disorder, it may be that they represent the different phases of the disorder in which certain people are more inclined to seek treatment. This issue remains open to empirical studies.

IMPAIRMENT AND COMPLICATIONS

Clinicians who work with traumatized populations are likely to observe many different manifestations of PTSD symptoms with their patients as well as varied constellations of collateral problems that reflect a patient's response to the experience of PTSD symptoms (e.g., self-medication; Keane et al., 1983, 1987), some underlying, preexisting psychopathology (e.g., personality disorder), and/or an environmental deficiency of some kind (e.g., inadequate social support, see Keane, Scott, Chavoya, Lamparski, & Fairbank, 1985; Solomon, Mikulincer, & Avitzur, 1988; Stretch, 1985; Wirtz & Harrell, 1987). Detailed (and ongoing) psychological assessment of trauma victims is essential to:

1. determine the presence and phase of the disorder (e.g., intrusive versus avoidant phase; see Horowitz, 1976; Keane et al., 1987)
2. specify the patient's unique manifestation of PTSD (e.g., does the patient experience more positive symptoms, such as greater reports of reexperiencing with concomitant high states of psychophysiological arousal, or more negative symptoms, such as a preponderance of avoidance and withdrawal behaviors; see Keane, 1989
3. identify and diagnose coexisting Axis-I and -II psychopathology (e.g., substance dependence, borderline disorder)
4. garner information about how other individuals in the patient's environment are affected by the patient's symptoms and coping style (e.g., occupational and personal relationships)
5. hypothesize interrelationships among the various factors 1–4 above determine and prioritize targets for psychological and possibly pharmacological interventions

Researchers have recently substantiated empirically the frequent presence of concurrent Axis-I and Axis-II disorders in people with PTSD (Kulka et al., 1988; Keane & Wolfe, in press). Most studies depicting such comorbidity have been conducted with samples of combat veterans with PTSD.

Sierles et al. (1983) interviewed 25 inpatients who carried a diagnosis of PTSD, as determined by structured interview using a modified version of the Schedule for Affective Disorders and Schizophrenia (SADS [Spitzer & Endicott, 1977]), in order to determine the coexistence of additional Axis-I and -II diagnoses. The data were striking: 84% of their patients studied carried at least one other diagnosis in addition to PTSD. The prevalence rates for the other diagnoses were as follows: 64% alcohol dependence, 48% antisocial personality disorder (ASPD), 20% drug dependence, and 72% reported a lifetime history of problems with depression. These results have been substantiated by several other comprehensive investigations (as part of larger epidemiological efforts; the NVVRS; Kulka et al., 1988; the ECA studies [Escobar et al., 1983]; Helzer et al., 1987; the CDC study, 1988; and in other outpatient veteran populations [Keane et al., 1987]; Sierles et al., 1986).

In studies of treatment-seeking patients, comorbidity rates range from 60% to 100% of all patients who met diagnostic criteria for PTSD. For example, in the majority of PTSD cases, some

form of substance dependence or abuse was also present (approximately 60% to 80% of the time), often functioning as a personal coping strategy that quells intrusive experiences, promotes sleep, and alleviates arousal states. A substantial number of combat-related PTSD patients have also been found to have a codiagnosis of antisocial personality disorder (approximately 20% to 40% of the time). These findings may indeed be a function of the Vietnam experience, where drafting soldiers did not yield a cross section of the young adult male population. Moreover, between 20% and 30% of these cases reported major affective disorder. Finally, 15% to 30% of cases manifested chronic dysthymia. Thus, careful diagnostic workups are crucial for developing proper treatment regimen for those PTSD patients who reach criteria for multiple disorders.

Cooccurring formal psychiatric diagnosis is one index of the level of impairment associated with PTSD. It is unclear at the present time whether such psychiatric disturbances are in some way part of the etiology of PTSD, or simply a collateral effect of the disorder in those individuals with a particular diathesis. Moreover, PTSD is associated with a variety of other dysfunctional behaviors and cognitions, as well as emotional complications that have serious implications for the patient's personal and social functioning.

The experience of being traumatized can have debilitating effects on an individual's interpersonal functioning. Wives of Vietnam veterans with combat-related PTSD, for example, report that their partners are more aggressive, less expressive, more avoidant and secretive, less trusting, and less willing to take on family responsibilities and maintain family structure (see Caroll, Rueger, Foy, & Donahoe, 1985; Roberts et al., 1982). Such a dysfunctional interpersonal environment takes a considerable toll on the patient's sense of personal efficacy as well as that of his or her significant others. The absence of familial or other social support is also a poor prognostic indicator for recovering from PTSD (Keane, Scott, Chavoya, Lamparski, & Fairbank, 1985).

Thus, some form of family or couples therapy often is indicated with traumatized patients and their families (Figley & Sprenkle, 1978; Silver, 1985). The patient and his or her significant others need gradually to take risks and learn skills for communicating openly and expressing feelings, as well as to learn skills to handle future stressors (e.g., parenting, limit setting, ensuring safety; Williams & Williams, 1987). Significant others also benefit from greater understanding of the broad reaching effects of trauma, the role the trauma plays in the victim's life, and the reason why PTSD symptoms are likely to be expressed at certain times.

It has been noted in both clinical and research contexts that combat-related PTSD is associated with problems that impair other aspects of personal and interpersonal functioning. These additional complications include suicidal ideation and gestures (as well as successful suicide), unemployment and financial difficulties, severe isolation, low frustration tolerance, fear of intimacy often masked by anger or indifference, sexual dysfunction, sleep disturbances, legal difficulties and possible imprisonment, substance abuse paranoid ideation, and hyperalertness and defensiveness often expressed by the storage of weapons in the home (Egendorf et al., 1981; Figley, 1978; Hearst, Newman, & Hulley, 1986; Nezu & Carnevale, 1987; Solomon & Mikulincer, 1987; Solomon, Mikulincer, & Avitzer, 1988; Walker, 1981; Wilson & Zigelbaum, 1983; Yaeger, Laufer, & Gallops, 1984).

Impairment in social functioning is not limited to veterans with combat-related PTSD. Rape victims, for example, in addition to experiencing symptoms of anxiety, fear, and depression (Ellis, Atkeson, & Calhoun, 1981; Kilpatrick et al., 1981), report many problems that have an impact on their social environments. These rape-related complications have been found to be suicidal ideation and attempts (Kilpatrick et al., 1985), difficulties being alone (Nadelson et al., 1982), feeling unsafe, distrustful yet dependent on significant others, often to the point of feeling burdensome (Kilpatrick et al., 1979; Resick et al., 1981), and sexual problems (Becker, Abel, & Skinner, 1979). Interestingly, rape victims report decreased satisfaction with a variety of sexual behaviors with the same frequency as nonvictims (Feldman-Summers, Gordan, & Meagher, 1979).

The degree of impairment as well as any personal and interpersonal complications associated with posttrauma adjustment vary considerably across individuals (Gleser et al., 1981; Kilpatrick et al., 1981; Kulka et al., 1988). It is noteworthy that the vast majority of individuals do not develop PTSD after experiencing extreme stressors. It appears that these individuals are probably not entirely asymptomatic but are coping better, a fact that is manifested in a more successful social adjustment and in the absence of seeking help for the problems they might experience (Hendin &

Hass, 1984; Wolfe & Keane, 1988). A variety of factors have been posited to account for such variance in posttrauma adjustment: age, sex, race, socioeconomic status, marital status, neurobiological factors, pretrauma adjustment, repertoire of coping skills, family history of psychopathology, the nature and extent of the trauma in objective terms, the person's appraisal of the stressful situation, behaviors during the trauma (e.g., acquiescence, abusive violence), and social support (Barlow, 1988; Card, 1987; Foy et al., 1987). Unfortunately, little is known about how these factors interact to determine level of impairment in PTSD. Much work remains to be done to account for patterns of posttrauma adjustment. Longitudinal research is clearly needed in this area.

Future theoretical models that account for level of posttrauma impairment in individuals will need to account for the possible interaction of a variety of personal and situational factors. Environmental factors such as the nature and extent of the trauma itself have been described. A useful scheme that can guide research into person variables responsible for adjustment posttrauma can be extrapolated from Mischel (1973); also see Evans and Litz (1987). These are construction competencies (e.g., a person's knowledge base, problem-solving abilities), encoding strategies (how stressful information is organized, abstracted, categorized, related to the self-schema, accessed, and utilized; see Chemtob et al., 1988), expectancies (both outcome and self-efficacy confidence judgments); values and preferences (e.g., judgments of the valence of key reinforcing and aversive stimuli; see Foa, Steketee, & Olasov Rothbaum, 1989, for a discussion of these factors in the development of PTSD); and self-regulatory systems and plans (coping style, arousal management ability, self-statements, appraisals, goals, selective attention and memory retrieval of personally relevant information, and metacognitive abilities or a person's awareness of his or her own cognitive processes and its effects on his or her behavior; see Litz & Keane, 1989, for a discussion of information processing factors in PTSD).

Finally, PTSD symptoms and their related effects show considerable variability within individuals over time. An individual can exhibit relatively good adjustment for some time after an experiencing a trauma, but then become increasingly symptomatic after additional stressful event. These precipitants have been observed clinically with aversive life stressors that may have a thematic connection to the original trauma (e.g., loss of a loved one, loss of employment, injury) and thus serve to reactivate memories of the extreme stressor.

DIFFERENTIAL DIAGNOSIS

Being accurate and comprehensive in assigning psychiatric diagnoses to individuals who have experienced very stressful life events is important in both clinical and research contexts. As can be gleaned from other sections of this chapter, the model PTSD patient will more than likely present with at least one other cooccurring Axis-I diagnosis. Thus clinicians need to cover a broad range of problem areas in their assessments and to be keen about differential as well as overlapping diagnoses. Broadly speaking, there are two key areas for clinicians to attend to in regard to differential diagnosis: What are the patient's characteristic (and reported) adjustment patterns following the event(s)? And are there any cooccurring diagnoses?

In regard to the first issue, it is important for the clinician to be aware of the several diagnostic categories that can be assigned to individuals who have experienced highly stressful life events. In terms of the current nosology, a person can be diagnosed with adjustment disorder, brief reactive psychosis, PTSD, and uncomplicated bereavement with or without a major depressive episode. Of course, knowledge about the diagnostic criteria for these various syndromes (see the DSM-III-R) will aid in differential diagnosis. Identification of the nature and extent of the stressor (e.g., was it "traumatic?"; see section on Clinical Presentation), a mental status exam (e.g., any signs of thought disorder?), as well as determination of the temporal parameters of the presenting complaint (e.g., how long has the problem lasted since the stressor?) are pieces of assessment information that are essential to this delineation process.

Coincident with determining the exact nature of a person's overall adjustment response to highly stressful events is the task of gathering information about cooccurring disturbances that may meet other formal Axis-I or Axis-II diagnostic criteria. Common cooccurring diagnoses are substance abuse or dependence, dysthymia, major depressive episode, panic disorder, and various manifestations of personality disorders. We have found that the SCID is a very useful diagnostic instrument that can determine the nature and extent of comorbidity in PTSD.

Since the diagnostic picture can often be very complex, it is extremely important for the clinician to adopt a working model of the interrelationships between the various presenting problems to facilitate treatment decisions. For example, is a PTSD patient's alcohol abuse functioning to reduce arousal and avoidance of memories of the trauma? If so, one might decide to treat the PTSD and expect the alcohol problem to abate. However, this is clearly not the only possible situation; it could be, for example, that the person has a positive family history of alcohol dependence, and it might be more prudent to treat this problem before addressing PTSD. Another example might be instructive: A person with PTSD might be experiencing a major depression with melancholia. This situation might call for a psychiatric consultation to begin a trial of antidepressant medication to energize the patient and perhaps "ready" him or her for the task of addressing PTSD.

CASE EXAMPLE

Bob is a 41-year-old, white Vietnam veteran who was referred to an outpatient clinic for evaluation by his family physician. He presented with marked anxiety symptoms and reported increased irritability and anger in interactions with his boss, wife, and three teenage daughters. His alcohol use had also increased in a parallel course with his anxiety. Bob indicated that his symptoms had little or no direct connection with his wartime experiences that occurred 20 years previously. Bob acknowledged that he had been restless since Vietnam but claimed that he had always been able to contain any symptoms. He stated that he never discussed his Vietnam experiences — good or bad — with anyone since his discharge. Bob had felt that he could best manage the pain that resulted from these experiences by forgetting about them. Besides, no one seemed to want to hear about his experiences when he ended his tour in February 1970.

Bob reported that his anxiety had escalated over the previous 6 months after his boss retired and was replaced by a younger man. The new boss was a recent college graduate with whom Bob had had several public disagreements. These disagreements caused him to be generally irritable, and this mood affected his interactions with his family. Added to this problem, Bob, normally a weekend beer drinker, began drinking both beer and whiskey heavily on weeknights and throughout the day on weekends. Typically, Bob slept 4 to 6 hours per night but now slept only 2 to 4 hours, and he reported this sleep as not restful and filled with disturbing dreams about work and his Vietnam experiences. With increasing anxiety and irritability, Bob worried that he was going to have a nervous breakdown or that he would explode. He sought treatment from a Veterans Affairs medical center.

A careful history from Bob, his wife, and his mother revealed that Bob was born and raised in a suburban neighborhood. The fourth of five children, Bob described his upbringing as happy and normal, except for an event at 13 when he and a friend discovered a decomposing body of a dead vagrant in an empty lot; he later used this experience as a benchmark to measure the repulsiveness of the injury and death he was to encounter in Vietnam. In high school, Bob had many friends, was a first-string player on the football team, and dated one girl for nearly three years. He occasionally drank beer, but only with friends on weekends, and he reported no drug use. Following his graduation in 1967, Bob enlisted in the Marines and eventually was assigned to combat duty in Vietnam. He served as an infantryman ("grunt") where he described his experience there as "one big search and destroy mission," being in the "bush" 9 out of 10 days and on operations lasting up to 30 days. While in Vietnam, he drank approximately a case of beer (24 cans) a month and smoked marijuana twice. Bob described his tour as involving firefights every few days and estimated that 75% of the men in his unit were combat casualties. He, himself, was wounded twice from shrapnel and was medically evacuated from combat once. Bob recalled that his most difficult memory occurred at the start of his tour, after the firebase on which he was posted was nearly overrun by soldiers of the North Vietnamese Army. A combat buddy was severely injured when a mortar landed nearby. After this episode, Bob recalled getting increasingly cold and numb to everything around him. Of the many events Bob recalled in the interviews, he had especially disturbing recollections of three episodes: Once he witnessed a captured Viet Cong soldier being pushed from a helicopter 400 feet above the ground during an interrogation. In another incident, he accidentally killed a man (suspected Viet Cong) and seriously injured two children when he fired upon them as they fled from an enflamed hut. Finally, while on a patrol Bob saw the Marine

ahead of him lose a leg and be blown skyward after stepping on a mine.

Bob describes his 36-hour return home from Vietnam as "scared and sweating in the jungle one day and strolling in town the next." While he was happy to be home, Bob was stunned by the extent of public outcry against the war. He also felt disillusioned by the official media portrayal of American wins and losses in Vietnam. He loved his family and friends but felt detached from them and was filled with a sense of isolation. Bob drank alcohol heavily during the first year back and alternated between unemployment and odd jobs for nearly two years before finding a job with the post office. During that period he married a woman whom he had known while in high school. Throughout their 17 years of marriage, Bob worked little at developing outside friendships but instead was alone or devoted time to his family.

At the time he sought treatment, Bob met the criteria for PTSD, substance abuse (alcohol), and dysthymic disorder. After the evaluation, Bob was taught relaxation skills and was given 12 sessions of implosive therapy. This treatment focused on repeated presentation in imagery of the traumatic events in a supportive, nonthreatening environment. He evidenced marked reductions in psychological distress as measured by self-report and psychological testing. His physiological reactivity to combat-related cues (visual and auditory presentations of combat stimuli) also showed a dramatic reduction. He reported a decrease in alcohol use and greater adjustment at work and home. At the end of treatment Bob was attending night school on a part-time basis to complete his bachelor's degree. Bob attributed the success he experienced to his addressing unresolved conflicts that stemmed from his involvement in Vietnam.

CHILDHOOD AND FAMILIAL ANTECEDENTS

Familial transmission of disorders is a characteristic that is shared by many mental health disturbances. Indeed, familial clustering of psychological disorders is one means of validating the existence of certain psychological disorders as distinct from other forms of psychological disorder (e.g., discriminating schizophrenia from depression; Robins & Guze, 1970). To date, only one study has been published on the prevalence of psychological disorder in families of PTSD individuals. Davidson, Swartz, Storck, Krishnan, and

Hammett (1985) studied patients with PTSD, major depression, and generalized anxiety disorder. The investigators found that 66% of the PTSD veterans had a positive family history of psychopathology, while depressed patients reported 79% positive histories, and generalized anxiety patients reported 93% prevalence, respectively. Unfortunately, this preliminary study has numerous limitations, including sampling methods and PTSD measurement ambiguity, and so conclusions must be tempered accordingly. Yet many interesting issues are raised by the findings.

Most theoretical formulations of psychological trauma speculate that anyone can be traumatized when presented with the right circumstances (Grinker & Spiegel, 1945; Horowitz, 1976). Individuals who have a specific psychological vulnerability (i.e., a positive family history) might be expected to develop PTSD with objectively less stress (i.e., they have a lower threshold). Moreover, at a constant level of stress exposure, these people with such a vulnerability would be expected to develop PTSD at a higher rate than those without such vulnerability. These hypotheses are consistent with the diathesis-stress view of psychopathology and the vulnerability conceptualization of schizophrenia initially formulated by Zubin and Spring (1977).

Especially with PTSD, the issue of vulnerability becomes more complicated because it is difficult to predict just what it is that might make one more likely to respond to extreme stress with PTSD symptomatology. Is it a genetic physiological inheritance, or is it a psychological or cognitive style that makes one susceptible to developing this disorder? At this time the specific substrate that is responsible for predisposing one to the disorder is not yet defined, and it is conceivable that the substrate might be either psychological or physiological or, even more complicated still, an interaction of the two.

The only study conducted on the familial issue is one that clearly indicates a lower prevalence of family disorder in PTSD than in other forms of psychopathology (Davidson et al., 1985). It seems clear from this study that a larger environmental component might be predicted when compared with the heredity component in twin studies or family studies or family studies on PTSD. Unfortunately, these studies have not yet been conducted, and the field is clearly in need of studies designed to address these questions.

Childhood antecedents, however, may play a greater role in our current understanding of the development of PTSD. In the finest mental health epidemiology study ever conducted in the United States, the NVVRS (Kulka et al., 1988) found that for Vietnam veterans who developed PTSD there is a risk factor of childhood antisocial activity. In this study of veterans, those people who had trouble in school, with authority, and at home were more likely to develop PTSD than were those veterans without such backgrounds. In drawing conclusions, however, it must be forthrightly stated that this was only one of the risk factors associated with PTSD. Not everyone with this background developed PTSD as a function of the war, and many people with very healthy and positive premorbid personalities did ultimately develop PTSD when exposed to overwhelming stress. Consistent with the comments made in the section of familial transmission, it seems clear from the NVVRS that those people who had a behavioral vulnerability were more likely to develop PTSD when exposed to extreme stress.

In summary, there is much work that remains to be done in understanding the precipitants of PTSD. Studies that rely exclusively upon retrospective review for evidence on pretrauma factors risk the development of systematic bias in the collection of data. Presently, the predisposing characteristics of PTSD await the collection of data on biological, experimental, and psychological dimensions.

SUMMARY

PTSD is a disorder associated with a broad range of problems highlighted by symptoms that relive parts of the traumatic event. The presence of these reliving experiences distinguishes PTSD from other anxiety disorders such as panic disorder, phobias, and generalized anxiety disorder. Moreover, PTSD can occur in still uncertain proportions of people exposed to massive stressors, such as combat, rape or other sexual assault, natural disasters, accidents involving motor vehicles (planes, cars, boats, trains), and other life-threatening experiences. PTSD is also found in observers of violence and in family members of those exposed to violence (mothers of children killed in automobile accidents by drunk drivers). This is true even though these individuals were not directly exposed to the extreme stressor. Because the diagnostic category of PTSD was for the first time formulated in the 1980 edition of the *Diagnostic and Statistical Manual of Mental Disorders* by the American Psychiatric Association, only recently have research findings begun to appear in the scientific literature. With the high prevalence rates of PTSD found in both the ECA study and the NVVRS, a growth in clinical and research attention can be expected over the next decade. It is hoped that many of the unanswered questions raised in this chapter will be among those that will soon be addressed.

REFERENCES

Adams, P. R., & Adams, G. R. (1984). Mount Saint Helen's ashfall: Evidence for a disaster stress reaction. *American Psychologist, 39*, 252–260.

American Psychiatric Association. (1980). *The diagnostic and statistical manual of mental disorders* (3rd ed.). Washington, DC: Author.

American Psychiatric Association. (1987). *The diagnostic and statistical manual of mental disorders* (3rd ed.). Washington, DC: Author.

Archibald, H. C., & Tuddenham, R. D. (1965). Persistent stress reactions after combat: A 20-year follow-up. *Archives of General Psychiatry, 12*, 475–481.

Atkeson, B. M., Calhoun, K. S., Resick, P. A., & Ellis, E. M. (1982). Victims of rape: Repeated assessment of depressive symptoms. *Journal of Consulting and Clinical Psychology, 50*, 96–102.

Barlow, D. E. (1988). *Anxiety and its disorders: The nature and treatment of anxiety and panic.* New York: The Guilford Press.

Baum, A., Gatchel, R. J., & Schaeffer, M. A. (1983). Emotional, behavioral, and physiological effects of chronic stress at Three Mile Island. *Journal of Consulting and Clinical Psychology, 51*, 565–572.

Becker, J. V., Abel, G. G., & Skinner, L. J. (1979). The impact of a sexual assault on the victim's sexual life. *Victimology: An International Journal, 4*, 229–234.

Black, J. L., & Keane, T. M. (1982). Implosive therapy in the treatment of combat related fears in a World War II veteran. *Journal of Behavior Therapy and Experimental Psychiatry, 13*, 33–40.

Blanchard, E. B., Kolb, L. C., Pallmeyer, T. P., & Gerardi, R. J. (1982). The development of a psychophysiological assessment procedure for post-traumatic stress disorder in Vietnam veterans. *Psychiatry Quarterly, 54*, 220–229.

Bromet, E., Schulberg, H. C., & Dunn, L. (1982). Reactions of psychiatric patients to the Three Mile Island nuclear accident. *Archives of General Psychiatry, 39*, 725–730.

Card, J. (1987). Epidemiology of PTSD in a national cohort of Vietnam veterans. *Journal of Clinical Psychology, 43*, 6–17.

Carroll, E. M., Rueger, D. R., Foy, D. W., & Donahoe, C. P. (1985). Vietnam combat veterans with posttraumatic stress disorder: Analysis of marital and cohabitating adjustment. *Journal of Abnormal Psychology, 94*, 329–337.

Chemtob, C., Roitblat, H., Hamada, R., Carlson, J., & Twentyman, C. (1988). A cognitive action theory of post-traumatic stress disorder. *Journal of Anxiety Disorders, 2*, 253–275.

Centers for Disease Control. (1988). Health status of Vietnam veterans. *Journal of the American Medical Association, 259*, 2701–2724.

Davidson, L. M., & Baum, A. (1986). Chronic stress and posttraumatic stress disorders. *Journal of Consulting and Clinical Psychology, 54*, 303–308.

Davidson, J., Swartz, M., Storck, M., Krishnan, R. R., & Hammett, E. (1985). A diagnostic and family study of posttraumatic stress disorder. *American Journal of Psychiatry, 142*, 90–93.

Derogatis, L. R. (1983). *SCL-90-R manual – II.* Towson, MD: Clinical Psychometric Research.

Dobbs, D., & Wilson, W. P. (1960). Observations on the persistence of traumatic war neurosis. *Journal of Mental and Nervous Diseases, 21*, 686–691.

Eaton, W. W., Sigal, J. J., & Weinfeld, M. (1982). Impairment in Holocaust survivors after 33 years: Data from an unbiased community sample. *American Journal of Psychiatry, 139*, 773–777.

Egendorf, A., Kadushin, C., Laufer, R. S., Rothbart, G., & Sloan, L. (1981). *Legacies of Vietnam: Comparative adjustment of veterans and their peers.* New York: Center for Policy Research.

Ellis, E. M. (1983). A review of empirical rape research: Victim reactions and response to treatment. *Clinical Psychology Review, 3*, 473–490.

Ellis, E. M., Atkeson, B. M., & Calhoun, K. S. (1981). An assessment of long-term reaction to rape. *Journal of Abnormal Psychology, 90*, 263–266.

Escobar, J. I., Randolph, E. T., & Puente, G., et al. (1983). Post-traumatic stress disorder in Hispanic Vietnam veterans: Clinical phenomenology and sociocultural characteristics. *The*

Journal of Nervous and Mental Disease, 171, 585–596.

Evans, I. M., & Litz, B. T. (1987). Behavioral assessment: A new theoretical foundation for clinical measurement and evaluation. In H. J. Eyesenck & I. Martin (Eds.), *Theoretical foundations of behavior therapy* (pp. 331–351). New York: Plenum Press.

Fairbank, J. A., Keane, T. M., & Malloy, P. F. (1983). Some preliminary data on the psychological characteristics of Vietnam veterans with posttraumatic stress disorder. *Journal of Consulting and Clinical Psychology, 51,* 912–919.

Feldman-Summers, S., Gordon, P. E., & Meagher, J. R. (1979). The impact of rape on sexual satisfaction. *Journal of Abnormal Psychology, 88,* 101–105.

Figley, C. R. (1978). Symptoms of delayed combat-stress among a college sample of Vietnam veterans. *Military Medicine, 143,* 107–110.

Figley, C. R., & Sprenkle, D. H. (1978). Delayed stress response syndrome: Family therapy indications. *Journal of Marriage and Family Counseling, 4,* 53–60.

Foa, E. B., Steketee, G., & Olasov Rothbaum, B. (1989). Behavioral/cognitive conceptualizations of post-traumatic stress disorder. *Behavior Therapy, 20,* 155–176.

Foy, D. W., Sipprelle, R. C., Rueger, D. B., & Carroll, E. M. (1984). Etiology of PTSD in Vietnam veterans: Analysis of premilitary, military, and combat exposure influences. *Journal of Consulting and Clinical Psychology, 52,* 79–87.

Foy, D. W., Carroll, E. M., & Donahoe, C. P. (1987). Etiological factors in the development of PTSD in clinical samples of Vietnam combat veterans. *Journal of Clinical Psychology, 43,* 17–27.

Foy, D. W., Resnick, H. S., Sipprelle, R. C., & Carroll, E. M. (1987). Premilitary, military, and postmilitary factors in the development of combat-related posttraumatic stress disorder. *The Behavior Therapist, 10,* 3–9.

Frederick, C. J. (1980). Effects of natural vs. human-induced violence upon victims. *Evaluation and Change* (Special Issue), 71–75.

Frye, J. S., & Stockton, R. A. (1982). Discriminant analysis of post-traumatic stress disorder among a group of Vietnam veterans. *American Journal of Psychiatry, 139,* 52–56.

Gallers, J., Foy, D. W., Donahoe, C. P., & Gold-farb, J. (1988). Posttraumatic stress disorder in Vietnam combat veterans: Effect on traumatic violence exposure and military adjustment. *Journal of Traumatic Stress, 1,* 181–192.

Gleser, G. C., Green, B. L., & Winget, C. (1981). *Buffalo Creek revisited: Prolonged psychosocial effects of disaster.* New York: Simon & Schuster.

Green, B., Grace, M., Lindy, J., Titchener, J., & Lindy, J. (1983). Levels of functional impairment following a civilian disaster: The Beverly Hills Supper Club fire. *Journal of Consulting and Clinical Psychology, 51,* 573–580.

Green, B. L., Lindy, J. D., & Grace, M. C. (1985). Posttraumatic stress disorder: Toward DSM-IV. *Journal of Nervous and Mental Disease, 173,* 406–411.

Grinker, R., & Spiegel, J. P. (1945). *Men under stress.* Philadelphia: Blakiston.

Hathaway, S. R., & McKinley, J. C. (1967). *Minnesota Multiphasic Personality Inventory: Manual for administration and scoring.* New York: Psychological Corporation.

Hearst, N., Newman, T. B., & Hulley, S. B. (1986). Delayed effects of the military draft on mortality: A randomized natural experiment. *The New England Journal of Medicine, 314,* 620–624.

Helzer, J. E., Robins, L. N., & McEvoy, M. A. (1987). Post-traumatic stress disorder in the general population. *The New England Journal of Medicine, 317,* 1630–1634.

Hendin, H., & Haas, A. P. (1984). Combat adaptations of Vietnam veterans without posttraumatic stress disorders. *American Journal of Psychiatry, 141,* 956–960.

Horowitz, M. (1976). *Stress response syndromes.* New York: Jason Aronson.

Keane, T. M. (1989). Post-traumatic stress disorder: Current status and future directions. *Behavior Therapy, 20,* 149–153.

Keane, T. M., Caddell, J. M., & Martin, B., et al. (1983). Substance abuse among Vietnam veterans with posttraumatic stress disorders. *Bulletin of Social Psychological Addictive Behavior, 2,* 117–122.

Keane, T. M., Caddell, J., & Taylor, K. (1988). Mississippi scale for combat-related post-traumatic stress disorder: Three studies in reliability and validity. *Journal of Consulting and Clinical Psychology, 56,* 85–90.

Keane, T. M., Fairbank, J. A., Caddell, J. M., & Zimering, R. T. (1989). Imposive (flooding) therapy reduces symptoms of PTSD in Vietnam combat veterans. *Behavior Therapy, 20*, 245–260.

Keane, T. M., Gerardi, R. J., Lyons, J. A., & Wolfe, J. (1986). The interrelationship of substance abuse and posttraumatic stress disorders: Epidemiological and clinical consideration. In M. Galanter (Ed.), *Recent developments in alcoholism* (Vol. 6). New York: Plenum Press.

Keane, T. M., Malloy, P. F., & Fairbank, J. A. (1984). Empirical development of an MMPI subscale for the assessment of combat-related posttraumatic stress disorder. *Journal of Consulting and Clinical Psychology, 52*, 888–891.

Keane, T. M., & Penk, W. (1988). The prevalence of post-traumatic stress disorder. Letter to the editor of *The New England Journal of Medicine, 318*, 1690–1691.

Keane, T. M., Scott, W. O., Chavoya, G. A., Lamparski, D. M., & Fairbanks, J. A. (1985). Social support in Vietnam veterans with post-traumatic stress disorder: A comparative analysis. *Journal of Consulting and Clinical Psychology, 53*, 95–102.

Keane, T. M., & Wolfe, J. (in press). Comorbidity in post-traumatic stress disorder: An analysis of community and clinical studies. *Journal of Applied Social Psychology*.

Keane, T. M., Wolfe, J., & Taylor, K. L. (1987). Post-traumatic stress disorder: Evidence for diagnostic validity and methods of psychological assessment. *Journal of Clinical Psychology, 43*, 32–43.

Kilpatrick, D. G., Best, C. L., Veronen, L. J., Amick, A. E., Vileponteaux, L. A., & Ruff, A. (1985). Mental health correlates of criminal victimization: A random community survey. *Journal of Consulting and Clinical Psychology, 53*, 866–873.

Kilpatrick, D. G., Resick, P. A., & Veronen, L. J. (1981). Effects of a rape experience: A longitudinal study. *Journal of Social Issues, 37*, 105–122.

Kilpatrick, D. G., Saunders, B. E., Veronen, L. J., Best, C. L., & Von, J. M. (1987). Criminal victimization: Lifetime prevalence, reporting to police, and psychological impact. *Crime and Delinquency, 33*, 479–489.

Kilpatrick, D. G., Veronen, L. J., & Resick, P. A. (1979). The aftermath of rape: Recent empirical findings. *American Journal of Orthopsychiatry, 49*, 658–669.

Kulka, R. A., Schlenger, W. E., Fairbank, J. A., Hough, R. L., Jordan, B. K., Marmar, C. R., & Weiss, D. S. (1988). *National Vietnam veterans readjustment study (NVVRS): Description, current status, and initial PTSD prevalence estimates.* Washington, DC: Veterans Administration.

Leopold, R. L., & Dillon, H. (1963). Psychoanatomy of a disaster: A long-term study of post-traumatic neurosis in survivors of a marine explosion. *American Journal of Psychiatry, 119*, 913–921.

Lifton, J. L., & Olsen, E. (1976). The human meaning of total disaster: The Buffalo Creek experience. *Psychiatry, 39*, 1–17.

Lindemann, E. (1944). Symptomatology and management of acute grief. *American Journal of Psychiatry, 101*, 141–148.

Litz, B. T., & Keane, T. M. (1989). Information processing in anxiety disorders: Application to the understanding of post-traumatic stress disorder. *Clinical Psychology Review, 9*, 243–257.

Logue, J. N., Melick, M. E., & Struening, E. L. (1981). A study of health and mental health status following a major disaster. *Research in Community and Mental Health, 2*, 217–274.

Madakasira, S., & O'Brien, K. F. (1987). Acute posttraumatic stress disorder in victims of a natural disaster. *The Journal of Nervous and Mental Disease, 175*, 286–290.

Malloy, P. F., Fairbank, J. A., & Keane, T. M. (1983). Validation of multimethod assessment of post-traumatic stress disorders in Vietnam veterans. *Journal of Consulting and Clinical Psychology, 51*, 488–494.

Mischel, W. (1973). Toward a cognitive social learning reconceptualization of personality. *Psychological Review, 80*, 252–283.

Nadelson, C. C., Notman, M. T., Zackson, H., & Gornick, J. (1982). A follow-up study of rape victims. *American Journal of Psychiatry, 139*, 1266–1270.

Nezu, A. M., & Carneval, G. J. (1987). Interpersonal problem solving and coping reactions of Vietnam veterans with post-traumatic stress disorder. *Journal of Abnormal Psychology, 96*, 155–157.

Ollendick, D. G., & Hoffman, S. M. (1982). Assessment of psychological reactions in disaster victims. *Journal of Community Psychology, 10*, 157–167.

Resick, P. A., Calhoun, K. S., Atkeson, B. M., & Ellis, E. M. (1981). Social adjustment in victims of sexual assault. *Journal of Consulting and Clinical Psychology, 49*, 705–712.

Roberts, W. R., Penk, W. E., Gearing, M. L.,

Robinowitz, R., Dolan, M. P., & Patterson, E. T. (1982). Interpersonal problems of Vietnam combat veterans with posttraumatic stress disorder. *Journal of Abnormal Psychology, 91*, 444–450.

Robins, E., & Guze, S. B. (1970). Establishment of diagnostic validity in psychiatric illness: Its application to schizophrenia. *American Journal of Psychiatry, 126*, 983–987.

Robins, L. N., Helzer, J. E., Croughan, J., & Ratcliff, K. (1981). National Institute of Mental Health Diagnostic Interview Schedule. *Archives of General Psychiatry, 38*, 381–389.

Schaeffer, M. A., & Baum, A. (1984). Adrenal cortical response to stress at Three Mile Island. *Psychosomatic Medicine, 46*, 227–237.

Seligman, M. E. (1974). *Learned helplessness.* San Francisco: W. H. Freeman.

Seligman, M. E., & Garber, J. (1980). *Human helplessness.* New York: Academic Press.

Shore, J., Tatum, E., & Vollmer, W. (1986). Psychiatric reactions to disaster: The Mount St. Helens experience. *American Journal of Psychiatry, 143*, 590–595.

Sierles, F. S., Chen, J., McFarland, R. E., & Taylor, M. A. (1983). Post-traumatic stress disorder and concurrent psychiatric illness. *American Journal of Psychiatry, 140*, 1177–1179.

Sierles, F. S., Chen, J. J., Messing, M. L., Besner, J. K., & Taylor, M. A. (1986). Concurrent psychiatric illness in non-Hispanic outpatients diagnosed as having posttraumatic stress disorder. *The Journal of Nervous and Mental Disease, 174*, 171–173.

Silver, S. M. (1985). The impact of post-traumatic stress disorder on families of Vietnam veterans. In C. R. Figley (Ed.), *Trauma and its wake.* New York: Brunner/Mazel.

Silverman, J. J. (1986). Post-traumatic stress disorders. *Advances in Psychosomatic Medicine, 16*, 115–140.

Smith, J. S., & Fisher, J. H. (1981). Special communications: Three Mile Island — the silent disaster. *Journal of the American Medical Association, 241*, 1656–1659.

Solomon, Z., & Mikulincer, M. (1987). Post-traumatic stress reactions, post-traumatic stress disorder, and social adjustment: A study of Israeli veterans. *Journal of Nervous and Mental Disorders, 175*, 277–285.

Solomon, Z., Mikulincer, M., & Avitzur, E. (1988). Coping, locus of control, social support, and combat-related posttraumatic stress disorder: A prospective study. *Journal of Personality and Social Psychology, 55*, 279–285.

Spielberger, C. D., Gorsuch, R. L., & Lushene, R. E. (1970). *Manual for the State-Trait Anxiety Interview (self-evaluation questionnaire).* Palo Alto, CA: Consulting Psychologists Press.

Spitzer, R. L., & Endicott, J. (1977). *Schedule for affective disorders and schizophrenia* (SADS) (3rd ed.). New York: Biometrics Research.

Spitzer, R. L., & Williams, J. B. W. (1985). *Structured clinical interview for DSM-III-R, patient version.* New York: Biometrics Research Department, New York State Psychiatric Institute.

Steketee, G., & Foa, E. B. (1987). Rape victims: Post-traumatic stress response and their treatment: A review of the literature. *Journal of Anxiety Disorders, 1*, 69–86.

Stretch, R. (1985). Post-traumatic stress disorder among US Army Reserve Vietnam and Vietnam-era veterans. *Journal of Consulting Clinical Psychology, 53*, 935–936.

Titchener, J. L., & Kapp, F. T. (1976). Family and character changes at Buffalo Creek. *American Journal of Psychiatry, 133*, 295–299.

Van der Kolk, B. A., Boyd, H., Krystal, J., & Greenburg, M. (1984). Post-traumatic stress disorder as a biologically based disorder: Implications of the animal model of inescapable shock. In B. A. Van der Kolk (Ed.), *Post-traumatic stress disorder: Psychological and biological sequelae.* Washington, DC: American Psychiatric Press.

Walker, J., & Nash, J. (1981). Group therapy in the treatment of Vietnam combat veterans. *International Journal of Group Psychotherapy, 31*, 376–389.

Wilkinson, C. B. (1983). Aftermath of a disaster: The collapse of the Hyatt Regency Hotel skywalks. *American Journal of Psychiatry, 140*, 1134–1139.

Williams, C. M., & Williams, T. (1987). Aftermath of a disaster: The collapse of the Hyatt Regency Hotel skywalks. *American Journal of Psychiatry, 140*, 1134–1139.

Wilson, J. P., Smith, W. K., & Johnson, S. K. (1985). A comparative analysis of PTSD among various survivor groups. In C. R. Figley (Ed.), *Trauma and its wake: The study and treatment of post-traumatic stress disorder* (pp. 142–172). New York: Brunner/Mazel.

Wilson, J. P., & Zigelbaum, S. D. (1983). The Vietnam veteran on trial: The relation of post-traumatic stress disorder to criminal behavior. *Behavioral Sciences and the Law, 4*, 69–84.

Wirtz, P. W., & Harrell, A. V. (1987). Effects of postassault exposure to attack-similar stimuli on long-term recovery victims. *Journal of Consulting and Clinical Psychology, 55*, 10–16.

Wolfe, J., & Keane, T. M. (1988). *Post-traumatic stress disorder and adjustment: In-country veteran survey*. Manuscript in preparation.

Yager, T., Laufer, R., & Gallops, M. (1984). Some problems associated with war experience in men of the Vietnam generation. *Archives of General Psychiatry, 41*, 327–333.

Zubin, J., & Spring, B. (1977). Vulnerability: A new view of schizophrenia. *Journal of Abnormal Psychology, 86*, 103–126.

CONDUCT DISORDER AND ANTISOCIAL PERSONALITY

EDITORS' COMMENTS

The diagnosis of conduct disorder in childhood augurs poorly for the future, given that at least 50% of children so diagnosed evince a full-fledged antisocial personality in adulthood. Once the symptoms in childhood extend beyond disobedience and unmanageable behavior, the course becomes chronic and unremitting. Impairment of function in childhood cuts across several settings, including school, home, and general interactions with age mates and adults. Already in childhood and adolescence the amoral and shallow personality features so central to adult antisocial personality can be clearly seen. The more flagrant childhood behaviors include stealing, firesetting, cruelty to animals, truancy, vandalism, and aggressive and destructive interactions with peers. In adulthood such dysfunction continues and expands, with considerable disorder in the individual's performance, whether it be in the military, at work, or in interpersonal relationships.

In adulthood the antisocial personality may turn to a life of crime. Indeed, antisocial personality is the most frequent psychiatric diagnosis given to individuals who are incarcerated. The vast majority of antisocial personalities are male, as are conduct-disordered children, again reflecting a link between the child and adult versions of the disorder. Although about half of the children diagnosed as conduct disordered do not become antisocial personalities when they reach adulthood, these individuals are at particular risk for other types of psychiatric disturbance.

Characteristically in childhood and later in adulthood, the antisocial personality is impulsive, experiences little guilt over his or her actions, has little regard for the rights and feelings of others, is not responsible, and functions in a manipulative manner.

Contrary to many of the other disorders described in this handbook, the longitudinal studies tracing the development and outcome of conduct disorder are excellent, methodologically sound, and most informative. Also, the family studies carried out in this area clearly show the intergenerational feature of the disorder, with the modeling influence of the father constituting a critical ingredient. Also contributory to the development of conduct disorder and antisocial personality is the genetic factor. But as usual it is difficult to tease apart genetic predisposition and modeling influences. However, the adoption studies, controlling for environmental influences, suggest that irrespective of the criminal proclivities of adoptive parents, biological children of noncriminals are least likely to display criminal behavior. By contrast, biological children of criminals who then lived with criminal parents were the most likely to evince criminal behavior. The most interesting aspect of such study involves biological children of criminals placed with noncriminal adoptive parents. These children fell between the other two groups with respect to eventual criminal behavior.

Some of the most fascinating findings about antisocial personalities concern the differences between them and "normals" with respect to neurological activity, physiological reactivity, and the usual efficacy of reinforcement and punishment. The documentation of such significant difference between antisocial and normals have led to theorizing that much of the behavior of antisocial personalities is driven by their need constantly to seek sensation and novelty in order to maintain some sense of homeostatic balance. Albeit interesting at the theoretical level, such notions have not resulted in pragmatic strategies for treating and preventing the pervasive sequelae of the disorder. Paradoxically, although a good bit more is known about conduct disorder and antisocial personality than many of the other disorders we consider here, the status of therapeutics is at a very primitive stage. Behavioral strategies show promise, at the very least when the conduct-disordered child is in a controlled setting, but once outside the confines of such control, the effects of operantly based and cognitively inspired treatments do not persist. Perhaps, then, the disorders should be considered as analogous to a chronic medical disease (with its usual vicissitudes), thus requiring constant vigilance and attention from the therapeutic community.

CHAPTER 21

CONDUCT DISORDER IN CHILDHOOD

Alan E. Kazdin

DESCRIPTION OF THE DISORDER

Conduct disorder includes a broad range of antisocial behaviors such as aggressive acts, theft, vandalism, firesetting, lying, truancy, and running away. Although these behaviors are diverse, their common characteristic is that they tend to violate major social rules and expectations. Many of the behaviors often reflect actions against the environment, including both persons and property.

Many symptoms of conduct disorder emerge in some form over the course of normal development. Fighting, lying, stealing, destruction of property, and noncompliance are relatively high at different points in childhood (Achenbach & Edelbrock, 1981; MacFarlane, Allen, & Honzik, 1954). For the most part, these behaviors diminish over time, do not interfere with everyday functioning, and do not predict untoward consequences in adulthood. There are several features of conduct disorder that make the behaviors clearly discrepant from what is seen in everyday life.

Conduct disorder refers to instances when the children or adolescents evince a pattern of antisocial behavior, when there is significant impairment in everyday functioning at home or school, or when the behaviors are regarded as unmanageable by significant others. Thus, the term conduct disorder is reserved here for antisocial behavior that is clinically significant and clearly beyond the realm of normal functioning. As antisocial behavior emerges, a wide range of consequences are evident, including disruptive relations with parents, teachers, and peers; poor school performance; and efforts to intervene in ways that themselves may be disruptive (e.g., transfer to new classrooms, schools, and neighborhoods). Clinically severe antisocial behavior is likely to bring the youth into contact with various social agencies. Mental health services (clinics, hospitals) and the criminal justice system (police, courts) are the major sources of contact for youths whose behaviors are identified as severe. Within the educational system, special services, teachers, and

Completion of this chapter was facilitated by a Research Scientist Development Award (MH00353) and a grant (MH35408) from the National Institute of Mental Health.

classes are often provided to manage such children on a daily basis.

CLINICAL PRESENTATION

The clinical presentation of conduct disorder is often very complex. The complexity derives from the range of dysfunctions that the child may evince and family and parent factors that may be involved as well. The behavioral problems that comprise conduct disorder are relatively clear because they usually refer to overt behavior with marked and stark consequences on the physical or interpersonal environment. More specifically, the behaviors usually reflect several characteristics. First, the behaviors, such as fighting, temper tantrums, stealing, and others, are relatively frequent. In some cases, the behaviors may be of a low frequency (e.g., firesetting), in which case intensity or severity, rather than frequency, is the central characteristic. Second, repetitiveness and chronicity of the behaviors are critical features. The behaviors are not likely to be isolated events or to occur within a brief period where some other influences or stressors (e.g., change in residence, divorce) is operative. Third, the breadth of the behaviors is central as well. Rather than an individual symptom or target behavior, there are usually several behaviors that occur together and form a syndrome or constellation of symptoms. Fourth, noncompliance and oppositional behavior are likely to be present. Although these behaviors do not have immediate deleterious effects, they are usually annoying and may have direct implications for how others (parents, teachers, and peers) interact (e.g., discipline) with the child.

Conduct disorder, as a syndrome, includes several core features, such as fighting, engaging in temper tantrums, theft, truancy, destroying property, defying or threatening others, and running away, among others (see Quay, 1986). Obviously, any individual child is not likely to show all of the symptoms. The notion that they are all part of a syndrome merely notes that they are likely to come in packages.

The characteristics of conduct disorder discussed to this point refer to features of the child. Yet, child characteristics cannot be divorced from characteristics of the parents and family. A variety of parent and family characteristics are associated with the dysfunction. Parents of antisocial youths are more likely to suffer from various psychiatric

disorders than are parents of children in the general population (Rutter et al., 1970). Criminal behavior and alcoholism, particularly of the father, are two of the stronger and more consistently demonstrated parental characteristics of conduct-disordered youths (Robins, 1966; Rutter & Giller, 1983; West, 1982).

Several features related to the interaction of parents with their children characterize families of conduct-disordered youths. Parent disciplinary practices and attitudes have been especially well studied. Parents of conduct-disordered youths tend to be harsh in their attitudes and disciplinary practices with their children (e.g., Farrington, 1978; Glueck & Glueck, 1968; McCord, McCord, & Howard, 1961; Nye, 1958). Conduct-disordered youths are more likely than normals and clinical referrals without antisocial behavior to be victims of child abuse and to be in homes where spouse abuse is evident (Behar & Stewart, 1982; Lewis, Shanok, Pincus, & Glaser, 1979). Lax, erratic, and inconsistent discipline practices for a given parent and between the parents also characterize families of children with conduct disorder. For example, severity of punishment on the part of the father and lax discipline on the part of the mother has been implicated in delinquent behavior (Glueck & Glueck, 1950; McCord et al., 1959). When parents are consistent in their discipline practices, even if they are punitive, children are less likely to be at risk for antisocial behavior (McCord et al., 1959).

Parents of antisocial children are more likely to give commands to their children, to reward deviant behavior directly through attention and compliance, and to ignore or provide aversive consequences for prosocial behavior (see Patterson, 1982). Fine-grained analyses of parent-child interaction suggest that antisocial behavior, particularly aggression, is systematically albeit unwittingly trained in the homes of antisocial children.

Supervision of the child, as another aspect of parent-child contact, has been frequently implicated in conduct disorder (Glueck & Glueck, 1968; Goldstein, 1984; Robins, 1966). Parents of antisocial or delinquent children are less likely to monitor their children's whereabouts, to make arrangements for their care when they are temporarily away from the home, or to provide rules in the home stating where the children can go and when they must return home (Wilson, 1980).

Dysfunctional family relations are manifested in several ways. Parents of antisocial youths, compared with parents of normal youths, show less acceptance of their children, less warmth, affection, and emotional support and report less attachment (Loeber & Dishion, 1983; McCord et al., 1959; West & Farrington, 1973). At the level of family relations, less supportive and more defensive communications among family members, less participation in activities as a family, and more clear dominance of one family member are also evident (Alexander, 1973; Hanson, Henggeler, Haefele, & Rodick, 1984; West & Farrington, 1973). In addition, unhappy marital relations, interpersonal conflict, and aggression characterize the parental relations of delinquent and antisocial children (see Hetherington & Martin, 1979; Rutter & Giller, 1983). Whether or not the parents are separated or divorced, it is the extent of discord that is associated with antisocial behavior and childhood dysfunction.

The present discussion does not exhaust the range of characteristics of parents and families of conduct-disordered youths. Other characteristics, such as mental retardation of the parent, early marriage of the parents, lack of parent interest in the child's school performance, and lack of participation of the family in religious or recreational activities have been found as well (Glueck & Glueck, 1968; Wadsworth, 1979). Many of the factors come in "packages." For example, family size, overcrowding, poor housing, poor parental supervision, parent criminality, and marital discord are likely to be related. Thus, although research can identify the influence of individual components, in practice they are invariably intertwined.

EPIDEMIOLOGY

Prevalence

The prevalence of conduct disorder is difficult to estimate given very different definitions that have been used and variations in rates for children of different ages, sex, socioeconomic class, and geographical locale. Estimates of the rate of conduct disorder among children have ranged from approximately 4% to 10% (Rutter, Cox, Tupling, Berger, & Yule, 1975; Rutter, Tizard, & Whitmore, 1970).

When rates are evaluated for specific behaviors that comprise conduct disorder and youths themselves report on their activities, the prevalence rates are extraordinarily high. For example,

among youths (ages 13 to 18) more than 50% admit to theft, 35% admit to assault, 45% admit to property destruction, and 60% admit to engaging in more than one type of antisocial behavior (such as aggressiveness, drug abuse, arson, vandalism) (see Feldman, Caplinger, & Wodarski, 1983; Williams & Gold, 1972). Even though it is difficult to pinpoint how many children might be defined as conduct disordered at a particular age, data consistently reveal that the problem is great by most definitions.

The extent of the problem is attested further by the utilization of clinical services by youths with antisocial behavior and their families. The rates of referrals of conduct disorder to clinical services are relatively high. Estimates have indicated that referrals to outpatient clinics for aggressiveness, conduct problems, and antisocial behaviors encompass from one third to one half of all child and adolescent cases (Gilbert, 1957; Robins, 1981).

Sex and Age Variations

Conduct disorder in children and adolescents varies as a function of sex (Gilbert, 1957; Robins, 1966). The precise sex ratio is difficult to specify because of varying criteria and measures of conduct disorder among the available studies. Nevertheless, antisocial behavior appears to be at least three times more common among boys (Graham, 1979). The sex differences are not merely due to biases in the referral process for identifying boys more than girls as problematic. Assessment of antisocial behavior through self-report reveals that male juveniles report higher rates of these behaviors than do females (Empey, 1982; Hood & Sparks, 1970).

Sex differences also are apparent in the age of onset of dysfunction. Robins (1966) found that the median age of onset of dysfunction for children referred for antisocial behavior was in the 8- to 10-year age range. Most (57%) boys had an onset before age 10 (median = 7 years old). For girls, onset of antisocial behavior was concentrated in the 14- to 16-year age range (median = 13 years old). Characteristic symptom patterns were different as well. Theft was more frequent as a basis of referral among antisocial boys than among antisocial girls. For boys, aggression was also likely to be a presenting problem. For girls, antisocial behavior was much more likely to include sexual misbehavior.

NATURAL HISTORY

Conduct disorder usually does not emerge *ex nihilo*. It is possible that antisocial behaviors may emerge as part of an adjustment reaction to specific stressors. However, usually the child's history conveys clear and predictable antecedents. Early and "subclinical" signs predict the later onset of conduct disorder. For example, teacher and peer measures of aggressiveness and unmanageability predict subsequent antisocial behavior (Glueck & Glueck, 1959; Mitchell & Rosa, 1981; West & Farrington, 1973). In addition, noncompliance and oppositional behavior appear to be initial behaviors that antedate conduct disorder (Loeber & Schmaling, 1985; Patterson, 1986). These behaviors are referred to as subclinical because they are not of the severity that lead to clinical referrals.

Although the history of individuals who are diagnosed as conduct disordered usually includes subclinical levels of such behavior, these behaviors are not invariably predictive of subsequent dysfunction. An obstacle for early detection is the fact that many children evince oppositional behavior and other antisocial behaviors (e.g., lying, stealing) but do not eventually evince the syndrome of conduct disorder. The waxing and waning of problematic behavior over the course of normal development makes early identification somewhat difficult.

Apart from early signs of antisocial behavior, there are other facets in the history of conduct-disordered youth that can be identified. Child temperament is one such sign. Temperament refers to those prevailing aspects of personality that show some consistency across situations and time. These aspects can be identified among children early in life. Differences in temperament are often based on such characteristics as activity of the child, emotional responsiveness, quality of moods, and social adaptability (Thomas & Chess, 1977). One dimension of temperament used to distinguish children is "easy to difficult" (Plomin, 1983). Easy children are characterized by positive mood, approach toward new stimuli, adaptability to change, and low-intensity reactions to new stimuli. Difficult children show the opposite pattern. Difficult children are more likely to be referred for treatment for aggressive behavior and tantrums than are easy children (Rutter, Birch, Thomas, & Chess, 1964). Thus, a difficult temperament is likely to characterize the history of youths eventually diagnosed as conduct disorder. The problem of relying on temperament is that a difficult temperament is likely to predict dysfunction in general, rather than to serve as a factor unique to antisocial behavior.

Additional factors in the history of antisocial youth are characteristics of the families from which they emerge, as discussed later. Antisocial child behavior emerges in the context of significant parent and family dysfunction. Thus, factors beyond characteristics of the child serve as factors that can predict the onset of antisocial behavior.

IMPAIRMENT AND COMPLICATIONS

The impairment and complications associated with antisocial behavior stem from the pervasiveness of the dysfunction and its correlates and stability over time. Apart from the antisocial, aggressive, and defiant behaviors, there are several correlates or associated features as well. Of the alternative symptoms that have been found among antisocial children, those related to hyperactivity have been the most frequently identified. These symptoms include excessive motor activity, restlessness, impulsiveness, and inattentiveness. In fact, as noted later, the cooccurrence of hyperactivity and conduct disorder has made their diagnostic delineation and assessment a topic of considerable research. Several other behaviors have been identified as problematic among antisocial youths, such as boisterousness, showing off, and blaming others (Quay, 1986). Many of these appear to be relatively mild forms of obstreperous behavior in comparison to aggression, theft, vandalism, or other acts that invoke damage to persons or property.

Youths with conduct disorder are likely to show dysfunction in diverse areas of their lives. Children with conduct disorder are also likely to suffer from academic deficiencies, as reflected in achievement level, grades, and specific skill areas, especially reading (e.g., Ledingham & Schwartzman, 1984; Sturge, 1982). Such children are often seen by their teachers as uninterested in school, unenthusiastic toward academic pursuits, and careless in their work (Glueck & Glueck, 1950). They are more likely to be left behind in grades, to show lower achievement levels, and to end their schooling sooner than their peers matched in age, socioeconomic status, and other demographic variables (Bachman, Johnston, & O'Malley, 1978; Glueck & Glueck, 1968).

The core symptoms of the dysfunction appear to begin a sequence of events that support continued dysfunction. Thus, failure to complete homework and possible truancy or lying are likely to decrease the attention of teachers to aid the student. Consequently, the initial dysfunctions at school are likely to portend further deterioration.

Poor interpersonal relationships are likely to correlate with antisocial behavior. Children who are high in aggressiveness or in other antisocial behaviors are rejected by their peers and show poor social skills (see e.g., Behar & Stewart, 1982; Carlson, Lahey, & Neeper, 1984). Such youths have also been found to be socially ineffective in their interactions with an array of adults (e.g., parents, teachers, and community members). Specifically, antisocial youths are less likely to defer to adult authority, to show politeness, and to respond in ways that promote further positive interactions (Freedman et al., 1978; Gaffney & McFall, 1981).

The correlates of antisocial behavior not only involve overt behaviors but also a variety of cognitive and attributional processes. Antisocial youths are deficient in cognitive problem-solving skills that underlie social interaction (see Dodge, 1985; Kendall & Braswell, 1985). For example, such youths are more likely than their peers to interpret gestures made by others as hostile and are less able to identify solutions to interpersonal problem situations and to take the perspective of others.

The poor prognosis of antisocial behavior leads to a variety of complications. The reason is that a large proportion of antisocial youths remain in continued contact with the mental health and criminal justice systems well into their adulthood. Over the course of their childhood and adolescence, antisocial youths are likely to be exposed to various forms of psychiatric and psychological treatment, family social work, juvenile adjudication and incarceration, and special education programs. Indeed, in light of the poor prognosis and continued contact with various social agencies, antisocial behavior has been identified as one of the most costly of mental disorders to society (Robins, 1981).

The poor prognosis for the individual is not the only source of complications. Antisocial behavior is not only stable over time within individuals but also within families. Antisocial behavior in childhood predicts similar behaviors in one's offspring (Huesmann, Eron, Lefkowitz, & Walder, 1984; Robins, 1981). The continuity is evident across multiple generations. Grandchildren are more likely to show antisocial behaviors if their grandparents have a history of these behaviors (Glueck

& Glueck, 1968). Thus, the social consequences of antisocial behavior may be perpetuated.

DIFFERENTIAL DIAGNOSIS

Diagnosis of Conduct Disorder

Diagnosis of conduct disorder as a specific clinical dysfunction in the *Diagnostic and Statistical Manual of Mental Disorders* (American Psychiatric Association, 1987) depends upon the presence of a number of symptoms. Specifically, to meet the criteria for conduct disorder, the individual must show any three of the following symptoms: (1) stealing without confrontation of a victim; (2) running away; (3) lying; (4) deliberate firesetting; (5) truancy; (6) breaking into someone's house, building, or car; (7) destroying property; (8) cruelty to animals; (9) forced sexual activity of another person; (10) use of a weapon; (11) often initiating fights; (12) stealing with confrontation of a victim; and (13) physical cruelty to people. The symptoms must be present for at least 6 months for the diagnosis to apply.

In the DSM-III-R, there are two major subtypes of conduct disorder, referred to as group type and solitary aggressive type. In the group type, the conduct problems occur primarily as a group activity in the company of friends who have similar problems and to whom the individual is loyal. Physical aggression may be present. Children are included in the solitary aggressive type if they show physically or verbally aggressive behavior. The behavior usually is initiated by the individual, rather than as part of group activity, and no attempt is made to conceal the behavior. The subtype notes that social isolation often may be evident.

Antisocial Behavior in Other Disorders

The diagnosis of conduct disorder is not entirely straightforward because characteristic behaviors may be evident in other diagnostic categories. Two diagnoses in particular are worth noting. The first is an adjustment disorder with disturbance of conduct. In the case of this disorder, the symptoms may be evident, but they usually can be traced to the onset of a particular stressor or change (e.g., divorce, loss of a relative) in the environment. The onset of symptoms within 3 months of the stressor would constitute an adjustment disorder. Symptom(s) such as increased fighting, vandalism, or truancy would be expected to decrease over time as the impact of the stressor attenuates. If the pattern continues, the diagnosis could be altered to conduct disorder.

Symptoms of conduct disorder also would be evident in conditions not due to a particular disorder. (Conditions not attributable to a specific mental disorder are referred to as V Codes in DSM-III. This coding system has been adopted from the International Classification of Diseases [WHO, 1979]. Parent-child problems [e.g., child abuse] or isolated antisocial behaviors of the child [e.g., fighting with the parent] might be categorized as a V code.) These conditions would include isolated acts rather than a pattern of antisocial behavior. Conflict between the parent and child would be the most common instance of one of these conditions. In such cases, the dysfunction is restricted in time and place and includes isolated symptoms rather than the more protracted syndrome.

Attention-Deficit Hyperactivity Disorder

Perhaps the most salient issue regarding differential diagnosis pertains to the relationship of ADHD to conduct disorder. The primary characteristics of Attention-Deficit Hyperactivity Disorder (ADHD) are persistent and excessive activity, distractibility, short attention span, and impulsivity (APA, 1987). Although not a core feature of the diagnosis, children with ADHD often show aggressive behavior, negativism, and other characteristics of conduct or oppositional disorder. Similarly, children who are characterized as aggressive or oppositional often are regarded as "hyperactive." Multivariate studies have shown that hyperactivity and aggression often emerge as separate factors (see Kazdin, 1987). Even so, children's scores on these factors (as evaluated from parent or teacher ratings) typically are correlated in the moderate range (r's = 0.40 to 0.60).

Current evidence suggests that many children who meet diagnostic criteria for conduct disorder may also meet criteria for attention-deficit disorder (ADD) with hyperactivity, the DSM-III equivalent to what is referred to in DSM-III-R as ADHD (see Prinz, Conner, & Wilson, 1981; Stewart, DeBlois, Meardon, & Cummings, 1980). The disorders can be distinguished and are associated with different background characteristics and prognoses (Loney, Kramer, & Milich, 1981; Loney, Langhorne, & Paternite, 1978). On the other hand, there is overlap as well that is important to recognize in discussing either disorder. In DSM-III-R, children who meet criteria can receive both diagnoses. It is not likely that the presence of one disorder would necessarily be confused with another. The diagnostic issue is the need for careful assessment to evaluate whether the criteria for each disorder are met.

CASE EXAMPLE

The diverse characteristics of antisocial children, the symptom constellations they present, and the situations from which they emerge can be illustrated by the case of Mitch, an 8-year-old boy who lived at home with his mother and one older and one younger brother. At home, he constantly fought with his brothers. The intensity of the fighting exceeded the usual boundaries of sibling interactions. On one occasion, Mitch stabbed his younger brother in the chest, and emergency treatment and a hospital stay were required. On another occasion, immediately preceding hospitalization, Mitch attacked a child in his class with a baseball bat. He hit the child twice, causing a broken arm. Apart from extreme aggressive acts at home and at school, he constantly defied authority and destroyed other children's property whenever he was angry. He argued frequently with his mother and would leave home for several hours at a time after an argument. On three occasions, he remained out overnight after arguments with his mother and could not be found by police. He stayed with friends on two occasions and stayed with his father (outside of the home) on the other occasion. Apart from his aggression and running away, he occasionally stole things from others. He stole purses from his teachers at school on two occasions within the year preceding his referral to the clinic. On each occasion, his mother found the purse in Mitch's closet and phoned the school to arrange for its return. Mitch denied that he had taken the purses.

Mitch was brought to the clinic because his mother felt she could no longer manage him and because his behavior seemed dangerous to her and her other children. Also, he had been recently suspended from school for 3 days because of a fight. Consequently, he was at home more than usual and engaged in more frequent and extreme aggressive behavior with his mother. Mitch's mother brought him to a clinic to seek treatment. The psychiatric evaluation at the clinic revealed that Mitch had become significantly more aggressive at home and at school in the past few months. His fighting, threats to others, and destruction of property all had seemed to worsen. Both the mother and Mitch's siblings had been physically injured. In addition, there was no consistent way to keep Mitch in the home at night. Based on the description of Mitch's recent behavior and in consultation with the mother, it was decided that Mitch should be hospitalized for a brief period to begin treatment and to help develop a program to integrate him back into school.

Several features of Mitch's home life and family are worth noting. Mitch lived with his mother. His mother and father were divorced 3 years earlier, when Mitch was 5 years old. Prior to the divorce, there had been considerable spouse and child abuse by the father. The father was a diagnosed alcoholic. When he came home inebriated, he often beat his wife and the children. On more than one occasion, he awakened one of the boys to beat them for not doing a chore like taking out the trash or washing the dishes. The mother and children moved to a women's shelter. This was followed by legal separation and divorce. The mother and boys eventually moved back into their home. The father remained nearby but did not seek further contact with the children after the divorce.

Mitch's mother worked part-time at a dry cleaners and also was on public assistance. She was at home in the afternoon and evenings when her children returned from school. Occasionally, her mother would help baby-sit for the children when she had to go to work and the children were home from school. Mitch's mother had a history of major depressive disorder, although she has been out of treatment for 2 years with no further episodes.

At school, Mitch was in the third grade. His academic performance and grades were consistently low. He had been placed in a special class for emotionally disturbed children because of his disruptive and aggressive behavior. Also, his high level of activity led to his being labeled as hyperactive. His level of intelligence, when tested, fell within the low normal range (full-scale IQ score of 92 on the Wechsler Intelligence Scale for Children — Revised, [WISC-R]). However, his work barely led to C grades in academic subjects because he missed so much class time and had such difficulty in completing his work.

General Comments

The case illustrates briefly the type and severity of problems that conduct disorder represents. The case underscores a few important points. First, the child engaged in rather severe behaviors. The problems were not merely failing to comply with his mother's requests, getting into arguments with

siblings, and not completing school work. Each of these behaviors was evident but did not serve as the primary basis for seeking professional attention. Second, the mother felt that the child was out of control and no longer manageable. The school also could not manage the child and had suspended Mitch for fighting. Third, the mother's situation was difficult to manage. She was a single parent, on welfare, with two other children to maintain and had a history of and was at risk for continued depression.

CONTINUITY AND DISCONTINUITY WITH ADULT PRESENTATION

The course and prognosis of antisocial behavior have been studied extensively and several different features have been identified. To begin with, among childhood disorders, conduct disorder tends to be relatively stable over time (Beach & Laird, 1968; Robins, 1978). The stability departs from many other disorders that often are age-specific and remit over the course of development. Thus, when children evince consistent antisocial behavior, such as aggressive acts toward others, it is unlikely that they will simply "grow out of it."

For the children who are diagnosed with conduct disorder and who are seen clinically for their antisocial behavior, the course and prognosis are relatively clear. Longitudinal studies have consistently shown that antisocial behavior identified in childhood or adolescence predicts a continued course of social dysfunction, problematic behavior, and poor school adjustment (e.g., Bachman et al., 1978; Gersten et al., 1976; Glueck & Glueck, 1968; Jessor & Jessor, 1977; McCord, McCord, & Zola, 1959). One of the most dramatic illustrations of the long-term prognosis of clinically referred children was the classic study by Robins (1966), who evaluated their status 30 years later. The results demonstrated that antisocial child behavior predicted multiple problems in adulthood. Youths who had been referred for their antisocial behavior, compared to youths with other clinical problems or matched normal controls, as adults suffered dysfunction in psychiatric symptoms, criminal behavior, physical health, and social adjustment. Several studies attest to the breadth of dysfunction of conduct-disordered children as they mature into adulthood. Table 21.1 highlights the characteristics that these children are likely to evince when they become adults.

Even though conduct disorder in childhood portends a number of other significant problems

Table 21.1. Long-Term Prognosis of Conduct-Disordered Youths: Overview of Major Characteristics Likely to be Evident in Adulthood

AREA OF FUNCTIONING	CHARACTERISTICS IN ADULTHOOD
1. Psychiatric status	Greater psychiatric impairment, including sociopathic personality, alcohol and drug abuse, and isolated symptoms (e.g., anxiety, somatic complaints); also, greater history of psychiatric hospitalization.
2. Criminal behavior	Higher rates of driving while intoxicated, criminal behavior, arrest records and conviction, and period of time spent in jail; greater seriousness of the criminal acts.
3. Occupational adjustment	Less likelihood of employment; shorter history of employment, lower-status jobs, more frequent change of jobs, lower wages, and greater dependence on financial assistance (welfare); served less frequently and performed less well in the armed services.
4. Educational attainment	Higher rates of dropping out of school, lower attainment among those who remain in school.
5. Marital status	Higher rates of divorce, remarriage, and separation.
6. Social participation	Less contact with relatives, friends, and neighbors; little participation in organizations such as church.
7. Physical health	Higher mortality rate; higher rate of hospitalization for physical (as well as psychiatric) problems.

Note: These characteristics are based on comparisons of clinically referred children identified for antisocial behavior relative to control clinical referrals or normal controls or from comparisons of delinquent and nondelinquent youths (see Bachman et al., 1978; Glueck & Glueck, 1950; Huesmann et al., 1984; Robins, 1966, 1978; Wadsworth, 1979).

in adulthood, not all antisocial children suffer impairment as adults. Nevertheless, data suggest that a high percentage of children are likely to suffer as adults. Across several different samples, Robins (1978) noted that among the most severely antisocial children, less than 50% become antisocial adults. Even though less than half of the children continue antisocial behavior into adulthood, the percentage is still quite high.

If diverse diagnoses are considered, rather than serious antisocial behavior alone, the picture of impairment in adulthood is much worse. Among children referred for antisocial behavior, 84% received a diagnosis of psychiatric disorder as adults (Robins, 1966). Although these diagnoses vary in degree of impairment (e.g., psychoses, neuroses), the data suggest that the majority of children with clinically referred antisocial behavior will suffer from a significant degree of impairment.

As already noted, not all antisocial youths become antisocial adults. Major factors that influence whether antisocial youths are likely to continue their behavior into adulthood include parent antisocial behavior, alcoholism, poor parental supervision of the child, harsh or inconsistent discipline practices, marital discord in the family, large family size, older siblings who are antisocial, and so on. The most significant predictors of long-

term outcome are characteristics of the child's antisocial behavior. Early onset of antisocial behaviors, antisocial acts evident across multiple settings (e.g., home and school), and many and diverse antisocial behaviors (e.g., several versus few, covert and overt acts) are the primary factors that predict untoward long-term consequences (Loeber & Dishion, 1983; Rutter & Giller, 1983).

SUMMARY

Conduct disorder is the diagnosis for serious antisocial behavior in childhood. However, the dysfunction can be considered lifelong. Early signs usually consist of disobedience and unmanageability. These appear to continue for some children and to emerge into more serious behavioral problems as evident primarily in aggression. A variety of related characteristics occur as well such as stealing, firesetting, vandalism, truancy, and others. The dysfunction continues into adulthood, although the diagnostic label changes (antisocial personality disorder in DSM-III-R). The continuity of the disorder is not only evident within the individual over the course of development but also within families across generations.

The significance of the diagnosis of conduct disorder is punctuated by the breadth of dysfunction in childhood, as reflected in diverse areas of functioning at home and at school and in interactions with adults and peers. The course for continued dysfunction is often set early. For example, early signs of antisocial behavior predict academic dysfunction. Poor academic performance generates its own untoward consequences that hinder subsequent social adjustment. The breadth of dysfunction continues into adulthood as reflected in work and home maladjustment. Already noted were the findings that not all youth with conduct disorder continue in their antisocial behavior into adulthood. Yet, those who avoid this particular path suffer from many other forms of dysfunction and maladjustment.

The longitudinal and transgenerational nature of the disorder raises many options for intervention. Children who evince signs of dysfunction and families whose children are at risk can be identified early for preventive interventions. Alternatively, young children who meet diagnostic criteria might be identified for treatment before the disorder leads to the deleterious consequences that follow. As yet, the point of effective intervention and the specific interventions that can controvert the pattern have not been identified.

REFERENCES

Achenbach, T. M., & Edelbrock, C. S. (1981). Behavioral problems and competencies reported by parents of normal and disturbed children aged four through sixteen. *Monographs of the Society for Research in Child Development, 46*(188).

Alexander, J. F. (1973). Defensive and supportive communications in normal and deviant families. *Journal of Consulting and Clinical Psychology, 40*, 223–231.

American Psychiatric Association. (1980). *Diagnostic and statistical manual of mental disorders* (3rd ed.). Washington, DC: Author.

American Psychiatric Association. (1987). *Diagnostic and statistical manual of mental disorders* (3rd ed. rev.). Washington, DC: Author.

Bachman, J. G., Johnston, L. D., & O'Malley, P. M. (1978). Delinquent behavior linked to educational attainment and post-high school experiences. In L. Otten (Ed.), *Colloquium on the correlates of crime and the determinants of criminal behavior*. Arlington, VA: The MITRE Corp.

Beach, C. F., & Laird, J. D. (1968). Follow-up study of children identified early as emotionally disturbed. *Journal of Consulting and Clinical Psychology, 32*, 369–374.

Behar, D., & Stewart, M. A. (1982). Aggressive conduct disorder of children. *Acta Psychiatrica Scandinavica, 65*, 210–220.

Carlson, C. L., Lahey, B. B., & Neeper, R. (1984). Peer assessment of the social behavior of accepted, rejected, and neglected children. *Journal of Abnormal Child Psychology, 12*, 189–198.

Dodge, K. A. (1985). Attributional bias in aggressive children. In P. C. Kendall (Ed.), *Advances in cognitive-behavioral research and therapy* (Vol. 4). Orlando, FL: Academic Press.

Empey, L. T. (1982). *American delinquency: Its meaning and construction*. Homewood, IL: Dorsey Press.

Farrington, D. P. (1978). The family backgrounds of aggressive youths. In L. A. Hersov, M. Berger, & D. Shaffer (Eds.), *Aggression and antisocial behaviour in childhood and adolescence*. Oxford: Pergamon Press.

Feldman, R. A., Caplinger, T. E., & Wodarski, J. S. (1983). *The St. Louis conundrum: The effective treatment of antisocial youths*. Englewood Cliffs, NJ: Prentice Hall.

Freedman, B. J., Rosenthal, L., Donahoe, C. P., Schlundt, D. G., & McFall, R. (1978). A social-behavioral analysis of skills deficits in delinquent and nondelinquent boys. *Journal of Consulting and Clinical Psychology, 46*, 1448–1462.

Gaffney, L. R., & McFall, R. M. (1981). A comparison of social skills in delinquent and nondelinquent adolescent girls using a behavioral role-playing inventory. *Journal of Consulting and Clinical Psychology, 49*, 959–967.

Gersten, J. C., Langner, T. S., Eisenberg, J. G., Simcha-Fagan, D., & McCarthy, E. D. (1976). Stability in change in types of behavioral disturbances of children and adolescents. *Journals of Abnormal Child Psychology, 4*, 111–127.

Gilbert, G. M. (1957). A survey of "referral problems" in metropolitan child guidance centers. *Journal of Clinical Psychology, 13*, 37–42.

Glueck, S., & Glueck, E. (1950). *Unravelling juvenile delinquency*. Cambridge, MA: Harvard University Press.

Glueck, S., & Glueck, E. (1959). *Predicting delinquency and crime*. Cambridge, MA: Harvard University Press.

Glueck, S., & Glueck, E. (1968). *Delinquents and nondelinquents in perspective.* Cambridge, MA: Harvard University Press.

Goldstein, H. S. (1984). Parental composition, supervision, and conduct problems in youths 12 to 17 years old. *Journal of the American Academy of Child Psychiatry, 23,* 679–684.

Graham, P. (1979). Epidemiological studies. In H. C. Quay & J. S. Werry (Eds.), *Psychopathological disorders of childhood* (2nd ed.). New York: John Wiley & Sons.

Hanson, C. L., Henggeler, S. W., Haefele, W. F., & Rodick, J. D. (1984). Demographic, individual, and family relationship correlates of serious and repeated crime among adolescents and their siblings. *Journal of Consulting and Clinical Psychology, 52,* 528–538.

Hetherington, E. M., & Martin, B. (1979). Family interaction. In H. C. Quay & J. S. Werry (Eds.), *Psychopathological disorders of childhood* (2nd ed.). New York: John Wiley & Sons.

Hood, R., & Sparks, R. (1970). *Key issues in criminology.* London: Weidenfeld & Nicholson.

Huesmann, L. R., Eron, L. D., Lefkowitz, M. M., & Walder, L. O. (1984). Stability of aggression over time and generations. *Developmental Psychology, 20,* 1120–1134.

Jessor, R., & Jessor, S. L. (1977). *Problem behavior and psychological development: A longitudinal study of youth.* New York: Academic Press.

Kazdin, A. E. (1987). *Conduct disorder in childhood and adolescence.* Newbury Park, CA: Sage Publications.

Kendall, P. C., & Braswell, L. (1985). *Cognitive-behavioral therapy for impulsive children.* New York: The Guilford Press.

Ledingham, J. E., & Schwartzman, A. E. (1984). A 3-year follow-up of aggressive and withdrawn behavior in childhood: Preliminary findings. *Journal of Abnormal Child Psychology, 12,* 157–168.

Lewis, D. O., Shanok, S. S., Pincus, J. H., & Glaser, G. H. (1979). Violent juvenile delinquents: Psychiatric, neurological, psychological, and abuse factors. *Journal of the American Academy of Child Psychiatry, 18,* 307–319.

Loeber, R., & Dishion, T. J. (1983). Early predictors of male delinquency: A review. *Psychological Bulletin, 94,* 68–99.

Loeber, R., & Dishion, T. J. (1984). Boys who fight at home and school: Family conditions influencing cross-setting consistency. *Journal of Consulting and Clinical Psychology, 52,* 759–768.

Loeber, R., & Schmaling, K. B. (1985). Empirical evidence for overt and covert patterns of antisocial conduct problems: A meta-analysis. *Journal of Abnormal Child Psychology, 13,* 337–352.

Loney, J., Kramer, J., & Milich, R. (1981). The hyperkinetic child grows up: Predictors of symptoms, delinquency, and achievement at follow-up. In K. Gadow & J. Loney (Eds.), *Psychosocial aspects of drug treatment for hyperactivity* (pp. 381–415). Boulder, CO: Westview Press.

Loney, J., Langhorne, J., & Paternite, C. (1978). An empirical basis for subgrouping the hyperkinetic/minimal brain dysfunction syndrome. *Journal of Abnormal Psychology, 87,* 431–441.

MacFarlane, J. W., Allen, L., & Honzik, M. P. (1954). *A developmental study of the behavior problems of normal children between 21 months and 14 years.* Berkeley: University of California Press.

McCord, W., McCord, J., & Howard, A. (1961). Familial correlates of aggression in nondelinquent male children. *Journal of Abnormal and Social Psychology, 62,* 79–93.

McCord, W., McCord, J., & Zola, I. K. (1959). *Origins of crime.* New York: Columbia University Press.

Mitchell, S., & Rosa, P. (1981). Boyhood behavior problems as precursors of criminality: A fifteen-year follow-up study. *Journal of Child Psychology and Psychiatry, 22,* 19–33.

Nye, F. I. (1958). *Family relationships and delinquent behavior.* New York: John Wiley & Sons.

Patterson, G. R. (1982). *Coercive family process.* Eugene, OR: Castalia.

Patterson, G. R. (1986). Performance models for antisocial boys. *American Psychologist, 41,* 432–444.

Plomin, R. (1983). Childhood temperament. In B. B. Lahey & A. E. Kazdin (Eds.), *Advances in clinical child psychology.* New York: Plenum Press.

Prinz, R., Connor, P., & Wilson, C. (1981). Hyperactive and aggressive behaviors in childhood: Intertwined dimensions. *Journal of Abnormal Child Psychology, 9,* 191–202.

Quay, H. C. (1986). Classification. In H. C. Quay & J. S. Werry (Eds.), *Psychopathological disorders of childhood* (3rd ed., pp. 1–34). New York: John Wiley & Sons.

Robins, L. N. (1966). *Deviant children grown up.* Baltimore: Williams & Wilkins.

Robins, L. N. (1978). Sturdy childhood predictors of adult antisocial behavior: Replications from longitudinal studies. *Psychological Medicine, 8*, 611–622.

Robins, L. N. (1981). Epidemiological approaches to natural history research: Antisocial disorders in children. *Journal of the American Academy of Child Psychiatry, 20*, 566–680.

Rutter, M., Birch, H. G., Thomas, A., & Chess, S. (1964). Temperamental characteristics in infancy and the later development of behavioral disorders. *British Journal of Psychiatry, 110*, 651–661.

Rutter, M., Cox, A., Tupling, C., Berger, M., & Yule, W. (1975). Attainment and adjustment in two geographical areas: I. The prevalence of psychiatric disorder. *British Journal of Psychiatry, 126*, 493–509.

Rutter, M., & Giller, H. (1983). *Juvenile delinquency: Trends and perspectives.* New York: Penguin Books.

Rutter, M., Tizard, J., & Whitmore, K. (Eds.). (1970). *Education, health and behaviour.* London: Longmans.

Stewart, M. A., DeBlois, C. S., Meardon, J., & Cummings, C. (1980). Aggressive conduct disorder children. *Journal of Nervous and Mental Disease, 168*, 604–610.

Sturge, C. (1982). Reading retardation and antisocial behaviour. *Journal of Child Psychology and Psychiatry, 23*, 21–31.

Thomas, A., & Chess, S. (1977). *Temperament and development.* New York: Brunner/Mazel.

Wadsworth, M. (1979). *Roots of delinquency: Infancy, adolescence and crime.* New York: Barnes & Noble.

West, D. J. (1982). *Delinquency: Its roots, careers and prospects.* Cambridge, MA: Harvard University Press.

West, D. J., & Farrington, D. P. (1973). *Who becomes delinquent?* London: Heinemann Educational Books.

Williams, J. R., & Gold, M. (1972). From delinquent behavior to official delinquency. *Social Problems, 20*, 209–229.

Wilson, H. (1980). Parental supervision: A neglected aspect of delinquency. *British Journal of Criminology, 20*, 203–235.

World Health Organization. (1979). *International classification of diseases, injuries, and causes of death* (9th ed.). Geneva: Author.

CHAPTER 22

ANTISOCIAL PERSONALITY DISORDER IN ADULTHOOD

Michael A. Milan

DESCRIPTION OF THE DISORDER

The current revision of the *Diagnostic and Statistical Manual of Mental Disorders* (American Psychiatric Association, 1987) identifies the essential feature of the antisocial personality disorder as a pattern of irresponsible and antisocial behavior beginning in childhood or early adolescence that continues into adulthood (p. 434). More specifically, the DSM-III-R diagnostic criteria for the disorder require that the individual be at least 18 years of age. The diagnostic criteria also require evidence of conduct disorder, as defined in the previous chapter (excepting as a clinical sign breaking into someone else's house, building, or car), with onset before 15 years of age. In addition, the diagnostic criteria for the disorder also require a pattern of irresponsible and antisocial behavior since 15 years of age as indicated by at least 4 of the following 10 characteristics:

1. Inability to sustain consistent work behavior, indicated by 6 months of unjustified unemployment within the past 5 years, repeated un-

explained absences, or abandonment of several jobs without realistic alternatives.
2. Failure to conform to social norms with respect to lawful behavior as indicated by repeatedly performing antisocial acts that are grounds for arrest.
3. Irritability and aggressiveness, as indicated by physical fights or assaults, including spouse or child beating.
4. Repeated failures to honor financial obligations, as indicated by defaulting on debts or failing to provide child support or support of other dependents.
5. Failure to plan ahead or impulsivity, as indicated by traveling from place to place in an unplanned manner or lacking a fixed address for a month or more.
6. Lack of regard for the truth, as indicated by repeated lying, uses of aliases, or "conning" others for pleasure or profit.
7. Recklessness regarding the safety of self or others, as indicated by driving while intoxicated or speeding.
8. If a parent or guardian, inability to function as a responsible parent, as indicated by mal-

307

nutrition of a child, a child's illness due to lack of minimal hygiene, failure to obtain medical care for a seriously ill child, a child's dependence on neighbors or nonresident relatives for food or shelter, failure to arrange for caretaking of a young child when away from home, or repeated squandering of money required for household necessities.

9. Failure to sustain at least one totally monogamous relationship for more than one year.
10. Lack of remorse, as evidenced by feelings of justification for having hurt, mistreated, or stolen from another.

The final requirement in the diagnosis of antisocial personality disorder is that the antisocial behavior must not occur exclusively during the course of schizophrenia or manic episodes.

While the most recent edition of the *Diagnostic and Statistical Manual* and its current revision (APA, 1980, 1987) apply the term antisocial personality disorder to the antisocial syndrome, the first two editions of the manual (APA, 1952, 1968) used the term sociopath. The change in terminology, as well as a change in the defining characteristics of the disorder, make it particularly difficult to compare earlier and later work in this area. Moreover, these difficulties have been compounded by some authors' use of other terms, such as psychopath, and other defining characteristics in their research and publications (e.g., Cleckley, 1941). As a consequence, the terms and defining characteristics of antisocial personality disorder, sociopath, and psychopath have been used interchangeably in discussions of the disorder. This chapter will use the term antisocial personality disorder when referring to the syndrome and the term antisocial when referring to individuals with that diagnosis. It should be noted, however, that the authors reviewed in this chapter may well have used other terms in their original works.

CLINICAL PRESENTATION

Clinical descriptions of individuals with the diagnosis of antisocial personality disorder are perhaps the most disparaging of all forms of psychopathology. For example, Karpman (1961) characterized antisocial individuals as callous and emotionally immature. He went on to describe them as two-dimensional people who are lacking in "real depth." Antisocials were said to exhibit only simple and "animal-like" emotional reactions, and then only as immediate responses to discomfort and frustration. Karpman added that they do not experience normal anxiety, although they may exhibit fear when their personal well-being is in immediate jeopardy. They were said to show poor judgment and to be motivated almost exclusively by their current needs and impulses. Karpman also described antisocials as creatures of the here-and-now who were indifferent to both the positive and negative long-term consequences of their acts. He concluded that such individuals often find themselves in trouble and that in their attempts to escape the troubles that they have created for themselves, antisocials create a plausible but contradictory system of lies, explanations, justifications, and promises, presented with a convincing sense of righteous indignation and personal integrity.

Craft (1965) agreed that the primary features of the antisocial personality disorder consisted of a tendency to act on impulse and a lack of feeling, affection, or love for others. Hare (1970) added that most clinical descriptions of antisocials have emphasized their egocentricity, lack of empathy, and inability to form warm, emotional relationships with others. This is in accord with the observations of Foulds (1965) and Buss (1966), who suggested that it is the antisocials' egocentricity and lack of empathy that underlie their tendency to treat individuals as objects rather than real people, and then feel no sorrow or guilt for having done so. They are therefore seen as individuals who either cannot or do not appreciate the feelings and perspectives of others. Because of such lack of empathy, antisocials are described as able to manipulate others as they would an inanimate object. In so doing, they may act to gratify their needs without either concerning themselves about the physical and emotional harm they will cause others, or accurately anticipating what others' reactions to them will be when they do so.

McCord (1982) painted a somewhat more sympathetic picture of individuals with the diagnosis of antisocial personality disorder, characterizing them as "lonely strangers" (p. 31) and postulating that their psychopathology does not involve a willful decision to do evil to others, but instead that they are in a real sense different from the rest of us. McCord suggested that antisocials have not been adequately socialized and are therefore not influenced by the values and norms of society. Moreover, they are not members of a deviant subculture that has rejected the values of the dominant culture. Instead, they have no allegiance to an individual or group other than themselves.

McCord (1982) also saw antisocials as unable to comprehend the feelings of empathy and compassion that individuals have for their fellow human beings and experience none themselves. They do, however, recognize that others do have such feelings, and will often play on those feelings in others in a manipulative fashion to achieve their own ends. As McCord pointed out, it should not be surprising that individuals without empathy and compassion for others do not experience feelings of guilt, shame, or remorse for the pain and anguish that they cause others. Indeed, Hare (1970) reports that it is this lack of guilt that is most influential in determining psychodiagnosticians' decisions concerning the diagnosis of antisocial personality disorder.

Finally, McCord (1982) saw antisocials as unable to maintain lasting emotional relationships with others. This includes relationships with parents, childhood friends, adult acquaintances, and spouses. While antisocials may feign these emotions, this is done for personal gain. The emotions, and the individuals to whom they are directed, are quickly abandoned when they are no longer useful. McCord's secondary characteristics of the antisocial personality disorder are impulsivity, aggressiveness, and a craving for excitement. While no one is immune to impulsivity, the impulsivity of the antisocials is qualitatively and quantitatively different from that of other individuals. In short, they tend to gratify their immediate and/or transient impulses without regard for the consequences to others and themselves for doing so. The aggression of many antisocials toward animals and their fellow humans is uncontrolled and typically manifest in more impersonal, unfocused, cruel, and purposeless ways than is that of others. Aggression appears to be a normal and appropriate way of life to antisocials. Finally, McCord noted that the craving for stimulation and entertainment is a human characteristic seen in even the youngest of children. Children have learned to control and gratify that craving in socially sanctioned ways while antisocials have apparently not mastered this developmental task and continue to seek and create an environment of constant change, dangerous excitement, and unpredictability.

Antisocial personality disorder overlaps with criminality, but not all individuals who would be diagnosed as showing an antisocial personality are criminals, and not all criminals would be diagnosed as showing an antisocial personality. Within the context of his discussion of the psychopath, Cleckley (with Thigpen, 1982) provided a detailed description of the impairment and complications experienced by those individuals, both criminal and noncriminal, whose behavior would justify the diagnosis of antisocial personality disorder. The clinical profile of the Cleckley psychopath consists of 16 characteristics (p. 204):

1. Superficial charm and good "intelligence"
2. Absence of delusions and other signs of irrational thinking
3. Absence of "nervousness" or psychoneurotic manifestations
4. Unreliability
5. Untruthfulness and insincerity
6. Inappropriate behavior that is inadequately motivated
7. Lack of remorse and shame
8. Poor judgment and failure to learn by experience
9. Shocking and vulgar behavior with intoxication and sometimes without
10. Empty suicidal threats
11. Pathologic egocentricity and incapacity to love
12. Sex life that is impersonal, trivial, and poorly integrated
13. General poverty in affective reactions
14. Unresponsiveness in general interpersonal relations
15. Specific lack of insight
16. Failure to follow any life plan

EPIDEMIOLOGY

As has been noted previously, the terms antisocial personality disorder, psychopath, sociopath, and sometimes criminal are used interchangeably in research into the origins and nature of antisocial behavior. Inconsistencies in definitions from study to study undoubtedly make it difficult to identify regularities in the etiology of the antisocial personality disorder. Nonetheless, certain findings of note have emerged. Robins, Helzer, Weissman, Orvaschel, Gruenberg, Bruche, and Regier (1984) reported the results of large-scale population surveys in three urban sites (Baltimore, New Haven, and St. Louis, MO) conducted between 1980 and 1982. The overall lifetime prevalence of the antisocial personality disorder ranged from 2.1% to 3.3%. Males were found to be between 4.1 and 7.8 times more likely than females to be diagnosed as showing the disorder. The lifetime prevalence ranged from 3.9% to 4.9% for males and from 0.5% to 1.2% for females.

Robins et al. (1984) found that the prevalence of antisocial personality disorder was highest in the inner city (5.7%), lower in the suburbs (3.1%), and lowest in small towns (2.4%). No consistent differences in prevalence were found between the races. College graduates showed a lower prevalence of the disorder than did nongraduates. The prevalence for college graduates ranged from 0.9% to 2.3%, while the prevalence for nongraduates ranged from 2.5% to 3.4%. Robins, Gentry, Munoz, and Martens (1977) reported that the antisocial personality is the third most commonly diagnosed disorder in psychiatric emergency rooms. Woodruff, Guze, and Clayton (1971) indicated that 15% of the males and 3% of the females receiving services in psychiatric outpatient clinics carry the diagnosis. Guze, Goodwin, and Crane (1969) found that the antisocial personality disorder is the most commonly diagnosed psychiatric disturbance in criminal populations.

Considerable effort has been devoted to the examination of the genetic etiology of the antisocial personality disorder. In an early study, Partridge (1928) traced the lineage of 50 antisocials and claimed to find that 24 had recent ancestors who also showed antisocial characteristics. More contemporary research in this area has involved studies of twin or adoptees. A third, more powerful, strategy involves the linkage of identifiable genetic traits with psychopathology. Although it was believed for a short time that the presence of an extra male chromosome (the 47, XYY abnormality) was associated with the disorder (e.g., Reid, 1978), there are no known genetic traits that are linked with the antisocial personality disorder (Cadoret, 1986).

Many of the twin and adoptee studies to be reported are not without methodological and interpretive difficulties. Nonetheless, certain regularities have emerged. The twin studies have focused more on delinquency and criminality than they have on the antisocial personality disorder. The findings to be reported are therefore only suggestive of the relationship between genetics and the disorder. In general, the twin studies are in accord with the position that individuals' genetic endowment can predispose them to antisocial behavior. For example, Christiansen (1977) examined the histories of a random sample of all twins born in Denmark during a 50-year period. He found that the probability of finding a criminal twin when the other twin was criminal (concordance) was approximately 0.50 for monozygotic (identical) twins and approximately 0.20 for dizygotic (fraternal) twins.

Eysenck and Eysenck (1978) reviewed nine twin studies and found that approximately 55% of the monozygotic twins were concordant for criminal antisocial behavior as compared to less than 15% of the dizygotic twins. Cloninger, Reich, and Guze (1978) presented complementary findings and estimated that the correlation of monozygotic heritability of criminality is approximately 0.70, while that of dizygotic heritability is slightly less than 0.30. While these and many other studies suggest a genetic basis for antisocial behavior, it must be remembered that identical twins are more likely to be treated the same by family, friends, and others than are fraternal twins and that the studies have assessed the heritability of criminality, not the antisocial personality disorder. The implication of twin studies for the heritability of the disorder is therefore unclear.

Adoption studies have attempted to control for environmental influences. In the most comprehensive study of the heritability of criminality to date, Mednick, Gabrielli, and Hutchings (1984) examined the relationship between criminality in biological and adoptive parents and criminality in all of Denmark's children adopted over a 27-year period. The biological children of criminals who were placed with adoptive criminal parents were most likely to engage in criminal behavior. The biological children of noncriminals were least likely to engage in criminal behavior, regardless of the criminality of the adoptive parents. The biological children of criminals who were placed with noncriminal adoptive parents fell midway between those groups. These and supplementary analyses performed by Mednick et al. indicate that the criminality of the biological parents is more important than the criminality of the adoptive parents in predicting outcome, suggesting a genetic contribution to criminal behavior.

Additional adoptive research suggests that the same relationships hold for parents and children with and without the antisocial personality disorder. For example, Schulsinger (1977) combined all personality disorders and found that the biological parents of adoptive children with those disorders were more likely to exhibit personality disorders than were the adoptive parents. Similarly,

Cadoret (1978) found that adoptees with histories of antisocial disorders in their family backgrounds were more likely to show the antisocial personality disorder than were adoptees without such histories. Although there are exceptions to these general findings, it does appear plausible that some individuals' genetic endowments contribute to or predispose them to antisocial behavior and the antisocial personality disorder. However, the relative weight of heredity and environment has not yet been examined in sufficient detail to even justify a cautious statement of their individual contributions to this serious disorder.

NATURAL HISTORY

The natural history of the antisocial personality is probably the least well-researched aspect of the disorder. The definition of the antisocial personality disorder requires that it originate as a conduct disorder, with onset before the age of 15 years. DSM-III-R (APA, 1987) notes that the earlier the onset of the conduct disorder in childhood, the more likely it is that the disorder will evolve into the antisocial personality disorder in adulthood.

One of the few longitudinal studies of antisocials was conducted by O'Neal, Robins, King, and Schaefer (1962), who followed 524 individuals who were initially seen as children at a child guidance center. Participants in the study were followed for as long as 30 years, with the ages of the participants at the end of the study ranging from 31 to 54 years. Most of the participants who met the criteria for the diagnosis of antisocial personality disorder at any time in their lives continued to show pronounced symptoms of the disorder at the end of the follow-up period. Many individuals showed some spontaneous improvement over the course of the study, and there were no ages at which improvement was not seen. However, for the small proportion of individuals in which pronounced improvement occurred, such improvement was most likely to be seen between 30 and 35 years of age. These findings support the observation that the antisocial personality disorder is a chronic and enduring condition. Although some individuals with the diagnosis may show marked improvements over time, most will show little or no change as they mature into their fifties and, perhaps, beyond.

Cross-sectional analysis of criminal behavior presents a somewhat different picture of the history of antisocial behavior. Uniform Crime Report data (Federal Bureau of Investigation, 1987) reveals that persons 20 years of age or younger account for more than one half the arrests for crimes against property and more than one third of the arrests for crimes against persons. Persons over the age of 50 years account for less than 5% of the arrests for crimes against property and persons. When differences in the size of age cohorts are controlled, persons under the age of 20 years are 16 times more likely than persons over the age of 50 to be arrested for the commission of a felony (Wilson & Herrnstein, 1985). Sturup (1968) presents similar cross-sectional data for offenders in Great Britain's correctional system. It therefore appears that while the symptoms of the antisocial personality disorder may not change over time, the commission of felony offenses resulting in arrests decrease in the older population groups. The degree to which the decrease in criminal behavior represents age-related and cohort-related differences is unclear.

Hare, McPherson, and Forth (1968) examined age and cohort effects on the criminal histories of antisocial and nonantisocial offenders. Participants were antisocial and nonantisocial prison inmates who volunteered for one of a series of psychophysiological studies conducted between 1964 and 1981. Cross-sectional analyses indicated the conviction rate (convictions per year) for the nonantisocial offenders declined steadily after the age of 25 years. The conviction rate for the antisocial offenders remained steady between 20 and 35 years of age and then began a sharp decline after the age of 35 years.

Hare et al. (1988) also performed a longitudinal analysis of criminal histories. These results are in general agreement with the cross-sectional analysis, but indicate that the decline in conviction rate begins after age 30 instead of after age 25 for the nonantisocial offenders and after age 40 instead of after age 35 for the antisocial offenders. Hare et al. also show that the antisocial offenders are more likely to be convicted of both violent and nonviolent offenses. However, the difference between the two groups was greatest for the nonviolent offenses, with the antisocial offenders committing many more nonviolent offenses relative to violent offenses than the nonantisocial offenders. These data indicate that many, but certainly not all, antisocial offenders turn away from criminal activities as they enter their forties. The work of O'Neal et al. (1962) suggests that the symptoms of the antisocial personality disorder continue unabated well after 40 years of age. This suggests that the older antisocial offenders continue to show antisocial behavior. However, the activities, either antisocial or prosocial, which antisocial offenders pursue when they turn away from crime, remain to be identified.

IMPAIRMENT AND COMPLICATIONS

Psychological research has examined several different aspects of the antisocial personality disorder. Much of this research appears to be based upon the assumption, stated or not, that there is an identifiable physiological defect in antisocials that explains the many ways in which they differ from normal individuals. Some of the earliest of this research focused on the electrical activity of the brains of antisocials. Hill and Watterson (1942) found that the electroencephalograms (EEGs) of 65% of the 66 antisocials he tested were characterized by abnormal slow-wave (theta) activity throughout the brain, while only 15% of a normal control group showed comparable slow-wave activity. There findings were replicated by Knott, Platt, Ashby, and Gottlieb (1953), who reported that somewhat more than half the 700 or more antisocials they examined showed abnormal EEG activity, with slow-wave activity the most common of the abnormalities found. Similarly, Arthur and Cahoon (1964) reported that approximately 55% of the 87 antisocials in their study showed some degree of EEG abnormality, most of it being slow-wave activity.

Another form of EEG abnormality that has captured some researchers' attention is the occurrence of positive spikes in the temporal lobe of the brain during sleep. Less than 5% of the general population show positive spikes (Hare, 1970). However, Kurland, Yeager, and Arthur (1963) reported that nearly 50% of the antisocials they tested showed positive spikes. Similarly, Niedermeyer (1963) found that positive spikes were present in the EEGs of nearly two thirds of the aggressive antisocials he examined.

While it is generally accepted that antisocials are more likely to show EEG abnormalities than are normals, the relationship between EEG abnormalities and antisocial behavior is unclear. Stafford-Clark, Pond, and Lovett-Doust (1951), Hill (1952), and Ellingson (1954) all reported that aggressive antisocials were more likely to show EEG abnormalities than were nonaggressive antisocials. These findings are contradicted, however, by the work of Ehrlich and Keogh (1956), who compared antisocials who did and did not show EEG abnormalities and found few differences of note. Similarly, Arthur and Cahoon (1964) reported no EEG differences between aggressive and nonaggressive antisocials. Finally, Kurland et al. (1963) observed that the majority of individuals who exhibit positive spiking in their EEGs do not show antisocial personality disorder symptomatology.

Based on the observation that slow-wave activity is characteristic of children's EEGs, some writers have theorized that the presence of slow waves in the EEGs of antisocials signifies immature and childlike cortical functioning (Hare, 1970, p. 32). This maturation retardation hypothesis is congruent with the seemingly childlike affect, behavior, and cognitions exhibited by many antisocials. Moreover, Robins (1966) reported that decreases in slow-wave activity coincided with decreases in symptomatology as antisocials passed into and through their forties. Finally, Kegan (1986) has looked at antisocials from the developmental perspective and concluded that their symptomatology reflects a developmental delay. As Bartol (1980) notes, however, the data on both the EEG activity of antisocials and the relationship of EEG activity and antisocial personality disorder symptomatology are incomplete and often contradictory. It is therefore premature to suggest that the causes of even some of the problems of antisocials may be attributed to maturational retardation or other cortical abnormalities that may be detected in the EEG.

A second series of studies has focused on the autonomic nervous system (ANS) activity of individuals with the diagnosis of antisocial personality disorder. Examination of resting level ANS activity has produced contradictory results. The early studies of Lindner (1942), Goldstein (1965), and Borkovec (1970) indicated that there were no differences between antisocials and others on measures of cardiac activity, respiration, and electrodermal activity. While more recent studies have confirmed that antisocials do not appear to differ from normals on measures of cardiac activity and respiration, those studies have also indicated that antisocials and normals do differ on measures of electrodermal activity. Hare (1968) reported that antisocials showed small but statistically significant decrements in the resting electrodermal activity and autonomic variability relative to the normal population. These findings have been confirmed by Aniskiewicz (1979), Dengerink and Bertilson (1975), and others, suggesting that antisocials exhibit a somewhat lower state of arousal than do others.

Other studies of antisocials' ANS activity have examined responsivity to stimulation. Hare (1968) found that antisocials' cardiac responsivity to repeated presentations of a stimulus adapts (decreases) more quickly than does that of normal controls. No differences between antisocials and normals were found for electrodermal and respiratory activity. Following his review of additional research on ANS reactivity, Hare (1970) concludes that antisocials also produce relatively small electrodermal responses in "lie detection" sessions and in situations others find stressful. He notes that antisocials also appear to show relatively rapid returns to baseline electrodermal activity after termination of stress exposure. The results of the research examining ANS activity during rest and in response to stimulation suggest, but by no means unequivocally demonstrate, that antisocials show lower levels of arousal and responsivity than do normals.

Quay (1965) recognized the implications of the ANS research for the antisocial personality disorder and theorized that much antisocial symptomatology may be attributed to an extreme form of stimulation seeking. Quay's theory holds that, at the physiological level, antisocials do not experience adequate stimulation from their environment. Antisocials must therefore compensate for their reduced level of stimulation by engaging in both a greater amount and greater range of exciting activities to maintain physiological stimulation at an optimal or homeostatic level. In support of this theory, Emmons and Webb (1974) found that both the Minnesota Multiphasic Personality Inventory and the Lykken Activity Preference Questionnaire indicated that antisocials are "pathological" stimulation seekers. Blackburn (1978) confirmed these findings in his comparison of antisocial and nonantisocial prisoners. This self-report information is complemented by the work of Wiesen (1965) (who reported that antisocials worked harder than normals to increase stimulation in a low-stimulation environment while normals worked harder than antisocials to reduce stimulation in a high-stimulation environment) and by the work of Chesno and Kilmann (1975) (who also reported confirmatory findings).

The final line of research to be discussed here has examined the relationship between learning and the antisocial personality disorder. In general, positive reinforcement (reward) studies have indi-cated that the learning performance of antisocials and normals do not differ (e.g., Bryan & Kapche, 1967). However, negative reinforcement (escape and avoidance) studies tend to indicate that antisocials learn more slowly and perform at a lower level than do normals (e.g., Lykken, 1955). Similarly, punishment studies tend to indicate that antisocials learn more slowly and perform at a lower level than do normals (e.g., Lykken, 1957; Scura & Eisenman, 1971). Finally, respondent (Pavlovian) conditioning studies tend to indicate that antisocials condition more slowly and perform at a lower level than do normals (e.g., Hare & Quinn, 1971; Ziskind, Syndulko, & Maltzman, 1978).

In a synthesis of the information on learning, personality, and the antisocial personality disorder, Eysenck (1952, 1964) has applied his general theory of personality to the understanding of the characteristics of antisocials. This understanding involves neuroticism and extraversion-introversion, two constitutional dimensions of personality that play a central role in Eysenck's theory. Eysenck (1964) reports research that indicates antisocials (and criminals) score high on neuroticism and extraversion. Eysenck (1964) also presents evidence that individuals who score high on extraversion are stimulation seekers and that individuals who score high on neuroticism are poor learners in respondent conditioning paradigms. More recent findings indicate that antisocials also score high on Eysenck's third dimension of personality, psychoticism (Eysenck & Eysenck, 1978).

Eysenck (1964; Eysenck & Eysenck, 1978) theorizes that antisocials' stimulation seeking leads them into exciting, and frequently undesirable, activities, and that the pairing of those activities with aversive stimulation when punishment is experienced does not lead to acquisition of aversive emotional responses that would otherwise occur when such activities are contemplated or engaged in on future occasions. Eysenck concludes that antisocials will therefore not refrain from engaging in antisocial activities when detection and punishment are improbable, because they have not acquired the range of conditioned aversive emotional responses that may be escaped or avoided by others only by turning away from the antisocial thoughts or activities. In essence, Eysenck has identified a mechanism through which individuals develop a "conscience" and has postulated that antisocials show defects that prevent or retard the family's and society's attempts to develop that conscience.

DIFFERENTIAL DIAGNOSIS

DSM-III-R (APA, 1987) points out that in the differential diagnosis of antisocial personality disorder, it is inappropriate to make the diagnosis in children. The diagnosis is limited to individuals who are at least 18 years of age. While children may show the symptoms of the disorder, the symptoms may lift spontaneously or evolve into other disorders. The diagnosis of conduct disorder should be considered for children showing the symptoms of the antisocial personality disorder. Many adult offenders show some, but not all, of the characteristics of the antisocial personality disorder. The diagnosis of adult antisocial behavior should be considered for individuals who do not meet all the criteria for the diagnosis of antisocial personality disorder and whose antisocial behavior cannot be attributed to other mental disorders.

DSM-III-R also notes that when alcohol or drug abuse and antisocial behavior begin in childhood and continue into adulthood, a psychoactive substance abuse disorder and antisocial personality disorder should both be diagnosed if the appropriate diagnostic criteria are satisfied. Both diagnoses are warranted regardless of the degree to which the antisocial behavior is a function of substance abuse (e.g., inability to sustain consistent work behavior because of alcohol intoxication, failure to honor financial obligations because earnings are spent on drugs, prostitution to support a habit). However, when antisocial behavior associated with substance abuse begins in adulthood, the diagnosis of antisocial personality disorder is inappropriate and should not be made unless other signs of the antisocial personality disorder were evident in childhood and continued into adult life.

Finally, DSM-III-R warns that persons with mental retardation, schizophrenia, and manic episodes may present with features of the antisocial personality disorder. Antisocial personality disorder may be diagnosed with mental retardation, schizophrenia, and manic episodes when there is a clear pattern of antisocial behavior that has continued since childhood. However, episodic antisocial behavior that occurs only during manic episodes does not justify the additional diagnosis of antisocial personality disorder.

Reexamination of the definition of the antisocial personality disorder reveals that it is possible for individuals with that diagnosis to have very few or even none of the defining characteristics in common. Despite these ambiguities, Gray and Hutchinson (1964) reported that 84% of the psychiatrists they surveyed considered the diagnostic category to be a meaningful one, and Spitzer, Forman, and Nee (1979) found that it is possible for clinicians using DSM-III criteria to diagnose the disorder reliably. Despite both the apparent importance of the disorder and the ability to diagnose it with reliability, some workers in the field have charged that it is nothing more than a "wastebasket" category into which a heterogeneous group of clinical types is placed, thereby impeding the search for a meaningful etiology, prognosis, or effective treatment (e.g., Lewis & Balla, 1975; Rotenberg, 1975). Others have agreed that the disorder is not a unitary construct, but have suggested that it may instead be composed of two or more subgroups of identifiable clinical phenomena (e.g., Lykken, 1957; Arieti, 1967).

Psychological testing may assist in the differential diagnosis of the antisocial personality disorder. In the United States, the MMPI is probably the most widely used of the objective diagnostic aids. Brantley and Sutker (1984) note that clinicians generally accept that the classical MMPI profile of the antisocial consists of elevated scores on both Scales 4 (psychopathic deviate) and 9 (hypomania). Megargee and Bohn (1979) presented data that individuals with elevations on Scales 4 and 9 do indeed typically meet the criteria for the diagnosis of antisocial personality disorder. They note, however, that individuals with this profile tend to be the nonaggressive antisocials. Megargee and Bohn present additional data indicating that antisocials who also show some elevation on Scales 6 (paranoia) and 8 (schizophrenia) tend to be the aggressive antisocials. Finally, they point out that individuals with an elevated Scale 2 (depression) and a Scale 4 spike tend to be the antisocials who are easily provoked to violence.

Additional subtypes of the antisocial personality disorder have been hypothesized. Lykken (1957) suggested that it is possible to distinguish between what have been called primary and secondary psychopaths, both of whom meet the diagnostic criteria for the antisocial personality disorder. He described primary psychopaths as individuals who exhibit little anxiety concerning the consequences of their behavior and are relatively unaffected by societal controls and sanctions. They are also seen as having poor prognoses for successful rehabilitation. Hill (1952) indicated that primary psychopathy is associated with a variety of electroencephalographic abnormalities.

Secondary psychopaths are described as not exhibiting these extreme deviations and are viewed as more amenable to rehabilitative efforts. Karpman (1961) also claimed to have identified two subtypes of psychopaths. The aggressive-predatory types were said to be aggressive and unfeeling predators, who took what they wanted. The passive-parasitic types were said to present themselves as needy and somewhat inadequate people, who then took advantage of and exploited the sympathy and help others offered to them.

Arieti (1967) suggested another two subtypes of antisocial personality disorders that were based upon intellectual level. These were the simple and complex sociopaths. The complex sociopaths were seen as individuals of at least average intelligence and judgment, who were able to circumvent society's mores successfully as they pursued and achieved their goals. The simple sociopaths were depicted as individuals of less than average intelligence who were unsuccessful in their antisocial endeavors. Arieti's notion that the antisocial personality disorder is not incompatible with success in American society has been elaborated by several writers. For example, Brantley and Sutker (1984) observed that the American culture appears to place considerable value on the use of interpersonal manipulation and individual power to overcome apparently insurmountable odds in the quest for financial gain or personal fame. It is unlikely, however, that many individuals who are properly diagnosed with the antisocial personality disorder will excel in modern society, if for no other reason than the diagnosis requires a long history of school and community problems that is incompatible with such success.

CASE EXAMPLE

Several authors (e.g., Bergman, 1968; Cleckley with Thigpen, 1982; Harrington, 1972; Potts et al., 1986; Yochelson & Samenow, 1976, 1977) have provided descriptions of individual cases of the antisocial personality disorder and/or its treatment. Unfortunately, discussion of approaches to the treatment of the disorder are beyond the scope of this chapter. However, a case example that typifies many aspects of the disorder will be presented. Although it is tempting to provide a description of one of the "notorious" but fortunately rare antisocials, such as David Berkowitz, Ted Bundy, Albert DeSalvo, David Essex, Gary Gilmore, Charles Manson, or Charles Starkweather (e.g., Leyton, 1986), Hare's (1970, pp. 1–4)

description of Donald S. exemplifies the criminal antisocials that are more likely to be encountered in clinical work and daily life.

When Donald S. was seen at age 30 as a subject in Hare's (1970) research program, he was just completing a 3-year prison term for escape and fraud. While serving a sentence for previous bigamy and forgery offenses, he had feigned illness and escaped from the prison hospital. While on escape, he committed the offenses that resulted in the second fraud conviction. Donald S. had represented himself to several religious organizations as an officer of an international philanthropic foundation. As such, he had enlisted their aid in a local fundraising campaign. In an effort to increase contributions in one such campaign, Donald S. arranged to be interviewed on a local television program. The interview was a great success and contributions increased by a considerable amount. Unfortunately, the success of the interview also resulted in portions of it being carried on national television. As a result, Donald S. was recognized, apprehended, and brought to trial.

Hare (1970) reported that during the trial it became apparent that Donald S. had no feelings of guilt for what he had done. He explained his behavior by claiming that his efforts undoubtedly induced people to give to all charities, not only to his false organization. He also observed that most people who gave to charities did so because they felt guilty about something in their past and therefore deserved to be bilked. Finally, he attempted to convince those whom he had defrauded that he had been unjustly accused and, in fact, persuaded several of those people to serve as character witnesses and plea for his release. After being released from prison, Donald S. applied for admission to a university and indicated in his application that he had been a research "colleague" of Hare. Shortly thereafter, Hare was contacted by a firm to which Donald S. had applied for employment because he had submitted Hare's name as a reference.

Donald S. was the youngest of three boys. His parents were middle class, and both his brothers grew up to lead normal, middle-class lives. Donald's father worked long hours, and when he was home he tended to be moody and to drink to excess. Donald's mother was a mild-mannered woman who tried to please her husband and prevent family strife. When she discovered that one of her children had engaged in some form of mischief, she typically did not deal with the problem directly but instead threatened to tell the boy's father. However, she usually did not follow through on the threat because she did not want to disturb her husband and disrupt the household. When Donald's father disciplined his children, it was typically in an inconsistent and punitive manner. Sometimes he would fly into a rage and beat a child, and at other times merely give a mild reprimand. The form of punishment seemed to be unrelated to the severity of the offense.

Hare (1970) indicated that Donald S. was a discipline problem as a child. He appeared to view rules and regulations a meaningless impediment to what he wanted to do and worked to circumvent them. He came to do this so skillfully that it was often difficult to prove that he had done so. Although his angelic appearance and manipulative ways usually got him what he wanted, on those occasions when he was thwarted he would typically first try affection and, if that did not work, throw a temper tantrum. On those occasions when Donald S. was about to be punished for a misdeed, he would typically concoct an explanatory lie that often shifted blame to a brother. If the big lie did not work, he would turn remorseful and contrite, promising to never do it again. If this did not work, he took his punishment in a sullenly defiant manner.

Donald S. had an undistinguished academic career despite his obvious intelligence. He was restless, easily bored, and often truant. His behavior while being observed by a teacher was usually acceptable. However, when not being observed he often got himself and others into trouble. Although suspected of being the instigator, he was skilled at avoiding blame or shifting it to someone else. His teachers described him as an "operator." As he matured, his misbehavior evolved from lying, cheating, and bullying smaller children to petty theft, gambling, alcohol, and making crude sexual advances toward younger girls and classmates. On one occasion he locked a girl in a shed after making a sexual advance toward her. Although she was not found for 16 hours, undoubtedly causing her family considerable anguish, Donald S. tried to avoid responsibility by first denying his involvement and then claiming that the girl had attempted to seduce him and that the door had locked "accidentally," and so on. He showed no signs of remorse for his behavior.

Donald S. was finally placed in a boarding school in an effort to control his behavior. He left the school at age 17, forged his father's name to a large check, and spent a year traveling the world, making his way by relying on his charm, attractiveness, and ability to deceive and manipulate others. As an adult, he held a succession of jobs, but only for short periods of time. He was charged with a variety of crimes, including theft, public intoxication, assault, and traffic violations. In most instances he was fined, placed on probation, or given a short sentence. Donald S. engaged in frequent and shallow sexual relationships. At age 22 he married a 41-year-old woman. This relationship was short lived, and he moved on to a succession of subsequent marriages, all bigamous.

The bigamous marriage that resulted in the imprisonment from which Donald S. escaped is of particular interest. He had been referred to a psychiatric facility for observation. His powers of persuasion, physical attractiveness, and sympathetic demeanor brought him to the attention of a female member of the professional staff who acted on his behalf. Following his release, they were married. Shortly thereafter, she refused to cover his gambling debts, and he forged her name to a check and left the marriage. He was apprehended, convicted, and sentenced to the term of imprisonment discussed at the beginning of this case example. Hare (1970) concluded by noting that Donald S. does not see anything wrong with what he has done over the years. He does not experience guilt, remorse, or shame for the way he uses others, or for the discomfort he causes them. He considers his course of action to be reasonable and appropriate despite its longer-term undesirable consequences for him. Moreover, those consequences have not dissuaded him from that course of action.

CHILDHOOD AND FAMILIAL CHARACTERISTICS

The general characteristics of the family and childhood backgrounds and experiences of individuals with the diagnosis of antisocial personality disorder have been presented within the context of the previous chapter's discussion of conduct disorders. What determines whether a child who showed a conduct disorder will grow up to be an adult who shows an antisocial personality disorder is far from clear. It is known, however, the single best predictor of the antisocial personality disorder in adulthood is the presence of antisociallike characteristics in childhood (e.g., Robins, 1978). Wolman (1987) has summarized the research on several other childhood and familial antecedents of the antisocial personality disorder. He pointed out that while lower socioeconomic status is correlated with antisocial behavior, Levy (1951) and Wolman (1973), among others, have noted that antisocials come from all socioeconomic strata. Indeed, Levy (1951) has distinguished between deprived antisocials, who have grown up in poverty, and indulged antisocials, who have grown up in affluence and luxury.

A more important correlate of the antisocial personality disorder appears to be the presence of the disorder in a parent (Archer, Sutker, White, & Orvin, 1978), most notably the father (Robins, 1966), who then serves as a model for antisocial behavior. Moreover, antisocial parents undoubtedly relate to their children in their own antisocial ways, which may well contribute to many of the other correlates of the disorder. For example, Wolman (1987) observed that there is a peculiar lack of warmth between parents and their children who grow up to be antisocials. He contended that the life histories of adult antisocials indicate that no one has ever cared for them and no one has ever loved them. Although these claims of continuous emotional neglect may be somewhat overstated, the early work of Bandura and Walters (1959) and O'Neal et al. (1982) is in accord with this observation. They reported that antisocial behavior is correlated with parental desertion, lack of support, and emotional deprivation.

Similarly, Greer (1964) found that 60% of the antisocials he examined experienced parental loss in comparison to 28% of the "neurotics" and 27% of the normals in his study. Craft, Stephenson, and Granger (1964) observed that the more severe the antisocial symptomatology, the more likely it is that parental loss has occurred. Oltman and Friedman (1967) added that the loss of the father and/or subsequent institutionalization are the conditions most closely associated with the disorder. It is not difficult to hypothesize that individuals who have not experienced strong emotional bonding early in their developmental histories will not easily form such bonds in later life (Harlow & Harlow, 1962), one of the distinguishing characteristics of the antisocials.

Wolman (1987) suggested that a lack of guidance on the part of parents is also related to the development of the antisocial personality disorder. He postulated that parents who do not set and impose limits are inconsistent and permissive, and do not teach what is right and wrong. These practices foster self-centered, amoral, and antisocial personality development, more of the distinguishing characteristics of the antisocials. Meyer (1980) indicated that two parenting styles

seem to be associated with the development of the antisocial personality disorder. As indicated previously, the first is the cold and distant parent. The second is the parent who administers rewards and punishment in such an inconsistent manner that it is impossible for the child to develop a sense of what is and is not appropriate.

Meyer's (1980) observations are supported by Fisher (1983), who highlighted the role of poor parental discipline and lax supervision in the development of the disorder. Finally, Wolman pointed out that family violence, directed at the child or at others, appears to be correlated with the development of the antisocial personality disorder. This observation is supported by Bandura (1973), who indicated that both verbal and physical parental attacks on children, as well as the threat of same, contribute to the formation of antisocial and violent behavior.

Additional childhood and familial characteristics that have been suggested as correlates of the antisocial personality disorder in adulthood include hyperactivity (Bartol, 1980), brain damage (McCord & McCord, 1964), family size (Fisher, 1984), thievery (Robins, 1966), and aggression (Sutker & King, 1984) as well as a host of others (e.g., Brantley & Sutker, 1984). It appears clear that the children who grow up to be antisocial are those who show some of the most disturbing affective, behavioral, and cognitive characteristics, are those who are raised in some of the most psychologically and socially damaging family conditions of which we are aware, and are some of those to whom government and the helping professions are either the most unwilling or most unable to provide assistance. The outcomes should not therefore be surprising.

SUMMARY

Much is known about the antisocial personality disorder. There is a general consistency in the clinical descriptions of the disorder, and a general agreement that individuals diagnosed with the disorder tend to be self-centered, lack a sense of responsibility, act on impulse, manipulate others, do not form meaningful interpersonal relationships, and do not experience guilt or shame for their actions. There is also general agreement that some individuals may be genetically predisposed to the disorder, and that those who show the disorder come from family backgrounds involving inconsistent and punitive parenting practices, a lack of warmth among family members, and the presence of an antisocial family member. In addition, there is general agreement that individuals diagnosed with the disorder tend to differ from normals in neurological activity and physiological reactivity, as well as in their responsivity to reinforcement and punishment.

Several theories have been advanced that seek to incorporate what is known about the antisocial personality disorder and explain the affect, behavior, and cognitions of individuals diagnosed with the disorder. In general, these theories have, to one degree or another, acknowledged the contributions of genetic endowment, early learning experience, and situational demands in their formulations of the disorder. There have been relatively few attempts, however, to move from theoretical formulation to effective prevention and rehabilitation. While there is certainly more to know than is now known about the disorder, it is also certainly time to apply what is now known to the development of programs to reduce the incidence of the disorder. Indeed, it may well be that the most productive settings in which to now formulate, test, and refine a theory of the antisocial personality disorder are in the very settings in which antisocials are found.

REFERENCES

American Psychiatric Association. (1952). *Diagnostic and statistical manual of mental disorders*. Washington, DC: Author.

American Psychiatric Association. (1968). *Diagnostic and statistical manual of mental disorders* (2nd ed.). Washington, DC: Author.

American Psychiatric Association. (1980). *Diagnostic and statistical manual of mental disorders* (3rd ed.). Washington, DC: Author.

American Psychiatric Association. (1987). *Diagnostic and statistical manual of mental disorders* (3rd ed. rev.). Washington, DC: Author.

Aniskiewicz, A. S. (1979). Autonomic components of vicarious conditioning and psychopathy. *Journal of Clinical Psychology, 35*, 60–67.

Archer, R. P., Sutker, P. B., White, J. L., & Orvin, G. H. (1978). Personality relationships between parents and adolescent offspring in inpatient treatment. *Psychological Reports, 42*, 207–214.

Arieti, S. (1967). *The intrapsychic self*. New York: Basic Books.

Arthur, R. G., & Cahoon, E. B. (1964). A clinical and electroencephalographic survey of psychopathic personality. *American Journal of Psychiatry, 120*, 875–882.

Bandura, A. (1973). *Aggression: A social learning perspective*. Englewood Cliffs, NJ: Prentice Hall.

Bandura, A., & Walters, R. H. (1959). *Adolescent aggression*. New York: The Ronald Press.

Bartol, C. R. (1980). *Criminal behavior: A psychosocial approach*. Englewood Cliffs, NJ: Prentice Hall.

Bergman, R. E. (Ed.). (1968). *The sociopath*. New York: Exposition Press.

Blackburn, R. (1978). Psychopathy, arousal, and the need for stimulation. In R. D. Hare & D. Schalling (Eds.), *Psychopathic behavior: Approaches to research* (pp. 157–164). New York: John Wiley & Sons.

Borkovec, T. (1970). Autonomic reactivity to stimulation in psychopathic, neurotic, and normal juvenile delinquents. *Journal of Consulting and Clinical Psychology, 35*, 217–222.

Brantley, P. J., & Sutker, P. B. (1984). Antisocial behavior disorders. In H. E. Adams & P. B. Sutker (Eds.), *Comprehensive handbook of psychopathology* (pp. 439–478). New York: Plenum Press.

Byran, J. H., & Kapche, R. (1967). Psychopathy and verbal conditioning. *Journal of Abnormal Psychology, 72*, 71–73.

Buss, A. H. (1966). *Psychopathology*. New York: John Wiley & Sons.

Cadoret, R. J. (1978). Psychopathology in adopted-away offspring of biologic parents with antisocial behavior. *Archives of General Psychiatry, 35*, 176–184.

Cadoret, R. J. (1986). Epidemiology of antisocial personality. In W. H. Reid, D. Dorr, J. I. Walker, & J. W. Bonner (Eds.), *Unmasking the psychopath* (pp. 28–44). New York: W. W. Norton.

Chesno, F., & Kilmann, P. (1975). Effects of stimulation intensity on sociopathic avoidance learning. *Journal of Abnormal Psychology, 84*, 144–150.

Christiansen, K. O. (1977). A preliminary study of criminality among twins. In S. A. Mednick & K. O. Christiansen (Eds.), *Biosocial bases of criminal behavior* (pp. 89–108). New York: John Wiley & Sons.

Cleckley, H. (1941). *The mask of sanity*. St. Louis: C. V. Mosby.

Cleckley, H., with Thigpen, C. H. (1982). *The mask of sanity*. St. Louis: C. V. Mosby.

Cloninger, C. R., Reich, T., & Guze, S. B. (1978).

Genetic-environmental interactions and antisocial behavior. In R. D. Hare & D. Schalling (Eds.), *Psychopathic behavior: Approaches to research* (pp. 225–237). New York: John Wiley & Sons.

Craft, M. (1965). *Ten studies into psychopathic personality*. Bristol, England: John Wright & Sons.

Craft, M., Stephenson, G., & Granger, C. (1964). A controlled trial of authoritarian and self-governing regimes with adolescent psychopaths. *American Journal of Orthopsychiatry, 34*, 543–554.

Dengerink, H. A., & Bertilson, H. S. (1975). Psychopathy and physiological arousal in an aggressive task. *Psychophysiology, 12*, 682–684.

Ehrlich S. K., & Keogh, R. P. (1956). The psychopath in a mental institution. *Archives of Neurology and Psychiatry, 76*, 286–295.

Ellingson, R. J. (1954). Incidence of EEG abnormality among patients with mental disorders of apparently nonorganic origin. *American Journal of Psychiatry, 111*, 263–275.

Emmons, T. D., & Webb, W. W. (1974). Subjective correlates of conditioned responsivity and stimulation seeking in psychopaths, normals, and acting-out neurotics. *Journal of Consulting and Clinical Psychology, 42*, 620.

Eysenck, H. J. (1952). *The scientific study of personality*. New York: Praeger.

Eysenck, H. J. (1964). *Crime and personality*. New York: Houghton Mifflin.

Eysenck, H. J., & Eysenck, S. B. G. (1978). Psychopathy, personality, and genetics. In R. D. Hare & D. Schalling (Eds.), *Psychopathic behavior: Approaches to research* (pp. 197–223). New York: John Wiley & Sons.

Federal Bureau of Investigation. (1987). *Uniform crime reports*. Washington, DC: U.S. Government Printing Office.

Fisher, D. (1983). Parental supervision and delinquency. *Perceptual and Motor Skills, 56*, 635–640.

Fisher, D. (1984). Family size and delinquency. *Perceptual and Motor Skills, 58*, 527–534.

Foulds, G. A. (1965). *Personality and personal illness*. London: Tavistock.

Goldstein, I. B. (1965). The relationship of muscle tension and autonomic activity to psychiatric disorders. *Psychosomatic Medicine, 27*, 39–52.

Gray, H., & Hutchinson, H. C. (1964). The psychopathic personality: A survey of Canadian psychiatrists. *Canadian Psychiatric Association Journal, 9*, 450–461.

Greer, S. (1964). Study of parental loss in neurotics and psychopaths. *Archives of General Psychiatry, 11*, 177–180.

Guze, S. B., Goodwin, D. W., & Crane, J. B. (1969). Criminality and psychiatric disorders. *Archives of General Psychiatry, 20*, 583–591.

Hare, R. D. (1968). Psychopathy, autonomic functioning, and the orienting response. *Journal of Abnormal Psychology, 73*(Monograph Supplement) Part 2, 1–24.

Hare, R. D. (1970). *Psychopathy: Theory and research*. New York: John Wiley & Sons.

Hare, R. D., McPherson, L. M., & Forth, A. E. (1988). Male psychopaths and their criminal careers. *Journal of Consulting and Clinical Psychology, 56*, 710–714.

Hare, R. D., & Quinn, M. J. (1971). Psychopathy and autonomic conditioning. *Journal of Abnormal Psychology, 77*, 223–226.

Harlow, H. F., & Harlow, M. K. (1962). Social deprivation in monkeys. *Scientific American*, 1–11.

Harrington, A. (1972). *Psychopaths*. New York: Simon & Schuster.

Hill, D. (1952). EEG in episodic psychotic and psychopathic behavior: A classification of data. *EEG and Clinical Neurophysiology, 4*, 419–442.

Hill, D., & Watterson, D. (1942). Electroencephalographic studies of the psychopathic personality. *Journal of Neurology and Psychiatry, 5*, 47–64.

Karpman, B. (1961). The structure of neurosis: With special differentials between neurosis, psychosis, homosexuality, alcoholism, psychopathy, and criminality. *Archives of Criminal Psychodynamics, 4*, 599–646.

Kegan, R. G. (1986). The child behind the mask: Sociopathy as developmental delay. In W. H. Reid, D. Dorr, J. I. Walker, & J. W. Bonner III (Eds.), *Unmasking the psychopath: Antisocial personality and related syndromes* (pp. 45–77). New York: W. W. Norton.

Knott, J. R., Platt, E. B., Ashby, M. C., & Gottlieb, J. S. (1953). A familial evaluation of the electroencephalogram of patients with primary behavior disorder and psychopathic personality. *EEG and Clinical Neurophysiology, 5*, 363–370.

Kurland, H. D., Yeager, C. T., & Arthur, R. J. (1963). Psychophysiologic aspects of severe behavior disorders. *Archives of General Psychiatry, 8*, 599–604.

Leyton, E. (1986). *Compulsive killers*. New York: New York University Press.

Levy, D. M. (1951). The deprived and indulged forms of psychopathic personality. *American Journal of Orthopsychiatry, 21*, 250–254.

Lewis, D. O., & Balla, D. (1975). Sociopathy and its symptoms: Inappropriate diagnosis in child psychiatry. *American Journal of Psychiatry, 132*, 720–722.

Lindner, R. (1942). Experimental studies in constitutional psychopathic inferiority. *Journal of Criminal Psychopathology, 3*, 252–276.

Lykken, D. T. (1957). A study of anxiety in the sociopathic personality. *Journal of Abnormal and Social Psychology, 55*, 6–10.

Lykken, D. T. (1955). A study of anxiety in the sociopathic personality. Doctoral dissertation, University of Michigan, Ann Arbor (University Microfilms, No. 55, 944). Cited in M. P. Feldman (1977), *Criminal behaviour: A psychological analysis*. London: John Wiley & Sons.

McCord, W. M. (1982). *The psychopath and milieu therapy*. New York: Academic Press.

McCord, W. M., & McCord, J. (1964). *The psychopath: An essay on the criminal mind*. Princeton, NJ: Van Nostrand.

Mednick, S. A., Gabrielli, W. F., & Hutchings, B. (1984). Genetic influences in criminal convictions. *Science, 224*, 891–894.

Megargee, E., & Bohn, M. (1979). *Classifying criminal offenders*. Beverly Hills, CA: Sage.

Meyer, R. G. (1980). The antisocial personality. In R. W. Woody (Ed.), *Encyclopedia of clinical assessment* (Vol. 1, pp. 190–198). San Francisco, CA: Jossey-Bass.

Niedermeyer, A. A. (1963). *Der Nervenarzt, 34*, 168. Cited in C. A. Bartol (1980), *Criminal behavior: A psychosocial approach*. Englewood Cliffs, NJ: Prentice Hall.

Oltman, J., & Friedman, S. (1967). Parental deprivation in psychiatric conditions. *Diseases of the Nervous System, 28*, 298–303.

O'Neal, P., Robins, L. N., King, L. J., & Schaefer, J. (1962). Parental deviance and the genesis of sociopathic personality. *American Journal of Psychiatry, 118*, 1114–1124.

Partridge, G. E. (1928). A study of fifty cases of psychopathic personality. *American Journal of Psychiatry, 7*, 953–973.

Potts, L. J., Barley, W. D., Jones, K. A., & Woodhall, P. K. (1986). Comprehensive inpatient treatment of a severely antisocial adolescent. In W. H. Reid, D. Dorr, J. I. Walker, & J. W. Bonner III (Eds.), *Unmasking the psychopath* (pp. 231–255). New York: W. W. Norton.

Quay, H. C. (1965). Psychopathic personality as pathological stimulation seeking. *American Journal of Psychiatry, 122*, 180–183.

Reid, W. H. (1978). Genetic correlates of antisocial syndromes. In W. H. Reid (Ed.), *The psychopath* (pp. 244–257). New York: Brunner/Mazel.

Robins, L. N. (1966). *Deviant children grow up*. Baltimore: Williams & Wilkins.

Robins, L. N. (1978). Sturdy childhood predictor of adult antisocial behavior: Replications from longitudinal studies. *Psychological Medicine, 8*, 611–622.

Robins, E., Gentry, D. A., Munoz, R. A., & Martens, S. (1977). A contrast of the three more common illnesses with the three less common in a study and 18-month follow-up of 314 psychiatric emergency room patients: II. Characteristics of patients with the three more common illnesses. *Archives of General Psychiatry, 34*, 269–281.

Robins, L., Helzer, J., Weissman, M., Orvaschel, H., Gruenberg, E., Bruche, J., & Regier, D. (1984). Lifetime prevalence of specific psychiatric disorders in three sites. *Archives of General Psychiatry, 41*, 949–958.

Rotenberg, M. (1975). Psychopathy, insensitivity, and sensitization. *Professional Psychology, 6*, 283–292.

Schulsinger, F. (1977). Psychopathy: Heredity and environment. In S. A. Mednick & K. O. Christiansen (Eds.), *Biosocial basis of criminal behavior* (pp. 109–141). New York: Gardner Press.

Scura, W. C., & Eisenman, R. (1971). Punishment learning in psychopaths with social and nonsocial reinforcers. *Corrective Psychiatry and Journal of Social Therapy, 17*, 58–71.

Spitzer, R. L., Forman, J. B., & Nee, J. (1979). DSM-III field trials: 1. Initial interrater diagnostic reliability. *American Journal of Psychiatry, 136*, 815–817.

Stafford-Clark, D., Pond, D., & Lovett-Doust, J. W. (1951). The psychopath in prison. *British Journal of Delinquency, 2*, 117–129.

Sturup, G. K. (1968). *Treating the "untreatable": Chronic criminals at Herstedvester*. Baltimore: The Johns Hopkins University Press.

Sutker, P. B., & King, A. R. (1984). Dissociative, somatoform, and personality disorders. In N. S. Endler & J. McV. Hunt (Eds.), *Personality and the behavioral disorders* (Vol. 2, pp. 771–807). New York: John Wiley & Sons.

Wiesen, A. E. (1965). *Differential reinforcing ef-*

fects of the onset and offset of stimulation on the operant behavior of normals, neurotics and psychopaths Doctoral Dissertation, University of Florida (Ann Arbor: University Microfilms). Cited in R. D. Hare (1970), *Psychopathology: Theory and research*. New York: John Wiley & Sons.

Wilson, J. Q., & Herrnstein, R. J. (1985). *Crime and human nature*. New York: Simon & Schuster.

Wolman, B. B. (1973). *Call no man normal*. New York: International University Press.

Wolman, B. B. (1987). *The sociopathic personality*. New York: Brunner/Mazel.

Woodruff, R. A., Guze, S. B., & Clayton, P. J. (1971). The medical and psychiatric implications of antisocial personality (sociopathy). *Diseases of the Nervous System, 32*, 712–714.

Yochelson, S., & Samenow, S. E. (1976). *The criminal personality: I. A profile for change*. New York: Jason Aronson.

Yochelson, S., & Samenow, S. E. (1977). *The criminal personality: II. The change process*. New York: Jason Aronson.

Ziskind, E., Syndulko, K., & Maltzman, I. (1978). Aversive conditioning in the sociopath. *Pavlovian Journal of Biological Science, 13*, 199–205.

MENTAL RETARDATION

EDITORS' COMMENTS

Unlike most of the other disorders discussed in this volume, mental retardation, by definition, always is first evident in childhood or adolescence (prior to age 18). In almost all cases, the condition continues into adulthood. However, although mental retardation is a lifelong condition, different periods in the life span yield different problems in adaptive behavior. Sensory and motor abilities, communication, and self-care skills are central during infancy and early childhood. However, during the school years more emphasis is placed on academic behavior and social interaction/peer relationships. Finally, in adulthood emphasis shifts to personal self-sufficiency, independence in community living, and vocational functioning. Intervention with intellectually impaired youngsters has been shown to yield a markedly improved prognosis, thus highlighting the importance of early detection and identification.

Both the American Psychiatric Association and the American Association of Mental Retardation have defined mental retardation utilizing three criteria: (1) significantly subaverage general intellectual functioning, (2) concurrent impairment in adaptive behavior, and (3) manifestation of the first and second criteria during the developmental period (before 18 years). The disorder is further defined by subtypes that reflect the extent of intellectual and adaptive functioning. Consideration of level of adaptive functioning is particularly important in diagnosing mild levels of mental retardation, where children easily can be misdiagnosed based on IQ scores alone (with more pervasive and severe intellectual impairment, deficits in adaptive functioning in almost all instances are shown concurrently).

As noted by Madle and Neisworth, it is not surprising that multiple etiologies have been identified for retardation, given that multiple factors form the basis for intelligence. Prenatal circumstances, such as maternal health problems and chromosomal disorder, account for the development of many retarded newborns. Also of etiological importance is maternal health during gestation and problems during labor and delivery. During infancy and childhood, injury is a chief source of retardation. In addition to these biologic factors, ineffective social and/or physical environments may play a role in the failure to develop an optional level of intelligence.

Because measures of infant development have been shown to correlate poorly with later childhood measures of intelligence, the clinician needs to be cautious in diagnosing retardation in instances of developmental lags. In addition, misinterpretation of a developmental lag can occur when the clinician is unaware of a specific sensory or motor deficit (e.g., hearing loss, neuromuscular disorders). Thus, examination of very young children by a competent physician is strongly advised prior to diagnosis and intervention with this age group.

Mental retardation may coexist with specific and/or pervasive developmental disorders. Specific developmental disorders are differentiated from retardation, in that there is a delay in the development of particular skills (e.g., reading, mathematics). However, there may be normal development in other areas. In pervasive developmental disorder, there are peculiar and bizarre responses to the environment that are not normal for any stage of development; in retardation, the child shows generalized delays in the development that appear at an earlier (normal) developmental period.

CHAPTER 23

MENTAL RETARDATION IN CHILDHOOD

A. Roland Irwin
Alan M. Gross

DESCRIPTION OF THE DISORDER

Mental retardation has been described in many different ways and from many different perspectives. It has been regarded as a test result, a symptom, an educational dilemma, and a source of public concern and anxiety (Crocker & Nelson, 1983). In addition to the obvious reference to deficiency of cognitive ability, the term itself has come to connote a variety of assumptions regarding origin, personal traits, segregation, and etiology, many of which have no factual base. However, the American Association on Mental Deficiency (AAMD) has done much to disdain implicit assumptions and discrepancies in definitions by promulgating what has now become the most widely employed definition of mental retardation: "refers to significantly subaverage general intellectual functioning existing concurrently with deficits in adaptive behavior, and manifested during the developmental period" (Grossman, 1983). This three-point definition has been adopted by the American Psychiatric Association in the *Diagnostic and Statistical Manual of Mental Disorders* (APA, 1987). All three parts of the definition are important to its intent of providing consistent diagnostics within a pragmatic framework.

Subaverage intellectual functioning is defined by first viewing intelligence quotients (IQ) as being normally distributed on a Gaussian curve. IQs are measured via one of the individually administered general intelligence tests, such as the Stanford-Binet and the Wechsler Intelligence Scale for Children. Performance two or more standard deviations below the mean is required for a diagnosis of mental retardation. Within this subaverage range of intellectual functioning, four levels of retardation are defined—mild, moderate, severe, and profound. Each level corresponds to a successive standard deviation below the mean. For example, mild retardation refers to performance between two and three standard deviations below the mean, moderate refers to performance between three and four standard deviations below the mean, and so on. If these categories are applied to the Stanford-Binet and the Wechsler, the IQ ranges shown in Table 23.1 would result.

As recommended by the American Psychiatric Association (1987), IQ scores should be thought to involve an error of measurement of 5 points in

Table 23.1. Levels of Mental Retardation as Measured by IQ.

	STANFORD-BINET	WECHSLER
Mild retardation	67–52	69–55
Moderate retardation	51–36	54–40
Severe retardation	35–20	39–25
Profound retardation	< 20	< 25

either direction. This allows exclusion of some individuals, whose IQ is slightly less than the two standard deviation cutoff for mild retardation, from the diagnosis of mental retardation, if clinical judgment is that adaptive behavior is either normal or minimally deficient.

The second criterion for diagnosis of mental retardation included in the AAMD definition is a deficit in adaptive behavior. This part of the definition is an acknowledgment that mental retardation has a personal and social feature as well as the previously emphasized intellectual aspect. Adaptive behavior generally refers to the degree to which an individual meets age and cultural standards of personal independence and social responsibility (Whitman & Johnston, 1987). In typical situations independence and social skills are commensurate with the individual's intellectual capacity. However, when quality of environment and social support are less than ideal, adaptive behavior may be underdeveloped relative to intellectual functioning. Alternatively, in certain situations, such as a developmentally delayed child with a particularly creative and energetic caretaker, the child's adaptive behavior may transcend her apparent intellectual deficiency.

Measurement of adaptive behavior presents the clinician a greater dilemma than that posed by the assessment of intelligence. This is due in part to the paucity of well-standardized, objective tests that have been developed for this purpose (Erickson, 1978), making clinical judgment a necessary adjunct. That one should always consider the child's age in the assessment of adaptive behavior is self-evident. Familiarity with normal socialization and independence abilities throughout the developmental period is necessary to make a relevant comparison.

Of those instruments that have been developed for measurement of adaptive behavior, the AAMD Adaptive Behavior Scale (Nihira, Foster, Shellhaas, & Leland, 1974) is one of the most widely accepted. This checklist is easily administered and

does not require special training in psychological testing. It contains two parts, the first of which consists of developmentally arranged items describing adaptive behaviors in ten different areas, such as language development, independent functioning (dressing, toilet use, etc.), and ability to use numbers and tell time. The examiner scores each item based on the subject's most advanced performance. The second part is a checklist covering 13 areas of maladaptive behavior and one section evaluating the use of medications. Another oft-used instrument for assessing adaptive behavior is the Vineland Adaptive Behavior Scales (Sparrow, Ballo, & Cicchetti, 1984). This instrument, also a checklist, measures adaptive behavior in four areas: communication, daily living skills, social skills, and motor skills.

The third part of the AAMD definition reserves the term mental retardation for conditions that are either congenital or arise during the developmental period. This separates it from other forms of intellectual deficiency such as dementia occurring during the senium.

CLINICAL PRESENTATION AND EPIDEMIOLOGY

When discussing epidemiology and clinical presentation of mental retardation one must straightway address the commonly asserted dichotomy between what have become known as the organic and cultural-familial forms of the disorder. Organic retardation refers to those cases in which the causative factor is an identifiable biological abnormality, often a chromosomal or metabolic disorder, or neurological damage due to toxins. These forms of retardation account for approximately 50% of all cases (APA, 1987). Cultural-familial retardation, which will be discussed shortly, encompasses all those cases for which no known specific biological factor can be identified. Although these two terms would seem to indicate that some forms of intellectual deficit are determined solely by biological or genetic factors while others are determined strictly by environment, this is likely not the case. As will be pointed out later, research suggests that intellectual capacity is determined by a combination of the two. This is true of all individuals, whether of normal intelligence or severely retarded.

The level of impairment for organic retardation usually ranges from moderated to profound. With the exception of a few rare genetically determined disorders such as phenylketonuria (PKU) and Tay-

Sach's disease, organic forms of retardation are no more prevalent in family members of the affected individual than in the general population (APA, 1987). Moreover, organic mental retardation occurs with equable frequency in the upper and lower socioeconomic classes. Diagnosis of organic forms of the disorder is usually established at birth or an early age. Some forms of biologically based retardation are distinguishable by visual inspection of anatomical features, while others require laboratory tests.

As previously stated, children whose intellectual impairment can be traced to a specific biomedical factor usually function in the range of moderate to profound retardation. Those in the moderate range account for roughly half of these cases. Academically, these moderately retarded children are usually unable to progress beyond the second grade level. With respect to adaptive behavior, they are often capable of communicating verbally during the preschool period, but have poor awareness of social conventions during this time (Sattler, 1982). During the school-aged period they can profit from social and occupational training and can learn adequate self-help skills. Moderate supervision is often required, however.

Those individuals classified as severely mentally retarded comprise about 7% of the mentally retarded population, or about one fourth of those for which there is an identifiable biological abnormality (APA, 1987). During preschool these children evince poor motor and speech development. Later in development, however, they may learn to talk and can acquire simple self-help skills.

The lowest-functioning subgroup, profound mental retardation, aggregates less than 1% of all cases of retardation. As preschoolers, these children display significant sensorimotor impairment, requiring a highly structured environment with constant supervision. Their ability to learn minimal self-care skills, even as adults, is limited. A few of these individuals acquire some speech or communication skills (Millon, 1969). Some sensorimotor development may take place during the school-aged and adult years, sometimes leading to development of very limited self-care skills. However, close supervision and custodial care will in almost all cases be a lifetime necessity.

Much ground has been gained regarding knowledge of biomedical origins of retardation since Down's syndrome, or trisomy 21, was first recognized as a chromosomal abnormality in 1959. Although there continue to be many forms of biologically based retardation for which specific causes have not yet been identified (such as some of the prenatal influence syndromes), etiology and even treatment of some forms have been discovered. The incidence rate of Down's syndrome is estimated at 1 per 1,000 births, making it the most frequently occurring autosomal chromosome abnormality in man (Pueschel, 1983). The child with Down's syndrome is most often moderately retarded with a recognizable phenotype due to the presence of a supernumary chromosome 21. According to Pueschel, it is thought that the excessive genetic material, through interaction with other gene functions, results in altered homeostasis leading to altered physical and central nervous system development. There have been more than 300 abnormal features described (Coleman, 1978). The most readily observable physical characteristics, those leading to ease in diagnosis, include a small skull, small nose with flattened bridge, upward-slanting eyes, small ears, protruding tongue, short neck, and small hands and short fingers.

According to Gerald and Meryash (1983), one of the most significant advances related to cytogenetic determinants of mental retardation in recent years was the discovery of what is now called the fragile X syndrome. This syndrome, which is named for a constricted region of the distal end of the X chromosome, also presents with well-characterized clinical features. Phenotypic features in the male include short stature, prominent forehead, large ears, midfacial hypoplasia, prominent mandible, and large hands and feet. These individuals evince a spectrum of intellectual capacity ranging from borderline intelligence to severe retardation, although most fall within the mild and moderate categories. The frequency of this new disorder is believed to be second only to trisomy 21 among chromosomal abnormalities causing significant intellectual impairment. It is more commonly seen as a source of intellectual impairment in males than females, thus partially accounting for the long-observed but not understood phenomenon of retardation being more prevalent in males than females.

Another sex chromosome abnormality, Turner's syndrome, in which the female has only one X chromosome for a total of 45, can cause intellectual deficits. About 20% of these individuals are mildly retarded, the impairment being strongly associated with space-form perceptual deficiencies (Erickson, 1978). A study by Alexander, Ehrhardt, and Money (1966) reported the mean Verbal IQ of 18 Turner's syndrome adults on the

WAIS to be 118, while the mean Performance IQ was 88. These individuals are usually diagnosed during adolescence when sexual development fails to occur.

Klinefelter's syndrome is a chromosomal anomaly in which the affected male has more than one X chromosome, in addition to the Y chromosome. This syndrome occurs in 1 per 450 male births, with mental retardation occurring in 25% to 50% of these cases (Jacobs & Strong, 1959). Impairment is usually mild.

There are a number of single-gene determined disorders that can result in developmental delay. These hereditary errors of metabolism, such as PKU and galactosemia, can produce a devastating cerebral handicap but are much less frequent than popular belief would indicate (Crocker & Nelson, 1983). PKU is a condition resulting from an inactive liver enzyme. It occurs approximately once in every 17,000 births and is detectable at birth by an inexpensive laboratory screening. Prevention of intellectual deficit is possible through dietary modification, if detected early. Galactosemia, even more rare than PKU, is a disorder involving the metabolism of galactose, derived from foods containing lactose. It also may be effectively treated. Yet another genetic disorder that may be inherited as a recessive condition is microcephaly, which usually results in severe mental retardation. Microcephaly is a condition in which head circumference is less than two standard deviations below the mean for a child's age and sex. Not all cases of microcephaly are genetically related. Some may be caused by infectious diseases, or drug and alcohol ingestion by the pregnant mother (Abuelo, 1983). Furthermore, not all cases of microcephaly result in mental retardation (Avery, Meneses, & Lodge, 1972).

Prenatal influence syndromes, or "birth defects," constitute an important background for developmental handicap. These are usually encountered as a variety of mild phenotypic anomalies in a child who also presents a developmental delay. It is assumed that the central nervous system has also been malformed. Most of these children are not identified as having one of the named syndromes. Crocker and Nelson (1983) include as topographical indicators the following: unusual palate shape, changes in position of the eyes and ears, small mandible, unusual feet, genital variation, and dermatoglyphics. Body growth is commonly slowed, and head circumference is sometimes small, but computed tomographic scannings of the central nervous system usually reveal normal findings. Etiology of these disorders is usually undetermined, with the exception of a few syndromes such as fetal alcohol syndrome, the result of recurrent maternal alcohol intoxication during the first or second trimester.

Perinatal factors such as intracranial hemorrhage and hypoxic-ischemic brain damage (asphyxia) are highly represented in the etiology of mental retardation (Lott, 1983). With the improvements of fetal monitoring techniques in the labor room and increasingly sophisticated intervention strategies for the troubled neonate, infant mortality rate has declined. It is conceivable that along with this decline, perinatal factors may become a more frequent cause of retardation. As pointed out by Lott, the quality of life for many of these sick neonates gives less reason for optimism than the survival itself. This should in no way cast a shadow on the efforts to improve upon infant survival rates. It does, however, point to the need for careful assessment of perinatal stresses that could have resulted in cerebral trauma, when searching for determinants of mental retardation.

As stated earlier, the organic forms of intellectual impairment account for approximately half of all cases of mental retardation. In the remaining cases, commonly called familial retardation, no known specific biological factor can be determined. Physical appearance is usually normal and impairment is most commonly in the mild range, with IQs between 50 and 70. There is often a familial pattern of similar degrees of deficit seen in parents and siblings of affected individuals (APA, 1987). This is contrary to what is found in organic forms of the disorder, where frequency is usually no greater in family members than in the normal population. The aforementioned exceptions to this rule include some of the genetically determined disorders (as opposed to chromosomal aberrations) and some forms of X linked mental retardation such as the fragile X syndrome.

The lower socioeconomic classes are overrepresented with cases of familial retardation. The reasons for this are not clear. However, this form of retardation may be associated with a lack of social, linguistic, and intellectual stimulation. Studies conducted in institutional settings in which infants were not afforded adequate amounts of interaction with others, or adequate variety of visual stimulation, demonstrated that developmental delay was a frequent occurrence in such settings and could easily be prevented (Casler, 1965). Furthermore, a number of intervention studies have demonstrated improvements in a variety of measures of intellectual ability following environmental enrichment. For example, Skeels (1966) claimed striking increases in IQ occurred when children were moved from an orphanage to more stimulating environments. Whimbey and Whimbey (1980) reported an experimental study that demonstrated higher IQs in children who were afforded a wide variety of stimulation to develop perceptual, motor, and language abilities than a control group of children from similar backgrounds. There is reason to believe that mildly retarded children are often the products of less than optimal environmental and psychological conditions, such as lack of reinforcement for learning and even the lack of opportunity to learn (Erickson, 1978). However, environmental deprivation does not completely account for familial retardation. For example, Achenbach (1974) found that the correlations between parents' and children's IQ scores remained about the same whether the children were raised by their biological parents or by adoptive parents. It is probably fair to conclude that mild mental retardation results from both genetic factors and poor quality of early childhood environment.

NATURAL HISTORY

Mental retardation is a disorder that, by its very nature, changes within the individual over time. Mentally retarded children behave as if passing through a developmental stage that would be normal for a child of an earlier chronological age. As the retarded child grows older, he develops new skills and learns new behavior patterns, thus changing the difficulties he may evince. Just as normal children change over time with respect to various abilities, strengths, and weaknesses, so does the child who is intellectually impaired.

Although behavioral and cognitive abilities may improve from childhood to adulthood, the measured degree of intellectual impairment (in terms of IQ) will obviously fail to reflect this improvement accurately. This is due to the fact that IQ is not a true quantitative measure, but one that portrays the individual's cognitive abilities relative to a cohort population. In addition, consistent improvement throughout development may be perceived as insignificant when the retarded individual is compared to normals who, by this age, have made drastic changes in terms of socialization and vocational skills.

Like most mental disorders, the level of impairment mental retardation bestows varies widely from one individual to the next. This variance, divided into the four categories of mild, moderated, severe, and profound, is a factor that partially determines the degree to which the disorder changes over the course of development from childhood to adulthood. The more severe forms of mental retardation are less likely to evince new behavior patterns through the developmental period because of their relatively diminished ability to benefit from instruction. Profoundly retarded children, for example, usually possess such a minimal capacity for learning that their adaptive behavior and cognitive capabilities will not change much from childhood to adulthood. Most will continue to require assistance in feeding, maintaining hygiene, toileting, and dressing and will develop minimal if any language capabilities.

Mildly retarded children are capable of developing, by adulthood, adaptive behaviors adequate for minimum self-support. The mildly retarded child with no biological etiology may even "outgrow" the diagnosis if exposed to a more stimulating environment and allowed more opportunities to learn. Moderately retarded children may also demonstrate considerable improvement over the course of development. Much progress has been made in teaching these individuals self-help skills such as using public transportation (Neef & Iwata, 1978) and cooking simple meals (Bellamy & Clark, 1977). Efforts have also been underway to improve social and vocational skills. Haring, Roger, Lee, Breen, and Gaylord-Ross (1986) taught moderately retarded children to initiate and expound on conversational topics. Wacker and Berg (1983) used picture prompts to teach complex vocational tasks to moderately retarded adolescents.

IMPAIRMENT AND COMPLICATIONS

The major source of impairment associated with the intellectual deficits of mental retardation is, by definition, restriction of adaptive behaviors. The degree of impairment of adaptive functioning is highly correlated with the degree of intellectual deficit. Thus, within the population of mentally retarded children there exists a wide variation in ability to function independently and demonstrate social responsibility. Children classified as mildly mentally retarded often evince adaptive behavior so similar to same-age normals that they require no closer supervision than do normal children

(Davison & Neale, 1982). These children can dress and feed themselves at an early age and may not present a significant child rearing problem until they begin to experience difficulty in school. They may develop communication and social skills during preschool and have minimal sensorimotor deficits. Academically, they often achieve sixth grade level by adolescence. The adaptive behavior of the remaining three subgroups (described previously) decreases progressively with level of intellectual capacity. The most severely impaired children are incapable of learning any self-help skills. They are unable to dress, feed, and toilet themselves, and thus require continuous care.

Two complications seen most often in severe and profound retardation are self-stimulation and self-injury. Self-stimulation refers to bizarre, repetitive or stereotypic behavior such as rocking and twirling. Although not necessarily harmful behaviors in and of themselves, they sometimes interfere with the teaching of other, more adaptive behaviors. Self-injury can take many different forms. Eye-gouging and biting are just two examples. These behaviors, which can be extremely difficult to eliminate, can often lead to serious physical harm.

There are other associated behavioral features, many of which are seen in moderate and mild retardation as well. Among these are overactivity, aggressiveness, and temper tantrums. Attention-deficit hyperactivity disorder and stereotypy/habit disorder are three to four times more common among children with mental retardation than in the general population (APA, 1987).

Children with biologically based intellectual impairment often have associated physical handicaps such as neuromuscular disorders, impairment of vision or hearing, and seizures.

Some people have voiced concern that anomalies of physical appearance associated with some forms of retardation may present a barrier to their attainment of near-normal life-styles. Rozner (1983) describes his and other plastic surgeons' efforts to improve the appearance and speech of children with Down's syndrome. Epicanthal folds of the eyelids, protruding tongue, chronically open mouth, upward slant of the eyes, midfacial hypoplasia, and abnormalities of dentition are some of the pathognomonic stigmata that Rozner asserts have been improved through surgery. These procedures are not without controversy, however. For some people the idea of facial plastic surgery for a child who may not have an actual

choice is repugnant. Pueschel, Monteiro, and Erickson (1986) point out a number of concerns, such as how will the surgical trauma affect the child, will surgery really make prejudices disappear, how will the child perceive the facial changes after surgery, and what will this mean to the child's self-image. They also point out that physicians and parents of Down's children differ drastically with respect to the extent to which each believe the children's facial features negatively affect their social development. Eighty-five percent of parents, but only 4% of physicians, see Down's children as well-accepted by society. Furthermore, data collected by Pueschel et al. (1986) show that 13% of parents, but 44% of physicians believe plastic surgery should be done on children with Down's syndrome. Given these data there is concern that the ultimate decision of whether or not to have plastic surgery may be unintentionally influenced by the biases of the physician.

DIFFERENTIAL DIAGNOSIS

Diagnosis of mental retardation can be either arduous or apparent, depending on the etiology and severity of the condition. Severe forms of the disorder, and those with obvious physical characteristics associated with a biological cause, are more easily recognized at an early age than cases of familial retardation. For example, Down's syndrome is apparent at birth though clear signs of cognitive impairment may not develop for several months. Profoundly retarded children, on the other hand, evince behavior patterns suggestive of cognitive handicap at a very early age, often within the first 2 or 3 months of life. Included among such behaviors are nonresponsiveness to contact, poor eye contact during feeding, diminished spontaneous activity, decreased alertness to voice or movement, irritability, and slow feeding (Crocker & Nelson, 1983). Although these signs should alert the practitioner to the possibility of mental retardation, it should be stressed that some of these behaviors could just as easily be indicative of another disorder, such as autism.

The less severely retarded infant will probably appear normal with respect to these potential red flags, but may demonstrate evidence of impairment during early childhood. The child may be slow to develop communication and self-help skills, and may have difficulty learning to interact with other children in age-appropriate play. Mildly retarded children usually pass undetected through infancy and preschool years. Difficulty with basic academic skills and application of appropriate reasoning and judgment, delayed development of interpersonal relationships, and inability to participate in group activities, are among the problems that can allude to the possibility of mental retardation (Millon, 1969).

In recent years much emphasis has been placed on the early recognition of cognitive handicap. Early intervention through environmental enrichment is now believed to be of pivotal importance to maximizing development of the retarded child. A number of screening devices have been developed to aid in early diagnosis. One such device is the Denver Developmental Screening Test, which assesses developmental level in five areas: gross and fine motor, adaptive behavior, language, and personal-social behavior. This test can be administered in less than 20 minutes, and has thus become a popular instrument among pediatricians. A more comprehensive instrument is the Bayley Scales of Infant Development, which consists of three major scales designed to measure mental skills, motor skills, and behavioral problems. It provides a more thorough evaluation by sampling a greater variety of behaviors, and is likely the most popular of all the infant tests (Schnell, 1983).

Although early detection and intervention are of paramount importance, extreme caution is warranted when interpreting the results of tests administered during infancy. A measured developmental lag should not automatically be equated with an absolute prediction of cognitive ability. It is well known that, in general, measures of infant development correlate poorly with measures of intelligence taken during later childhood. However, cases of significant development lag can serve to alert the clinician to possible cognitive compromise. In these cases, monitoring the child's further development with a watchful eye for additional signs of developmental delay is suggested. Cases of extreme delay in early development (e.g., a mental-age score of less than 4 months obtained by an 8-month-old on the Bayley) may be assumed to have greater predictive validity concerning later intelligence, and thus warrant early intervention (Holden, 1972).

Reason for caution when interpreting developmental lag in infancy stems not only from the generally poor predictive validity concerning later childhood intelligence, but also from the fact that such developmental delay may be the result of specific sensory and/or motor defects. Lack of alertness and poor response to speech can be due to hearing loss. Severe visual impairment in the infant is associated with a lack of curiosity, prolonged mouthing of objects, and delayed walking. Slow motor development, which is often seen in retarded children, can also be the result of a neuromuscular disorder which is unaccompanied by mental retardation (Baroff, 1974). Hypotonia, for example, is a disorder which results in delayed motor development but does not produce mental retardation. Cerebral palsy also causes motor impairment and may or may not result in concomitant cognitive deficit. Given these possible confounds concerning early detection of intellectual impairment, the clinician would be remiss to diagnose mental retardation and commence with intervention prior to examination by a physician, particularly in a very young child.

Provided clinicians follow the diagnostic guidelines set forth by the AAMD and outlined in the DSM-III-R, few diagnostic errors should occur. According to the DSM-III-R, mental retardation should be diagnosed regardless of the presence of another disorder, such as pervasive developmental disorder or a specific developmental disorder. In specific developmental disorders there is a delay in development of certain skills such as arithmetic or, more commonly, reading, but development is normal in other areas. In pervasive developmental disorder many basic functions such as development of social skills and language are out of sequence or occur at slower rates. In addition, there are peculiar speech patterns and bizarre responses to various aspects of the environment that are not normal for any stage of development. In contrast, the mentally retarded child shows generalized delays in development, but behaves as if he were passing through an earlier normal period of development. Mental retardation may coexist with a specific development disorder, and frequently coexists with pervasive developmental disorder.

Concurrent with the recent emphasis of early recognition of developmental delay has been an emphasis on determining a variety of factors that place the infant at risk for cognitive impairment. Although the presence of risk factors does not indicate that mental retardation is inevitable, knowledge of these factors can serve to alert the clinician of the increased likelihood of cognitive impairment and thus aid in early diagnosis. These risk factors can be divided into physical factors, demographic factors, and those involving the psychological environment (Erickson, 1978). Included among the physical risk factors are a number of maternal infections such as rubella and syphilis. Prenatally contracted rubella results in mental retardation in 25% of the cases (Chess, Korn, & Fernandez, 1971). A wide variety of drugs and addictive substances have been shown to be potential causes of mental retardation, and thus present risk factors when consumed by the pregnant mother. Other physical factors linked to mental retardation include low birth weight (Crocker & Nelson, 1983), poor postnatal nutrition (Stoch & Smythe, 1976), anoxia, perinatal and postnatal head injury (Healy, Herman, & Rubin, 1983), and lead and mercury poisoning (Graef, 1983).

Demographic variables related to risk of mental retardation include age and socioeconomic status of the mother, and sex of the infant. Teenage mothers and women over age 35 are at greater risk of having a retarded child (Erickson, 1978), with particular concern surrounding chromosomal abnormalities. Cognitive deficits are more likely among children from lower socioeconomic classes. It should be noted that socioeconomic status is likely related to many physical factors such as nutrition, and to the psychological environment. Being male can be an added risk when associated with other risk factors because mental retardation is twice as common in males than in females (Haskins, 1986). This is due in part to the more numerous chromosomal abnormalities affecting males.

Risk factors involving the psychological environment are more difficult to ascertain. Theoretically, a child with optimal biological makeup who is deprived of much environmental stimulation will become mentally retarded. As pointed out earlier, many studies have alluded to the possible detrimental effects of deprivation of certain kinds of interaction with the environment. The problem then becomes one of determining just what kind of environmental interaction is important. Birch and Gussow (1970) found that retarded children of lower socioeconomic status were more likely to come from large families living in small houses than nonretarded children of similar socioeconomic status. This would seem to indicate that less individual parental attention and crowded living conditions may be a risk factor. Erickson asserts that environments that fail to provide adequate models for learning and opportunity to learn cognitive skills may constitute a risk for mental retardation.

CASE EXAMPLES

Case 1

David S. is a 7-year, 6-month-old boy who was referred for treatment by his first grade teacher because of deficits in academic skills and behavior problems at school and home. Ms. S., David's mother, provided information about his developmental history, current family situation, and behavior problems at home. Ms. S. is a single parent with seven children, David being the middle child. They live in a three-bedroom house that is in a state of disrepair, with a leaky roof and poor heating. Ms. S. is currently unemployed and has not maintained gainful employment in several years, partly because of frequent bouts with depression. She has few social supports and no family in the surrounding area. Although she appeared concerned about David's academic and behavioral difficulties, Ms. S. seemed overwhelmed with other concerns pertaining to her family's financial situation.

Ms. S. reported that her pregnancy with David was normal and delivery was uncomplicated. Most of his developmental milestones were unremarkable. David crawled at 8 months, walked at 11 months, and was toilet trained at about 2 years of age. His language development was slightly delayed, however.

In response to questions regarding David's behavior at home, Ms. S. stated that his behavior has been more difficult to handle than that of her other children. He frequently exhibits temper tantrums while playing with his siblings, or when some restriction has been placed on him by his mother. He is noncompliant to many directives made by Ms. S. Ms. S. reported that her main forms of discipline are spanking and scolding, although she admitted that sometimes she becomes exhausted and gives in to his tantrums. David possesses social skills that allow him to make friends. He is capable of engaging in structured play that requires rule-following, and can initiate such activities. He plays with neighborhood children but often is involved in skirmishes related to his difficulty with respecting the rights of other children.

David's academic and behavior problems at school were identified by interviewing his teacher. She revealed that he has been unable to master many of the basic skills necessary for classroom achievement such as understanding and following instructions. Relative to other students in his first grade class, he has difficulty maintaining attention to tasks and tends to respond to questions impulsively without considering all alternatives. He is noncompliant to classroom rules and does not respond to disciplinary measures usually successful with other children. Socially, his behavior closely resembles that described at home. He does interact with other children, but has some difficulty getting along because of frequent tantrums and an unwillingness to give in to the desires of other children.

David was observed on 3 consecutive days, in class and on the playground at school. He exhibited frequent noncompliance in the classroom. For example, he had to be repeatedly told to join in group activities and sometimes appeared deliberately to respond incorrectly when given a directive. He was frequently inattentive and off-task during group instruction and independent work. He was easily distracted from his work, either by staring outside through the window, or playing with his pencil and eraser. David's behavior on the playground was consistent with his teacher's description of his social interactions. He did engage in group play, but was involved in skirmishes more often than the other children.

A psychoeducational assessment was conducted, which included the Stanford-Binet Intelligence Scale and the Peabody Individual Achievement Test (Dunn & Markwardt, 1970). Adaptive behavior was assessed via the Vineland Adaptive Behavior Scales (Sparrow, Balla, & Cicchetti, 1984). David listened to the instructions and appeared to try hard during the assessment. However, his short attention span required the assessment to be extended over two sessions. David's performance on the Stanford-Binet resulted in an IQ of 65. No areas of significantly superior or inferior ability were evident. On the Peabody he received a total test standard score of 69, with relatively consistent performance across the areas of mathematics, reading, spelling, and general information. David's mother served as informant for completion of the Vineland. He achieved an Adaptive Behavior Composite standard score of 69. Close inspection of the individual items revealed that David's major difficulties involve maladaptive behaviors involving social living, although his daily living and motor skills were also mildly deficient.

Given the apparent normalcy of David's physical history, it is probable that his current behavior and academic difficulties are a product of the less than ideal environment in which he lives. He had probably been afforded minimal positive interaction with his mother, who lacked the requisite skills to handle his problems in a positive way. Intervention with David began with a parent training program to assist Ms. S. in the contingency management of David's temper outbursts and general noncompliance. Briefly, this program emphasized increasing positive reinforcement of desirable behavior, appropriate ways of giving directives, and the use of time out. A home-based contingency management program was also implemented whereby David could earn rewards at home for improved class participation and task completion. His teacher was encouraged to praise David when he stayed on task with individual class assignments and participated in group classroom activities. It was also recommended that David be considered for enrollment in his school's special education program. David demonstrated improvement with respect to his temper tantrums and noncompliance within a few weeks, and soon after improved in class participation and completion of in-class assignments.

Case 2

Brad B. is a 17-year-old boy referred because of maladaptive behaviors he was engaging in at home and at his school for retarded children. Brad was diagnosed with Down's syndrome at birth. He displayed the characteristic small, low-set ears, small hands and short fingers, upward-slanting eyes, and small skull.

Brad was the third child born to a family of three children. Both his parents had maintained stable employment that allowed the family a comfortable, middle-class life-style. His two older sisters had enjoyed academic success in high school and were currently enrolled in college courses.

Mrs. B. reported that her pregnancy and delivery with Brad were normal. However, she and Mr. B. were both in their late thirties when Brad was conceived. As expected, most of Brad's developmental milestones were delayed. He crawled at 12 months, walked at 24 months, and began talking in phrases at 28 months. By 3 years of age he was eating with a spoon. Toilet training was delayed more than expected based on the developmental rate of most other behaviors. He did not become fully continent (diurnally) until 6 years of age.

Both of Brad's parents were dedicated to maximizing his academic and adaptive behavior accomplishments. They had consistently engaged him in cognitively stimulating activities throughout his childhood. At age 14 they enrolled Brad in a day school for mildly and moderately retarded children, where he was taught such self-help skills as counting money, telling time, and washing clothes.

Mr. and Mrs. B. brought Brad to the clinic seeking assistance in dealing with two problematic behaviors in which he had engaged with increasing frequency over the last 6 months: flushing socks down the toilet and self-stimulation of his genitals in public. He had always been fascinated with the toilet, but never attempted to flush articles of clothing until one day he accidentally dropped a sock in the toilet. It appeared that flushing socks was rewarding for Brad, as he became very excited and reported to his parents this "new discovery." Despite numerous attempts at punishing this behavior through removal of personal objects and privileges, Brad continued to flush socks about twice a week.

Brad began self-stimulating (rubbing the crotch of his pants) 8 months prior to the referral. This behavior presented a problem because he lacked the ability to discriminate between situations in which it would and would not be appropriate. He frequently self-stimulated in the presence of others, although he did not appear to be seeking attention. The self-stimulation eventually became an impulsive or habitual behavior that Brad appeared to emit without full awareness. Like the sock-flushing behavior, attempts to punish it proved futile.

Treatment of the self-stimulation involved reinforcement of an incompatible behavior (placing his thumbs through his belt loops), with the problem behavior itself serving as the discriminative stimulus. After repeated attempts to punish Brad systematically for flushing socks failed, it was discovered that he was only flushing dirty socks. He was then taught to wash them in the washing machine instead, a routine that appeared to be a greater reward than flushing.

CONTINUITY AND DISCONTINUITY WITH ADULT PRESENTATION

By definition mental retardation is always first evident during childhood or adolescence, and in most cases continues into adulthood. As such, childhood and adulthood mental retardation are identical disorders with different manifestations that are a result of development. Factors such as etiology, familial pattern, prevalence, and sex ratio are roughly equivalent for the two.

SUMMARY

Mental retardation refers to subaverage intellectual functioning concurrent with deficiencies in adaptive behavior detectable before age 18. The causes of this disorder range from deprivation of the psychological environment to a plethora of potential biological influences. For many cases, however, the etiology remains a mystery. Impairment may be either mild, allowing the individual a near-normal lifestyle, or completely incapacitating.

Tremendous progress has been made toward the treatment of mental retardation, and some forms of the disorder are now preventable through dietary measures and genetic counseling. Much emphasis has been placed on teaching mentally retarded children self-care and cognitive skills. As a result, fewer children are requiring institutionalization and custodial care. With the advent of group homes and sheltered workshops, more retarded adults are able to assume greater independence and responsibility for their economic needs.

The dramatically improved prognosis for intellectually impaired children who receive treatment underscores the need for early recognition of the disorder. Risk factors have been identified to alert the clinician of an increased likelihood that mental retardation may develop. However, the presence of such risks does not necessitate the presence of mental retardation at a later age.

REFERENCES

Abuelo, D. N. (1983). Genetic disorders. In J. L. Matson & J. A. Mulick (Eds.), *Handbook of mental retardation* (pp. 105–120). Elmsford, NY: Pergamon Press.

Achenbach, T. (1974). *Developmental psychopathology*. New York: The Ronald Press.

Alexander, D., Ehrhardt, A. A., & Money, J. (1966). Pediatric multiphasic program: Preliminary description. *American Journal of Diseases in Children, 142*, 161–107.

American Psychiatric Association. (1987). *Diagnostic and statistical manual of mental disorders* (3rd ed. rev.). Washington, DC: Author.

Avery, G. B., Meneses, L., & Lodge, A. (1972). The clinical significance of "measurement microcephaly." *American Journal of Diseases of Children, 123*, 214–217.

Baroff, G. S. (1974). *Mental retardation: Nature, cause, and management*. Washington, DC: Hemisphere.

Bellamy, G. T., & Clark, G. (1977). Picture recipe cards as an approach to teaching severely and profoundly retarded adults to cook. *Education and Training of the Mentally Retarded, 12*, 69–73.

Birch, H. G., & Gussow, J. D. (1970). *Disadvantaged children: Health, nutrition, and school failure*. New York: Harcourt Brace Jovanovich.

Casler, L. (1965). The effects of tactile stimulation on a group of institutionalized infants. *Genetic psychology monographs, 71*, 137–175.

Chess, S., Korn, S., & Fernandez, P. (1971). *Psychiatric disorders of children with rubella*. New York: Brunner/Mazel.

Coleman, M. (1978). Down's syndrome. *Pediatric Annals, 7*, 90–103.

Crocker, A. C., & Nelson, R. P. (1983). Major handicapping conditions. In M. D. Levine, W. B. Carey, A. C. Crocker, & R. T. Gross (Eds.), *Developmental-behavioral pediatrics* (pp. 756–769). Philadelphia: W. B. Saunders.

Davison, G. C., & Neale, J. M. (1982). *Abnormal psychology* (3rd ed.). New York: John Wiley & Sons.

Erickson, M. T. (1978). *Child psychopathology*. Englewood Cliffs, NJ: Prentice Hall.

Graef, J. W. (1983). Environmental toxins. In M. D. Levine, W. B. Carey, A. C. Crocker, & R. T. Gross (Eds.), *Developmental-behavioral pediatrics* (pp. 427–439). Philadelphia: W. B. Saunders.

Gerald, P. S., & Meryash, D. L. (1983). Chromosomal disorders other than Down syndrome. In M. D. Levine, W. B. Carey, A. C. Crocker, & R. T. Gross (Eds.), *Developmental-behavioral pediatrics* (pp. 346–353). Philadelphia: W. B. Saunders.

Grossman, H. J. (Ed.). (1983). *Classification in mental retardation*. Washington, DC: American Association on Mental Deficiency.

Haring, T. G., Roger, B., Lee, M., Breen, C., & Gaylord-Ross, R. (1986). Teaching social language to moderately retarded handicapped students. *Journal of Applied Behavior Analysis, 19*, 159–171.

Haskins, R. (1986). Social and cultural factors in risk assessment and mild mental retardation. In D. C. Farran & J. D. McKinney (Eds.), *Risk in intellectual and psychosocial development* (pp. 29–60). Orlando, FL: Academic Press.

Healy, A., Herman A. H., & Rubin, I. L. (1983). Perinatal stresses. In M. D. Levine, W. B. Carey, A. C. Crocker, & R. T. Gross (Eds.), *Developmental-behavioral pediatrics* (pp. 390–403). Philadelphia: W. B. Saunders.

Holden, R. H. (1972). Prediction of mental retardation in infancy. *Mental Retardation, 10*, 28–30.

Jacobs, P. A., & Strong, J. A. (1959). A case of human intersexuality having possible XXY sex-determining mechanism. *Nature, 183*, 302–303.

Lott, I. T. (1983). Perinatal factors in mental retardation. In J. L. Matson & J. A. Mulick (Eds.), *Handbook of mental retardation* (pp. 97–103). Elmsford, NY: Pergamon Press.

Millon, T. (1969). *Modern psychopathology: A biosocial approach to maladaptive learning and functioning*. Philadelphia: W. B. Saunders.

Neef, N. A., Iwata, B. A., & Page, T. J. (1978). Public transportation training: In vivo versus classroom instruction. *Journal of Applied Behavior Analysis, 11*, 331–334.

Nihira, K., Forster, R., Shellhaas, M., & Leland, H. (1974). *AAMD adaptive behavior scale, 1974 revision*. Washington, DC: American Association on Mental Deficiency.

Pueschel, S. M. (1983). The child with Down syndrome. In M. D. Levine, W. B. Carey, A. C. Crocker, & R. T. Gross (Eds.), *Developmental-behavioral pediatrics* (pp. 353–362). Philadelphia: W. B. Saunders.

Pueschel, S. M., Monteiro, L. A., & Erickson, M. (1986). Parents' and physicians' perceptions of facial plastic surgery in children with Down's syndrome. *Journal of mental deficiency research, 30*, 71–79.

Rozner, L. (1983). Facial plastic surgery for Down's syndrome. *Lancet, 833*, 1320–1323.

Sattler, J. M. (1982). *Assessment of children's intelligence and special abilities* (2nd ed.). Boston: Allyn & Bacon.

Schnell, R. R. (1983). Standardized psychological testing. In M. D. Levine, W. B. Carey, A. C. Crocker, & R. T. Gross (Eds.), *Developmental-behavioral pediatrics* (pp. 1004–1021). Philadelphia: W. B. Saunders.

Skeels, H. M. (1966). Adult status of children with contrasting early life experiences. *Monograph of the Society for Research in Child Development, 31* (serial no. 3).

Sparrow, S., Balla, D. A., & Cicchetti, D. V. (1984). *Vineland adaptive behavior scales*. Circle Pines, MN: American Guidance Service.

Stoche, M. B., & Smythe, P. M. (1976). Fifteen year developmental study of severe undernutrition during infancy on subsequent physical growth and intellectual functioning. *Archives of Disorders in Children, 51*, 327–342.

Wacker, D. P., & Berg, W. K. (1983). Effects of picture prompts on the acquisition of complex vocational tasks by moderately retarded adolescents. *Journal of Applied Behavior Analysis, 16*, 417–433.

Whimbey, A., & Whimbey, L. S. (1980). *Intelligence can be taught*. New York: E. P. Dutton.

Whitman, T. L., & Johnston, M. B. (1987). Mental retardation. In M. Hersen & V. B. Van Hasselt (Eds.), *Behavior therapy with children and adolescents* (pp. 184–223). New York: John Wiley & Sons.

CHAPTER 24

MENTAL RETARDATION IN ADULTHOOD

Ronald A. Madle

In spite of the long history of mental retardation as a field, the condition has been differentiated from various forms of mental illness only since about the eighteenth century (Scheerenberger, 1983). It is evident, however, that individuals with marked intellectual delay were treated with scorn and persecution throughout much of history. Until recently they were often exterminated or served as court jesters, servants, and the like. At times they were considered to be "possessed by Satan." Even benign views of mental retardation stressed the hopelessness of the condition.

The earliest positive treatment of the retarded is generally traced to the late eighteenth century (Scheerenberger, 1983). With John Locke's introduction of environment as a major force in human development, Itard (1932) reacted to the discovery of a feral child with optimism and asserted that the child could be "civilized." While this thrust would eventually become the dominant approach, there continued to be throwbacks. In the late nineteenth century, for example, the belief emerged that all retardation was inherited and could be eradicated. The retarded were sterilized and segregated from society in institutions in order to eliminate this "scourge." Some societies (Nazi Germany) even systematically destroyed the retarded.

The earliest attempts to define mental retardation stressed the failure of the retarded to adapt to the demands of society. With the introduction of intelligence testing, the cognitive abilities of the retarded gained primacy. Most modern definitions, however, treat both intellectual and adaptive behavior delays as conjoint elements in defining this disorder, although there continues to be debate on the issue (e.g, Burack, Hodapp, & Zigler, 1988; Zigler & Balla, 1982).

Retardation by definition always originates prior to adulthood, although many adults are retarded since the condition is chronic and typically persists throughout the life span. Only recently has there been significant attention to retardation during the adult portion of the life span (e.g., Matson & Marchetti, 1988; Seltzer & Krauss, 1987). Most attention has been to the characteristics, needs, and treatment of the infant, child, and adolescent. As a consequence, much of what is known about the characteristics of the adult mentally retarded individual still must be extrapolated from study of children and adolescents.

DESCRIPTION OF THE DISORDER

The most widely accepted contemporary definition of mental retardation is that of the American Association on Mental Retardation (AAMR, formerly the American Association on Mental Deficiency). This definition, which closely resembles others, indicates that mental retardation " . . . refers to significantly subaverage general intellectual functioning resulting in or existing concurrently with deficits in adaptive behavior and manifested during the developmental period" (Grossman, 1983, p. 11). The stress is explicitly on delayed levels of behavioral performance without reference to actual or presumed cause. The most outstanding characteristic of the disorder is clearly the generalized delay in a wide range of behavioral domains (Madle, 1983).

The AAMR definition consists of three key elements. The first is that the individual must display *significantly subaverage general intellectual functioning*. This is defined as an IQ score on a widely accepted, standardized intelligence test, generally a Wechsler or Binet scale, which is two or more standard deviations below the mean (approximately below IQ 70). The second major criterion is that *impairment in adaptive behavior* is evidenced. The individual must display significant lags in areas such as academic learning, personal independence, and social responsibility to receive the label. The last element in the definition requires that both intellectual and adaptive functioning impairments must be identified during the developmental period (before age 18). This specifically rules out the inclusion of individuals who "regress" during adulthood, perhaps due to trauma, psychiatric disorder, or senility. Such individuals, while displaying similar characteristics, are not considered mentally retarded.

CLINICAL PRESENTATION

Mental retardation is an overall state of impairment recognizable in an individual's behavior, rather than a single syndrome. It manifests itself in an array of intellectual and behavioral deficiencies. As noted by Esquirol in 1828,

> Idiocy is not a disease but a condition in which the intellectual faculties are never manifested or have never been developed sufficiently to enable the idiot to acquire such an amount of knowledge as persons of his own age, and placed in similar circumstances with himself, are capable of receiving. (cited in Szymanski & Crocker, 1985, p. 1635)

Mentally retarded adults are a heterogeneous group. In fact, persons classified as mentally retarded generally may have little in common beyond the label assigned and the overall intellectual and adaptive delay in comparison to their age mates. Mentally retarded adults range from those who are nearly totally dependent on others for their care to others who may function intellectually and behaviorally nearly as well as "normal" persons. The most obvious aspect presented to the clinician is the variation of adaptive behavior impairment, as well as a level of cognitive functioning below the norm.

Levels of Retardation

AAMR defines four levels of retardation. While these levels are defined primarily in terms of intellectual functioning, the most clinically outstanding impairment is in *adaptive behavior*. These four levels—mild, moderate, severe, and profound—are shown in Table 24.1, which also summarizes key levels of adaptive functioning at each level during adulthood.

The mildly retarded, with Stanford-Binet IQs between 52 and 68, show the least degree of impairment. In fact, many of these individuals differ relatively little from others of their age and may be undetectable by the general public. Often they will not be identified as mentally retarded until sometime in elementary school and will "lose" the label when they enter adulthood. With IQs ranging from 36 to 51, the moderately retarded evidence increased difficulty in acquiring and performing tasks taken for granted by most people. At this level the individual's self-management skills become increasingly limited. They do not achieve an independent adjustment and will always require some degree of supervision. Delays at the severely (IQ 20–35) and profoundly (IQ under 20) retarded levels become markedly more pronounced in essentially all areas of functioning. The severely and profoundly retarded will always require much supervision. Individuals at this level often display many stereotyped, repetitive behaviors, and are frequently institutionalized.

Table 24.1. Degree of Impairment by Level of Retardation

LEVEL OF RETARDATION	MAJOR DOMAIN OF ADAPTIVE FUNCTIONING
Mild IQ 52–68 MA 8–11	*Self-management.* Full self-care skills; often function independently; many benefit from assistance with activities of daily living; may need another person to serve as an "advisor." *Language.* Both receptive and expressive skills limited but generally adequate for day-to-day purposes. *Academics.* May read simple informational materials; unlikely to read for pleasure; money skills limited to simple addition and subtraction; need much assistance with budgeting and simple money management. *Employment.* Capable of regular, unskilled employment; may achieve assistant status in a trade. *Social Roles.* May have friends, marry, and raise children; function in various community roles such as voting; increased contact with legal system.
Moderate IQ 36–51 MA 6–8	*Self-management.* Have basic self-care skills; do not achieve an independent adjustment; will always require some degree of supervision. *Language.* Generally functional for communication; intelligibility of speech may be much impaired. *Academics.* Do not achieve functional reading and money skills. *Employment.* Do not generally work at the regular level of employment but can work productively in sheltered workshops. *Social Roles.* Do not generally fill roles such as spouse and parent; are capable of friendships with the opposite sex; do not fulfill ordinary community functions.
Severe IQ 20–35 MA 4–6	*Self-management.* Do not function independently; many can acquire some self-help skills (e.g., feeding, dressing, toileting). *Language.* Understanding likely to be much better than expressive language; speech often poorly articulated; difficult to understand. *Academics.* No functional reading or number skills. *Employment.* May be capable of some useful work either at sheltered workshop or work activity levels; more likely to be attending day activity center. *Social Roles.* Do not generally fulfill adult social roles; have some peer relationships; generally relate to other adults in a child-like fashion; perform no community roles.
Profound IQ <20 MA <4	*Self-management.* Will always require supervision; may acquire some rudimentary self-care skills; mobility often impaired due to sensory or motor problems. *Language.* Better receptive than expressive language; little or no speech. *Academics.* No reading, writing, or number skills. *Employment.* Usually unable to perform any useful work; with intensive training may achieve a work-activity level of productivity. *Social Roles.* Do not fulfill any adult social roles; may appear as social isolates; pay little attention to others except as it relates to their own needs.

Cognitive, Learning, and Social/ Personality Characteristics

While overall adaptive behavior delays are the most salient feature in the mentally retarded, certain cognitive, learning, and social/personality differences are commonly noted, particularly in the mildly to moderately retarded. The presence of cognitive differences in retardation is generally acknowledged, and the nature of these differences has been an area of long-standing disagreement (Zigler & Balla, 1982). Some psychologists (e.g., Spitz, Ellis) advocate a *deficit* model, while others (e.g., Zigler) contend that a *developmental* model is more appropriate. The deficit model suggests

some basic processes (such as some aspect of memory) operate differently or more poorly than in normal individuals. In the *developmental* model, however, cognitive processes are seen as operating the same as those in normal children with the same mental age; any differences are attributed to motivational factors. More recently attempts have been made to combine these models into a unified theory of retardation (e.g., Detterman, 1987; Sternberg & Spear, 1985). No matter which model is accurate, the mentally retarded do evidence differences from similar-aged peers in various cognitive functions, as discussed in the paragraphs that follow.

There is little difference in the operation of principles governing the acquisition, maintenance, and extinction of simple responses, as well as in simple memory functions (e.g., Denny, 1964; Ellis, McCartney, Ferretti, & Cavalier, 1977; Estes, 1970). Landesman-Dwyer and Butterfield (1983) note this is hardly surprising since these principles are derived from cross-species experimentation where classical conceptions of intelligence would vary widely. The exception to this finding, of course, is when gross central nervous system damage is involved (see Landesman-Dwyer & Sackett, 1978).

The most outstanding cognitive differences are in "higher-level" reasoning (Landesman-Dwyer & Butterfield, 1983). On intelligence tests, for example, a relative strength typically is evidenced on *nonverbal* tasks, that is, those involving motor responses with minimal verbal expression. The exception to this is in the more severely retarded where perceptual and motor impairments are frequently encountered. Verbal tasks that require reasoning and judgment are generally difficult for retarded individuals at all levels of functioning.

Many of the cognitive differences between the retarded and nonretarded adult are the same as those noted between normal children and adults. Retarded individuals show substantial difficulties in learning new behaviors and discriminations, as well as in problem solving (Ingalls, 1978). Retarded individuals, for example, tend to overlook readily available cues that would help them solve problems; that is, they have difficulty focusing on relevant stimuli from an array of distractors (Hallahan & Reeve, 1980). This was initially reported by Zeaman and House (1963) who discovered an "attentional deficit" where the retarded do not readily focus on relevant dimensions in a multidimensional discrimination learning problem. This may be because of an inability to organize input systematically so that they are confused and overwhelmed by useless informational "noise." Such difficulty with attending to environmental cues likely contributes to the common observation that even when new learning takes places it either fails to generalize to new situations or overgeneralizes into inappropriate situations (Spitz, 1963).

Retarded individuals normally show little transfer of learning strategies from one problem to similar new ones. Harter (1967) noted that the retarded acquire *learning sets* in a series of successive problems — which are widely regarded as an important index of learning ability — more slowly than normal individuals. Zeaman and House (1963) even suggested that a reverse type of learning set ("failure set") is often seen in which subjects were unable to solve easy problems after having been exposed to a series of difficult problems. Clinically this "failure set" is noticed as a pronounced reaction to failure or a lack of motivation.

Effective information processing also requires the flexible use of an array of strategies. The failure to accomplish this is a major source of many deficiencies. The mentally retarded also tend to perform less adequately on tasks requiring planning and foresight (e.g., Spitz & Winters, 1977). When confronted with a problem, they tend not to plan strategies and ask strategic questions that would help them to gain relevant information. Heal and Johnson (1970) suggested that this is largely a result of a marked inhibitory deficit. Success in solving problems is aided by a reflective rather than impulsive style, which requires inhibition of the initial response. Another noticeable problem is the failure to use active problem-solving strategies such as the invention of mediational sentences or images. Even though they are capable of using such strategies when instructed, their typical approach to problem solving is passive (e.g., Ellis et al., 1977). Similar difficulties are seen in the use of strategies such as rehearsal or organizational "chucking" in memory tasks.

Examination of personality and motivational characteristics requires an understanding of social influences on the retarded person. Numerous characteristics are often evidenced by the retarded but these are also typical of nonretarded individuals exposed to the same types of conditions, especially those of a similar "mental age." While most research available on personality and motivation of the mentally retarded has been conducted with children, clinical experience suggests the findings apply equally to the retarded adult.

Typically mentally retarded children, adolescents, and young adults consistently exhibit higher anxiety levels than do the nonretarded (Silverstein, 1970). This should be expected given the difficulties that these individuals face on a day-to-day basis. Another related characteristic is that the retarded tend to have heightened positive and negative reaction tendencies toward adults (Zigler, 1966a, b). On the one hand they possess increased desire to interact with "adults," which is even enhanced in retarded individuals who are in deprived settings (e.g., institutions, isolated community settings). At the same time, they exhibit increased reluctance and wariness about this interaction based on the frequency of past disappointing and punishing contacts they have had. Many have come to expect failure as a way of life and have learned to defend themselves against it. This results in an individual who shows substantial conflicts in interactions with others.

Increased exposure to failure situations of course tends to modify motivation. A variety of ways to deal with what Noonan and Barry (1967) have called "success deprivation" may be adopted. Given the more common experience of failure, the retarded individual becomes distrustful of his or her own abilities, seeing less likelihood of succeeding in new situations. As a result the mentally retarded have been typified as having a predominant motivation to "avoid failure" rather than to "achieve success." They learn to expect failure and react impassively when it occurs; they make stereotyped responses that display a lack of effort and involvement; they avoid situations where failure may occur; they may develop unrealistic excuses and defenses to explain their defects; or they accept low levels of success that intellectually normal individuals would not tolerate. Their measured self-concept, not surprisingly, is typically lower than that of nonretarded individuals.

Overall, retarded individuals display a marked dependence on the environment in their motivation. Haywood (1968) demonstrated that the retarded are less motivated by the intrinsic, self-actualizing aspects of a task and more by extrinsic factors such as money. Along the same lines, the retarded are typically described as having a greater external than internal locus of control. Zigler and his associates (e.g., 1966a, b) have described the tendency of the retarded to depend upon external cues as guides to action. This tendency to be more suggestible has been termed "outer-directedness." Many of these characteristics taken together result in the retarded person being very dependent upon others.

EPIDEMIOLOGY

Traditionally, the estimated prevalence of retardation has been set at 2% to 3% of the general population. This figure is derived from predictions based on the normal distribution of intelligence, which would predict 2.28% of the population with IQs two or more standard deviations below the mean (Dingman & Tarjan, 1960). Statistical statements concerning the prevalence of this condition tend to be erroneous however. They are based on faulty assumptions, such as (1) only IQ affects the diagnosis, (2) the diagnosis is always made in infancy and does not change, and (3) mortality rates are similar to those in the general population (Tarjan, Wright, Eyman, & Keeran, 1973). Because identification of mental retardation relies on impairments in both intelligence and adaptive behavior, identification at numerous points, individuals losing the diagnosis, and increased mortality in the more severely impaired, the 3% figure is in reality too high.

The estimate also relies on a two-group model of retardation in which the first group — cultural-familial — includes those individuals whose functioning is predicted by the normal distribution of intelligence. Most of these cases are mildly to moderately retarded. The figure of 2.28% prevalence is only correct if the actual correlation between adaptive behavior and intelligence is perfect. The estimated population correlation of these two measures actually is between 0.4 and 0.6 (Harrison, 1987). This suggests that only about 0.3% to 0.55% of the population would meet both criteria. The second group — organically based — present gross clinical/somatic etiologies. Individuals in this group usually are severely to profoundly retarded and appear to overlay the normal curve with an IQ distribution with a mean of 32 (SD = 5).

Empirical surveys provide minimal clarification. In a review of 60 studies conducted between 1894 and 1958, Wallin (1958) found prevalence estimates ranging from 0.05% to 13% of the population. Reviews of more recent epidemiological studies (Conley, 1973; McLaren & Bryson, 1987) also show considerable variation in overall prevalence rates. It appears that when the criterion of adaptive behavior is considered in epidemiological surveys, the prevalence is typically estimated at about 1% (Tarjan et al., 1973). This is especially true during adulthood when many of the mildly retarded have "blended into" society and a number of biologically involved individuals have died (up to 68% of the more severely impaired are expected to die by age 20; Herbst & Baird, 1984). Of this overall number, approximately 89% are mildly retarded, with the remaining levels showing progressively lower prevalence rates (moderate 7%, severe 3%, and profound 1%).

No matter what the more accurate prevalence rate is, it is only an average. The prevalence of retardation is substantially affected by factors such as age, race, sex, socioeconomic status, and ethnic group membership (e.g., Conley, 1973; Reschly & Jipson, 1976). Most of the variation in prevalence rates is accounted for by cases of mild retardation; the prevalence of severe retardation tends to be more evenly distributed across these factors.

A number of familial factors have been shown to result in higher rates of retardation. These include the low measured intelligence of the mother and large family size, very young mothers or mothers over age 35, and the presence of a retarded sibling. There have also been consistent variations in prevalence found with individual characteristics. Somewhat higher prevalence rates are found among males, generally at a rate of about 2 to 1 (Conley, 1973). Racial group membership also has a bearing, with the prevalence of retardation among blacks, for example, being strikingly higher than in whites. Much of this variation, however, is probably due to cultural factors associated with race. Of particular relevance to adult retardation is the consistent finding that prevalence is affected by age in epidemiological studies. The general pattern is one in which prevalence is about 1% during the preschool years, shows an increase at school entry age, with a sharp increase from about 10- to 14-years-old, followed by a decline during the postschool years back to approximately 1% (Conley, 1973). Overall, in fact, it is generally believed that 1% is the best estimate of the prevalence of adult retardation.

Social class is particularly linked to variations in prevalence. Lemkau and Imre (1969), for example, found that individuals from the lowest of five social classes were almost 13 times as likely to be identified as retarded than those from the highest three classes. It is the relationship between social class and retardation that is thought to be responsible for the higher rates of retardation in the economically disadvantaged and ethnic minorities (Maloney & Ward, 1979). Additionally, there is a consistent finding of increased rates of retardation among rural as opposed to urban populations (Conley, 1973).

Many of the retarded experience additional physical or emotional handicaps that greatly complicate their vocational, social, and academic adjustment. The epidemiology of these will be explored in greater detail in a later section.

NATURAL HISTORY

As indicated earlier, retardation is a chronic condition that, at least at the more severe levels, continues to be displayed by the individual throughout the life span. The more mildly retarded, however, may acquire the label (as opposed to the condition) sometime during elementary school and once again lose it in the postschool years.

One aspect of the natural history of mental retardation is the area of "mental growth." The likely pattern in the mentally retarded is that "mental age" increments proceed at a slower rate than in the normal population and reaches an asymptote at a lower point (Fisher & Zeaman, 1970). As with normal individuals, however, information acquisition continues well into the adult years.

The most significant element of natural history in retardation are the changes in various aspects of adaptive behavior. As indicated in the AAMR definition of adaptive behavior, different portions of the life span emphasize differing elements of adaptive behavior (Grossman, 1983). During infancy and early childhood, the key aspects tend to be the acquisition of sensory and motor capabilities, self-care skills, and communication. During the school years, however, more stress is placed on the traditional academic-learning cluster of adaptive behavior, along with social interaction and peer relationships. On moving into adulthood we see the emphasis move to personal self-sufficiency and independence in community living and vocational adjustment.

Various studies of the developmental course of adaptive behavior have been reported (e.g., Eyman & Arndt, 1982; Schlottmann & Anderson, 1982). In what is perhaps the most comprehensive report, Eyman and Widaman (1987) studied the changes in adaptive behavior of over 30,000 retarded individuals, by level of retardation and placement setting, across the life span. In contrast to most earlier studies, Eyman and Widaman (1987) employed a semilongitudinal methodology to approximate a full longitudinal follow-up of individuals. Individuals from both institutional and community settings showed significant growth during the early years of development followed by a leveling off or, occasionally, a decline in abilities. As the level of retardation became more severe, the growth curves flattened out. That is, there was a continued acquisition of adaptive behavior throughout the life span, although at a slower rate and with a lower asymptote with lower intelligence. Obviously the development of adaptive behavior in this population is a slow process but does generally continue well into adult years. Eyman and Arndt (1987) did caution about too literal an interpretation of the flatter growth curves for the more severely impaired since the test-retest interval for the study was 4 years; prior research suggested that at least 6 years follow-up is needed to obtain reliable changes in profoundly retarded clients (Silverman, Silver, Sersen, & Lubin, 1986).

Another aspect of natural history includes the previously noted decrease in the number of mildly intellectually retarded individuals who lose the diagnosis of mental retardation. In some cases this is due to the gradual acquisition of adaptive behaviors that allow them to function adequately in society. At other times, and perhaps most frequently, it is because the reduced environmental demands for academic functioning permit an improved behavior-environment match. The findings of Edgerton and Bercovici (1976) are an example of this phenomenon. They found that many marginally competent retarded adults are able to learn "passing behaviors" to cloak their handicap. Many also showed remarkable gains in adaptive behavior over a 12-year time span.

IMPAIRMENT AND COMPLICATIONS

While the adaptive impairments resulting from mental retardation are inevitably visible by the school years, retardation has always been at least implicitly associated with the failure to function independently as an adult. Once the adult years are reached, the primary impairments in the mildly impaired relate to difficulties in self-management (maintenance of a home, budgeting, etc.), gaining and holding employment, and maintaining normative adult social roles (friend, spouse, parent, etc.). At the more impaired levels, all of these problems are magnified and additional complications such as associated physical disorders are common. These problems are often magnified during adulthood, when almost three quarters of those who were in school as educable mentally retarded receive no further services (Richardson, Koller, Katz, & McLaren, 1984).

Independence and Self-management

Dependence on other family members for day-to-day existence is the cultural norm at earlier ages, but the young adult is expected to become independent. At the mild level this often happens. The evidence is generally overwhelming that somewhere between 50% to 80% of mildly retarded adults can be expected to achieve an independent adjustment (e.g., Bell, 1976; Richardson, 1978). Of course, the adjustment may be marginal, but it is generally independent.

Such independence, however, is rare for the more severe degrees of retardation. In follow-up studies of former students in trainable classes (IQ range about 30 to 50), at least one quarter were institutionalized, with the remaining living with their families (e.g., Saenger, 1957; Stanfield, 1973). Few were productively employed or were

involved outside the home. While these individuals are not independent, more recently they are able to function in such nonfamily community residential settings as group homes. At the severe and profound levels of retardation, many of the individuals are either institutionalized or are placed in intensive community residences. Their self-management skills are so deficient that they would be unable to exist left to their own resources.

Employment

All levels of employment are found with retarded individuals. Mildly retarded adults are capable of regular employment, usually in unskilled jobs. Many unskilled jobs exist is our culture, particularly in the service industry (e.g., fast-food restaurants). Becker (1976), for example, surveyed job preparation programs for the retarded and found the majority being trained for roles such as janitor, dishwasher, kitchen helper, maid, and similar occupations. While these are the lowest-paying jobs, providing little economic security, they do allow productive employment. When individuals have difficulty holding jobs, it is usually due to low productivity and motivation (i.e., work habits) rather than social incompetence or behavior problems (e.g., Nitzberg, 1970).

At the more severe levels of retardation the nature of employment changes. There is a heavy emphasis on sheltered rather than regular employment (sheltered workshops and work activity centers). While Conley (1976) suggested that productive jobs are possible for persons with IQs as low as 40, special training procedures allow even more impaired individuals to function in productive employment. With severely and profoundly retarded persons, however, it is unlikely that the skills and persistence needed for productive employment can be acquired. Day activity centers, where simulated employment and prevocational activities are provided, become the most common meaningful daily activities for these individuals.

Social Roles

In adult life, a number of social roles, with culture-specific behavioral expectations, are held by retarded persons. Mildly retarded individuals function in all these roles: family members, friends, spouses, parents. However, their social lives seem to be more isolated, and fewer of them have opposite-sex friends, marry, or have children. When they do have children, they typically encounter significant problems in both interpersonal relations and child rearing (Koller, Richardson, & Katz, 1988). While moderately retarded adults have friends and may have opposite-sex interests, they are less likely to marry (Koller et al., 1988) and often lead socially isolated lives. Most of their leisure time may be in isolated activities such as watching TV or walking alone in the neighborhood (Stanfield, 1973). In the severely and profoundly retarded, there may be difficulty in entering into even "friend" relationships. These individuals continue to relate to normal adults in a childlike manner or even show little or no interest in others.

At all levels there is usually little involvement in the broader community in areas such as civic responsibilities (voting, community work, etc.). At the mild level there is also an increased likelihood of trouble with the criminal justice system. The proportion of retarded persons in prison exceeds that of the general population (MacEachron, 1979), although this may be largely due to the greater vulnerability of this group.

Associated Impairments

The mentally retarded, particularly the more severely impaired, display increased risks for a number of associated conditions. Conroy and Derr (1971) reported such increased risks from a nationwide survey of retarded persons in both community and institutional settings. High percentages of individuals had ambulation problems (42.3%), gross or fine motor upper limb problems (42.2% and 43.9%). Speech, hearing, and visual impairments were also common (54.9%, 15%, and 26.8%). Other common neurological disorders with this group include cerebral palsy and epilepsy. Conley (1973) reported that approximately 2% of retarded individuals are cerebral palsied which is ten times higher than among the nonretarded. The prevalence of cerebral palsy varies substantially with level of retardation; the severely retarded showed about seven times the prevalence of cerebral palsy as the more mildly impaired. About 0.5% to 2% of nonretarded individuals have epilepsy, while the rate in the mentally retarded is at least doubled. Conroy and Derr (1971) reported as many as 17.8% of the retarded have at least some history of epilepsy. The occurrence of epilepsy is fairly constant across levels of retardation. McLaren and Bryson (1987) also reported greatly increased risks for these conditions in their epidemiological review.

The prevalence of psychiatric disorders in the mentally retarded is unclear. While some individuals feel that psychiatric disturbances are uncommon in this population, others have indicated higher rates than in the normal population. Reiss, Levitan, and Szysko (1982) have indicated that the frequency of psychiatric disorders is difficult to ascertain because of a phenomenon call *diagnostic overshadowing* where the primary diagnosis of retardation often results in no other diagnostic categories being assigned. Most comprehensive reviews suggest a rate of psychiatric impairment in the low 40s (e.g., Conley, 1973; Conroy & Derr, 1971; Matson & Barrett, 1982a).

Several studies have examined prevalence rates of finer-grained diagnoses. Richardson, Katz, Koller, McLaren, and Rubinstein (1979), for example, found that 22% of a group of 222 mentally retarded young adults showed neurotic problems (e.g., anxiety), while another 20% showed conduct and antisocial problems. Matson and Barrett (1982b) also contend that the retarded show substantial rates of clinical, as well as subclinical, depression. Romanczyk and Kistner (1982) reviewed information on psychosis in the retarded and concluded that, in spite of methodological problems and practitioner biases that the retarded cannot be schizophrenic, the prevalence of schizophrenia at least equals and possibly exceeds that in the normal population.

While the empirical data on psychiatric disorders in the retarded are cloudy at the present, it appears likely that they occur at relatively high rates. Such a phenomenon would be congruent with some of the characteristics mentioned earlier (e.g., increased anxiety, positive and negative reaction tendencies), as well as the diminished adaptive skills in coping with the stresses encountered on a daily basis.

DIFFERENTIAL DIAGNOSIS

While the three-element AAMR definition has been generally accepted, there continue to be alternative definitions, as well as debate on the definitions. One area of disagreement is on whether adaptive behavior should be considered as a criterion for the diagnosis. Some (e.g., Clausen, 1972; Zigler, Balla, & Hodapp, 1984) have argued that diagnosis of retardation should be limited to subaverage IQ only since the reliability and validity of current adaptive behavior instruments is not well established. On the other hand, Mercer (1973) contends that since retardation is a sociological label that refers to role-specific cultural expectations, adaptive behavior is a critical factor in the decision to label someone as mentally retarded. The behavioral model of retardation, as put forth by Bijou (1966), also stressed the adaptive aspects of mental retardation and paid minimal attention to the intellectual aspects.

However, as currently defined, the diagnosis of mental retardation requires consideration of both the intellectual and adaptive behavior functioning of the individual. Definitions require that intelligence be assessed through a well-normed, individualized measure of intelligence. Typically at the adult level this requires an IQ of below 70 on the *Wechsler Adult Intelligence Scale-Revised* or below 68 on the *Stanford-Binet Intelligence Scale*. Additionally, the impairment in the overall IQ should reflect substantial weaknesses in most aspects of intelligence rather than very deficient functioning in only a few areas.

Especially at the mild level of retardation it is then essential that diagnosis be based on the demonstrated impairment of adaptive behavior. While such assessment may be based on clinical judgment, more recently psychometrically derived scales measuring adaptive behavior have been employed. One of the earliest of these, which still receives considerable use, is the *AAMR Adaptive Behavior Scale* (Nihira, Foster, Shellhaas, & Leland, 1975). One continuing criticism of this scale, however, is that it was inadequately normed by using only mentally retarded individuals. This, of course, makes a determination of deviation from the population mean continue to rely primarily on clinical judgment. More recently, several scales have become available that do provide normative information based on the general population. These include the *Vineland Adaptive Behavior Scale* (Sparrow, Balla, & Cicchetti, 1984) and the *Scales of Independent Behavior* (Bruininks, Woodcock, Weatherman, & Hill, 1984). While these are among the most popular scales, many additional adaptive behavior instruments can be found in Harrison (1987).

Since retardation is assessed without regard to actual or presumed etiology (Grossman, 1983), it is very likely that additional diagnoses may be used in addition to retardation. The key element in differential diagnosis at the adult level centers on the "age of onset" of the diminished intellectual and adaptive skills. Individuals with various other diagnoses such as schizophrenia also display the essential impairments present in retardation. While the issue is somewhat arbitrary, the individual who is actively psychotic, or who shows diminished capabilities after treatment for a psychosis, would only be labeled mentally retarded when the impairment occurred prior to 18 years of age.

CASE EXAMPLES

With the great heterogeneity in cognitive and behavioral functioning, as well as etiologies of mental retardation, the presentation of one case could hardly represent the condition. To portray the diversity better, we will present several cases that sample some of the common levels of functioning and associated conditions.

Born to working-class parents in a large city, *Sally* is now 47 years old. She was the oldest of three children. Her birth and development were relatively uneventful, although her parents reported she was somewhat slow learning to talk. While Sally showed some difficulty with learning to read in school, she mostly received passing grades. In seventh grade, however, she began to have difficulty with the legal and social services systems for being promiscuous. Upon testing it was found that Sally's IQ was in the high-mild (IQ = 67) range of retardation. As this was in the 1940s when institutions were the primary alternative for the retarded, Sally was committed as "incorrigible" and mildly retarded to an all-female public institution.

Sally had great difficulty adjusting to the restrictive environment of an institutional setting and quickly became a "behavior problem." She constantly attempted to "elope" and was always agitating other residents of the facility. During the day, she was required to work in the farm fields to contribute to her upkeep in the facility. With the increased attention to habilitation in the late 1960s, Sally was moved to the kitchen of the facility for her work assignments, and she learned skills in simple cooking and cleaning. With the increased responsibility she received, much of the rebellious, antisocial behavior gradually disappeared.

As part of the institution's community placement program, Sally was placed with a family in a nearby small town where she continued to work in the kitchen at the facility, now getting paid the minimum wage. After several years Sally progressed to the point where she was able to move into her own apartment as well as hold a job in a local fast-food restaurant. She now is able to live in the community with minimal assistance from others, and, in fact, very few individuals are aware of her past diagnosis as mildly retarded.

Harry is age 30 and the son of a factory worker and his spouse in a small Pennsylvania town. Around age 3 Harry's parents became concerned that he was not progressing as quickly as they thought he should be; he only said a few sentences and still was not toilet trained. At that time their physician suspected that Harry was mentally retarded and referred him for evaluation. Upon testing he was found to be moderately intellectually retarded (IQ = 52). In addition to the expected problems Harry encountered in elementary school, he soon became difficult for his parents to handle. He was becoming aggressive with his younger brother and also had acquired a fascination with the trains that passed on a nearby track. Many times his parents found him playing on the tracks; once they had to pull him from the path of an oncoming train.

At the point of despair, Harry's parents voluntarily committed him to a state institution at the recommendation of the local Mental Health/ Mental Retardation Service Unit. At the facility Harry's playing around the train track was eliminated (due to lack of opportunity), but be began walking in front of cars. He was enrolled in classes for the trainable mentally retarded conducted by the regional special education unit. As he grew in size to 6′ 1″ by age 18, his aggression increasingly became a problem and required numerous behavioral programs to deal with it. At age 18, his program was expanded to include vocational programming in an on-campus sheltered workshop.

In the past several years Harry's aggression ceased to be a problem, and he was able to maintain a sheltered work level of productivity. Last year Harry was released from the institution and placed in a group home with six clients and a sheltered workshop in his original community.

Sam is a 35-year-old severely retarded male (IQ = 32) who lives in a building on the grounds of a private residential facility. He is minimally toilet trained and is able to feed himself. His social behaviors are very limited, and he displays poor articulation. Most of his day is spent in a central programming area with 12 other clients and 2 staff. Here attempts are made to train functional skills such as simple survival word recognition and improved social interaction skills.

Periodically Sam leaves the central area to receive intensive training in the use of a communica-

tion board that allows him to communicate better with others. He also has sessions with a physical therapist who is working on his gait problem. In Sam's living area the staff also work on improving Sam's dressing skills and mealtime behaviors. He is now able to remove all types of clothing and put on a pullover shirt independently.

Sam has lived in the private facility since he was 3 years old. When he was born to a 39-year-old middle-class mother he was diagnosed with Down's syndrome (trisomy 21), a genetic disorder characterized by an extra chromosome. The family's physician recommended institutionalization as soon as possible since Sam would be very retarded. While this is no longer common practice (since Down's syndrome children no longer have such a limited prognosis), it was so at the time. He displays the characteristic stigmata of an individual with Down's syndrome such as a round head shape, almond-shaped eyes, and protruding tongue.

Teresa is a 23-year-old profoundly retarded female with many associated problems. She is nonverbal and has a distorted spine which causes her to lean to the side. She has a severe seizure disorder and would have daily grand mal seizures if medication had not been able to control them. Teresa is aware of the activity around her but seems to understand little of what it means. Much of her day is spent pounding on a piano in the living area when she is not engaged in some basic self-care skill training. While she can be engaged in activities to improve her self-care behaviors under supervision, she will never progress beyond a toddler level of development. Her retardation was traced to severe anoxia at birth leading to substantial neurological damage.

CHILDHOOD AND FAMILIAL ANTECEDENTS

Not a simple trait like eye color, intelligence is considered to be a composite of myriad capabilities. Thus, intelligence has a more stable polygenetic basis, wherein whole networks of genes are involved. This complex gene base makes possible a wide range of expressions (phenotypes) but also suggests multiple points where things can go awry. Further, given a "normal" genetic makeup, numerous biologic and environmental circumstances can act to impair intelligence. In view of the multiple foundation for intelligence, it is not surprising that multiple etiologies have been identified for retardation. Of course, both biologic and psychosocial (nature and nurture) factors are implicated. A convenient way to organize these causative factors is by *when* they impinge on development. The usually pre-, peri-, and postnatal periods may be more completely identified as including circumstances at conception, during pregnancy, at birth, and during neonatal, infancy, and early childhood periods.

Conception

Prenatal circumstances are preeminent in the etiology of retardation that has a clear biologic referent. Starting at conception, concerns include parents' health status and intactness of their genetic material. Health problems of the mother may have a significant influence on the quality of the fetus. Frequent health concerns include high blood pressure, chronic kidney disease, juvenile-onset of diabetes, and prolonged use of certain medications and drugs. Any of these and other health circumstances can result in complications for the fetus or neonate; impaired intellectual functioning can be one of the outcomes of such complications.

Chromosomal disorders may be present in either parent and, of course, are a major cause of identifiable syndromes associated with retardation. Chromosomal errors include too few or too many chromosomes, missing or additional material (although normal number), and aberrations in the sex chromosome. Chromosomal problems may occur in 1% of all births and perhaps 10% of the recognized mental retardation syndromes. Fortunately, most of these chromosomal errors are detectable from blood samples of prospective parents. Exposure to radiation, chemicals, and potent drugs can damage the genetic material of would-be parents, and these sources of peril are becoming major contemporary concerns.

Conception and the immediate events thereafter are particularly vulnerable times. Maternal age (i.e., age of the available ova), parent health, presence of certain drugs, and the particular genetic shuffle contributed by each parent are major concerns to be considered. Provided with genetic risk information and counseling, couples must make the difficult decision to conceive or not. If unfortunate information is provided *after* conception, the decision to consider a therapeutic abortion is more agonizing, fraught with ethical, religious, psychological, and financial consequences.

Pregnancy

Assuming an intact genetic endowment, mental retardation may be caused by problems encountered during gestation resulting in improper development of or damage to the brain or spinal cord. Again, certain maternal health problems are clearly related. As mentioned previously, a diabetic (or even prediabetic) mother may engender problems. Large for gestational age infants (over 10 pounds) may be a concern, necessitating cesarean delivery to avert an otherwise difficult and prolonged labor. The neonate may have trouble with self sugar regulation, resulting in a low blood sugar level that imperils nerve tissue. Fetal nutrition must be monitored closely when the mother is carrying more than one child. Discordant twins may result from inadequate nutrition, with one twin suffering very low birth weight with associated risks. Maternal nutrition during the course of pregnancy must include adequate calories and protein to assure fetal brain development. Serious deficits in the mother's diet can produce irreversible fetal damage.

Kidney disease is also related to fetal malnutrition, with associated very low birth weight, prematurity, and organ damage. Other major hazards during pregnancy include exposure to certain disastrous infections, toxins, and radiation. The perils of rubella, herpes, chicken pox, syphilis, toxoplasmosis, and other (preventable or treatable) infections are well documented. Fortunately, Rh disease affecting the second child is no longer a significant problem given today's preventative measures and chemical means to prevent sensitization of the Rh negative mother.

Birth

Labor and delivery often entail several hours during which the infant is vulnerable to physical trauma, deficient oxygen supply, and infection; trauma may result from prolonged or difficult labor, especially when the mother's pelvis is too small, the fetus drops in an abnormal position, or there is forceps damage. Further, medications (analgesics and anesthetics) used to ease a difficult delivery may require emergency measures with a neonate who fails to breathe as a result of the crossing of these medications into the infant's blood.

Numerous inborn errors of metabolism are responsible for a large portion of more severe levels of retardation. It is now possible to identify and treat numerous metabolic disorders through controlled diets and medications. The well-known early identification and treatment of phenylketonuria illustrates how corrective measures may avert otherwise certain retardation. Finally, other congenital defects may result in retardation. Myelomeningocele (the most frequent birth defect) often produces hydrocephaly with resulting brain injury. Very early surgical correction can preclude the most severe motor and brain impairment.

Biologic factors can be specified in about 25% of the entire population labeled retarded (Grossman, 1983). Persons with moderate and severe levels of retardation are characterized by "organicity," with identifiable syndromes in about half of such cases. Typically, more severe levels of retardation include associated disorders of other organs, chronic illness, and development disabilities.

Infancy and Early Childhood

It is clear that numerous organic factors are related to the etiology of retardation. Yet in the case of most persons labeled "retarded," there is no apparent genetic or biological defect. In fact, using the classification system of "mild," "moderate," and "severe to profound," no clear biologic basis for retardation can be identified in about 75% of cases. Practically all these cases are usually within the mildly retarded range. Further, the vast majority of mildly retarded persons are of subaverage socioeconomic status (SES).

It should be pointed out, also, that it is rare to find a higher-SES child with an IQ of less than 80, unless an organic syndrome is apparent (Kushlick & Blunden, 1974). In fact, "the relationship of measured intelligence to socioeconomic level is one of the best documented findings in mental test history" (Tyler, 1965, p. 336), with a correlation of 0.70 between intelligence and SES. One is immediately tempted to place blame on defects of the environment, and yet most children from poor backgrounds are not retarded. Thus, it seems reasonable that where environmental variables are involved, they may interact with constitutional factors of the parents or child to produce retardation. Since children vary in their biological characteristics, some may be more vulnerable to less than optimal environments.

Low socioeconomic circumstances are strongly related to retardation through several possible mechanisms. The family's ability to provide adequate childhood nutrition may result from not enough money or nutritional knowledge. Likewise, children of impoverished families are at greater risk for retardation resulting from childhood diseases (such as poliomyelitis, mumps, measles). This risk is almost 100% preventable through early immunization and prompt treatment. Inappropriate parenting and high levels of family stress are also clearly related to conditions of inadequate income levels to raise children.

Unfortunately, injury is a chief source of brain injury and retardation during infancy and early childhood. Automobile accidents, drowning, and falls are major causes of head injury (about 2 million cases per year). Physical abuse and neglect undoubtedly impair intellectual development but, like most psychosocial factors, cannot be assessed as easily as biologic factors. Nevertheless, since most retardation has no identifiable biological basis, psychosocial factors may be responsible in several ways. As mentioned, economic factors may reduce the quality of early care. Parenting practices may be extremely inadequate for providing the stimulus and response opportunities needed to facilitate development.

By now, it is common knowledge that children require stimulation for proper development. Likewise, many events in the environment (experiences for the child) may or may not be effective stimulation for the child, depending on when and how they are presented. Thus what may be an effective developmental stimulus for a certain child at a given time may not be for another child or the same child at a different time.

We can identify at least two broad categories of ineffective environments with respect to their effects. First, certain environmental events such as trauma, hunger, and separation from loved ones can temporarily disrupt a child's ongoing functioning. This will be reflected in lower test scores, developmental quotients, clinical assessment, and so on. But these effects are usually easily reversed and have little or no long-range impact. It is the second type of ineffective environment with which we are primarily concerned. Repeated trauma, sustained hunger, and prolonged reduction in necessary stimulation may bring about more basic changes in intelligence that are difficult to reverse. Stimulus novelty, discrepancy, figure-ground contrast, and variety are all aspects of stimulation that can make a difference. It is quite conceivable that many home environments, especially those in which the socioeconomic circumstances are low, may actually provide less effective stimulation than a well-managed institution.

The importance of a quality physical environment for the optimal development of intelligence is frequently emphasized. But equally important is the nature of social interactions with parents, caregivers, teachers, or ward attendants that can be a crucial determininant in the child's progress. The uncaring, too busy, or unknowledgeable parent or ward attendant may fail to provide the social experiences conducive to intellectual growth. In addition to poverty itself, the presence of a large number of children in a family may make it impossible for parents to provide sufficient stimulation for each child. Research in child development is convincing that early, quality adult-child interaction is essential in fostering adequate development.

Many "readiness capabilities" are present in the normal infant that permit it to interact progressively with, and benefit from, the environment. A snowball effect becomes evident, with the infant *able* to learn more because it previously has learned more (the "rich-get-richer" phenomenon). Thus, it becomes most important to assure that the young child is not without the enabling skills that are necessary for subsequent learning. Child development authorities have suggested a number of critical infant abilities (e.g., Appleton, Clifton, & Goldberg, 1975). These abilities can be seen as competencies to look for in infants and as targets for instruction if they are not present. Some of the more important skills directly and indirectly related to the development of intelligence are (1) the ability to observe, pay attention to, and notice discrepancies; (2) persistence at tasks and the use of problem-solving strategies; (3) the ability to imitate, anticipate consequences, and take another's perspective; (4) skill in exploring, manipulating objects, and controlling body position; and (5) competence in communication, especially vocalization and, later, verbalization. Children seriously lacking in these skills or in opportunities to develop them are at risk for delay or impairment of intelligence.

SUMMARY

Adults with the condition known as mental retardation show a wide variety of behavioral characteristics and etiologies. Most outstanding in this disorder is the delayed levels of intellectual and adaptive behaviors that are evident to differing degrees at the various levels of retardation. While much mythology still surrounds the condition (e.g., "the retarded are dangerous"), the past decade has seen increased attention to the adult portion of the life span. Additional emphasis has been placed on moving retarded individuals from sterile institutional environments to community settings, as well as creating more humane and treatment-oriented institutions. Greater attention is also being paid to developing service systems that will improve the employability of the retarded adult, such as the supported employment model (Rusch, 1986).

Treatment and training of the mentally retarded, which began with Itard (1932), has seen increased activity in the past 25 years. This has been largely due to the growth of behavioral approaches, which are the treatment of choice with most retarded individuals (e.g., Madle & Neisworth, 1989). The application of behavioral technology has greatly improved the lives of many retarded adults, especially the more severely impaired, giving them skills in basic self-care, improved communication skills, and meaningful daily activities, as well as eliminating many associated behavior problems.

REFERENCES

Appleton, T., Clifton, R., & Goldberg, S. (1975). The development of behavioral competence in infancy. In F. D. Horowitz (Ed.), *Review of child development research* (Vol. 4). Chicago: University of Chicago Press.

Becker, R. L. (1976). Job placement training for retarded youth. *Mental Retardation, 14*, 7–11.

Bell, N. J. (1976). IQ as a factor in community lifestyle of previously institutionalized retardates. *Mental Retardation, 14*, 29–33.

Bijou, S. W. (1966). A functional analysis of retarded development. In N. R. Ellis (Ed.), *International review of research in mental retardation* (Vol. 1). New York: Academic Press.

Bruininks, R. H., Woodcock, R. W., Weatherman, R. F., & Hill, B. K. (1984). *Scales of independent behavior*. Allen, TX: DLM Teaching Resources.

Burack, J. A., Hodapp, R. M., & Zigler, E. (1988). Issues in the classification of mental retardation: Differentiating among organic etiologies. *Journal of Child Psychology and Psychiatry, 29*, 765–779.

Clausen, J. A. (1972). Quo vadis, AAMD. *Journal of Special Education, 6*, 51–60.

Conley, R. W. (1973). *The economics of mental retardation*. Baltimore: The Johns Hopkins University Press.

Conley, R. W. (1976). Mental retardation—An economist's approach. *Mental Retardation, 14*, 20–24.

Conroy, J. W., & Derr, K. E. (1971). *Survey and analysis of the habilitation and rehabilitation status of the mentally retarded with associated conditions*. Washington, DC: U.S. Department of Health, Education, and Welfare.

Denny, M. R. (1964). Research in learning performance. In H. Stevens and R. Heber (Eds.), *Mental retardation*. Chicago: University of Chicago Press.

Detterman, D. K. (1987). Theoretical notions of intelligence and mental retardation. *American Journal of Mental Deficiency, 92*, 2–11.

Dingman, H. F., & Tarjan, G. (1960). Mental retardation and the normal distribution curve. *American Journal of Mental Deficiency, 64*, 991–994.

Edgerton, R. B., & Bercovici, S. M. (1976). The cloak of competence: Years later. *American Journal of Mental Deficiency, 80*, 485–497.

Ellis, N. R., McCartney, J. F., Ferretti, R. P., & Cavalier, A. R. (1977). Recognition memory in mentally retarded persons. *Intelligence, 3*, 310–317.

Estes, W. K. (1970). *Learning theory and mental development*. New York: Academic Press.

Eyman, R. K., & Arndt, S. (1982). Life-span development of institutionalized and community-based mentally retarded persons. *American Journal of Mental Deficiency, 86*, 342–350.

Eyman, R. K., & Widaman, K. F. (1987). Life-span development of institutionalized and community-based mentally retarded persons, revisited. *American Journal of Mental Deficiency, 91*, 559–569.

Fisher, M. A., & Zeaman, D. (1970). Growth and decline of retardate intelligence. In N. R. Ellis (Ed.), *International review of research on mental retardation* (Vol. 4). New York: Academic Press.

Grossman, H. J. (Ed.). (1983). *Classification in mental retardation*. Washington, DC: American Association on Mental Deficiency.

Hallahan, D. P., & Reeve, R. E. (1980). Selective attention and distractibility. In B. K. Keogh (Ed.), *Advances in special education: 1. Basic constructs and theoretical orientations*. Greenwich, CT: JAI Press.

Harrison, P. L. (1987). Research with adaptive behavior scales. *The Journal of Special Education, 21*, 37–68.

Harter, S. (1967). Mental age, IQ, and motivational factors in the discrimination set learning performance of normal and retarded children. *Journal of Experimental Child Psychology, 5*, 123–141.

Haywood, H. C. (1968). Motivational orientation of overachieving and underachieving elementary school children. *American Journal of Mental Deficiency, 75*, 661–667.

Heal, L. W., & Johnson, J. T., Jr. (1970). Inhibition deficits in retardate learning and attention. In N. R. Ellis (Ed.), *International review of research in mental retardation* (Vol. 4). New York: Academic Press.

Herbst, D. S., & Baird, P. A. (1984). Survival rates and causes of death among persons with nonspecific mental retardation. In J. M. Berg (Ed.), *Perspectives and progress in mental retardation: 2. Biomedical aspects*. Baltimore: University Park Press.

Ingalls, R. P. (1978). *Mental retardation: The changing outlook*. New York: John Wiley & Sons.

Itard, J. M. G. (1932). *The wild boy of Aveyron* (George and Muriel Humphrey, Trans.). New York: Appleton-Century-Crofts.

Koller, H., Richardson, S. A., & Katz, M. (1988). Peer relationships of mildly retarded young adults living in the community. *Journal of Mental Deficiency Research, 32*, 321–331.

Kushlick, A., & Blunden, R. (1974). The epidemiology of mental subnormality. In A. M. Clarke and A. B. D. Clarke (Eds.), *Mental deficiency: The changing outlook* (3rd ed.). London: Methuen.

Landesman-Dwyer, S., & Butterfield, E. C. (1983). Mental retardation: Developmental issues in cognitive and social adaptation. In M. Lewis (Ed.), *Origins of intelligence* (2nd ed.). New York: Plenum Press.

Landesman-Dwyer, S., & Sackett, G. P. (1978). Behavioral changes in non-ambulatory, profoundly mentally retarded individuals. In C. E. Meyers (Ed.), *Quality of life in severely retarded people: Research foundations for improvement*. Washington, DC: American Association on Mental Deficiency.

Lemkau, P. V., & Imre, P. D. (1966). Results of a field epidemiologic study. *American Journal of Mental Deficiency, 73*, 858–863.

MacEachron, A. E. (1979). Mentally retarded offenders: Prevalence and characteristics. *American Journal of Mental Deficiency, 84*, 165–186.

Madle, R. A. (1983). Mental retardation: General learning dysfunction. In J. T. Neisworth, R. M. Smith, and F. M. Hunt (Eds.), *The exceptional child: A functional approach* (2nd ed.). New York: McGraw-Hill.

Madle, R. A., & Neisworth, J. T. (1989). Behavioral approaches to retardation. In A. S. Bellack, M. Hersen, and A. E. Kazdin (Eds.), *International handbook of behavior modification and behavior therapy* (2nd ed.). New York: Plenum Press.

Maloney, M. P., & Ward, M. P. (1979). *Mental retardation and modern society*. New York: Oxford University Press.

Matson, J. L., & Barrett, R. P. (Eds.). (1982a). *Psychopathology in the mentally retarded*. New York: Grune & Stratton.

Matson, J. L., & Barrett, R. P.(1982b). Affective disorders. In J. L. Matson and R. P. Barrett (Eds.), *Psychopathology in the mentally retarded*. New York: Grune & Stratton.

Matson, J. L., & Marchetti, A. (1988). *Developmental disabilities: A life-span perspective*. Philadelphia: Grune & Stratton.

McLaren, J., & Bryson, S. E. (1987). Review of recent epidemiological studies of mental retardation: Prevalence, associated disorders, and etiology. *American Journal on Mental Retardation, 92*, 243–254.

Mercer, J. R. (1973). *Labeling the mentally retarded*. Berkeley: University of California Press.

Nihira, K., Foster, R., Shellhaas, M., & Leland, H. (1975). *AAMD Adaptive Behavior Scale*. Monterey, CA: Publishers Test Service.

Nitzberg, J. (1970). Casework with mentally retarded adolescents and young adults and their families. In M. Schreiber (Ed.), *Social work and mental retardation*. New York: Day.

Noonan, J. R., & Barry, J. R. (1967). Performance of retarded children. *Science, 156*, 171.

Reiss, S., Levitan, G. W., & Szysko, J. (1982). Emotional disturbance and mental retardation: Diagnostic overshadowing. *American Journal of Mental Deficiency, 86*, 567–574.

Reschly, D. J., & Jipson, F. J. (1976). Ethnicity, geographic locale, age, sex, and urban-rural residence as variables in the prevalence of mild retardation. *American Journal of Mental Deficiency, 81*, 154–161.

Richardson, S. A. (1978). Careers of mentally retarded young persons: Services, jobs, and interpersonal relations. *American Journal of Mental Deficiency, 82*, 349–358.

Richardson, S. A., Katz, M., Koller, H., McLaren, L., & Rubinstein, B. (1979). Some characteristics of a population of mentally retarded young adults in a British city: A basis for estimating some service needs. *Journal of Mental Deficiency Research, 23*, 275–283.

Richardson, S. A., Koller, H., Katz, M., & McLaren, L. (1984). Career paths through mental retardation services: An epidemiological perspective. *Applied Research in Mental Retardation, 5*, 53–67.

Romanczyk, R. G., & Kistner, J. A. (1982). Psychosis and mental retardation: Issues of coexistence. In J. L. Matson and R. P. Barrett (Eds.), *Psychopathology in the mentally retarded*. New York: Grune & Statton.

Rusch, F. R. (1986). *Competitive employment issues and strategies*. Baltimore: Brookes.

Saenger, G. (1957). *The adjustment of severely retarded adults in the community*. Albany, NY: Interdepartmental Health Resources Board.

Scheerenberger, R. C. (1983). *A history of mental retardation*. Baltimore: Brookes.

Schlottmann, R. S., & Anderson, V. H. (1982). Developmental changes of institutionalized mentally retarded children: A semi-longitudinal study. *American Journal of Mental Deficiency, 87*, 277–281.

Seltzer, M. M., & Krauss, M. W. (1987). *Aging and mental retardation: Extending the continuum*. Washington, DC: American Association of Mental Deficiency.

Silverman, W. P., Silver, E. J., Sersen, E. A., & Lubin, R. A. (1986). Factors related to adaptive behavior changes among profoundly retarded, physically disabled persons. *American Journal of Mental Deficiency, 87*, 347–350.

Silverstein, A. B. (1970). The measurement of intelligence. In N. R. Ellis (Ed.), *International review of research in mental retardation* (Vol. 4). New York: Academic Press.

Sparrow, S. S., Balla, D. A., & Cicchetti, D. V. (1984). *Vineland Adaptive Behavior Scales*. Circle Pines, MN: American Guidance Service.

Spitz, H. H. (1963). Field theory in mental deficiency. In N. R. Ellis (Ed.), *Handbook of mental deficiency*. New York: McGraw-Hill.

Spitz, H. H., & Winters, E. H. (1977). Tic-tac-toe performance as a function of maturation level of retarded adolescents and nonretarded children. *Intelligence, 1*, 108–117.

Stanfield, J. S. (1973). Graduation: What happens to the retarded child when he grows up? *Exceptional Children, 39*, 458–552.

Sternberg, R. J., & Spear, L. C. (1985). A triarchic theory of mental retardation. In N. R. Ellis and N. W. Bray (Eds.), *International review of research in mental retardation* (Vol. 13). New York: Academic Press.

Szymanski, L. S., & Crocker, A. C. (1985). Mental retardation. In H. I. Kaplan and B. J. Sadock (Eds.), *Comprehensive textbook of psychiatry/IV* (Vol. 2, pp. 1635–1671). Baltimore: Williams & Wilkins.

Tarjan, G., Wright, S. W., Eyman, R. K., & Keeran, C. J. (1973). Natural history of mental retardation: Some aspects of epidemiology. *American Journal of Mental Deficiency, 64*, 609–617.

Tyler, L. E. (1965). *The psychology of human differences* (3rd ed.). New York: Appleton-Century-Crofts.

Wallin, J. E. (1958). Prevalence of mental retardates. *School and Society, 86*, 55–56.

Zeaman, D., & House, B. J. (1963). The role of attention in retardate discrimination learning. In N. R. Ellis (Ed.), *Handbook of mental deficiency*. New York: McGraw-Hill.

Zigler, E. (1966a). Mental retardation: Current issues and approaches. In L. W. Hoffman and M. L. Hoffman (Eds.), *Review of child development research* (Vol. 2). New York: Russell Sage Foundation.

Zigler, E. (1966b). Research on personality structure in the retardate. In N. R. Ellis (Ed.), *International review of research in mental retardation* (Vol. 1). New York: Academic Press.

Zigler, E., & Balla, D. (1982). *Mental retardation: The developmental-difference controversy*. Hillside, NJ: Lawrence Erlbaum Associates.

Zigler, E., Balla, D., & Hodapp, R. M. (1984). On the definition and classification of mental retardation. *American Journal of Mental Deficiency, 89*, 215–230.

ALCOHOL ABUSE AND ALCOHOL DEPENDENCE

EDITORS' COMMENTS

Alcoholism in adulthood over the years has received a tremendous amount of attention from clinicians and researchers alike, eventuating into a large knowledge base as to the genetic and familial antecedents, biological and physiological effects, personality characteristics, course, and to some extent its treatment. It is only more recently, however, that parallel attention has been accorded to alcohol abuse in children and adolescents. Study of the antecedents of adult alcoholism is of considerable import, given that in primary alcoholics drinking may begin from 12 to 14 years of age, with actual intoxication occurring from 14 to 18 years of age. Unfortunately, the long-term studies following childhood and adolescent drinkers into adulthood have not been carried out at this point. Such studies, of course, would have major ramifications with respect to preventative and rehabilitation programs at various developmental levels.

The parallel chapters in this section, as those in other sections of the handbook, clearly reflect that much more is known about the adult version of the disorder. However, some basic facts about drinking in childhood and adolescence are available. To begin with, in one study reported in De Blassie's Chapter 25, 28% of 13,000 upper-level high school students surveyed appeared to have some sort of drinking problem. Albeit perhaps a high estimate, the effect of alcohol on the adolescent's life is far-ranging, and includes truancy, general decline of interest in old friends and extracurricular activities, moodiness, fatigue, unkempt appearance, and general deterioration of all interpersonal relationships. Also, alcohol is considered to be the gateway drug to still more pernicious substances, such as marijuana, heroin, cocaine, and the large variety of the extant hallucinogens.

The list of impairment and complications of alcohol abuse in adolescence is extensive. For example, drinking is implicated in 50% of accidents, homicides, and suicides committed by adolescents. In addition, lying, cheating, acts of delinquency, and affective symptoms are common concomitants of alcohol abuse.

In adulthood the list of impairment and complications is even greater, given the chronicity of the problem. The numerous problems listed in Warnock and Goodwin's Chapter 26 appear under the rubrics of gastrointestinal complications, nutritional deficiencies, neurological and psychiatric complications, suicide, social complications, vocational complications, and accidents. Indeed, as chronicity increases in adulthood, no area of the alcoholic's life is spared. Furthermore, the expected life span of the alcoholics is significantly reduced, due to medical illness, accidental death, or suicide.

Warnock and Goodwin, in the chapter, document very nicely the childhood and familial antecedents of adult alcoholism, citing in support data adduced from family studies, twin studies, adoption studies, and investigations delineating biological markers. But, as already noted, fewer data are available tracing the path of the adolescent alcoholic on a prospective basis. Undoubtedly such studies will be carried out by future investigators.

CHAPTER 25

ALCOHOL ABUSE IN CHILDHOOD

Richard R. DeBlassie

DESCRIPTION OF THE DISORDER

Beginning in the mid-1970s and continuing through the present, alcohol has been the single most abused drug in adolescent culture (Belkin, 1988). The adolescent problem drinker is likely to have a high absentee rate, appear intoxicated in class, and fall behind in school work. It is not uncommon to find a flask of alcohol concealed on the person of the student, and the student may even imbibe during the class itself, so strong is the drive and so weak the control.

Finn (1986) suggests that perhaps because we do not, or cannot, agree on why youth engage in alcohol abuse, there is also no consensus in our society regarding the level of concern we should have about this relatively commonplace youthful behavior. He goes on and enumerates six distinct schools of thought regarding the nature and seriousness of youthful drunkenness: (1) intoxication is a symptom or "signpost" of problem drinking, (2) drunkenness is a warning signal of incipient or future problems, (3) why youngsters get drunk is the critical variable, (4) intoxication can be judged in the context of cultural norms, (5) inebriation is

one of other social changes in the past 20 years, and (6) drunkenness is in large measure an innocuous expression of boisterousness and most will "mature out" of this as they get older.

Alcohol, a powerful depressant, can cause both physical and psychological dependence and may lead to brain and liver damage. Alcohol use by adolescents tends to increase dramatically as they get older. Beer is by far their favorite beverage of abuse, followed by wine and hard liquor (Towers, 1987). Most adolescents are introduced to alcohol by experimenting with beer. Drinking to intoxication, or being "bombed" or "smashed," is a common occurrence among frequent adolescent users of alcohol. Alcohol is a major problem for young drinkers, often leading to the use of other drugs (Towers, 1987).

CLINICAL PRESENTATION

Finn (1986) suggested that it is much more justifiable to conclude that youths who get drunk are problem drinkers, rather than alcoholics. Blane and Hewitt (1977) support this contention in a study of 13,000 junior and senior high students

355

conducted nationally, in which they found that almost 28% of the adolescents surveyed had a drinking problem. These researchers defined a "problem" as getting drunk four or more times during one year or having one or more problems with family members, friends, school, or the law as a result of drinking. Towers (1987) suggested that, depending on the severity of the adolescent's abuse, certain telltale signs may become apparent, including

1. Truancy, class cutting
2. Declining interest in extracurricular activities
3. Dropping old friends or hanging out with new ones
4. Unexpected mood swings, unprovoked hostility, fights, or vehement arguments
5. Vehemently defending the right to drink or get high, resisting talking or hearing about alcohol
6. Dramatic changes in physical appearance
7. Exhibiting obvious signs of alcohol use such as bottles
8. Slurred or incoherent speech; always tired
9. Deterioration of the youth's relationship with members of his or her family. (pp. 61–63)

In a similar vein, a pamphlet disseminated by the Christophers of New York (Christopher News Notes, 1986) notes that indications of possible alcohol (and other drug) abuse include

1. Decline in grades
2. A lack of interest in former activities
3. A tendency to be sullen and uncommunicative
4. Neglect of personal hygiene
5. Insomnia or excessive sleep
6. Poor motor coordination, slurred speech, or inability to concentrate
7. A need for more spending money, or disappearance of money or valuables

Approaching adolescent alcohol abuse from a symptomatic point of view with respect to actual alcohol imbibing behavior, Zucker and Harford (1981) classified adolescent drinking levels into six drinking categories:

1. Nondrinkers—don't drink or drink less than once a year.
2. Infrequent drinkers—drink once a month at most and drink lightly.
3. Light drinkers—drink once a month at most and drink medium amounts (2–4 drinks) per typical drinking occasion or drink no more than 3–4 times a month and drink small amounts.
4. Moderate drinkers—drink at least once a week and drink small amounts per typical drinking occasion or drink 3–4 times a month and drink

medium amounts per typical drinking occasion or drink no more than once a month and drink large amounts (5+ drinks) per typical drinking occasion.
5. Moderate-heavier drinkers—drink at least once a week and drink medium amounts per typical drinking occasion or drink 3–4 times a month and drink large amounts per typical drinking occasion.
6. Heavier drinkers—drink at least once a week and drink large amounts per typical drinking occasion. (p. 976)

The results of Zucker and Harford's (1981) study (which are reported later in this chapter under the section Epidemiology) indicated that these categories of drinking behavior were indeed valid.

Using a drinking classification scheme similar to Zucker and Harford's, Barnes and Welte (1986) surveyed 27,335 seventh to twelfth grade students in New York State and found that 71% were drinkers and 13% were heavy drinkers (i.e., they drank at least once a week and typically consumed 5 or more drinks per occasion). They concluded that the heavy drinking student (the abuser) could be characterized by frequent school misconduct, first becoming drunk at an early age, having a greater number of friends who get drunk weekly, parental approval of drinking, poor grades in school, being an older adolescent, and being male and white.

King (1980) approached the adolescent alcohol abuser from a characterization of the social and emotional needs of the young alcohol abuser. She discussed three areas of social and emotional growth that she felt are central to examining the phenomenon of teenage alcohol abuse. First, she suggested that alcohol abuse is only one of the many forms of behavior that may be exhibited by deviant youth, that all deviant youth suffer from a low level of self-esteem, and that the deviant behavior represents an attempt to deal with this inadequacy. The young person who unwisely chooses to abuse alcohol often does so as a result of low self-regard, not having experienced the feelings of security and acceptance in childhood that are essential to his or her development of self-esteem. Thus, having a strong need for acceptance by others, such a person may allow peer pressure to dictate the decision to imbibe. Second, alcohol abusers frequently refuse to accept self-responsibility for their actions. Thus, young abusers assign responsibility for drinking to peers, teachers, parents, or simply boredom and the desire for "kicks." Finally, for many young abusers of alcohol, excessive drinking becomes a means of withdrawal from the pressures of adolescence. They resort to ineffective coping skills that are both nonproductive and self-destructive, but nonetheless serve as one means of handling distress.

EPIDEMIOLOGY

Experts call alcohol abuse the most serious drug problem among adolescents, and it is estimated that 3.3 million aged 14 to 17 abuse alcohol (Christopher News Notes, 1986). The incidence and extent to which adolescent alcohol abuse exists appear to be of broad proportions. In support of this, Horton (1985), for example, reported that children are beginning alcohol use at an early age, the average beginning age purportedly being 12.5 years. He also reported that one half of high school students are classified as regular drinkers, one of three drinks heavily at least once a week, one of four students in high school has a serious drinking problem, and that approximately 4 million youth under the age of 17 are treated for alcohol abuse. Teen drinkers, according to Sherouse (1985), account for nearly 50% of all fatal automobile accidents.

Several sources have corroborated the prevalence of considerable alcohol abuse by adolescents. The National Council on Alcoholism (1988), for example, reports that:

1. About 90% of high school students are heavy drinkers or problem drinkers (drinking at least once a week with five or more drinks per drinking occasion).
2. Fifteen percent of high school students are heavy drinkers or problem drinkers (drinking at least once a week with five or more drinks per drinking occasion).
3. Thirty-one percent of high school students are considered to be alcohol misusers (drunkenness at least six times per year).
4. Twenty-five percent of high school students are abstainers.
5. Six percent of high school students are daily users of alcohol.
6. Forty-one percent of all seniors took five or more drinks in a row in the prior two weeks before the survey.
7. The most popular drink among teenagers is beer.
8. Alcohol is the most widely used drug among teenagers.

9. The average age that kids begin to drink is 13.
10. Teenage girls are drinking almost as much as teenage boys.
11. Evidence suggests that problem drinkers started drinking at a younger age than nonproblem drinkers. Earlier use of alcohol among teenagers may increase the potential for developing alcoholism later. (p. 1)

Finn (1986) reports that

1. Twenty-five percent of all seventh graders report getting drunk one or more times a year.
2. Twenty-three percent of high school students report that they get drunk four or more times a year; approximately 5% get drunk at least once a week.
3. As many as half of all college students on some campuses get drunk at least 12 times a year and perhaps 1 out of every 15 as often as once a week. (p. 37)

Zucker and Harford (1981), according to a national survey conducted in 1980, concluded that:

1. By the time that children reach the age of 13, approximately 30% of the boys and 22% of the girls are drinkers and that by age 18, 92% of the boys and 73% of the girls are drinkers.
2. Sex differences are present throughout the age grades; boys are more likely than girls to be drinkers at all ages and are somewhat more likely to be heavier drinkers at older ages (17 and 18).
3. Adolescents from blue-collar families are somewhat less likely to be drinkers than are adolescents from white-collar families.
4. In general, the likelihood of heavier drinking among adolescents is inversely related to their parents' educational level.
5. Adolescents from the Northeast are more likely to be drinkers than those from other regions of the country.

Finally, Forney, Forney, Davis, Van Hoose, Cafferty, and Allen (1984), in a discriminant analysis performed on a sample of 1,715 sixth and eighth grade students, found that

1. Children who were light or frequent drinkers tended to have fathers who were light or frequent drinkers and that children who did not drink or infrequently drank tended to have

mothers who did not drink or infrequently drank.

2. Whites generally drank more than nonwhites and males more than females.

3. The interaction of grade and mother's drinking pattern is quite noticeable for the frequent drinkers. For the sixth grade frequent drinkers, the mothers also tended to be frequent drinkers. However, for the eighth grade frequent drinkers, the mothers tended to be nondrinkers.

4. There is a tendency for the rural students to be heavier drinkers than urban students.

5. There was not a significantly larger number of frequent and heavy drinkers from broken homes. (pp. 353-354)

NATURAL HISTORY

The effects of alcohol abuse by teenagers has a number of inherent dangers, especially if treatment is not undertaken. Famularo and Stone (1985) suggest a relationship between early onset alcohol abuse and the developmental of major affective disorders in adolescence, antisocial behaviors, and poor school performance. Deykin, Levy, and Wells (1980) support this notion of alcohol abuse as contributing to depression. They state:

Alcohol as well as many drugs are depressogens, the repeated use of which produces both the subjective feelings of depression and the neurovegetative signs such as sleep and appetite disturbance, cognitive impairment, and decreased energy characteristic of the depressed syndrome. (p. 178)

That prolonged use of alcohol in adolescents can affect cognitive functioning is corroborated by Mitic (1980), who states: "Alcohol, especially in large quantities, can affect cognitive process such as memory and recall and thereby enable the individual to avoid or repress thinking about his failure" (p. 204).

Bartimole and Bartimole (1987) in examining the long-term effects of teenage alcohol abuse conclude that

1. Alcohol has no nutritive value at all; it inhibits the digestive system and may rob the body of necessary nutrients.

2. Since alcohol is, in reality, a poison, it adversely affects the body from the first sip; brain damage occurs with each ingestion of alcohol. Admittedly, the damage, with limited intake of

alcohol, is negligible, but those who frequently drink large volumes of liquor suffer deeper brain damage, which is irreversible.

3. Particularly dangerous is the ingestion of alcohol in concert with other drugs, especially depressants. It falls to the liver to filter out the alcohol and depressants from the bloodstream. The combination of alcohol and depressants can lead to serious illness, or even death.

4. The heart is susceptible to the effects of alcohol abuse, too. Abnormalities in heart rhythm and pumping action may occur, and may be life-threatening.

5. Finally, prolonged and extreme use of alcohol may cause psychological and/or physical dependency. Withdrawal symptoms for those trying to quit the drug are extreme: body tremors, severe sleep difficulties, digestive problems, and delerium tremens.

Thus, it appears that alcohol abuse in adolescence can, from a historical/developmental perspective, eventuate in several serious consequences if not cared for and treated as early as possible. It appears that a teenager does not have to be labeled or diagnosed as an "alcoholic" in order for some of the aforementioned consequences to occur. It, therefore, becomes contingent upon parents, schools, and other community agencies to convince teenagers to learn to be able to discipline, and limit, themselves regarding alcohol. Teenagers who learn to control their alcohol intake are more likely to be responsible drinkers as adults. Prevention and treatment/intervention programs should be considered and implemented for those who are positions to come into contact with alcohol abusing teenagers.

IMPAIRMENT AND COMPLICATIONS

Alcohol and other drugs, according to Griswold-Ezekoye, Klumpfer, and Bukoski (1986) may cause problems associated with acute use (e.g., auto accidents), chronic use (e.g., cirrhosis), and a behavioral pattern of chronic use called dependency. These same writers conclude that alcohol is associated with more than 50% of the reported cases of the three major causes of death for youth: accidents, homicides, and suicides. In 1982 alone, 9,263 teenagers died in alcohol-related auto accidents.

In an article titled "Questions and Answers About Teenage Alcohol and Abuse," published by the National Institute on Alcohol Abuse and Alcoholism (no date and in the public domain), several factors are discussed regarding the implications of teenage alcohol abuse.

1. Adolescent drinking is related to involvement in other delinquent acts (e.g., lying, cheating, stealing, skipping school).
2. Feelings of isolation, unstable relationships with friends, inadequate social skills, transient and undefined values, difficulty making decisions, an exaggerated desire for independence, and a lack of self-control are often found among young problem drinkers.
3. Youthful problem drinkers are also found to engage in and be more tolerant of deviance, attach less importance to religion, and put more value on self-determination and autonomy from parents.
4. Teenage alcohol abusers often experience familial relationships that are filled with stress, physical abuse, and psychological abuse, or indifference; low levels of self-esteem, problems relating to self-acceptance, unstable identity, and low awareness of their own emotions and inner experience; and a lack of self-control.
5. Alcohol is also implicated in thousands of adolescent drownings, violent injuries and deaths, and injuries from fire.

Downs, Flanagan, and Robertson (1985–86), in a study dealing with labeling and rejection of adolescent heavy drinkers, found the following:

1. The label of "heavy drinker" resulted in widespread overt avoidance of the "heavy drinker" by the other adolescents.
2. This overt avoidance resulted in labeled heavy drinkers having a restricted social world consisting primarily of other heavy drinkers.
3. A substantial minority of nondrinkers/moderate drinkers will continue to reject an adolescent who changes from a heavy drinker to a nondrinker.
4. Adolescents recovering from alcohol abuse may face widespread rejection by other adolescents.
5. Posttreatment adolescents may benefit from placement in a social world different from that prior to treatment.

Horton (1985) suggests that a number of myths need to be debunked about adolescent alcohol use/abuse that, if not, will tend to perpetuate impairment of such youth and present serious complications. He argues that:

> The most dangerous myth is that alcohol use is a rite of passage into adult society. . . . Another myth that needs to be overcome is that only particular types of students will get into trouble with alcohol. . . . Among other myths that retard our abilities to reduce or eliminate adolescent alcohol abuse are the ones that one can be too young to have an alcohol problem; that it is acceptable for boys but not girls to try alcohol; that getting drunk once is a learning experience that will preclude later heavy drinking; that drinking alcohol demonstrates masculinity; that intoxication is humorous; and that drunks are happy drunks. (pp. 6–7)

Johnson, O'Malley, and Bachman (1984) suggested that among preadolescents, use of "gateway" substances (tobacco, alcohol, and marijuana) is rare. However, as young people progress through adolescence, more and more experiment with and begin regularly using these and other substances. Because drug use progresses in a predictable order—young people use the gateway drugs before they use hard drugs (cocaine, PCP, heroin)—it appears that one of the complications of adolescent alcohol abuse is the strong possibility that this may lead to the abuse of the harder drugs as they progress chronologically.

Adolescent depression, alcohol, and drug abuse with respect to a sample of 414 college students aged 16 to 19 years was studied by Deykin, Levy, and Wells (1980). The aforementioned association between early and repeated drunkenness ("problem drinking") and other drug abuse was corroborated. In addition, alcohol abuse was associated with the prevalence of major depressive disorder (MDD), but not with other psychiatric disorders. The onset of MDD almost always preceded alcohol or substance abuse, suggesting the possibility of self-medication as a factor in the development of adolescent alcohol abuse.

DIFFERENTIAL DIAGNOSIS

One perspective from which to view teenage intoxication is that youths who get drunk on more than an experimental basis have a drinking problem or are alcoholics. There are, according to Finn (1986), important differences between problem drinking and alcoholism among adolescents (e.g., most problem drinkers typically not only drink less often than alcoholics, they can drink in moderation if they feel the situations call for staying sober; alcoholics tend to be psychologically dependent). He concludes that youngsters who got drunk, no matter how frequently, cannot be considered alcoholics unless they have lost control over their drinking and have become physiologically and emotionally addicted to alcohol. With reference to a diagnosis, he states that "repeated drunkenness *by itself* cannot warrant a *diagnosis* of alcoholism unless: (a) it has persisted over a considerable period of time, (b) the drunken episodes occur frequently, and (c) the drinker is unable to consume alcohol in moderation" (p. 39). The U.S. Department of Health, Education, and Welfare (1974) reported alcohol abuse in relation to teenagers (or adults) as:

> Repeated episodes of intoxication or heavy drinking which impairs health, or consistent use of alcohol as a coping mechanism in dealing with the problems of life to a degree of serious interference with an individual's effectiveness on the job, at home, in the community or behind the wheel of a car. (p. 1)

A classic and one of the earliest studies dealing with alcohol misuse by adolescents was that by MacKay (1961). The following diagnostic indicators were found in the personalities of his sample of teenagers: "frequent signs of hostility in the family, lack of control, a basic feeling of anxiety and pervasive depression, unfulfilled dependent needs, impulse control was weak, expectation of loss in all relationships, and the need to belong very strong" (p. 126).

The *Diagnostic and Statistical Manual of Mental Disorders* (American Psychiatric Association, 1987), also known as the DSM-III-R, unfortunately does not allude to alcohol abuse per se with respect to adolescents. The only reference to adolescent alcohol abuse in DSM-III-R is as follows:

> Alcohol dependence and abuse are often associated with use and abuse of other psychoactive drugs, including cannabis, cocaine, heroin, amphetamines, and various sedatives and hypnotics. Frequent and often simultaneous use of alcohol plus several of the above substances is most commonly seen in adolescents and people under 30. (p. 173)

Finally, Bartimole and Bartimole (1987) suggest the following as symptomatic of adolescent alcohol abuse: a sense of isolation; poor relationships with friends; an overstated desire for independence; a lack of willpower; high stress; and uncertain values, goals, and priorities accompanied by low levels of self-esteem and self-acceptance.

CASE EXAMPLE

George, a 16-year-old high school sophomore, had been arrested with a charge of driving while intoxicated (DWI). He had recently received his young driver's permit and decided to "celebrate" his accomplishment by inviting a couple of his friends "for a few beers down by the river." Earlier in the day he had discovered a twenty-dollar bill in his mother's purse and decided that he should take it "for some future use." After school he and his friends convinced a young adult (age 21), who was loitering around the school, to buy them three six-packs of beer by offering to pay him five dollars.

George and his friends went to his home, borrowed his mother's car under the pretense of having to go to the local mall to purchase a pair of shoes, and proceeded to drive to the river. The three teenagers spent about 2 hours on the riverbank indulging themselves in their beer. At about six o'clock that evening they decided they should go home, at which time George drove the car onto the highway that would take them home. Once they had driven about a mile they noticed a spotlight aimed at them while simultaneously hearing the shrill of a siren. George pulled the car over to the side of the highway and was approached by a highway patrolman, who asked him for his license and proof of insurability for the car, both of which George readily presented. The patrolman told George that he was driving beyond the speed limit and at the same time swerving the vehicle in a very dangerous way. George did not protest and subsequently was given a written citation and asked to appear at the municipal court within 2 weeks.

Since George appeared quite inebriated and neither of his friends (who were both cited for drinking alcoholic beverages while underage) could drive, the patrolman called George's father and told him about his condition and recommended that he or someone come by and drive George and his friends to their homes. George's father, while very angry at George's behavior, nevertheless agreed to pick up the three teenagers and drive them home.

This episode had been the fifth time that George had been caught in an infraction involving use of alcoholic beverages. Over the past 2 years he had been suspended from school for having alcoholic beverages on his person or hidden in his school locker on four different occasions. Although George's parents were very angry at the latest involvement with drinking, they decided that talking to George about this incident while he appeared to be inebriated would serve little purpose and, therefore, decided to wait until the next day to confront him and talk about it.

George had begun experimenting with alcoholic beverages when he was 14 years old and in the eighth grade. He had been talking one day with several of his friends who shared with him that they had tried beer and whiskey several times and had "gotten a real buzz out of them" and that he should try them. Although George had been taught that it was wrong to engage in imbibing alcohol at his age, he decided that since many of his friends partook of alcohol, as did his parents, he could see no reason why he shouldn't "take a slug" once in a while. Besides, if he didn't his friends would ridicule him and call him a "weirdo." George's parents were completely unaware that his drinking behavior had begun at such an early age until the school principal called them and revealed to them that some liquor had been found in his locker, which resulted in his first suspension from school. Once this incident occurred, they agreed that from time to time they noticed that their liquor supply had dwindled somewhat but had decided that each of them had taken it. No suspicion had fallen upon George or onto his three older siblings. After George's fourth suspension from school, they were advised by the school counselor that he had a serious drinking problem. He referred to George as a moderate to heavy drinker since George had admitted that he imbibed at least once a week. The doses varied from medium to large amounts, depending on how George felt and the situation he was in with respect to being with friends or simply not feeling good about himself. George's parents were incredulous, insisting that George was a good boy and that they had never smelled any liquor on him nor seen him inebriated. Their denial of George's "drinking problem" continued until his arrest with a charge of DWI.

George's parents accompanied him to the municipal court hearing and made no attempt to contest the charge. Thus, George was found guilty and placed on juvenile probation for one year, with the added condition that he and his parents agree to seek professional help to what George's parents now conceded was indeed a drinking problem. George agreed to this, but after being told by his parents that they had set an appointment with a local specialist in adolescent alcohol problems, he became belligerent and stated that he was reluctant to go to a "shrink" because he

really didn't have a problem. Following a very intense confrontation and a threat by his parents to turn George in to the authorities for failing to fulfill one of the conditions of the probation, he finally, though reluctantly, decided that he would go, but only under the condition that he would just go and listen to what the psychologist had to say. He should not be expected, he revealed to his parents, to share anything about himself with them or with the psychologist.

George was the youngest of four siblings (three boys and one girl). The first three siblings were 2 years apart, while George was 6 years younger than his youngest sibling. His father was a engineer, while his mother was a real estate broker. Both were highly successful in their careers, enjoyed a wide circle of friends, and were highly respected in their community. They entertained frequently at home and always served cocktails, employing a bartender for this purpose. Parental expectations of all four children were quite high although, as the youngest, George was given a bit more latitude than his siblings. Tension in the atmosphere at home caused George to be confused regarding his parents' expectations. Sibling confrontations, peer pressure, and a general sense of worthlessness led him to try imbibing liquor in order to "get a buzz;" he found this quite enjoyable in terms of "being high" and being able to deal with his problems. Besides, he had easy access to alcoholic beverages at home and no one would suspect or know that he had indulged. He had learned from his peers to carry a breath freshener to camouflage the smell of alcohol.

Initially, the psychologist encountered resistance and denial regarding a drinking problem in George's case. His parents also exhibited some denial about the seriousness of George's problem. Three months into therapy, the psychologist experienced a breakthrough on George's part, which was modeled somewhat on the cooperation that he observed his parents were giving to the psychologist. During ensuing sessions, a number of issues evolved, including George's feeling of worthlessness and his inability to deal with his parents' expectations, peer ridicule and pressure, sibling rivalry, and feeling of being alone in such a large high school atmosphere. From time to time during therapy, George would confess that he had imbibed anywhere from small to large amounts of liquor. Each time he revealed this to the psychologist in the presence of his parents, they would take this as a setback and become extremely angry with George. He explained to them and to the psychologist that his friends would harass him when he refused their offer of liquor, and so, to stay in their good graces, he would also take a few drinks.

In spite of these "setbacks" the psychologist assured George and his parents (who, as a result of family therapy, ceased their drinking activities) that progress was occurring, especially as a result of the therapy and George's attending a young people's AA group. For George, who is still in therapy, the prognosis appears quite good, although some regression still occurs.

CONTINUITY AND DISCONTINUITY WITH ADULT PRESENTATION

This section attempts to deal with the question of how alcohol abuse in adolescence relates to a continuance or to the development of alcohol abuse in adulthood. The question of teenage alcohol abuse as a warning signal of future problem drinking or alcoholism is dealt with by Finn (1986). He suggests that drunken behavior on the part of many teenagers may be viewed by some as a sign that a youngster may have an emotional or genetic predisposition toward problem drinking or alcoholism. He goes on to state,

> There are several million problem drinkers in the country, and studies indicate that many adult males who abuse alcohol engaged in drunken behavior as youngsters and at a generally earlier age than adults who do not have drinking problems. . . . However, we have no way of knowing whether there is a cause and effect relationship between youthful intoxication and problems with alcohol later in time. It is possible that adult problem drinkers and alcoholics would still abuse alcohol even if they had been prevented or discouraged from getting drunk as youngsters. In addition, many teenagers and young adults who get drunk do *not* become problem drinkers as adults. . . . Thus, the "warning theory" turns out to involve a "false alarm" in a significant number of cases. (p. 41)

The Comptroller General of the United States (1979), in discussing youth problem drinking, corroborated Finn's finding: "Young people who drink heavily may not perceive themselves as problem drinkers, and there is no conclusive evidence that adolescent problem drinking problems persist in later life" (p. 3).

In a slightly different vein, Black (1979), in re-

ferring to children of alcoholics (i.e., children exposed to alcoholism), observed:

> We need to explore the dynamics of the child exposed to alcoholism. Typically, parents and professionals do not acknowledge the need for bringing children into the treatment program, except to treat a behavioral or disciplinary problem or to assist in a confrontation among family members. The tendency is to focus on a problem child who is often stereotyped as a potential future alcoholic. . . . I believe, however, that the child with behavioral problems in the alcoholic home is in the minority. (p. 123)

In support of the foregoing, Barnes (1979) in discussing teenage drinking, suggested:

> From the data, what may be expected to be youth's [teenage abusers] relation to beverage alcohol in the future? Prediction is a difficult, hazardous, and frustrating art. Longitudinal designs necessary to detect shifts in the prevalence and patterns of alcohol usage are beset with numerous conceptual, methodological, and practical difficulties. Consequently, alcohol surveys of young people have typically been carried out at one point in time in a specified geographical locale. (p. 387)

Globetti (1982), in dealing with teenage drinking, stated,

> Investigations up to this time have not sought to prove that teenagers who have complications with their use of alcohol are fledgling or incipient alcoholics. What they have shown is that problem drinking among youth does show characteristics and signs that approximate profiles of adult alcoholics. Only recently do we have some indication that adult problem drinking may in fact be predicted from early drinking behavior. However, it is still too early to specify what network of variables discriminate those teenagers who will be responsible drinkers from those who will be problem drinkers in later life. (p. 210)

Thus, while pointing out the possibility of predicting adult problem drinking from early drinking behavior, and to some degree disagreeing with Finn (1986), the Comptroller General of the United States (1979), and Black (1979), Globetti, nevertheless, appears to express some caution with respect to making any final conclusions about the question prematurely.

It would appear, then, that it is somewhat precarious to make any predictions or inferences about adult alcoholic abuse from alcohol abuse behaviors observed during teenage years.

SUMMARY

Although alcohol is the single most abused drug in childhood and adolescence, there appears to be a question in our society with regard to how much concern should be shown about this common phenomenon. There are, nevertheless, several theories regarding the nature and seriousness of youthful intoxication. Also, the physical and psychological effects of alcohol on youth are well known.

There are a number of symptoms (high truancy, unexpected mood swings, slurred speech, etc.) that are highly indicative of "alcoholic behavior." Researchers have successfully classified youthful alcoholic drinking into various categories, ranging from "nondrinkers" to "heavier drinkers," and they have reported the average beginning age of alcoholic use is 12.5 years. Several sources have consensually agreed on the prevalence of alcohol abuse by adolescents.

The extent to which alcohol abuse is begun early by teenagers has been shown to have a relationship with the development of major affective disorders in adolescence, which result in serious consequences if not cared for or treated early on. However, research is cautious in pointing out that it is somewhat questionable to attempt to predict adult alcohol abuse from alcohol abuse encountered in adolescence.

REFERENCES

American Psychiatric Association. (1987). *Diagnostic and statistical manual of mental disorders* (3rd ed. rev.). Washington, DC: Author.

Barnes, G. M. (1979). A perspective on drinking among teenagers with special reference to New York State studies. *Journal of School Health, 45*, 386–389.

Barnes, G. M., & Welte, J. W. (1986). Patterns and predictors of alcohol among 7–12 grade students in New York State. *Journal of Studies on Alcohol, 47*, 53–62.

Bartimole, C. R., & Bartimole, J. E. (1987). *Teenage alcoholism and substance abuse: Causes, consequences, and cures.* Hollywood, FL: Frederick Fell.

Belkin, G. (1988). *Introduction to counseling* (2nd ed.). Dubuque, IA: William C. Brown.

Black, C. (1979). Children of alcoholics. *Alcohol Health and Research World, 21*, 23–28.

Blane, H. T., & Hewitt, L. E. (1977). *Alcohol and youth: An analysis of the literature, 1960–1975.* Springfield, VA: National Institute on Alcohol Abuse and Alcoholics.

Christoper News Note. (1986). *Dying to do drugs.* New York: The Christopers.

Comptroller General of the United States. (1979). *Report to Congress on the drinking driver problem—what can be done about it?* Washington, DC: U.S. General Accounting Office.

Deykin, E. Y., Levy, S. C., & Wells, V. (1980). Adolescent depression and drug abuse. *American Journal of Public Health, 77*(2), 178–182.

Downs, W. R., Flanagan, J. C., & Robertson, (1985–86). Labeling and rejection of adolescent heavy drinkers: Implications for treatment. *The Journal of Applied Social Sciences, 10*(1), 1–9.

Famularo, R., & Stone, K. (1985). Pre-adolescent alcohol abuse and dependence. *American Journal of Psychiatry, 142*(10), 1187–1189.

Finn, P. (1986). Teenage drunkenness: Warning signal, transient boisterousness, or symptom of social change? In C. M. Felsted (Ed.), *Youth and alcohol abuse: Readings and resources* (pp. 36–51). Phoenix, AZ: The Oryx Press.

Forney, M. A., Forney, P. D., Davis, H., Van Hoose, J., Cafferty, T., & Ailen, H. (1984). A discriminant analysis of adolescent problem drinking. *Journal of Drug Education, 4*(4), 347–355.

Globetti, G. (1982). Teenage drinking. In N. J. Estes & M. E. Heinmann (Eds.), *Alcoholism: Development, consequences, and interventions* (2nd ed.). St. Louis: C. V. Mosby.

Griswald-Ezekoye, S., Klumpfer, K. L., & Bukoski, W. J. (1986). *Childhood and chemical abuse: Prevention and intervention.* New York: The Haworth Press.

Horton, L. (1985). *Adolescent alcohol abuse.* Bloomington, IN: Phi Delta Kappa.

Johnson, L. O., O'Malley, P. M., & Bachman, J. G. (1984). *Highlights from drugs and American high school students 1975–1983.* Rockville, MD: U.S. Department of Health and Human Services, National Institute on Drug Abuse.

King, S. (1980). Young alcohol abusers: The challenge of prevention. *Journal of Drug Education, 10*(3), 233–238.

McKay, J. R. (1961). Clinical observations or adolescent problem drinkers. *Quarterly Journal of the Study of Alcohol, 22*(37), 124–134.

Mitic, W. R. (1980). Alcohol use and self-esteem

of adolescents. *Journal of Drug Education,* *10*(3), 197–208.

National Council on Alcoholism. (1988). *Facts on teenage drinking.* NY: Author.

Rachel, J. V., Williams, J. R., Brehm, M. L., Cavanaugh B., Moore, R. P., & Eckerman, N. C. (1975). *A national study of adolescent drinking behavior, attitudes and correlates.* Springfield, VA: National Technical Information Service (for the National Institute on Alcohol Abuse and Alcoholism).

Sherouse, D. (1985). *Adolescent drug and alcohol abuse handbook.* Springfield, IL: Charles C Thomas.

Towers, R. L. (1987). *Student drug and alcohol abuse.* Washington, DC: National Education Association of the United States.

U.S. Department of Health, Education, and Welfare (1974). *Alcohol and health: New knowledge.* Second report to the U.S. Congress, Washington, DC: U.S. Government Printing Office.

Zucker, R. S., & Harford, T. C. (1981). *National study of the demography of adolescent drinking practices in 1980.*

CHAPTER 26

ALCOHOL DEPENDENCE IN ADULTHOOD

Julia K. Warnock
Donald W. Goodwin

DESCRIPTION OF THE DISORDER

The revised third edition of the American Psychiatric Association's *Diagnostic and Statistical Manual of Mental Disorders* (American Psychiatric Association, 1987) distinguishes between psychoactive substance use disorder, such as alcohol dependence and alcohol abuse, and psychoactive substance-induced organic mental syndrome (see section on Impairment and Complication). The diagnosis of alcohol dependence syndrome requires the features of continued use of alcohol despite adverse consequences, generally of a physiological, behavioral, cognitive, or social nature. The definition of alcohol abuse and alcohol dependence as used in DSM-III (APA, 1980) were widely considered inadequate. Thus, in the DSM-III-R, new criteria for alcohol dependence were developed. In addition, alcohol abuse became a residual category for noting maladaptive patterns of alcohol use that have never met the criteria for dependence. Tables 26.1 and 26.2 list the criteria specified in DSM-III-R for differentiating psychoactive substance dependence from abuse.

Alcohol, like the general anesthetics, depresses the nervous system. The central nervous system effects of alcohol are generally proportionate to the level of blood concentration. Table 26.3 gives the criteria for alcohol intoxication. These symptoms can be more severe with higher levels of alcohol in blood, culminating in coma at approximately 400 mg/dl and respiratory center paralysis and death at approximately 500 mg/dl.

CLINICAL PRESENTATION

The clinical presentation of the patient with an alcohol addiction is dependent on when in the course of the illness he presents. Often during the initial phase of the illness the indications of an alcohol problem can be gained only by obtaining a thorough social and medical history. Corroborated reports from the patient, family, and friends are frequently required to verify information regarding the patient's job or school performance, marital harmony, trouble with legal or police systems, and accidents. These social and legal problems are more frequently associated with alcoholics than with nonalcoholics.

Patients who admit to having such problems

Table 26.1. Diagnostic Criteria for Psychoactive Substance Dependence

A. At least 3 of the following:

1. Substance often taken in larger amounts or over a longer period than the person intended.

2. Persistent desire or one or more unsuccessful efforts to cut down or control substance use.

3. A great deal of time spent in activities necessary to get the substance (e.g., theft), taking the substance (e.g., chain smoking), or recovering from its effects.

4. Frequent intoxication or withdrawal symptoms when expected to fulfill major role obligations at work, school, or home (e.g., does not go to work because hung over, goes to school or work "high," intoxicated while taking care of his or her children), or when substance use is physically hazardous (e.g., drives when intoxicated).

5. Important social, occupational, or recreational activities given up or reduced because of substance use.

6. Continued substance use despite knowledge of having a persistent or recurrent social, psychological, or physical problem that is caused or exacerbated by the use of the substance (e.g., keeps using heroin despite family arguments about it, cocaine-induced depression, or having an ulcer made worse by drinking).

7. Marked tolerance: need for markedly increased amounts of the substance (i.e., at least a 50% increase) in order to achieve intoxication or desired effect, or markedly diminished effect with continued use of the same amount.

Note: The following items may not apply to cannabis, hallucinogens, or phencyclidine (PCP):

8. Characteristic withdrawal symptoms (see specific withdrawal syndromes under psychoactive substance-induced organic mental disorders).

9. Substance often taken to relieve or avoid withdrawal symptoms.

B. Some symptoms of the disturbance have persisted for at least 1 month, or have occurred repeatedly over a longer period of time.

Criteria for Severity of Psychoactive Substance Dependence:

Mild: Few, if any, symptoms in excess of those required to make the diagnosis, and the symptoms result in no more than mild impairment in occupational functioning or in usual social activities or relationships with others.*

Moderate: Symptoms or functional impairment between "mild" and "severe."

Severe: Many symptoms in excess of those required to make the diagnosis, and the symptoms markedly interfere with occupational functioning or with usual social activities or relationships with others.*

In Partial Remission: During the past 6 months, some use of the substance and some symptoms of dependence.

In Full Remission: During the past 6 months, either no use of the substance, or use of the substance and no symptoms of dependence.

*Because of the availability of cigarettes and other nicotine-containing substances and the absence of a clinically significant nicotine intoxication syndrome, impairment in occupational or social functioning not necessary for a rating of severe nicotine dependence.

Reprinted with permission from the *Diagnostic and Statistical Manual of Mental Disorders. Third Edition, Revised.* Copyright 1987 American Psychiatric Association.

should be questioned further about any relationship alcohol could play regarding the patient's social and/or behavioral problems. Additional sources of information are needed, because alcoholics frequently minimize the amount of alcohol they drink and the magnitude of their social difficulties. Medical complaints that may be associated with the early phase of alcoholism include gastrointestinal disturbance, insomnia, diarrhea, and impotence (Holt, Skinner, & Israel, 1981). More commonly, however, there are no laboratory indices or physical stigmata marking the early phase of the disease. The best approach is for the physician to have a high index of suspicion, coupled with a sensitive and thorough approach to history taking (Liskow & Goodwin, 1986).

Goodwin and Guze (1989) note that those suffering from alcoholism are preoccupied with obtaining large enough quantities of alcohol sufficient to produce intoxication over long periods. It is especially true in the early stages of alcoholism that patients may deny their obsession or attempt to rationalize their need by asserting that they drink no more than their friends or acquaintances. As part of their defense, alcoholics tend to spend their time with other heavy drinkers. Further, "as alcoholism progresses and problems from drinking become more serious, alcoholics may drink alone, sneak drinks, hide the bottle, or take other measures to conceal the seriousness of their condition" (p. 177).

The medical, social, occupational, psychological, or legal problems caused or exacerbated by

Table 26.2. Diagnostic Criteria for Psychoactive Substance Abuse

A. A maladaptive pattern of psychoactive substance use indicated by at least one of the following:
   1. continued use despite knowledge of having a persistent or recurrent social, occupational, psychological, or physical problem that is caused or exacerbated by use of the psychoactive substance;
   2. recurrent use in situations in which use is physically hazardous (e.g., driving while intoxicated).

B. Some symptoms of the disturbance have persisted for at least 1 month or have occurred repeatedly over a longer period of time.

C. Never met the criteria for Psychoactive Substance Dependence for this substance.

Reprinted with permission from the *Diagnostic and Statistical Manual of Mental Disorders. Third Edition, Revised.* Copyright 1987 American Psychiatric Association.

drinking become more apparent as the disease progresses (see the section on Impairment and Complications in DSM-III-R). And as the disease progresses, the addicted patient likely presents for medical care or treatment. Referral for treatment occurs when the illness progresses to the point that the patient, the family member or friends, the authorities, the employer, or the physician feel compelled to attempt to intervene because of the adverse consequences. Interestingly, 91% of 10,758 consecutive individuals who sought admission to an alcoholism inpatient treatment unit did so following referral by family, friends, or other patients, or in response to media announcements. Less than 10% of these patients were referred to hospitals for alcohol treatment by physicians (Mendelson, Babor, Mello, & Pratt, 1986).

The late stage of alcoholism has certain physical stigmata associated with a long history of alcohol abuse. Goodwin and Guze (1989) suggest that physicians are in a unique position to rate the following clinical signs of the disease:

1. Arcus senilis — a ringlike opacity of the cornea — occurs commonly with age, causes no visual disturbance, and is considered an innocent condition. The ring forms from fatty material in the blood. Alcohol increases fat in the blood, and more alcoholics are reported to have the ring than their contemporaries who do not drink heavily.
2. A red nose (acne rosacea) suggests that the owner has a weakness for alcoholic beverages. Some people with red noses, however, are teetotalers or even rabid prohibitionists and resent the insinuation.
3. Red palms (palmar erythema) are also suggestive, but not diagnostic, of alcoholism.
4. Cigarette burns between the index and middle fingers or on the chest and contusions and

Table 26.3. Diagnostic Criteria for Alcohol Intoxication

A. Recent ingestion of alcohol (with no evidence suggesting that the amount was insufficient to cause intoxication in most people).

B. Maladaptive behavioral changes (e.g., disinhibition of sexual or aggressive impulses, mood lability, impaired judgment, impaired social or occupational functioning).

C. At least one of the following signs:
   1. slurred speech
   2. incoordination
   3. unsteady gait
   4. nystagmus
   5. flushed face

D. Not due to any physical or other mental disorder.

Reprinted with permission from the *Diagnostic and Statistical Manual of Mental Disorders. Third Edition, Revised.* Copyright 1987 American Psychiatric Association.

bruises should raise suspicions of recent alcoholic stupor.

5. Painless enlargement of the liver may suggest a larger alcohol intake than the liver can handle. Severe, constant upper abdominal pain and tenderness radiating to the back indicates pancreatic inflammation, which is sometimes caused by alcohol.

6. Reduced sensation and weakness in the feet and legs may occur from excessive drinking. (p. 180)

EPIDEMIOLOGY

In 1985 the federal government (U.S. Government Public Health Reports, 1985) studied the drinking habits of more than 30,000 households. Drinkers were divided into abstainers, moderate drinkers, and heavy drinkers. A moderate drinker was defined as one who drank from 4 to 13 drinks per week with a heavy drinker averaging 2 or more drinks per day or over 14 drinks per week. One drink was defined as a 1½-ounce highball, a bottle of beer, or 4 ounces of wine. The researchers found that heavy drinkers were concentrated in the highest income groups (families with incomes greater than $50,000 per year) and among whites. Other studies, such as the survey by Cahalan, Cisin, and Crossley (1969), found conflicting evidence with higher drinking rates noted among blue-collar workers and urban blacks. The Cahalan et al. (1969) study also suggested that more drinkers live in cities and suburbs than in rural regions and small towns. Religion also predicted whether a person was a drinker. Most urban Jews and Episcopalians drank on occasion; however, fewer than half of rural Baptists were noted to drink.

Another survey from the National Institute of Mental Health (Robins et al., 1984) found alcohol abuse and dependence to be the leading lifetime diagnosis of 15 DSM-III psychiatric diagnoses. In the three sites of St. Louis, New Haven, and Baltimore, alcohol abuse or dependence had a lifetime prevalence rate of 18.1%, 11.5%, and 13.7%, respectively. Alcohol abuse and dependence had a significant male predominance in all three sites. Also, the age group of 25 to 44 was similar in having the largest percentage of individuals with alcohol abuse and dependence. Additionally, the inner-city environment was associated with a higher rate of the disorder than the rural or suburban areas. Robins, Murphy, and Breckenridge (1968) noted that urban blacks begin drinking at an earlier age than did whites of comparable socioeconomic status. Female alcoholics have been studied much less than their male counterparts (Haver, 1986), but generally speaking women begin heavy drinking at a later age than do men (Goodwin, 1971; Pemberton, 1967). However, the 18- to 30-year-old female age group tends to be the heaviest consumers and may be increasing in proportion (Martin & Casswell, 1988).

Goodwin and Guze (1989) have made the following comments on the epidemiology of alcoholism.

In the United States, blacks in urban ghettos appear to have a particularly high rate of alcohol-related problems; whether rural blacks have comparably high rates of alcohol problems is unknown (Maddox & Williams, 1968; Robins et al., 1968). American Indians are also said to have high rates of alcoholism (Dozier, 1966), but this does not apply to all tribes, and books have been written debunking the "firewater myth" (Guze, 1976; Leland, 1976). Orientals, on the other hand, generally have low rates of alcoholism.

Alcoholism is a serious problem in France and Russia (Sadoun, Lolli, & Silverman, 1965). Although Italy, like France, is a "vinocultural" country (where wine is a popular beverage), it is commonly asserted that Italians have a lower rate of alcoholism than the French (Bales, 1946; Lolli, Serianni, Golder, & Luzzato-Fegiz, 1958). The evidence for this is scant, however. Estimates of alcoholism rates are usually based on cirrhosis rates and admissions to psychiatric hospitals for alcoholism. France has the highest cirrhosis rate in the world, but Italy also has a high rate, suggesting that alcoholism may be more common in Italy than is generally assumed. Ireland has a relatively low cirrhosis rate, despite its reputation for a high rate of alcoholism. According to de Lint and Schmidt (1971), there is a positive correlation between per capita consumption of alcohol and cirrhosis rates. If cirrhosis rates are a reliable indicator of the extent of alcoholism in a particular country, then both cirrhosis and alcoholism are correlated with the total amount of alcohol consumed by the population of that country. Cirrhosis rates themselves are probably somewhat unreliable, and estimates of the prevalence of alcoholism in different countries tend to change from time to time as new information is obtained (Popham, 1970).

Alcohol problems are correlated with a history of school difficulty (Mayfield, 1968). High school dropouts and individuals with a record of frequent truancy and delinquency appear to have a particularly high risk of alcoholism.

No systematic studies have explored the relationship between occupation and alcoholism, but cirrhosis data suggest that individuals in certain occupations are more vulnerable to alcoholism than those doing other types of work. Waiters, bartenders, longshoremen, musicians, authors, and reporters have relatively high cirrhosis rates; accountants, mail carriers, and carpenters have relatively low rates (de Lint & Schmidt, 1971). (pp. 174–175)

NATURAL HISTORY

The natural history of any disorder is best understood by investigating individuals with the disorder from a longitudinal prospective. Frequently, the research on alcoholism is flawed methodologically. Studies often lack controls, are retrospective rather than prospective in design, and are inadequate in terms of follow-up. Another complicating factor in the study of alcoholism is the lack of consensus of a definition of the illness among investigators. In spite of these limitations some perspective about the various courses of the natural history of alcoholism may be gleaned.

One factor that plays a role in the natural history of alcoholism is the sex of the patient. The rates of men who are heavy drinkers range from 15% to 22% as compared to 3% to 6% for women (Ferrence, 1980), making the ratio of men to women approximately 3 : 1 to 7 : 1. In men, the onset of the disorder and course may be more insidious and the alcoholic may not be fully aware of his dependency on alcohol until his thirties, typically not presenting for treatment until his late thirties or forties (Drew, 1968; Schuckit, 1985). Spontaneous remission is not uncommon (Schuckit, 1985). Evidence suggests that the course of the disorder appears more variable in women. Especially likely in women is a history of major affective disorder (Helzer & Pryzbeck, 1988; Schuckit, Pitts, Reich, King, & Winokur, 1969). Spontaneous remission in women apparently is less frequent (Goodwin, 1971; Pemberton, 1967).

Age is a variable related to the clinical subgroups of alcoholism as described by Cloninger (1987). Type I alcoholism begins typically after the age of 25 and is associated with loss of control, guilt, and fear about dependence on alcohol. This type of heavy drinker is not typically associated with fighting and arrests as part of the natural history. The Type II alcoholic, on the other hand, has an onset before age 25, and is associated with frequent impulsive-aggressive behavior, such as fighting or reckless driving after drinking. This Type II alcoholic is associated with antisocial personality traits, having frequent spontaneous alcohol-seeking behaviors and little guilt or fear

about alcohol dependence. Individuals over the age of 65 rarely become alcoholic.

Several studies have found that selected childhood personality traits are predictive of later alcohol abuse. These investigators have found that premorbid traits associated with antisocial personality such as overactivity, impatience, aggression (Knop, Teasdale, Schulsinger, & Goodwin, 1985; Robins, 1966; Vaillant, 1983) and high novelty seeking, low harm avoidance, and low reward dependence (Cloninger, Sigvardsson, & Bohman, 1988) are predictive of alcohol abuse in young adults. Cloninger et al. (1988) describe individuals high in novelty seeking as impulsive, quick tempered, and distractible, whereas low-novelty individuals are rigid, reserved, and attentive to details. Low–harm-avoidance traits characterize individuals who are uninhibited, carefree, and energetic; high–harm-avoidance individuals are described as cautious, pessimistic, and apprehensive worriers. Individuals high in reward dependence are characterized as sensitive to social cues, sympathetic, and sentimental. Low-reward dependent individuals are socially detached and emotionally aloof. Additionally, other childhood personality variables, such as passivity and dependence (Block, 1971) and low novelty seeking, high harm avoidance, and high reward dependence (Cloninger et al., 1988) are predictive of Type I or later onset alcohol abuse.

Schuckit (1985) discusses the natural history of primary alcoholism. Primary alcoholism is defined by Schuckit (1985) as serious alcohol problems occurring in an individual with no preexisting major psychiatric diagnosis. This type of alcoholic may take his or her first drink at age 12 to 14, and become intoxicated for the first time at age 14 to 18. Typically during the late twenties major problems related to alcohol begin to confront the individual. However, the patient usually does not enter treatment until about age 40. The usual age of death is between 55 and 60 years, with the leading causes of death being heart disease, cancer, accident, and suicide. Perhaps as many as 10% to 30% of individuals who meet criteria for alcoholism will learn to abstain or to become asymptomatic drinkers without treatment intervention.

While the natural history of the primary alcoholics, as discussed earlier, follows a fluctuating clinical course, this may be particularly true of those alcoholic individuals who also have another psychiatric diagnosis. Guze, Cloninger, Martin, and Clayton (1986) note, in their investigation of 500 psychiatric clinic patients, that alcoholism was associated with depression, mania, antisocial personality, Briquet's syndrome, and drug dependence. However, in the identified alcoholic probands, alcoholism was the only psychiatric disorder found to be increased among first-degree relatives. The authors speculated that perhaps it was the associated psychiatric conditions in the alcoholic individual that increased the likelihood that the patient sought psychiatric help.

The disease of alcoholism fits the pattern of a chronic relapsing illness. There are often periods of remission and exacerbation, with a wide spectrum of drinking patterns. Because of the diversity in clinical course, it is the emphasis on the problems caused by alcohol that provides the basis for diagnosing alcoholism.

IMPAIRMENT AND COMPLICATIONS

Alcoholism is defined by the problems it creates. The impairment, complications, and symptoms inevitably overlap. For present purposes, medical, psychiatric, and social complications will be considered separately.

Medical Complications

Mendelson et al. (1986) investigated the prevalence of medical disorders for 10,758 consecutive admissions of middle-class American men and women for inpatient alcoholism treatment in eight states. Approximately 70% of the men and 73% of the women had significant medical problems in addition to the diagnosis of alcoholism. The medical complications of alcoholism may be directly related to the short-term or accumulated effects of alcohol intake or associated indirectly with abuse. Examples of the latter may include accidents or neglect of other medical problems.

Gastrointestinal Complication
Numerous complications of the upper gastrointestinal tract are associated with alcoholism, including parotid gland enlargement, increased incidence of esophageal cancer, esophageal varies, chronic antral gastritis, hemorrhagic gastritis, and Mallory-Weiss tears. Alcoholic pancreatitis may develop after 10 to 15 years of heavy alcohol abuse. This is a chronic form of pancreatitis associated with permanent changes in structure and function. This may result not only in abdominal pain and vomiting during an acute relapse, but

also more chronic difficulties, such as pancreatic insufficiency, glucose intolerance, ascites, and pseudocysts.

Liver damage is one of the most serious medical complications of alcoholism. Development of the fatty liver, which may be precirrhotic in the alcoholic, is a reversible condition mediated by the increased NADH/NAD ratio that occurs during ethanol oxidation. The clinical presentation is generally benign and asymptomatic. Alcoholic hepatitis, on the other hand, presents with jaundice, anorexia, right upper quadrant pain, hepatomegaly, fever, and increased liver function tests. In particular, the SGOT/SGPT ratio is greater than one in a majority of patients with alcoholic hepatitis.

The primary physical signs and symptoms in cirrhosis include jaundice, weight loss, anorexia, and weakness. Associated manifestations symptomatic of cirrhosis may include gynecomastia, palmar erythema, asterixis, variceal hemorrhage, ascites, testicular atrophy, and hepatic encephalopathy. Goodwin and Guze (1989) note the following:

> It appears that cirrhosis results from the combined effect of alcohol and diet plus other factors, possibly including heredity. Human and animal studies indicate that a single large dose of alcohol combined with a diet rich in fat produces a fatty liver (Lieber, 1968; Wallgren & Barry, 1970). Conversely, alcohol together with fasting can result in a fatty liver. Most patients with Laennec's cirrhosis in Western countries are excessive drinkers. Most severe alcoholics, however, do not develop cirrhosis; probably less than 10 percent. (p. 185)

Nutritional Deficiencies
Malnutrition frequently is associated with alcoholism and may be responsible for some of the most serious disabilities. Ethanol can also impair the intestinal absorption of vitamins, including thiamine. Thiamine deficiency contributes to the Wernicke-Korsakoff syndrome or the alcohol amnestic syndrome (Table 26.4).

Table 26.4. Diagnostic Criteria for Alcohol Amnestic Disorder

A. Amnestic syndrome following prolonged, heavy ingestion of alcohol.

B. Not due to any physical or other mental disorder.

Reprinted with permission from the *Diagnostic and Statistical Manual of Mental Disorders. Third Edition, Revised.* Copyright 1987 American Psychiatric Association.

The acute Wernicke stage consists of ocular disturbances (nystagmus and sixth nerve palsy), ataxia, and confusion. Typically, these symptoms resolve in several days, but the disease may progress to a chronic brain syndrome—Korsakoff's psychosis. The most characteristic feature of Korsakoff's psychosis is the short-term memory loss. The Wernicke-Korsakoff syndrome is associated with necrotic lesions of the mammillary bodies, dorsal medial nucleus of the thalamus, and other brainstem areas. Immediate thiamine administration corrects early Wernicke signs and may prevent development of an irreversible alcohol amnestic disorder (Korsakoff-type dementia). However, once the dementia is established, it is noted that thiamine does not usually help alleviate symptoms (Goodwin, 1989).

The fat-soluble vitamins such as A, D, and K may be deficient in the alcoholic because of decreased dietary intake or decreased absorption resulting from steatorrhea. Deficiency of vitamin A has been linked to abnormal dark adaptation and hypogonadism (Korsten & Lieber, 1985).

Folate deficiency is the most common cause of megaloblastic anemia in malnourished alcoholics. Severe folate deficiency can result in granulocytopenia and thrombocytopenia. Diagnostic confirmation involves measuring the red cell folate levels, a reflection of tissue stores.

Other Medical Complications

Long-term alcohol abuse can cause serious destruction of skeletal and cardiac muscle fibers. In the alcoholic with cardiomyopathy, there is also a deposition of fat and scar tissue that leads to a symmetric cardiomegaly with the associated signs and symptoms of congestive heart failure. A decrease in plasma testosterone is associated with alcohol use, and hypogonadism has long been associated with alcoholic cirrhosis.

Psychiatric Complications

Alcoholism is associated with dementia, alcohol withdrawal, alcohol withdrawal delirium, alcohol hallucinosis, and suicide. Many of the cognitive deficits found in alcoholics undergoing detoxification have been noted to be reversible (Goodwin, 1989). A diagnosis of dementia associated with alcoholism is made if the criteria in Table 26.5 are met. Even though intelligence quotient scores do not appear to be significantly lowered with heavy alcohol use, there may be functional impairment in perceptual-motor tasks,

Table 26.5. Diagnostic Criteria for Dementia Associated with Alcoholism

A. Dementia following prolonged, heavy ingestion of alcohol and persisting at least 3 weeks after cessation of alcohol ingestion.

B. Exclusion, by history, physical examination, and laboratory tests, of all causes of dementia other than prolonged heavy use of alcohol.

Reprinted with permission from the *Diagnostic and Statistical Manual of Mental Disorders. Third Edition, Revised.* Copyright 1987 American Psychiatric Association.

nonverbal abstraction, and problem solving that varies directly with the amount of alcohol intake (West, 1984).

Withdrawal Effects

The term "uncomplicated alcohol withdrawal" (Table 26.6) refers to withdrawal symptoms that are unaccompanied by delirium. The most common withdrawal symptom is tremulousness, which usually occurs a few hours after cessation of drinking. Irritability, delusions, and insomnia are common. If transitory hallucinations occur, they usually begin 12 to 24 hours after drinking stops.

Alcohol Withdrawal Delirium

Alcohol withdrawal delirium refers to a more serious manifestation of the withdrawal syndrome associated with marked autonomic hyperactivity, delirium, and frequently intercurrent medical illness (Table 26.7). For a diagnosis of alcohol withdrawal delirium, gross memory disturbance should be present, in addition to other withdrawal symptoms, such as agitation and vivid hallucinations. Classically, the delirium begins 2 or 3 days after drinking stops. The physician should be alert to medical illness, such as hepatic decompensation, pneumonia, subdural hematoma, pancreatitis, and fractures during the presence of a delirium.

Chronic Alcoholic Hallucinosis

Chronic alcoholic hallucinosis (Table 26.8) refers to the persistence of hallucinations, usually auditory, for long periods after other abstinence symptoms subside and after the patient has stopped heavy drinking. Chronic alcoholic hallucinosis is a rare disorder. After 75 years of debate concerning its etiology, whether drinking actually produces the condition has not been resolved.

Table 26.6. Diagnostic Criteria for Uncomplicated Alcohol Withdrawal

A. Cessation of prolonged (several days or longer) heavy ingestion of alcohol or reduction in the amount of alcohol ingested, followed within several hours by coarse tremor of hands, tongue, or eyelids, and at least one of the following:
1. nausea or vomiting
2. malaise or weakness
3. autonomic hyperactivity (e.g., tachycardia, sweating, elevated blood pressure)
4. anxiety
5. depressed mood or irritability
6. transient hallucinations or illusions
7. headache
8. insomnia

B. Not due to any physical or other mental disorder, such as alcohol withdrawal delirium.

Reprinted with permission from the *Diagnostic and Statistical Manual of Mental Disorders. Third Edition, Revised.* Copyright 1987 American Psychiatric Association.

Suicide

Suicide is an important psychiatric complication of alcoholism. Hirschfeld and Davidson (1988) report the risk of suicide among alcoholics as about 15%; additional risk factors for suicide among alcoholics include being male, divorced or widowed, a history of prior suicide attempt, recent job changes, and disruption of a close interpersonal relationship.

Social Complications

Accidents and Violence

The consumption of alcohol substantially increases the chances of death or injury in accidents. West (1984) estimates that about 70% of deaths as a result of falls, 83% of deaths by fire, and 50% to 69% of drownings in the United States are related to drinking alcohol on the part of the victims. He further concludes that alcohol intoxication is involved in 65% of child abuse cases, 70% of serious assaults, 80% of homicides, 50% of forcible rapes, and 72% of robberies annually.

Motor Vehicle Accidents

Motor vehicle accidents involving drunken drivers costs the nation more than $5 billion annually. It has been reported that individuals with drinking problems comprise 48% of drivers responsible for their own fatal injuries, 41% of those who survived but were responsible for another's fatality, and 31% of those who fatally injured a pedestrian (West, 1984).

Table 26.7. Diagnostic Criteria for Alcohol Withdrawal Delirium

A. Delirium developing after cessation of heavy alcohol ingestion or a reduction in the amount of alcohol ingested (usually within 1 week).

B. Marked autonomic hyperactivity (e.g., tachycardia, sweating).

C. Not due to any physical or other mental disorder.

Reprinted with permission from the *Diagnostic and Statistical Manual of Mental Disorders. Third Edition, Revised.* Copyright 1987 American Psychiatric Association.

Table 26.8. Diagnostic Criteria for Alcohol Hallucinosis

A. Organic hallucinosis with vivid and persistent hallucinations (auditory or visual) developing shortly (usually within 48 hours) after cessation of or reduction in heavy ingestion of alcohol in a person who apparently has alcohol dependence.

B. No delirium as in alcohol withdrawal delirium.

C. Not due to any physical or other mental disorder.

Reprinted with permission from the *Diagnostic and Statistical Manual of Mental Disorders. Third Edition, Revised.* Copyright 1987 American Psychiatric Association.

DIFFERENTIAL DIAGNOSIS

Each alcoholic patient should have a good psychiatric and developmental history — corroborated by family members — a mental status examination, and a physical examination, including a neurological evaluation. Alcoholics are at increased risk for a wide range of psychiatric and medical conditions, including hypoglycemia (Freinkel & Arky, 1966), a subdural hematoma, or infectious diseases. Excessive use of alcohol may produce a wide range of psychiatric symptoms that simulate other psychiatric disorders. Schuckit (1983) has cautioned that the alcoholic can present with symptoms *resembling* major affective disorders, schizophrenia, organic mental disorders, and primary drug abuse. Moreover, heavy alcohol intake can exacerbate the symptoms of other primary psychiatric syndromes, including the primary affective disorders, schizophrenia, and antisocial personality. The prudent clinician refrains from making an additional psychiatric diagnosis while the patient is drinking heavily or is in the process of alcohol withdrawal.

The concept of dual diagnoses, that is, alcoholics who have a coexisting psychiatric diagnosis, has received recent emphasis. Guze et al. (1986) found, in their comparison of female alcoholics versus nonalcoholic probands from a psychiatric clinic, that the alcoholism was significantly associated with secondary depression (60% vs. 24.7%), Briquet's syndrome (37.8% vs. 18.3%), antisocial personality (17.8% vs. 4.3%), and drug dependence (17.8% vs. 2.5%). Similarly, alcoholism in the male probands was significantly associated with secondary depression (52.1% vs. 20%), secondary mania (4.2% vs. 0.0%), and antisocial personality (25.4% vs. 12.4%). Penick, Powell, Liskow, Jackson, and Nickel (1988) found at the intake hospitalization of 241 male veteran alcoholics that 43.7% were positive for alcoholism only, 30% for alcoholism and one additional psychiatric syndrome, 17.6% for alcoholism and two additional syndromes, and 8.8% for alcoholism and three or more additional syndromes. At follow-up one year later, 51.7% were positive for alcoholism only, 26.7% for alcoholism and one additional psychiatric syndrome, 13.2% for alcoholism and two additional syndromes, and 8.3% for alcoholism and three or more additional syndromes.

Helzer and Pryzbeck (1988) examined the comorbidity between alcohol abuse and dependence, other substances of abuse and nonsubstance psychiatric disorders in a sample of 20,000 persons drawn from the general population. The strongest degree of association, in descending order, was with antisocial personality (ASP), then with drug abuse/dependence, and finally with mania. More specifically, the diagnosis of ASP was almost four times more common among male alcoholics than in the general population. Women alcoholics were 12 times more likely to carry the additional diagnosis of ASP than were women in the general population. The association between alcoholism and major depression in this study was less striking, but interesting in that male alcoholics were only slightly more likely to have a diagnosis of depression than men in the general population (5% vs. 3%), whereas female alcoholics had a 19% chance of receiving the diagnosis of depression compared to 7% of women in general.

Critics of the dual diagnosis argue that these studies have not been conducted on alcohol-free patients. That is, only in alcoholics who have abstained from alcohol for a period of time can possible coexisting psychiatric disorders be diagnosed because many of the associated signs and symptoms lessen or resolve with several weeks or months of abstinence. Brown and Schuckit (1988), for example, found that 42% of primary male alcoholics entering inpatient treatment appeared significantly depressed by a Hamilton rating (≥ 20). Only 6% of these patients remained depressed after four weeks of abstinence. Longitudinal studies are needed following a period of abstinence to separate the factors involved in this issue of psychiatric comorbidity in the alcoholic patient.

CASE EXAMPLES

Case 1

The natural history of alcoholism may vary depending upon the sex, family history, and culture of the individual. Some alcoholics, females to a larger degree than males, may have their diagnosis and treatment complicated by also suffering from an affective disorder.

The 53-year-old wife of a business executive learned that her husband was having an affair. Formerly, she was a moderate-to-light social drinker. Now, she began drinking early in the daytime, wine at first and later vodka. Her personal appearance and housework were neglected. She made numerous tipsy calls to family and friends, causing a great deal of embarrassment for the family. When her husband agreed to abandon the mistress, she forgave him, but their relationship continued to deteriorate.

At first she successfully hid her drinking, but the husband found empty bottles in the trash and full ones concealed in closets and drawers. He consulted a physician who referred them to a marriage therapist. While the drinking problem quickly emerged, so did the history of depressive symptoms. Abstinence became a condition for therapy. The drinking stopped, but her depressive symptoms persisted. Her family history was strongly positive for mood disorders, and, as a college senior, she had missed a semester because of depression. She was referred to a psychiatrist, who successfully treated the depression with supportive psychotherapy and medication. At follow-up her marital problems were much improved and her drinking consisted of an occasional glass of wine.

Case 2

Alcohol is one of the few psychoactive drugs that can produce classical amnesia. Nonalcoholics, when drinking, may also experience this amnesia but much less often than do alcoholics. Goodwin (1989) notes that these periods of amnesia or blackouts are particularly distressing to alcoholics, because they may fear that while intoxicated they have unknowingly harmed someone or behaved imprudently.

A 53-year-old vice president of a large corporation became distressed by a recent divorce and separation from his family. He fell into a pattern of having increasingly longer lunch hours. Time spent in a bar sitting in pensive silence or chatting with other customers increased. Previously a two-martini lunchtime drinker, his intake increased to four or five martinis followed by wine with his lunch. He developed a high tolerance for alcohol and could return to his office without seeming intoxicated.

On a Friday afternoon, following one of these "lunch" episodes he did not make it back to the office. Instead, he awoke the next morning in his own bed but with no recollection of events for the preceding day. He was frightened. Where had he been? What had he done? How did he get home? Where was his car? He became panicked by the prospect that he had harmed someone, perhaps in a car accident. He walked out to the garage. He

found his car. He checked to see whether there were dents. There were none. He was relieved but still uneasy. He continued to feel guilty that he had committed some terrible crime that he could not remember.

Later the bartender informed him that he had drunk steadily through the afternoon but did not seem intoxicated when he left the bar in the late afternoon with a woman. His memory remained a blank. He was so shaken by the experience that he swore off alcohol. Several years later at follow-up, he was still abstinent.

Case 3

Patterns of drinking are variable, and no one particular pattern is exclusively associated with alcoholism. But with heavy drinking withdrawal symptoms are predictable with discontinuation. The following is an example of uncomplicated alcohol withdrawal.

A 30-year-old newspaper reporter started drinking with friends one evening after work and continued to drink through the evening, falling asleep in the early morning hours. On awakening, he had a strong desire to drink again and decided not to go to work. Food did not appeal to him, and instead, he had several Bloody Marys. Later, he went to a local tavern and drank beer through the afternoon. He met some friends and continued drinking into the evening.

The pattern of drinking through the day persisted for the next 7 days. On the eighth morning, he tried to drink a morning cup of coffee and found that his hands were shaking so violently he could not get the cup to his mouth. He managed to pour some whiskey into a glass and drank as much as he could. His hands became less shaky, but now he was nauseated and began having dry heaves. He felt ill and intensely anxious and decided to call a doctor friend. The doctor recommended hospitalization.

On admission, the patient had a marked resting and exertional tremor of the hands, and his tongue and eyelids were tremulous. He also had feelings of internal tremulousness. Lying in the hospital bed, he found the noises outside his window unbearably loud and began seeing visions of animals and, on one occasion, a dead relative. He was terrified and called a nurse, who gave him a tranquilizer. He became quieter, and his tremor was less pronounced. At all times, he realized that the visual phenomena were imaginary. He always knew where he was and was oriented otherwise. After a few days, the tremor disappeared, and he no long hallucinated. He still had trouble sleeping, but otherwise felt back to normal and vowed never to drink again (Goodwin & Guze, 1989, pp. 188–189).

Case 4

One of the most striking cases observed in medicine is a patient suffering from the amnestic syndrome due to chronic alcoholism and thiamine deficiency.

A 48-year-old divorced housepainter is admitted with a history of 30 years of heavy drinking. He had two previous admissions for detoxification, but the family states that he has not had a drink in several weeks and shows no sign of alcohol withdrawal. He looks malnourished, however, and, on examination, is found to be ataxic and to have a bilateral sixth cranial nerve palsy. He appears confused and mistakes one of the physicians for a dead uncle.

Within a week, the patient walks normally, and there is no sign of a sixth nerve palsy. He seems less confused and can now find his way to the bathroom without direction. He remembers the names and birthdays of his siblings, but has difficulty naming the past five presidents.

More strikingly, he has great difficulty in retaining information for longer than a few minutes. He can repeat back a list of numbers immediately after he has heard them, but a few minutes later, he does not recall being asked to perform the task. Shown three objects—keys, comb, and ring—he cannot recall them 3 minutes later. He does not seem worried about this lack of recall. Asked if he can recall the name of his doctor, he replies, "certainly," and proceeds to call the doctor "Dr. Masters" (not his name), whom he claims he first met in the Korean War. He tells a long untrue story about how he and "Dr. Masters" served as fellow soldiers in the Korean War.

The patient is calm, alert, friendly. One could be with him a short period and not realize he has a severe memory impairment because of his intact immediate memory and spotty, but sometimes impressive, remote memory. Thus, his amnesia is largely anterograde. Although high doses of thiamine are used in his treatment, his short-term memory deficit persists and appears to be irreversible (Goodwin & Guze, 1989, pp. 186–187).

CHILDHOOD AND FAMILIAL ANTECEDENTS

Adolescent Drinking

Two important studies give estimates of alcohol use in adolescence. The University of Michigan's Institute for Social Research published the results of surveys of high school seniors from 1975 to 1988 on the topic of substance use for 11 classes of drugs, including alcohol (Johnston, O'Malley, & Bachman, 1988). The recent 1988 survey yielded important results concerning alcohol use among high school students. The proportion of students having five or more drinks in a row during the prior two weeks declined significantly from 38% to 35%. This is down from a high of 41% in 1983. Daily use of alcohol declined from a peak of 5.9% in 1979 to 4.8% in 1984, with no further decline through 1987. The other comprehensive survey of U.S. teenagers' drinking behavior was collected by members of the Research Triangle Institute. The survey was based on a nationwide probability sample of all junior and senior high school students in 48 states and the District of Columbia (Rachal et al., 1980). Their definition of problem drinking included frequency of drunkenness (four or more times in the past year) and reported negative consequences in two or more life areas (friends, school, dates, police, family, and driving). According to this definition of problem drinking, 27% of 13,122 students were problem drinkers. Donovan, Jessor, and Jessor (1983) note that little is actually known about the continuity of problem drinking between adolescence and adulthood. In their longitudinal study, they found that of the 1972–1973 adolescent problem drinkers, 53% of the high school sample men, and 70% of the high school sample women were nonproblem drinkers in 1979 at follow-up.

Children and adolescents with alcoholic first-degree relatives are at increased risk for developing alcoholism. Of course, members of a family share a common environment as well as common genes. While the evidence is accumulating for the genetic factors (Family Studies and Biological Markers in DSM-III-R), environmental factors must be considered in the etiology of alcoholism. Niven (1984) indicates that some family studies have shown that at least 45% of the alcoholic subjects did *not* have an alcoholic parent or other relative. Thus, for children and adolescents, certain environmental factors may influence the expression and severity of alcohol dependence. It is difficult to determine the relative contribution of hereditary or environmental factors, and the familial studies thus far cannot explain the absence of alcoholism in some offspring of alcoholics.

Family Studies

Goodwin and Guze (1989) have summarized the historical development of family studies related to alcoholism.

> Every family study of alcoholism regardless of country of origin has shown much higher rates of alcoholism among the relatives of alcoholics than in the general population. According to a number of studies, about 25 percent of fathers and brothers of alcoholics are themselves alcoholics (Cotton, 1979; Goodwin, 1981).
>
> Not everything that runs in families is inherited, however. Speaking French, for example, runs in families and is not inherited. How does one separate nature from nurture in familial illnesses?
>
> Two methods are used in psychiatric research. One is to compare identical and fraternal twins. If identical twins are more often concordant for alcoholism than fraternal twins, this would point to a genetic influence. Another way is to study adopted persons who have alcoholism in the biological family but not in the family of upbringing. Both approaches have been applied to alcoholism. Here, briefly, are the results.
>
> **Twin Studies.** A Swedish investigator (Kaij, 1960) found that identical twins were significantly more concordant for alcoholism than were fraternal twins, the more severe the alcoholism the greater the difference. . . . A [second] study, in England (Murray, Clifford, & Gurlin, 1983), showed no difference between identical and fraternal twins. The most recent study (Hrubec & Omenn, 1981) involved analyzing a large number of Veterans Administration records. The results supported a genetic factor; identical twins were more often concordant for alcoholism than fraternal twins. . . .
>
> **Adoption Studies.** The first adoption study of alcoholism was published in 1944 (Roe, 1944). It showed no difference in drinking behavior between children of alcoholics and children of nonalcoholics, both in their early twenties. The sample size was small and no criteria were presented for the diagnosis of alcoholism. It was not clear whether the biological parents were alcoholic by today's definition.
>
> A small flurry of adoption studies began in the early 1970s, ushered in by a study comparing adult half-siblings of alcoholics with adult full-siblings (Schuckit, Goodwin, & Winokur, 1972). The assumption behind the study was that if genetic factors were important, full-siblings would more often be alcoholic than half-siblings. This

did not prove to be the case. However, the study did find that half-siblings, predictably, were from broken families, and this afforded the opportunity to compare the incidence of alcoholism in offspring with alcoholism in biological parents and in parents of upbringing. Having a biological father who was alcoholic was highly correlated with alcoholism in the sons, but there was no correlation with alcoholism in the surrogate fathers. The study, in short, failed to prove its central hypothesis but ended up as a kind of adoption study suggesting that biological factors were more important than environmental factors in producing alcohol problems.

> In the decade after the half-sibling study, the results from three separate adoption studies in Denmark, Sweden, and the United States (Iowa) were published (Bohman, 1978; Cadoret & Gath, 1978; Goodwin, Schulsinger, Hermansen, Guze, & Winokur, 1973). The studies produced remarkably similar findings: (1) sons of alcoholics were three to four times more likely to be alcoholic than were sons of nonalcoholics, whether raised by their alcoholic biological parents or by nonalcoholic adoptive parents; (2) sons of alcoholics were no more susceptible to nonalcoholic adult psychiatric disturbances (e.g., depression, sociopathy) than were sons of nonalcoholics where both groups were raised by nonalcoholic adoptive parents. The Iowa study (Cadoret & Gath, 1978; Cadoret, Cain, & Grove, 1979) did find a higher rate of childhood conduct disorder in the male offspring of alcoholics, an association later supported by several studies that have documented a history of hyperactive syndrome or conduct disorder in the childhood of alcoholics (Goodwin, Schulsinger, Hermansen, Guze, & Winokur, 1975).
>
> The results regarding female alcoholism were more equivocal. In the Danish study (Goodwin, Schulsinger, Knop, Mednick, & Guze, 1977), 4 percent of the daughters of alcoholics were alcoholics, but so were 4 percent of the control women, introducing the possibility that adoption could contribute to alcoholism. A low rate of alcoholism in the adopted-out daughters of alcoholics was found in the Swedish study (Bohman, 1978; Bohman, Sigvardsson, & Cloninger, 1981), although subsequent analysis revealed a correspondence between alcoholism in the biological mothers and alcoholism in the adopted-out daughters (Cloninger, Bohman, & Sigvardsson, 1981). (pp. 190–192)

Biological Markers

In light of the evidence that alcoholism is a familial disorder, investigators are searching for biological markers suggestive of genetic influences. Several lines of neurophysiological investigation indicate significant differences between high-risk subjects with a family history of alcoholism and low-risk individuals. Utilizing various cognitive paradigms, the amplitude of the late positive component (P3) of the event-related potential (ERP) was found to be significantly reduced in abstinent alcoholics compared to controls (Begleiter, Porjesz, & Tenner, 1980; Porjesz, Begleiter, Bihari, & Kissin, 1987). ERPs are computer-averaged brain waves measuring electrophysiological reactions to stimuli. The amplitude deficits in the P3 voltage of the ERP were observed not only in chronic alcoholics abstinent for two to five years, but the low-voltage pattern was also found to be present in young nondrinking sons of alcoholics. Thus, it appears that the deficits in P3 voltage of the ERP may antecede the onset of chronic alcohol abuse and may be present in males at high risk for alcoholism (Begleiter, Porjesz, Bihari, & Kissin, 1984). These results have been replicated in different laboratories (O'Conner, Hesselbrock, Tasman, & DePalma, 1987; Steinhauer, Hill, & Zubin, 1987).

Other lines of investigation that show promise of potential biological markers for a predisposition to alcoholism involve the resting state electroencephalographic (EEG) activity. Male alcoholics demonstrate excessive high-frequency EEG activity and appear deficient in levels of slow waves. In one study children of alcoholics manifested excessive fast EEG activity compared to male controls (Gabrielli et al., 1982). Further investigation revealed that sons of alcoholics showed greater increases of slow-wave activity and greater decreases of fast-wave activity after alcohol ingestion than did control subjects (Pollock et al., 1983).

Studies of monoamine oxidase (MAO), an enzyme involved in the degradation of central nervous system neurotransmitters, have yielded interesting results. While several studies have reported low MAO levels, measured in blood platelets, in alcoholics compared to controls (Major & Murphy, 1978; Wiberg, Gottfries, & Oreland, 1977), the finding may be specific for a certain subclassification of alcoholics. Some investigators (von Knorring, Bohman, von Knorring, & Oreland, 1985) have found that platelet MAO levels were significantly lower in the Type II alcoholics as compared to the Type I. Von Knorring et al. (1985) describe Type I alcoholism as characterized by the onset of heavy drinking after the age of 25 years with no signs of social complications such as violence while intoxicated or legal difficulties. Type II alcoholism has an onset before the age of 25 years, with at least two instances of social complications such as violence while intoxicated, legal difficulties, or family conflicts because of exces-

sive alcohol abuse. Note the similarity of the Type I and Type II alcoholics as described by Cloninger (1987). (See the Natural History section of DSM-III-R.) It is quite exciting to speculate on the research in this field. As this disease becomes deciphered, more specific statements can be made regarding biological markers, prognosis, treatment, and perhaps preventive measures.

SUMMARY

Alcoholism is a disease with medical, social, occupational, psychological, and legal consequences. The disease has a natural history with manifest complications that reflect the interactions of predisposing biological and behavioral factors in conjunction with environmental precipitating factors (Begleiter & Porjesz, 1988). The differential diagnosis can be complicated by the fact that long-term excessive use of alcohol may produce a host of psychiatric symptoms that may simulate a variety of psychiatric disorders. In turn, heavy alcohol intake can exacerbate the symptoms of primary psychiatric syndromes. Armed with the evidence that alcoholism is a familial disorder, investigators are presently vigorously searching for biological markers to decipher the possible etiologies of the disorder of alcoholism.

REFERENCES

American Psychiatric Association. (1980). *Diagnostic and statistical manual of mental disorders* (3rd ed.). Washington, DC: Author.

American Psychiatric Association. (1987). *Diagnostic and statistical manual of mental disorders* (3rd ed. rev.). Washington, DC: Author.

Bales, R. F. (1946). Cultural differences in rates of alcoholism. *Quarterly Journal on Studies of Alcohol, 5*, 480.

Begleiter, H., & Porjesz, B. (1988). Potential biological markers in individuals at high risk for developing alcoholism. *Alcoholism: Clinical and Experimental Research, 12*, 488–493.

Begleiter, H., Porjesz, B., Bihari, B., & Kissin, B. (1984). Event-related brain potentials in boys at risk for alcoholism. *Science, 225*, 1493–1496.

Begleiter, H., Porjesz, B., & Tenner, M. (1980). Neuroradiological and neurophysiological evidence of brain deficits in chronic alcoholics. *Acta Psychiatrica Scandanavia, 62*(Suppl. 286), 3–13.

Block, J. (1971). *Lives through time.* Berkeley, CA: Bancroft Books.

Bohman, M. (1978). Some genetic aspects of alcoholism and criminality: A population of adoptees. *Archives of General Psychiatry, 35,* 269–276.

Bohman, M., Sigvardsson, S., & Cloninger, R. (1981). Maternal inheritance of alcohol abuse: Cross-fostering analysis of adopted women. *Archives of General Psychiatry, 38,* 965–969.

Brown, S. A., & Schuckit, M. A. (1988). Changes in depression among abstinent alcoholics. *Journal of Studies on Alcohol, 49,* 412–417.

Cadoret, R. J., Cain, C. A., & Grove, W. M. (1979). Development of alcoholism in adoptees raised apart from alcoholic biologic relatives. *Archives of General Psychiatry, 37,* 561–563.

Cadoret, R. J., & Gath, A. (1978). Inheritance of alcoholism in adoptees. *British Journal of Psychiatry, 132,* 252–258.

Cahalan, D., Cisin, I. H., & Crossley, W. M. (1969). American drinking practices: A national survey of behavior and attitudes. *Monograph No. 6.* New Brunswick, NJ: Rutgers University Center of Alcohol Studies.

Cloninger, C. R. (1987). Neurogenic adaptive mechanisms in alcoholism. *Science, 236,* 410–416.

Cloninger, C. R., Bohman, M., & Sigvardsson, S. (1981). Inheritance of alcohol abuse: Cross-fostering analysis of adopted men. *Archives of General Psychiatry, 36,* 861–868.

Cloninger, C. R., Sigvardsson, S., & Bohman, M. (1988). Childhood personality predicts alcohol abuse in young adults. *Alcoholism: Clinical and Experimental Research, 12,* 494–505.

Cotton, N. S. (1979). The familial incidence of alcoholism: A review. *Journal of Studies on Alcoholism, 40,* 89–116.

Donovan, J. E., Jessor, R., & Jessor, L. (1983). Problem drinking in adolescence and young adulthood: A follow-up study. *Journal of Studies on Alcoholism, 44,* 109–137.

Dozier, E. P. (1966). Problem drinking among American Indians: The role of socio-cultural deprivation. *Quarterly Journal of Studies on Alcohol, 27,* 72–87.

Drew, L. R. H. (1968). Alcoholism as a self-limiting disease. *Quarterly Journal of Studies on Alcohol, 29,* 956–967.

Ferrence, R. G. (1980). Sex differences in the prevalence of problem drinking. In O. J. Kalant (Ed.), *Research advances in alcohol and drug problems* (Vol. 5, pp. 125–201). New York: Plenum Press.

Freinkel, N., & Arky, R. A. (1966). Effects of alcohol on carbohydrate metabolism in man. *Psychosomatic Medicine, 28,* 551–563.

Gabrielli, W. F., Mednick, S. A., Volavka, J., Pollock, V. E., Schulsinger, F., & Itil, T. M. (1982). Electroencephalograms in children of alcoholic fathers. *Psychophysiology, 19,* 404–407.

Goodwin, D. W. (1971). Blackouts and alcohol-induced memory dysfunction. In N. K. Mellow & J. H. Mendelson (Eds.), *Recent advances in studies of alcoholism: An interdisciplinary symposium* (pp. 508–536). Washington, DC: U.S. Department of Health, Education, and Welfare.

Goodwin, D. W. (1981). *Alcoholism: The facts.* New York: Oxford University Press.

Goodwin, D. W. (1989). Alcoholism. In H. I. Kaplan & B. J. Sadock (Eds.), *Comprehensive textbook of psychiatry* (5th ed.). Baltimore: Williams & Wilkins.

Goodwin, D. W., & Guze, S. B. (1989). *Psychiatric diagnosis* (4th ed.). New York: Oxford University Press.

Goodwin, D. W., Schulsinger, F., Hermansen, L., Guze, S. B., & Winokur, G. (1973). Alcohol problems in adoptees raised apart from alcoholic biological parents. *Archives of General Psychiatry, 28,* 238–242.

Goodwin, D. W., Schulsinger, F., Hermansen, L., Guze, S. B., & Winokur, G. (1975). Alcoholism and the hyperactive child syndrome. *Journal of Nervous and Mental Disorders, 160,* 349–353.

Goodwin, D. W., Schulsinger, F., Knop, J., Mednick, S., & Guze, S. B. (1977). Alcoholism and depression in adopted-out daughters of alcoholics. *Archives of General Psychiatry, 34,* 751–755.

Guze, S. B. (1976). *Criminality and psychiatric disorders.* New York: Oxford University Press.

Guze, S. B., Cloninger, C. R., Martin, R., & Clayton, P. (1986). Alcoholism as a medical disorder. *Comprehensive Psychiatry, 27,* 501–510.

Haver, B. (1986). Female alcoholics: I. Psychosocial outcome six years after treatment. *Acta Psychiatrica Scandinavica, 74,* 102–111.

Helzer, J. E., & Pryzbeck, T. R. (1988). The co-occurrence of alcoholism with other psychiatric disorders in the general population and its impact on treatment. *Journal of Studies on Alcoholism, 49*, 219–224.

Hirschfeld, R. M. A., & Davidson, L. (1988). Clinical risk factors for suicide. *Psychiatric Annals, 18*, 628–635.

Holt, S., Skinner, H. A., & Israel, Y. (1981). Early identification of alcohol abuse: II. Clinical and laboratory indicators. *Canadian Medical Association Journal, 124*, 1279–1295.

Hrubec, Z., & Omenn, G. S. (1981). Evidence of genetic predisposition to alcoholic cirrhosis and psychosis: Twin concordances for alcoholism and its biological end points by zygosity among male veterans. *Alcoholism: Clinical Experimental Research, 5*, 207–215.

Johnston, L. D., O'Malley, P. M., & Bachman, J. G. (1988). *Illicit drug use, smoking, and drinking by America's high school students, college students, and young adults, 1975–1987.* (National Institute on Drug Abuse, DHHS Publication No. ADM 89-1602). Washington, DC: U.S. Government Printing Office.

Kaij, L. (1960). *Studies on the etiology and sequels of abuse of alcohol.* Lund, Sweden: University of Lund.

Knop, J., Teasdale, T. W., Schulsinger, R., & Goodwin, D. W. (1985). A prospective study of young men at high risk for alcoholism: School behavior and achievement. *Journal of Studies on Alcohol, 46*, 273–278.

Korsten, M. A., & Lieber, C. S. (1985). Medical complications of alcoholism. In J. H. Mendelson & N. K. Mills (Eds.), *The diagnosis and treatment of alcoholism* (2nd ed., pp. 21–64). New York: McGraw-Hill.

Leland, J. (1976). *Firewater myths.* New Brunswick, NJ: Rutgers University Center of Alcohol Studies.

Lieber, C. S. (1968). Metabolic effects produced by alcohol in the liver and other tissues. *Advances in Internal Medicine, 14*, 151–199.

Lint, J. de, & Schmidt, W. (1971). The epidemiology of alcoholism. In Y. Israel & J. Mardones (Eds.), *Biological basis of alcoholism* (pp. 423–442). Toronto: Wiley-Interscience.

Liskow, B., & Goodwin, D. W. (1986). Alcoholism. In G. Winokur & P. Clayton (Eds.), *The medical basis of psychiatry* (pp. 190–211). Philadelphia: W. B. Saunders.

Lolli, G., Serianni, E., Golder, G. M., & Luzzatto-Fegiz, P. (1958). *Alcohol in Italian culture.* Monograph No. 3, Yale Center of Alcohol Studies. Glencoe, IL: Free Press.

Maddox, G. L., & Williams, J. R. (1968). Drinking behavior of Negro collegians. *Quarterly Journal of Studies on Alcohol, 29*, 117–129.

Major, L. F., & Murphy, D. L. (1978). Platelet and plasma amine oxidase activity in alcoholic individuals. *British Journal of Psychiatry, 132*, 548–554.

Martin, C., & Casswell, S. (1988). Types of female alcoholics: A multivariate study. *Journal of Studies on Alcohol, 49*, 273–280.

Mayfield, D. G. (1968). Psychopathology of alcohol: I. Affective charge with intoxication. *Journal of Nervous and Mental Disease, 146*, 314–321.

Mendelson, J. H., Babor, T. F., Mello, N. K., & Pratt, H. (1986). Alcoholism and prevalence of medical and psychiatric disorders. *Journal of Studies on Alcoholism, 47*, 361–366.

Murray, R. M., Clifford, C., & Gurlin, H. M. (1983). Twin and alcoholism studies. In M. Galanter (Ed.), *Recent developments in alcoholism* (pp. 25–46). New York: Gardner Press.

Niven, R. G. (1984). Alcohol in the family. In L. J. West (Ed.), *Alcoholism and related problems* (pp. 91–109). Englewood Cliffs, NJ: Prentice Hall.

O'Conner, S., Hesselbrock, V., Tasman, A., & DePalma, N. (1987). P3 amplitudes in two distinct tasks are decreased in young men with a history of paternal alcoholism. *Alcohol, 4*, 323–330.

Pemberton, D. A. (1967). A comparison of the outcome of treatment in female and male alcoholics. *British Journal of Psychiatry, 113*, 367–373.

Penick, E. C., Powell, B. J., Liskow, B. I., Jackson, J. O., & Nickel, E. (1988). The stability of coexisting psychiatric syndromes in alcoholic men after one year. *Journal of Studies on Alcohol, 49*, 395–405.

Pollock, V. E., Volavka, J., Goodwin, D. W., Mednick, S. A., Gabrielli, W. F., Knop, J., & Schulsinger, F. (1983). The EEG after alcohol administration in men at risk for alcoholism. *Archives of General Psychiatry, 40*, 857–861.

Popham, R. E. (1970). Indirect methods of alcoholism prevalence estimation: A critical evaluation. In R. E. Popham (Ed.), *Alcohol and alcoholism* (pp. 294–306). Toronto: University of Toronto Press.

Porjesz, B., Begleiter, H., Bihari, B., & Kissin, B. (1987). Event-related brain potentials to high incentive stimuli in abstinent alcoholics. *Alcohol, 4*, 274–283.

Rachal, J. V., Guess, L. S., Hubbard, R. L., Maisto, S. A., Cavanaugh, E. R., Waddell, R., & Benrud, C. H. (1980). *Adolescent drinking behavior: 1. The extent and nature of adolescent alcohol and drug use, 1974 and 1978 national sample studies*. Research Triangle Park, NC: Research Triangle Institute.

Robins, L. N. (1966). *Deviant children grown up: A sociological & psychiatric study of sociopathic personality*. Baltimore: Williams & Wilkins.

Robins, L. N., Helzer, J. E., Weissman, M. M., Orvaschel, H., Gruenber, E., Burke, J. D., & Regier, D. A. (1984). Lifetime prevalence of specific psychiatric disorders in three sites. *Archives of General Psychiatry, 41*, 949–958.

Robins, L. N., Murphy, G. E., & Breckenridge, M. B. (1968). Drinking behavior of young negro men. *Quarterly Journal of Studies on Alcohol, 29*, 657–684.

Roe, A. (1944). The adult adjustment of children of alcoholic parents raised in foster homes. *Quarterly Journal of Studies on Alcohol, 5*, 378–393.

Sadoun, R., Lolli, G., & Silverman, M. (1965). *Drinking in French culture*. Monographs of the Rutgers Center of Alcohol Studies, 5. New Haven, CT: Yale College and University Press.

Schuckit, M. A. (1983). Alcoholism and other psychiatric disorders. *Hospital and Community Psychiatry, 34*, 1022–1027.

Schuckit, M. A. (1985). Treatment of alcoholism in office and outpatient settings. In J. H. Mendelson & N. K. Mello (Eds.), *The diagnosis and treatment of alcoholism* (pp. 295–324). New York: McGraw-Hill.

Schuckit, M. A., Goodwin, D. W., & Winokur, G. (1972). A study of alcoholism in half-siblings. *American Journal of Psychiatry, 128*, 1132–1136.

Schuckit, M., Pitts, F. N., Jr., Reich, T., King, L. J., & Winokur, G. (1969). Alcoholism. *Archives of Environmental Health, 18*, 301–306.

Steinhauer, S., Hill, S. Y., & Zubin, J. (1987). Event related potentials in alcoholics and their first degree relatives. *Alcohol, 4*, 307–314.

U.S. Government. (1985). *Public Health Reports, 101*, 593–598.

Vaillant, G. E. (1983). Natural history of male alcoholism: V. Is alcoholism the cart or the horse to sociopathy? *British Journal of Addiction, 78*, 317–326.

Knorring, A. L. von, Bohman, M., Knorring, L. von, & Oreland, L. (1985). Platelet MAO activity as a biological marker in subgroups of alcoholism. *Acta Psychiatrica Scandinavica, 72*, 51–58.

Wallgren, H., & Barry, H. (1970). *Actions of alcohol* (Vol. I). Amsterdam: Elsiever.

West, L. J. (1984). Alcoholism and related problems: An overview. In L. J. West (Ed.), *Alcoholism and related problems: Issues for the American public* (pp. 1–26). Englewood Cliffs, NJ: Prentice Hall.

Wiberg, A., Gottfries, C. G., & Oreland, L. (1977). Low platelet monoamine oxidase activity in human alcoholics. *Medical Biology, 55*, 181–186.

OBESITY

EDITORS' COMMENTS

Obesity in the adult population has been a focus of attention for many years. The problem most certainly is widespread, with 10% to 50% of the population defined as overweight, depending upon the criteria used. In recent years, much of the focus in this area has shifted to children. Meyers, Klesges, and Bene, in Chapter 27, note that this shift to children is due to the intractability of the adult obese; it is hoped that greater success will be achieved with modifying the problem in youngsters.

There is clearly a relationship between childhood and adulthood obesity, with obese youngsters showing a greatly increased risk of becoming obese adults. In fact, nearly three quarters of obese children will become obese adults.

Perhaps the most serious complications arising from obesity are the associated medical problems that may result in increased mortality. In addition to significant health problems, the social stigma and negative psychosocial consequences that result can be psychologically devastating.

The clinical presentation of obesity in children and adults is quite similar, in terms of dietary intake, lack of exercise, and absence of additional psychopathology. By contrast, however, the obese adult generally is more concerned than the obese child about dieting and weight loss.

Family studies have indicated that obesity runs in families, although such studies, obviously, are not capable of separating the environmental from the genetic influences. Genetic studies, including twin and adoptee investigations, support the hypothesis that there is a genetic component involved in the transmission of obesity. However, what is inherited (i.e., body size, number of fat cells, efficiency of fat storage, metabolism) requires further investigation.

Obesity not infrequently is associated with bulimia, an eating disorder included in DSM-III-R. Therefore, care should be taken to review the clinical criteria for this condition when assessing the obese individual. Moreover, especially among children, attention should be paid to possible endocrine and oncologic problems that have obesity as a consequence or secondary characteristic (e.g., Cushing's syndrome).

CHAPTER 27

OBESITY IN CHILDHOOD

Andrew W. Meyers
Robert C. Klesges
Cheryl R. Bene

In 1967 Richard Stuart reported an impressively successful behavioral treatment of adult obesity. However, since that time, attempts to treat adult obesity have generally been disappointing. Weight losses in adult obesity programs have been small, longer-term maintenance of those losses has been poor, and variability in response to treatment has been great (Brownell & Wadden, 1986). The intractability of adult obesity has served to focus interest on methods for identifying and treating obesity in children.

Theoretically, a concentration on obese children presents health professionals and social scientists with several potential advantages. Parents and caregivers typically have the opportunity and the control to modify child behavior. Developing patterns of food intake and physical activity are more easily influenced (Klesges et al., 1983). Finally, biological factors that presumably contribute to adult weight status may still be in developmental process (Hirsch & Knittle, 1970).

While definitional issues in childhood obesity are complex, there is general agreement that the prevalence of obesity in American children is high and probably increasing (Dietz, 1987). Obesity in

children is consistently related to increases in a number of cardiovascular risk factors, respiratory disease, and accidents. Further, overweight children tend to become overweight adults (Charney, Goodman, McBride, Lyon, & Pratt, 1976).

These factors argue for an increased understanding of childhood obesity and its relation to adult obesity and related health risks. In this chapter we will discuss issues central to this task. We begin with definitional issues surrounding childhood obesity. A review of current evidence on epidemiology, physiological and psychological complications, and differential diagnosis will be followed by a summary of the major causal theories of childhood obesity. The relationship between child and adult obesity and contemporary clinical approaches to obesity in children will be presented. The chapter will conclude with a composite case study that will serve to illustrate the major issues in this area.

DESCRIPTION OF THE DISORDER

Researchers who study children and childhood problems typically view obesity as having a highly desirable outcome variable. That is, "being normal weight" can be agreed upon as the preferable, standard measure of outcome in intervention studies. For assessment and descriptive studies, obesity can presumably be objectively and carefully measured. As a result, the reader may be surprised to learn that there is little consistency in the literature regarding the determination of body weight.

Probably the most commonly used method of evaluating whether or not an adult is obese has been some percentage (usually 20% or more) above "ideal body weight," based on the Metropolitan Life Insurance tables 1959 or 1983 norms. While the use of these norms in adults continues to be hotly debated and criticized (e.g., Schulz, 1986), no norms for children are provided because the Metropolitan Life Insurance Company was most concerned with identifying ideal body weights associated with longevity (Metropolitan Life, 1983, 1959).

However, the concept of using an ideal body weight with children has been employed commonly in the childhood obesity literature. Ideal body weight is usually defined as the statistical average based on height/weight standards (e.g., Department of Health, Education, and Welfare, 1977; Jelliffe, 1966), and obesity is then defined as at least 20% above that level (e.g., Epstein et al., 1988). Defining obesity as present in those who exceed the 75th or 85th percentile of that standard is also regularly used (e.g., Garn & Clark, 1976; Klesges et al., 1983, 1984).

Childhood obesity has also been defined as a derivative of weight and height. Common transformations include the ponderal index (weight/height^3), the body mass, or quetelet, index (weight/height^2), the pirquet index (height^3/weight), and the livi index (weight^3/height). These equations were originally designed as measures that would correlate more highly with body fat in adults (Straw & Rodgers, 1985). To our knowledge, however, no studies have adequately validated these equations in preschool- and school-aged children, so their use (other than for descriptive purposes) in classifying childhood obesity is questionable.

The foregoing methods of quantifying obesity are based on a determination of body weight. There are also a large number of methods of assessing body fat. These include densitometry, hydrostatic testing (underwater weighing), bioelectric impedence, and skinfold calipering (Straw & Rodgers, 1985). Many of the more elaborate, and most reliable, procedures (e.g., hydrostatic testing) have rarely been tested in children, given

their obtrusiveness and potential discomfort (Klesges et al., 1988). By far the most popular, and the method most easily "implemented" with children is an estimate of body fat through the use of skinfold calipers (Straw & Rodgers, 1985). Fortunately, nationally normed data on children are available (DHEW, 1977), but only for triceps skinfold. Both the percentile or percentage above ideal body weight and triceps skinfold should be obtained to present an accurate picture of the obese child.

EPIDEMIOLOGY

Given the large number of methods used to define obesity, the use of different populations, and different assessment methodologies, it may not be surprising to learn that estimates of the prevalence of childhood obesity vary greatly. While it is generally agreed that prevalence rates are higher in girls than in boys and prevalence increases with age, estimates of childhood obesity range from 2% to 32% (Brownell, 1986). In a summary of the literature, Brownell (1986) concluded that actual prevalence was in the 10% to 25% range. Interestingly, the most comprehensive and probably the best conducted study indicates that the prevalence of obesity in children is increasing (Dietz, 1987; Dietz, Gortmaker, & Sobol, 1985). Defining obesity as a triceps skinfold greater than the 85th percentile, Dietz and Gortmaker (1985) assessed children and adolescents participating in cycles II and III of the National Health Examination Survey. Each cycle provided an approximate sample size of 7,000 children representing a good cross section of the United States. Over the 15-year period between cycles, the prevalence of obesity increased by approximately 40% in both children and adolescents.

The prevalence of obesity appears to covary with a number of demographic and family variables. In a comprehensive review of the relationship between socioeconomic status (SES) and obesity, Sobal and Stunkard (1989) reported a strong direct relationship between SES and obesity in both adults and children in developing nations (i.e., as social class increases, obesity increases). In developed countries (e.g., the United States, Canada), there appears to be an inverse relationship between SES and obesity for women. For men, however, a "bimodal distribution" was observed, with roughly half the studies finding a positive and half finding a negative relationship. For children, however, no consistent relationship between SES and obesity was found.

Childhood obesity is probably best predicted by

the number of biologic parents who are obese. While both environmental (Garn & Clark, 1976) and genetic (Stunkard et al., 1986) arguments have been raised, it is clear that obesity runs in families. Children with two obese parents have two to three times the triceps skinfold thickness of children of two lean parents (Garn & Clark, 1976). An infant is much more likely to become obese as an adult if his or her parents were both obese (51% vs. 20% if both parents were thin). The probability of obesity in a child also increases as a function of the number of other obese family members (Garn et al., 1981). Childhood obesity may also be inversely related to family size (Jacoby et al., 1975).

Family interactional patterns appear to play a role in childhood obesity. Parents who prompt, or overly encourage, eating in children are much more likely to have an obese child (Klesges et al., 1983, 1986). Parents who prompt and encourage physical activity in children are less likely to have an obese child (Klesges et al., 1984, 1986). Those who encourage a lot of eating are unlikely to encourage physical activity in their children (Klesges et al., 1986). Parental modeling of eating behavior may also have an effect on children's subsequent eating behavior (Harper & Sanders, 1975).

Finally, it appears that there may be a relationship between obesity and television viewing (Dietz & Gortmaker, 1985; Palumbo & Dietz, 1985). Utilizing data from the National Health Examination Survey (*ns* = 2,153–6,965), these investigators found significant cross-sectional and longitudinal evidence for a link between obesity and the amount of television viewing. However, this relationship was much stronger for older (12 to 17 years) compared to younger (6 to 11 years) children, and the relationship between television viewing and obesity appeared to strengthen as the degree of obesity increased.

NATURAL HISTORY

Several studies have assessed the question of whether childhood obesity predicts adult obesity. There is overwhelming evidence that while adult obesity does not necessarily start in childhood, obesity that starts in childhood strongly tracks (persists) and strongly predicts adult obesity. Fisch et al. (1975) in a study of 1,786 children, found that 78% of the obese children studied at age 4 were still obese at age 7. Charney et al. (1976) assessed the heights and weights of 355 adults between the ages of 20 and 30 years and compared them to pediatric records. They found that the

best predictor of adult obesity was weight attained during the first 6 months of life. Thirty-six percent of those exceeding the 90th percentile at 6 months of age were overweight as adults, compared to 14% of the average weight infants. Shapiro et al. (1984) found that the degree of tracking in obesity was age related, with obesity at 3 to 4 years of age predicting later obesity much better than obesity at 1 to 2 years of age. Abraham et al. (1971) reported that 80% of overweight children become overweight adults, and Stunkard and Burt (1967) estimated that if an overweight child has not achieved a normal weight status by late adolescence, the odds against he or she doing so as an adult were 28 to 1.

It appears that the strength of the relationship between childhood and adult obesity depends on how early obesity is detected in the child. Epstein (1986) recently summarized four large-scale investigations (total sample size = 8,410) of the relationship between childhood (6 months to 13 years of age) and adulthood obesity. Epstein (1986) concluded that "The percentage of obese children who become obese adults is 14 percent in infancy, 41 percent at age 7, and about 70 percent at 10 to 13 years of age. The relative risk at these three ages increases from 2.33 to 3.73 to 6.55. While normal-weight children can become obese adults, keeping a child thin throughout development will reduce the relative risk of the child becoming an obese adult" (p. 161).

It also appears that the correlation between child and adult obesity increases as a function of the severity of the obesity (Dietz, 1987). It has been estimated that approximately 1.5 years of weight maintenance is needed (to allow height to increase and relative weight to decrease) for each 20% increment of excess weight (Dietz, 1983). A Swedish study (Borjeson, 1962) reported that about 30% of boys who were 120% of ideal body weight achieved ideal body weight over a seven-year period. In contrast, not a single child whose weight was in excess of 160% of ideal body weight achieved a normal weight within this period of time.

Not only does childhood obesity persist into adulthood, spontaneous remission rates for obesity are extremely low. An early study (Stunkard & McLaren-Hume, 1959) reported that most obese people do not enter treatment for obesity, most who enter do not lose weight, and most who lose weight regain it. A review published more recently (Brownell, 1982) concluded that the cure rate for obesity is less than that for many forms of cancer.

In conclusion, it appears that few health-related

indices (e.g., blood pressure, cholesterol levels, activity patterns) track as well as obesity. Once an obese child reaches adolescence, the probability of becoming an obese adult is very high and the probability of spontaneous remission is very low. These data strongly underscore the need for the development of more effective weight control programs for children delivered in a cost-effective manner.

IMPAIRMENT AND COMPLICATIONS

The relationship between adult obesity and myriad health problems is extremely well documented. Overweight in adults is associated with increased morbidity and mortality for both males and females (Bray, 1987). While chronic degenerative disease processes in children rarely result in death, childhood obesity is related to increases in a number of cardiovascular risk factors (Berenson, 1980). Further, the developing overweight child may be even more vulnerable than the obese adult to a variety of psychosocial stereotypes and the concomitant discrimination, reduced life options, and loss of self-esteem.

Hypertension

Elevated blood pressure in adults is related to the occurrence of cardiovascular disease (Kannel, 1978). An association between high blood pressure, morbidity, and mortality also exists early in life. Heyden, Bertel, Hames, and McDonough (1969) found that 25% of obese hypertensive adolescents experienced a serious cerebrovascular or cardiovascular event within 7 years of initial testing.

Available evidence generally indicates that obese children have higher blood pressures than their normal weight peers. Both Londe, Bourgoyne, Robson, and Goldring (1971) and Rames, Clarke, Connor, Reiter, and Tauer (1978) reported that over 50% of hypertensive children but less than one sixth of their normotensive peers were obese. Obese adolescents were found to have significantly higher blood pressure than nonobese adolescents (de Castro et al., 1976). Significant correlations have been established between subscapular skinfold (Court, Hill, Dunlop, & Bolton, 1974), triceps skinfold (Lauer, Connor, Leaverton, Reiter, & Clark, 1975), weight (Voors, Foster, Frerichs, Webber, & Berenson, 1976), and children's blood pressure levels. Finally, childhood obesity is a significant predictor of increasing

blood pressure over a 4-year period (Lauer, Anderson, Beaglehole, & Burns, 1983).

Cholesterol

A high level of total plasma cholesterol, with elevated low-density lipoproteins and depressed high-density lipoproteins, is an independent risk factor in the development of cardiovascular disease (Kannel, 1978; Voors et al., 1982). However, the relationship between body fat measures and serum cholesterol and triglycerides in children and adolescents in weak (Coats & Thoresen, 1980). Clarke, Morrow, and Morse (1970), Coates, Jeffery, Slinkard, Killen, and Danaher (1978), Florey, Uppal, and Lowy (1976), and Lauer et al. (1975) reported significant but modest correlations among measures of body weight and body fat and measures of total cholesterol and triglycerides. In contrast, a robust negative relationship between weight and high-density lipoproteins in adolescents has been reported (Coates et al., 1978), and a strong positive association between changes in body fat and low-density lipoproteins in children ages 5 to 12 has been observed (Freedman et al., 1985). This suggests that obesity in children and adolescents may affect lipoprotein ratios and that assessment of total serum cholesterol must consider this specific finding.

Diabetes

The relationship among obesity, hyperinsulinism, carbohydrate intolerance, and diabetes in children is not firmly established. Martin and Martin (1973) found that 28% of unselected obese children given oral glucose had chemical diabetes and an additional 26% demonstrated an impairment of carbohydrate tolerance—prevalence rates similar to those of obese adults. These detrimental effects were more likely to occur in children over the age of 9. Similarly, Drash (1973) evaluated 18 grossly obese adolescents and reported that all subjects revealed marked hyperinsulinism and 39% were carbohydrate intolerant.

Other Physical Complications

It is widely believed that obese children are more likely to suffer from respiratory problems than are normal weight children. Tracey, De, and Harper (1971) compared the health records of obese and nonobese children between the ages of 3 months and 2 years and found reliable differences in the occurrence of respiratory illness. Thirty-nine percent of the obese children in the sample experienced a respiratory illness during the 6-month observation period while such problems were observed in only 22% of the nonobese control group. Pulmonary function problems due to impaired work capacity of the lungs have also been identified in obese children (Burwell, Robin, Whaley, & Bickelman, 1956).

The evidence of a relationship between cancer and obesity in children is sketchy, though documentation of hematological and immunological impairment associated with obesity exists (Bray, 1986). Chandra and Kutty (1980) reported that a significantly greater percentage of obese children (38%) showed impairment in cell-mediated immune response. Finally, obese children appear to be even more vulnerable to accidents than their normal weight peers. For example, Wilmore and Pruitt (1972) found that obese boys suffered accidental burns more frequently than did nonobese boys.

Social Rejection

Existing evidence suggests that adolescent and adult obesity is related to discrimination in college admissions (Canning & Mayer, 1966), upwardly mobile marriages (Elder, 1969), and employment (Larkin & Pines, 1979). Many social scientists have contended that the psychosocial consequences of childhood obesity are equally severe (LeBow, 1984). A number of studies have asked both children and adults to rate obese children against other groups thought to be unattractive. Richardson, Hastorf, Goodman, and Dornbush (1961) asked a sample of 10- and 11-year-old children from across the United States to rate the likeability of pictures of a nondisabled, nonobese child, an obese child, and four disabled children (e.g., facial disfigurement, missing hand). All child raters, regardless of demographic category, rated the obese child least liked. These findings have been confirmed in other studies using adult raters (Goodman, Richardson, Dornbush, & Hastorf, 1963) and both adult and disabled child raters (Maddox, Back, & Liederman, 1968). These findings are typically interpreted in terms of the raters' judgment of obese children's responsibility for their condition (Bray, 1986).

Sociometric ratings of obese children have produced a more confusing picture than ratings of physical appearance. Hammer (1981; cited in Jarvie, Lahey, Graziano, & Framer, 1983), working with third graders, found a preference for the average weight child relative to the obese child. However, the ratings of the obese child reflected less liking rather than disliking. Staffieri (1967) reported that both thin and heavy 6- to 10-year-old children received fewer positive nominations than did those with a moderate body build. Sallade (1973) found no evidence of differential preference for obese children among third, fifth, eighth, and eleventh graders.

In two studies from our research group, little evidence was found for discrimination against the obese child. Cohen, Klesges, Summerville, and Meyers (1989) evaluated the influence of relative weight on sociometric nominations and rankings by first, third, and fifth graders. The only weight-related differences involved first grade overweight males who received fewer liking nominations than did other males and overweight females and third grade males who were rated lower than were other males. No weight differences were found for measures of dislike. Wilkin, Meyers, Cohen, and Klesges (1988), working with the same age groups, found no significant body weight influences. The latter investigation extended this analysis to behavioral observations of social interaction during the school lunch period. Again, there were no significant differences between obese and nonobese children. Peer group sociometry, using different sociometric measures across a wide age range of children, has produced little evidence of an active social discrimination of the obese child.

Self-esteem

If a social stigma against the obese does operate, one would expect the self-esteem of the obese child to suffer. Indeed, Sallade (1973) did find a more negative self-concept among obese as opposed to nonobese third, fifth, eighth, and eleventh graders. In contrast, three studies distinguished no differences in self-esteem due to weight. Wadden, Foster, Brownell, and Finley (1984) examined third through eighth grade children and found no self-esteem differences between weight groups. Similar results were reported in a population of 7- to 12-year-olds though deficits in physical self-esteem were noted (Mendelson & White, 1982). Finally, Kaplan and Wadden (1986) failed to find self-esteem differences between obese and average weight 9- to 18-year-old black children. In summary, we have little evidence to support the conclusion that childhood obesity is related to self-esteem or self-concept problems.

Psychopathology

The assumption that obesity and psychopathology are linked has a long history in both the adult and child literature (Wadden & Stunkard, 1987). Wadden and Stunkard reviewed 12 studies that found mildly elevated levels of depression, hypochondriasis, hysteria, and impulsivity in obese adults. However, these studies consistently failed to employ adequate control groups (e.g., nonobese patients seeking treatment for a physical disorder) or strictly defined diagnostic criteria. Indeed, when Halmi, Long, and Stunkard (1980) examined 86 morbidly obese adults using stringent diagnostics, no differences in prevalence of psychiatric disorders were found between the obese and the nonobese. Further support for this finding comes from the classic Midtown Manhattan study (Moore, Stunkard, & Srole, 1962) and several large-scale European studies (see Wadden & Stunkard, 1987) that identified only weak or no relationships between psychopathology and weight.

Similar findings are apparent for obese children. In Salade's (1973) study, no social adjustment or personality adjustment differences were identified. Karpowitz and Zeis (1975) found no weight-related differences in a population of 12- to 15-year-olds on measures of personal problems and locus of control. Finally, body image disturbances are thought to be common among the obese (Stunkard & Mendelson, 1967). However, Stunkard and Burt (1967) were unable to distinguish body image problems in obese and nonobese teenage girls. Orthodontic braces, glasses, and pigtails were identified as frequently as weight as a source of concern over physical characteristics.

While current evidence supports the existence of a negative stereotype concerning the obese child, the effects of this stereotype are less clearly delineated. Sociometric ratings have not identified the obese child as "more disliked," but there has been some evidence for fewer "liked" nominations. No differences in behavioral interaction between obese and nonobese children have been reported. Contrary to hypotheses, neither measures of self-esteem nor psychopathology have distinguished children of different weight.

Extant research may not, as yet, have identified those factors that mediate the relationship among overweight and the psychological variables of interest. Stunkard and Burt (1967) have stressed the importance of peers in the adolescent's quest to cope with obesity. Certainly family and the close social network will also have an impact on the obese child. A negative stereotype of childhood obesity may function to the extent that the obese child and his or her significant others believe the stereotype (Meyers & Craighead, 1984).

DIFFERENTIAL DIAGNOSIS

Childhood obesity results from excess caloric intake relative to energy expenditure. Yet, there exist some medical syndromes associated with excess adiposity that need to be differentiated from simple obesity. Careful attention should be given to the initial clinical interview in which relevant information must be gathered to exclude these disorders from consideration in the etiology of the child's obesity. Appropriate medical referrals should be made when any of these medical conditions are suspected.

Obesity is a secondary characteristic to some congenital disorders and to a handful of acquired endocrine and oncologic problems that manifest themselves in the first few years of life. Among the acquired disorders that have obesity as an associated characteristic, Cushing's syndrome is well documented. This syndrome is an endocrine disorder that results from abnormally high levels of blood cortisol from hyperfunctioning of the adrenal cortex. The syndrome is rare in pediatric populations relative to its frequency in adulthood, but it has been found to occur neonatally and is three times more prevalent in females than males (Rudolph, Hoffman, & Axelrod, 1987). Prominent characteristics of this syndrome are obesity, hypertension, and short stature. Growth is usually severely retarded, with most of the children falling below the third percentile for height. Abnormal fat deposition is characteristic; obesity is localized to the trunk and abdomen while the extremities remain a normal size (Rudolph et al., 1987).

Cushing's can manifest in several forms. Most (85%) of the cases appear as Cushing's syndrome; these arise in young children (7 years of age or younger) as the result of adrenocorticol tumors. In children 7 years or older, Cushings disease, which has a slightly different etiology but manifests similar symptomology, is the most common form of this syndrome (Nelson, Behrman, & Vaughan, 1987). This particular form of the syndrome is the result of bilateral hyperphasia of the adrenals. At the age of 7 years and older the syndrome occurs equally in males and females. The generally accepted physical signs of both syndromes include a rounded face, prominent flushed cheeks (moon facies), a doubled chin, and cervical fat pads resulting in a "buffalo hump." Abnormal masculinization, facial and bodily hair, acne, and deepening of the voice may be present. Thinning of the skin and purplish striae on the hips, abdomen, and thighs are also common manifestations of the disease (Rudolph et al., 1987). Cushing's disease or syndrome should be suspected in obese children of short stature or decelerating growth rate presenting with hypertension, moon facies, and/or purplish striae (Nelson et al., 1987).

Frohlich's syndrome, also an acquired condition, is caused by lesions of the hypothalamus affecting the anterior lobe of the pituitary. Pituitary damage results in observed sexual abnormalities and hypothalamic lesions disrupt the appetite control center. As a result, these children are obese and hypogonadic. The syndrome is also very rare and presents varying symptomatology depending upon the age of onset. Other anomalies, such as brain damage secondary to tumor, trauma, or infection, can also result in obesity, but these occur quite infrequently.

Among the congenital disorders resulting in obesity, the Prader-Labhart-Willi syndrome is relatively uncommon, occurring once per 10,000 births (Nelson et al., 1987). This disorder is often referred to as the "H3O syndrome" because of its prominent characteristics: hypotonia, hypomentia, hypogonadism, and obesity (Bray et al., 1983). Similar to the other syndromes discussed here, this disorder is characterized by obesity, short stature, and mild to moderate mental retardation. These children possess almond-shaped eyes and small hands and feet. They are hypotonic and often have feeding difficulties at birth. By the age of 2 or 3, they develop insatiable appetites, which often lead to very resourceful food-seeking behaviors and obesity (Rudolph et al., 1987). Behavior problems, temper tantrums (Dietz, 1987), and an inability to control emotions are often seen (Magalini, 1971). Central nervous system disorder is postulated but has not been substantiated. The etiology of the disorder remains controversial, yet the manifestations suggest abnormal hypothalamic functioning (Rudolph et al., 1987).

Myelodysplasia is the second most common of the congenital disorders related to obesity, and it occurs in 1 per 1,000 live births (Dietz, 1987). This disorder is characterized by atrophy of the muscles in the lower extremities. Loss of lean tissue from the large muscle groups in the lower body results in a decreased resting metabolic rate. According to Dietz (1987), the obesity occurs mainly because the lowered energy requirements can easily go unrecognized.

Neonatal screenings detect congenital hypothyroidism in 1 per every 4,000 live births (Rudolph et al., 1987). Although it has often been assumed that many obese children have thyroid dysfunction, most children do not become obese because of hypothyroidism. Nelson et al. (1987) report that the presence of hypothyroidism among obese children probably does not exceed its prevalence in the general pediatric population.

Childhood obesity has been associated with Mauriac's, Laurence-Moon-Biedl's, Carpenter's, Alstrom's, and Down's syndromes; these also occur at low rates and are even less well documented. Many of these disorders with syndromatic obesity are related to endocrine abnormalities. The resultant obesity can be differentiated from the occurrence of simple obesity by characteristics such as short stature, retarded bone development, hypogonadism, and mental retardation. Children with simple obesity are usually taller than average, begin sexual maturation early, and have advanced bone development (Nelson et al., 1987; Rudolph et al., 1987).

Consistent with adult obesity, all childhood obesity is due to disrupted energy balance. Although there are at least a dozen medical syndromes that have obesity as a frequent or associated feature, they account for less than 5% of all cases of pediatric obesity (Rudolph et al., 1987).

ETIOLOGY

Despite the vast number of investigations that have sought genetic, biochemical, physiological, and environmental causes of childhood obesity (Brownell, 1982; Keesey, 1980; Stunkard et al., 1986), the identification of a cause, or causes, of obesity remains elusive. The demographic and familial correlates of obesity, as well as the strong recent evidence of a genetic influence on childhood obesity (Stunkard et al., 1986), actually are correlates and not causes of obesity. That is, the laws of thermodynamics certainly apply to weight gain and obesity, and only energy intake versus expenditure can have a direct impact on weight gain (Garrow, 1978). Genetics, for example, might predispose a person toward increased eating, decreased physical activity, lowered metabolism, or some combination of the three. We will now look at the evidence for possible direct causes of childhood obesity (namely, dietary intake, physical activity, metabolic rate).

Dietary Intake

The relationship between diet and obesity has long been of interest to nutrition researchers. However, the results of the vast majority of studies of nutrition and obesity fail to find overweight–normal weight differences on measures of dietary intake either in adults or children (e.g., Huenemann, 1974; Berenson et al., 1979), and if differences are found (e.g., Johnson et al., 1956), they appear in a paradoxical direction with obese individuals eating less. An example of the failure to find overweight–normal weight differences in self-reported dietary intake comes from the HANES I survey (Braitman et al., 1985). Directly addressing the problem of poor methodologies and inadequate sample sizes, these investigators analyzed a sample of 6,219 nonpregnant adults whose diets were not restricted or influenced by illness, drugs, or pregnancy. Highly trained interviewers administered a standardized 24-hour dietary recall to all subjects. Diets were cross-checked by a food frequency form for the preceding three months. Results indicated that neither the caloric intake nor the caloric intake adjusted for physical activity levels and age was higher in the obese subjects.

One possible explanation of these results is that the obese are systematically biasing their reports of dietary intake. To evaluate this possibility, we recently completed two investigations (Klesges et al., 1988; Myers et al., 1988) where we compared the accuracy of self-reports of obese versus normal weight subjects. Individuals (Myers et al., 1988) or families with either a normal weight or obese child (Klesges et al., 1988) were brought to a laboratory, ostensibly to take part in a study unrelated to dietary intake. After completing questionnaires, they were offered a free lunch at a university cafeteria. Although subjects thought they were left alone to dine, a number of research assistants were carefully and unobtrusively obtaining dietary intake information on these subjects. Plate waste was saved and weighed. Subjects then returned to the laboratory to "finish the assessment." The next day, all subjects were contacted and asked about dietary intake information for the previous day, using a standardized 24-hour dietary recall methodology. Results indicated that obesity status of the individual had no impact on

the accuracy of the recalled information in either investigation.

Physical Activity

There appears to be general consensus, at least with children, that the overweight children are more sedentary than are their normal weight counterparts (Myres & Yeung, 1979; Weil, 1977; Wooley et al., 1979). For example, in an early study of physical activity and obesity, Bullen et al. (1964) assessed the physical activity of 109 obese and 72 nonobese adolescent girls engaged in sports activities at summer camp. On the basis of approximately 27,000 behavioral observations, the obese group was far less physically active. Waxman and Stunkard (1980) found that obese boys were far less active than were their nonobese brothers inside the home, slightly less active outside the home, and equally active at school. Thus, the literature appears to consistently record, with a few notable exceptions (e.g., Stunkard & Pestka, 1962; Wilkinson et al., 1977), reliable differences in physical activity between obese and nonobese children. While there is general agreement regarding obese–nonobese differences in physical activity, there is less agreement regarding the interpretation of these findings. That is, it is not known whether lower levels of physical activity in the obese are a cause or a consequence of obesity.

Metabolic Rate

Metabolic rate is an important, and often overlooked, variable in energy imbalances because approximately 75% of total energy expenditure comes in the form of metabolism (Bernstein et al., 1983; Ravussin et al., 1984). Thus, even a small change in metabolic rate can place a person at high risk for weight gain. While the majority of metabolic studies conducted to date have been with adults, the results of well-conducted investigations indicate that total energy expenditure (typically measured for 24 hours in a whole room indirect calorimeter) is higher in obese subjects (Blaza & Garrow, 1983; Prentice et al., 1986). If the results are expressed per kilogram of fat-free mass, the values obtained in lean and obese subjects are the same (Prentice et al., 1986). The thermic effect of food (the metabolic cost of eating) appears to be less pronounced, or blunted, in obese people (Jequier, 1987). Since resting metabolic rate (and total energy expenditure) is higher in the obese and it accounts for a much greater number of calories burned relative to the thermic effect of food, it is not clear how important this energy difference is, with reviews coming to different conclusions as to the significance of these findings (Garrow, 1981; Jequier, 1987).

While the results of cross-sectional studies of obese–normal weight differences in metabolic rate are equivocal, two recent prospective studies indicate that metabolism may indeed play a role in the weight gain process. Ravussin et al. (1988) measured 24-hour energy expenditure in 95 adults and reported that total energy expenditure significantly, but modestly ($r = -0.39$, $p < 0.0001$), correlated with changes in body weight over a 2-year period. The risk of gaining 16.5 or more pounds was 400% higher in persons with energy expenditures 200 kcal or less below predicted levels compared with persons with energy expenditures 200 kcal or more above predicted values. In a study with infants born to either normal weight ($n = 6$) or overweight ($n = 12$) mothers, Roberts et al. (1988) reported that total energy expenditure (measured by a doubly labeled water technique) at 3 months of age was 21% lower in infants who became overweight at 12 months of age ($p < 0.05$). Thus, it appears that a low total energy expenditure is one risk factor for later weight gain.

To conclude this section, it appears that possible energy balance differences between obese and normal weight children are probably subtle and very complex. Additional prospective studies of the impact of dietary intake, physical activity, and metabolic rate on accelerated weight gain are critically needed.

CLINICAL INTERVENTION

Treatment of the obese child has only recently received the attention given to adult obesity. Through the mid-1970s traditional treatments, including inpatient starvation, appetite suppressants, nutrition counseling, and exercise prescriptions produced limited weight loss, high attrition, high relapse, and negative emotional effects. By the mid-1980s, comprehensive behaviorally based interventions, employing behavioral, cognitive, family, and biological components, had demonstrated somewhat more promising results (Brownell, 1984). Epstein (1986) concluded that contemporary behavioral treatments for childhood obesity were superior to nonbehavioral interventions and control groups. Further, children receiving these treatments were significantly less obese than were controls 5 years after their weight loss effort (Epstein, Wing, Koeske, & Valoski, 1987).

While broad-based behavioral approaches to childhood obesity have achieved some promising results, the active components of these programs have yet to be identified. Comprehensive weight loss programs typically strive for dietary change and increases in physical activity through parental and family involvement, child management, self (often parent-assisted)-monitoring, behavioral contracting, stimulus control strategies, and social and cognitive skill development (Epstein, 1986; Graves, Meyers, & Clark, 1988).

Diet and Exercise

Obesity and weight change are complex biobehavioral phenomena. However, weight loss still must involve a reduction of kilocalories consumed relative to energy expended. In the obese, child dietary restriction presents the dual responsibility of reducing food consumption without impairing the child's nutritional intake and physical growth. Perhaps the most innovative diet for children is Epstein's (1986) "traffic light diet," which divides foods into red (restrict), yellow (consume with caution), and green (acceptable) categories. These categories are based on calories per serving relative to nutritional value and utilize self-monitoring and reinforcement components. Epstein and his colleagues have employed this diet regimen in several successful child weight loss programs (Epstein & Wing, 1987).

Increases in physical activity and exercise may be the most beneficial step one can take in a weight loss effort. Bullen et al. (1964), Corbin and Pletcher (1968), and Waxman and Stunkard (1980) reported that obese children were less physically active than were the nonobese. In response to these data, Epstein has attempted successfully to increase programmed exercise and life-style physical activity (e.g., walking to school; Epstein, et al., 1985). Recently, Epstein, Wing, Valoski, and Devos (1988) reported that, at a 5-year follow-up, children who showed the largest long-term reduction in relative weight and the lowest initial physical fitness level demonstrated the greatest improvements in fitness.

Parental Involvement

Perhaps the most impactful component in childhood obesity treatment programs is parental involvement. Clearly parents exert great influence on children's habit formation and this fact is high-lighted by Klesges's evidence that parental offers of food, and less encouragement and more discouragement of physical activity, were correlated with children's relative weight (Klesges et al., 1983, 1984).

A number of studies have attempted to improve parents' general and weight-related child management skills. Both Aragona, Cassady, and Drabman (1975) and Israel, Stolmaker, and Andrian (1985) presented evidence that such training within a behavioral weight loss program for children was beneficial. Unfortunately, the results of evaluations of more broadly defined parental involvement in childhood obesity treatment have been equivocal (Clark, Meyers, Coyne, & Perkins, 1984; Epstein & Wing, 1987). For example, Aragona et al. (1975) and Epstein, Wing, Koeske, Andrasik, and Ossip (1981) conducted treatment programs that demonstrated the value of parental involvement while Kingsley and Shapiro (1977) found no difference in child weight loss due to parent's participation.

The difficulty in evaluating the role of parents in children's weight loss may be due largely to the tremendous variability in the way researchers operationalize the concept of parental involvement. Parental attendance with the overweight child (Kingsley & Shapiro, 1977), parental attendance in sessions separate from the child (Brownell, Kelman, & Stunkard, 1983), parental participation through printed handouts and homework (Kirschenbaum, Harris, & Tomarken, 1984), and actual parental participation in the weight loss effort (Epstein et al., 1981) have all been examined. Israel, Stolmaker, Sharp, Silverman, and Simon (1984) have distinguished two parental roles in child weight loss: weight loss participants versus helper. Our own work suggests that parental involvement is not a dichotomous variable; parents surely differ in the amount of encouragement, support, and effort that they invest in their child's weight loss program (Clark et al., 1984). Some parents in our studies relinquished self-monitoring and other responsibilities to the child, some assisted the child, while others did all assignments for the child. Accounting for varying degrees of parental involvement may be central to understanding child weight loss.

Another variable that confounds conclusions concerning parental participation is the child's age or developmental stage. Will parental involvement be equally beneficial for the 5-year-old and the 15-year-old? While no clear-cut answer to this question exists, common sense suggests that it will not. Epstein (1986) has proposed a multiple-stage treatment model that gradually, across the age range, shifts responsibility for program components from the parent to the child. During the first 5 years of life control of the program is left to parents. From 5 to 8 years the program continues to focus on parent management, but the increasingly social child is trained to handle social situations that affect weight. Increasing responsibility is granted to the 8- to 12-year-old, including self-monitoring and goal setting. Programs for adolescents closely resemble adult weight loss interventions. Parents are called on for support, but care must be taken not to conflict with the adolescent's striving for independence.

Future Treatment Directions

In addition to the developmental and family issues in weight loss interventions for children, at least two other areas deserve research consideration. Brownell (1984) has advocated the treatment of childhood obesity in the schools. The school setting presents the advantages of reaching large numbers of children at low-cost, continuous, and long-term contact with participants and a nonmedical, educational model of intervention.

Interventions in the school hold open the possibility of prevention-oriented programs. Prevention activities possess some clear advantages over treatment efforts (Meyers & Schleser, 1981), yet little prevention work has been done in childhood obesity. In what may be the only meaningful study on obesity prevention in children, Piscano, Lichter, Ritter, and Siegal (1978) presented 80 parents of 3-month-old infants a nutritionally balanced diet regimen for their children. This group was compared with 50 infants fed a conventional diet. At 3 years of age the control group showed a 25.5% prevalence of overweight while the treatment group exhibited a significantly lower 1.3% prevalence rate. The study suffers from lack of random assignment, subject selection bias, failure to control for nonspecific treatment effects, and failure to confirm the application of the independent variable; however, the results are quite impressive and worthy of further exploration.

CASE EXAMPLE

Robert Wilson, an 11-year-old white male was seen at an urban university behavioral medicine clinic. He was brought in by his parents because they were concerned about their son's continuing weight gain, increasing lethargy, and social isolation. At the time of the initial visit Robert was 5′ 4″ and weighed 170 lb, placing him above the 95th percentile for relative weight. He also ranked above the 95th percentile for body fat based on his triceps skinfold measure of 27 mm. Robert was fair skinned, with bright red hair, and was dressed neatly. During the first interview Robert appeared shy and quiet, and he initially avoided eye contact. Mrs. Wilson answered most of the questions, but Robert expressed himself well and eventually made appropriate eye contact when questions were addressed directly to him. Robert was currently doing well in school and reported liking history and English. According to his teacher's reports, Robert was a diligent A student with an above-average IQ. He appeared to be psychologically well adjusted and had no history of behavioral or psychosocial problems. Mr. Wilson expressed frustration over his son's weight problem, but both of the parents appeared supportive and genuinely concerned about their child's social, psychological, and physical welfare.

Mrs. Wilson was a registered nurse working days at a local hospital. Mr. Wilson worked full time as a salesman, and occasionally in the evenings as a security guard. The parents' work schedule forced Robert's 14-year-old brother to supervise Robert and his 5-year-old sister after school. The parents' combined income placed them in the upper-middle socioeconomic class. Robert's father, a former football player, was a tall obese man (6′ 4″ 250 lbs). His mother was approximately 30 pounds overweight. Both of Robert's siblings were normal weight. There was some jealousy between Robert and his older brother who excelled in athletic and extracurricular activities.

Mrs. Wilson claimed the she and her husband had a good relationship and described it as a "traditional marriage." She cooked, cleaned, and waited on her husband when he returned home at night. The father described himself as a sports enthusiast and reported enjoying relaxing with a snack in front of the television in the evenings. Robert was also an avid television watcher, spending most of his afternoons and evenings watching television. Robert admired his father and was particularly sensitive to his comments. He looked forward to the evenings when he and his father could spend time together. Eating was encouraged in the family and used as a form of entertainment. His mother would inadvertently encourage Robert to eat more than his siblings by giving him larger portions because he was "such a big boy." She also liked to participate in the family television hour by serving ice cream or making snacks for other family members. In addition, family events were generally spectator sports that involved no direct physical activity.

Robert was slightly overweight as a toddler but had been gaining weight rapidly over the last year. His mother reported that he began putting on weight about the time that his best friend moved away. Robert was not engaged in any athletic or social activities outside of school. Although Robert was described as being awkward and clumsy as a child, he had been actively involved in football and some school and church activities with his friend up until the last year. His mother reported that Robert appeared quieter and sad after his friend left, and he became more awkward and gradually withdrew from sports.

Robert's father had always actively encouraged his son's participation in athletics. As Mr. Wilson became disappointed in Robert's weight and change of interests, the relationship between Robert and his father became increasingly strained. He would verbally encourage his son to diet, lose weight, and exercise. Robert was very sensitive to his father's comments but was unable to lose the weight on his own. As Robert's weight increased and his father's attempts to help appeared ineffective, Mr. Wilson gradually withdrew from the weight loss effort.

At school Robert was very quiet and was often teased because of his weight and red hair. He would follow along with the group but had no close friends at home or in the neighborhood. Robert reported that books were his friends and that he liked to read and ate out of boredom and when watching television. He stated that he enjoyed spending time with his father.

Mrs. Wilson had unsuccessfully tried to restrict Robert's diet several times in the past. In general, Robert would sabotage his mother's efforts. She frequently found him sneaking food from the freezer and bribing his younger sister to sneak out dessert for him. He also was quite manipulative of his mother's emotions and would appear sad and rejected when placed on a diet. After 1 to 2 weeks of such behavior, Mrs. Wilson would usually give in and loosen the dietary restriction, which eventually led to Robert's having full access to the foods of his choice. In addition, Mrs. Wilson would inadvertently encourage Robert's eating behavior by asking him to taste new recipes and by insisting that he clean his plate. Regardless of "cheating," Robert would lose approximately 5 pounds with each diet, but regain it quickly once his mother stopped the program.

For the week prior to the initial treatment session, Robert's mother assisted him in keeping a 7-day food and activity diary, in which Robert recorded everything that he consumed over the week, any physical activities that he engaged in, and the amount of time spent in various physical activities. Reports from his mother and the diary confirmed that Robert was a relatively inactive child. He spent most of his time in quiet activities — reading books, watching television, putting together models — and would occasionally attend a Wednesday night youth church meeting where refreshments were served. His caloric intake (1,500 calories/day) was slightly above average for his age and sex. The nutrient composition of his diet was analyzed, and it revealed that Robert's diet consisted of several calorically dense foods with a high sugar and saturated fat content.

Although Robert's dietary habits and inactivity could explain his weight increase over the last year, it was not completely clear whether his inactivity and lethargy were a result of his obesity or if it were associated with some type of endocrine or metabolic disturbance. Thus, to rule out the possibility of any medical problems, Robert's parents gave consent to obtain past medical records, and a referral was made for Robert to have a physical examination prior to any psychological treatment. The physician's exam showed no evidence of any endocrine or metabolic disturbances and indicated that other than his obesity, Robert was generally healthy. At the time of the exam, Robert was borderline hypertensive (which was believed to be the result of his weight status); he had a slightly elevated level of serum cholesterol and low-density lipoproteins, but there was no evidence of any respiratory problems. The physician also indicated that moderate dietary restriction seemed a reasonable option for weight control.

Initial treatment sessions focused on the development of a comprehensive behavioral intervention that would involve both the parents and other siblings. The goal of the program was to increase Robert's physical activity and gradually reduce his caloric intake by parent-assisted self-monitoring, stimulus control strategies, and operant procedures. Family cohesiveness was viewed as an asset, and the entire family was involved to facilitate the treatment. A primary goal was for the entire family to adopt a healthy diet regimen. In this way,

Robert's meals did not need to be prepared separately, so he did not feel isolated. Robert was placed on a contingency management program. He monitored his food intake daily, and his mother checked this over with him. Dietary restriction was accomplished by a gradual reduction of empty calories from the diet: carbonated beverages were replaced with diet beverages, whole milk was replaced by skim milk, and fruits were given as treats in place of sweets.

The initial plan worked well for the first few weeks, before it was observed that Robert was having his sister sneak food for him again. Robert contracted with his mother that he would record all the foods he ate, and he could earn points for keeping complete records, holding his junk food to a minimum, and keeping his caloric intake below a target level. At the end of the week, Robert could redeem points for a new book or an activity of his choice with his father.

Free time after school remained an inactive period and a high-risk time for Robert to overeat. His mother prepared nutritious snacks and left them for the children to have when they returned home. The time without adult supervision was also restructured. Robert was encouraged to pick an activity to do 3 days a week after school. The purpose of this was threefold: (1) to select a behavior that was incompatible with eating, (2) to increase caloric expenditure, and (3) to increase Robert's social circle. Robert's siblings were also involved to maintain a family effort. Robert became involved in Cub Scouts and another community activity where he eventually made some new friends.

One obstacle of treatment was to get Mr. Wilson to participate in increasing his activity with Robert without placing high demands for athletic competence. Additional time was also spent on teaching the parents to lessen their offers of food and to encourage daily living as well as sport-related physical activity.

After 16 weeks of treatment, Robert had lost 14.9 pounds. He lost an initial 5.5 pounds in the first 2 weeks, but weight loss tapered off to approximately 0.7 lbs/wk. Skinfold thickness reduced to 24 mm, and low-density lipoprotein levels declined substantially. This treatment was a moderate success, and the contingency management program was to be extended by Robert and his parents until they reached his eventual goal. Robert was seen once a month thereafter to monitor progress during the initial stages of maintenance. One year after treatment, Robert had grown to 5′ 5.5″ and weighed 155 lbs. Based on relative weight, Robert remained above the 70th percentile, but his progress was considered good, since he continued to maintain a slow, steady weight reduction. In addition, he had increased the probability that his weight loss would be maintained by changing his eating behaviors and increasing his activity level.

CONTINUITY AND DISCONTINUITY WITH ADULT PRESENTATION

To our knowledge, no study has ever longitudinally evaluated the clinical presentation of obesity from childhood to adulthood. However, a number of studies have assessed clinical issues in the obese both in children and in adults. As indicated elsewhere, there is clear evidence that obese children are likely to become obese adults (Charney et al., 1976). Furthermore, what is observed is a general and consistent lack of clinical differences in the adult and child obese. Dietary intakes, relative to the nonobese, consistently show no differences in both children and adults (Berenson et al., 1979; Braitman et al., 1985). Levels of physical activity appear to be lower in the obese child than in the nonobese child (Waxman & Stunkard, 1980), and recent evidence indicates the levels of aerobic activity, but not other types of physical activity, are negatively related to body fat in adults (Klesges et al., 1988). The obese child does not appear to be at increased risk for psychological and psychosocial disorders (Coates & Thoresen, 1980); neither is the obese adult, although concerns about dieting and weight loss are more prevalent in the obese adult (Klesges, 1984). In summary, it appears that few differences distinguish the presentation of obesity in children from that in adults.

SUMMARY

Increasing evidence on the intractability of adult obesity has served to focus attention on the assessment and treatment of childhood obesity. Concentration on the obese child offers several potential advantages. Increased control of child behavior, developing patterns of food intake and physical activity, and early impact on biological processes that contribute to the overweight condition all may benefit the weight loss effort.

Although body weight can be carefully and objectively measured, there is no consensus on the definition of childhood obesity. We recommend using percentage above ideal body weight and tri-

ceps skinfold measurement corrected for age and gender. Confusion over the definition of childhood obesity has made prevalence rates difficult to identify. Different estimates place the figure between 10% and 25% of the population, and recent surveys suggest that this figure may be increasing.

The single best predictor of childhood obesity is probably the number of biological parents who are obese. The probability of obesity also increases as a function of the number of other family members who are obese. Further, interactional patterns in families appear to play a role in the child's obese condition. Parents who prompt, or overly encourage, eating in children are much more likely to have an obese child, while parents who prompt and encourage physical activity in children are less likely to have an obese child.

As in adult obesity, there are relationships between overweight and a number of cardiovascular risk factors in children. Childhood obesity is related to elevated blood pressures and low-density lipoproteins, carbohydrate intolerance, and respiratory illness. While there is evidence of a negative social stereotype of obese children, the effects of that stereotype on self-esteem, social interaction, and child psychopathology are unclear.

There is little evidence of dietary differences between obese and nonobese children. However, extant research appears to support the observation that the obese child is less physically active than his or her normal weight peer. The impact of metabolic rate on weight status is equivocal, but recent evidence suggests that low total energy expenditure may be a risk factor for later weight gain. Several medical syndromes or disease states are related to excess adiposity in children, though these conditions appear to account for an exceptionally small number of obesity cases.

The need for effective childhood obesity treatment programs is underscored by the finding that obesity that starts in childhood strongly predicts adult obesity. Current evaluations of obesity treatment for children indicate that broad-based cognitive/behavioral treatments for childhood obesity are superior to nonbehavioral interventions and control groups. This superiority has been maintained at 5-year follow-up assessments. While the results of such programs reveal promise, the active components of these interventions have yet to be identified. Further investigation of the role of dietary change, physical activity, parental and family involvement, child management, self- and parental monitoring, behavioral contracting, stimulus control strategies, and social and cognitive skill development is warranted.

REFERENCES

Abraham, S., Collins, G., & Nordsieck, M. (1971). Relationship of childhood weight status to morbidity in adults. *Public Health Reports, 86,* 273–284.

Aragona, J., Cassady, J., & Drabman, R. (1975). Treating overweight children through parental training and contingency contracting. *Journal of Applied Behavior Analysis, 8,* 269–278.

Berenson, G. S. (1980). *Cardiovascular risk factors in children: The early natural history of atherosclerosis and essential hypertension.* New York: Oxford University Press.

Berenson, G. S., Blonde, C. V., Farris, R. P., Foster, T. A., Frank, G. C., Srinivasan, S. R., Voors, A. W., & Webber, L. S. (1979). Cardiovascular disease risk factor variables during the first year of life. *American Journal of Diseases in Children, 122,* 1049–1057.

Bernstein, R. S., Thornston, J. C., Yang, M. U., Wang, J., Redmond, A. M., Pierson, R. N., Pi-Sunyer, F. X., & Itallie, T. B. (1983). Prediction of the metabolic rate in obese patients. *American Journal of Public Health, 37,* 595–602.

Blaza, S., & Garrow, J. S. (1983). Thermogenic response to temperature, exercise, and food stimuli in lean and obese women, studied by 24 hr. direct calorimetry. *British Journal of Nutrition, 49,* 171–180.

Borjeson, M. (1962). Overweight children. *Acta Paediatrica Scandivica, 51*(Suppl. 132).

Braitman, L. E., Adlin, E. V., & Stanton, J. L., Jr. (1985). Obesity and caloric intake: The National Health and Nutrition Examination Survey of 1971–1975 (HANES I). *Journal of Chronic Diseases, 38,* 727–732.

Bray, G. A. (1986). Effects of obesity on health and happiness. In K. D. Brownell & J. P. Foreyt (Eds.), *Handbook of eating disorders: Physiology, psychology, and treatment of obesity, anorexia, and bulimia* (pp. 3–44). New York: Basic Books.

Bray, G. A. (1987). Overweight is risking fate: Definition, classification, prevalence, and risks. In R. J. Wurtman & J. J. Wurtman (Eds.), *Human obesity* (pp. 14–28). New York: The New York Academy of Sciences.

Bray, G. A., Dahms, W. T., Swerdloff, R. H., Fiser, R. H., Atkinson, R. L., & Carrel, R. E. (1983). The Prader-Willi Syndrome: A study of 40 patients and a review of the literature. *Medicine, 62,* 59–80.

Brownell, K. D. (1982). Obesity: Understanding and treating a serious, prevalent and refractory disorder. *Journal of Consulting and Clinical Psychology, 50,* 820–840.

Brownell, K. D. (1984). New developments in the treatment of obese children and adolescents. In A. J. Stunkard & E. Stellar (Eds.), *Eating and its disorders: Association for research in nervous and mental disease* (Vol. 62, pp. 175–183). New York: Raven Press.

Brownell, K. D. (1986). Social and behavioral aspects of obesity. In N. A. Krasnegor, J. D. Arasteh, & M. F. Cataldo (Eds.), *Child health behavior: A behavioral pediatrics perspective* (pp. 310–324). New York: John Wiley & Sons.

Brownell, K. D., Kelman, S. H., & Stunkard, A. J. (1983). Treatment of obese children with and without their mothers: Changes in weight and blood pressure. *Pediatrics, 71,* 515–523.

Brownell, K. D., Stunkard, A. J., & Albaum, J. M. (1980). Evaluation and modification of exercise patterns in the natural environment. *American Journal of Psychiatry, 137,* 1540–1545.

Brownell, K. D., & Wadden, T. A. (1986). Behavior therapy for obesity: Modern approaches and better results. In K. D. Brownell & J. P. Foreyt (Eds.), *Handbook of eating disorders: Physiology, psychology, and treatment of obesity, anorexia, and bulimia* (pp. 180–197). New York: Basic Books.

Bullen, B. A., Reed, R. R., & Mayer, J. (1964). Physical activity of obese and nonobese adolescent girls appraised by motion picture sampling. *American Journal of Clinical Nutrition, 14,* 211–223.

Burwell, C. S., Robin, E. D., Whaley, R. D., & Bickelman, A. G. (1956). Extreme obesity associated with alveolar hypoventilation—a Pickwickian syndrome. *American Journal of Medicine, 21,* 811–818.

Canning, H., & Mayer, J. (1966). Obesity—its possible effect on college acceptance. *The New England Journal of Medicine, 275,* 1172–1174.

Chandra, R. K., & Kutty, K. M. (1980). Immunocompetence in obesity. *Acta Paediatrica Scandinavica, 69,* 25–30.

Charney, E., Goodman, H. C., McBride, M., Lyon, B., & Pratt, R. (1976). Childhood antecedents of adult obesity: Do chubby infants become obese adults? *The New England Journal of Medicine, 295,* 6–9.

Clark, L., Meyers, A. W., Coyne, T., & Perkins, S. C. (1984). *Childhood obesity treatment: The role of the children's age and parental involvement*. Paper presented at the Association for the Advancement of Behavior Therapy, Philadelphia.

Clarke, R. P., Morrow, S. B., & Morse, E. H. (1970). Interrelationships between plasma lipids, physical measurements, and body fatness of adolescents in Burlington, Vermont. *American Journal of Clinical Nutrition, 23*, 754–763.

Coates, T. J., Jeffery, R. W., Slinkard, L. A., Killen, J., & Danaher, B. (1978). *Frequency of contact and monetary incentives in weight reduction with adolescents*. Paper presented at the Association for the Advancement of Behavior Therapy, Chicago.

Coates, T. J., & Thoresen, C. E. (1980). Obesity among children and adolescents: The problem belongs to everyone. In B. Lahey & A. Kazdin (Eds.), *Advances in child clinical psychology* (Vol. 3, pp. 215–264). New York: Plenum Press.

Cohen, R., Klesges, R. C., Summerville, M., & Meyers, A. W. (1989). A developmental analysis of the influence of body weight on the sociometry of children. *Addictive Behaviors, 14*, 473–476.

Corbin, C. B., & Pletcher, P. (1968). Diet and physical activity patterns of obese and non-obese elementary school children. *The Research Quarterly, 39*, 922–928.

Court, J. M., Hill, G. J., Dunlop, M., & Bolton, T. (1974). Hypertension in childhood obesity. *Australian Pediatric Journal, 10*, 296–300.

Castro, F. J. de, Biesbroeck, R., Erikson, C., Farrell, P., Leong, W., Murphy, D., & Green, R. (1976). Hypertension in adolescents. *Clinical Pediatrics, 15*, 24–26.

Department of Health, Education, and Welfare. (1977). *National Center for Health Statistics growth curves for children: Birth to 18 years*. (DHEW Publication No. 78-1650).

Dietz, W. H. (1983). Childhood obesity: Susceptibility, cause, and management. *Journal of Pediatrics, 103*, 676–686.

Dietz, W. H. (1987). Childhood obesity. In R. J. Wurtman & J. J. Wurtman (Eds.), *Human obesity* (pp. 47–54). New York: The New York Academy of Sciences.

Dietz, W. H., & Gortmaker, S. L. (1985). Do we fatten our children at the television set? Obesity and television viewing in children and adolescents. *Pediatrics, 75*, 807–812.

Dietz, W. H., Gortmaker, S. L., & Sobol, A. M. (1985). Trends in the prevalence of childhood and adolescent obesity in the United States. *Pediatric Research, 19*, 198A.

Drash, A. (1973). Relationship between diabetes mellitus and obesity in the child. *Metabolism, 22*, 337–344.

Elder, G. H. (1969). Appearance and education in marriage mobility. *American Sociological Review, 34*, 519–533.

Epstein, L. H. (1986). Treatment of childhood obesity. In K. D. Brownell & J. P. Foreyt (Eds.), *Handbook of eating disorders: Physiology, psychology, and treatment of obesity, anorexia, and bulimia* (pp. 159–179). New York: Basic Books.

Epstein, L. H., Koeske, R., Wing, R. R., & Valoski, A. (1988). The effect of family variables on child weight change. In B. G. Melamed, K. A. Matthews, D. K. Routh, B. Stabler, & N. Schneiderman (Eds.), *Child health psychology* (pp. 63–74). Hillsdale, NJ: Lawrence Erlbaum Associates.

Epstein, L. H., & Wing, R. R. (1987). Behavioral treatment of childhood obesity. *Psychological Bulletin, 101*, 331–342.

Epstein, L. H., Wing, R. R., Koeske, R., Andrasik, R., & Ossip, D. (1981). Child and parent weight loss in family-based behavior modification programs. *Journal of Consulting and Clinical Psychology, 49*, 647–685.

Epstein, L. H., Wing, R. R., Koeske, R., & Valoski, A. (1985). A comparison of lifestyle exercise, aerobic exercise, and calisthenics on weight loss in obese children. *Behavior Therapy, 16*, 651–665.

Epstein, L. H., Wing, R. R., Koeske, R., & Valoski, A. (1987). Long-term effects of family-based treatment of childhood obesity. *Journal of Consulting and Clinical Psychology, 55*, 91–95.

Epstein, L. H., Wing, R. R., Valoski, A., & Devos, D. (1988). Long-term relationship between weight and aerobic fitness change in children. *Health Psychology, 7*, 47–53.

Fisch, R. O., Bilek, M. K., & Ulstrom, R. (1975). Obesity and leanness at birth and their relationship to body habitus in later childhood. *Pediatrics, 56*, 521–527.

Florey, C. du V., Uppal, S., & Lowy, C. (1976). Relation between blood pressure, weight, and plasma sugar and serum insulin levels in school children aged 9–12 years in Westland, Holland. *British Medical Journal, 1*, 1368–1371.

Freedman, D. S., Burke, G. L., Hasha, D. W., Srinivasan, S. R., Cresanta, J. L., Webber, L.

S., & Berenson, G. S. (1985). Relationship of changes in obesity to serum lipid and lipoprotein changes in childhood and adolescence. *Journal of the American Medical Association, 254*, 515–520.

Garn, S. M., Bailey, S. M., Solomon, M. A., & Hopkins, P. J. (1981). Effects of remaining family members on fatness prediction. *American Journal of Clinical Nutrition, 34*, 148–153.

Garn, S. M., & Clark, D. C. (1976). Trends in fatness and the origins of obesity. *Pediatrics, 57*, 443–456.

Garrow, J. S. (1978). Problems in measuring human energy balance. In *Assessment of energy metabolism in health and disease* (pp. 2–5). Columbus, OH: Ross Laboratories Press.

Garrow, J. S. (1981). Thermogenesis and obesity in man. In P. Bjorntorp, M. Cairella, & A. N. Howard (Eds.), *Recent advances in obesity research III* (pp. 208–215). London: J. Libbey.

Goodman, N., Richardson, S. A., Dornbush, S. M., & Hastorf, A. H. (1963). Various reactions to physical disabilities. *American Sociological Review, 28*, 429–435.

Graves, T., Meyers, A. W., & Clark, L. (1988). An evaluation of parental problem-solving in the behavioral treatment of childhood obesity. *Journal of Consulting and Clinical Psychology, 56*, 246–250.

Halmi, K. A., Long, M., & Stunkard, A. J. (1980). Psychiatric diagnosis of morbidly obese gastric bypass patients. *American Journal of Psychiatry, 137*, 470–472.

Harper, L. V., & Sanders, K. M. (1975). The effect of adults eating on young children's acceptance of unfamiliar food. *Journal of Experimental Child Psychology, 20*, 206–214.

Heyden, S., Bertel, A. G., Hames, C. G., & McDonough, J. R. (1969). Elevated blood pressure levels in adolescents. *Journal of the American Medical Association, 209*, 1683–1698.

Hirsch, J., & Knittle, J. L. (1970). Cellularity of obese and nonobese human adipose tissue. *Federation Proceedings, 29*, 1516–1521.

Huenemann, R. L. (1974). Environmental factors associated with preschool obesity. *Journal of the American Dietetic Association, 64*, 480–487.

Israel, A. C., Stolmaker, L., & Andrian, C. A. G. (1985). The effects of training parents in general child management skills on a behavioral weight loss program for children. *Behavior Therapy, 16*, 169–180.

Israel, A. C., Stolmaker, L., Sharp, J. P., Silver-

man, W. K., & Simon, L. G. (1984). An evaluation of two methods of parental involvement in treating obese children. *Behavior Therapy, 15*, 266–272.

Jacoby, A., Altman, D. G., Cook, J., & Holland, W. W. (1975). Influence of some social and environmental factors on the nutrient intake and the nutritional status of school children. *British Journal of Preventive and Social Medicine, 29*, 116–120.

Jarvie, G. L., Lahey, B., Graziano, W., & Framer, E. (1983). Childhood obesity and social stigma: What we know and what we don't know. *Developmental Review, 3*, 237–273.

Jeliffe, D. B. (1966). *The assessment of nutritional status of the community*, (WHO Monograph 3). Geneva: World Health Organization.

Jequier, E. (1987). Energy utilization in human obesity. In R. J. Wurtman & J. J. Wurtman (Eds.), *Human obesity* (pp. 73–83). New York: The New York Academy of Sciences.

Johnson, M. L., Burke, B. S., & Mayer, J. (1956). Relative importance of inactivity and over-eating in the energy balance of obese high schools girls. *American Journal of Clinical Nutrition, 4*, 37–44.

Kannel, W. B. (1978). Status of coronary heart disease risk factors. *Journal of Nutrition Education, 10*, 10–14.

Kaplan, K. M., & Wadden, T. A. (1986). Childhood obesity and self-esteem. *Journal of Pediatrics, 109*, 367–370.

Karpowitz, D. H., & Zeis, F. R. (1975). Personality and behavior differences of obese and nonobese adolescents. *Journal of Consulting and Clinical Psychology, 43*, 886–891.

Keesey, R. E. (1980). A set-point analysis of the regulation of body weight. In A. J. Stunkard (Ed.), *Obesity* (pp. 144–165). Philadelphia: W. B. Saunders.

Kingsley, R. G., & Shapiro, J. (1977). A comparison of three behavioral programs for the control of obesity in children. *Behavior Therapy, 8*, 30–36.

Kirschenbaum, D. S., Harris, E. S., & Tomarken, A. J. (1984). Effects of parental involvement in behavioral weight loss therapy for preadolescents. *Behavior Therapy, 15*, 485–500.

Klesges, R. C. (1984). Obesity and personality: Global versus specific measures? *Behavioral Assessment, 6*, 347–356.

Klesges, R. C., Coates, T. J., Brown, G., Sturgeon-Tillisch, J., Moldenhauer-Klesges, L. M., Holzer, B., Woolfrey, J., & Vollmer, J.

(1983). Parental influences on children's eating behaviors and relative weight. *Journal of Applied Behavior Analysis, 16*, 371–378.

Klesges, R. C., Coates, T. J., Moldenhauer-Klesges, L. M., Holzer, B., Gustavson, J., & Barnes, J. (1984). The FATS: An observational system for assessing physical activity in children and associated parent behavior. *Behavior Assessment, 6*, 333–345.

Klesges, R. C., & Hanson, C. L. (1988). Determining the environmental causes and correlates of childhood obesity: Methodological issues and future research directions. In N. A. Krasnegor, G. D. Grave, & N. Krechmer (Eds.), *Childhood obesity: A biobehavioral perspective* (pp. 92–118). Caldwell, NJ: Telford Press.

Klesges, R. C., Hanson, C. L., Eck, L. H., & Durff, A. (1988). Accuracy of self-reports of food intake in obese and normal weight individuals: II. The effects of parental obesity on children's dietary intake. *American Journal of Clinical Nutrition, 48*, 1252–1256.

Klesges, R. C., Malott, J. M., Boschee, P. F., & Weber, J. M. (1986). The effects of parental influences on children's food intake, physical activity, and relative weight. *International Journal of Eating Disorders, 5*, 335–346.

Klesges, R. C., Wilder, M., Somes, G., Alpert, B., & Klesges, L. M. (1988). The reliability and validity of multi-site skinfold assessments in preschool children. *Journal of Medicine and Science in Sports and Exercise*.

Larkin, J. C., & Pines, H. A. (1979). No fat persons need apply: Experimental studies of the overweight stereotype and hiring preferences. *Sociology of Work and Occupations, 6*, 312–327.

Lauer, R. M., Anderson, A. R., Beaglehole, R., & Burns, T. L. (1983). Factors related to the tracking of blood pressure in children: U.S. National Center for Health Statistics Health Examination Surveys Cycles II and III. *Hypertension, 6*, 307–314.

Lauer, R. M., Connor, W. E., Leaverton, P. E., Reiter, M. A., & Clark, W. R. (1975). Coronary heart disease risk factors in children: The Muscatine study. *Journal of Pediatrics, 86*, 697–700.

LeBow, M. D. (1984). *Child obesity: A new frontier of behavior therapy*. New York: Springer.

Londe, J., Bourgoyne, J. J., Robson, A. M., & Goldring, D. (1971). Hypertension in apparently normal children. *Journal of Pediatrics, 78*, 569–577.

Maddox, G. L., Back, R. K., & Liederman, V. R. (1968). Overweight and social deviance and disability. *Journal of Health and Social Behavior, 9*, 287–298.

Magalini, S. (1971). *Dictionary of medical syndromes*. Philadelphia: J. B. Lippincott.

Martin, M. M., & Martin, A. (1973). Obesity, hyperinsulinism, and diabetes mellitus in childhood. *Journal of Pediatrics, 82*, 192–201.

Mendelson, B. K., & White, D. R. (1982). Relation between body self-esteem and self-esteem of obese and normal children. *Perceptual and Motor Skills, 54*, 899–905.

Metropolitan Life Insurance Company. (1959). New weight standards for men and women. *Statistical Bulletin of the Metropolitan Life Insurance Company, 40*, 1.

Metropolitan Life Insurance Company. (1983). 1983 Metropolitan height and weight tables. *Statistical Bulletin of the Metropolitan Life Insurance Company, 64*, 3.

Meyers, A. W., & Craighead, W. C. (1984). *Cognitive behavior therapy with children*. New York: Plenum Press.

Meyers, A. W., & Schleser, R. (1981). Behavioral community psychology. In W. E. Craighead, A. Kazdin, & M. Mahoney (Eds.), *Behavior modification: Principles, issues and applications* (2nd ed., pp. 479–501). Boston: Houghton Mifflin.

Moore, M. E., Stunkard, A. J., & Srole, L. (1962). Obesity, social class and mental illness. *Journal of the American Medical Association, 181*, 962–966.

Myers, R. J., Klesges, R. C., Eck, L. H., Hanson, C. L., & Klem, M. L. (1988). Accuracy of self-reports of food intake in obese and normal weight individuals: I. The effects of obesity on self-reports of dietary intake. *American Journal of Clinical Nutrition, 48*, 1258–1251.

Myres, A. W., & Yeung, D. I. (1979). Obesity in infants: Significance, etiology, and prevention. *Canadian Journal of Public Health, 70*, 113–119.

Nelson, W. E., Behrman, R. E., & Vaughan, V. C. (1987). *Nelson textbook of pediatrics* (13th ed.). Philadelphia: W. B. Saunders.

Palumbo, F. M., & Dietz, W. H. (1985). Children's television: Its effect on nutrition and cognitive development. *Pediatric Annals, 14*, 793–801.

Piscano, J. C., Lichter, H., Ritter, J., & Siegal, A. P. (1978). An attempt at prevention of obesity in infancy. *Pediatrics, 61*, 360–364.

Prentice, A. M., Black, A. E., Coward, W. A., Davies, H. L., Goldberg, G. R., Murgartroyd, P. R., Ashford, J., Swayer, M., & Whitehead, R. G. (1986). High-levels of energy expenditure in obese women. *British Journal of Medicine, 292*, 983–987.

Rames, L. K., Clarke, W. R., Connor, W. E., Reiter, M. A., & Tauer, R. M. (1978). Normal blood pressures and the evaluation of sustained blood pressure elevation in childhood: The Muscatine study. *Journal of Pediatrics, 86*, 245–251.

Ravussin E., Burnard, B., Schutz, Y., & Jequier, E. (1984). Twenty-four-hour energy expenditure and resting metabolic rate in obese, moderately obese, and control subjects. *American Journal of Clinical Nutrition, 35*, 566–573.

Ravussin, E., Lillioja, S., Knwoler, W. C., Christin, L., Freymond, D., Abbott, W. G. H., Boyce, V., Howard, B. V., & Bogardus, C. (1988). Reduced rate of energy expenditure as a risk factor for body-weight gain. *The New England Journal of Medicine, 318*, 467–472.

Richardson, S. A., Hastorf, A. H., Goodman, N., & Dornbush, S. M. (1961). Cultural uniformity in reaction to physical disabilities. *American Sociological Review, 90*, 44–51.

Roberts, S. B., Savage, J., Coward, W. A., Chew, B., & Lucas, A. (1988). Energy expenditure and intake in infants born to lean and overweight mothers. *The New England Journal of Medicine, 318*, 461–466.

Rudolph, A. M., Hoffman, J. I. E., & Axelrod, S. (1987). *Pediatrics* (18th ed.). Norwalk, CT: Appleton & Lange.

Sallade, J. (1973). A comparison of the psychological adjustment of obese vs. non-obese children. *Journal of Psychosomatic Research, 17*, 89–96.

Schulz, L. O. (1986). Obese, overweight, desirable, ideal: Where to draw the line in 1986? *Journal of the American Dietetics Association, 86*, 1702–1704.

Shapiro, L. R., Crawford, P. B., Clark, M. J., Pearson, D. L., Raz, J., & Huenemann, R. L. (1984). Obesity prognosis: A longitudinal study of children from the age of 6 months to 9 years. *American Journal of Public Health, 74*, 968–972.

Sobal, J., & Stunkard, A. J. (1989). Socioeconomic status and obesity: A review of the literature. *Psychological Bulletin, 105*, 260–275.

Staffieri, J. R. (1967). A study of social stereotype of body type image in children. *Journal of Personality and Social Psychology, 7*, 101–104.

Straw, M. K., & Rogers, T. (1985). Obesity assessment. In W. W. Tryon (Ed.), *Behavioral assessment in behavioral medicine* (pp. 19–65). New York: Springer.

Stuart, R. S. (1967). Behavioral control of overeating. *Behaviour Research and Therapy, 5*, 357–365.

Stunkard, A. J., & Burt, V. (1967). Obesity and body image: II. Age at onset of disturbances in body image. *American Journal of Psychiatry, 123*, 1443–1447.

Stunkard, A. J., & McLaren-Hume, M. (1959). The results of treatment for obesity. *Archives of Internal Medicine, 103*, 79–85.

Stunkard, A. J., & Mendelson, M. (1967). Obesity and body image: I. Characteristics of disturbances in the body image of some obese persons. *American Journal of Psychiatry, 123*, 1296–1300.

Stunkard, A. J., & Pestka, J. (1962). The physical activity of obese girls. *American Journal of Diseases in Children, 103*, 116–121.

Stunkard, A. J., Sorensen, T. I. A., Hanis, C., Teasdale, T. W., Chakraborty, R., Schull, W. J., & Schulsinger, F. (1986). An adoption study of human obesity. *The New England Journal of Medicine, 314*, 193–198.

Tracey, V. V., De, N. C., & Harper, J. R. (1971). Obesity and respiratory infections in infants and young children. *British Medical Journal, 1*, 16–18.

Voors, A. W., Foster, T. A., Frerichs, R. R., Webber, L. S., & Berenson, G. S. (1976). Studies of blood pressures in children, ages 5–14 years, in a total biracial community: The Bogalusa heart study. *Circulation, 54*, 319–327.

Voors, A. W., Harsha, D. W., Webber, L. S., Radhakrishnamurthy, B., Simavasan, S. R., & Berenson, G. S. (1982). Clustering of anthropometric parameters, glucose tolerance, and serum lipids in children with high and low B- and pre-B-lipoproteins. *Atherosclerosis, 2*, 346–355.

Wadden, T. A., Foster, G. D., Brownell, K. D., & Finley, E. (1984). Self-concept in obese and normal weight children. *Journal of Consulting and Clinical Psychology, 52*, 1104–1105.

Wadden, T. A., & Stunkard, A. J. (1987). Psychopathology and obesity. In R. J. Wurtman & J. J. Wurtman (Eds.), *Human obesity* (pp. 14–28). New York: The New York Academy of Sciences.

Waxman, M., & Stunkard, A. J. (1980). Caloric

intake and expenditure of obese boys. *Journal of Pediatrics, 96*, 187–193.

Weil, W. B. (1977). Current controversies in childhood obesity. *Journal of Pediatrics, 91*, 175–187.

Wilkin, N., Meyers, A. W., Cohen, R., & Klesges, R. C. (1988). *An assessment of peer ratings and behavioral interactions of obese and nonobese children.* Manuscript in preparation. Memphis State University, Department of Psychology, Memphis, TN.

Wilkinson, P., Parklin, J., & Pearloom, G. (1977). Energy intake and physical activity in obese children. *British Medical Journal, 1*, 756.

Wilmore, D. W., & Pruitt, B. J. (1972). Fat boys get burned. *Lancet, 2*, 631–632.

Wooley, S. C., Wooley, O. W., & Dyrenforth, S. R. (1979). Theoretical, practical, and social issues in behavioral treatments of obesity. *Journal of Applied Behavior Analysis, 12*, 3–25.

CHAPTER 28

OBESITY IN ADULTHOOD

William J. Fremouw
Diana Damer
Martha E. Smith

DESCRIPTION AND CLINICAL PRESENTATION

Obesity is the biological condition of excessive body fat. The typical American adult male's body is composed of 14% percent fat, while the average adult female has 24% body fat (Stuart & Davis, 1972). Depending on the criteria used, 10% to 50% of the population is obese (Bray, 1987). While defining and measuring obesity may appear to be straightforward, it is not. Measures of body fat are difficult to obtain and interpret. The only direct means to assess body fat is to analyze carcass composition. Since this is almost impossible, the following indirect methods are typically used.

Height-Weight Measures

The most common method of measuring obesity (as summarized by Brownell, 1981) has been the distribution of weights at given heights. The 1960 and 1983 Metropolitan Life Insurance Company weight tables are the most widely used (see Table 28.1). Based on pooled data from 25 insurance companies and 4.5 million people who ap-

plied for insurance, the weights associated with the longest longevity were determined (Stanley Kranczer, personal communication, July 14, 1988).

Using these tables, obesity is typically defined as a minimum of 20% above the ideal weight for a particular height. Using this criterion, approximately 30% of men and 40% of women between 40 and 49 years old are obese (Metropolitan Life Insurance Company, 1983). Height-weight tables can sometimes be misleading if they are used as the sole indicator of a weight problem. For example, a person may exceed the ideal weight for his or her height and yet not meet the criteria for obesity. Often athletes who are particularly muscular are overweight for their height, although their body fat content is below the norm. They may be heavier than the ideal because muscle, instead of fat, comprises a disproportionate amount of their body weight (Fremouw & Heyneman, 1983).

It should be noted that the ideal weights are neither average weights nor the weights physicians recommend. Instead, they are the weights at which mortality was lowest. This standard of measurement is limited in the following ways: (1) the

Table 28.1.   1983 Metropolitan Life Insurance Company Weight Table by Height and Small, Medium, or Large Frame

| MEN | | | | | | | | | | WOMEN | | | | |
| HEIGHT | | SMALL FRAME | MEDIUM FRAME | LARGE FRAME | | HEIGHT | | SMALL FRAME | MEDIUM FRAME | LARGE FRAME |
FEET	INCHES					FEET	INCHES			
5	2	128–134	131–141	138–150		4	10	102–111	109–121	118–131
5	3	130–136	133–143	140–153		4	11	103–113	111–123	120–134
5	4	132–138	135–145	142–156		5	0	104–115	113–126	122–137
5	5	134–140	137–148	144–160		5	1	106–118	115–129	125–140
5	6	136–142	139–151	146–164		5	2	108–121	118–132	128–143
5	7	138–145	142–154	149–168		5	3	111–124	121–135	131–147
5	8	140–148	145–157	152–172		5	4	114–127	124–138	134–151
5	9	142–151	148–160	155–176		5	5	117–130	127–141	137–155
5	10	144–154	151–163	158–180		5	6	120–133	130–144	140–159
5	11	146–157	154–166	161–184		5	7	123–136	133–147	143–163
6	0	149–160	157–170	164–188		5	8	126–139	136–150	146–167
6	1	152–164	160–174	168–192		5	9	129–142	139–153	149–170
6	2	155–168	164–178	172–197		5	10	132–145	142–156	152–173
6	3	158–172	167–182	176–202		5	11	135–148	145–159	155–176
6	4	162–176	171–187	181–207		6	0	138–151	148–162	158–179

Weights at ages 25–59 based on lowest mortality. Weight in pounds according to frame (in indoor clothing weighing 5 pounds, shoes with 1-inch heels).

Weights at ages 25–59 based on lowest mortality. Weight in pounds according to frame (in indoor clothing weighing 3 pounds, shoes with 1-inch heels).

subject selection was biased because only insured people were measured, (2) males outnumbered females and whites outnumbered blacks, (3) the subjects were classified arbitrarily for body frame, and (4) all persons were weighed in shoes and clothes (Stanley Kranczer, personal communication, July 14, 1988).

Height and weight measures have been used in various combinations as indices of obesity. The two ratios most commonly used are weight-height and BMI, body mass index: weight (kg)/height^2 (m). Keys, Fidanza, Karvonen, Kimura, and Taylor in Brownell (1981) compared these measures with the more direct measurements of density and skinfold thickness and found the BMI to be most valid. According to Bray (1976), height-weight and the BMI are the best measures, although an additional measure of fatness such as skinfold thickness may be useful.

Skinfold Thickness

The estimation of total body fat by measuring skinfold thickness is acceptable to many researchers (Bray, 1976; Franzini & Grimes, 1976). However, unless the evaluator is very experienced in the use of skinfold calipers, the reliability is very low (Womersley & Durnin, 1973). Obesity standards for skinfolds have been developed by

Seltzer and Mayer (1965) using the triceps site and by Durnin and Womersley (1974) using the sum of skinfolds obtained from the triceps, biceps, subscapular (below shoulder blade), and suprailiac sites (over pelvic bone). Bray (1976) recommends using at least two sites when measuring skinfolds.

Body Circumferences and Diameters

Formulas for estimating body fat from measurements of distances around the neck, chest, waist, hips, and thighs and the diameters or distances between the shoulders or hips have been devised by Behnke and Wilmore in Brownell (1981). These measurements tend to be more reliable than skinfolds and are as accurate for obese as for lean persons.

Somatotyping

To classify people as endomorphic, mesomorphic, or ectomorphic, Sheldon (1954) employed pictures of individual persons. These represent relatively crude estimations and require extensive training in order to achieve reliability. They can be useful, however, for making rapid judgments of weight in studies where subjects are unaware they are being observed (Brownell, Stunkard, & Albaum, 1980).

Density

Because a submerged object displaces its own weight in water, fat estimates can be obtained by submerging the body in water. Using conversion tables and equations that take into account the average density of fat and nonfat body constituents, the amount of body fat is then calculated. This method, hydrostatic weighing, is one of the more rigorous procedures for assessing body fat. It is valid except in cases where body fat distribution is unusual, as is sometimes the case with athletes. Because expensive and sensitive equipment is required, its use is limited.

Overall, obesity is typically first defined by weight at least 20% greater than the height-weight norms. The body mass index is then calculated. If available, more direct measures of body fat such as skinfold thickness or hydrostatic weight are then used to supplement the traditional weight-based definitions of obesity.

EPIDEMIOLOGY

Obesity is one of the most serious and prevalent medical and psychological problems of modern society. Estimates of its prevalence range from 10–50%, depending upon the criteria used to define obesity (Bray, 1987). The second National Health and Nutrition Survey (NHANES II) found that approximately 26% of adult Americans between the ages of 20 to 75 years were overweight. In this survey, "overweight" was defined by a body mass index calculated by dividing weight in kilograms by weight in meters squared. Men are considered to be overweight if their BMI is greater than or equal to 27.8. They are classified as severely overweight if their BMI is greater than or equal to 31.1. Similarly, the cutoff indices for women are 27.3 and 32.3, respectively (VanItallie, 1985).

According to another classification scheme, adults are considered to be overweight if their body weight exceeds their ideal weight by 20% or more. Ideal weight is considered to be the midpoint of the recommended weight range for an individual's gender, height, and body frame as shown in the 1983 Metropolitan Life Insurance Company table (Metropolitan Life, 1983). According to this classification, adults are described as being mildly, moderately, or severely obese if their body weights are 20% to 40% overweight, 41% to 100% overweight, or more than 100% overweight, respectively (Stunkard, 1984). The percentages of 20% overweight and 40% over-

weight closely correspond to the previously mentioned BMI cutoff indices for defining overweight and severely overweight (VanItallie, 1985).

Of the approximately 34 million Americans who are classified as being overweight, it is interesting to note their distribution in the population in terms of gender, age, race, and socioeconomic status (Table 28.2). On the average, the prevalence of overweight among females is greater than that among males (Bray, 1987). There is an increase in prevalence of overweight among both white and black men between the ages of 20 and 54, after which the prevalence begins to decrease. Among white women, the prevalence of overweight increases through age 74, whereas it levels off at age 55 among black women (VanItallie, 1985).

Racial differences in body weight are also found among American adults. The prevalence of overweight is greater among black men than white men between the ages of 35 and 54. Overweight is much more common among black women than white women at all ages. In fact, the percentage of overweight among black women between the ages of 45 and 54 is twofold that of white women in this age range (VanItallie, 1985).

Socioeconomic factors also play a role in the prevalence of overweight. Women below the poverty line have a much higher prevalence of overweight than do women in higher social classes. However, interestingly, men above the poverty line actually have a slightly higher prevalence of overweight relative to men below the poverty line (VanItallie, 1985). Although these results raise the question of a possible confound between race and social class, since the greatest percentage of overweight is among black women below the poverty line, statistical analyses revealed that race and social status were independent predictors of overweight (Landis, Stanich, Freeman, & Koch, 1976).

NATURAL HISTORY

Only 5% of all obesity can be attributed to underlying physical disorders such as brain damage, endocrine dysfunction, and hereditary diseases (VanItallie, 1977). The remaining 95% of obesity may be caused by a number of different factors. One focus of research has been life-styles, including chronic overeating and inactivity, which can lead to obesity (VanItallie & Campbell, 1972). There are a variety of highly palatable foods, especially those high in fat and sugar content, which are readily available in our society. These types of foods have been shown to create obesity in labora-

Table 28.2. NHANES II Data on Prevalence of Overweight in Men and Women According to Age, Race, and Social Class

	MEN		WOMEN	
AGE	WHITES	BLACKS	WHITES	BLACKS
20–24	12.7%	5.5%	9.6%	23.7%
25–34	20.9%	17.5%	17.9%	33.5%
35–44	28.2%	40.9%	24.8%	40.8%
45–54	30.5%	41.4%	29.9%	61.2%
55–64	28.6%	26.0%	34.8%	59.4%
65–74	25.8%	26.4%	36.5%	60.8%

	MEN		WOMEN	
AGE	POVERTY	NONPOVERTY	POVERTY	NONPOVERTY
20–24	7.5%	12.8%	10.5%	11.5%
25–34	20.3%	20.5%	30.8%	18.4%
35–44	24.0%	29.3%	49.1%	23.7%
45–54	28.5%	31.4%	54.1%	30.3%
55–64	26.0%	27.8%	44.1%	35.5%
65–74	20.9%	25.8%	46.1%	37.0%

From VanItallie (1985).

tory animals. Sclafani and Springer (1976) fed rats a "supermarket" diet, including chocolate chip cookies, salami, cheese, bananas, marshmallows, milk chocolate, and peanut butter. At least seven foods were available at any one time, and the food choices were changed frequently to maintain variety. After a 2-month period, these rats had gained 269% more weight than had control animals fed only Purina Chow. This diet of "supermarket" foods may similarly lead to the development of obesity in humans.

Another variable that may contribute to the onset of obesity is inactivity. According to the U.S. Department of Agriculture, the incidence of obesity today is higher than it was in 1910, yet caloric intake is approximately 5% less. A major factor that might account for this inconsistency is that overall level of activity has decreased with the increase in automation (Stern, 1984). Once an individual becomes obese, there is evidence to suggest that inactivity contributes to its maintenance. Chirico and Stunkard (1960) found that obese men and women walked less than normal weight adults during their routine daily activities. Obese men walked, on the average, four miles per day, whereas men of normal weight walked six miles per day. Obese women walked, on the average, two miles per day, whereas those of normal weight walked five miles per day. Since it is often difficult

for obese individuals to engage in physical activity, a vicious cycle is created. The more fat an individual gains, the less active he or she becomes, further contributing to the obese state. Thus, inactivity may play an important role in both the development and maintenance of obesity.

Another approach to the pathogenesis of obesity hypothesizes that obese individuals are biologically programmed to be fat. The amount of fat stored in the body is a product of the number and size of the fat cells. Nisbett (1972) postulated that the number of adipocytes in the body is determined by heredity and early nutritional experiences and is permanently fixed by adolescence. Overeating during this critical period results in a permanent elevation in fat cell number, while weight loss or gain following this period results only in a change in size but not number of adipocytes. Hirsch and Knittle (1970) identified two subtypes of obesity from morphologic studies of adipose tissue. Early onset obesity is characterized by an increase in fat cell number or hyperplasia, whereas adult onset obesity is characterized by an increase in cell size or hypertrophy. Bjorntorp and his colleagues (1975) studied 10 hyperplastic obese women and 11 hypertrophic obese women who were placed on a 1,100 kcal/day diet until weight loss failure occurred. While the enlarged fat cells decreased to the size of the fat cells of controls, the fat cell number remained unchanged. Therefore, the hypertrophic obese subjects ended their diet with a normal percentage of body fat, while the hyperplastic subjects remained obese. These results suggest that early onset or hyperplastic obesity is more refractory than is adult onset or hypertrophic obesity.

Dieting is by far the most commonly used method of achieving weight loss among obese individuals. Millions of dollars are spent each year on low-calorie diet foods and liquid formulas, appetite suppressants, fad diets, and other diet programs (Stuart & Davis, 1972). Ironically, it is possible that dieting may actually be a critical factor in maintaining the obese state. An increasing number of studies are examining the effects of weight cycling, or repeated dieting attempts with subsequent regain. One study examined the metabolic effects of weight cycling among laboratory animals (Brownell, Greenwood, Stellar, & Shrager, 1986). Sprague-Dawley type rats were given ad libitum access to a high-fat diet until they became obese. They were then put on a diet and refed for two cycles of weight loss and regain. Results showed that weight was lost during the second cycle at only half the rate and was regained at three times the rate of the first cycle. Furthermore, these rats had a significantly elevated number of fat cells and a significantly higher percentage of body fat. These results show that weight cycling increases metabolic efficiency among laboratory animals. There is also evidence to suggest that humans who repeatedly diet and regain may also experience this increased metabolic efficiency (Brownell, 1988). Weight cycling may, therefore, contribute to the maintenance of obesity by slowing the metabolic rate to a point that makes a negative energy balance virtually impossible to achieve.

Dieting often proves unsuccessful for reasons other than an increased efficiency in energy expenditure. Restricted food intake is associated with chronic hunger and a compelling drive to eat. Individuals who develop a restrained eating pattern are at high risk for binge eating. Pyle, Mitchell, and Eckert (1981) found that overeating began after a period of dieting in 30 out of 34 patients. Similarly, Hawkins and Clement (1980) reported that degree of dietary restraint was significantly correlated with severity of binge eating. Therefore, the evidence indicates that dieting, so commonly utilized by overweight people, is associated with adverse biological and psychological reactions that help to perpetuate obesity.

IMPAIRMENT AND COMPLICATIONS

Medical Consequence of Obesity

Obesity has long been associated with serious medical problems such as coronary disease. The second National Health and Nutrition Examination Survey (NHANES II) found that the risk of hypertension among overweight individuals is three times higher than for nonoverweight individuals. The risk is greatest among overweight persons aged 20 to 44 years who are 5.6 times more likely to develop hypertension than are nonoverweight persons in the same age group. The risk of hypercholesterolemia is 1.5 times greater among overweight than among nonoverweight persons. The relative risk increases to 2.1 times higher among overweight individuals who are 20 to 44 years (VanItallie, 1985). Obesity has also been associated with impairments in pulmonary functions, gall bladder disease, trauma to the weight-carrying joints, dermal abnormalities, proteinuria, endocrine abnormalities, and cancer (Bray, 1985).

Some studies have indicated that it is the excess accumulation of adipose tissue in the abdominal region, rather than total body fat mass, that increases the risk for cardiovascular disease (Bjorntorp, 1985). Abdominal obesity (large stomach-thin hips and thighs, often called a beer belly), which is most common in men, has been associated with more complications than gynoid obesity (characterized by thin abdomin-large hips and thighs often described as a pear-shaped distribution typically found in women) (Vague, 1956). It appears that when the waist/hip ratio exceeds 1.0 in men or 0.8 in women, the risk for ischaemic heart disease, stroke, or premature death increases (Bjorntorp, 1985). These studies suggest that those obese persons with excess fat in the abdominal region are at greatest risk for developing cardiovascular risk factors and disease than people whose excess fat is on the hips and legs.

Obesity is associated with an increase in mortality for both males and females. Data from the American Cancer Society on more than 750,000 individuals showed a curvilinear increase in mortality with increasing weight. The relationship of mortality and overweight was almost linear above a BMI of 25 kg/m^2 (Lew & Garfinkel, 1979). Similar results were found in the Build Study (Society of Actuaries, 1979) and in the Framingham Study (Hubert, Feinleib, McNamara, & Castelli, 1983).

In a prospective study by the American Cancer

Society, mortality ratios for major diseases were computed in relation to overweight. Diabetes was associated with the highest mortality ratio for overweight men and women. The mortality rates were five times greater for men and nearly eight times greater for women who were 40% or more overweight. Ratios were also computed for digestive diseases (men, 3.99; women, 2.29), cerebral vascular lesions (men, 2.27; women, 1.52), coronary heart disease (men, 1.95; women, 2.07), and cancer (men, 1.33; women, 1.55). Mortality rates by cancer site were highest among overweight men for colon-rectal and prostate cancer. Overweight women had higher mortality rates from cancer of the endometrium, uterus, gall bladder, cervix, ovary, and breast (Garfinkel, 1985).

Social and Psychological Consequences of Obesity

Many obese persons suffer adverse psychosocial consequences due to the pervasive negative attitudes toward obesity in modern society (Allon, 1982). Evidence shows that the obese are discriminated against in many aspects of their lives. One study found that obese high school students were accepted into high-ranking colleges less frequently than were normal weight students, even though the groups did not differ in qualifications or application rates (Canning & Mayer, 1966). Roe and Eickwort (1976) reported that 16% of employers surveyed reported that they would not hire obese women under any circumstances. When children were shown pictures of an obese child, a normal weight child, and children with various disabilities, the obese child was consistently chosen as the least likable (Goodman, Dornbusch, Richardson, & Hastorf, 1963). Even health care providers described their obese patients as "weak-willed, ugly, and awkward" (Maddox & Liederman, 1969).

Despite this strong prejudice and discrimination in our society, obese persons generally do not show greater psychological disturbances, including depression, anxiety, and low self-esteem, than do normal weight persons (Wadden & Stunkard, 1985). However, one problem characteristic of obese persons appears to be a negative body image (Wadden & Stunkard, 1985). Some obese persons feel that their bodies are grotesque, and they become preoccupied with their weight (Stunkard & Mendelson, 1961). Body image disturbance is most common in young women of middle to upper-middle social classes in which the stigma of obesity is quite strong (Stunkard & Burt, 1967).

Although psychological disturbances have been found among some obese persons, these may be the result of dieting rather than the obese state per se. Dieting has long been associated with adverse emotional reactions, including depression, anxiety, and irritability. These responses are more common among persons with childhood onset obesity and among the severely obese (Stunkard & Rush, 1974). Halmi, Stunkard, and Mason (1980) found that 41% of severely obese patients experienced moderate to severe depression, 53% experienced moderate to severe anxiety, and 64% experienced moderate to severe irritability while dieting. Only a minority of these patients did not experience negative responses to weight loss attempts. In addition to these psychological disturbances, dieting may also lead to binge eating and bulimia (Polivy & Herman, 1985).

The adverse psychological and behavioral disturbances among obese persons appear to be a result, at least in part, of their restrained eating patterns. However, it is also possible that those obese persons who are most disturbed by their weight are the ones most likely to diet. This issue of cause and effect still needs to be resolved.

DIFFERENTIAL DIAGNOSIS

Technically, obesity is the biological state of excessive body fat. It is not a psychiatric diagnosis included in the *Diagnostic and Statistical Manual of Mental Disorders* (American Psychiatric Association, 1987). However, obesity is often associated with eating disorders because of shared behavioral patterns and problems such as overconcern with body shape or weight. Anorexia nervosa and bulimia nervosa are the two most commonly diagnosed adult eating disorders. A person cannot experience anorexia nervosa and obesity concurrently because anorexia nervosa requires a body weight of 15% below the norm for age and height, while obesity begins with body weight 20% above the norm.

Bulimia nervosa does not have a weight criterion and can occur among obese individuals. According to the DSM-III-R, bulimia nervosa has the following characteristics:

1. Recurrent episodes of binge eating (rapid consumption of a large amount of food in a discrete period of time)

2. A feeling of lack of control over eating behavior during the eating binges
3. The person regularly engages in either self-induced vomiting, use of laxatives or diuretics, strict dieting or fasting, or vigorous exercise in order to prevent weight gain
4. A minimum of two binge eating episodes a week for at least three months
5. Persistent overconcern with body shape and weight. (pp. 68–69)

Gormally (1984) described the assessment and treatment of obese bulimics. Bulimia nervosa can be evaluated by a clinical interview that addresses each of these diagnostic criteria. In addition, self-report questionnaires such as Smith and Thelen's Bulimia Test (BULIT, 1984) can be used to assess the presence and severity of bulimia nervosa by someone who is obese. A minimum score of 102 is the usual cutoff for defining clinically severe bulimia.

CASE EXAMPLE

Behavioral approaches to the treatment of obesity have grown rapidly since Stuart and Davis's pioneering work in the 1960s. The following study presents case material demonstrating a comprehensive behavioral program for the treatment of obesity, combined with a self-imposed protein-sparing diet (Linn, 1976). This latter approach requires dieters to consume daily only 4 to 8 fluid ounces of predigested liquid protein formula along with vitamins and mineral supplements until the desired weight loss is achieved. The behavior change program, which had focused on changing food selection, eating styles, and stimulus-controlled aspects of eating, had been implemented for 25 weeks before the liquid protein diet regimen was initiated by the client. The following case study was presented by Kattell, Callahan, Fremouw, and Zitter (1979), as an example of a successful weight loss program that integrated behavior change procedures with a more radical fasting approach.

The client, Sharon, was a 34-year-old married mother of two children. Sharon reported that she had normal weight as a child, adolescent, and young adult. After the birth of the two children, she had gained approximately 50 pounds that she had been unable to lose through her own dieting efforts. At the beginning of the treatment program, she was 62 inches tall and weighed 178 pounds. Based on the Metropolitan Scale, she was 42.4% overweight and had a body mass index of 32.36.

Sharon had no other serious health problems based on a recent medical physical. She had no history of psychiatric care or substance abuse. There were no health problems causing or arising from her current obesity. Sharon had a stable marriage and reported no unusual life changes or stresses at the time treatment began. She did not work outside of the home.

Her family history showed that both parents were of normal weight and that her siblings were described as being average weight. Her history of adult onset fits the hypertrophic type of obesity.

Assessment Procedures

Sharon completed a daily self-monitoring form of all food consumed. Based on Stuart and Davis (1972), the diary required her to record the antecedents to eating (location, time of day, hunger, emotionality, and details of the act), duration of the eating episode, and the amount of food and type of food consumed. Diary entries were completed immediately following any eating episode. Data from these diaries were scored to determine the percentage of eating episodes taking place in designated, appropriate eating places such as a dining room or kitchen. Also, the percentage of snacks that were "appropriate" (contained 150 calories or fewer and were separated from any other snacks by at least 3 hours). These daily data were transformed to mean weekly percentages. Sharon was weighed each week on a medical balance beam scale to determine her weight.

Treatment

Figure 28.1 presents the six phases of the treatment program and corresponding body weight. The treatment began with a 7-week baseline during which the baseline for body weight, designated eating place, and appropriate snack percentages were determined on a weekly basis. The treatment began with Sharon being instructed to modify the antecedents to her eating behavior as follows:

1. Use an appropriate place to eat each meal and snack
2. Engage in no competing activities while eating, such as reading or watching television
3. Keep as many snacks out of sight and out of easy access within the home as possible
4. Make available lower-calorie snacks

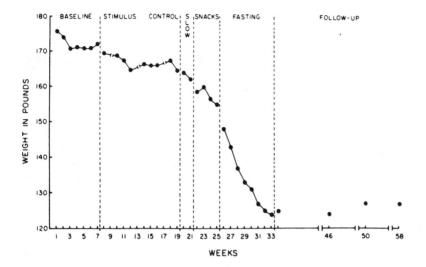

Figure 28.1. Subject's weight during treatment and 6 months of follow-up.

5. Remove serving containers from the dining room before starting a meal.

These stimulus control procedures were based on Stuart and Davis's prior work and reduce the number and types of antecedents for eating within the house such as the sight of high-calorie foods lying out on the counter.

During the third phase, Sharon was directed to eat more slowly by placing her utensils or hand-held food down after every third bite and to insert two delays of a least 2 minutes duration into the evening meal. By slowing the rate of eating, the client has more time to digest the food and become satiated without overeating. Approximately 15 minutes are needed from the time the food is consumed until it begins to reduce hunger. Therefore, eating more slowly is designed to reduce the total number of calories consumed before hunger begins to remit.

The final phase of the formal behavioral training consisted of providing Sharon with instructions for preplanning more appropriate low-calorie snacks. A snack menu was designed in which she would select 150-calorie snacks from 3″ × 5″ cards containing complete descriptions of approximately 20 low-calorie snacks that she enjoyed. Each morning she chose two cards at random as her daily snack menu.

After 25 weeks of baseline and treatment conditions, Sharon expressed strong disappointment with her rate of weight loss. Although she had lost 20 pounds, she wished for more rapid weight loss. Against the recommendation of the therapist, she then began the diet described by Robert Linn in the *Last Chance Diet* (1976). On this diet she consumed approximately 360 calories per day in a form of a liquid protein concentrate. For the next 8 weeks she consumed no other calories than the liquid protein diet. She agreed to be under a physician's supervision to monitor her for any medical complications. Each week she met with her therapist to be weighed, to discuss her problems with this strict diet, and to discuss her eventual return to eating.

After 8 weeks of this modified fast, Sharon reintroduced food gradually for the next 2 weeks until she was again consuming 1,200 to 1,600 calories. At the end of the fast, Sharon had achieved her goal weight of 125 pounds. She was seen regularly for follow up for 6 months to assess her body weight and eating behaviors.

Overall, the combination of the behavioral change program and modified fast was successful. As summarized in Figure 28.1, Sharon lost 53 pounds from baseline to Week 33. Her follow-up data showed that she regained only 3 pounds and was only 2% overweight.

Figure 28.2 presents behavioral data collected from the self-monitoring forms. These data demonstrate that Sharon changed at least two specific eating behaviors before and maintained those changes after her modified fast. During baseline, she ate at a designated eating place 61%. Following stimulus control instruction, she maintained 100% compliance with eating in an appropriate designated area.

During baseline Sharon consumed appropriate

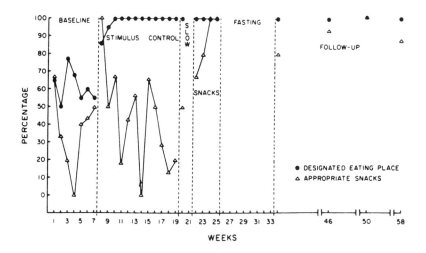

Figure 28.2. Percentage of eating episodes in designated eating place and percentage of snacks that were appropriate.

low-calorie snacks only 36% of episodes. Her follow-up data showed that her choice of snacks improved to over 80% appropriate low-calorie snacks.

Objectively, Sharon's is an example of a very successful weight loss program, changing from 42.4% overweight to 2% overweight. She experienced no negative psychological problems of anxiety, depression, or marital distress, which are sometimes reported with major changes in body weight. Equally important, Sharon was able to maintain her posttreatment body weight for at least six months and did not show the weight rebound of the yo-yo dieters. Overall, this is a very successful program that combined both behavior change techniques and a modified fast regimen. Prior to initiation of the modified fast, Sharon had already made major changes in her eating habits and food selection. This is considered the key of her long-term success, in that she had acquired the appropriate healthy eating habits that allowed her to maintain her new body weight. This combination of approaches is now being pursued by other researchers because of its promise to make substantial changes in obesity with hope for successful maintenance (Wadden, Smoller, & Stunkard, 1987).

CHILDHOOD AND FAMILIAL ANTECEDENTS

Hereditary factors may exert influence on obesity through channels such as body size, number of fat cells, efficiency of fat storage, and metabo-lism. One source of evidence for a genetic origin of human obesity comes from comparisons of monozygotic and dizygotic twins. Stunkard, Foch, and Hrubec (1986) conducted a twin study of human obesity and found the concordance rates for different degrees of overweight were twice as high for monozygotic twins (61% at 15% overweight, 44% at 40% overweight) as for dizygotic twins (31% at 15% overweight, 0% at 40% overweight). Height, weight, and body mass index were all highly heritable both at 20 years of age ($r = 0.80$, $r = 0.78$, and $r = 0.77$, respectively) and at a 25-year follow-up ($r = 0.80$, $r = 0.81$, and $r = 0.84$, respectively).

Comparisons of adoptees with their biological and adopted parents provide further evidence for genetic components of obesity. Stunkard et al. (1986) divided 540 Danish adoptees into four weight classes: thin, median weight, overweight, and obese. They found a strong relationship between the weight class of the adoptees and the body mass index of their biological parents. There was no apparent relationship, however, between the weight class of the adoptees and the body mass index of their adoptive parents. In the overweight and obese adoptee weight classes, 41% of the biologic mothers and 49% of the biologic fathers were overweight, as compared to 35% of the adoptive mothers and 45% of the adoptive fathers. In the thin adoptee weight class, 18% of the biologic mothers and 35% of the biologic fathers were overweight, as compared to 34% of the adoptive mothers and 57% of the adoptive fathers.

Although the Danish adoptee study makes a

significant contribution to the obesity literature, it has received a great deal of criticism. Dietz (1986) claims that any variant of weight for height correlates as well with relative leg length and lean body mass as with fat. Therefore, it is impossible to conclude that comparable body mass index reflects similar degrees of obesity; it may instead only indicate the heritability of frame size. Hartz (1986) argues that Stunkard et al.'s (1986) conclusion that "family environment alone has not apparent effect" in determining adult obesity is based on the fact that they found no association between the obesity of the children and that of their adoptive parents. The underlying assumption is that the degree of obesity in parents reflects the likelihood that family environment caused the obesity. The accuracy of this assumption has not yet been tested. For some families, the contrary may be true. For example, parents who have struggled with obesity themselves may take particular cautions to ensure that their children do not suffer the same fate.

Other evidence suggests that the level of fatness is not simply hereditary and additive (Garn, 1986). For example, spouses resemble each other in fatness levels. This could be the result of cohabitation or people may simply tend to choose partners of comparable body size. Furthermore, parent-child and sibling correlations of fatness actually increase during the growing years, which might reflect effects of communal living. Parent-child fatness correlations also decrease after children move out, and family members still living together show simultaneous changes in fatness (Garn, 1986). These patterns of fatness within families suggest that nongenetic effects must be given serious attention. Systematic similarities have thus been demonstrated among genetically related individuals living together, genetically unrelated individuals living together (such as spouses), and genetically related individuals living apart (adoptees and biological parents). These findings indicate that both heredity and environment are potentially great influences on the development of obesity.

A number of parental and family factors may affect childhood obesity. For instance, a child with one overweight parent has a 40% chance of becoming overweight; if a child has two obese parents, the chances increase to 80% (Bray, 1976). This could be attributed to environmental as well as genetic factors. Parental weight may also interact with child weight to influence the development of childhood obesity. Fifty-one percent of

obese infants with obese parents become obese adults, compared to 20% of obese infants with thin parents (Charney, Goodman, McBride, Lyon, & Pratt, 1976). Furthermore, the weight of other family members may affect childhood obesity. Garn, Bailey, Solomon, and Hopkins (1981) found that if all other family members in a four-member nuclear family were lean, 3.2% of the boys and 5.4% of the girls were obese. However, if the remaining family members were all obese, then 27.5% of the boys and 24.1% of the girls were obese. Family size has been shown to be an important risk factor for childhood obesity. Jacoby, Altman, and Cook (1975) indicated that obesity is inversely related to family size. That is, the relative risk of an only child being obese is 2.2 times as great as a child in a family with four children. It is 1.52 times as great if two-child families are compared with families with four or more children.

The notion that the obese child plays a special role in maintaining equilibrium in a distressed or dysfunctional family has received increased attention. Beck and Terry (1985) found that obese families perceive their homes as more conflictual and less cohesive, less interested in social and cultural activities, and less organized compared to normal weight families. Obese parents, compared to non-obese parents, also described themselves as more controlling and their families as less independent. Ganley (1986) suggests that the adoption of a systematic approach may help advance the research and treatment of obesity.

Energy expenditure (EE) and resting metabolic rate (RMR) have been the target of many obesity studies. Bogardus et al. (1986) found that RMR is a familial trait and it is independent of differences in fat-free mass, age, and sex. However, more studies are needed to determine whether the familial component of the resting metabolic rate is a contributing factor in obesity. Griffiths and Payne (1976) studied energy expenditure in the children of fat and thin parents using continuous heart rate monitoring. There were no significant differences in body weight between the two groups at the time of measurement; however, children of obese parents had significantly reduced total daily energy expenditure. This is an important study, as it is the first demonstration of differences in metabolism preceding the development of obesity in children genetically and environmentally at risk for obesity.

Roberts, Savage, Coward, Chew, and Lucas (1988) studied infants of 6 lean and 12 overweight mothers who were recruited soon after birth. They observed no significant difference between infants who became overweight by the age of 1 year (50% of infants born to overweight mothers and none of those born to lean mothers) and those who did not, with respect to weight, length, skinfold thickness, metabolic rate of 0.1 and 3 months of age, and metabolizable energy intake at 3 months. However, total energy expenditure at 3 months of age was 20.7% lower in the infants who became overweight than in the infants who did not. This difference could account for the mean difference in weight gain. These results suggest that reduced energy expenditure, particularly physical activity, significantly contributed to weight gain in the first year of the life in infants born to overweight mothers.

Using a respiratory chamber, Ravussin et al. (1988) measured 24-hour energy expenditure in 95 southwestern American Indians. They found that energy expenditure adjusted for body composition, age, and sex, correlated with the rate of change in body weight over a 2-year follow-up period ($r = -0.39$, $p < 0.001$). The estimated probability of gaining more than 7.5 kg in body weight was four times greater in persons with a low adjusted 24-hour energy expenditure (200 kcal per day below predicted values) than in persons with a high 24-hour energy expenditure (200 kcal per day above predicted values, $p < 0.01$). In a group of 94 siblings from 36 families, values for adjusted 24-hour energy expenditure aggregated in families (intraclass correlation = 0.48). The authors concluded that a low rate of energy expenditure may be an important factor in the aggregation of obesity in families.

Johnson, Burke, and Mayer (1956) interviewed 28 obese high school girls and 28 matched controls to determine daily calorie intake and physical activity. Activities were divided into classes according to EE. Obese girls spent 4 hours per week in "active sports and other strenuous acts" as compared to the 11 hours that normal girls spent in these activities. Obese girls also consumed fewer calories per day than normals. Thus, deficiency in energy expenditure and not excessive eating were associated with childhood obesity in this group.

Stunkard has examined the physical activity of obese adults by means of a pedometer. In a study of 15 obese women and 15 controls, Dorris and Stunkard (1957) found that the obese women walked an average of 2 miles per day as compared to 4.9 miles per day for the controls. Similarly, Chirico and Stunkard (1960) found that 25 obese

men walked an average of 3.7 miles per day as compared to 6 miles per day walked by the 25 nonobese controls. Thus, obese adults also show an energy expenditure deficit.

Donahoe, Lin, Kirschenbaum, and Keesey (1984) studied 10 overweight women in a behavioral treatment program over an 18-week period consisting of three consecutive phases: baseline, diet only, and diet and exercise. The RMR was lowered during the diet phase by an amount twice that expected on the basis of weight loss. Exercise, however, increased the RMR to a level appropriate to the dieter's current body weight. This suggests that exercise may help to offset the energy conserving metabolic consequences of dieting.

The preceding studies suggest that low energy expenditure plays an important role in the development and maintenance of obesity. Recent findings on energy expenditure suggest that it may be more predictive of obesity and weight gain than energy intake and, in some cases, metabolic rate.

Obesity in childhood is linked with an increased risk of becoming an obese adult. Studies have shown that 2.33 times more obese infants than nonobese infants become obese adults (Charney et al., 1976), 41% of obese 7-year-old children become obese adults compared with 11% of normals (Stark, Atkins, Wolff, & Douglas, 1981), and 74% of obese 10- to 13-year old boys and 72% of obese girls become obese vs. 31% and 11% for normals (Abraham & Nordsieck, 1960). Obese infants tend to remain obese as adolescents and as adults more often than chance would allow, and the older the obese child, the more likely he or she is to become an obese adult.

SUMMARY

Obesity is the biological condition of excessive body fat. It is not a diagnosis included in the DSM-III-R; however, it is often associated with eating disorders because of shared behavioral patterns such as overconcern with body shape or weight. Depending upon the criteria used, 10% to 50% of the population is obese. The most widely used measure of excess weight has been the distribution of weights at given heights. The 1983 Metropolitan Life Insurance Company weight tables are the best known. Using these tables, obesity is typically defined as a minimum of 20% above the ideal weight for a particular height.

Obesity has long been associated with serious medical problems such as coronary disease, gall bladder disease, cancer, and increased mortality.

In addition, many persons suffer adverse psychosocial consequences due to pervasive negative attitudes toward obesity in modern society.

Systematic similarities have been demonstrated among genetically related individuals living together, genetically unrelated individuals living together (such as spouses), and genetically related individuals living apart (adoptees and their biological parents). These findings indicate that both heredity and environment are potentially great influences on the development of obesity.

Recent studies have demonstrated that low energy expenditure plays an important role in the development and maintenance of obesity. In fact, evidence suggests that it may be more predictive of obesity and weight gain than energy intake and, in some cases, metabolic rate.

REFERENCES

Abraham, S., & Nordsieck, M. (1960). Relationship of excess weight in children and adults. *Public Health Reports, 75*, 263–273.

Allon, N. (1982). The stigma of overweight in everyday life. In B. B. Wolman (Ed.), *Psychological aspects of obesity: A handbook* (pp. 130–174). New York: Van Nostrand Reinhold.

American Psychiatric Association. (1987). *Diagnostic and statistical manual of mental disorders* (3rd ed. rev.). Washington, DC: Author.

Beck, S., & Terry, K. (1985). A comparison of obese and normal weight families' psychological characteristics. *The American Journal of Family Therapy, 13*(3), 55–59.

Bjorntorp, P. (1985). Obesity and the risk of cardiovascular disease. *Annals of Clinical Research, 17*, 3–9.

Bjorntorp, P., Carlgren, G., Isaksson, B., Krotkiewski, M., Larsson, B., & Sjostrom, L. (1975). Effect of an energy reduced dietary regimen in relation to adipose tissue cellularity in obese women. *American Journal of Clinical Nutrition, 28*, 445–452.

Bogardus, C., Lillija, S., Ravussin, E., Abbott, W., Zawadzki, J. K., Young, A., Knowler, W. C., Jacobowitz, R., & Moll, P. P. (1986). Familial dependence of the resting metabolic rate. *The New England Journal of Medicine, 315*, 96–100.

Bray, G. A. (1976). *The obese patient.* Philadelphia: W. B. Saunders.

Bray, G. A. (1985). Complications of obesity. *Annals of Internal Medicine, 103*, 1052–1062.

Bray, G. A. (1987). Overweight is risking fate: Definition, classification, prevalence, and risks. *Annals of the New York Academy of Sciences, 499*, 14–28.

Brownell, K. (1988, January). Yo-yo dieting: Repeated attempts to lose weight can give you a hefty problem. *Psychology Today, 20*, 22–23.

Brownell, K. D. (1981). Assessment of eating disorders. In D. H. Barlow (Ed.), *Behavioral assessment of adult disorders* (pp. 329–404). New York: Guilford Press.

Brownell, K. D., Greenwood, M. R. C., Stellar, E., & Shrager, E. E. (1986). The effects of repeated cycles of weight loss and regain in rats. *Physiology & Behavior, 38*, 459–464.

Brownell, K. D., Stunkard, A. J., & Albaum, J. M. (1980). Evaluation and modification of exercise patterns in the natural environment. *American Journal of Psychiatry, 13*(12), 1540–1545.

Canning, H., & Mayer, J. (1966). Obesity—Its possible effects on college admissions. *The New England Journal of Medicine, 275*, 1172–1174.

Charney, M., Goodman, H. C., McBridge, M., Lyon, B., & Pratt, R. (1976). Childhood antecedents of adult obesity: Do chubby infants become obese adults? *The New England Journal of Medicine, 295*, 6–9.

Chirico, A. M., & Stunkard, A. J. (1960). Physical activity and human obesity. *The New England Journal of Medicine, 263*, 935–940.

Dietz, W. H. (1986, July). Adoption study of obesity [letter to the editor]. *The New England Journal of Medicine*, 128–129.

Donohoe, C. P., Lin, D. H., Kirschenbaum, D. S., & Kessey, R. E. (1984). Metabolic consequences of dieting and exercise in the treatment of obesity. *Journal of Consulting and Clinical Psychology, 52*(5), 827–836.

Dorris, R. J., & Stunkard, A. J. (1957). Physical activity: Performance and attitudes of a group of obese women. *American Journal of the Medical Sciences, 233*, 622–628.

Durnin, J. V. G. A., & Womersley, J. (1974). Body fat assessed from total body density and its estimation from skinfold thickness: Measurements on 481 men and women aged from 16 to 72 years. *British Journal of Nutrition, 32*, 77–97.

Franzini, L. R., & Grimes, W. B. (1976). Skinfold measures as the criterion of change in weight control studies. *Behavior Therapy, 7*, 256–260.

Fremouw, W. J., & Heyneman, N. E. (1983). Obesity. In M. Hersen (Ed.), *Outpatient behavior therapy* (pp. 173–202). New York: Grune & Stratton.

Ganley, R. M. (1986). Epistemology, family patterns, and psychosomatics: The case of obesity. *Family Process, 25*, 437–451.

Garfinkel, L. (1985). Overweight and cancer. *Annals of Internal Medicine, 103*, 1034–1036.

Garn, S. M. (1986). Family-line and socioeconomic factors in fatness and obesity. *Nutrition Reviews, 44*(12), 381–386.

Garn, S., Bailey, S., Solomon, M., & Hopkins, P. (1981). Effect of remaining family members on fatness prediction. *American Journal of Clinical Nutrition, 34*, 148–153.

Goldbourt, U., & Medalie, J. H. (1974). Weight-height indices. *British Journal of Prevention and Social Medicine, 28*, 116–126.

Goodman, N., Dornbusch, S. M., Richardson, S. A., & Hastorf, A. H. (1963). Variant reactions to physical disabilities. *American Sociology Review, 28*, 429–435.

Gormally, J. (1984). The obese binge eater: Diagnosis, etiology and clinical issues. In R. Hawkins, W. Fremouw, & P. Clement (Eds.), *The binge-purge syndrome*. New York: Springer.

Griffiths, M., & Payne, P. R. (1976). Energy expenditure in small children of obese and nonobese parents. *Nature, 260*, 698–700.

Halmi, K. A., Stunkard, A. J., & Mason, E. E. (1980). Emotional responses to weight reduction by three methods: Gastric bypass, jejunoileal bypass, diet. *American Journal of Clinical Nutrition, 33*, 446–451.

Hartz, A. (1986, July). Adoption study of obesity [letter to the editor]. *The New England Journal of Medicine*, 129.

Hawkins, R. C., & Clement, P. F. (1980). Development and construct validation of a self-report measure of binge eating tendencies. *Addictive Behaviors, 5*, 219–226.

Hirsch, J., & Knittle, J. L. (1970). Cellularity of obese and nonobese human adipose tissue. *Federation Proceedings, 29*, 1516–1521.

Hubert, H. B., Feinleib, N., McNamara, P., & Castelli, W. (1983). Obesity as an independent risk factor for cardiovascular disease: A 26 year follow up of participants in the Framingham Heart Study. *Circulation, 67*, 968–977.

Jacoby, A., Altman, D. G., & Cook, J. (1975). Influence of some social and environmental factors on the nutrient intake and the nutritional status of school children. *British Journal of Prevention and Social Medicine, 29*, 116–120.

Johnson, M. L., Burke, B. S., & Mayer, J. (1956). Relative importance of inactivity and overeating in the energy balance of obese high school girls. *American Journal of Clinical Nutrition, 4*(1), 37–44.

Kattell, A., Callahan, E. J., Fremouw, W. J., & Zitter, R. C. (1979). The effects of behavioral treatment and fasting on eating behavior and weight loss: A case study. *Behavior Therapy, 10*, 579–587.

Landis, J. R., Stanich, W. M., Freeman, J. L., & Koch, G. G. (1976). A computer program for the generalized chi-square analysis of categorical data using weighted least squares (GENCAT). *Computer Programs in Biomedicine, 6*, 196–231.

Lew, E. A., & Garfinkel, L. (1979). Variations in mortality by weight among 750,000 men and women. *Journal of Chronic Diseases, 32*, 563–576.

Linn, R. (1976). *The last chance diet*. New York: Bantam Books.

Maddox, G. L., & Liederman, V. (1969). Overweight as a social disability with medical implications. *Journal of Medical Education, 44*, 214–220.

Metropolitan Life Insurance Company. (1983). 1983 Metropolitan height and weight tables (1974). *Statistical Bulletin of the Metropolitan Life Insurance Company, 64*, 2–9.

Nisbett, R. E. (1972). Hunger, obesity, and the ventromedical hypothalamus. *Psychological Review, 79*, 433–453.

Polivy, J., & Herman, C. P. (1985). Dieting and binging: A causal analysis. *American Psychologist, 40*, 193–201.

Pyle, R. L., Mitchell, J. E., & Eckert, E. D. (1981). Bulimia: A report of 34 cases. *Journal of Clinical Psychiatry, 42*, 60–64.

Ravussin, E., Lillioja, S., Knowler, W. C., Christin, L., Freymond, D., Abbott, W. G. H., Boyce, V., Howard, B. V., & Bogardus, C. (1988). Reduced rate of energy expenditure as a risk factor for body weight gain. *The New England Journal of Medicine, 318*(8), 467–472.

Roberts, S. B., Savage, J., Coward, W. A., Chew, B., & Lucas, A. (1988). Energy expenditure and intake in infants born to lean and overweight mothers. *The New England Journal of Medicine, 318*(8), 461–466.

Roe, D. A., & Eickwort, K. R. (1976). Relationships between obesity and associated health factors with unemployment among low income women. *Journal of the American Medical Women's Association, 31,* 193–194, 198–199, 203–204.

Sclafani, A., & Springer, D. (1976). Dietary obesity in adult rats: Similarities to human obesity syndromes. *Physiology and Behavior, 17,* 461–471.

Seltzer, C. C., & Mayer, J. (1965). A simple criterion of obesity. *Postgraduate Medicine, 38,* 101–107.

Sheldon, W. H. (1954). *Atlas of men.* New York: Harper & Brothers.

Smith, M. C., & Thelen, M. H. (1984). Development and validation of a test of bulimia. *Journal of Counseling and Clinical Psychology, 52,* 863–872.

Society of Actuaries and Association of Life Insurance Medical Directors of America. (1979). *Build Study of 1979.* Chicago: Author.

Stark, D., Atkins, E., Wolff, D. H., & Douglas, J. W. B. (1981). Longitudinal study of obesity in the National Survey of Health and Development. *British Medical Journal, 283,* 12–17.

Stern, J. S. (1984). Is obesity a disease of inactivity? In A. J. Stunkard & E. Stellar (Eds.), *Eating and its disorders* (pp. 131–139). New York: Raven Press.

Stuart, R. B., & Davis, B. (1972). *Slim chance in a fat world: Behavioral control of obesity.* Champaign, IL: Research Press.

Stunkard, A. J. (1984). The current status of treatment for obesity in adults. In A. J. Stunkard & E. Stellar (Eds.), *Eating and its disorders* (pp. 157–173). New York: Raven Press.

Stunkard, A. J., & Burt, V. (1967). Obesity and the body image: II. Age at onset of disturbances in the body image. *American Journal of Psychiatry, 123,* 1443–1447.

Stunkard, A. J., Foch, T. T., & Hrubec, Z. (1986). A twin study of human obesity. *Journal of the American Medical Association, 256*(1), 51–54.

Stunkard, A. J., & Mendelson, M. (1961). Disturbances in body image of some obese persons. *Journal of the American Dietetic Association, 38,* 328–331.

Stunkard, A. J., & Rush, J. (1974). Dieting and depression reexamined: A critical review of reports of untoward responses during weight reduction for obesity. *Annals of Internal Medicine, 81,* 526–533.

Stunkard, A. J., Sorensen, T. I. A., Hanis, C., Teasdale, T. W., Chakraborty, R., Schull, W. J., & Schulsinger, F. (1986). An adoption study of human obesity. *The New England Journal of Medicine, 314*(4), 193–198.

Vague, J. (1956). The degree of masculine differentiation of obesity as a factor determining predisposition to diabetes, atherosclerosis, gout, and uric calculous disease. *American Journal of Clinical Nutrition, 4,* 20–26.

VanItallie, T. B. (1977, February). *Diet related to killer disease* (Vol. II). Hearings before the Select Committee on Nutrition and Human Needs of the United States Senate, Ninety-fifth Congress (First Session), Part 2, Obesity, 44.

VanItallie, T. B. (1985). Health implications of overweight and obesity in the United States. *Annals of Internal Medicine, 103,* 983–988.

VanItallie, T. B., & Campbell, R. B. (1972). Multidisciplinary approach to the problem of obesity. *Journal of the American Dietetic Association, 61,* 385–390.

Wadden, T. A., Smoller, J. W., & Stunkard, A. J. (1987). In W. G. Johnson (Ed.), *Advances in eating disorders.* Greenwich, CT: JAI Press.

Wadden, T. A., & Stunkard, A. J. (1985). Social and psychological consequences of obesity. *Annals of Internal Medicine, 103,* 1062–1067.

Womersley, J., & Durnin, J. V. G. A. (1973). An experimental study on the variability of measurement of skinfold thickness on young adults. *Human Biology, 45,* 281–292.

AFTERWORD

In this volume we have set out to provide a longitudinal perspective on the study of psychopathology. A longitudinal or life-span approach to psychiatric illness is relatively recent. Historically, study of adult psychopathology predominated, with little attention paid to disturbed children and adolescents. Conceptualizations of psychopathology in these young populations portrayed children and adolescents as "miniature adults" who essentially experienced the same illnesses as their adult counterparts. Until recently, the DSM system for classifying mental disorders continued this trend by using the same categories for both child and adult populations and by failing to utilize developmental "modifiers" for the diagnostic criterion. With the advent of DSM-III in 1980 (and, more recently, DSM-III-R in 1987), childhood disorders gained more attention in their own right. Indeed, a section of the manual was devoted exclusively to disorders that have their onset in childhood or adolescence, and developmental modifiers were added to a number of criteria for a variety of "adult" disorders.

A longitudinal approach to psychopathology acknowledges that, as normal development shows characteristic patterns and changes from childhood to adolescence, and adolescence to adulthood, so does the development of psychopathological conditions. We have explored the similarities and differences between childhood, adolescent, and adult presentations for the various disorders, as well as the continuity of the disorders over time. As for the commonalities and differences of presentation at different ages, for the most part the hallmarks of the various disturbances remain intact. However, significant developmental differences have been highlighted and need to be considered when evaluating the major diagnostic entities in different age groups. Evidence of continuity over time for the disorder is less frequently documented. However, follow-up data that currently are available suggest that a child or adolescent at risk moves to adulthood at risk, although the specific constellation of symptoms for the same disorder may vary according to the developmental period.

Cross-sectional, longitudinal, familial, and genetic studies address the types of issues that have been underscored in this book. Data from such investigations, when available, have been presented. However, such studies tend to be costly and time-consuming, thus possibly accounting for a less than optimal database from which to draw current conclusions. An increased respect has been emerging for a life-span approach to psychopathology, and for studies of this type, which should result in continued expansion in this direction. Such data are warranted in order for us to fine-tune our interventions and, ultimately, move toward prevention. We look forward to these developments with eager anticipation and hope that this volume may provide the needed impetus in that direction.

AUTHOR INDEX

SUBJECT INDEX

ABOUT THE EDITORS
AND CONTRIBUTORS

ABOUT THE EDITORS

Michel Hersen (Ph.D.) is professor of Psychiatry and Psychology at the University of Pittsburgh School of Medicine. He is past president of the Association for Advancement of Behavior Therapy. He has coauthored and coedited 62 books, including *Single Case Experimental Designs*, published by Pergamon Press. He has also published more than 172 scientific journal articles and is coeditor of several psychological journals, including *Behavior Modification*, *Clinical Psychology Review*, *Journal of Anxiety Disorders*, *Journal of Family Violence*, and *Journal of the Multihandicapped Person*. Dr. Hersen is the recipient of several research grants from the National Institute of Mental Health, the Department of Education, the National Institute of Disabilities and Rehabilitation Research, and the March of Dimes Birth Defects Foundation.

Cynthia G. Last (Ph.D.) is associate professor of Psychology and director of the School Phobia Program in the Department of Psychology at Nova University. With Dr. Hersen, she is editor and founder of the *Journal of Anxiety Disorders*.

She has coauthored and coedited eight books including: *Child Behavior Therapy Casebook*, *Handbook of Anxiety Disorders*, *Handbook of Child Psychiatric Diagnosis*, and *Anxiety Disorders in Children*. Dr. Last is the recipient of several research grants from the National Institute of Mental Health to study anxiety disorders in children and adolescents. She has published numerous journal articles and book chapters on the assessment, diagnosis, and treatment of anxiety disorders in both child and adult populations.

ABOUT THE CONTRIBUTORS

Cheryl R. Bene (M.A., Memphis State University, 1988) is presently completing her Ph.D. in clinical psychology at Memphis State University. Her research and clinical interests are in the areas of Restraint Theory, mechanisms of obesity, and weight management. Ms. Bene is presently completing a clinical internship at the Medical College of South Carolina.

T. P. Berney (M.B., University of Birmingham, 1969) is a consultant in the Child Psychiatry of

Handicap at the Fleming Nuffield Unit, Newcastle upon Tyne and Prudhoe Hospital. His particular interests are in the areas of epilepsy and autism.

Dudley David Blake (Ph.D., State University of New York at Albany, 1987) works as a staff research clinical psychologist at the National Center for Post-Traumatic Stress Disorder, Behavioral Science Division, Boston VAMC and is a Co-director of the Behavioral Consultation Program at the Boston VA Medical Center. Dr. Blake's clinical research interests include PTSD assessment and treatment, and the study of pretrauma factors (family concordance and social adjustment) in PTSD.

Gabrielle A. Carlson (M.D., Cornell University Medical College, 1968) did her psychiatric training at Washington University in St. Louis, National Institute of Mental Health, Bethesda and University of California, Los Angeles. She is currently the director of the Division of Child and Adolescent Psychiatry at SUNY Stony Brook. Her research interests and publications (including one book) have focused on the phenomenology of bipolar disorder initially in adults and ultimately in adolescents and children.

Brian L. Cook (D.O., College of Osteopathic Medicine and Surgery, 1976) is Assistant Professor of Psychiatry at the University of Iowa College of Medicine, and Staff Psychiatrist at the Department of Veterans Affairs Medical Center in Iowa City, Iowa. His major research interests include affective disorders, alcoholism, and anxiety disorders. Dr. Cook has authored and coauthored a number of articles and chapters in his areas of research interest.

Diana Damer (B.A., William and Mary College, 1987) is a doctoral student in the Department of Psychology at West Virginia University with an interest in health psychology.

Richard R. DeBlassie (Ed.D. University of Arizona, 1967) is interim head and professor, Department of Counseling and Educational Psychology, New Mexico State University. He has authored and coauthored 150 professional journal articles and seven books in the area of counseling, childhood, and adolescence. He has been the recipient of several training grants from the National Institute of Mental Health in the area of training research and evaluation specialists.

Paul M. G. Emmelkamp is professor of Clinical Psychology & Psychotherapy and head of the Department of Clinical Psychology at the University of Groningen, the Netherlands. He serves on the editorial board of a number of behavioral and cognitive therapy journals and is editor of the *Annual Series of European Research in Behaviour Therapy*. He is the author and (co)editor of 10 books and has authored numerous articles and chapters on anxiety, phobias, psychopathology, assessment, and (failures in) behavior therapy. He is past president of the European Association of Behaviour Therapy and chairman of the Dutch Collaborative Program of Experimental Psychopathology.

Spencer Eth (M.D., University of California, Los Angeles, 1976) is the acting chief of Psychiatry at the West Los Angeles VA Medical Center. He is also an assistant professor of Psychiatry at the UCLA School of Medicine and a clinical associate professor of Psychiatry at the University of Southern California School of Medicine. Dr. Eth has been active in the field of psychotraumatology and has coedited Post-Traumatic Stress Disorder in Children, published by the American Psychiatric Press in 1985.

Greta Francis (Ph.D., Virginia Polytechnic Institute and State University, 1986) completed a postdoctoral research fellowship at Western Psychiatric Institute and Clinic. She joined the faculty at Brown University in 1988. She currently is an assistant professor in the Department of Psychiatry and Human Behavior based at the Emma Pendleton Bradley Hospital. Her clinical and research interests include anxiety and affective disorders in children and adolescents.

William J. Fremouw (Ph.D., University of Massachusetts, 1974) is a professor of Psychology at West Virginia University where he is the director of Clinical Training. He is a diplomate in forensic psychology from the American Board of Professional Psychology. His current interests are forensic psychology and health psychology.

Donald W. Goodwin (M.D., University of Kansas, 1964) is professor and chairman of Psychiatry at the University of Kansas. He has written numerous articles on psychiatric disorders, especially alcohol dependence. In 1988 he published three books: *Is Alcoholism Heredi-*

tary?, *Alcohol and the Writer*, and *Psychiatric Diagnosis* (coauthored with Samuel B. Guze).

Alan M. Gross (Ph.D., Washington State University) is associate professor of psychology at the University of Mississippi. His research interests include behavioral pediatrics, child behavior therapy, and self-management. He has been the editor of *Behavior Therapist* and is currently on the editorial boards of *Behavior Modification* and *Behavioral Medicine Abstracts*. He has recently edited, with Ronald Drabman, the *Handbook of Clinical Behavioral Pediatrics*. Dr. Gross is the recipient of several NIH grants.

Laura E. Hess (M.S.) is a doctoral candidate in the department of Human Development and Family Studies at Pennsylvania State University. Her dissertation research involves an examination of the relationships between family structural and functional change and early adolescent adjustment across home, school, and peer contexts.

Rudolf Hoehn-Saric (M.D.) is associate professor of Psychiatry and director of the Psychiatric Outpatient Services and the Anxiety Disorders Clinic in the Department of Psychiatry and Behavioral Sciences, Johns Hopkins University School of Medicine. His research, conducted conjointly with Daniel R. McLeod, focuses on psychological, physiological, and pharmacological aspects of anxiety disorders. He has authored numerous publications and is on the editorial board of the *Journal of Anxiety Disorders*.

Rose M. Huntzinger (Ph.D., 1989, Virginia Polytechnic Institute and State University) is currently completing a post-doctoral fellowship in pediatric neuropsychology.

A. Roland Irwin (M.S., Northeast Louisiana University) is a doctoral candidate in clinical psychology at the University of Mississippi.

Alan E. Kazdin (Ph.D., Northwestern University, 1970) is professor of Psychology at Yale University and director of the Child Conduct Clinic of the Yale Psychological Services. Currently, he is editor of the *Journal of Consulting and Clinical Psychology* and *Psychological Assessment*. His work focuses on childhood psychopathology, particularly the assessment and treatment of antisocial behavior and depression. Recent publications include *Child Psychotherapy: Developing and Identifying Effective Treatments* and *Conduct Disorder in Childhood and Adolescence*.

Terence M. Keane (Ph.D., State University of New York at Binghamton, 1978) is chief of Psychology Service at the Boston VA Medical and Outpatient Clinic; director of the National Center for Post-traumatic Stress Disorder, Behavioral Sciences Division; and professor of Psychiatry (Psychology) at Tufts University School of Medicine. He has written numerous articles for scientific journals and many book chapters primarily on the assessment and treatment of psychological trauma. His research is supported by the Department of Veterans Affairs and the National Institute of Mental Health.

Martin B. Keller (M.D., Cornell University Medical School) is director of Outpatient Psychiatry at Massachusetts General Hospital in Boston, and associate professor of Psychiatry, Harvard Medical School. Dr. Keller is a principal investigator in the National Institute of Mental Health Collaborative Study on the Psychobiology of Depression, a long-term, naturalistic, prospective follow-up study of depressed patients and their first degree relatives. He has authored and coauthored over 100 articles and chapters on affective disorders and other psychiatric conditions.

Robert L. Klesges (Ph.D., University of Wyoming, 1980) is currently an associate professor of Psychology at Memphis State University and an associate professor of Pediatrics and Biostatistics/Epidemiology at the University of Tennessee, Memphis. His major area of research interest is in obesity assessment and the relationship between smoking and body weight. He has published extensively in psychology, medicine, nutrition, and exercise journals and is a three-time contributor to the Surgeon General's Report on Smoking and Health. He is currently on six editorial boards and reviews for four study sections at the National Institutes of Health.

Israel Kolvin (M.D., F.R.C. Psych) was previously professor of Child and Adolescent Psychiatry of the University of Newcastle upon Tyne and director of the Human Development Unit. He is now professor of Child and Family Mental Health at the Royal Free Hospital and the Tavistock Institute, London. He has researched widely in the field of epidemiology. His interests in clinical research have been the psychosis of childhood and depression. He has recently jointly completed a book entitled *Continuities of Deprivation*.

Richard M. Lerner (Ph.D., City University of New York, 1971) is professor of Child and Adolescent Development at Pennsylvania State University. He is the author or editor of more than 20 books and over 150 articles and chapters. Dr. Lerner is on the editorial board of numerous journals, is the editor of the *Journal of Research on Adolescence*, the associate editor of the *International Journal of Behavioral Development*, and coeditor of the annual series *Life-Span Development and Behavior*. His current research involves a longitudinal study of early adolescent development.

Michael R. Liebowitz (M.D., Yale University, 1969) is associate professor of Clinical Psychiatry at Columbia University and director of the Anxiety Disorders Clinic at the New York State Psychiatric Institute. He serves on the editorial board of the *Journal of Anxiety Disorders* and the *Journal of Personality Disorders*. His principal areas of interest have been in diagnosis, pathophysiology, and treatment of anxiety and affective disorders.

Brett T. Litz (Ph.D., State University of New York at Binghamton, 1987) is a staff research clinical psychologist at the National Center for Post-Traumatic Stress Disorder, Behavioral Science Division, Boston VAMC, and a clinical instructor in psychiatry at Tufts University School of Medicine. Dr. Litz has published in the area of information processing in PTSD and is currently doing research in this area supported by the Department of Veterans Affairs.

Ronald A. Madle (Ph.D., Pennsylvania State University, 1975) is director of Staff Development and Program Evaluation at Laurelton Center, a residential facility for mentally retarded adults. He is also adjunct assistant professor of Human Development at the Pennsylvania State University and is currently completing postdoctoral study in school psychology at the same location. Dr. Madle, a fellow of the American Association on Mental Retardation, has authored or coauthored over 50 book chapters, articles, and professional papers in the areas of mental retardation, behavior modification, staff development, and school psychology.

F. Dudley McGlynn (Ph.D., University of Missouri – Columbia, 1968) is professor and chairman of the Department of Behavioral Science at the University of Missouri – Kansas City School of Dentistry. He has been affiliated with Mississippi State University and with the University of Florida. Dr. McGlynn has written extensively in the areas of behavioral fear therapy and behavioral medicine in dentistry. He serves on the editorial boards of six journals.

Daniel R. McLeod (Ph.D.) is assistant professor of Psychiatry in the Department of Psychiatry and Behavioral Sciences, Johns Hopkins University School of Medicine. His research, conducted conjointly with Rudolf Hoehn-Saric, focuses on psychological, physiological, and pharmacological aspects of anxiety disorders. He has published several papers in the fields of anxiety disorders and psychopharmacology. Dr. McLeod currently has a research grant from the NIAAA to study relationships between alcohol and anxiety.

Daniel W. McNeil (Ph.D., University of Alabama, 1982) is assistant professor in the Department of Psychology at Oklahoma State University. He completed a postdoctoral experience in behavioral medicine and dentistry research at the University of Florida. Dr. McNeil has written in the areas of dental and social anxiety with an emphasis on bioinformational networks in emotional imagery.

Andrew W. Meyers (Ph.D., Pennsylvania State University, 1974) is professor of Psychology and director of the Center of Applied Psychological Research at Memphis State University. He has published extensively in the areas of behavioral medicine, sport psychology, and children's problem solving. Dr. Meyers is currently associate editor of *Behavior Therapy* and he is on the editorial boards of *Cognitive Therapy and Research*, *Journal of Exercise and Sport Psychology*, and *Journal of Applied Sport Psychology*.

Michael A. Milan (Ph.D., University of Florida, 1970) is professor of Clinical Psychology and director of Graduate Studies at the Georgia State University, Atlanta, Georgia. He is the past president of the American Association for Correctional Psychology and a former member of the editorial board of *Criminal Justice and Behavior*. Dr. Milan's primary areas of interest are behavior modification and therapy and crime and delinquency. He is the author, coauthor, or coeditor of two books, several book chapters, and numerous articles including *Correctional Rehabilitation and Management: A Psychological Approach* (with Teodoro Ayllon) and *Handbook of Social Skills Training and Research* (with Luciano L'Abate).

Randall L. Morrison (Ph.D., University of Pittsburgh, 1982) is scientist, Department of Mental Health at the American Medical Association and associate professor in the Department of Psychiatry at the Medical College of Pennsylvania at EPPI. He has authored and coauthored numerous articles and chapters, primarily in the areas of schizophrenia, psychosocial treatments for chronic psychiatric patients, and marital and family violence. He is coeditor of *The Handbook of Family Violence* and *Medical Factors for Psychological Disorders: A Handbook for Psychologists*. He is on the editorial boards of the *Journal of Family Violence* and *Behavior Modification*. Dr. Morrison is the recipient of several grants from the National Institute of Mental Health.

John T. Neisworth (Ph.D., University of Pittsburgh) is professor of Special Education and director of the Early Intervention Program at Penn State University. He has authored or coauthored 14 text and reference books, including *Modifying Retarded Behavior*, *The Exceptional Child*, *The Young Exceptional Child*, and *Linking Developmental Assessment and Early Intervention*. He also is coauthor of two major instruments: A System to Plan Early Childhood Services (SPECS) and Responsibility and Independence Scales for Adolescents (RISA). He is cofounder and current coeditor of *Topics in Early Childhood Special Education* and is on the editorial board of several journals. His current research interests focus on empirically based instruction and the treatment utility of assessment.

Wendy B. Nelles is a doctoral candidate in clinical psychology at The University at Albany, State University of New York. She is currently completing her internship at the Tufts New England Medical Center—Boston V.A. Consortium. Her research interests are in the area of developmental psychopathology, and she is currently investigating issues in resiliency and competency in children.

Katherine Nitz (M.S.) is pursuing her doctoral degree in the Department of Child Clinical Psychology at George Washington University. Her research interests include testing of a "goodness of fit" model of person-context relations with regard to early adolescent temperament.

Thomas H. Ollendick (Ph.D., Purdue, 1971) is currently professor of Psychology and director of Clinical Training at Virginia Polytechnic Institute and State University. His clinical and research interests center on social learning theory and its role in the understanding, prediction, and control of diverse child and adolescent behavior problems.

Caroly S. Pataki (M.D., New York University School of Medicine, 1981) is assistant professor of Psychiatry (Child) at the State University of New York at Stony Brook. She is also the Medical Director of the Children's Psychiatric Inpatient Service at SUNY at Stony Brook University Hospital.

Judith L. Rapoport (M.D., Harvard University, 1959) is the chief of the Child Psychiatry Branch, National Institute of Mental Health. She is the author of *The Boy Who Couldn't Stop Washing*, a New York Times' Best seller. She has published over 100 articles and 3 books in her major fields of research interest: psychiatric diagnosis, hyperactive children, biological aspects of child psychiatry, pediatric psychopharmacology, and obsessive compulsive disorder.

Franklin R. Schneier (M.D., Cornell University, 1983) is a National Institute of Mental Health research fellow at the Anxiety Disorders Clinic of New York State Psychiatric Institute and a research fellow at Columbia University. His research interests include diagnostic and treatment issues in anxiety disorders.

Wendy K. Silverman (Ph.D., Case Western Reserve University, 1981) is associate professor of Psychology and Director of the Child and Adolescent Fear and Anxiety Treatment Program at the Center for Stress and Anxiety Disorders, The University at Albany, State University of New York. Dr. Silverman's research interests are in the child clinical area, focusing particularly on the assessment and treatment of the childhood anxiety disorders. She is the recipient of a FIRST award from the National Institute of Mental Health to conduct a treatment outcome study for childhood phobia.

Lori A. Sisson (Ph.D.) is a research clinical psychologist at the Western Pennsylvania School for Blind Children and adjunct clinical instructor in Psychiatry at the University of Pittsburgh School of Medicine. Her major clinical and research interests include development and evaluation of community referenced behavior management and skills training procedures with children and adolescents who have multiple disabilities.

Martha E. Smith (Ph.D., West Virginia University, 1987) is a staff psychologist at the Community Hospital and Rehabilitation Center, Missoula, Montana. Her interests are in rehabilitation and health psychology.

Jenelle Sobotka (Pharm. D., University of Iowa, 1989) is a clinical pharmacist at the Department of Veterans Affairs Medical Center In Iowa City, Iowa. Her major research interests involve epidemiologic studies of quality assurance within an academic medical center. Her projects involve mainly pharmacologic issues in psychiatry and infectious disease.

Cyd C. Strauss (Ph.D., University of Georgia, 1983) is clinical assistant professor at the University of Florida and director of the Center for Children and Families in Gainesville, Florida. Her research interests are in the area of childhood psychopathology, with particular interest in anxiety disorders in children and adolescents. Dr. Strauss has authored and coauthored numerous articles and chapters in the area of childhood anxiety disorders. She serves on the editorial board of *Journal of Anxiety Disorders*.

Susan E. Swedo (M.D., Southern Illinois University School of Medicine, 1980) is a senior staff fellow in the Child Psychiatry Branch. Her major research and clinical interests are: adolescent suicide, behavioral research in adolescent medicine, adolescent obesity, teenage parenthood, and obsessive compulsive disorder.

Michael E. Thase (M.D., Ohio State University, 1979) is associate professor of Psychiatry, director of the Mood Disorders Module, and associate director of the Mental Health Clinical Research Center at the University of Pittsburgh School of Medicine and the Western Psychiatric Institute and Clinic. Dr. Thase is the author or coauthor of over 80 referred articles and chapters. His primary

research interests include the assessment and differential therapeutics of affective disorders.

Bruce A. Thyer (Ph.D., University of Michigan, 1982) is an associate professor of Social Work at the University of Georgia and an associate clinical professor with the Department of Psychiatry and Health Behavior at the Medical College of Georgia. He has authored numerous articles in the field of anxiety disorders, including "Treating Anxiety Disorders" (Sage, 1987). He is on the editorial boards of the *Journal of Anxiety Disorders*, the *Journal of Applied Behavior Analysis*, the *Journal of Behavior Therapy and Experimental Psychiatry*, and *Behavior and Social Issues*. He is currently secretary/treasurer for the Division of the Experimental Analysis of Behavior of the American Psychological Association.

Julie H. Wade (M.S., University of Pennsylvania, 1978) is currently a research associate at the Medical College of Pennsylvania at EPPI where she coordinates a research project examining the social skills of individuals with schizophrenia.

Julia K. Warnock (M.D., University of Tennessee, 1984; Ph.D., University of Kansas, 1977) is assistant professor of Psychiatry at the University of Kansas Medical Center where she is director of the Adult Outpatient Psychiatry clinic. Her main areas of teaching and research include psychiatric diagnosis, especially mood disorders and psychopharmacology. She has written articles on biofeedback, stress management, ECT, and adverse dermatologic side-effects of psychotropic medications. She has also coauthored book chapters on alcohol dependence and genetics.

George Winokur (M.D., University of Maryland, 1947) is The Paul W. Penningroth professor and head, Department of Psychiatry, University of Iowa. His major areas of teaching and research include manic–depressive disease and alcoholism, genetics and epidemiology, and studies of natural history of psychiatric illness. He serves on the editorial board of the *Archives of General Psychiatry*, *Annals of Clinical Psychiatry*, *Biological Psychiatry*, *European Archives of Psychiatry and Neurological Sciences*, and the *Journal of Affective Disorders* (of which he is one of the two chief editors). Recent publications have been concerned with clinical and follow-up differences between schizoaffective disorder, bipolar illness, and unipolar depression.

Joanne Wunder (B.A., Boston University) is senior research analyst in the Department of Psychiatry at Massachusetts General Hospital/Harvard Medical School. Ms. Wunder has worked with Dr. Martin Keller's Boston-based research group for the past four years, and has coauthored with Dr. Keller several articles, chapters, and monographs on affective disorders. Ms. Wunder has also done graduate work in psychology at Northeastern University.

Joel Yoeli (Ph.D., University of Denver, 1982) is former director, regional unit for research assessment and treatment of autism at Eitanim Psychiatric Hospital in Israel. He is currently on staff at the Fleming Nuffield Unit for child psychiatry and psychology, implementing psychological input into the multidisciplinary assessment and treatment of autistic children and adolescents.

Pergamon General Psychology Series

Editors: **Arnold P. Goldstein,** Syracuse University
Leonard Krasner, Stanford University &
SUNY at Stony Brook

*Out of print in original format. Available in custom reprint edition.